TRADE
CURRENCIES
AND FINANCE

TRADE CURRENCIES AND FINANCE

Morris Goldstein

Peterson Institute for International Economics, USA

NEW JERSEY · LONDON · SINGAPORE · BEIJING · SHANGHAI · HONG KONG · TAIPEI · CHENNAI · TOKYO

Published by

World Scientific Publishing Co. Pte. Ltd.
5 Toh Tuck Link, Singapore 596224
USA office: 27 Warren Street, Suite 401-402, Hackensack, NJ 07601
UK office: 57 Shelton Street, Covent Garden, London WC2H 9HE

Library of Congress Cataloging-in-Publication Data
Names: Goldstein, Morris, 1944– author.
Title: Trade, currencies and finance / Morris Goldstein,
  Peterson Institute for International Economics, USA.
Description: New Jersey : World Scientific Publishing, [2017]
Identifiers: LCCN 2016055407 | ISBN 9789814749572 (hard cover)
Subjects: LCSH: International trade. | Foreign exchange. |
  Banks and banking, International--Law and legislation.
Classification: LCC HF1379 .G655 2017 | DDC 332/.042--dc23
LC record available at https://lccn.loc.gov/2016055407

British Library Cataloguing-in-Publication Data
A catalogue record for this book is available from the British Library.

Copyright © 2017 by World Scientific Publishing Co. Pte. Ltd.

All rights reserved. This book, or parts thereof, may not be reproduced in any form or by any means, electronic or mechanical, including photocopying, recording or any information storage and retrieval system now known or to be invented, without written permission from the publisher.

For photocopying of material in this volume, please pay a copying fee through the Copyright Clearance Center, Inc., 222 Rosewood Drive, Danvers, MA 01923, USA. In this case permission to photocopy is not required from the publisher.

Desk Editor: Tay Yu Shan

Typeset by Stallion Press
Email: enquiries@stallionpress.com

Printed in Singapore

About the Author

Photo Credit: Jeremey Tripp

Morris Goldstein, non-resident Senior Fellow at the Peterson Institute for International Economics, has held several senior staff positions at the International Monetary Fund, including Deputy Director of Research from 1987 to 1994. From 1994 to 2010, he held the Dennis Weatherstone Senior Fellow position at the Peterson Institute. He has written extensively on international economic policy. He is the author of *Banking's Final Exam: Stress Testing and Bank-Capital Reform* (2017, forthcoming), *Managed Floating Plus* (2002), *The Asian Financial Crisis: Causes, Cures, and Systemic Implications* (1998), *The Case for an International Banking Standard* (1997), *The Exchange Rate System and the IMF: A Modest Agenda* (1995), co-editor of *Debating China's Exchange Rate Policy* (2008), *Private Capital Flows to Emerging Markets after the Mexican Crisis* (1996), co-author of *The Future of China's Exchange Rate Policy* (2009) with Nicholas R. Lardy, co-author of *Controlling Currency Mismatches* *in Emerging Markets* (2004) with Philip Turner, co-author of *Assessing Financial Vulnerability: An Early Warning System for Emerging Markets* with Graciela Kaminsky and Carmen Reinhart (2000), and project director of *Safeguarding Prosperity in a Global Financial System: The Future International Financial Architecture* (1999) for the Council on Foreign Relations Task Force on the Future of the International Financial Architecture.

Contents

About the Author   v

Introduction   xiii
By Morris Goldstein

Part I: **Foreign Trade**   1

1. Income and Price Effects in Foreign Trade   3

   By Morris Goldstein and Mohsin S. Khan
   Morris Goldstein and Mohsin S. Khan, "Income and Price Effects in Foreign Trade," Reprinted from Ronald W. Jones and Peter Kenen (editors), Handbook of International Economics, Vol 2, pp. 1041–1105, Copyright (1985) with permission from Elsevier.

2. The Supply and Demand for Exports: A Simultaneous Approach   83

   By Morris Goldstein and Mohsin S. Khan
   Morris Goldstein and Mohsin S. Khan, "The Supply and Demand for Exports: A Simultaneous Approach," The Review of Economics and Statistics, 60:2 (April, 1978),

pp. 275–286. © 1978 by the President and Fellows of Harvard College. Used with permission of the publisher.

3. Prices of Tradable and Nontradable Goods in the Demand for Total Imports — 105

By Morris Goldstein, Mohsin S. Khan, and Lawrence H. Officer

Morris Goldstein, Mohsin S. Khan, and Lawrence H. Officer, "Prices of Tradable and Nontradable Goods in the Demand for Total Imports," The Review of Economics and Statistics, 62:2 (May, 1980), pp. 190–199. © 1980 by the President and Fellows of Harvard College. Used with permission of the publisher.

Part II: Currency Regimes, Exchange Rate Policy and International Policy Coordination — 125

4. Market-Based Fiscal Discipline in Monetary Unions: Evidence from the US Municipal Bond Market — 127

By Morris Goldstein and Geoffrey Woglom

Morris Goldstein and Geoffrey Woglom, "Market-Based Fiscal Discipline in Monetary Unions: Evidence from the U.S. Municipal Bond Market," in Mathew Canzoneri, Vittorio Grilli, and Paul Masson, (editors), Establishing a Central Bank: Issues in Europe and Lessons from the US," Cambridge University Press, 1992.

5. A Guide to Target Zones — 165

By Jacob A. Frenkel and Morris Goldstein

"A Guide to Target Zones" by Jacob A. Frenkel and Morris Goldstein. Reprinted from Vol. 33, No. 4 (December 1986) International Monetary Fund Staff Papers. Copyright © 1986 by the International Monetary Fund. Used with permission of the publisher.

6. Managed Floating Plus 207

 By Morris Goldstein
 "Managed Floating Plus" from Managed Floating Plus, by Morris Goldstein, pp. 43–75 (2002). Peterson Institute for International Economics. Used with permission of the publisher.

7. The Rationale for, and Effects of, International Economic Policy Coordination 241

 By Jacob A. Frenkel, Morris Goldstein, and Paul R. Masson
 Jacob A. Frenkel, Morris Goldstein, and Paul R. Masson, "The Rationale for, and Effects of International Economic Policy Coordination," in William Branson, Jacob A. Frenkel, and Morris Goldstein (editors), International Policy Coordination and Exchange Rate Fluctuations, pp. 9–55 (1990). University of Chicago Press and NBER. Used with permission of the publishers.

Part III: Banking, Financial Crises and Financial Regulation 299

8. Banking Crises in Emerging Economies: Origins and Policy Options 301

 By Morris Goldstein and Philip Turner
 "Banking Crises in Emerging Economies: Origins and Policy Options", by Morris Goldstein and Philip Turner. Copyright © 1996 by Bank for International Settlements. Used with permission of the publisher.

9. An International Banking Standard: The Time is Ripe 365

 By Morris Goldstein
 Morris Goldstein, "An International Banking Standard: The Time is Ripe," in George C. Kaufman (editor), Research in Financial Services: Private and Public Policy, Volume 9, pp. 99–106. Copyright © 1997 by JAI Press Inc., Emerald Group Publishing Limited. Used with permission of the publisher.

x   Contents

10. Origins of the Crisis   375

   By Morris Goldstein
   "Origins of the Crisis" from The Asian Financial Crisis: Causes, Cures, and Systemic Implications by Morris Goldstein, pp. 1–22 (1998). Peterson Institute for International Economics. Used with permission of the publisher.

11. Methodology and Empirical Results   397

   By Morris Goldstein, Graciela Kaminsky and Carmen Reinhart
   "Methodology" and "Empirical Results" from Assessing Financial Vulnerability by Morris Goldstein, Graciela L. Kaminsky and Carmen M. Reinhart, pp. 11–44 (2000). Peterson Institute for International Economics. Used with permission of the publisher.

12. Measuring Currency Mismatch and Aggregate Effective Currency Mismatch   437

   By Morris Goldstein and Philip Turner
   "Measuring Currency Mismatch: Beyond Original Sin" and "Aggregate Effective Currency Mismatch" from Controlling Currency Mismatches in Emerging Markets by Morris Goldstein and Philip Turner, pp. 21–56 (2004). Peterson Institute for International Economics. Used with permission of the publisher.

13. The Case for an Orderly Resolution Regime for Systemically-Important Financial Institutions   483

   By Rodgin Cohen and Morris Goldstein
   "The Case for an Orderly Resolution Regime for Systemically-Important Financial Institutions" by Rodgin Cohen and Morris Goldstein. Copyright © 2009 by The Pew Charitable Trusts. Used with permission of the publisher.

14. The 2014 EU-Wide Bank Stress Test Lacks Credibility   503

    By Morris Goldstein
    "The 2014 EU-wide bank stress test lacks credibility" by Morris Goldstein. Copyright © 2014 by VOX, CEPR's Policy Portal. Used with permission of the publisher.

Part IV: IMF Policies   509

15. Evaluating Fund Stabilization Programs with MultiCountry Data: Some Methodological Pitfalls   511

    By Morris Goldstein and Peter Montiel
    "Evaluating Fund Stabilization Programs with Multicountry Data" by Morris Goldstein and Peter Montiel. Reprinted from Vol. 33 No. 2 (June 1986) International Monetary Fund Staff Papers. Copyright © 1986 by International Monetary Fund. Used with permission of the publisher.

16. IMF Structural Programs   553

    By Morris Goldstein
    Morris Goldstein, "IMF Structural Programs," in Martin Feldstein (editor), Economic and Financial Crises in Emerging Market Economies, pp. 363–437 (2003). University of Chicago Press and NBER. Used with permission of the publishers.

17. The Fund Appears to be Sleeping at the Wheel   639

    By Morris Goldstein and Michael Mussa
    "The Fund appears to be sleeping at the wheel" by Morris Goldstein and Michael Mussa. Originally published in the Financial Times, October 2, 2005.

18. Currency Manipulation and Enforcing the Rules
of the International Monetary System 643

By Morris Goldstein
"Currency Manipulation and Enforcing the Rules of the
International Monetary System" by Morris Goldstein from
Reforming the IMF for the 21st Century, Edwin M. Truman,
editor, pp. 141–155 (April 2006). Peterson Institute for
International Economics. Used with permission of the publisher.

Part V: China's Exchange Rate Policies 661

19. Two-Stage Currency Reform for China 663

By Morris Goldstein and Nicolas Lardy
"Two-Stage Currency reform for China" by Morris Goldstein
and Nicholas Lardy. Originally published in the Wall Street
Journal, September 12, 2003.

20. China's Exchange Rate Policy Dilemma 667

By Morris Goldstein and Nicholas Lardy
Morris Goldstein and Nicholas Lardy, "China's Exchange
Rate Policy Dilemma," American Economic Review, Vol 96,
No. 2, pp. 422–426, 2006. Used with permission of the publisher.

21. Challenges Facing the Chinese Authorities Under the
Existing Currency Regime 677

By Morris Goldstein and Nicholas Lardy
Morris Goldstein and Nicholas Lardy, "Challenges Facing the
Chinese Authorities Under the Existing Currency Regime," in
Morris Goldstein and Nicholas Lardy, The Future of China's
Exchange Rate Policy, pp. 27–82 (2009). Peterson Institute
for International Economics. Used with permission of the publisher.

Introduction to Trade, Currencies, and Finance

Morris Goldstein

The 21 papers collected in this volume were written between 1978 and 2014. About three-quarters of the papers were collaborations with a wonderful and talented group of co-authors, many of which remain good friends today.

By choice, the included papers encompass the different outlets for my writings — from very short editorials (op-eds) on economic controversies of the day (published in financial newspapers), to technical empirical papers based on more formal hypothesis testing (published in leading economic journals), to much longer analyses of macroeconomic policy questions (published in conference volumes or my own books).

Taken as a group, the collected papers shine a light on many of the important research and policy issues in international economics over the past 40 years or so. I believe that those issues remain highly relevant today. In this Introduction, I identify several key questions that are addressed in each of the 21 papers. The papers are divided up into five subject areas: (i) foreign trade; (ii) currency regimes, exchange rate policy, and international policy coordination; (iii) banking, financial crises, and financial regulation; (iv) IMF policies; and (v) China's exchange rate policies.

PART I: FOREIGN TRADE

Chapter 1: Goldstein and Khan on Income and Price Effects in Foreign Trade

- How should the time-series behavior of imports and exports be modeled? How should the model for manufactured goods (imperfect substitutes) differ from the model for primary commodities (perfect substitutes)?
- Is the sum of long-run price elasticities of demand for imports and exports in advanced economies large enough to allow an exchange rate depreciation to improve the trade balance (is the Marshall-Lerner condition usually satisfied)?
- Are short-run price elasticities of demand for imports and exports much smaller than long-run ones; what about differences is short-run versus long-run income elasticities of demand for imports and exports?
- What are representative estimates of the effect of import price changes on aggregate domestic price indices?

Chapter 2: Goldstein and Khan on The Supply and Demand for Exports

- Is it reasonable to assume an infinite export price-elasticity of supply for an individual country?
- How should an export supply equation best be specified, and can export supply and demand be integrated in a simultaneous approach?
- What are representative estimates of the export elasticity of supply for advanced economies?

Chapter 3: Goldstein, Khan, and Officer on Prices of Tradable and Nontradable Goods in the Demand for Imports

- Is it justifiable in specifying the demand for imports to include only one relative price, namely, that between imports and domestic tradable goods, and to ignore the prices of nontradable goods
- If one did want to drop this assumption of "separability" and test for the influence of nontradable goods prices on import demand, how would one construct an index of nontradable goods prices?

Introduction to Trade, Currencies, and Finance xv

- Do empirical import-demand equations for advanced economies justify leaving out the price of nontradable goods?

PART II: CURRENCY REGIMES, EXCHANGE RATE POLICY, AND INTERNATIONAL POLICY COORDINATION

Chapter 4: Goldstein and Woglom on Market-Based Fiscal Discipline in Monetary Unions

- What constraints should be placed on national fiscal polices in a currency union?
- Can market-based fiscal discipline (a rising default premium on the debt of the member-country running excessive fiscal deficits) be expected to rein-in fiscal policy excesses?
- What insights into this market-discipline issue can be gleaned from estimating the relationship between the cost of borrowing and the measures of default risk in the US municipal bond market?

Chapter 5: Frenkel and Goldstein on A Guide to Target Zones

- What is meant by a target-zone approach to exchange rate management?
- What are the perceived deficiencies in the other exchange rate systems that have motivated a call for the adoption of target zones?
- How would target zones (allegedly) remedy these deficiencies?
- What factors are behind the skepticism over and opposition to target zones?

Chapter 6: Goldstein on Managed Floating Plus

- What are the key characteristics of a "managed floating plus" exchange rate regime for emerging-market economies with high capital mobility?
- Why are all three components of this regime (that is, managed floating, inflation targeting, and measures to discourage currency mismatching) necessary to make it function effectively?
- What advantages for emerging economies does a managed floating plus currency regime possess over the competition (adjustable pegs, crawling bands, currency boards, and dollarization)?

Chapter 7: Frenkel, Goldstein, and Masson on The Rationale for, and Effects of, International Policy Coordination

- Why is international policy coordination beneficial?
- What are the main barriers to effective international policy coordination?
- What is the appropriate range and depth of economic policies to be coordinated?
- What are the leading alternatives mechanisms for coordination and what are their pros and cons?
- Judging from simulations with multi-country models (e.g., the IMF's MULTIMOD model) what are the effects of international policy coordination?

PART III: BANKING, FINANCIAL CRISES, AND FINANCIAL REGULATION

Chapter 8: Goldstein and Turner on Banking Crises in Emerging Economies

- Why do banking crises in developing countries merit particular attention?
- What are the leading factors contributing to the high incidence of banking crises in developing countries?
- What are the policy options for strengthening banking systems in these countries?

Chapter 9: Goldstein on An International Banking Standard

- Why is an international banking standard needed?
- What guidelines should be included in such a standard?
- Who would set the standard?
- How would compliance with the standard be monitored and encouraged?

Chapter 10: Goldstein on The Origins of the (Asian Financial) Crisis

- Which countries were at the eye of the Asian financial crisis of 1997-98?
- What were the multiple origins of this crisis?

Introduction to Trade, Currencies, and Finance   xvii

Chapter 11: Goldstein, Kaminsky, and Reinhart on Methodology and Empirical Results (for an early warning system for emerging economies)

- What guidelines should influence the design of an early-system for forecasting currency and banking crises in emerging economies?
- Why is the "signals approach" the preferred methodology for forecasting currency and banking crises in our sample of 25 emerging economies over the 1970-1995 period (with 1996 and 1997 reserved for out-of-sample exercises)?
- What should the 15 early-warning indicators tested in this early-warning exercise be?
- How should the optimal thresholds for each indicator be estimated?
- Which early-warning indicators proved to be the best ones based on their in-sample and out-of-sample forecasts?

Chapter 12: Goldstein and Turner on Measuring Currency Mismatch

- How should currency mismatch be defined?
- Why is "original sin" a poor measure of currency mismatch?
- Why is our new measure of "aggregate effective currency mismatch" an advance over earlier measures of currency mismatch?
- Are large negative currency mismatches either leading or contemporaneous with currency and banking crises in emerging economies over the 1994-2002 period?

Chapter 13: Cohen and Goldstein on The Case for an Orderly Resolution Regime for Systemically-Important Financial institutions

- Why is a new Orderly Resolution Regime (ORR) for Systemically-Important Financial Institutions (SIFIs) needed?
- Will a New ORR be over-used and will it increase moral hazard going forward?
- How should an ORR for SIFIs be designed?

Chapter 14: Goldstein on Why the 2014 EU-Wide Bank Stress Test Lacks Credibility

- What were the four key findings of the 2014 EU-wide stress test and accompanying Asset Quality Review (AQR)?
- Why were these findings not credible?
- Why was this test a missed opportunity for the ECB to gain credibility as the Single Supervisor for Europe's largest banks?

PART IV: IMF POLICIES

Chapter 15: Goldstein and Montiel on Evaluating Fund Stabilization Programs with MultiCountry Data: Some Methodological Pitfalls

- How have the effects of Fund (IMF) stabilization programs been estimated in the past?
- Why do the "before-after" approach and the "control group approach" yield estimates of program effects that differ from "true" program effects?
- How can a "modified control-group approach" remove sample-selectivity bias and produce a non-biased estimate of program effects when the selection of program countries is non-random?
- What operational issues need to be confronted when using the modified control group approach?

Chapter 16: Goldstein on IMF Structural Programs

- What are "structural policies"?
- Why has there been active debate on the scope and intrusiveness of IMF policy conditionality over structural policies since the 1997-1998 Asian financial crisis?
- What would alternative mandates for the Fund imply about the intrusiveness of structural policy conditionality?
- What has the structural content of Fund policy conditionality and its effectiveness been?
- Have the product of the number of Fund structural policy conditions and the effectiveness of those conditions been roughly equal to a constant?

Introduction to Trade, Currencies, and Finance   xix

- What are the alternative approaches to streamlining Fund structural policy conditionality?

Chapter 17: Goldstein and Mussa on the Fund Sleeping at the Wheel

- Has the Fund been asleep at the wheel on its most fundamental responsibility, namely, firm surveillance over its members' exchange rate policies?
- Why was large-scale, prolonged, one-way intervention in exchange markets by several Asian economies (and particularly by China) – to resist meaningful appreciation of their currencies in 2004-2006 – contrary to their responsibilities as members of the IMF?
- Why should the international community insist that the IMF does its assigned job as the vigorous, competent, unbiased, international umpire for exchange rate policies?

Chapter 18: Goldstein on Currency Manipulation and Enforcing the Rules of the International Monetary System

- Why are international codes of conduct on exchange rate policies needed?
- Why are several popular arguments denying that currency manipulation took place over the 2004-2006 period seriously flawed?
- What is the evidence that China was engaging in currency manipulation over the 2004-2006 period?
- What can be done to reduce the frequency and scale of currency manipulation?

PART V: CHINA'S EXCHANGE RATE POLICIES

Chapter 19: Goldstein and Lardy on Two-Stage Currency Reform for China

- How could the circle (in 2003) be squared that seemingly called for three objectives: a near term revaluation of the yuan, greater stability of the yuan in the medium term, and greater flexibility and market determination of the yuan down the road?

- Imagine (in 2003) a two-step reform of China's currency regime. Step one would consist of a medium-size (15-25%) revaluation of the yuan, a widening of the currency band (to 5-7% from less than 1%), and a switch from a unitary peg to the dollar to a three-currency basket peg. Step two would be adoption of a managed float. Would such a two-step reform process solve China's currency dilemma?
- Why was this two-step currency reform superior to the alternatives favored (in 2003) by both the Chinese government and the US government?

Chapter 20: Goldstein and Lardy on China's Exchange Rate Policy Dilemma

- Was the currency reform announced by China on July 21, 2005 a meaningful change, and if not, why not?
- Was the Chinese RMB undervalued (in 2005), and if so, by how much?
- What problems did the 2005 currency regime pose for China and the global economy?
- What was constraining China's willingness and ability to deal with the shortcomings of its currency regime and what would be a reasonable compromise solution?

Chapter 21: Goldstein and Lardy on Challenges Facing the Chinese Authorities under the Existing (2009) Currency Regime

- Was the RMB highly undervalued at the end of 2007?
- How did an increasingly undervalued exchange rate, a rapidly expanding current account surplus, and a concomitant accelerating buildup of foreign exchange reserves pose challenges for the independence of monetary policy, the rebalancing of the sources of economic growth, efforts to reform China's banking system, and China's external adjustment?
- Would an RMB appreciation have had much effect on China's global current-account adjustment?

I have enjoyed very much writing working on this set of papers over the past 40 years. I hope you the reader will enjoy reading them.

February 2017

Part I
Foreign Trade

Chapter 1

Income and Price Effects in Foreign Trade*

Morris Goldstein and Mohsin S. Khan

1. INTRODUCTION

Few areas in all of economics, and probably none within international economics itself, have been subject to as much empirical investigation over the past thirty five years as the behavior of foreign trade flows. Reasons for this unusual degree of attention are not hard to find. First, the data base is a rich one.[1] Statistics on the value of imports and exports extend over long time periods and can be disaggregated by commodity and by region

---

*The views expressed are the sole responsibility of the authors and do not necessarily reflect the views of the IMF. We are grateful to Jacques Artus, William Branson, Robert Cumby, Michael Dooley, David Folkerts–Landau, John Helliwell, William Hemphill, Peter Kenen, Malcolm Knight, Anne McGuirk, and Tim Padmore for helpful comments on an earlier draft.

[1] The availability of trade data was surely a contributing factor to the advanced nature of the early empirical work on trade models. It is sufficient to note that by 1957 there already existed, inter alia: (i) at least 42 books and articles containing estimates of income and price elasticities for imports and exports [see Cheng's (1959) survey]; (ii) several superb methodological criticisms [Orcutt (1950), Harberger (1953)] that explained why estimated price elasticities could differ from the true elasticities; and (iii) at least one complete simultaneous model of import demand and supply [Morgan and Corlett (1951)], actually estimated by limited-information maximum likelihood methods, that displays the authors' awareness of many of the methodological issues that still entertain current research.

of origin or destination to a relatively fine level.[2] Second, the underlying theoretical framework for the determination of trade volumes and prices is a familiar one from consumer demand and production theory, and can make do with relatively few explanatory variables, most of which have accessible empirical counterparts. Third, the estimated income and price elasticities of demand and supply have seemingly wide application to a host of important macro-economic policy issues, including but not limited to: the international transmission of changes in economic activity and prices, the impact of both expenditure-reducing (monetary and fiscal) policies and expenditure-switching (exchange rate, tariff, subsidy) policies on a country's trade balance, the welfare and employment implications of changes in own or partner-countries' trade restrictions, and the severity of external balance constraints on domestic policy choices.

In this chapter the aim is to identify, summarize, and evaluate the main methodological and policy issues that have surrounded the estimation of trade equations. By "trade equations" we mean equations for the time-series behavior of the quantities and prices of merchandise imports and exports,[3] and as the title of the chapter suggests, we focus explicitly on the role played by income and prices in the determination of these trade variables.

Our task is made easier by the admirable coverage of the early empirical literature and of many specific topics in trade modelling in previous survey papers. Indeed, trade surveys have appeared at least once every five years since 1959. Early (1936–57) estimates of income propensities and price elasticities have been surveyed and evaluated by Cheng (1959) and by Prais (1962). Early world trade models are discussed in Taplin (1973), and more recent multi-country models are compared and analyzed by Deardorff and Stern (1977) and by Fair (1979). Special mention should be made of the comprehensive trade surveys of Leamer and Stern (1970), Magee (1975), and Stern *et al.* (1976). The Leamer and Stern (1970) book has, among other things, a lucid discussion of the time-series estimation of import and export demand relationships. In this chapter we have tried to update and expand upon their analysis of methodological issues; in particular; we devote more attention to

---

[2] Branson (1980), for example, in his paper on trends in U.S. international trade, present data on U.S. trade balances by end-use commodity that extend back to 1925.
[3] Empirical work on international trade in services (or "invisibles") is still quite limited; see Bond (1980) and the references cited therein.

supply relationships.[4] Magee's (1975) trade survey is the broadest one available, encompassing methodological questions, empirical evidence, pure trade and monetary theory, and associated policy issues. We inevitably therefore cover some of the same ground but we have tried to minimize duplication.[5] Finally, Stern *et al.* (1976) have provided an exhaustive annotated bibliography of price elasticity studies in international trade spanning the 1960–1975 period, as well as summary tables of "median" price elasticities broken down by commodity group and by country. We offer our own updated "consensus" price and income elasticities which partially reflect Stern *et al.*'s (1976) findings but which also give higher weights to what we regard as the better quality estimates.[6]

The plan of the chapter is as follows. Section 2 addresses the main methodological issues in the specification of trade models. This is basically a discussion about what variables ought in theory to be included in demand and supply functions for imports and exports, what choices and compromises have to be made in the measurement of these variables, and what light existing evidence throws on the choice among competing specifications. Section 3 is concerned with what we call econometric issues in trade modelling. The subjects covered are the treatment of dynamics and time lags, aggregation, simultaneity, and stability of the relationships concerned. Section 4 turns to the empirical estimates of income and price elasticities themselves and to the policy implications of those estimates. Summary tables are constructed from recent empirical studies to illustrate the revealed "consensus", or lack of it, on (i) long-run price and income elasticities of demand for total merchandise

---

[4] We have placed much less emphasis than Leamer and Stern (1970) on the theory and measurement of the elasticity of substitution in international trade and on index number problems associated with aggregation. Further, we do not deal at all with constant-market-share analysis of export growth.

[5] Specifically, we have provided only passing reference to Orcutt's (1950) criticisms of estimated price elasticities; to conflicts between Keynesian, absorption, and monetary approaches to the balance of payments; to estimates of the effects of tariff reductions on trade, and to earlier world trade models. Instead, we have substituted discussions of econometric issues involved with modelling of trade relationships, factors responsible for inter-country differences in price elasticities, feedback effects of exchange rate changes on domestic prices, and conflicts between specifications of demand and supply in trade models and those currently in vogue elsewhere in macroeconomics.

[6] Like the other trade surveys, our review of the empirical evidence concentrates on industrial-country trade. An up-to-date survey of empirical trade models for developing countries still waits to be written.

imports and exports; (ii) the difference between short-run and long-run price elasticities of demand; (iii) price and activity elasticities for broad commodity classes of imports; (iv) supply price elasticities for exports, (v) the so-called "pass-through" of exchange rate changes onto the domestic currency prices of imports and exports; (vi) the elasticity of export price with respect to domestic prices (or labor costs) and competitors' export prices; and (vii) the "feedback" effect of exchange rate changes on domestic prices. Drawing on this evidence, broad conclusions are advanced on the effectiveness of devaluation. Section 5 offers some concluding observations as well as suggestions for further research.

2. SPECIFICATION ISSUES IN TRADE MODELLING

How should the time-series behavior of imports and exports be modelled? In our view, the appropriate model depends on, among other things, the type of good being traded (perfectly homogeneous primary commodities versus highly differentiated manufactured goods), on the end-use to which the traded commodity is being put (whether for final consumption or as a factor input), on the institutional framework under which trade takes place (an economy where resources are allocated via relative prices versus one where administrative controls play the predominant role in allocation), on the purpose of the modelling exercise (forecasting versus hypothesis testing), and sometimes even on the availability of data (e.g. if reliable data exist on trade values but not on volumes).

Nevertheless, it still makes sense as a framework for the discussion of particular specification issues to set out the two general models of trade that have dominated the empirical literature, namely, the imperfect substitutes model and the perfect substitutes model. Since most trade studies have dealt with aggregate imports (exports), the two models have often been viewed as competitors. Once disaggregation is admitted, however, there is no reason why the two models should not be seen as complements — one dealing with trade for differentiated goods, and the other with trade for close — if not perfect — substitutes.[7]

---

[7] Clark (1977) is one of the few studies that actually follows this guideline.

2.1. The Imperfect Substitutes Model

The key underlying assumption of the imperfect substitutes model is that neither imports nor exports are perfect substitutes for domestic goods. Support for this assumption comes from two sources. First, there is the (debating) argument that *if* domestic and foreign goods were perfect substitutes, then one should observe: (i) either the domestic or foreign good swallowing up the whole market when each is produced under constant (or decreasing) costs [Magee (1975)]; and (ii) each country as an exporter or importer of a traded good but not both [Rhomberg (1973)]. Since both of these predictions are counter to fact at both the aggregate and disaggregated level, i.e. one normally observes the coexistence of imports and domestic output and the flourishing of two-way trade, the perfect substitutes hypothesis can be rejected. The second bit of evidence is more direct. A large number of empirical studies [Kreinen and Officer (1978), Isard (1977b), Kravis and Lipsey (1978)] have shown that, even at the most disaggregated level for which comparable data can be gathered, there are significant and nontransitory price differences for the "same" product in different countries (after translation into a common currency), as well as between the domestic and export prices of a given product in the same country. In short, the "law of one price" does *not* seem to hold either across or within countries, except perhaps for standard commodities such as wheat or copper that are sold on international commodity exchanges.[8] It would appear therefore that finite price elasticities of demand and supply can in fact be estimated for most traded goods.

In eqs. (1)–(8) below, we present a "bare-bones" imperfect substitutes model of country i's imports from, and exports to, the rest of the world(*):

$$I_i^d = f(Y_i, PI_i, P_i), \quad f_1, f_3 > 0, \quad f_2 < 0, \tag{1}$$

$$X_i^d = g(Y^*e, PX_i, P^*e), \quad g_1, g_3 > 0, \quad g_2 < 0, \tag{2}$$

$$I_i^s = h[PI^*(1+S^*), P^*], \quad h_1 > 0, \quad h_2 < 0, \tag{3}$$

$$X_i^s = j[PX_i(1+S_i), P_i], \quad j_i > 0, \quad j_2 < 0, \tag{4}$$

$$PI_i = PX^*(1+T_i)e, \tag{5}$$

---

[8]The validity of the law of one price (net of transport costs and other impediments to trade) for these primary commodities is usually assumed rather than tested; see however McCloskey and Zecher (1976) who found support for it in price movement during the period 1870–1913.

$$PI^* = PX_i(1 + T^*)/e, \tag{6}$$

$$I_i^d = I_i^s e, \tag{7}$$

$$X_i^d = X_i^s. \tag{8}$$

These eight equations determine the quantity of imports demanded in country i (I_i^d), the quantity of country i's exports demanded by the rest of the world (X_i^d), the quantity of imports supplied to country i from the rest of the world (I_i^s),[9] the quantity of exports supplied from country i to the rest of the world (X_i^s), the domestic currency prices paid by importers in the two regions (PI_i and PI^*), and the domestic currency prices received by exporters in two regions (PX_i, PX^*). The exogenous variables are the levels of nominal income in the two regions (Y_i, Y^*), the price of (all) domestically produced goods in the two regions (P_i, P^*), the proportional tariff (T_i, T^*) and subsidy rates (S_i, S^*) applied to imports and exports in the two regions, and the exchange rate (e) linking the two currencies (expressed in units of country i's currency per unit of the rest-of-the world's currency).

The main characteristics of the imperfect substitutes model can be summarized as follows. In accordance with conventional demand theory, the consumer is postulated to maximize utility subject to a budget constraint.[10] The resulting demand functions for imports and exports thus represent the quantity demanded as a function of the level of (money) income in the importing region, the imported good's own price, and the price of domestic substitutes. For aggregate imports or exports, the possibilities of inferior goods and of domestic complements for imports are typically excluded, so that income elasticities (f_1 and g_1) and cross-price elasticities of demand (f_3 and g_3) are assumed to be positive,[11] whereas the own-price elasticities of demand (f_2 and g_2) are of course expected to be negative. Most often, the additional assumption is made that the consumer has no money illusion,

---

[9] This is, of course, the supply of exports of the rest of the world to country i.

[10] When the importer is a producer and when imports are intermediate goods that are inputs to the domestic technology, the demand for imports can analogously be derived by maximizing production subject to the producer's cost constraint. In that case, the resulting import demand function will have as its arguments the price of imports, the price of the domestic (composite) input, and the level of domestic gross output; for example, see Burgess (1974), and Kohli (1982).

[11] Less assurance about the signs of the income elasticity and cross-price elasticities is warranted when the demand equations are disaggregated by commodity or by region of origin or destination of the trade flow; see Magee (1975, p. 179).

so that a doubling of money income and all prices leaves demand constant, i.e. $f_1 + f_2 + f_3 = 0$, $g_1 + g_2 + g_3 = 0$. In its most common form, such homogeneity of the demand function is expressed by dividing the right-hand-side of eq. (1) by P_i so that the two arguments of the demand function become the level of *real* income (Y_i/P_i) and the relative price of imports (PI_i/P_i). In this simple model, only current income matters for import (export) demand, and no distinction is made between secular or cyclical income movements or between transitory and permanent income. Also note from eqs. (5) and (6) that the price of imports relevant for import demand is the landed domestic-currency price inclusive of all charges (tariffs, transportation, etc.) actually paid by the purchaser.

When we leave the two-country model for the *n*-country real world, the symmetry between the import demand eq. (1) and the export demand eq. (2) disappears. This is because a country's total imports face competition only from domestic producers, whereas a country's total exports face competition not only from domestic producers in the importing region but also from "third country" exporters to that region. Indeed, the conventional practice in specifying export demand equations is to assume that the dominant relative price competition occurs among exporters. Thus, the only relative-price term that typically appears is the ratio of the export price to competitors' export prices (PX_c) adjusted for exchange rate change, i.e. ($PX_i/PX_c \cdot e$).[12] In much of the empirical literature, the estimation of price effects on export demand has in fact been carried out within an "elasticity of substitution" framework. The demand equation then takes the form:

$$X_i^d/X^{d*} = v(PX_i/PX^* e), \quad v' < 0, \tag{2'}$$

where X^{d*} is the demand for exports to the rest of the world from third countries. One deficiency of eq. (2') compared to eq. (2), especially as regards aggregate exports, is that the former implicitly assumes that the income elasticities of demand for exports from country i and for those from third countries are the same in the rest of the world.[13] As there is no a priori reason

---

[12]This restriction is often rationalized by the fact that industrial countries are their own principal competitors, so that PX_i/PX_c and PX_i/P_i will move together so long as domestic prices (P) and export prices (PX) are linked within countries.

[13]See Leamer and Stern (1970). For further analysis of the concept of "elasticity of substitution," see Richardson (1973).

for this to hold, imposing such a restriction without first testing it is likely to involve some misspecification.

The specification of the two supply eqs. (3) and (4) are identical, with the quantity supplied assumed to be a positive function of the own price and a negative function of the price of domestic goods in the exporting country. Imposition of homogeneity on the supply function is equivalent to the restriction that $-h_1 = h_2$ in eq. (3), and $-j_1 = j_2$ in eq. (4). Although the theory of export supply is still very much a contested and unresolved subject in empirical trade work, the basic idea behind eqs. (3) and (4) is a simple one. The supply of exports will increase with the profitability of producing and selling exports. Therefore, the domestic price index (P) serves a dual role in the supply functions. First, for a given level of the export price, the profitability of producing exports falls when factor costs in the export industries increase. As these factor costs are likely to move with the general level of domestic prices, P serves as a proxy for them. Second, to the extent that resources involved in exportables production can be transferred to other uses or that the export price of a given good can be kept different from the domestic price, the relative profitability of selling exports falls with an increase in domestic prices.[14] At the aggregate level, the domestic price index includes prices of tradable goods (PT) sold at home as well as the price of nontradables (PNT), i.e. $P = xPT + (1-x)PNT$, where x is the weight of tradables in domestic consumption. Thus, the aggregate export supply functions (3) and (4) accommodate supply substitution between the home and export market for a given tradable good in the manner of the price-discriminating monopolist, as well as substitution between production of all tradables and nontradables.

Note that the relevant own price in the export supply functions is the price actually received by the exporter, inclusive of any subsidies (S) or other incentives or penalties for exporting, and that the price is expressed in domestic currency terms. This latter seemingly innocuous point carries one significant implication. Even if the country is "small" in the sense that it cannot affect

---

[14]The model described by eqs. (1)–(8) does not really explain *why* domestic prices should not equal export prices. In the literature, the three main explanations for such a divergence are different demand elasticities in the home and export market, different cost structures for home and export production, or simply distortions in the market.

the *foreign* currency prices of either its imports or its exports, it can still affect its export volume to the extent that it can affect the *internal* profitability of producing and/or selling exportables. For example, even in a situation where import demand is very price inelastic ($f_2, f_3 \approx 0$), where exports must carry the same foreign currency price everywhere ($PX_i/PX_c e = 1$), and where the export price cannot be separated from the domestic price of tradables ($PX/PT = 1$), a devaluation can nevertheless have some potency (aside from expenditure-reducing effects) via its impact on the internal terms of trade between exports and nontradables (PX/PNT).

An advantage of presenting the supply side as well as the demand side of the imperfect substitutes model is to make it plain that the relationship between quantities and prices is, at least in theory, simultaneous. Despite this fundamental point, strongly emphasized in the trade literature of the 1950s [Orcutt (1950), Harberger (1953)], the bulk of the time-series work on import and export equations has addressed the supply side only by assumption. Specifically, the prevailing practice has been to assume that the supply-price elasticities for imports and exports [i.e. h_1 in eq. (3) and j_1 in eq. (4), respectively] are infinite. The great allure of such an assumption is that it permits satisfactory estimation of the import and export demand eqs. (1) and (2) by single-equation methods, since PI_i and PX_i can then be viewed as exogenous; conversely, if the supply elasticities are less than infinite, one should either estimate the full structural simultaneous model or solve for and estimate the reduced-form expressions for quantities and prices as functions of only the exogenous variables in the system. We shall have more to say on the simultaneity issue later. For now, it is sufficient to argue that the infinite supply-elasticity assumption is more defensible for a country's imports than for its exports. The rest of the world may well be able to increase its supply of exports to a single country without an increase in price, but it is less likely that even a large single country can increase its total export supply at a constant price unless there exists a large pool of unemployed resources in the export industry itself or elsewhere in the economy.

Our final comments on the imperfect substitutes model are caveats about the true "exogeneity" of at least one key exogenous variable (namely, domestic prices), about the legitimacy of an export supply function under conditions of less than perfect competition, and about the "equilibrium" or market-clearing property of the model.

On the first point, there is by now a considerable body of empirical evidence [see Goldstein (1980), Kenen and Pack (1979), and Section 4] that suggests that domestic prices (P_i), export prices in domestic currency terms (PX_i) and money wages rates are each strongly influenced by exchange rate changes (Δe) and by changes in foreign export prices (ΔPX^*), especially in small, highly-open economies with wage indexation schemes. The implication of such domestic price "feedback" effects, i.e. lack of exogeneity for P_i in eqs. (1)–(4), is that high price elasticities offer no guarantee that devaluation or other expenditure-switching policies will actually be effective in altering a country's trade balance.[15] If P_i rises by close to, or equal to, the same proportion as PI_i and PX_i in eqs. (1) and (4) respectively, then the *relative* price changes induced by such policy actions will be small.

A second caveat is that export supply functions, like eqs. (3) and (4), can in theory exist independently of the demand functions only under conditions of perfect competition [Basevi (1973)]. Only under perfect competition is it legitimate to regard the export price as exogenous, that is as beyond the influence of the quantity supplied by any individual exporting country. For this reason, many trade researchers have chosen instead to work with reduced-form export price equations where the quantity of exports does not appear at all. Following the empirical literature on domestic pricing under imperfect competition [e.g. Eckstein and Fromm (1968)], some such as Clark (1977) have assumed that the export price is set as a "markup" (λ) on the level of normal unit labor cost (Z),[16] with the size of the markup varying positively with the state of excess demand at home ($Y_i/\bar{Y}_i$) and abroad ($Y^*/\bar{Y}^*$), and with the level of competitors' export prices (PX_c)[17]:

$$PX_i = \lambda(Z, Y_i/\bar{Y}_i, Y^*/\bar{Y}^*, PX_c), \quad \lambda_1, \lambda_2, \lambda_3, \lambda_4 > 0. \qquad (4')$$

---

[15] We abstract here from the expenditure-reducing role of exchange rates or tariffs via their effect on the real value of money balances; on this latter role, see Frenkel and Johnson (1976).

[16] Normal unit labor cost is usually defined as the wage rate divided by the trend or normal level of real output per man hour.

[17] Another route is to derive the export price from the profit-maximizing conditions for a discriminating monopolist [see Artus (1977)]. The resulting estimating equation for PX, however, is usually quite similar to the one obtained from the markup model.

Note that eq. (4′) has many similarities to the reduced-form equation that would emerge from solving the *structural* demand and supply eqs. (2) and (4) for PX_i in terms of only the exogenous variables. This also explains why there has often been some confusion about whether the explanatory variables in export price equations like eq. (4′) represent supply or demand influences.

Turning to the equilibrium characteristic of the imperfect substitutes model as represented in eqs. (7) and (8), the implicit assumption is that prices move to equate supply and demand in each time period. This assumption, however, can be viewed as inconsistent with much of modern pricing theory, which argues that there are costs to changing prices in imperfectly competitive markets and that firms consequently will want to balance the costs of changing prices against the costs of other adjustment measures, such as changing inventories (stocks), unfilled orders (queues), and output itself [e.g. Hay (1970)].[18] This literature on "sticky prices" carries two suggestions for the specification of the imperfect substitutes trade model. One is that if the market-clearing property of the model is to be retained, then nonprice rationing variables should be included in both the demand and supply equations so that price changes alone are not responsible for market-clearing and the "full" or "effective" price actually faced by buyers and sellers governs demand and supply.[19] A second alternative solution is to postulate that observed trade quantities and prices reflect markets in "disequilibrium" and accordingly, then to specify what the adjustment mechanisms are. For example, one can postulate that export prices respond to excess demand while export quantities respond to excess supply, or vice versa [Goldstein and Khan (1978)]; alternatively, one can argue that observed quantities and prices represent the lower of export demand or supply and then use recent econometric techniques [Fair and Kelejian (1974), Minford (1978)] to identify which observations correspond to periods of excess supply and which to excess demand. In short, the equilibrium characterization of the imperfect substitutes model is only one of several possibilities.

---

[18] Such price stickiness is regarded as a key factor in recent explanations of both exchange rate "overshooting" and the failure of purchasing power parity to work in the short run [see Dornbusch and Jaffee (1978)].

[19] By the "full" or "effective" price, we mean the observed price plus other implicit costs (e.g. waiting times, storage costs) paid by buyers and sellers.

2.2. The Perfect Substitutes Model

Even though the imperfect substitutes model has been the mainstay of empirical work on trade equations, there are at least three reasons for examining the perfect substitutes model as well. First, despite many man-made impediments to arbitrage such as tariffs, quotas, and special preferential trading relationships, there is no denying that there are homogeneous commodities (wheat, copper, sugar, etc.) that are traded on organized international commodity markets at a common price (net of transportation and interest costs and expressed in terms of a common currency). For such "standard" commodities, a framework is needed where demands and supplies do not depend on price differentials between domestic and foreign goods. Second, it is possible that international differences in the methodology of constructing price statistics (e.g. weighting patterns, survey methods, index number formulae) can lead to observed international price differences for a given good or bundle of goods that understate the true degree of substitutability. In other words, some traded industrial goods may be closer substitutes than the (imperfect) price statistics would suggest. Third and finally, there may be insights about price and income elasticities for imports and exports that emerge from a perfect substitutes framework that do not when goods are assumed to be imperfect substitutes.

Equations (9)–(16) below constitute a simple perfect substitutes model of trade for our representative country i:

$$D_i = 1(P_i, Y_i), \quad 1_1 < 0, \quad 1_2 > 0 \tag{9}$$

$$S_i = n(P_i, F_i), \quad n_1 > 0, \quad n_2 < 0 \tag{10}$$

$$I_i = D_i - S_i, \tag{11}$$

$$X_i = S_i - D_i, \tag{12}$$

$$PI_i = P_i = PX_i = e \cdot P_w, \tag{13}$$

$$D_w = \sum_{i=1}^{m} D_i, \tag{14}$$

$$S_w = \sum_{i=1}^{m} S_i, \tag{15}$$

$$D_w = S_w. \tag{16}$$

In this perfect substitutes model, D_i is the total quantity of traded goods demanded in country i; S_i is the supply of traded goods produced in country i; I_i and X_i are the quantities of country i's imports and exports; PI_i, PX_i, P_i, and P_w are the import, export, domestic, and world prices of traded goods; D_w and S_w are the world demand and supply of traded goods; and Y_i and F_i are money income and factor costs in country i.

For the purposes of this chapter there are three main features of the perfect substitutes model. First, contrary to the imperfect substitutes model, there are no separate import demand or export supply functions. Instead, the demand for imports and the supply of exports represent the "excess" demand and "excess" supply respectively for domestic goods; see eqs. (11) and (12). This means that estimating or forecasting import demand or export supply for a perfectly substitutable good is really a matter of forecasting domestic demand and domestic supply, with imports or exports emerging as the residual. In practice, this often turns out to be more difficult than it sounds because estimates of domestic demand and supply elasticities are usually harder to obtain than those for imports or exports, and because the primary commodities that best fit the perfect substitutes mold are usually subject to "stock" as well as "flow" demand (with the former requiring specifications of price expectation schemes). Second, and again in contrast to the imperfect substitutes model, once we abstract from transportation costs and other trade barriers (e.g. tariffs) and express all prices in a common currency, then there is only one traded goods price in the perfect substitutes model (i.e. $P_t = PI_i = PX_i = P_w$); furthermore, this (world) price is determined by the interaction of *world* supply and *world* demand for the traded good.[20] Put in other words, country i will only be able to affect the world price of the traded good to the extent that it can affect either world supply or world demand. In general, it can be shown [Isard (1977a), Clark (1977)] that in the absence of inventory and backlog changes, a country's ability to influence the world price of a homogeneous good will depend (positively) on both its share of world consumption (imports) and world production (exports) and on the value of its own price elasticities of

---

[20] Once nontraded goods are admitted, however, their prices (PNT) would enter the aggregate demand equation (9) with a positive sign. Similarly, once disaggregation is permitted, prices of "other" traded goods may enter the demand equation. Still, the essence of the model is that the same product, as long as it is freely traded, should carry the same price everywhere.

demand and supply for that good.[21] If the country is too "small" to affect the world price of the traded good, then an increase in domestic supply will reduce import demand directly (without any change in price). In contrast, the same increase in domestic supply in the imperfect substitutes model would reduce import demand via its effect on P_i and hence on the relative price of imports, PI_i/P_i; see eq. (1).

Yet a third noteworthy feature of the perfect substitutes model is that it yields several implications for inter-country differences in price elasticities of supply and demand for imports and exports that do not emerge from the imperfect substitutes model. Specifically, using eqs. (12) and (13) and employing standard definitions of price elasticities of demand and supply, it is possible to relate the price elasticity of demand for imports (ε_I^d) and the price elasticity of supply for exports (ε_x^s) to the domestic demand ($1_1 < 0$) and supply-price elasticities ($n_1 > 0$) of eqs. (9) and (10) as follows:[22,23]

$$\varepsilon_I^d = \frac{D_i}{I_i} \cdot 1_1 - \frac{S_i}{I_i} n_1, \tag{17}$$

$$\varepsilon_x^s = \frac{S_i}{X_i} n_1 - \frac{D_i}{X_i} 1_1. \tag{18}$$

Equation (17) states that the price elasticity of demand for imports (ε_I^d) of a homogeneous good will be positively related to the (absolute) values of the domestic demand and supply price elasticities, and negatively related to the shares of imports in domestic demand and in domestic production of the good. This proposition has often been advanced by "elasticity optimists" to support the claim that import price elasticities of demand can be high even for relatively inelastic products, and the more so the more closed the economy, namely when the ratios I_i/D_i and I_i/S_i are low. As noted by Magee (1975), at least the former implication of eq. (17) seems to be consistent with empirical evidence

---

[21] To see this, take the total differentials of eqs. (15) and (16), set $D_w = S_w$, and solve for d P_w.
[22] These derivations can be found in most international economics textbooks; for example, see Kreinin (1979).
[23] If an income term is added to the supply eq. (10), it is similarly possible to relate the income elasticity of demand for imports to income elasticities of demand and supply for domestic goods and to the shares of imports in domestic demand and in total supply; see Magee (1975, p. 189).

in the sense that estimated import price elasticities of demand typically exceed estimated domestic price elasticities of demand.[24]

Turning to eq. (18), it similarly suggests that the export supply elasticity (ε_x^s) will be positively related to the (absolute) value of the domestic demand price elasticity and negatively to the supply price elasticity and the shares of exports in domestic demand and in total supply of the good. Unfortunately, comparable estimates of domestic and export supply elasticities simply do not exist, so it is not possible to draw any conclusions as to whether the latter are larger than the former.

Finally, if we let the quantity of world exports (X_w) equal the sum of country i's exports (X_i) and the exports of the rest of the world (X^*), country i's export price elasticity of demand $(\varepsilon_x^d)_i$ can be related to the export price elasticity of demand $(\varepsilon_x^d)_w$ and to the export price elasticity of supply $(\varepsilon_x^s)^*$ in the rest of the world:

$$(\varepsilon_x^d)_i = (X_w/X_i)(\varepsilon_x^d)_w - (X^*/X_i)(\varepsilon_x^s)^* \tag{19}$$

The implication of eq. (19) is again on the side of the "elasticity optimists", for even if the global export price elasticity of demand for a homogeneous good is relatively small, a single country's export price elasticity of demand can be high if it has a small share in world exports. Note, however, that if one views eqs. (17), (18) and (19) as a group, then a country cannot simultaneously have (relatively) large demand price elasticities for imports and exports and a large supply price elasticity for exports unless it is both relatively closed to imports and exports *and* maintains a relatively small share of world exports.[25] The United States, for example, would meet the first criterion but not the second, while the smaller European countries such as Belgium and the Netherlands would meet the second criterion but not the first.

2.3. Choice of Variables

With the general outlines of the imperfect and perfect substitutes models in mind, we next consider the empirical variables that have been used as the

---

[24] Compare the domestic price elasticities of demand in Houthakker and Taylor (1970) with the import price elasticities for the United States in Houthakker and Magee (1969), Stern *et al.* (1976), and Clark (1977).

[25] The question of inter-country differences in price and income elasticities is discussed at greater length in Section 4.

appropriate counterparts to the theoretical ones. The discussion is selective rather than exhaustive, concentrating upon what we regard as the most important issues.

2.3.1. *Dependent variables*

As indicated earlier, conventional trade models, like the demand and production theories on which they are based, treat import (export) quantities or prices but not their product as the dependent variables. Trade data, however, are oblivious to this theoretical nicety and are most readily available in value terms. This means that an appropriate deflator has to be found to convert the value data back into its quantity and price components. This problem takes on considerable difficulty and complexity when dealing with the large number of products that comprise a country's aggregate imports and exports. One encounters all the usual problems associated with constructing price indices, namely those related to current or base period weights, quality change, changing composition of products within broader goods categories, etc. along with the additional requirement of reasonable comparability across countries.

The best deflator would of course be the actual transactions or contractual prices for imports (PI) and exports (PX) themselves. Indices based on such international transactions prices do exist but their country, product, and time-period coverage are as yet quite limited.[26] In brief, these price data are restricted to only a few major industrial countries, the time-series seldom extends beyond a ten year period, only some manufactured goods are included, and exports are much better represented than imports.

Faced with the absence of comprehensive data on PI and PX, empirical trade researchers have relied on two second-best but more widely available price deflators, namely unit value indices (PUV) and wholesale price

---

[26]The NBER export price series constructed by Kravis and Lipsey (1971, 1974, 1978) cover machinery, transport equipment, metals, and metal products for the time periods 1957–53, 1961–57, 1962–61, 1963–62, and 1964–63. The indices were calculated for the United States, the United Kingdom, Germany, and on a more partial basis for Japan and the Common Market as a whole. Official export price series are also produced by Germany and Japan, but Kravis and Lipsey (1974) raise some doubts about their quality. Finally, trade price indices for the United States have recently become available [Bureau of Labor Statistics (1980)] for some manufactured products over the 1970–79 period.

indices (PWH).[27] Unit value indices are calculated by dividing the value of imports (exports) by the physical quantities of imports (exports). While perfectly legitimate for a single product, this procedure yields spurious price indices when quite different products are combined in one index. For example, when the commodity composition of imports changes, a unit value index will change even if all "true" prices of the component import products remain unchanged. Similarly, because unit value indices are not fixed-weight indices, a price increase accompanied by a decrease in quantity demanded automatically lowers that good's weight in the index. Wholesale prices escape this latter problem but include some goods often regarded as nontradables, use domestic rather than international weights for the tradable goods, and refer to list rather than transaction prices.[28] Also, as suggested earlier, the domestic and export price for a given product can diverge for nontrivial time periods reflecting various types of market imperfections.

If PWH and PUV are conceded to have drawbacks as representations of true import and export prices, how significant are these drawbacks likely to be? Kravis and Lipsey (1974) have provided some answers to this question by comparing movements of PWH and of PUV with their series on international transactions prices for manufactured exports (PX). In short, they found that: (i) there was a statistically significant positive relationship between PX and PWH and between PX and PUV but that this relationship was considerably closer ($R^2 = 0.47$) in the first case than in the second ($R^2 = 0.06$); (ii) the relationship between PX and PWH was much closer for some countries (the United States, the United Kingdom), than for others (Germany, Japan); and (iii) the relationship between PX and PWH was not noticeably closer for time spans longer than one year than for one-year periods.

A related but perhaps more central question for this chapter is how poor measures of PI and PX will affect the estimated price elasticities of demand and supply. Two cases need to be distinguished. The first case is where the dependent variable (I or X) is correctly measured but there is

---

[27] Unit value indices are published in the IMF's *International Financial Statistics* (IFS) for practically all IMF member countries. They typically extend back to the early 1950s, and cover total imports and total exports. The coverage and availability of domestic wholesale price indices are similar to those of unit value indices.

[28] The consumer price index and the gross domestic product deflator also have serious deficiencies as proxies for traded goods prices; see Goldstein and Officer (1979).

measurement error in the import or export price data. In this situation, we have a standard errors in variables problem [Kmenta (1971)], and we get the standard results, namely, the estimated coefficient on *PI* or *PX* will be biased toward zero.[29] Consistent with this diagnosis, Kravis and Lipsey (1974) found that replacement of *PWH* with *PX* in a conventional export elasticity-of-substitution equation [like eq. (2′) above] led to estimated elasticities that were roughly twice as high, as well as to significantly higher explanatory power for the equation itself. The second case, which is probably the predominant one in practice, is where an improperly measured *PI* or *PX* series is used to deflate an error-free import or export *value* variable, as well as for the explanatory price variable. Here, negative correlation will be introduced between the errors in the dependent variable and the errors in the explanatory price variable, with the result that the estimated price elasticity will be biased toward minus one [Kemp (1962a), Kravis and Lipsey (1974), Magee (1975)]. It therefore suggests some suspicion of unitary price elasticity estimates from studies where both the dependent and independent variables are derived using *PWH* or *PUV*.

The next relevant question is what options are available to the empirical trade researcher facing poor import and export price data. At one extreme, trade equations can be specified with the value of imports (exports) as the dependent variable [e.g. Branson (1968)]. Since the volume price elasticity of demand is equal to the value elasticity minus one, this procedure still permits estimation of the former. Also, if the purpose of the exercise is to estimate or forecast only the value of imports, this procedure has obvious advantages over trying to explain two component series of poor quality. Its main disadvantage is that the determinants of price and volume are different, and a single equation therefore carries the danger that the estimated coefficients will represent some unknown interaction of supply and demand influences. At the other end of the spectrum, one can work with the widely available price proxies (*PUV, PWH*), accept the danger of biased estimates, and exercise due caution on the ranges of the true elasticities. This has been the route followed in the most of the studies on total imports (exports) simply because the better quality export or import price data are not available at high levels of aggregation; also, some researchers [Beenstock and Minford (1976)] have

---

[29]This was one of the arguments used by Orcutt (1950) to support his position that true price elasticities of demand for imports exceeded the estimated ones.

argued that component measurement errors may at least partially cancel out at high levels of aggregation. Intermediate options include restricting hypothesis-testing on demand and supply elasticities to goods for which the better quality price data are available [e.g. Artus and Sosa (1978)]; replacing import unit values with a weighted index of exporters' domestic wholesale prices [e.g. Clark (1977)]; relaxing the homogeneity restriction on relative import (export) prices as a concrete response to the larger assumed measurement error in import or export prices than in either the domestic price index or the exchange rate [e.g. Ahluwalia and Hernandez-Cata (1975)]; and using the exchange rate and the tariff rate to generate the local-currency price of imports as a substitute for the unit value index [e.g. Mutti (1977)].

2.3.2. *Income and other scale variables*

In our exposition of the imperfect substitutes model, the demands for imports and exports were treated as positive functions of the level of real income in the importing regions. While this has overwhelmingly been the conventional practice in empirical work, alternative and/or additional "scale" variables have frequently been proposed for both aggregate and disaggregated demand functions. In addition, scale variables have also found their way into the export supply function.

2.3.2.1. Import demand

There are at least three conscious choices to be made in the specification of the scale variable in the aggregate import demand equation[30]: (i) should one use

---

[30]When the dependent variable in the import demand function is disaggregated by type of commodity, prevailing practice is to make an accommodating disaggregation adjustment in the scale variable so as to get a better fix on the particular component of aggregate income or expenditure that shifts the demand for that commodity. For example, Deppler and Ripley (1978) use real consumption expenditure as the scale variable in the import volume equation for foods and beverages, an average of output in manufacturing and real final domestic demand for manufactures in the equation for manufactures, etc. If the existing disaggregated import functions can be criticized it is not for failing to select an appropriate scale variable for a particular type of imports but rather for doing only that. Thus, import demand functions for primary products seldom distinguish between flow and stock demand; functions for investment goods make little effort to model expected output or to specify longer lag structures appropriate to capital goods; import functions for durable goods typically find no place for habit formation, etc. For discussion and estimates of disaggregated trade equations, see Kreinin (1967), Stone (1979), Deppler and Ripley (1978), and Rhomberg and Boissonneault (1965).

real income or real expenditure; (ii) if real income is chosen, should cyclical and secular movements in real income be treated separately; and (iii) how should "life-cycle" or "permanent/transitory" consumption patterns be handled in import demand.

(i) *Real income versus real expenditure.* The issue here is whether domestic demand for foreign goods (imports) should properly be related to domestic demand for all goods, i.e. to expenditure, or rather to the sum of domestic demand for domestic goods and the foreign demand for domestic goods (exports), i.e. to income. Micro demand theory offers little guidance since it typically constrains expenditure to equal income. In the empirical literature, the choice between these two scale variables has usually been made on grounds of consistency with the implicit or explicit overall model of balance-of-payments adjustment. Specifically, real expenditure has been favored in a monetary-oriented framework because it can be related to the difference between actual and real money balances, thereby assuring a direct role for money in trade and balance-of-payments adjustment [see, for example, Aghevli and Khan (1980)]. In contrast, the Keynesian preference for real income follows naturally from the foreign-trade multiplier, income-driven view of balance-of-payments adjustment.[31] Rather surprisingly, there has been practically no attempt to choose between these two alternative scale variables on empirical grounds (e.g. goodness-of-fit criterion).[32]

(ii) *Secular versus cyclical real income.* In our prototype import demand eq. (1), movements in real income (Y_i/P_i) were assumed to have the same effect on the quantity of imports demanded regardless of whether these movements represented trend (secular) or cyclical variations about that trend. This assumption has been challenged in empirical work. First, there is the argument alluded to earlier, that prices do not act to clear markets, especially during periods of excess demand. Instead, periods of excess demand are said to be characterized by longer domestic waiting times, less availability and

---

[31] Prevailing practice treats the monetary and Keynesian (cum elasticity) models of balance-of-payments adjustment as alternatives, but they can clearly be reconciled in a more general model of balance-of-payments adjustment.

[32] An exception is the study by Brillembourg (1975) for three Latin American countries — Colombia, Ecuador, and Venezuela. He found that real expenditure, along with relative prices and quantitative rationing variables, produced a better explanation of import demand than did an analogous specification using real income.

higher costs of credit, and less vigorous pursuit of new orders by suppliers — a consequence of which is that consumers increasingly turn to foreign suppliers [Gregory (1971)]. For these reasons, the cyclical income elasticity of demand for imports is expected to exceed the secular elasticity. The second challenge, which complements the first one, is that the secular income elasticity of demand for imports is best viewed within a perfect substitutes framework as equal to the difference between the domestic production and consumption of importables [Johnson (1958), Magee (1975)]. This suggests not only that the secular elasticity may be less than the cyclical income elasticity but also that the secular elasticity might even be *negative* under certain conditions.[33]

Our reading of the empirical evidence on cyclical versus secular income elasticities can be summarized as follows. First, when trend (or potential) real income and cyclical real income are included in the import demand equation at the same time, both usually appear with positive and statistically significant coefficients [Clark (1977), Lawrence (1978)]; the same verdict applies to import demand equations where real income and capacity utilization appear jointly [Branson (1968), Hooper (1976, 1978)]. Second, there is some tendency for the estimated cyclical elasticities to exceed the secular elasticities [Deppler and Ripley (1978)], but there are enough exceptions [Khan and Ross (1975), Geraci and Prewo (1980)] to cast serious doubt on the final outcome. Third, since Magee's (1975) reluctant conclusion that he could not find any negative estimates of secular income elasticities for total imports, some have appeared [e.g. Khan and Ross (1975)], but it is by no means clear how these should be interpreted since they presumably mix together import substitution, tastes, and other structural factors. Fourth, if one grants the case that nonprice rationing of imports occurs during cyclical upswings, it is still an open question as to whether cyclical income variables are the best way to measure these effects [e.g. Gregory (1971) prefers estimated waiting times as a rationing proxy]. Fifth, more recent studies [e.g. Hooper (1976, 1978)] have moved in the desirable direction of including cyclical income abroad as well as

---

[33] As indicated in Magee (1975, p. 189), the condition for a negative income elasticity is $(DI/SI) < (E_Y^s/E_Y^d)$, where E_Y^s and E_Y^d are the domestic income elasticities of supply and demand respectively, and DI and SI are the domestic demand for and supply of importables, respectively.

at home in the demand equation to capture *relative* nonprice rationing costs. If prices do not clear markets at home, they probably do not abroad either.

(iii) *Permanent and transitory income.* As is well known, the distinction between current income and "permanent" or "life-cycle income" is at the core of modern consumption theory [see Dornbusch and Fisher (1978) for a lucid summary]. Since imports represent consumption by domestic residents of foreign goods, it is surprising that so little attention has been given to this distinction in the specification of the aggregate import demand function.[34]

Potential application of permanent income or life-cycle concepts to the aggregate import demand function raises the following points and puzzles. To begin, one motivation for the permanent income and life-cycle models was to explain the greater slope of the long-run consumption function in the United States, compared to the short-run function. As indicated earlier, however, most empirical trade studies find a higher income elasticity for imports from cyclical income than from potential or trend income. This suggests that cyclical non-price rationing effects predominate over permanent/transitory consumption differences. Second, it needs to be acknowledged that the key operational problem central to testing of both the permanent and life-cycle income hypotheses — how best to relate expected future income to current and past observed income — still seems to be unresolved in the literature. In addition to the econometric problems associated with generating permanent income via use of fixed distributed lags [see Lucas (1976)], there is the additional problem in import functions that one may not want to impose the same lag distribution on all the explanatory variables.[35] Third,

---

[34] A notable exception is the recent study by Geraci and Prewo (1980) where cyclical and trend components of real income are given transitory and permanent income interpretations and where the estimated permanent income elasticity exceeds the transitory income elasticity in four out of the five sample countries. Also, note that the case for making permanent/transitory income distinctions does not apply to "separable" or "allocative" import functions where the decision of how much to consume is treated separately from the decision of how to allocate total consumption between imports and domestic goods.

[35] Hall (1978) has offered a way around these problems by proposing tests of the permanent income and life-cycle models that concede from the outset that none of the right-hand-side variables is exogenous; specifically, the test involves determining whether all variables other than consumption lagged one period have nonzero coefficients in a regression equation for current consumption. The rub is that this approach may reveal little about the true structural relation between consumption and its determinants.

and operating in the opposite direction, the joint finding that only current income is usually significant in import demand functions and that there is an apparent structural instability in the behavior of income elasticities of demand for imports [Hooper (1978), Stern *et al.* (1979)] is suggestive of some pay-off from trying alternative representations of real income. Similarly, one can note the considerable measure of success achieved by Sachs (1981) in using an inter-temporal life-cycle savings/investment framework to explain the pattern of current account positions after the oil shocks of the 1970s. In sum, there would seem to be plenty of room and reason for experimenting with other specifications of real income in the aggregate import demand function to bring it closer into line with the treatment of aggregate consumption in the domestic empirical literature.

2.3.2.2. Export supply

The application of income and other scale variables in work on export supply (or pricing) has been less intensive, but two issues merit discussion: (i) the roles of trend income and trend exports in export supply, and (ii) the effects of cyclical income or demand changes on the supply of exports.

(i) *Trend income.* The basic argument for including trend income in the export supply function is that a country or industry's ability and willingness to supply exports will not be fully captured by the ratio of export prices to domestic prices (or factor costs) but will depend also on the output capacity of the economy as a whole. Put in other words, secular changes in the level of aggregate real output will be accompanied by advances in factor supplies, infrastructure, and total factor productivity that will lead to an increase in export supply at any given level of export prices. When such a trend output variable has been added to a conventional total export supply function [like eq. (4)], the results have been encouraging. Goldstein and Khan (1978) found that trend income appeared with the expected positive sign and was statistically significant in their equations for total exports in all eight industrial countries in their sample. Similarly, Geraci and Prewo (1980) found a significant positive effect for potential output in all five of their country export-supply equations.

(ii) *Trend exports.* This is a variable that has not been considered in the empirical export-supply literature but one that should be if export supply functions are to be compatible with some of the recent theoretical literature on aggregate supply. At the center of this new neoclassical supply literature [see Lucas (1973), Sargent (1976)] is the so-called "surprise" supply function. The basic idea is that actual supply (Y) will exceed normal or trend supply ($\bar{Y}$) only to the extent that current price (P) exceeds the expected price (P^e).[36]

Application of the "surprise" supply function to exports is attractive for at least three reasons. First, it does not stretch the imagination unduly to think of the domestic price as a reasonable measure of the expected export price. Exporters know from experience that there will be *temporary* periods for which export prices will depart from domestic prices, but $PX = P_i$ in the long run and on average; hence P_i can serve as good predictor of PX.[37] Second, when $P^e = P$ (i.e. $P = PX$), where P^e is the expected price level, then the surprise supply function implies that actual (current) export supply will equal trend exports. This seems preferable to the implication of the standard supply function (4) that export supply will be constant when $PX = P$. Third, if trend exports and trend real output move closely together, then those empirical results that find a significant positive role for trend output in total export supply would likewise be consistent with a positive significant role for trend exports. In any case, this strikes us as a promising area for future research.

(iii) *Cyclical income effects.* Most of the empirical work in this area is based on the twin premises that when domestic demand pressure increases, selling in the home market becomes more profitable than selling abroad, and that this increased profitability is *not* fully captured by movements in the ratio of domestic to export prices. This cyclical tilt toward the domestic market might reflect the better quality of domestic customers (e.g. larger purchase volume, stronger brand allegiance) or a perceived higher risk associated with export sales. In any event, the prediction is that the quantity of resources devoted to export production and the quantity of goods offered to the export market will decline when domestic income rises above trend. Operationally, the implication is that a cyclical income or other scale variable ought to be added to the export supply equation.

---

[36] A stochastic (error) term is usually included in the supply function, but it need not concern us here.

[37] In cases where the data contradict the hypothesis that $PX = P$ on average, one could still retain the surprise supply function by: (i) using a time-series model to generate the "expected" ratio of PX to P; (ii) by using deviation of the actual from the expected ratio to measure "surprises" in relative export prices; and (iii) by relating export quantity surprises to relative export price surprises.

Review of the existing empirical evidence on the export supply effects of domestic demand pressure prompts the following conclusions and observations. First, Mintz's (1967) finding, based on non-econometric tests for the United States, that cyclical upturns are associated with decreases in export quantities and increases in export prices has been supported by later econometric studies for the United States and other industrial countries [Artus (1973) (1977), Clark (1977), Hooper (1976) (1978), Winters (1976), Dunlevy (1979)]. Second, no consensus has yet emerged on whether the positive export price effect of domestic demand expansions is larger or smaller than the negative export quantity effect. Ballpark estimates are that a 10 percent increase in the capacity utilization rate would in the long run reduce the quantity of exports supplied by 3–5 percent [Artus (1973), Dunlevy (1979)] and increase the export price by a similar percentage [Artus (1977)]; there are wide inter-country differences, however, around these central quantity and price elasticities. Third, one of the main channels by which domestic demand pressure reduces the quantity of exports is via the former's effect on lengthening delivery delays and hence on weakening the exporting country's nonprice competitive position [Ball *et al.* (1966), Artus (1973)]; this is sometimes referred to as the "pull" effect of domestic demand pressure and it suggests that domestic cyclical income variables play a role in the foreign demand for exports as well.

2.3.3. *Relative prices*

Whereas the choice for scale variables is usually which *one* among many to pick, the problem for relative prices is rather which *ones* to exclude so as to keep the number of price terms small enough for estimation purposes while still capturing the dominant sources of demand or supply substitution.

2.3.3.1. Aggregate import demand

A country's total imports face potential competition from two broad categories of domestically produced goods, namely tradables and nontradables.[38] This means that an unrestricted demand equation for imports would have three prices — import prices (PI_i), domestic tradable prices (PT_i) and domestic

---

[38] If exports and domestic tradables carry different prices, then exports constitute a third separate source of competition for imports.

nontradable prices (PNT_i). In the empirical literature, the typical practice has been to *assume* that the demand for imports is independent of the price of nontradables, and the rationale is that the consumer engages in a two-step decision process. In step one, he allocates his expenditure between all tradable and nontradable goods on the basis on his income and the relative price of tradables to nontradables. In the second step, he allocates his expenditure on tradable goods (given at step one) between imports and domestic tradables. By virtue of such "separability" in consumption, only one relative price — namely that between imports and domestic tradables — need appear in the import demand equation. PNT is relevant therefore only for the demand for all tradables. In short, combining such separability with homogeneity, the import demand function takes the form

$$I_i^d = \gamma(Y_i/PT_i, PI_i/PT_i), \quad \gamma_1' > 0, \quad \gamma_2' < 0. \qquad (1')$$

The problem is that when the researcher moves to estimate eq. (1'), he immediately faces the problem that price indices for domestic tradables as such do not exist. Conventional procedure is therefore to use one of two readily available proxies, namely the wholesale price index (PWH) or the implicit deflator of gross domestic product ($PGDP$). However, both these indices contain nontrivial shares of products that might reasonably be considered as nontradables [Goldstein and Officer (1979)]. The consequence is that, in actual estimation of eq. (1'), the cross-price elasticity of demand for imports is constrained to be identical as between domestic tradable and nontradable goods. Thus, the PNT that was excluded by theory comes in by the back door of data availability.

Goldstein *et al.* [1980], using price indices for tradable and nontradable goods constructed from data on current and constant dollar GDP by industry of origin,[39] found that the price of nontradable goods was not a significant determinant of the demand for total imports in the majority of industrial countries in their sample. This finding supports the "separability" assumption typically made in aggregate import demand studies. Second, both Goldstein *et al.* (1980) and Murray and Ginman (1976), the latter working only with

---

[39]The tradable sector consists of agriculture, mining, and manufacturing. All other industries in which GDP originates are classified as nontradables; see Goldstein and Officer (1979) for a more detailed discussion of this data base on tradable/nontradable prices and real output.

U.S. data, report that the cross-price elasticity of demand for imports is higher, as expected, with respect to the price of domestic tradables than the price of nontradables.

Similarly, the estimated price elasticities of demand for imports generally turn out to be larger and more significant when the price of tradables is used as the denominator of the relative price variable than when a general domestic price index inclusive of nontradables ($PGDP$) is employed.[40]

2.3.3.2. Disaggregated import demand

Once imports or exports are disaggregated by type of commodity and/or by country of origin or destination, the number of potential competitors for imports of type i from country j increases dramatically. Therefore, some more systematic and explicit scheme has to be adopted to permit estimation or derivation of the own-and cross-price elasticities of demand.

The most popular solution to this problem, reflected in most recent world trade models [Samuelson (1973), Hickman and Lau (1973), Deppler and Ripley (1978), Artus and McGuirk (1981), Geraci and Prewo (1980)], is due to a pioneering contribution by Armington (1969). The building blocks of the Armington model can be summarized as follows.[41]

First, all commodities are distinguished by kind and by place of production. Types of commodities (called "goods") correspond to rather broad commodity classifications, such as nontradables, manufactures, raw materials, etc. Goods produced by different countries are called "products". Thus French and German manufactures are the same good but are different products. Products are assumed to be imperfect substitutes for one another.

---

[40]Turning from the domestic to the import price, it is important to note that tariffs should be included in the domestic-currency price of imports. Unhappily, inclusion of tariff rates is still the exception rather than the rule in the empirical literature, despite the fact that the average ad-valorem tariff on industrial-country imports has been changing (falling) over the past few decades [IBRD (1981)] and the evidence [e.g. Kreinin (1961)] that tariff changes do have sizeable effects on import demand. Quantitative restrictions on imports should similarly be taken into account in import demand although there is no obvious method of measuring them. See Brillembourg (1975), Khan (1974), Hemphill (1974), and Weisskoff (1979) for alternative approaches to measuring the effect of price and quantity restrictions on imports.

[41]Our description of the Armington model follows Branson (1972), Rhomberg (1973), and Artus and McGuirk (1981), but in a much more condensed form.

Second, the import demand for a product is determined in a "separable" two-step manner. In step one, the consumer determines his demand for the goods family to which a product belongs on the basis of his income, the good's price, and the prices of other goods. In step two, he determines his demand for that product on the basis of his overall demand for that good (given at step one) and of the ratio of the product's price to the weighted average of the prices of other products in that same goods family.

Third, by assuming that the elasticities of substitution between all pairs of products in the same goods family are identical and constant in any market, it is possible to characterize the allocative or distribution function in step two as

$$I^d_{1ij}/I^d_{1i} = b_{ij}^{\phi_{ij}}(P_{1ij}/P_{1i})^{-\phi_{ij}}, \tag{20}$$

where I^d_{1ij} is the quantity of imports demanded in country i of good 1 exported by country j (that is of product ij) I^d_{1i} is the quantity of good 1 demanded in country i from all sources of supply, b_{ij} is the base period quantity share of country j in total imports of good 1 by country i, P_{ij} is the price of product ij, P_{1i} is the price of good 1 in country i (equal to a weighted average of product prices within good 1), and ϕ_{ij} is the elasticity of substitution for product ij.

Fourth, and most important, this framework permits the derivation of formulae for both the direct (d_{ij}) and cross price (c_{ij}) elasticities of demand for imports of any product into country i from any exporting country j using only three pieces of information: (i) the share of each exporter in the importing country's total demand for that good (S_{ij}); (ii) the elasticity of substitution for products within that goods family (ϕ_{ij}); and (iii) the own-price elasticity of demand in the importing country for that good (n_{i1}).[42] Trade share parameters (S_{ij}'s) can be readily obtained from published *OECD* or *IMF* sources on the direction of trade. The elasticities of substitution (ϕ_{ij}) and price elasticities of demand (n_{1j}) are less straightforward to acquire but usual practice is to base them on available published studies.

The Armington methodology has at least three appealing features. It provides an extremely economical and consistent method for estimating

---

[42] Following Branson (1972, p. 29), the direct (d_{ij}) and cross-price elasticities of demand (c_{ij}) by country i for product ij can be expressed as:

$$d_{ij} = -|\phi_{ij} - S_{ij}(\phi_{ij} - n_{i1})|, \tag{20a}$$
$$c_{ij} = S_{ij}(\phi_{ij} - n_{i1}). \tag{20b}$$

all the bilateral and multilateral direct and cross-price effects of a single or simultaneous set of traded goods price changes. For this reason, the methodology has been extensively used to estimate the trade balance effects of a hypothetical or actual set of currency realignments [Armington (1970), Branson (1972), Artus and Rhomberg (1973), Artus and McGuirk (1981)]. Furthermore, the methodology itself is quite flexible, as evidenced by its subsequent application to export supply functions [Geraci and Prewo (1980)] and to trade in intermediate goods [Clements and Theil (1978)]. Finally, the model yields some interesting implications for intercountry differences in price elasticities. Specifically, in the usual case when the elasticity of substitution (ϕ_{ij}) is larger in absolute value than the price elasticity of demand for the respective goods class (n_{1i}), the model implies that countries with larger market shares should have a relatively low own-price elasticities of demand for their goods and a relatively high cross-price elasticities of demand [Branson (1972), Tables 4 and 5, and eqs. (20a) and (20b)]. The rationale is that if a country has a small market share, a decrease in its relative price increases its sales principally by taking away business from other exporters; but if it already has a major share of the market, price declines increase its sales only if the size of the market itself grows.

At the same time, it is also clear that the Armington model is not without problems. One is in choosing the right level of aggregation for the goods categories. If these are defined too narrowly, the separability assumption is likely to be violated; if they are very broadly defined, the assumptions governing estimates of the elasticity of substitution (i.e. identical income elasticities) are likely to be violated. Another caveat is that the Armington model is just a methodology for computing direct and cross-price elasticities of demand, and the estimates derived from it will only be as good as the estimates of ϕ_{ij} and n_{1i} on which the former are based. Estimates of elasticities of substitution abound in the literature, but much less is known about the price elasticities for broad goods classes.

3. ECONOMETRIC ISSUES IN TRADE MODELLING

In proceeding from the theoretical models outlined in the previous section to actual estimation of trade relationships, several important econometric issues have to be addressed. The particular issues we consider in this section are:

dynamics and the treatment of lags, aggregation, simultaneity, and the stability of the relationships over time.[43] While this list by no means exhausts all the econometric issues, it nevertheless covers the major ones. Careful attention to these issues is a prerequisite for doing quantitative work on the subject.[44]

For expositional convenience, the analysis here is conducted only for the case of the import demand function. It is a simple matter to translate the discussion to the case of export demand, and in general to the supply functions for imports and exports as well. Specific issues relating to the latter are dealt with separately as the analysis requires.

3.1. Dynamics and Time Lags

Thus far, the basic demand and supply equations for imports and exports have been presented as "equilibrium" relationships, without any reference to time units. In the real world, however, the presence of adjustment costs and of incomplete information implies that the adjustment of dependent variables to explanatory ones will not be instantaneous, i.e. importers and exporters will not always be on their long-run demand and supply schedules. Gauging the pattern and length of such time lags is important not only for obtaining

---

[43] Two particular issues which we do not cover here are homogeneity and the appropriate functional form of the estimating equation. The subject of homogeneity of demand and supply equations has been discussed by Leamer and Stern (1970) and tests of the postulate that the functions are homogeneous of degree zero in prices have been performed by Murray and Ginman (1976), Mutti (1977), and Goldstein *et al.* (1980), among others. In the last study, it is shown that the homogeneity postulate is generally accepted for import demand equations of most industrial countries. Insofar as the functional form is concerned, Khan and Ross (1977) provide a description of the Box and Cox (1964) methodology that can be used to determine empirically whether the function should be specified in linear or log-linear terms, and further show that log-linear specification is preferable for import demand equations in the cases of Canada, Japan and the United States. This finding was confirmed by Boylan, Cuddy, and O'Muircheartaigh (1980) for three smaller European countries — Ireland, Denmark and Belgium. An interesting recent paper by Honda and Ohtani (1980) jointly tests for homogeneity and the appropriate functional form by generalizing the procedure adopted by Khan and Ross (1977).

[44] It is probably fair to argue that researchers in the international trade sphere have been more conscious of econometric problems and pitfalls than those in most other areas of applied economics. This sensitivity can be traced back to the seminal paper of Orcutt (1950) which highlighted the various methodological issues involved in estimating import and export equations, and which still serves as a continuing guide and conscience to anyone engaged in empirical research on trade.

forecasts of imports and exports but also for evaluating many policy issues related, for example, to changes in tariffs, exchange rates, and so on.

What is at issue, then, is not whether lags ought to be incorporated in trade equations but rather how best to do so. A simple approach to the modelling of dynamic trade behavior is to specify the equation within the framework of a general distributed-lag model with geometrically declining weights. This has come to be known popularly as the "Koyck" model, which for the specific case of import demand is written as:[45]

$$I_t = \beta \sum_{j=0}^{\infty} (1-\beta)^j I_{t-j}^d. \tag{21}$$

The parameter β measures the response of actual imports to the demand for imports and is bounded (0,1). If actual imports are equal to the desired level, β will equal unity; in contrast, a value of zero for the β implies that equilibrium is never reached. The average or mean-time lag in adjustment can be calculated as $(1-\beta)/\beta$.

There are two particular variants of the general function (21) that are typically employed in trade studies. First, the partial-adjustment model which states that imports adjust to the difference between the demand for imports and actual imports in the previous period:

$$\Delta I_t = \beta \left[I_t^d - I_{t-1} \right]. \tag{22}$$

By substituting for I_t^d one obtains a reduced form equation that differs from the equilibrium model of eq. (1) simply by the addition of a lagged imports term. A second variant of the Koyck model is one where demand and supply depend not on actual prices but rather on some notion of "expected" prices. If expectations are formed according to the adaptive-expectations model of Cagan (1956), one obtains an equation fairly similar to that yielded by the partial-adjustment model (22).

Estimates of import and export equations using some type of Koyck formulation have been made by Houthakker and Magee (1969), Magee (1970), and Goldstein and Khan (1976). These have shown that while adjustment is

---

[45] While we write the model in linear terms, it should be remembered that it could be defined in log-linear terms.

not instantaneous, the lags are fairly short, with most of the effect occurring within four quarters or so. For example, Goldstein and Khan (1976) estimated the average lag in total import demand to be between two and four quarters for a group of seven industrial countries; while in another study [Goldstein and Khan (1978)], the same authors found that the average lag for total exports ranged between one and five quarters.

Provided due care is paid to the error structure in the estimation equations, geometric lag models are relatively straightforward to estimate and the results are easily interpreted. However, such specifications do have certain fundamental features which may not be fully acceptable. First, and by definition, these models assume that the largest effect of any change in the explanatory variables occurs in the initial period. In contrast, it could be argued that the true lag effect builds up gradually over time and declines after that. In other words, the appropriate lag pattern could be an inverted "v" shape (or even a more complicated distribution) rather than the steadily declining lag pattern emerging from the Koyck-lag models. Some adjustment can be made to the general geometric distributed-lag model to allow for this, for example by permitting the first few lagged terms to be unrestricted, but in doing so one loses the theoretical rationales of the partial-adjustment and adaptive expectations models.

Another more serious problem with such models is that the lag in the response of the dependent variable is assumed to be the *same* irrespective of whether the change in imports is due to variation in prices or in the scale variable. It has been argued [for example by Magee (1975)] that there is no reason for the time response to be the same for all explanatory variables. Further, the lag that is estimated could be a combination of different lag patterns on the different explanatory variables. In this connection, the relatively short average lag that has been found in empirical studies using Koyck lags could primarily reflect a short real income lag that is not really valid for prices. A number of writers have argued that the delayed response of imports and exports due to recognition lags, decision lags, delivery lags, replacement lags, and production lags,[46] is likely to be quite different depending on the explanatory variable that initiates the response. While there appears to be some agreement that the effect of real income or other scale variables is largest in the initial

---

[46] See Junz and Rhomberg (1973) for a discussion of these different types of lags.

period and declines rapidly thereafter, there is much less of a consensus on the proper distributed-lag pattern for price changes. For this reason, it is generally not appropriate to impose a geometrically declining pattern a priori.

These problems with Koyck lags have led to the wide use of polynomial (Almon) lag models in estimating trade equations. Such formulations avoid the imposition of a uniform lag pattern on all the explanatory variables and permit less stringent restrictions on the shape of that lag distribution. The results from such experiments have been, to say the least, quite mixed. In general, the lag pattern associated with the scale variable has been quite similar to that yielded by the geometric lag model, but the responses of imports and exports to price changes have displayed a variety of lag patterns. Some writers [e.g. Heien (1968) and Samuelson (1973)] have found that the effect on imports of a relative price change decays steadily over time, with about 75 percent of the effect taking place in the first year and the remainder occurring in the following year. Others [e.g Buckler and Almon (1972), Clark (1977)] found a bell-shaped or inverted "v" pattern for relative price changes. Applying the polynomial lag approach to aggregate import equations for twelve industrial countries, Goldstein and Khan (1976) discovered that the weights of the lag structure declined steadily in half the cases and either increased over time or took on the inverted bell shape in the other half. Interestingly, it was also found that the statistical significance of the relative price term was substantially lower than when a geometric lag structure was imposed.

Since polynomial lags allow for more flexibility than Koyck lags, they are perhaps better able to represent the reaction of the dependent variable to changes in the exogenous variables. However, the shape and form of the lag pattern is dependent on the degree of the polynomial, on whether end-point constraints are imposed and if so in what way, and on the number of lags included. Naturally, the researcher cannot be expected to go through all possible permutations so that some degree of subjective prefiltering is invariably present in the lag forms selected. This makes it difficult to determine whether the reported lag structure is the result of a number of preliminary tests with the selection based on some criteria of goodness-of-fit, or whether it simply reflects the priors of the researcher. Furthermore, one often finds such lag structures, particularly those from models utilizing higher-order polynomials and a large number of lags, yielding signs on the coefficients for some of the lagged values that are clearly at variance with theoretical expectations [Minford

(1978)]. While some rationalization of such results is typically provided, the arguments seem somewhat strained, since sign-switching of the coefficients of lagged values of the variables is extremely difficult to justify theoretically.

Some compromise between the geometric and polynomial lag models can be made by incorporating the main advantages of the two, although to our knowledge this has not yet been done in trade equations. Hall and Sutch (1967), for example, suggest that the initial part of the lag distribution be represented by a low-order polynomial and the latter part by a Koyck distribution. In the more general case, separate low-order polynomials could be applied to the scale and price variables, with a common geometric lag structure being applied after some point in time. This would yield a model that was more flexible than the Koyck-type model, yet at the same time avoid many of the problems associated with polynomial lags.

Another worrisome problem is that the estimated lag distributions in trade equations do not seem to be independent of the unit of observation. In other words, one can obtain strikingly different results for the same model depending on whether the unit observation of the data is monthly, quarterly, or annual. This is the familiar time-aggregation problem in econometrics. It is possible, for example, that the very long lags (up to six years) on relative prices reported by some researchers [Junz and Rhomberg (1973)] are simply a consequence of their use of pooled time-series cross-section data. Some relief from this time-aggregation problem could perhaps be obtained by considering the methods of estimation proposed by Sims (1971) and Wymer (1972). These methods, which essentially involve the discrete-time approximation of continuous-time models, yield estimates of lags that are apparently independent of the unit of observation. As far as we can ascertain, there has again as yet been no effort made in this direction.

Finally, it would seem that there is also considerable potential in the application of the techniques of time series analysis to trade relationships. This methodology, associated with the names of Box and Jenkins (1970), is very powerful in identifying and estimating general distributed-lag relationships. The techniques of *ARIMA* models and transfer functions are now widely available and thus can be readily applied. The principal advantage of such an approach is that it involves a minimum of arbitrariness in the choice of the lag distribution, as the data itself is allowed to determine the form and length of the lag process.

In sum, the issue of timing is clearly a very crucial one in the estimation of trade relationships and has received a great deal of attention. Unfortunately, despite the energy expended on the topic, the issue is far from settled. We do not know the length of the lags involved and we are as yet unclear on how lag patterns ought to be modelled. Additional work in this area should still pay large positive marginal returns.

3.2. Aggregation

Since trade data are available on a disaggregated basis for most countries, it is relevant to ask two related questions.[47] First, is it necessary to estimate disaggregated relationships and then combine them to obtain an aggregate estimate? Second, if the answer to the first question is in the affirmative, how should the aggregate values for the elasticities be derived from the estimates of the components?

The general guideline for disaggregation is quite simple. If the effect of the determining variables is exactly the same as between the aggregate and disaggregated groups, or if the relationship between the components and aggregate explanatory variables is a stable one, then one can be indifferent between the aggregate and disaggregated equations.[48] If these basic preconditions are not satisfied, however, and they are unlikely to be satisfied in any realistic situation, disaggregation is always better, as the estimates obtained directly from the aggregate relationship are likely to be biased. This point was made persuasively by Orcutt (1950) for the case of price elasticities. In aggregate trade equations, goods with relatively low price elasticities can display the largest variation in prices and therefore exert a dominant effect on the estimated aggregate price elasticity, thereby biasing the estimate downwards. The same problem can in principle arise with respect to the scale variable, although here it is typically less serious.

---

[47] We deal here only with disaggregation over commodities, not over regions. The latter form of disaggregation can be viewed as another way of disaggregating by commodities, since certain regions trade in certain types of commodities. The other main rationale for regional disaggregation is to give expression to the assumed particular import demand behavior of developing countries; see, for example Rhomberg and Boissoneault (1965).
[48] See Madalla (1977).

The relationship between the parameters obtained from estimates of disaggregated equations and those from the aggregate equation has been defined rigorously by Theil (1954). In the case of the aggregate import-demand equation, for example, the parameters of real income and prices will depend not only on the corresponding parameters of the disaggregated relationship but also on the parameters of the other included variables. In other words, the aggregate real income coefficient will be a weighted average of the disaggregated real income coefficients and the weighted average of the disaggregated price coefficients. Unless all the disaggregated coefficients are equal, estimation of the aggregate relationship, by ignoring this interaction, will result in specification bias.

Concern with the issue of aggregation bias has led to a number of empirical studies that use disaggregated import and export data. In most such studies, the disaggregation tends to be limited to a standard one-digit *SITC* classification, although some studies [Kreinin (1967), Khan (1975), and Stone (1979)] have been able to disaggregate more finely. Estimates of income and price elasticities for disaggregated commodity categories are examined in Section 4, and it is sufficient here to note that these elasticities differ across commodity groups, with price elasticities higher for manufactures than for non-manufactures. The activity or income elasticity of demand for manufactures also appears to be higher than those for the other groups, but perhaps less markedly.

If one accepts the view that disaggregation is usually warranted, how should one proceed to obtain aggregate elasticities from the disaggregated estimates? For a linear functional form of the equation, this is a relatively simple matter of taking the weighted average of the disaggregated estimates, with the weights being the shares of the components in the total. In the log-linear case, it has been demonstrated by Barker (1970) that one has to adjust the component elasticities by the variation in the component real incomes and prices relative to the variation in their respective aggregates. This ratio is generally referred to as the "distribution" factor. Thus, in the log-linear specification, a weighted average of the disaggregated import elasticities would equal the "true" elasticities only if the distribution factors were equal to one or if they were uncorrelated with the other terms. While it may be plausible to assume that these distribution factors for real income approximate unity, there is less reason to suppose that component price indices move exactly in proportion to the total price index. Both Magee (1975) and Khan (1975) found that import price elasticities calculated after adjusting for the distribution factor turned out to be significantly *lower* than those obtained utilizing the simple weighted average method.

Finally, it should be mentioned that while disaggregation may be preferable in principle, there has been some controversy on its merits in practice. If the disaggregated data are accurate and the component equations well specified, then disaggregation always results in more information. But Grunfeld and Griliches (1960) and Aigner and Goldfeld (1974) make the point that disaggregated data are generally subject to larger measurement errors than are aggregate data, and further that disaggregated functions are more likely to be misspecified than aggregate relationships. In such a case, it may be advisable to estimate the aggregate relationship. Essentially, the argument revolves around predictability, that is, whether predictions from a model using aggregate data are more accurate than those derived from disaggregated data. If the forecast errors from the disaggregated estimates cancel each other out, then disaggregation makes no difference. If such cancelling-out does not occur, the sum of forecast errors may be larger than those obtained from the aggregate relationship. Edwards and Orcutt (1969) show via simulation experiments that predictions from disaggregated data are much better than those from aggregated data, but this finding is challenged by Aigner and Goldfeld (1973) who show that this supposed superiority of disaggregated models cannot be generalized.

3.3. Simultaneity

As demonstrated by Orcutt (1950) and Prais (1962) among others, price elasticities in trade relationships can be seriously biased by simultaneity between quantities and prices. Thus, single-equation estimates of the price elasticities of demand and supply can be weighted averages of the "true" demand and supply elasticities and consequently can be biased downward. More formally, simultaneity implies correlation between the determining variables in an equation and the error term, which violates one of the conditions for the use of classical least squares analysis [Orcutt (1950), Harberger (1953), Kmenta (1971)]. The basic conditions under which one can proceed to estimate, say, a demand equation that would be free of such bias are either that the price elasticity of supply is infinite, or that the demand function is stable while the supply function shifts around.[49]

---

[49] For a formal analysis, see Madalla (1977) and Leamer (1981).

When such assumptions cannot be made, there are basically two options. The first is to solve the model to obtain the reduced form, and then estimate that by ordinary least squares. Provided that the model is just identified, one can recover the price and income elasticities of demand and supply from the estimates of the reduced-form equations. However, one seldom has the luxury of having a just-identified model to work with, so that the latter step is often not possible. For example, Amano's (1974) study of export behavior of industrial countries eliminates the problems created by simultaneity, but the over-identified nature of the model prevents one from calculating either the demand *or* supply price elasticities. An alternative approach is to estimate the model using simultaneous equation methods. The earliest attempt at simultaneous estimation of trade equations is contained in the impressive study by Morgan and Corlett (1951), who estimated import demand and supply functions for various commodities by limited-information maximum-likelihood methods. While the results were quite poor, their approach was correct conceptually, and it has properly served as a model for later research. More recent studies, using techniques such as two-stage least squares or instrumental variables, include those by Rhomberg and Boissoneault (1965), Basevi (1973), Khan (1974), Artus (1975) and Gylfason (1978). It is not possible in many of these cases to derive the supply-price elasticity, but the procedure adopted does correct for simultaneity.

Explicit export-supply functions have been incorporated into export demand models by Magee (1970), Gylfason (1978) and Goldstein and Khan (1978).[50] The last study formulates a two-equation model of exports and estimates the complete model simultaneously by full-information maximum-likelihood methods. All three studies introducing a supply function for exports found that this extension tended to raise the estimated price elasticity of demand (vis-a-vis the OLS estimates), a result that can be explained by the less-than-infinite supply-price elasticities found in these studies. Goldstein and Khan (1978), for example, report the latter as ranging from 1.1 to 6.6 for a group of seven industrial countries.

---

[50] Simultaneous estimation of import relationships has rarely been undertaken, although here one would probably be justified in assuming that, in all but a few large countries, the price of imports is unaffected by variations in an individual country's demand. For two such attempts to estimate import supply equations, see Magee (1970) and Gylfason (1978).

Given the accumulated evidence, it would seem that simultaneity is not a problem that can be dealt with by assumption, particularly in relation to exports. Rather, the correct procedure is to formulate a complete model, test it, and then decide whether the price variable in the demand equation can be treated as exogenous. It needs to be recognized, however, that this procedure is laborious and there is always a risk of misspecification attached to the construction of complete models. Fortunately, there are certain statistical tests, such as the regression specification error test (RESET) due to Ramsey (1969), and the specification tests developed by Hausmann (1978), that can be applied in a single-equation context. These tests are quite powerful in detecting a nonzero mean disturbance that may be caused by omitted variables, incorrect functional form, or simultaneous-equation bias. Another option that has not been explored in the trade literature is to utilize the so-called "causality tests" due to Granger (1969) and Sims (1972), which enable one to test for feedback relations between variables.[51]

3.4. Stability of Trade Relationships

Whether a regression relationship varies or is stable over time is obviously important from both a predictive and an analytical point of view. Forecasts can be accurate only if the underlying equation on which they are based is unchanging. Similarly, determining the effects of changes of exogenous variables with any degree of confidence also requires that the parameters of the function be invariant over time. Changes in the basic relationship can be either gradual or sudden, and in either case the resulting parameters will be biased and inconsistent if allowance is not made for such shifts. There are in fact good reasons for expecting that trade relationships are subject to both types of changes. Gradual changes in the elasticities can come about as the pattern of trade changes during the process of economic development or as the result of changes in government trade policies. Sudden shocks such as changes in the exchange rate or exchange rate regime, or large oil price increases can also fundamentally alter the basic demand or supply relationships.

Yet another potential reason for instability of the parameters is the so called "quantum effect", originally suggested by Orcutt (1950). It is argued that the

---

[51] In other words, if there were no contemporaneous relationship between the variables in question one could be justified in estimating the model by classical least squares methods.

price elasticity of demand for imports will be larger for large price changes than for small price changes. The rationalization for this quantum effect is that the price change must be large enough to overcome buyer inertia and the costs related to switching suppliers [see, for example, Liu (1954)]. Its chief implication is that estimates of elasticities based on a sample containing both large and small price changes will not be equally applicable in other situations where large or small price changes predominate.

The statistical procedures used to test for stability have typically involved the introduction of dummy variables to isolate the point at which the structural shift is suspected of taking place, and/or splitting the sample at this point and estimating the relevant functions for the two sub-periods. The latter approach was adopted by Kemp (1962b) for the case of Canadian imports. Estimating the import equation for sub-periods 1929–1939 and 1947–1955, Kemp (1962b) found that the income elasticity doubled in size. Magee (1972) used a similar approach on a bilateral model for U.S. imports and exports, and reported significant changes in both the price and income elasiticities as between the periods 1951–1960 and 1961–1969. Stability tests of a similar type have also been performed by Rhomberg and Boissoneault (1965) and Ahluwalia and Hernandez–Cata (1975) for U.S. exports and imports, respectively, and by Heien (1968) on import equations for a group of industrial countries.

More formal test to determine the constancy of the regression relationship over time have been conducted by Hooper (1978) and Stern *et al.* (1979). Hooper (1978) applied the standard approach of splitting the sample at the point where the shift is assumed to have occurred, and then proceeded to test whether the shift was statistically significant by using the F-test developed by Chow (1960).[52] The results of that exercise indicated that the demand for U.S. nonagricultural exports had been relatively stable for the period under consideration, but that the U.S. nonoil import demand function had been unstable. Hooper (1978) then introduced additional variables into the import

---

[52] An interesting search procedure was adopted by Hooper (1978) to determine the point of change in the relationship. It basically involves the estimation of export and import volume equations for the U.S. over a 24-quarter segment, then moving this segment along the overall sample (1957–77) year by year and repeating the estimation. Changes in the elasticities can be visually identified and the equations re-estimated for the sub-periods determined by this search procedure.

demand function in a (partially successful) attempt to reduce the instability. This latter step, namely correcting in some way for the shift in the relationship, is rarely undertaken, so that the effort is to be commended.[53]

Identifying the point where a break in the relationship occurs is almost always a difficult task. Recently, however, new tests of stability have been developed, principally by Brown *et al.* (1975), that require no more information than is already contained in the data. Such tests have recently been applied to the case of the demand for aggregate U.S. imports and exports by Stern et al. (1979) over the period 1956–1976. The set of tests chosen, however, while powerful in detecting haphazard or nonsystematic shifts in the function, are not really suitable for the testing of gradual or secular changes. Brown et al. (1975) consider other tests more appropriate for the latter case, and it is advisable to employ the complete battery of tests instead of choosing a particular sub-set of such tests.[54]

The evidence on the quantum effect is somewhat mixed. The initial test of this hypothesis, conducted by Liu (1954), found the coefficient on a squared relative price-change variable in a equation for U.S. imports to be significantly different from zero and therefore concluded that the large/small price change distinction was a valid one, with large changes tending to raise the price elasticity. Goldstein and Khan (1976) tested the same quantum effect hypothesis for 12 industrial countries by allowing alternatively the import price elasticity and the speed of adjustment to vary with the size of the relative price change. They found no evidence that the price elasticity of demand for imports varied with the size of the price change, or that importers adjusted faster when faced with larger than "normal" price changes. These results, which held up when the tests were conducted at a lower level of disaggregation and with alternative lag structures, supported the more indirect tests reported by Magee (1975). In sum, notwithstanding Liu's (1954) results, there does not seem to be strong empirical support at this point for the quantum effect.

---

[53] Some other work has also been done on introducing the suspected cause of instability directly into the regression relationship. For example, Hooper and Kohlhagen (1978) introduce an exchange rate uncertainty variable into trade equations. A time trend to capture secular changes is also frequently employed.

[54] The reason for using several tests in combination is because departures from constancy of parameters may show up in different ways and the various tests may not be equally powerful in detecting the particular kind of departure encountered.

4. ESTIMATES OF PRICE AND INCOME ELASTICITIES AND RELATED POLICY ISSUES

In this section we turn from questions of methodology to a presentation of the actual econometric estimates of price, income (activity), pass-through, and feedback elasticities, and to the policy issues associated with the size and time patterns of those elasticities. In order of appearance, we consider: (i) price and income elasticities of demand for imports and exports; (ii) the price elasticity of supply for exports, the pass-through of exchange rate changes onto local-currency prices of imports and exports, and the elasticities of export price with respect to domestic costs and competitors' export prices; and (iii) the (feedback) elasticity of domestic prices with respect to changes in import prices and exchange rates. Following that, we offer some observations on the effectiveness of devaluation in improving a country's balance of payments.

To aid in the presentation of the empirical evidence, we have constructed summary tables of estimates for each of the elasicity parameters mentioned above. In selecting the entries for these tables, we have been guided by three considerations. First, because many interesting policy questions relate to inter-country differences in elasticities, we have given priority to multi-country studies since they usually use the same equation specification across countries. Second, to minimize duplication with earlier trade surveys [Magee (1975), Stern et al. (1976)], we have emphasized recent contributions (post 1973) and have seldom included estimates made prior to 1969. Third, we make no pretense of having compiled an exhaustive list of estimates but we have tried to cover the studies most frequently cited in the literature as well as those recent studies that, in our view, rest on the most solid methodological ground.

4.1. Price and Income Elasticities of Demand for Imports and Exports

As indicated earlier, most of empirical trade work has been confined to the estimation of demand functions for imports and exports that closely resemble eqs. (1) and (2) of the imperfect substitutes model. Tables 1–4 provide a condensed picture of the relative price and income elasticities that have emerged from these empirical studies.

Four broad conclusions stand out. First, the sum of the long-run (greater or equal to 2 years) price elasticities of demand for imports and exports invariably

Table 1: Long-run Price Elasticities of Demand for Total Exports and Imports: Representative Estimates From Recent Studies

	Total Exports									
Country	Houthakker-Magee (1969)	Goldstein-Khan (1978)	Hickman-Lau (1973)	Beenstock-Minford (1976)	Amano et al.[a] (1981)	Basevi (1973)	Samuelson (1973)	Adams et al. (1969)	Gylfason (1978)	Stern et al. (1976)
Austria	n.a.	n.a.	−0.93	n.a.	n.a.	n.a.	−1.21	n.a.	...	−0.93
Belgium	...	−1.57	−1.02	−0.84	n.a.	n.a.	−1.14	...	...	−1.02
Canada	−0.59	n.a.	−0.84	−1.00	−0.33	−0.59	−1.10	−0.23	...	−0.79
Denmark	−0.56	n.a.	−1.28	n.a.	n.a.	n.a.	−1.06	n.a.	n.a.	−1.28
France	−2.27	−1.33	−1.09	−1.59	−0.34	n.a.	−1.28	−1.06	...	−1.31
Germany	−1.25	−0.83	−1.04	−1.90	−0.29	−1.68	−1.12	−0.65	−0.38	−1.11
Italy	−1.12	−3.29	−0.93	−1.91	−0.30	−0.72	−1.29	−0.25	−1.91	−0.93
Japan	−0.80	...	−0.50	−3.00	−0.81	−2.38	−1.04	−0.71	−2.13	−1.25
Netherlands	...	−2.72	−0.95	−2.10	n.a.	−2.39	−1.07	−0.59	−0.88	−0.95
Norway	...	n.a.	−0.80	n.a.	n.a.	n.a.	−1.16	n.a.	n.a.	−0.81
Sweden	−0.47	n.a.	−1.99	n.a.	n.a.	−1.92	n.a.	n.a.	n.a.	−1.96
Switzerland	−0.58	n.a.	−1.01	n.a.	n.a.	n.a.	−1.51	n.a.	n.a.	−1.01
United Kingdom	−1.24	−1.32	−1.27	−1.47	−0.08	−0.71	−1.28	−0.48	−0.32	−0.48
United States	−1.51	−2.32	−1.38	n.a.	−0.32	−1.44	−1.13	−0.60	−0.62	−1.41

Table 1: (Continued)

Country	Total Imports								
	Houthakker-Magee (1969)	Adams et al. (1969)	Taplin (1973)	Goldstein-Khan (1980)	Beenstock Minford (1976)	Samuelson (1973)	Gylfason (1978)	Stern et al. (1976)	Armington (1970)	Geraci and Prewo (1980)
Austria	n.a.	n.a.	n.a.	−0.82	n.a.	−1.42	−1.21	−1.32	−1.37	n.a.
Belgium	−1.02	−0.61	−0.65	−0.48	−2.90	...	−2.57	−0.83	−1.11	n.a.
Canada	−1.46	−0.62	−1.59	−0.20	−2.50	−1.29	...	−1.30	−1.30	n.a.
Denmark	−1.66	n.a.	−0.85	−0.42	n.a.	−0.23	n.a.	−1.05	−1.26	n.a.
France	...	−0.81	−0.39	n.a.	−1.31	−0.79	−0.46	−1.80	−1.53	−0.33
Germany	−0.24	−0.85	−0.61	−0.25	−0.74	−0.92	−1.36	−0.88	−1.48	−0.60
Italy	−0.13	...	−1.03	−0.45	−0.88	−1.01	−0.32	−1.03	−1.42	n.a.
Japan	−0.72	...	−0.81	n.a.	−1.21	...	...	−0.78	−1.47	−0.72
Netherlands	...	−0.24	−0.02	n.a.	...	...	−1.65	−0.68	−1.13	n.a.
Norway	...	n.a.	−1.20	n.a.	n.a.	...	n.a.	−1.19	−1.19	n.a.
Sweden	−0.79	n.a.	−0.76	−0.84	n.a.	−0.80	n.a.	−0.79	−1.30	n.a.
Switzerland	−0.84	n.a.	−1.10	n.a.	n.a.	...	n.a.	−1.22	−1.35	n.a.
United Kingdom	−0.21	...	−0.22	...	...	...	...	−0.65	−1.38	−0.79
United States	−1.03	−1.16	−1.05	−1.12	−1.04	...	−1.12	−1.66	−1.73	−1.23

[a] Unweighted average of (correctly-signed) estimates in Table 1–2.
... indicates zero or wrong-signed coefficient on relative prices.

Income and Price Effects in Foreign Trade   47

Table 2: Short-run versus Long-run Price Elasticities of Demand for Imports and Exports: Representative Estimates

Investigator	(1) Short-run (0–6 Months) Price Elasticity	(2) Long-run (>2 Years) Price Elasticity	(3) Ratio of Long-run to Short-run Elasticity	(4) Time Period (in Years) for 50% of Final Price Effect	(5) Total Length (in Years) of Lag Distribution	(6) Type of Distributed Lag	(7) Level of Aggregation	(8) Type of Equation
(1) Hooper (1976)	−0.42	−0.54	1.3	<0.25	2	Polynomial	U.S. nonfuel imports	Standard import demand
	−0.17	−0.79	4.6	1.00	2	Polynomial	U.S. nonagricultural exports	Standard export demand
(2) Lawrence (1978)	−0.14	−1.52	10.8	1 – 1.5	2	Polynomial	U.S. imports of manufactures	Standard import demand
	−0.17	−1.85	10.8	1 – 1.5	2	Polynomial	U.S. exports of manufactures	Standard export demand
(3) Deppler and Ripley (1978)	−0.50	−0.97	1.9	≈1.0	3.5	Discrete	Imports of manufactures (unweighted average, 14 industrial countries)	Standard import demand
	−0.80	−1.40	1.7	≈1.0	3.5	Discrete	Exports of manufactures (unweighted average, 14 industrial countries)	Standard export demand
(4) Beenstock and Minford (1976)	−0.50	−1.18	2.4	0.5 – 1.0	up to 5	Polynomial	Total imports unweighted average, 9 industrial countries	Standard import demand
	−0.70	−1.73	2.5	0.5 – 1.0	up to 5	Polynomial	Total exports, unweighted average, 8 industrial countries	Standard export demand

(*Continued*)

Table 2: (Continued)

Investigator	(1) Short-run (0–6 Months) Price Elasticity	(2) Long-run (>2 Years) Price Elasticity	(3) Ratio of Long-run to Short-run Elasticity	(4) Time period (in Years) for 50% of Final Price Effect	(5) Total Length (in Years) of Lag Distribution	(6) Type of Distributed Lag	(7) Level of Aggregation	(8) Type of Equation
(5) Goldstein and Khan (1978)	−0.76	−1.35	1.8	<0.25	∞	Koyck	Total exports, unweighted average, 8 industrial countries	Standard export demand
(6) Taplin (1973)	−0.32	−1.33	4.2	>5.0	∞	Koyck	Total exports, pooled, cross-section for industrial countries	Elasticity of substitution framework
(7) Heien (1968)	−0.77	−0.93	1.2	<1	3	Variety	Total imports, unweighted average, 11 industrial countries	Standard import demand
(8) Junz and Rhomberg (1973)	−1.52	−3.88	2.5	2	5	Discrete	Manufactured exports pooled, cross-section 13 industrial countries	Elasticity of substitution framework
(9) Artus and Sosa (1978)	−0.07	−0.77	11.0	n.a.	3	Discrete	13 industrial countries Exports of nonelectrical machinery (3 industrial countries)	Elasticity of substitution framework
(10) Hickman and Lau (1973)	−0.63	−0.95	1.5	—	—		Total exports of 25 industrial countries	Elasticity of substitution framework

Table 3: Long-run Activity Elasticities for Total Exports and Total Imports

	Total Exports					
	(1)	(2)	(3)	(4)	(5)	(6)
Country	Houthakker-Magee (1969)	Basevi (1973)	Goldstein-Khan (1978)	Deppler-Ripley (1978)[a,b]	Balassa (1979)[c]	Wilson-Takacs (1979)
Austria	n.a.	n.a.	n.a.	1.08	2.04	n.a.
Belgium	1.87	1.29	1.68	1.03	1.98	n.a.
Canada	1.41	1.15	n.a.	0.69	1.89	1.97
Denmark	1.69	n.a.	n.a.	1.08	1.82	n.a.
France	1.53	n.a.	1.69	0.70	2.04	2.14
Germany	0.91	1.33	1.80	1.11	2.27	1.59
Italy	2.68	1.18	1.96	1.12	2.07	n.a.
Japan	3.55	1.62	4.22	1.45	2.00	n.a.
Netherlands	1.88	0.85	1.91	0.65	1.91	n.a.
Norway	1.59	n.a.	n.a.	0.75	1.82	n.a.
Sweden	1.75	1.22	n.a.	1.14	1.93	n.a.
Switzerland	1.47	n.a.	n.a.	0.82	n.a.	n.a.
United Kingdom	1.00	0.61	0.92	0.90	2.20	1.75
United States	0.99	0.92	1.01	1.32	2.02	2.15

	Total Imports						
	(1)	(2)	(3)	(4)	(5)	(6)	(7)
Country	Houthakker-Magee (1969)	Taplin (1973)	Goldstein-Khan (1976)	Samuelson (1973)	Adams et al. (1969)	Geraci-Prewo (1980)	Wilson-Takacs (1979)
Austria	n.a.	1.04	n.a.	1.08	n.a.	n.a.	n.a.
Belgium	1.94	1.27	1.75	1.38	1.21	n.a.	n.a.
Canada	1.20	1.18	n.a.	0.95	0.90	n.a.	1.87
Denmark	1.31	1.08	0.84	1.38	n.a.	n.a.	n.a.
France	1.66	1.30	1.28	1.45	1.32	1.57	1.07
Germany	1.85	1.35	1.52	1.17	1.34	1.42	1.46
Italy	2.19	1.26	1.83	1.86	1.35	n.a.	n.a.
Japan	1.23	1.12	1.30	1.26	0.93	0.77	1.69
Netherlands	1.89	1.27	2.04	1.56	1.35	n.a.	n.a.
Norway	1.40	0.90	1.01	1.63	n.a.	n.a.	n.a.
Sweden	1.42	1.02	1.33	1.13	n.a.	n.a.	n.a.
Switzerland	2.05	1.25	n.a.	1.46	1.07	n.a.	n.a.
United Kingdom	1.45	1.24	1.78	1.46	1.07	2.24	2.57
United States	1.68	1.81	1.84	1.89	0.76	1.53	4.03

[a] Refers to manufactured exports only.
[b] Refers to cyclical changes in real income.
[c] Refers to trend (permanent) real income.

Table 4: Long-run Price and Activity Elasticities for Disaggregated Import Categories: Some Representative Estimates

Commodity categories	Deppler-Ripley (1978)[a]	Taplin (1973)[b]	Basevi (1973)[c]	Clark (1977)[c]	Ball-Marwah (1962)[d]	Houthakker-Magee (1969)[d]	Barker (1976)[e]	Stern et al. (1976)[f]	Theil and Clements (1978)[g]
Price elasticities									
Foods and beverages (SITC0 + 1)	−0.34	−0.57	−0.55	−1.14	−0.47	−0.18 to −1.28	−0.13 to −0.18	−0.78	−0.58
Raw materials (SITC2 + 4)	—	−0.63	−0.13	−1.25	−0.83	−1.18[h]	−0.44[h]	−0.50	−0.95
Fuels (SITC3)	—	−0.63	−0.04	—	n.a.	—	—	−0.96	n.a.
Manufactures and misc. goods (SITC5-9)	−0.97	−1.23	−0.71	−4.72	−1.98	−1.8 to −4.0	−1.37	−1.34	−1.16 to −1.4
Activity elasticities									
Foods and beverages (SITC0 + 1)	2.83	0.84	1.08	0.38	0.96	0.30 to 1.28	1.12 to 1.16	n.a.	0.14
Raw materials (SITC2 + 4)	0.32	0.75	0.83	0.96	1.15	0.61[h]	1.91[h]	n.a.	0.25
Fuels (SITC3)	1.22	0.96	1.40	—	n.a.	—	—	n.a.	n.a.
Manufactures and misc. goods (SITC5-9)	1.27	1.44	1.46	2.60	2.07	1.11	1.99	n.a.	0.28 to 0.32

[a] Unweighted average, 14 industrial countries.
[b] Unweighted average, 25 industrial or semi-industrial countries.
[c] Unweighted average, 10 industrial countries.
[d] United States.
[e] United Kingdom.
[f] Median estimate, all industrial countries.
[g] Pooled, cross-section for 13 industrial countries.
[h] Raw materials plus fuels.

exceeds one for industrial countries (Table 1).[55] Thus, if the Marshall–Lerner condition (together with infinite supply elasticities) is regarded as the dividing line between elasticity optimists and pessimists, we read Table 1 as firmly in the camp of the elasticity optimists. On the import side, Harberger's (1957) judgment of 25 years ago that the price elasticity of import demand for a typical country "... lies in or above the range of -0.5 to -1.0" still seems on the mark; his corresponding consensus export price elasticity of "... near or above -2" appears somewhat on the high side (a range of -1.25 to -2.50 would be our consensus estimate) but would be consistent with those studies that either estimate export price elasticities of demand in a simultaneous framework [e.g. Goldstein and Khan (1978)] or employ long lag distributions on the export price variable [e.g. Beenstock and Minford (1976)]. In short, the estimates in Table 1 suggest that over a period of two to three years, relative prices do play a powerful role in the demand for total imports and exports.[56] As such, the potential contribution of expenditure-switching policy instruments (the exchange rate, tariffs and subsidies) to trade balance adjustment is a strong one.

The second conclusion, brought out forcefully in Table 2, is that *short-run* (0–6 months) price elasticities of demand for imports and exports are considerably smaller than the long-run elasticities. The considerable variation across studies in the estimated shape and length of the lag distribution on relative prices makes it hazardous to offer specific estimates of the relationship

---

[55] The only borderline case in Table 1 is the United Kingdom; here however, the results of other econometric studies [Barker (1976), Winters (1976)] strongly suggest that when U.K. imports and exports are disaggregated by commodity class, the aggregate price elasticities of demand increase significantly, suggesting that aggregation bias is perhaps a more serious problem in trade equations for the United Kingdom than in those for other countries.

The low estimated export price elasticities obtained in the recent study by Amano et al. (1981) for the seven major industrial countries are not so easy to dismiss. Until further work is done, we will not be able to tell whether these reflect some unusual features of their sample period (1971–1977), or specification and estimation differences, or a true secular decline in the price elasticities themselves.

[56] The range of estimated price elasticities in Table 1 is quite wide, and Kohli (1982) has shown how large differences in price elasticities can result from seemingly small differences in the definition of the scale and domestic price variables (e.g. real national income versus real national product) even when derived form the *same* structural model; further these differences in elasticities across alternative definitions of the right-hand-side variables increase with the size of the country's foreign trade sector.

between short-run and long-run elasticities.[57] Nevertheless, the evidence in Table 2 would not be inconsistent with the judgment that long-run price elasticities are roughly twice as high as short-run ones, and that about 50 percent of the final relative price adjustment takes place within a one-year period.

This marked difference between short-run and long-run price elasticities of demand carries at least two policy implications.[58] One is that the trade balance response to devaluation can follow a pattern described by the "*J* curve". The value of the trade balance can worsen in the short run in response to devaluation because of low short-run price elasticities of demand and the tendency for import prices to rise more rapidly in local currency terms than export prices. Over time, the price elasticities of demand grow larger and export prices catch-up with import prices, with the result that the initial deterioration in the trade balance is halted and then reversed. Nevertheless, the preverse initial response of the trade balance can frequently last for say four to five quarters and it can amount to as much as 10 percent of the local-currency value of imports [Spitaeller (1980)].

The second and most significant implication of low short-run price elasticities is that short-run changes in countries' trade balances will then be dominated by real income movements at home and abroad. A comparison of the short-run price elasticities in Table 2 with the income elasticities of demand in Table 3, reveals that for periods up to one year in length, the sum of income elasticities for imports and exports is anywhere from two to four times larger than the respective sum of price elasticities. Consistent with this conclusion, most detailed analyses of short to medium-term changes in current account positions among major industrial countries [e.g. Wallich (1978), Truman (1978)] point to differential real income movements across countries as the key explanatory factor.

---

[57] As illustrated in Table 2, three of the troubling aspects of the estimates of time lags on relative prices are: (i) the tendency for the estimated long-run price elasticities to vary positively with the *assumed* length of the lag distribution; (ii) the tendency for studies based on pooled time-series and cross-section data [e.g. Junz and Rhomberg (1973)] to yield much longer lags than those based on time-series data for single countries; and (iii) the tendency for the polynomial lags to yield longer average lags than either the Koyck or discrete unconstrained distributed lag formulations.

[58] This subsection draws heavily on arguments presented in Goldstein (1980).

Our third broad conclusion, based on the estimates shown in Table 3, is that income elasticities of demand for a representative industrial country fall in the range of 1 to 2 on both the import and export sides. This carries two implications. The first is that in the absence of secular increases in the relative price of imports, one should expect the shares of imports and exports in GNP (in real terms) to be rising over time. Evidence collected by Salant (1977, Tables 2 and 3) shows that this is just what has been happening, at least for industrial countries as a group since the late 1940s. The second implication is more controversial and relates to differences across countries in the relationship between income elasticities of demand for exports versus imports. If the income elasticity of demand for a country's imports is significantly larger than that for its exports, then the country confronts an unpalatable choice: either grow at the same rate as its trading partners and accept a secular deterioration in its balance, or to opt for external balance and accept a slower growth rate than its trading partners.[59]

This issue of unequal income elasticities first attracted attention in the empirical literature in the paper by Houthakker and Magee (1969), where the authors found that the income elasticity for Japan's exports was substantially higher than that for its imports, whereas the United Kingdom and the United States were in the opposite category — a finding that seemed to be consistent with the strong trade account performance of Japan and the weak performances of the United Kingdom and the United States during much of the 1960s. As shown in Table 3, subsequent multi-country econometric studies have on balance replicated this inter-country pattern of income elasticities.[60] Still, serious questions have been raised about both the existence and interpretation of the Houthakker-Magee income-elasticity effect. On the first count, Hooper (1978) has advanced the argument that the observed

---

[59] If income elasticities for imports and exports are the same, then conventional trade models of course yields the implication that a country which grows faster than its trading partners will suffer a deterioration in its trade balance. Indeed, such nonsynchronization of growth rates is typically at the root of most explanations for large switches in current account positions; e.g. see Truman (1978), Lawrence (1978), Wallich (1978).

[60] An exception is the recent study by Balassa (1979). This study however uses a constant-market-shares approach to export modelling and this renders the "apparent" income elasticities derived from it noncomparable in a strict sense with income elasticities from traditional export demand equations.

high estimated income-elasticity of demand for U.S. imports reflects the positive correlation between U.S. income growth and a relevant omitted variable, namely, supply capacity in the exporting countries, particularly the newly-industrialized developing countries. Under normal circumstances, such increases in supply capacity would be reflected in export prices and hence in U.S. import prices. In this case however, so Hooper (1978) argues, these exports contained many new products with zero or unduly low weights in the standard price indices; hence, this supply effect was not reflected in recorded movements in U.S. import prices. When a supply proxy for foreign production is included in the U.S. import demand function along with the normal arguments, the estimated income elasticity of demand drops from above two to somewhere between 1.3 and 1.7. This still leaves the income elasticity for U.S. nonoil imports above that for U.S. nonagricultural exports (1.2) but the difference is no longer substantial. Similar views that the high estimated income elasticity for Japanese exports may really be picking up the influence of some collinear omitted variable have often been put forward but less success has been achieved in identifying just what that omitted variable could be.

A second challenge to the Houthakker-Magee thesis is that it neither differentiates between the trade balance effects of secular versus cyclical income movements nor does it account for the (positive) effect of secular income movements on export supply. Bazdarich (1979), for example, has noted that cyclical increases in U.S. GNP have generally been associated with deterioration in the U.S. trade balance and dollar depreciation whereas increases in potential or trend GNP have had the opposite effect. Perhaps more interesting, Geraci and Prewo (1980) found that while the long-run income elasticity of demand for U.S. imports was high (1.5), it was low relative to the long-run export *supply* elasticity with respect to trend real income (2.5). Similarly, the trend-income demand elasticity for imports was low relative to the trend-income supply elasticity for exports for Japan, whereas the two elasticities were quite close together for France, Germany, and the United Kingdom. Although Geraci and Prewo (1980) interpret their findings as consistent with persistent trade surpluses by the United States (1958–1974) and Japan, their results could still be compatible with the Houthakker-Magee thesis if it was export demand rather than export supply that was the constraint on actual exports during the sample period.

A final criticism of the Houthakker-Magee hypothesis, and indeed of all income-based trade models, is that the analysis is too partial-equilibrium in nature. One branch of the criticism, as represented in recent papers by McKinnon (1978), Artus (1979), and Sachs (1981), reminds us of Alexander's (1952) fundamental insight that the current account surplus must be equal to the difference between income and expenditure or, to what is the same thing, to the difference between savings and investment.[61] Application of this "absorption view" to the observed current account imbalances of the 1970s yields the conclusion that the observed imbalances reflected inter-country differences in the incentives to savings and investment [Artus (1979)] and inter-country differences in shifts in investment induced in turn by inter-country differences in permanent income [Sachs (1981)]. Note that the two approaches (income and absorption) need not be incompatible if, as suggested in Section 2, conventional import and export demand equations use permanent or life-cycle income as the scale variable rather than current income.

Our fourth broad conclusion is based on the estimates shown in Table 4. There are significant differences in both price and income elasticities of demand across commodity groups. More particularly, the price elasticity of demand for manufactures is significantly larger than that for nonmanufactures.[62] Within nonmanufactures, price elasticities for raw materials and fuels appear to be larger than those for food and beverages, but the differences do not seem large. In the case of the activity elasticities, the comparisons are clouded by the use of different activity variables across commodity groups but, on balance, we again see a higher elasticity for manufactures (especially if estimates of the activity elasticity for fuels do not reflect recent conservation efforts). The chief implication of these inter-commodity differences in income and price elasticities is that differences in the commodity structure of trade can lead both to differences across countries in price and income elasticities for their total

---

[61] Another branch of criticism comes from the monetary approach [Frenkel and Johnson (1976)] which predicts that countries with high growth rates of real income will run balance-of-payments surpluses because of the positive effect of higher real income on the demand for real money balances.

[62] We have restricted Table 4 to imports because most export demand equations for nonmanufactures omit any relative price term, implying that the price elasticity for these goods is either zero or infinite.

imports and exports and to differences in elasticities as between the exports and imports of a single country.

But differences in the commodity composition of trade are not the only explanation for the observed inter-country differences in price elasticities of demand. In fact, two other explanations have already been alluded to in Section 2, namely differences in the share of imports in total domestic demand and supply, as in eq. (17) of the perfect substitutes model, and differences in the share of imports in total domestic demand, as derived from eq. (20) of the Armington model. Yet another explanation, which is highlighted in an interesting recent study by Goldsbrough (1981), is that price elasticities are much smaller for intra-firm trade (trade among affiliates of the same firm) than for conventional trade, and that the share of intra-firm trade in total trade differs across countries.[63] Given the resources that have been devoted to estimating price elasticities and the implications of inter-country differences in these elasticities for, say, the required change in exchange rates needed to remove existing trade imbalances, a strong case can be made for doing more research on competing explanations for inter-country differences in price elasticities.[64]

---

[63] Still a fourth explanation is Vernon's (1966) "product cycle" which implies that the size of a country's price elasticities will depend on its stage in the product cycle, i.e. on whether it is exporting new and technologically-intensive manufactured goods (early stage) or exporting or importing these goods once their production has become standardized (later stage). Price elasticities are expected to be low in the early stage of the product cycle and high in the later stages. The same theory also implies differences in price elasticities as between a single country's exports and imports [Magee (1975)].

[64] As an initial modest step in this direction, we performed some simple rank correlations between the ordinal rankings of countries by size of price elasticity, as indicated by the studies in Table 1, and the ordinal rankings that emerge alternatively from differences in the commodity structure of imports and from differences in the share of imports in total domestic demand and supply. For the commodity structure model, we assigned each country the same import price elasticity of demand for each of the four broad commodity groups listed in Table 4. In this way, cross-country differences in the price elasticity of demand for total imports reflect solely cross-country differences in the structure (value shares) of imports across commodities. Similarly, by using eq. (17) of the perfect substitutes model, and by assigning each country the same price elasticities of demand (1_1) and supply (n_1) for importables, we were able to generate cross-country differences in the price elasticity of demand for total imports (ε_I^d) that reflect solely cross-country differences in the shares of imports in domestic demand (I_i/D_i) and in domestic supply (I_i/S_i). The commodity structure model yielded considerably higher correlation with the econometric results than did the perfect substitutes (or the Armington) model.

4.2. Supply Elasticities, Import and Export Pass-throughs, and Export Price Determination

Despite over thirty years of econometric work on trade equations, it does not take a very large table to present a reasonably comprehensive list of existing estimates of the price elasticity of supply for exports.[65] Table 5 presents those estimates, most of which come from export supply functions similar to those presented in the imperfect substitutes model of Section 2 [eq. (4)].

Although the supply-elasticity estimates show somewhat more variation across studies than did the demand-price elasticities, the following conclusions emerge from Table 5. First, excluding the United States, the supply-price elasticity for the total exports of a representative industrial country appears to be in the range of one to four. The supply elasticity for U.S. exports is probably considerably higher than that, perhaps even reaching ten to twelve. Second, there is a tendency in the empirical results for the estimated export supply elasticity to vary *positively* with the size of the exporting country (as measured say by its real GNP) and *negatively* with the ratio of export openness. Gylfason (1978), for example, reports a rank correlation of 0.66 between his estimates of export supply elasticities and the real GNP of the sample countries, and one of −0.43 between the supply elasticities and the ratios of exports to GNP.[66] The relatively high degrees of export openness of Germany and the United Kingdom may explain why their estimated supply-price elasticities are smaller than might be expected on the basis of their size alone. A third conclusion is that supply-price elasticities for disaggregated exports are higher than those for total exports. This is consistent with a priori reasoning, as resources for expanding production of total exports can come only from the import-competing or nontradable sector, whereas resources for expanding exports of one industry can come from other export industries as well. The fourth but more tentative conclusion is that time lags in the adjustment of export supply to price changes are longer than those on the demand side [Geraci and Prewo (1980)]. This

---

[65] As regards estimates of supply-price elasticities for imports, even a table is unnecessary. In the recent literature, we know only of Magee's (1970) estimate for U.S. imports of finished manufactures and Gylfason's (1978) estimates of imports supply for some industrial countries.

[66] In a similar vein, Magee (1970) suggests that a back-of-the-envelope method for estimating a country's supply-price elasticity for total exports is to multiply the ratio of GNP to exports by two. He derives this formula from the observation that his estimated supply-price elasticity for U.S. exports is roughly twice the ratio of U.S. GNP to exports.

Table 5: Estimates of Long-run Supply-price Elasticity for Exports

Investigator	Supply-price Elasticity	Level of Aggregation	Country
(1) Magee (1970)	11.5	Total exports	United States
(2) Goldstein and Khan (1978)	6.6	Total exports	United States
	4.6	Total exports	Germany
	2.5	Total exports	Netherlands
	1.9	Total exports	France
	1.4	Total exports	United Kingdom
	1.2	Total exports	Belgium
	1.1	Total exports	Italy
(3) Dunlevy (1979)	2.1	Exports of manufactures	United States
	0.7	Total exports	United Kingdom
(4) Basevi (1973)	3.8	Exports of chemicals and fertilizers to U.S.A.	Canada
	4.9	Exports of minerals and metals to world (less U.S.A.)	Canada
(5) Artus and Sosa (1978)	4.6	Exports of nonelectrical machinery	Germany
	4.2	Exports of nonelectrical machinery	United Kingdom
	3.1	Exports of nonelectrical machinery	United States
(6) Gylfason (1978)	2.4	Total exports	United States
	1.7	Total exports	Japan
	1.4	Total exports	Netherlands
	0.8	Total exports	Germany
	0.8	Total exports	United Kingdom
	0.5	Total exports	Italy
(7) Geraci and Prewo (1980)	12.2	Total exports	United States
	6.7	Total exports	Japan
	4.6	Total exports	Germany
	1.4	Total exports	United Kingdom

may reflect the larger start-up costs associated with export production, different skill requirements in export production than in the rest of the economy, or the greater degree of uncertainty associated with selling abroad rather than domestically.

Because the evidence on export supply elasticities is so meagre, the policy implications that one can draw from this evidence are likewise thin. The observation that export supply elasticities differ significantly across countries does suggest, however, that export subsidies and other incentives to exporting will not yield the same export supply responses across countries. In other words, even if comprehensive codes could be legislated and enforced that would equalize export subsidies across countries, some countries (most likely the larger, less open ones) would still get more export-supply response than others.

Another implication, and one that relies only on the conclusion that export supply elasticities are less than infinite, is that export prices in domestic currency will move to offset some (or even all) of the effect of a change in the exchange rate on the foreign-currency price of exports. In other words, the "pass-through" of exchange rate changes into export price changes (in foreign currency terms) will be less than complete.[67] The consequence for the trade balance effect of an exchange rate change, however, depends on the size of the price elasticity of demand for exports.[68] If the demand elasticity is greater than or equal to unity, a lower supply elasticity reduces the effect of an exchange rate change on the value of the trade balance; alternatively, when demand is inelastic, a lower supply elasticity enlarges the effects of an exchange rate change. The often-cited conclusion that devaluation can still be effective when the sum of the demand elasticities is less than unity so long as supply elasticities are less than infinite [e.g. Gylfason (1978)], is just an implication of this general result. The reasoning for this result is no different than in domestic applications of price theory: an inelastic supply curve produces a larger price

---

[67] Branson (1972, p. 21) shows that the percentage change in export prices in foreign currency terms (dPX/PX) associated with a percentage change in the exchange rate (de/e), call it k, can be expressed as:

$$k = (dPX/PX)/(de/e) = (1 - (\varepsilon_x^d/\varepsilon_x^s))^{-1},$$

where ε_x^d and ε_x^s are the demand-price and supply-elasticities for exports, respectively. Note that since $-\infty \leq \varepsilon_x^d \leq 0$ and $\infty \leq \varepsilon_x^s \leq 0$, an infinite supply elasticity for exports implies full "pass-through" ($k = 1$) of exchange rate changes into export price changes, whereas a zero export supply elasticity implies no pass through ($k = 0$); by analogy, note also that when the demand elasticity is infinite, $k = 0$, whereas $k = 1$ when the demand elasticity is zero.

[68] The case for imports is symmetrical to that for exports.

Table 6: Estimates of Import and Export Price Changes (in Domestic Currency Terms) in Response to a 10 Percent Devaluation

	Spitaeller (1980)				Kreinin (1977)	Robinson et al. (1979)	
	Import Prices		Export Prices		Import Prices	Export Prices	
	6 Months	2 Years	6 Months	2 Years	2 Years	6 Months	2 Years
Belgium	10.2	10.2	6.8	6.8	9.0	13.8	13.8
Canada	10.1	10.1	6.7	9.5	n.a.	4.5	8.9
France	8.3	10.3	5.3	5.9	n.a.	7.1	7.1
Germany	7.3	7.3	1.7	2.6	6.0	7.7	9.3
Italy	10.9	10.9	8.7	10.5	10.0	9.9	9.9
Japan	11.5	11.5	5.9	5.9	8.0	12.1	6.5
Netherlands	6.6	11.6	6.8	6.8	n.a.	5.7	6.0
Sweden	10.2	10.2	2.3	4.8	n.a.	10.1	10.1
United Kingdom	9.3	10.6	3.5	5.6	n.a.	7.9	7.9
United States	7.1	10.2	3.2	3.2	5.0	5.8	5.8

increase for a given rightward shift of the demand curve than an elastic one, and the impact of that price increase on the *value* of sales depends on whether demand is elastic or not. Since the weight of the evidence in Table 1 is that demand price elasticities are greater than unity in the long run, we interpret the lower-than-infinite export supply elasticities as a factor that will *diminish* the trade balance effects of exchange rate changes.

An alternative to inferring the size of export and import-price pass-throughs from estimates of demand and supply price elasticities is to estimate these pass-throughs directly by regressing import or export prices on exchange rates. One strong advantage of this latter approach is that if high-frequency data (monthly, quarterly) are used, the results can tell us something useful about the *timing* of the response of import and export prices to exchange rate changes.

Table 6 presents some representative estimates of import and export-price responses (pass-throughs) to a hypothetical 10 percent devaluation in the country's currency. Three features of the evidence in Table 6 merit explicit mention. First, there is a marked tendency for import prices to rise more quickly (in domestic currency) than export prices in response to devaluation; the contrast is particularly evident in the short run (six months) but still holds, albeit to a lesser degree, in the medium run (two years). As suggested earlier, this type of price behavior, in combination with low short-run price elasticities of demand, are what accounts for the "*J*-curve" response of the trade balance to a devaluation. Second, time lags in the import-price pass-through are short; typically the effect is complete in six months, except perhaps for the largest industrial countries which have significant buying power on the international market. Thus, Spitaeller (1980) finds that import prices rise by the full extent of the devaluation in all countries except Germany, whereas Kreinin (1977) finds significant departure from full passthrough only for the United States and Germany. Recalling our preceding discussion of supply elasticities, the finding of full import price pass-through is consistent with the proposition that import supply elasticities are large relative to both import demand elasticities and export-supply elasticities, particularly over the short term. Full import price pass-through also implies that countries cannot count on much slippage between exchange rate changes and import price changes as a moderating factor in the domestic price feedback effects of exchange rate changes. A third feature of the evidence in Table 6 is the larger degree of export price pass-through in the smaller more-open industrial countries than in the larger less-open ones. For example, Robinson *et al.*'s (1979) estimates suggest that within two years of a devaluation, the domestic currency price of total exports will rise so as to offset nearly 100 percent of the devaluation for small open economies (e.g. Sweden, Austria, Belgium), 70–90 percent for medium-sized economies (e.g. France, Germany, Italy, the United Kingdom), and roughly 60 percent for large, relatively-closed economies (Japan, the United States). Spitaeller's (1980) export pass-through estimates are lower but convey a similar cross-country pattern.[69] The clear message is that the larger less-open countries will, ceteris paribus, be able to hold the initial competitive export-price advantage obtained by devaluation longer than the smaller more-open industrial countries [Goldstein (1980)].

Table 7 provides some complementary evidence on export price determination but this time drawing on empirical studies where imperfect competition

---

[69] Other empirical work on export price pass-throughs also shows that the size of the pass-through falls with the share of manufactures in total exports, implying that those countries with high shares of manufactures in total exports will be able to retain the competitive price advantage from devaluation longer than those with relatively high shares of primary commodities in total exports.

Table 7: Elasticity of Export Prices of Manufactures with Respect to Domestic Prices or Wage Costs and Competitors' Export Prices

Country	Deppler-Ripley (1978)		Artus (1974)		Samuelson (1973)	
	Unit labor Costs	Competitors' Prices	Wage Rates	Competitors' Prices	Domestic Prices	Competitors' Prices
Austria	...	1.02	n.a.	n.a.	...	0.21
Belgium	0.51	0.44	n.a.	n.a.	...	0.78
Canada	0.49	0.46	n.a.	n.a.	0.67	...
Denmark	0.26	0.66	n.a.	n.a.	0.36	0.46
France	0.56	0.40	0.71	0.41	0.42	0.59
Germany	0.57	0.40	0.58	0.36	0.38	...
Italy	0.19	0.44			...	0.80
Japan	0.58	0.58	0.42	0.54	...	0.60
Netherlands	...	0.24	n.a.	n.a.	0.15	0.56
Norway	...	1.31	n.a.	n.a.	...	0.96
Sweden	...	0.99	n.a.	n.a.	0.39	0.83
Switzerland	...	0.32	n.a.	n.a.	1.05	...
United Kingdom	0.42	0.51	0.62	0.11	0.82	0.27
United States	1.53	...	0.85	0.09	0.99	0.19

is the maintained hypothesis. In these studies, the "mark-up" export price equation [e.g. eq. (4′)] replaces the export supply model [e.g. eq. (4)]. The two determinants of export price that are accorded major importance in Table 7 are competitors' export prices and domestic factor costs. The interesting thing about the estimated elasticities of export price with respect to these two determinants is not so much their absolute size as their relative size across different groups of countries.[70] Here, we find a consistent pattern. The smaller more-open countries apparently base their export prices on competitors' export prices; conversely, the larger less-open countries apparently use domestic factor costs or prices as the prime mover of export prices. Theoretical justifications for this finding are presented in Deppler and Ripley (1978) and Beenstock

---

[70]The reader may note that the elasticity of export price with respect to competitors' export prices often differs from the elasticity with respect to the exchange rate, even though in theory they should be equal. Spitaeller (1980) provides a case for unequal elasticities in terms of the shares of different currencies used in invoicing exports and imports. More general implications of alternative mixes of invoice currencies are analyzed in Magee (1973) and Magee and Rao (1980).

and Minford (1976), among others. The basic idea is that the relative weight given to competitors' export prices (PX_C) in export price determination will vary positively with the price elasticity of demand for the country's exports and with the slope of the marginal cost curve for producing exportables. Small countries, so the argument goes, with their small shares of world trade and limited domestic factor supplies, face both nearly perfect competition for their exports and sharply rising marginal costs in export production; hence, export prices follow competitors' prices with an elasticity close to one. At the other end of the spectrum are the large countries with their higher trade shares (and assumed higher degree of monopoly power) and larger production bases that together mean lower demand price elasticities for their exports and flatter marginal cost curves; this translates in turn into export price formation that is dominated by domestic factor cost behavior. Other factors that can influence the relative contributions of competitors' prices and domestic costs are the degree of specialization of exports (more specialization reduces the weight of PX_c), the degree of capacity utilization (higher utilization increases the weight of PX_c), and the share of exportables in total production (a higher export share increases the weight of PX_c).

In sum, the imperfect-competition export price models imply that countries can be classified as either "price makers" (price-transmitters) or "price takers" (price-receivers) on the basis of the structural characteristics that govern the demand and supply elasticities for their exports. While these characteristics need not be fully captured by size and degree of openness, the empirical results do identify the larger less-open industrial countries as the ones with the most latitude in export pricing and hence, also with the greatest potential for holding on longest to the export price advantage conferred by devaluation. These models also highlight the importance of the domestic cost and price feedback effects of exchange rate changes for relative traded goods prices. It is to this latter topic that we now turn.

4.3. Domestic Price Feedback Effects of Import Price Changes

Table 8 presents some representative estimates of the effect of import price changes on the three most widely-used aggregate domestic price indices (i.e. the consumer price index, the wholesale price index, and the GDP deflator). The tale told by Table 8 and the associated empirical literature can be summarized as

Table 8: Estimates of the Elasticity of Domestic Prices with Respect to Changes in Import Prices

	Consumer Prices		Wholesale Prices	GDP Deflator
	Dornbusch and Krugman (1976)	Spitaeller (1980)	Beenstock and Minford (1976)	Artus and McGuirk (1981)
Canada	0.20	0.24	0.28	0.17
France	0.16	0.32	0.28	0.23
Germany	0.03	0.08	0.23	0.22
Italy	0.28	0.36	—	0.16
Japan	0.24	n.a.	0.20	0.14
United Kingdom	0.19	0.20	—	0.27
United States	0.14	0.16	0.05	0.14

follows.[71] First, import price changes do have a sizeable effect on the domestic price level in industrial countries. A consensus estimate would be that a 10 percent change in import prices leads eventually to a change in domestic prices of anywhere from 1.5 to 4.0 percent for a "representative" industrial country.[72] In this regard, Bruno (1978) in a pooled cross-section time-series regression for 16 OECD countries over the 1972–1976 period, found that each 10 percent change in import prices was associated with a 1.8 percent change in consumer prices. Second, time lags in the pass-through of import price changes onto domestic price changes are longer than those associated with the pass-through of exchange rate changes into import price changes, but most studies find that roughly half of the final domestic price effect takes place within one year. Where long lags are apparent, they are usually explainable in terms of institutional arrangements that limit the frequency with which wages can be renegotiated to take account of unexpected developments in the cost of living, exchange rate-induced or otherwise. Third, there are large differences

---

[71] In addition to the studies listed in Table 8, estimates of the effect of import price changes on domestic prices can be found in Goldstein (1977), and Hooper and Lowry (1979).

[72] From time to time the argument has been made that positive changes in import prices have a greater proportionate effect on domestic prices than negative ones, thereby leading to a progressive "ratcheting-up" of domestic prices in the face of exchange rate fluctuations. The arguments and empirical evidence for such a "ratchet effect" have been examined by Goldstein (1977), who finds little support for it. A somewhat more sympathetic verdict is offered by Kenen and Pack (1979).

across countries in the effect of import price changes on domestic prices, with the United States clearly being at the low end of the spectrum among the seven major industrial countries, and with the United Kingdom, France, and Italy at the upper end. Furthermore, if some of the smaller more-open industrial countries (e.g. Belgium, the Netherlands) were included in Table 8, it is possible that they would show even larger domestic price feedbacks. The very low estimated feedback elasticity for Germany's consumer prices is surprising in view of Germany's size and openness; in this respect, the feedback estimates for Germany's wholesale prices and its GDP deflator are probably more reliable.

If the domestic price effect of import price changes is significant and varies across countries, we can next ask what determines the size of that effect? Theory and empirical work suggest four principal factors: (i) the substitutability between imported and domestic goods in consumption and production; (ii) the share of imports in final expenditure or total output; (iii) the elasticity of factor prices, particularly money wages, with respect to actual (or expected) domestic price changes; and (iv) the elasticity of domestic prices with respect to changes in factor prices (again, principally money wages). The higher are each of these parameters, the greater will be the elasticity of domestic prices with respect to import price changes.[73]

If imports were perfect substitutes for domestic goods, then the domestic price equation would be a simple one; the only explanatory variable would be import prices and it would carry an estimated coefficient of unity [Isard (1977b)]. As indicated earlier, however, in our discussion of the "law of one price", the empirical literature has rejected the perfect substitutes hypothesis. This means that import price increases and decreases can still generate "sympathetic" and "disciplinary" effects respectively on domestic prices of similar goods, but that these effects are likely to be much smaller than unity [Kravis and Lipsey (1978)].[74]

Where imports represent inputs to production, standard production theory predicts that the elasticity of domestic prices with respect to import prices should be approximated by the (value) share of imports in total output, at

---

[73] See Goldstein (1974), Ball *et al.* (1977) and Bruno (1978).
[74] de Melo and Robinson (1981) show how the degrees of demand and supply substitution also affect the domestic price effects of changes in tariff and (export) subsidy rates.

least in the case of a Cobb-Douglas production function; [Ball *et al.* (1977)].[75] Thus, ceteris paribus, the more "import-open" the economy, the greater should be the domestic price effects of import price changes. Further, since countries differ much more with regard to the sizes of their import shares [Salant (1977)] than to either labor's share in total output or the response of money wages to domestic inflation, it is likely that this first factor is the dominant source of the inter-country variation in the elasticity of domestic prices with respect to import prices that we observe in the empirical studies.[76]

If there was some money illusion in the 1950s and 1960s, there does not seem to be any left in the 1970s and 1980s, to judge from the unitary coefficient on expected inflation rates now commonly found in aggregate wage equations [Santomero and Seater (1978)]. But this does not mean that the money wage response to domestic price changes is the same in all countries. In some countries money wages are formally indexed to the cost of living on practically a one-for-one basis; in other countries indexation is used but with a price index that specifically omits changes in the terms of trade; in other countries recourse has sometimes been made to incomes policies that guarantee labor an increased real wage; and in still others, indexation itself is prohibited.[77] All of this, plus differences across countries in the basic bargaining power of unions vis-à-vis employers, leads to differences in what Sachs (1980) calls the degree of "real wage resistance" among countries. Where indexation is widespread and where downward real wage resistance is strong, the domestic price effects of import price changes will likewise be strong.

What then are the policy implications of this feedback effect of import price changes on domestic prices? In our view, there are two major ones. The first is that the feedback effects can sharply diminish the *real* exchange rate changes that result from nominal exchange rate changes, and thereby

---

[75] Note that substitutability still counts here, but it is the substitution in production between imports and other factor inputs (labor, capital) that matters, not that between similar final goods in expenditure.

[76] Bruno (1978) dissents on this point. He finds small inter-country/differences in the effect of *PI* on *P* within a pooled time-series cross-section framework, and explains this by arguing that countries are more similar in the share of tradables in production and consumption than import or export data suggest.

[77] A good review of inter-country differences in indexation practices can be found in Braun (1976).

sharply reduce the expenditure-switching effects of such exchange rate changes even in the face of both reasonably high demand and supply elasticities for imports and exports and of supporting macroeconomic policies that keep a firm handle on the level of demand. Artus and McGuirk (1981) use the Fund's multilateral exchange rate model to contrast the trade balance effects of a 10 percent devaluation under low and high domestic price feedbacks. For the low feedback simulation, the elasticities of wages and the cost of capital with respect to the cost-of-living index are 0.5 and 0.3, respectively; in the high feedback simulation, these two elasticities jump to 0.85 and 0.70, respectively. Holding everything else constant, the trade balance effects with high domestic price feedback turn out to be only 60 percent as large as those with low feedback. In short, high domestic price feedback makes exchange rate changes less effective.[78,79]

The second implication of domestic price feedbacks arises out of their timing. Because the domestic price effects of exchange rate changes typically appear much before the resource allocation effects (due to low short-run price elasticities of demand and supply), there is a sense in which the "costs" of devaluation come before the "benefits".[80] This timing problem can act as a serious obstacle to devaluation itself.

4.4. Overview of the Effectiveness of Exchange Rate Changes

Since so much of the empirical trade literature over the past thirty years has focused on estimating price elasticities to determine whether devaluation "works" (i.e. improves the current account), it could seem appropriate to conclude this section with some broad generalizations on the effectiveness of exchange rate changes.

---

[78] Indeed, some observers [e.g. Lewis (1976)] have gone farther. They argue that with floating rates the domestic price feedback effects of exchange rate changes induce further depreciation of the exchange rate, thereby drawing high inflation countries into a "vicious circle" of high inflation and exchange rate depreciation, and low-inflation countries into a "virtuous circle" of price stability and exchange rate appreciation. This argument however neglects the role of excess money balances in driving both the inflation rate and the exchange rate, as well as other factors that help to put a check on the circle; see Bilson (1979), and Goldstein (1980).
[79] We speak here only of the expenditure-switching role of exchange rate changes. Even if domestic prices to rise by the full extent of the devaluation, the current account may improve as economic agents reduce expenditure to restore their desired level of real money balances.
[80] Of course, the same argument implies that benefits precede the costs in the case of revaluation.

(1) Relative prices matter. There is nothing in the empirical evidence on price elasticities themselves to indicate that their magnitude would be a barrier to successful devaluation over a time period of two to three years. Recent efforts to isolate the medium-term expenditure-switching effects of exchange rate changes [e.g. Artus and McGuirk (1981)] suggest that a 10 percent devaluation, along with low domestic price feedback, would improve the trade balance of a representative industrial country by somewhere between 4 and 10 percent of the initial value of trade; the corresponding figure for high domestic feedback would be roughly half that large. In this sense, we interpret the existing empirical evidence as endorsing Harberger's (1957) conclusion that "... the price mechanism works powerfully and pervasively in international trade".

(2) The short run is not, however, the same as the medium or long run. For time periods up to six months or perhaps even a year, the low trade volume response combined with the more rapid rise in local currency import prices than in export prices can quite commonly produce a deterioration in the trade balance of the depreciating country. In a similar vein, the domestic price feedback effects of exchange rate changes will appear before the resource allocation effects. In small, relatively open, highly-indexed economies, a 10 percent devaluation might well yield a 5 percent rise in the cost of living within a year.

(3) Relative prices are not the only things that matter. Whatever the price elasticities of demand and supply for imports, exports, tradables, and nontradables, it is worth remembering the lesson of the absorption approach that an improvement in the current account requires a reduction in expenditure relative to income; likewise, the monetary approach reminds us that there is a capital account as well as a current account, and that an exchange rate-induced excess demand for real money balances, if permitted to arise, can be satisfied from either channel. Both of these lessons are relevant for interpreting case histories of exchange rate changes [Laffer (1977), Miles (1979)]. In our view, before/after trade balance comparisons that indicate that devaluation does not work are typically instead examples of: lack of supporting expenditure-reducing policies (usually the offsetting of the positive effect of devaluation on the demand for real money balances by expansions in the money supply), of longer-term incentive patterns that favor expenditure over saving, of faster adjustment speeds in asset than in goods markets that cause devaluation to

work via the capital rather than the current account, or of accompanying trade policies that swamp the goods market effect of devaluation. In such circumstances, it is easy for the association between nominal exchange rate changes and current account imbalances to look weak even in the long run.

(4) Countries are different. While we read the empirical evidence as supportive of the effectiveness of exchange rate changes, we do not read it as supportive of *equal* effectiveness across countries. Differences in the commodity composition of trade, in degrees of import and export openness, in the degree of capacity utilization, in the degree of real wage resistance, and in the efficacy of monetary and fiscal policies all count. Although it is difficult to generalize on the basis of just one or two characteristics, it is our impression that the larger, less-open industrial countries face smaller domestic price feedbacks and can hold on to more of the initial competitive price advantage conferred by exchange rate changes than the smaller, more-open countries. Consistent with this, world trade models typically show a higher trade balance elasticity with respect to the exchange rate for the former group than for the latter.[81] These inter-country differences in the effectiveness of devaluation may also explain why countries often hold different views on the optimal degree of exchange rate flexibility.

5. CONCLUDING OBSERVATIONS

In some respects, empirical work on the time-series behavior of foreign trade flows has changed little over the past thirty years. The major thrust of this literature is still by and large single-equation studies that regress import or export volumes on the level of real economic activity at home or abroad and on relative traded goods' prices, with attention closely focused on the estimated income and price elasticities of demand. Despite the dramatic improvement in estimation techniques and capabilities, our review of the empirical evidence also did not uncover any indication that there have been dramatic changes in the sizes of these elasticities themselves over this period. While harder to document, we likewise suspect that the uses to which these elasticities are put are still pretty much the same, with forecasts of trade balances under

---

[81] See Artus and McGuirk (1981).

alternative growth and inflation paths and simulations of the expenditure-switching effects of exchange rate changes leading the way. Finally, most of the major methodological pitfalls in the specification and estimation of trade models that currently preoccupy researchers had already been identified by the early 1950s.

But all of this should not convey the impression that we have learned little of late about income and price effects in foreign trade. As illustrated in the previous three sections, noteworthy advances have been registered in understanding, inter alia, the determinants of export supply and export prices, the role of nonprice rationing in both import demand and export supply, the domestic price feedback effects of exchange rate changes, differences between short-run and long-run price elasticities of demand and between secular and cyclical income elasticities, the theoretical framework appropriate for computing all the own and cross-price elasticities of demand associated with a set of multilateral relative price changes for traded goods, the practical consequences for estimated price and income elasticities of measurement error in the price data, improper aggregation across commodity groups, ignoring the simultaneity between trade volumes and trade prices, and of the possibility of instability in the basic relationships.

At the same time, it is also apparent from our survey of the literature that existing empirical work is subject to some serious criticisms and that significant gaps remain to be filled by future research. To be more specific, there is in our view still a tendency for empirical trade work to be isolated from what is happening in macroeconomic theory. Two prominent examples of this isolation are the neglect of "permanent" or "life-cycle" income constructs in aggregate import and export demand functions and the absence of "expected" prices from export supply functions. Given the maintained hypothesis that imports and exports are (imperfect) substitutes for domestic goods, it does not make sense to have one theory of consumption or of aggregate supply for domestically-produced goods and another quite different one for imports and exports. Also, application of these concepts to trade models would help to remedy another shortcoming of this literature, namely the tendency for intertemporal considerations to be almost exclusively backward-looking rather than forward-looking.

A second broad area in which existing trade models come up short is in the integration of the real and financial sectors, i.e. in the interaction of goods and asset markets. Such integration would not be necessary if partial-equilibrium trade models were used only to answer partial-equilibrium questions. These trade models, however, are frequently employed to answer general-equilibrium questions that impinge on asset markets as well as goods markets, such as what would be the current account repercussions of exchange rate changes or of across-the-board tariff reductions. Such questions can be restricted by assumption to expenditure-switching effects in the goods market (i.e. one can assume that the authorities act to hold the overall level of final domestic demand constant), but it would be useful to know more about the implications for other macro variables, even under a constant-expenditure policy. This need not mean that trade models, if they are to be useful, should be appendages of large-scale economy-wide macro models; but it does suggest that we need to know more about to how the scale and relative price variables in trade equations are influenced by traditional macro policy instruments (monetary and fiscal policy) and how slower speeds of adjustment in goods than in asset markets will affect the short- and medium-run response of trade flows to internal and external price and income shocks.

Closer to the traditional pastures of trade modelling, we still see a significant pay-off to additional econometric work on time lags in export and import volume equations. As discussed in Sections 3 and 4, the existing literature has not yet produced anything approaching a consensus on the mean lag in the response of trade volumes to relative price changes despite, many studies on just that subject. More concretely, we have suggested ways in which the better qualities of geometric and polynomial distributed lags might be combined for this purpose; similarly, it would be worthwhile applying recent advances in time-series estimation to get a better handle on these lags. But better econometric methods alone are not likely to be sufficient. We will simultaneously need to learn more about the institutional factors (currency invoicing, lags between orders and deliveries, productions lags, etc.) that give rise to these lags so that we can have some solid priors to rely on in the estimation. Econometric advances in recent years can also be fruitfully applied in dealing with the issues of simultaneity and stability that still arise in the area of applied trade. We would certainly recommend that such techniques, discussed at length in Section 3, be utilized in future research on foreign trade relationships.

Our final priority area for future research is in the area of inter-country differences in price and income elasticities of demand and supply for traded goods. As suggested in Sections 2 and 4, there are many potential explanations for such observed inter-country differences (some relating to the commodity structure of trade, others to shares of imports and exports in domestic consumption and production or in world imports and exports, others to product cycles for new products, etc.), but very little has yet been done on testing these competing explanations. Since differences in elasticities across countries are often as crucial for assessing the trade impacts of income and price changes as the absolute sizes of the elasticities themselves, research on the former topic strikes us as important for understanding these impacts.

Morris Goldstein and Mohsin S. Khan, "Income and Price Effects in Foreign Trade," Reprinted from Ronald W. Jones and Peter Kenen (editors), Handbook of International Economics, Vol 2, pp. 1041–1105, Copyright (1985) with permission from Elsevier.

REFERENCES

Adams, F.G., et al. (1969), An econometric analysis of international trade (Organization for Economic Cooperation and Development, Paris).

Aghevli, B. and M.S. Khan (1980), "Credit policy and the balance of payments in developing countries", in: W.L. Coats and D.R. Khatkhate, eds., Money and monetary policy in less-developed countries (Pergamon Press, Oxford) 685–711.

Ahluwalia, I. and E. Hernandez-Cata (1975), "An econometric model of U.S. merchandise imports under fixed and fluctuating exchange rates, 1959–73", IMF Staff Papers, 22:791–824.

Aigner, D.J. and S.M. Goldfeld (1973), "Simulation and aggregation: A reconsideration", Review of Economics and Statistics, 55:114–118.

Aigner, D.J. and S.M. Goldfeld (1974), "Estimation and prediction from aggregate data when aggregates are measured more accurately than their components", Econometrica, 42:113–134.

Alexander, S.S. (1952), "Effects of devaluation on a trade balance", IMF Staff Papers, 2:263–278.

Amano, A. (1974), Export price behavior in selected industrial countries, unpublished (Kobe University, Japan).

Amano, A., A. Muruyama and M. Yoshitomi (1981), A three-country linkage model (Economic Planning Agency, Tokyo).

Armington, P.S. (1969), "A theory of demand for products distinguished by place of production", IMF Staff Papers, 26:159–178.

Armington, P.S. (1970), "Adjustment of trade balances: Some experiments with a model of trade among many countries", IMF Staff Papers, 27:488–526.

Artus, J.R. (1973), "The short-run effects of domestic demand pressure on export delivery delays for machinery", Journal of International Economics, 3:21–36.

Artus, J.R. (1977), "The behavior of export prices for manufactures", in: P.B. Clark, D.E. Logue and R.J. Sweeney, eds., The effects of exchange rate adjustments (U.S. Treasury, Washington, D.C.), 319–340.

Artus, J.R., (1979), Persistent surpluses and deficits on current account among major industrial countries, unpublished (IMF, Washington, D.C.).

Artus, J.R. and A.K. McGuirk (1981), "A revised version of the multilateral exchange rate model", IMF Staff Papers, 28:275–309.

Artus, J.R. and R.R. Rhomberg (1973), "A multilateral exchange rate model, IMF Staff Papers", 20:591–611.

Artus, J.R. and S.C. Sosa (1978), "Relative price effects on export performance: The case of nonelectrical machinery", IMF Staff Papers, 25:25–47.

Balassa, B. (1979), "Export composition and export performance in the industrial countries, 1953–71", Review of Economics and Statistics, 61:604–607.

Ball, R.J. and K. Marwah (1962), "The U.S. demand for imports, 1948–1958", Review of Economics and Statistics, 44:395–401.

Ball, R.J., J.R. Eaton and M.D. Steuer (1966), "The relationship between United Kingdom export performance in manufactures and the internal pressure of demand", Economic Journal, 76:501–518.

Ball, R.J., T. Burns and J. Laury (1977), "The role of exchange rate changes in balance of payments adjustment: The United Kingdom case", Economic Journal, 87:1–29.

Barker, T.S. (1970), "Aggregation error and estimates of the U.K. import demand function", in: K. Hilton and D.E. Heathfield, eds., The econometric study of the United Kingdom (London), 115–145.

Barker, T.S. (1976), "Imports", in: T.S. Barker, ed., Economic structure and policy (Chapman and Hall, London), 162–176.

Basevi, G. (1973), "Commodity trade equations in project LINK", in: R. Ball, ed., The international linkage of national economic models (North-Holland, Amsterdam) 227–281.

Bazdarich, M. (1979), "Has a strong U.S. economy meant a weak dollar"? Federal Reserve Bank of San Francisco Economic Review, Spring:35–46.

Beenstock, M. and P. Minford (1976), A quarterly econometric model of trade and prices 1955–72, in: M. Parkin and G. Zis, eds., Inflation in open economies (Manchester University Press, Manchester).

Bilson, J.F.O. (1979), "The 'vicious circle' hypothesis", IMF Staff Papers, 26:1–37.

Bond, M.E. (1980), "The world trade model: invisibles", IMF Staff Papers, 26:257–333.

Boylan, T.A., M.P. Cuddy and J. O'Muircheartaigh (1980), "The functional form of the aggregate import demand equation: A comparison of three European economies", Journal of International Economics, 10:561–566.

Box, G.E.P. and D.R. Cox (1964), "An analysis of transformations", Journal of the Royal Statistical Society, 26, Series B: 211–243.

Box, G.E.P. and G.M. Jenkins (1970), Time series analysis: Forecasting and control (Holden-Day, San Francisco).

Branson, W.H. (1968), A Disaggregated model of the U.S. balance of trade, Staff Economic Studies No. 44, Board of Governors of the Federal Reserve System, February.

Branson, W.H. (1972), "The trade effects of the 1971 currency realignments", Brookings Papers on Economic Activity, 15–69.

Branson, W.H. (1980), "Trends in United States international trade and investment since World War II", in: M. Feldstein, ed., The American economy in transition (National Bureau of Economic Research, Chicago), 183–257.

Braun, A. (1976), "Indexation of wages and salaries in developed economies", IMF Staff Papers, 23:226–271.

Brillembourg, A. (1975), "Specification bias in the demand for imports: The case of the Granco-lombian countries", April, unpublished (IMF, Washington, D.C.).

Brown, R.L., J. Durbin and J.M. Evans (1975), "Techniques for testing the constancy of regression relationships over time", Journal of the Royal Statistical Society, 37, Series B:149–163.

Bruno, M. (1978), "Exchange rates, import costs, and wage-price dynamics", Journal of Political Economy, 86:379–404.

Buckler, M. and C. Almon (1972), Imports and exports in an input-output model, Research Memorandum No. 38, Maryland Inter-Industry Forecasting Project.

Bureau of Labor Statistics (1980), Comparisons of United States, German and Japanese export price indexes (Washington, D.C.).

Burgess, D.F. (1974), "Production theory and the derived demand for imports", Journal of International Economics, 4:103–117.

Cagan, P. (1956), "The monetary dynamics of hyperinflation", in: M. Friedman, ed., Studies in the quantity theory of money (University of Chicago Press, Chicago), 25–117.

Cheng, H.S. (1959), "Statistical estimates of elasticities and propensities in international trade — a survey of published studies", IMF Staff Papers, 7:107–158.

Chow, G.C. (1960), "Tests of equality between subsets of coefficients in two linear regressions", Econometrica, 28:591–605.

Clark, P.B. (1977), "The effects of recent exchange rate changes on the U.S. trade balance", in: P.B. Clark, D.E. Logue and R.J. Sweeney, eds., The effects of exchange rate adjustments (U.S. Treasury, Washington, D.C.), 201–236.

Clements, K.W. and H. Theil (1978), "A simple method of estimating price elasticities in international trade", Economic Letters, 1:133–137.

Deardorff, A.V. and R.M. Stern (1977), "International economic interdependence: Evidence from econometric models", unpublished (University of Michigan, Ann Arbor, Mich.).

de Melo, J. and S. Robinson (1981), "Trade policy and resource allocation in the presence of product differentiation", Review of Economics and Statistics, 63: 169–177.

Deppler, M.C. and D.M. Ripley (1978), "The world trade model: Merchandise trade", IMF Staff Papers, 25:147–206.

Dornbusch, R. and S. Fischer (1978), Macroeconomics (McGraw-Hill, New York).

Dornbusch, R. and D.M. Jaffee (1978), "Purchasing power parity and exchange rate problems: Introduction", Journal of International Economics, 8:157–162.

Dornbusch, R. and P. Krugman (1976), "Flexible exchange rates in the short run", Brookings Papers on Economic Activity, 1:143–185.

Dunlevy, J.A. (1979), "Export demand, export supply, and capacity pressure: A simultaneous equations study of American and British export performance", unpublished (Auburn University).

Eckstein, O. and G. Fromm (1968), "The price equation", American Economic Review, 68:1159–1183.

Edwards, J.B. and G.H. Orcutt (1969), "Should aggregation prior to estimation be the rule?", Review of Economics and Statistics, 51:409–420.

Fair, R.C. (1979), "On modelling the economic linkages among countries", in: R. Dornbusch and J.A. Frenkel, eds., International economic policy — Theory and evidence (The Johns Hopkins University Press, Baltimore), 209–238.

Fair, R.C. and H.H. Kelejian (1974), "Methods of estimation for markets in disequilibrium: A further study", Econometrica, 52:177–190.

Frenkel, J.A. and H.G. Johnson eds. (1976), The monetary approach to the balance of payments (Allen and Unwin, London).

Geraci, V.J. and W. Prewo (1980), "An empirical demand and supply model of multilateral trade", March, unpublished (University of Texas, Texas).

Goldsbrough, D.J. (1981), "International trade of multinational corporations and its responsiveness to changes in aggregate demand and relative prices", IMF Staff Papers, 28:573–599.

Goldstein, M. (1974), "The effect of exchange rate changes on wages and prices in the United Kingdom", IMF Staff Papers, 21:694–739.

Goldstein, M. (1977), "Downward price inflexibility, ratchet effects and the inflationary impact of import price changes", IMF Staff Papers, 24:569–612.

Goldstein, M. (1980), "Have flexible exchange rates handicapped macroeconomic policy?", Special Papers in International Economics, No. 14 (Princeton University).

Goldstein, M. and M.S. Khan (1976), "Large versus small price changes and the demand for imports", IMF Staff Papers, 23:200–225.

Goldstein, M. and M.S. Khan (1978), "The supply and demand for exports: A simultaneous approach", Review of Economics and Statistics, 60:275–286.

Goldstein, M. and L.H. Officer (1979), "New measures of prices and productivity for tradable and nontradable goods", Review of Income and Wealth, 25:413–427.

Goldstein, M., M.S. Khan and L.H. Officer (1980), "Prices of tradable and nontradable goods in the demand for total imports", Review of Economics and Statistics, 62:190–199.

Granger, C.W.J. (1969), "Investigating causal relations by econometric models and cross-spectral methods", Econometrica, 37:424–438.

Gregory, R. (1971), "United States imports and internal pressure of demand", American Economic Review, 61:28–47.

Grossman, G.M. (1981), "Import competition from developed and developing countries", unpublished (Princeton University, Princeton, N.J.).

Grunfeld, Y. and Z. Griliches (1960), "Is aggregation necessarily bad?", Review of Economics and Statistics, 42:1–13.

Gylfason, T. (1978), "The effect of exchange rate changes on the balance of trade in ten industrial countries", October, unpublished (IMF, Washington D.C.).

Hall, R.E. (1978), "Stochastic implications of the life cycle-permanent income hypothesis: Theory and evidence", Journal of Political Economy, 86:971–988.

Hall, R.E. and R.C. Sutch (1967), "A flexible infinite distributed lag", paper presented at The Econometric Society Meetings.

Harberger, A.C. (1953), "A structural approach to the problem of import demand", American Economic Review, 43:148–159.

Harberger, A.C. (1957), "Some evidence on the international price mechanism", Journal of Political Economy, 65:506–521.

Hausman, J.A. (1978), "Specification tests in econometrics", Econometrica, 46:1251–1272.

Hay, G. (1970), "Production, prices, and inventory theory, American Economic Review", 60:531–545.

Heien, D.M. (1968), "Structural stability and the estimation of international import price elasticities", Kyklos, 21:695–712.

Hemphill, W.L. (1974), "The effect of foreign exchange receipts on imports of less developed countries", IMF Staff Papers, 21:637–677.

Hickman, B. and L. Lau (1973), "Elasticities of substitution and export demand in a world trade model", European Economic Review, 4:347–380.

Honda, Y. and K. Ohtani, (1980), "The joint specification of functional form and relative price restriction in the aggregate import demand equation", unpublished (Kobe University, Japan).

Hooper, P. (1976), "Forecasting U.S. export and import prices and volumes in a changing world economy", International Finance Discussion Paper No. 99, Board of Governors of the Federal Reserve System, December.

Hooper, P. (1978), "The stability of income and price elasticities in U.S. trade, 1957–1977", International Finance Discussion Paper No. 119, Board of Governors of the Federal Reserve System, June.

Hooper, P. and S. Kohlhagen (1978), "The effect of exchange rate uncertainty on the prices and volume of international trade", Journal of International Economics, 8:438–511.

Hooper, P. and B. Lowry (1979), "The impact of dollar depreciation on the U.S. price level: An analytical survey of empirical estimates", International Finance Discussion Paper No. 128, Board of Governors of the Federal Reserve System.

Houthakker, H.S. and S.P. Magee (1969), "Income and price elasticities in world trade", Review of Economics and Statistics, 51:111–125.

Houthakker, H.S. and L.D. Taylor (1970), Consumer demand in the United States: Analyses and projections (Harvard University Press, Cambridge).

International Bank for Reconstruction and Development (1981), World Development Report 1981 (Washington, D.C.).

Isard, P. (1977a), "The price effects of exchange-rate changes", in: P.B. Clark, D.E. Logue and R.J. Sweeney, eds., The effects of exchange rate adjustments (U.S. Treasury, Washington, D.C.), 369–388.

Isard, P. (1977b), "How far can we push the 'law of one price'?", American Economic Review, 67:942–948.

Johnson, H.G. (1958), International trade and economic growth; Studies in pure theory (Allen and Unwin, London).

Junz, H.B. and R.R. Rhomberg (1965), "Prices and export performance of industrial countries, 1953–63", IMF Staff Papers, 12:224–269.

Junz, H.B. and R.R. Rhomberg (1973), "Price competitiveness in export trade among industrial countries", American Economic Review, 63:412–418.

Kemp, M.C. (1962a), "Errors of measurement and bias in estimates of import demand parameters", Economic Record, September:369–372.

Kemp, M.C. (1962b), "The demand for Canadian imports: 1926–55" (University of Toronto Press, Toronto).

Kenen, P.B. and C. Pack (1979), "Exchange rates and domestic prices: A survey of the evidence", Research Memorandum, International Finance Section, (Princeton University, Princeton).

Khan, M.S. (1974), "Import and export demand in developing countries, IMF Staff Papers", 21:678–693.

Khan, M.S. (1975), "The structure and behavior of imports of Venezuela", Review of Economic and Statistics, 57:221–224.

Khan, M.S. and K.Z. Ross (1975), "Cyclical and secular income elasticities of the demand for imports", Review of Economics and Statistics, 57:357–361.

Khan, M.S. and K.Z. Ross (1977), "The functional form of the aggregate import equation", Journal of International Economics, 7:149–160.

Kohli, U.R. (1982), "Relative price effects and the demand for imports", Canadian Journal of Economics, May:205–219.

Kmenta, J. (1971), Elements of econometrics (Macmillan, New York).

Kravis, I.B. and R.E. Lipsey (1971), Price competitiveness in world trade (NBER, New York).

Kravis, I.B. and R.E. Lipsey (1974), "International trade prices and price proxies", in: N. Ruggles, ed., The role of the computer in economic and social research in Latin America (NBER, New York), 253–268.
Kravis, I.B. and R.E. Lipsey (1978), "Price behavior in the light of balance of payments theories", Journal of International Economics, 8:193–246.
Kreinin, M.E. (1961), "Effects of tariff changes on the prices and volume of imports", American Economic Review, 51:297–329.
Kreinin, M.E. (1967), "Price elasticities in international trade", Review of Economics and Statistics, 49:510–516.
Kreinin, M.E. (1977), "The effect of exchange rate changes on the prices and volume of foreign trade", IMF Staff Papers, 24:207–329.
Kreinin, M.E. (1979), International economics (Harcourt Brace Jovanich, New York).
Kreinin, M. and L.H. Officer (1978), "The monetary approach to the balance of payments: A survey", Studies in International Finance No. 43 (Princeton University).
Laffer, A.B. (1977), "Exchange rates, the terms of trade, and the trade balance", in: P.B. Clark, D.E. Logue, and R.J. Sweeney, eds., The effects of exchange rate adjustments (U.S. Treasury, Washington, D.C.), 32–44.
Lawrence, R. (1978), "An analysis of the 1977 U.S. trade deficit", Brookings Papers on Economic Activity, 1:159–190.
Leamer, E.E. (1981), "Is it a demand curve, or is it a supply curve? Partial identification through inequality constraints", Review of Economics and Statistics, 63:319–327.
Leamer, E.E. and R.M. Stem (1970), Quantitative international economics (Allyn and Bacon, Boston).
Lewis, P. (1976), "The weak get weaker with floating rates", New York Times, October 10.
Liu, T.C. (1954), "The elasticity of U.S. import demand: A theoretical and empirical reappraisal", IMF Staff Papers, 3:416–441.
Lucas, R.E. (1973), "Some international evidence on output-inflation trade-offs", American Economic Review, 63:326–334.
Lucas, R.E. (1976), "Econometric policy evaluation", in: K. Brunner and A. Meltzer, eds., The Phillips curve and labor market (North-Holland, Amsterdam).
Maddala, G.S. (1977), Econometrics (McGraw-Hill, New York).
Magee, S.P. (1970), "A theoretical and empirical examination of supply and demand relationships in U.S. international trade", unpublished, (Council of Economic Advisers, Washington, D.C.).
Magee, S.P. (1972), "Tariffs and U.S. trade", unpublished (Council of Economic Advisers, Washington, D.C.).
Magee, S.P. (1973), "Currency contracts, pass-through, and devaluation", Brookings Papers on Economic Activity, 1:303–323.
Magee, S.P. (1975), "Prices, income and foreign trade: A survey of recent economic studies", in: P.B. Kenen, ed., International trade and finance: Frontiers for research (Cambridge University Press, Cambridge).

Magee, S.P. and R. Rao (1980), "Vehicle and nonvehicle currencies in international trade", American Economic Review, 70:368–373.
McCloskey, D.N. and J.R. Zecher (1976), "How the gold standard worked, 1980–1913", in: J.A. Frenkel and H.G. Johnson, eds., The monetary approach to the balance of payments (Allen and Unwin, London), 357–385.
McKinnon, R. (1978), "Exchange rate instability, trade imbalances, and monetary policies in Japan and the United States", unpublished (Stanford University, Stanford, CA.).
Miles, M.A. (1979), "The effects of devaluation on the trade balance and the balance of payments: Some new results", Journal of Political Economy 87:600–620.
Minford, P. (1978), Substitution effects, speculation and exchange rate stability (North-Holland, Amsterdam).
Mintz, I. (1967), Cyclical fluctuations in the exports of the United States since 1879, Studies in Business Cycles No. 15 (NBER, New York).
Morgan, D.I. and W.J. Corlett (1951), "The influence of price in international trade: A study in method", Journal of the Royal Statistical Society 114, Series A:307–358.
Murray, T. and P. Ginman, (1976), "An empirical examination of the traditional aggregate import demand model", Review of Economics and Statistics, 58:75–80.
Mutti, J.H. (1977), "The specification of demand equations for imports and domestic substitutes", Southern Economic Journal, 44:68–73.
Okun, A. (1975), "Inflation: Its mechanics and welfare costs", Brookings Papers on Economic Activity, 2:351–501.
Orcutt, G. (1950), "Measurement of price elasticities in international trade", Review of Economics and Statistics, 32:117–132.
Prais, S.J. (1962), "Econometric research in international trade: A review", Kyklos, 15:560–577.
Ramsey, J.B. (1969), "Tests for specification errors in classical least-squares regression analysis", Journal of the Royal Statistical Society, 31, Series B:350–371.
Rhomberg, R.R. (1973), "Towards a general trade model", in: R.J. Ball, ed., The international linkage of national economic models (North-Holland, Amsterdam), 9–20.
Rhomberg, R.R. and L. Boissonneault (1965), "The foreign sector", in: The Brookings quarterly econometric model of the United States, (Rand McNally, Chicago), 375–406.
Richardson, J.D. 1973, "Beyond (but back to?) the elasticity of substitution in international trade", European Economic Review, 4:381–392.
Robinson, P., T. Webb and M. Townsend (1979), "The influence of exchange rate changes on prices: A study of 18 industrial countries", Economica, 46:27–50.
Sachs, J. (1980), "Wage indexation, flexible exchange rates, and macroeconomic policy", Quarterly Journal of Economics, 94:731–748.
Sachs, J. (1981), "The current account and macroeconomic adjustment in the 1970s", Brookings Papers on Economic Activity, 1:201–268.

Salant, W. (1977), "International transmission of inflation", in: L. Krause and W. Salant, eds., Worldwide inflation (Brookings Institution, Washington), 167–226.
Samuelson, L. (1973), "A new model of world trade", OECD Occasional Studies (Organization for Economic Cooperation and Development, Paris).
Sargent, T.J. (1976), "The observational equivalence of natural and unnatural rate theories of macroeconomics", Journal of Political Economy, 84:631–640.
Santomero, A. and J. Seater (1978), "The inflation-unemployment trade-off: A critique of the literature", Journal of Economic Literature, 16:499–544.
Sims, C. (1971), "Discrete approximations to continuous time distributed lags in econometrics", Econometrica, 39:545–564.
Sims, C. (1972), "Money, income, and causality", American Economic Review, 62:540–552.
Spitaeller, E. (1978), "A model of inflation and its performance in the seven main industrial countries, 1958–76", IMF Staff papers, 25:254–277.
Spitaeller, E. (1980), "Short-run effects of exchange rate changes on terms of trade and trade balance", IMF Staff Papers, 27:320–348.
Stern, R.M., J. Francis and B. Schumacher (1976), Price elasticities in international trade — An annotated bibliography (Macmillan, London).
Stern, R.M., C.F. Baum and M.N. Greene (1979), "Evidence on structural change in the demand for aggregate U.S. imports and exports", Journal of Political Economy, 87:179–192.
Stone, Joe A. (1979), "Price elasticities of demand for imports and exports: Industry estimates for the U.S., the E.E.C. and Japan", Review of Economics and Statistics, 61:117–123.
Taplin, G.B. (1973), "A model of world trade", in: R.J. Ball, ed., The international linkage of national economic models (North-Holland, Amsterdam), 177–223.
Theil, H. (1954), Linear aggregation of economic relations (North-Holland, Amsterdam).
Theil, H. and K.W. Clements (1978), "A Differential Approach to U.S. Import Demand", Economics Letters, 1:249–254.
Truman, E. (1978), "Balance-of-payments adjustment from a U.S. perspective: The lessons of the 1970's", unpublished (Board of Governors of the Federal Reserve System, Washington, D.C.).
Vernon, R. (1966), "International Investment and International Trade in the Product Cycle", Quarterly Journal of Economics, 80:191–207.
Wallich, H. (1978), "Reflections on the U.S. balance of payments", Challenge March/April, 34–40.
Weisskoff, R. (1979), "Trade, protection and import elasticities for Brazil", Review of Economics and Statistics, 51:58–66.

Wilson, J.F. and W. Takacs (1979), "Differential responses to price and exchange rate influences in the foreign trade of selected industrial countries", Review of Economics and Statistics, 51:267–279.

Winters, L.A. (1976), "Exports", in: T.S. Barker, ed., Economic structure and policy (Chapman and Hall, London), 131–161.

Wymer, C.E. (1972), "Econometric estimation of stochastic differential equation systems", Econometrica, 40:565–577.

Chapter 2

The Supply and Demand for Exports: A Simultaneous Approach

Morris Goldstein and Mohsin S. Khan*

Section I. INTRODUCTION

Empirical studies of international trade flows have generally concentrated on the formulation and estimation of demand relationships for imports and exports, e.g., see the studies by Houthakker and Magee (1969), Taplin (1973), and Hickman and Lau (1973). Supply relationships have typically been handled by assumption, the usual practice being to assume that the export and import supply price elasticities facing any individual country are infinite. While the assumption of an infinite price elasticity seems reasonable a priori in the case of the world supply of imports to a single country, this assumption carries far less intuitive appeal when applied to the supply of exports of an individual country. That is, unless idle capacity exists in the export (or domestic) sector, or more generally, unless export production is

---

*International Monetary Fund

The views expressed in this paper are not necessarily those of the IMF. The authors are grateful to Bijan Aghevli, Jacques Artus, Andrew Crockett, Robert Heller, Max Kreinin, Rudolf Rhomberg, and two anonymous referees for helpful comments on an earlier draft, and to Fernando Santos for competent research assistance. An earlier version of this paper was presented at the Third World Congress of the Econometric Society, Toronto, August 1975.

Received for publication August 13, 1976. Revision accepted for publication November 12, 1976.

subject to constant or increasing returns to scale, it is unlikely that an increase in the world demand for a country's exports can be satisfied without any increase in the price of its exports (at least in the short run).[1]

In the relatively few cases where a supply function for exports has actually been specified,[2] it has usually not been possible to obtain an estimate of the supply price elasticity either because the relevant structural parameters could not be recaptured from the reduced-form estimating equation, or because the structural supply equation itself did not posit a direct relationship between the quantity of exports supplied and export prices.[3] For example, the recent study by Amano (1974) on the export behavior of ten industrial countries contains explicit export demand and export supply functions but the over-identified nature of that model prevents one from obtaining estimates of either the demand or the supply-price elasticities. Similarly, the studies by Ball *et al.* (1966), Suss (1974), and Artus (1970) deal directly with the supply of exports, or more precisely with the effect of domestic demand pressure on export behavior, but these are models of the short-run adjustment process that do not yield estimates of the price elasticity of export supply.

The primary purpose of this study is to investigate the price responsiveness of both export demand and export supply using quarterly data on the aggregate exports of eight industrial countries for the period 1955–1970. Two relatively simple models of export demand and supply are introduced and these models are then estimated simultaneously so as to eliminate any bias arising from the two-way relationship between export quantities and export prices. Since we estimate the structural equations directly, estimates of both the demand and supply price elasticities are obtained for each of the following eight countries in our sample: Belgium, France, Germany, Italy, Japan, the Netherlands, the United Kingdom, and the United States. In general, our empirical results

---

[1] This of course assumes that the entire increase in demand cannot be satisfied from inventories.
[2] For good general discussions of export supply functions, see Basevi (1973), Rhomberg (1973), and Leamer and Stern (1970). Also, see Morgan and Corlett (1951) for an early attempt to provide simultaneous estimates of export demand and export supply.
[3] An exception is the 1964 study by Rhomberg and Boissonneault (1964) that contains a structural export supply function similar to the one employed here. The price elasticities of export supply and export demand are not, however, estimated simultaneously in that study as they are here. In addition, the studies differ in a number of other respects including, inter alia, the degree of country aggregation, the use of annual versus quarterly data, the time periods under study, and the proxy used for export capacity in the export supply equation.

suggest that estimates of demand-price elasticities for (aggregate) exports can be substantially different when export supply relationships are explicitly taken into account.

The plan of the paper is as follows: Section II introduces the basic theory behind each of the models that are to be estimated. The results obtained from estimating the structural demand and supply equations are presented and discussed in section III. The study's principal conclusions appear in section IV. Data definitions and sources are given in the appendix.

Section II. THEORETICAL SPECIFICATION OF THE EXPORT FUNCTIONS

In this section, two versions of a basic model of export quantity and price determination are considered. The first model, which we refer to as the "equilibrium" model, makes the simplifying assumption that there are no lags in the system so that the adjustment of export quantities and prices to their respective equilibrium values is instantaneous; in a quarterly model such as ours, this would mean that all adjustment takes place within a one-quarter period. In the second model, which we label the "disequilibrium" model, we relax the above assumption and admit the possibility that adjustment of actual to equilibrium values may take place with some delay. Therefore, in the disequilibrium model, excess demand and supply are allowed to emerge and to affect the prices and quantities of exports.

A. *Equilibrium Model*

The world demand for an individual country's exports is specified in log-linear form as follows:

$$\log X_t^d = a_0 + a_1 \log (PX/PXW)_t + a_2 \log YW_t \qquad (1)$$

where

$$X^d = \text{quantity of exports demanded}$$
$$PX = \text{price of exports}$$
$$PXW = \text{weighted average of the export prices}$$
$$\text{of the country's trading partners}$$

YW = weighted average of the real incomes of the country's trading partners.

Since equation (1) is specified in logarithms, a_1 and a_2 are the (relative) price and real income elasticities (of export demand), respectively. It is expected that a_1 will be negative and a_2 positive.[4]

The supply of exports is specified as a log-linear function of the relative price of exports (i.e., the ratio of export prices to domestic prices) and of an index of the productive capacity of the country:

$$\log X_t^s = \beta_0 + \beta_1 \log (PX/P)_t + \beta_2 Y_t^* \qquad (2)$$

where

X^s = quantity of exports supplied
PX = price of exports
P = domestic price index
Y^* = logarithm of an index of domestic capacity.

Equation (2) embodies the hypothesis that as the price of exports rises relative to domestic prices, production for export becomes more profitable and, hence, exporters will supply more. In addition, exports are posited to rise, *ceteris paribus*, when there is an increase in the country's capacity to produce. We therefore expect both β_1 and β_2 to be positive in the results. The equation can be normalized for the price of exports, PX_t to yield[5]

$$\log PX_t = b_0 + b_1 \log X_t^s + b_2 Y_t^* + b_3 \log P_t \qquad (3)$$

---

[4] It should be noted that while the sign of the real income elasticity (a_2) is usually assumed to be positive, it need not necessarily be so. For example, if the exports of a country were simply a residual demand by the rest of the world, i.e., the difference between world production and consumption of importables, then a_2 could be negative if increases in world income were associated with faster growth in the production than in the consumption of importables. For a fuller treatment of this argument, see Magee (1975) and Khan and Ross (1975).

[5] Since we are going to estimate the model simultaneously, each of the equations should have the appropriate endogenous variable on the left-hand side. This, however, is only a matter of convenience since the estimates of the parameters are invariant with respect to the normalization procedure when a system method of estimation is employed.

where

$$b_0 = -\frac{\beta_0}{\beta_1}; \quad b_1 = \frac{1}{\beta_1}; \quad b_2 = -\frac{\beta_2}{\beta_1};$$

and

$$b_3 = \frac{\beta_1}{\beta_1}.$$

Since $\beta_1, \beta_2 > 0$, we expect that

$$b_1 > 0; \quad b_2 < 0; \quad b_3 > 0.$$

The parameter β_1, which is the price elasticity of the supply of exports, can be obtained from (3) by calculating $(b_1)^{-1}$. As b_1, tends to zero, β_1, will tend to infinity.

Equations (1) and (3) constitute the equilibrium model, and estimates of the structural parameters can be obtained by estimating these two equations simultaneously.[6] In order to obtain the effect of solely exogenous variables on the quantity and price of exports, we can solve the two equations to obtain the reduced-forms:

$$\log X_t = \frac{a_0 + a_1 b_0}{D} - \frac{a_1}{D} \log PXW_t + \frac{a_2}{D} \log YW_t$$

$$+ \frac{a_1 b_2}{D} Y_t^* + \frac{a_1 b_3}{D} \log P_t \qquad (4)$$

$$\log PX_t = \frac{b_0 + a_0 b_1}{D} - \frac{a_1 b_1}{D} \log PXW_t$$

$$+ \frac{a_2 b_1}{D} \log YW_t + \frac{b_2}{D} Y_t^* + \frac{b_3}{D} \log P_t. \qquad (5)$$

Since $D = 1 - a_1 b_1$ and is positive, we expect the reduced-form coefficients to have the pattern of signs shown in Table 1.

B. *Disequilibrium Model*

In order to introduce the possibility of disequilibrium behavior into the export model, we utilize the adjustment mechanism outlined by Houthakker and Taylor (1970). In this model, exports are assumed to adjust to the difference

---

[6] Assuming $X_t^d = X_t^s = X_t$, and the addition of stochastic error terms.

Table 1: Reduced-form Coefficients: Equilibrium Model

	$\log PXW_t$	$\log YW_t$	Y_t^*	$\log P_t$
$\log X_t$	+	+	+	−
$\log PX_t$	+	+	−	+

between demand for exports in period t and the actual flow in the previous period:[7]

$$\Delta \log X_t = \gamma[\log X_t^d - \log X_{t-1}] \tag{6}$$

where γ is the coefficient of adjustment (assumed positive) and Δ is a first-difference operator, $\Delta \log X_t = \log X_t - \log X_{t-1}$.

The adjustment function (6) assumes that the quantity of exports adjusts to conditions of excess demand in the rest of the world, and therefore, the price of exports is determined in the exporting country.[8]

---

[7] The model, (6), is an approximation to a theoretical dynamic model expressed in continuous time:

$$\frac{d}{dt} \log X(t) = \gamma \left[\log X^d(t) - \log X(t)\right], \quad \gamma > 0. \tag{6a}$$

The Houthakker-Taylor discrete approximation corresponding to (6a) is

$$\Delta \log X_t = \gamma [M \log X_t^d - M \log X_t] \tag{6b}$$

where $M = 0.5(1 + L)$ and L is a lag-operator, $LX_t = X_{t-1}$. Sargan (1975) has shown that though the estimates from (6b) are biased, the bias is known and will generally be small if the eigenvalues of (6b) are small.

Equation (6a) is a relationship with a lag structure that has exponentially declining weights, as its deterministics part can be written as

$$\log X(t) = \int_0^\infty \gamma e^{-\gamma \theta} \log X^d(t - \theta)\, d\theta.$$

[8] An alternative function could be specified where the change in export quantity is related to excess supply so that excess demand would determine the change in the price of exports. Experiments with this alternative model yielded markedly inferior results as compared to the results of the model considered here. This suggests in turn that the supply side of the export market may have a more monopolistic market structure than the demand side, and that exporters are price-setters rather than price-takers. Of course, in reality both export quantity and export price may adjust to excess demand so that the alternative adjustment functions discussed above should be considered as approximations.

By substituting equation (1) into (6) we obtain an estimating equation for exports:

$$\log X_t = c_0 + c_1 \log (PX/PXW)_t + c_2 \log YW_t + c_3 \log X_{t-1} \quad (7)$$

where $c_0 = \gamma a_0$, $c_1 = \gamma a_1$, $c_2 = \gamma a_2$, and $c_3 = 1 - \gamma$. Based on the expected signs of the parameters a_1, a_2, and γ, we would expect that

$$c_1 < 0; \quad c_2 > 0; \quad c_3 > 0.$$

The mean time lag in the adjustment of exports is equal to γ^{-1} and can be calculated from the parameters of equation (7) as $(1 - c_3)^{-1}$.

Since the quantity of exports is specified as adjusting to excess demand, the price of exports adjusts to conditions of excess supply[9]:

$$\Delta \log PX_t = \lambda[\log X_t - \log X_t^s], \quad \lambda > 0 \quad (8)$$

where λ is the coefficient of adjustment. In this framework an increase in excess supply will lower the price of exports, and conversely for a decrease.

Substituting equation (2) into (8) and solving for $\log PX_t$ we obtain

$$\log PX_t = d_0 + d_1 \log X_t + d_2 \log P_t + d_3 Y_t^* + d_4 \log PX_{t-1} \quad (9)$$

where

$$d_0 = \frac{-\lambda \beta_0}{1 + \lambda \beta_1}, \quad d_1 = \frac{\lambda}{1 + \lambda \beta_1},$$

$$d_2 = \frac{\lambda \beta_1}{1 + \lambda \beta_1}, \quad d_3 = \frac{-\lambda \beta_2}{1 + \lambda \beta_1},$$

and

$$d_4 = \frac{1}{1 + \lambda \beta_1}.$$

Since $\beta_1 > 0$, $\beta_2 > 0$, and $\lambda > 0$, we expect that $d_1 > 0$; $d_2 > 0$; $d_3 < 0$; $d_4 > 0$.

---

[9] We also considered an alternative model where export prices adjust to excess supply *and* to competitor's export prices. The latter variable, however, did not perform very well in the empirical work and therefore we deal only with the simpler specification shown in equation (8).

Table 2: Reduced-form Coefficients: Disequilibrium Model

	$\log PXW_t$	$\log YW_t$	Y_t^*	$\log P_t$	$\log PX_{t-1}$	$\log X_{t-1}$
$\log X_t$	+	+	+	−	−	+
$\log PX_t$	+	+	−	+	+	+

The reduced-form equations obtained from equations (7) and (9) are:

$$\log X_t = \frac{c_0 + c_1 d_0}{D'} - \frac{c_1}{D'} \log PXW_t$$

$$+ \frac{c_2}{D'} \log YW_t + \frac{c_1 d_3}{D'} Y_t^* + \frac{c_1 d_2}{D'} \log P_t$$

$$+ \frac{c_1 d_4}{D'} \log PX_{t-1} + \frac{c_3}{D'} \log X_{t-1} \tag{10}$$

$$\log PX_t = \frac{d_0 + d_1 c_0}{D'} - \frac{c_1 d_1}{D'} \log PXW_t$$

$$+ \frac{c_2 d_1}{D'} \log YW_t + \frac{d_3}{D'} Y_t^* + \frac{d_2}{D'} \log P_t$$

$$+ \frac{d_4}{D'} \log PX_{t-1} + \frac{c_3 d_1}{D'} \log X_{t-1} \tag{11}$$

where $D' = 1 - c_1 d_1$. Based on the signs of the structural parameters we expect the reduced form coefficients to carry the signs shown in Table 2.

Section III. RESULTS

The equilibrium and disequilibrium models outlined in the previous section were estimated for the eight countries listed in the introduction. The estimator used was Full-Information Maximum Likelihood (FIML). This estimator requires specification of the complete model and utilizes all a priori restrictions on the system to estimate the structural coefficients simultaneously by maximizing the likelihood function of the model. On the basis of asymptotic theory, FIML appears to be the best estimator. It should be pointed out that this estimator can be highly sensitive to small changes in specification and/or data. For the equilibrium model we used a linear FIML estimator (except for the case of Japan where we used Two Stage Least Squares [TSLS]).

For the disequilibrium models, however, due to the nonlinear restrictions on parameters, we used a nonlinear FIML estimator in all eight cases.

Tables 3 and 4 show the estimates for the equilibrium and disequilibrium models, respectively. In each of the tables are shown the values of the estimated coefficients and, in parentheses below each, the ratio of the estimated coefficients to their respective standard errors. This ratio can be interpreted as following a "quasi-T" distribution, though strictly speaking its distribution is asymptotic normal. The coefficient of determination, R^2, is also calculated for the individual equations although its meaning in simultaneous models is at best ambiguous.[10] The same reservation also applies to the standard error of the estimate, S.E., that is presented. We have not reported any test of autocorrelation, such as the Durbin-Watson statistic, since the properties of these tests are not clear in simultaneous models when one is using a full-information estimator.[11] In Table 4 (the disequilibrium model) we also report the estimated values (along with their respective t-ratios) of the individual parameters.

A. *Equilibrium Model*

As can be seen in Table 3, the estimated price elasticity in the export demand equation (1) carries the expected negative sign and is significantly different from zero (at the usual 5% level) in all the countries in our sample except Japan.[12] In six of the eight countries studied — namely, Belgium, France, Italy, the Netherlands, the United Kingdom, and the United States, the estimated price elasticity is also greater than unity. This implies a fairly large response of exports to changes in relative prices. These price elasticity results differ rather markedly from the results obtained by some earlier investigators for the same group of countries. For example, Houthakker and Magee (1969) found a significantly negative relationship between exports and relative export prices only in the cases of France and the United States. In a similar vein, the export

---

[10] This is because it is not bounded (0, 1) but ($-\infty$, 1) so that small values are not an indication of a "poor" fit.

[11] Since preliminary tests on the individual equations did not indicate any serious problem with autocorrelation we assumed that the errors were independent.

[12] In the case of Japan, the price elasticity of demand had an (unexpected) positive sign and was significantly different from zero. We do not regard this as a credible result.

Table 3: Structural Equation Estimates: Equilibrium Model
(Total Exports: Quarterly Data, 1955–1970)

Belgium
1. $\log X_t = -3.085 - 1.572 \log (PX/PXW)_t + 1.683 \log YW_t$
   $\quad\quad\quad\quad (8.15) \quad (2.63) \quad\quad\quad\quad\quad\quad (20.91)$
   $R^2 = 0.971; \quad \text{S.E.} = 0.043$

2. $\log PX_t = 5.887 + 0.815 \log X_t - 3.233\ Y_t^* + 2.156 \log P_t$
   $\quad\quad\quad\quad\ (6.33) \quad (3.21) \quad\quad\quad (3.84) \quad\quad (4.76)$
   $R^2 = 0.881; \quad \text{S.E.} = 0.015$

France
1. $\log X_t = -3.156 - 1.334 \log (PX/PXW)_t + 1.693 \log YW_t$
   $\quad\quad\quad\quad (18.67) \quad (5.91) \quad\quad\quad\quad\quad\quad (51.57)$
   $R^2 = 0.977; \quad \text{S.E.} = 0.056$

2. $\log PX_t = 2.242 + 0.528 \log X_t - 1.242\ Y_t^* + 1.217 \log P_t$
   $\quad\quad\quad\quad\ (5.89) \quad (3.45) \quad\quad\quad (5.73) \quad\quad (7.92)$
   $R^2 = 0.831; \quad \text{S.E.} = 0.033$

Germany
1. $\log X_t = -3.744 - 0.831 \log (PX/PXW)_t + 1.805 \log YW_t$
   $\quad\quad\quad\quad (19.36) \quad (4.31) \quad\quad\quad\quad\quad\quad (46.30)$
   $R^2 = 0.915; \quad \text{S.E.} = 0.042$

2. $\log PX_t = 2.337 + 0.219 \log X_t - 1.216\ Y_t^* + 0.497 \log P_t$
   $\quad\quad\quad\quad\ (4.30) \quad (2.55) \quad\quad\quad (3.18) \quad\quad (3.96)$
   $R^2 = 0.813; \quad \text{S.E.} = 0.010$

Italy
1. $\log X_t = -4.482 - 3.290 \log (PX/PXW)_t + 1.964 \log YW_t$
   $\quad\quad\quad\quad (8.76) \quad (8.54) \quad\quad\quad\quad\quad\quad (17.81)$
   $R^2 = 0.957; \quad \text{S.E.} = 0.081$

2. $\log PX_t = 9.129 + 0.891 \log X_t - 2.897\ Y_t^* + 1.038 \log P^t$,
   $\quad\quad\quad\quad\ (4.30) \quad (2.55) \quad\quad\quad (3.18) \quad\quad (4.41)$
   $R^2 = 0.817; \quad \text{S.E.} = 0.021$

Japan
1. $\log X_t = -15.020 + 2.471 \log (PX/PXW)_t + 4.228 \log YW_t$
   $\quad\quad\quad\quad (10.02) \quad (2.17) \quad\quad\quad\quad\quad\quad (13.26)$
   $R^2 = 0.942; \quad \text{S.E.} = 0.083$

2. $\log PX_t = 3.232 + 0.346 \log X_t - 0.910\ Y_t^* + 0.864 \log P_t$
   $\quad\quad\quad\quad\ (2.25) \quad (1.45) \quad\quad\quad (2.97) \quad\quad (2.12)$
   $R^2 = 0.840; \quad \text{S.E.} = 0.022$

Netherlands
1. $\log X_t = -4.187 - 2.728 \log (PX/PXW)_t + 1.905 \log YW_t$
   $\quad\quad\quad\quad (26.94) \quad (4.89) \quad\quad\quad\quad\quad\quad (62.23)$
   $R^2 = 0.950; \quad \text{S.E.} = 0.034$

2. $\log PX_t = 5.490 + 0.4004 \log X_t - 1.293\ Y_t^* + 0.715 \log P_t$
   $\quad\quad\quad\quad\ (19.30) \quad (5.57) \quad\quad\quad (7.91) \quad\quad (7.15)$
   $R^2 = 0.854; \quad \text{S.E.} = 0.017$

(Continued)

Table 3: (Continued)

United Kingdom	1.	$\log X_t = 0.435 - 1.323 \log (PX/PXW)_t + 0.918 \log YW_t$ $\qquad\qquad (2.58)\quad (6.70)\qquad\qquad\qquad (27.04)$ $R^2 = 0.954;\qquad \text{S.E.} = 0.027$
	2.	$\log PX_t = 2.502 + 0.691 \log X_t - 1.447\, Y_t^* + 1.213 \log P_t$ $\qquad\qquad\; (12.69)\;\; (7.68)\qquad\quad (7.06)\qquad\; (8.55)$ $R^2 = 0.830;\qquad \text{S.E.} = 0.077$
United States	1.	$\log X_t = -0.039 - 2.319 \log (PX/PXW)_t + 1.010 \log YW_t$ $\qquad\qquad\; (0.23)\quad (5.08)\qquad\qquad\qquad (29.43)$ $R^2 = 0.941;\qquad \text{S.E.} = 0.061$
	2.	$\log PX_t = 2.438 + 0.152 \log X_t - 0.366\, Y_t^* + 0.690 \log P_t$ $\qquad\qquad\; (12.94)\;\; (3.19)\qquad\quad (7.59)\qquad\; (4.16)$ $R^2 = 0.845;\qquad \text{S.E.} = 0.018$

price elasticities computed by Hickman and Lau (1973) for these countries tend to be considerably smaller than the elasticities estimated by us. A more detailed comparison of our equilibrium (demand price) elasticities with those of both Houthakker-Magee (1969) and Hickman-Lau (1973) as well as with the estimates obtained by us using Ordinary Least Squares (OLS), is given in Table 5. In short, our results point to an important role for relative prices in determining the world demand for these countries' exports.

The estimated income elasticities in Table 3 have the expected positive signs and are significantly different from zero at the 1% level in the equations for all eight countries.[13] In contrast to the price elasticities of demand, the estimated income elasticities tend to be very similar to the ones obtained by Houthakker and Magee (1969) for this group of countries. The inter-country pattern of income elasticities observed by Houthakker and Magee, where the exports of the United States and the United Kingdom have a relatively low, and the exports of Japan a relatively high, income elasticity is also evident in our results. It might be noted that the export demand equations all seem to be quite well specified judging by the values of the R^2s obtained.[14]

---

[13] As a caveat, it should be noted that the export demand model used here does not allow one to distinguish secular from cyclical effects in the income elasticity; for an empirical treatment of this issue, see Khan and Ross (1975).

[14] Recall our discussion about the use of the R^2 statistic — it is bounded $(-\infty, 1)$ so that values close to unity are still a fairly good indicator of the goodness-of-fit of the *individual* equation.

Table 4: Structural Equation Estimates: Disequilibrium Model
(Total Exports: Quarterly Data, 1955–1970)

Belgium
1. $\log X_t = -2.094 - 0.035 \log (PX/PXW)_t + 0.979 \log YW_t + 0.484 \log X_{t-1}$
   $\quad\quad\quad\quad (4.59)\quad\quad (0.17)\quad\quad\quad\quad\quad\quad (4.96)\quad\quad\quad\quad (4.84)$
   $\gamma = 0.516;\quad a_1 = -0.068;\quad a_2 = 1.898$
   $\quad (5.16)\quad\quad\quad\quad (0.16)\quad\quad\quad\quad (30.27)$
   $R^2 = 0.991;\quad\text{S.E.} = 0.040$

2. $\log PX_t = 1.712 + 0.162 \log X_t + 0.268 \log P_t - 0.532\, Y_t^* + 0.732 \log PX_{t-1}$
   $\quad\quad\quad\quad\quad (5.45)\quad\quad (4.17)\quad\quad\quad\quad (3.65)\quad\quad\quad\quad (5.38)\quad\quad\quad\quad (10.00)$
   $\lambda = 0.221;\quad \beta_1 = 1.653;\quad \beta_2 = 3.285$
   $\quad (3.85)\quad\quad\quad\quad (2.75)\quad\quad\quad\quad (8.40)$
   $R^2 = 0.635;\quad \text{S.E.} = 0.023$

France
1. $\log X_t = -2.633 - 1.109 \log (PX/PXW)_t + 1.408 \log YW_t + 0.171 \log X_{t-1}$
   $\quad\quad\quad\quad (7.93)\quad\quad (5.62)\quad\quad\quad\quad\quad\quad (8.63)\quad\quad\quad\quad (1.81)$
   $\lambda = 0.829;\quad a_1 = -1.338;\quad a_2 = 1.697$
   $\quad (8.78)\quad\quad\quad\quad (5.36)\quad\quad\quad\quad (44.27)$
   $R^2 = 0.979;\quad \text{S.E.} = 0.056$

2. $\log PX_t = 0.969 + 0.244 \log X_t + 0.336 \log P_t - 0.459\, Y_t^* + 0.664 \log PX_{t-1}$
   $\quad\quad\quad\quad\quad (5.12)\quad\quad (3.35)\quad\quad\quad\quad (4.61)\quad\quad\quad\quad (4.14)\quad\quad\quad\quad (9.10)$
   $\lambda = 0.367;\quad \beta_1 = 1.379;\quad \beta_2 = 1.882$
   $\quad (3.06)\quad\quad\quad\quad (2.82)\quad\quad\quad\quad (12.20)$
   $R^2 = 0.937;\quad \text{S.E.} = 0.037$

Germany
1. $\log X_t = -0.947 - 0.251 \log (PX/PXW)_t + 0.399 \log YW_t + 0.809 \log X_{t-1}$
   $\quad\quad\quad\quad (3.30)\quad (1.79)\quad\quad\quad\quad\quad\quad (3.21)\quad\quad\quad\quad (12.32)$
   $\gamma = 0.191;\quad a_1 = -1.317;\quad a_2 = 2.091$
   $\quad (2.91)\quad\quad\quad\quad (1.39)\quad\quad\quad\quad (13.76)$
   $R^2 = 0.996;\quad \text{S.E.} = 0.029$

2. $\log PX_t = 0.271 + 0.041 \log X_t + 0.051 \log P_t - 0.099\, Y_t^* + 0.949 \log PX_{t-1}$
   $\quad\quad\quad\quad\quad (2.57)\quad\quad (2.06)\quad\quad\quad\quad (0.99)\quad\quad\quad\quad (2.94)\quad\quad\quad\quad (18.48)$
   $\gamma = 0.043;\quad \beta_1 = 1.245;\quad \beta_2 = 2.411$
   $\quad (2.15)\quad\quad\quad\quad (0.78)\quad\quad\quad\quad (8.31)$
   $R^2 = 0.925;\quad \text{S.E.} = 0.008$

Italy
1. $\log X_t = -2.393 - 1.016 \log (PX/PXW)_t + 0.952 \log YW_t + 0.569 \log X_{t-1}$
   $\quad\quad\quad\quad (4.82)\quad\quad (4.35)\quad\quad\quad\quad\quad\quad (5.74)\quad\quad\quad\quad (8.70)$
   $\gamma = 0.431;\quad a_1 = -2.356;\quad a_2 = 2.206$
   $\quad (6.60)\quad\quad\quad\quad (5.00)\quad\quad\quad\quad (16.13)$
   $R^2 = 0.998;\quad \text{S.E.} = 0.032$

2. $\log PX_t = 1.625 + 0.123 \log X_t + 0.251 \log P_t - 0.473\, Y_t^* + 0.749 \log PX_{t-1}$
   $\quad\quad\quad\quad\quad (3.83)\quad\quad (1.96)\quad\quad\quad\quad (2.48)\quad\quad\quad\quad (3.38)\quad\quad\quad\quad (7.41)$
   $\lambda = 0.165;\quad \beta_1 = 2.038;\quad \beta_2 = 3.845$
   $\quad (2.11)\quad\quad\quad\quad (1.31)\quad\quad\quad\quad (3.40)$
   $R^2 = 0.571;\quad \text{S.E.} = 0.030$

(Continued)

Table 4: (*Continued*)

Japan	1.	$\log X_t = -4.058 + 0.066 \log (PX/PXW)_t + 1.211 \log YW_t + 0.668 \log X_{t-1}$ $(4.89)(0.39)(5.02)(10.19)$ $\lambda = 0.332;\quad a_1 = 0.199;\quad a_2 = 3.642$ $(5.07)(0.39)(22.65)$ $R^2 = 0.997;\quad \text{S.E.} = 0.039$
	2.	$\log PX_t = 0.128 + 0.072 \log X_t - 0.009 \log P_t - 0.099\ Y_t^* + 1.008 \log PX_{t-1}$ $(1.21)(2.71)(0.16)(2.56)(20.03)$ $\lambda = 0.072;\quad \beta_1 = -0.112;\quad \beta_2 = 1.383$ $(2.81)(0.16)(4.42)$ $R^2 = 0.887;\quad \text{S.E.} = 0.015$
Netherlands	1.	$\log X_t = -2.243 - 1.263 \log (PX/PXW)_t + 1.015 \log YW_t + 0.471 \log X_{t-1}$ $(5.83)(3.36)(5.85)(5.08)$ $\gamma = 0.529;\quad a_1 = -2.389;\quad a_2 = 1.920$ $(5.70)(3.38)(44.61)$ $R^2 = 0.992;\quad \text{S.E.} = 0.037$
	2.	$\log PX_t = 3.468 + 0.269 \log X_t + 0.644 \log P_t - 1.009\ Y_t^* + 0.356 \log PX_{t-1}$ $(4.87)(3.95)(4.48)(4.88)(2.48)$ $\lambda = 0.756;\quad \beta_1 = 2.394;\quad \beta_2 = 3.753$ $(1.76)(4.03)(7.79)$ $R^2 = 0.881;\quad \text{S.E.} = 0.050$
United Kingdom	1.	$\log X_t = 0.506 - 1.174 \log (PX/PXW)_t + 0.896 \log YW_t + 0.006 \log X_{t-1}$ $(2.88)(5.99)(11.56)(0.07)$ $\gamma = 0.994;\quad a_1 = -1.181;\quad a_2 = 0.902$ $(11.54)(6.07)(26.74)$ $R^2 = 0.947;\quad \text{S.E.} = 0.040$
	2.	$\log PX_t = 0.553 + 0.248 \log X_t + 0.212 \log P_t - 0.369\ Y_t^* + 0.788 \log PX_{t-1}$ $(3.81)(5.28)(3.69)(5.00)(13.76)$ $\lambda = 0.314;\quad \beta_1 = 0.854;\quad \beta_2 = 1.489$ $(4.18)(4.52)(17.99)$ $R^2 = 0.979;\quad \text{S.E.} = 0.016$
United States	1.	$\log X_t = -0.030 - 1.262 \log (PX/PXW)_t + 0.603 \log YW_t + 0.405 \log X_{t-1}$ $(0.21)(3.36)(6.63)(4.49)$ $\gamma = 0.595;\quad a_1 = -2.123;\quad a_2 = 1.014$ $(6.59)(3.42)(20.31)$ $R^2 = 0.945;\quad \text{S.E.} = 0.054$
	2.	$\log PX_t = 0.527 + 0.067 \log X_t + 0.268 \log P_t - 0.179\ Y_t^* + 0.732 \log PX_{t-1}$ $(4.12)(2.67)(3.72)(4.34)(10.13)$ $\lambda = 0.092;\quad \beta_1 = 3.998;\quad \beta_2 = 2.662$ $(2.63)(2.10)(4.06)$ $R^2 = 0.886;\quad \text{S.E.} = 0.049$

The estimates of the export supply relationship (3) also yield useful information. The estimated coefficient of exports, $\hat{b}_1$, is positive and significantly different from zero in seven of the eight equations, implying a positively-sloped supply function for exports in each of these countries. The exception was Japan where the estimated coefficient on exports was not significantly

Table 5: Comparison of Estimated Export Price Elasticities of Demand: Total Exports

Country	Goldstein-Khan[a]	Houthakker-Magee[b]	Hickman-Lau[c]	Goldstein-Khan[d]
Belgium	−1.57	+0.42	−0.67	0.05
France	−1.33	−2.27	−0.96	−1.01
Germany	−0.83	+1.70	−0.76	−0.52
Italy	−3.29	−0.03	−0.71	−1.11
Japan	+2.47	−0.80	−0.46	0.07
Netherlands	−2.73	−0.83	−0.72	−0.47
United Kingdom	−1.32	−0.44	−1.05	−0.94
United States	−2.32	−1.51	−1.06	−2.13

[a] Estimates taken from Table 3. Period = 1955–1970; quarterly data; estimation method = FIML.
[b] Estimates taken from Houthakker and Magee (1969), Table 1, p. 113. Period = 1951–1966; annual data; estimation method = OLS.
[c] Estimates taken from "static model," Hickman and Lau (1973), Table 5, p. 375; export price elasticities derived from estimates of elasticity of substitution. Period = 1961–1969; annual data; estimation method = OLS.
[d] Period = 1955–1970; quarterly data; estimation method = OLS. Complete results are available from the authors upon request.

different from zero — a finding that can be interpreted as suggesting that Japanese export production is infinitely elastic with respect to relative prices. As mentioned previously, one can obtain an estimate of the aggregate export supply elasticity with respect to price from the estimated version of equation (3) by calculating $(b_1)^{-1}$. These computed elasticities are given in Table 6, and as can be seen, they show a rather wide variation across countries,[15] for example, if we exclude Japan, the elasticities range from a low of 1.1 for Italy to a high of 6.6 for the United States. Unfortunately, there are very few estimates of

---

[15] Other things being equal, one might expect the export supply-price elasticity to be larger, the smaller the relative size of the export sector (vis-á-vis the domestic sector), i.e., the smaller the relative size of the export sector, the easier it should be to expand export production by drawing away resources from the domestic sector. Apart from the United States, which has the highest estimated supply elasticity and the lowest ratio of exports to GDP (about 4.0% in 1963), there seems to be no clear relationship between relative "openness" and the estimated export supply elasticities. For the seven countries (excluding Japan), the 1963 ratios of exports to GDP were as follows: Belgium (35.0%), France (9.8%), Germany (15.1%), Italy (10.1%), the Netherlands (34.4%), the United Kingdom (14.4%), and the United States (4.0%). A rank correlation test between openness and the export elasticity yielded a coefficient of only 0.18.

Table 6: Estimated Export Price Elasticities of Supply
(Total Exports: Quarterly Data, 1955–1970)

Country	Supply Elasticity β_1
Belgium	+1.2
France	+1.9
Germany	+4.6
Italy	+1.1
Japan	$+\infty$
Netherlands	+2.5
United Kingdom	+1.4
United States	+6.6

Note: Estimates taken from equilibrium model, Table 3.

export supply elasticities available in the literature with which to compare the estimates given in Table 6. Those estimates that are available suggest, as do our estimates, that export supply elasticities are smaller for the European countries than for the United States. For example, Rhomberg and Boissonneault (1964) obtained an aggregate export supply elasticity of 2.5 for a group of 17 European countries using annual data for the period 1949–62. This is quite close to our estimates of supply elasticities for the European countries. For the United States, Rhomberg and Boissonneault obtained a supply elasticity of 15 while Magee (1975) reports an estimate of 11.5 for total U.S. exports — both of which are obviously much higher than our estimate of nearly 7. With so little empirical work available, the absolute size of the estimated supply elasticities, if not their approximate ordinal ranking across countries, should be regarded as tentative.

The performance of the capacity variable (Y^*) is in accordance with the theory, with the coefficient being significant in all eight cases. The domestic price variable appears with the expected positive sign and is also significantly different from zero at the 1% level.[16] The fits of the supply equations are uniformly poorer than those for the export demand equations, but this seems to be the usual case with equations that attempt to explain the behavior of export prices (see Amano, 1974).

---

[16] However, this coefficient was close to its expected value of unity in only three cases, namely, Italy, Japan, and the United Kingdom.

B. *Disequilibrium Model*

The short-run price elasticities of demand, shown in Table 4, are negative and significantly different from zero at the 5% level in the results for France, Italy, the Netherlands, the United Kingdom, and the United States. As expected, the short-run price elasticities are smaller than the equilibrium price elasticities shown in Table 3. The same result is true of the short-run versus the equilibrium income elasticities. The coefficient on lagged exports is significantly different from zero, implying a degree of dynamic adjustment, in the equation for six of the eight countries (the exceptions are France and the United Kingdom). At the same time, the average time lag for adjustment of exports to changes in the independent variables is estimated to be quite short — the mean time lag ranges from about 1 quarter for the United Kingdom to a little over 5 quarters for Germany. These average lag calculations may, however, primarily reflect a short lag on the real income variable and the limitation of the partial-adjustment model, which imposes the same (declining) geometrically-weighted lag distribution on all the explanatory variables.[17] In this regard, it is interesting to note that some of the studies that have found very long lags in export behavior have been export market-share studies where only relative prices (and not world real income) appear as explanatory variables.[18] The fits of the disequilibrium demand equations appear to be good, but this is to be expected in models using a Koyck-type lag structure (i.e., a lagged dependent variable).

Turning to the disequilibrium export supply results, the coefficient of exports has the expected positive sign in all eight cases and is significantly different from zero. Domestic prices have a positive and significant effect on export prices in all countries except Germany and Japan. Productive capacity has a significantly negative effect in all countries. The coefficient of lagged export prices is quite large and highly significant in all equations suggesting that this variable is capturing a good part of the dynamics of changes in export prices.[19]

---

[17] We did not experiment with alternative lag formulations, for example, polynomial lags, due to the difficulty of handling such formulations in a simultaneous framework. Discrete lags on the relative prices and exports variables would have eliminated the simultaneity in the model. For these reasons, we restricted our analysis only to geometric lags.

[18] See Junz and Rhomberg (1973).

[19] Rather than being a meaningful result, this may of course be simply due to autocorrelation in the model.

Table 7: Estimated Export Price Elasticities of Supply

Country	Supply Elasticity β_1
Belgium	+1.6
France	+1.3
Germany	+1.2
Italy	+2.0
Japan	−0.1
Netherlands	+2.3
United Kingdom	+0.8
United States	+3.9

Note: Estimates taken from disequilibrium model, Table 4.

Estimates of the price elasticity of supply, $\hat{\beta}_1$, calculated from the disequilibrium model are shown in Table 7. Again, as in the estimates reported in Table 6 for the equilibrium model, there is considerable inter-country variation, with the United States having the largest elasticity and the United Kingdom the smallest. The disequilibrium model yielded higher estimated supply price elasticities than did the equilibrium model for Belgium and Italy, while for the cases of France, Germany, Netherlands, the United Kingdom and the United States, the opposite held true. The rank correlation coefficient between openness and the elasticities in Table 7 (excluding Japan) was 0.11, thus showing an even weaker relationship than was evident from the equilibrium model.

It is not clear from our results which version of the model, equilibrium or disequilibrium, is superior. On conventional statistical grounds, i.e., goodness-of-fit, the models seem equally well-specified as the R^2s are very similar. On a priori grounds, the disequilibrium model has the distinct advantage that it permits time lags to occur in the adjustment of actual to equilibrium values. On the other hand, the supply price elasticities obtained from the equilibrium, model seem more credible than those from the disequilibrium model; e.g., the relatively low supply elasticity for Germany and the relatively high one for Italy in the disequilibrium model appear dubious. In short, we must remain agnostic on the question of whether an equilibrium or disequilibrium version of the export model is more appropriate.

The reduced forms of the two models, expressing the endogenous variables in terms of the exogenous (and lagged endogenous) variables, were calculated from the structural equation estimates of Tables 3 and 4. In dynamic analysis terms, the reduced-form coefficients are called "impact multipliers" and they measure the immediate response of the endogenous variables to changes in the exogenous variables. With very few exceptions, the reduced-form coefficients displayed the expected signs indicated in Tables 1 and 2.[20]

For the disequilibrium case we also tested for the dynamic stability of the estimated models by calculating their respective eigenvalues. These eigenvalues were calculated from the endogenous part of the structural model:

$$\log X_t - \hat{\gamma}\hat{a}_1 \log PX_t - (1 - \hat{\gamma}) \log X_{t-1} = 0 \tag{12}$$

$$\log PX_t - \frac{\hat{\lambda}}{1 + \hat{\lambda}\hat{\beta}_1} \log X_t - \frac{1}{1 + \hat{\lambda}\hat{\beta}_1} \log PX_{t-1} = 0. \tag{13}$$

The values of the eigenvalues obtained from the models for each of the eight countries are shown in Table 8. It can be shown analytically that the eigenvalues of the model can have two real parts or one real part with a complex

Table 8: Eigenvalues of Disequilibrium Model

Country	Eigenvalue			Damping Period (Quarters)
	Real	Imaginary	Modulus	
Belgium	0.726	—	0.726	1.38
	0.545	—	0.545	1.83
France	0.465	—	0.465	2.15
	0.192	—	0.192	5.20
Germany	0.870	±0.054	0.872	1.15
Italy	0.585	±0.189	0.615	1.63
Japan	1.022	—	1.022	0.98
	0.662	—	0.662	1.51
Netherlands	0.309	±0.173	0.354	2.83
United Kingdom	0.609	—	0.609	1.64
	0.006	—	0.006	166.67
United States	0.558	—	0.558	1.79
	0.489	—	0.489	2.05

---

[20]The reduced-form results for both the equilibrium and disequilibrium models are available from the authors upon request.

conjugate.[21] In the table we present also the modulus of the eigenvalues and the damping period (or average time lag).

The results show that with the exception of the case of Japan, all the calculated moduli are less than unity, and thus we conclude that the estimated disequilibrium models are dynamically stable. The cause of instability in the Japanese results can be traced easily to the positive sign obtained for the price elasticity of demand, $\hat{a}_1$.[22]

Section IV. CONCLUSION

Previous studies on the behavior of exports have tended to ignore the simultaneous relationship between the quantity of exports and their price. In this study we have taken explicit account of this simultaneity by specifying well-defined models of export demand and supply and by estimating these models simultaneously on quarterly aggregate export data for eight industrial countries over the 1955–70 period.[23]

Our empirical results indicated, inter alia, that export price elasticities of demand are probably considerably larger than those obtained previously by other researchers for this group of countries. This result, in combination with estimates of the price elasticities of demand for (aggregate) imports,[24] would suggest that the Marshall-Lerner condition for stability would be easily satisfied for almost all the countries in our sample.[25] Our estimated income

---

[21] The eigenvalue will have a complex conjugate if

$$2(1 - \hat{\gamma})(1 + \hat{\lambda}\hat{\beta}_1) > 1 + |(1 - \hat{\gamma})(1 + \hat{\lambda}\hat{\beta}_1)|^2 + 4|\hat{\gamma}a_1(1 - \hat{\gamma})\hat{\lambda}|.$$

[22] It is interesting to note that even with this positive sign the eigenvalue is only barely greater than unity.

[23] It is worth noting that the period 1955–70 was one of fixed exchange rates for most of the countries in our sample, the notable exceptions being the revaluations for the Netherlands (1961) and Germany (1961, 1969), and the devaluations for the United Kingdom (1967) and France (1957, 1958, 1969). In projecting our results to the period of managed floating, care would need to be taken to account for any significant changes in either exchange rate uncertainty or relative price variability.

[24] For estimates of the price elasticities of demand for imports for the same countries, see Goldstein and Khan (1976).

[25] We must remain agnostic on the Marshall-Lerner conditions for Japan since our estimates of the relevant price elasticities were insignificant on the import side (see Goldstein and Khan, 1976) and significant but incorrectly signed on the export side.

elasticities tended to be very similar to those obtained in earlier studies and here we, like Houthakker and Magee (1969), found evidence that the (world) income elasticities for both U.S. and U.K. exports were considerably lower than those for other countries; in contrast, the estimated world income elasticity for Japanese exports was particularly high relative to other industrial countries. Although the simultaneous nature of our models prevented us from experimenting with alternative lag formulations, our estimates using a Koyck-type distributed lag suggested that the adjustment of exports to changes in the independent variables was neither instantaneous nor very long (i.e., usually less than one year). The estimated dynamic models were also found (with one exception) to be stable.

APPENDIX

Data Definitions and Sources

All data are quarterly, seasonally adjusted, for the period 1955–1970 and are taken from two sources:

a. International Monetary Fund, *International Financial Statistics*
b. Organization for Economic Cooperation and Development, *Main Economic Indicators*

All data are expressed in domestic currency units.

X = index of the volume of exports, 1960 = 100. Source b.
PX = index of the unit value of exports, 1960 = 100. Source b.
P = index of wholesale prices, 1960 = 100. Source a.
PXW = "world" export price index, 1960 = 100. This series was calculated using the method described by Houthakker and Magee (1969), the world price facing country j is

$$PXW_j = \sum_i \alpha_{ji} \sum \beta_{ik} PX_k$$

$$i = 1, \ldots, 18$$

$$k = 1, \ldots, 17$$
$$\sum \alpha_{ji} = 1, \quad \sum \beta_{ik} = 1.$$

where α_{ji} is the weight of market i in exporter j's exports to 18 countries, and β_{ik} is the share of supplier k (not equal to i or j) in market i relative to the 17 non-j suppliers. PXW is, therefore, the weighted average of the prices of 18 competitors in each of the 18 markets. The weights are calculated on the basis of 1955–1970 averages.

$YW =$ "world" real income expressed as an index, 1960 = 100. This series was calculated as

$$YW_j = \sum_i \alpha_{ji} Y_i$$
$$i = 1, \ldots, 18$$
$$\sum_i \alpha_{ji} = 1$$

where Y_i is an index of real income in country i. This series was calculated first as an annual series (due to lack of quarterly data on real income in a large number of countries), and then converted to a quarterly basis by using a quadratic interpolation method; see Goldstein and Khan (1976), appendix II.

$Y^* =$ log of trend of real income on a quarterly basis.

Morris Goldstein and Mohsin S. Khan, "The Supply and Demand for Exports: A Simultaneous Approach," *The Review of Economics and Statistics*, 60:2 (April, 1978), pp. 275–286. © 1978 by the President and Fellows of Harvard College. Used with permission of the publisher.

REFERENCES

Amano, Akichiro, "Export Price Behavior in Selected Industrial Countries," Kobe University, Japan, unpublished, 1974.

Artus, Jacques, "The Short-Run Effects of Domestic Demand Pressure on British Export Performance," IMF *Staff Papers* 17 (July 1970), 247–274.

Ball, R. J., J. R. Eaton, and M. D. Steuer, "The Relationship between United Kingdom Export Performance in Manufactures and the Internal Pressure of Demand," *Economic Journal* 76 (Sept. 1966), 501–518.

Basevi, Giorgio, "Commodity Trade Equations in Project LINK," in R. Ball (ed.), *The International Linkage of National Economic Models* (Amsterdam: North-Holland Publishing Company, 1973), 227–281.

Goldstein, Morris, and Mohsin S. Khan, "Large Versus Small Price Changes and the Demand for Imports," IMF *Staff Papers* 23 (Mar. 1976), 200–225.

Hickman, Bert G., and Lawrence J. Lau, "Elasticities of Substitution and Export Demand in a World Trade Model," *European Economic Review* 4 (Dec. 1973), 347–380.

Houthakker, Hendrik S., and Stephen P. Magee, "Income and Price Elasticities in World Trade," this REVIEW 51 (May 1969), 111–125.

Houthakker, Hendrik S., and Lester D. Taylor, *Consumer Demand in the United States* (Cambridge: Harvard University Press, 2nd edition, 1970).

Junz, Helen B., and Rudolf R. Rhomberg, "Price Competitiveness in Export Trade among Industrial Countries," *American Economic Review* 63 (May 1973), 412–418.

Khan, Mohsin S., and Knud Z. Ross, "Cyclical and Secular Income Elasticities of the Demand for Imports," this REVIEW 57 (Aug. 1975), 357–361.

Leamer, Edward E., and Robert M. Stern, *Quantitative International Economics* (Boston: Allyn and Bacon, 1970).

Magee, Stephen P., "Prices, Income and Foreign Trade: A Survey of Recent Economic Studies," in P. B. Kenen (ed.), *International Trade and Finance: Frontiers for Research* (Cambridge: Cambridge University Press, 1975), 175–252.

Morgan, D. J., and W. J. Corlett, "The Influence of Price in International Trade: A Study in Method," *Journal of the Royal Statistical Society*, series A, (Part III) (1951), 307–358.

Rhomberg, Rudolf R., "Towards a General Trade Model," in R. J. Ball (ed.), *The International Linkage of National Economic Models* (Amsterdam: North-Holland Publishing Company, 1973), 9–20.

Rhomberg, Rudolf R., and Lorrette Boissonneault, "Effects of Income and Price Changes on the U.S. Balance of Payments," IMF *Staff Papers* 11 (Mar. 1964), 59–122.

Sargan, J. D., "Some Discrete Approximations to Continuous Time Stochastic Models," *Journal of the Royal Statistical Society* 34 series B (1975), 74–90.

Suss, Esther, "The Effect of Economic Activity on Exports," International Monetary Fund, unpublished, July 1974.

Taplin, Grant, "A Model of World Trade," in R. J. Ball (ed.), *The International Linkage of National Economics Models* (Amsterdam: North-Holland Publishing Company, 1973), 177–223.

Chapter 3

Prices of Tradable and Nontradable Goods in the Demand for Total Imports

Morris Goldstein, Mohsin S. Khan, and Lawrence H. Officer*

I. INTRODUCTION

EMPIRICAL studies of the demand for total imports typically relate the quantity of imports to the importing country's level of real income (or real expenditure) and to the ratio of the price of imports to the price of domestic import substitutes.[1] In specifying and measuring just what these (imperfect) domestic import substitutes are, two general guidelines have been followed.

First, despite the fact that both domestic tradable and nontradable goods are potential competitors with imports in the consumer's budget, it has been *assumed* in empirical investigations that the demand for imports is

---

*International Monetary Fund, International Monetary Fund, and Michigan State University, respectively.

Received for publication September 15, 1978. Revision accepted for publication March 16, 1979.

An earlier version of this paper was presented at the Econometric Society Meetings, New York, December 1977.

The authors are grateful to Ken Clements, Andrew Crockett, Robert Heller, John Suomela, and two anonymous referees for helpful comments. Kellett Hannah and Fernando Santos provided competent research assistance. The views expressed are the sole responsibility of the authors.

[1] See Leamer and Stern (1970) and Magee (1975) for good discussions of the traditional import demand equation.

independent of the price of nontradable goods.[2] In particular, consumers are viewed implicitly as engaging in a two-step decision process. In the first step, they allocate their expenditure between (all) tradable goods and nontradable goods on the basis of, inter alia, the relative price of these goods. In the second step, they allocate their expenditure on tradable goods (given from step one) between imports and domestic tradables. The practical upshot of such "separability" in consumption is that it justifies including only *one* relative price — namely, that between imports and domestic tradables — in the aggregate import equation.[3]

The price of nontradable goods is thus relevant only for the demand for all tradables.

Second, when it comes actually to representing the relative price of imports, researchers have run into the problem that price indices for domestic tradables as such do not exist. The usual practice has then been to use either of two readily available proxy variables, namely, the wholesale price index or the implicit deflator of gross domestic product (GDP).[4] While it is recognized, at least by some observers (e.g., Leamer and Stern (1970)), that the presence of nontradable goods in these indices constrains the price elasticity of demand for imports to be identical as between (domestic) tradable and nontradable goods, this deficiency has been viewed either as a minor one, or as one that can be avoided only by recourse to disaggregation of the data.[5]

---

[2] A nontradable good is one that is not *internationally* traded for any relevant range of variation in relative prices.

[3] According to Goldman and Uzawa (1964), strong separability is defined as the independence of the marginal rate of substitution between goods in the same or in different branches relative to the quantities consumed in a third branch. In other words, strong separability implies that the allocation of goods (factors of production) within each branch is determined only by relative goods (factors) prices within that branch. The first important practical applications of separability in trade equations were made by Armington (1969) and Gregory (1971).

[4] Houthakker and Magee (1969), Taplin (1973), Samuelson (1973), and Khan and Ross (1975) all use the wholesale price index as the domestic price variable in their multicountry studies of aggregate import demand. Goldstein and Khan (1976) and Helen (1968) are examples of studies that use the GDP deflator as the domestic price variable in the total import equation.

[5] Leamer and Stern (1970) state: "When aggregate imports is the dependent variable, the use of only the price index for GNP in the price relative involves the assumption that imports substitute generally the same with all domestic goods. Such an assumption is rarely warranted, and the procedure will surely impair the price relative's explanatory power. This is again a problem of aggregation... (pp. 14–15).

The purpose of this paper is to formulate a general import function in which the prices of imports, tradable goods, and nontradable goods enter as arguments. This function is then tested utilizing new price indices (of our own construction) of tradable and nontradable goods. From the resulting estimates we can ascertain whether the price of nontradable goods is relevant empirically in the determination of the demand for imports. We then proceed further and undertake two additional tests. First, we investigate the effect of constraining the price elasticities of imports with respect to tradable and nontradable goods to be equal, namely, through the use of the GDP deflator as the sole domestic price variable in the equation. Second, we test the equation excluding the price of nontradable goods, leaving only the ratio of the price of imports to the price of tradable goods as the relative price variable. In brief, we find that imports are unaffected by variations in the price of nontradable goods for seven of the ten countries considered, and that the statistical properties of the estimated price elasticities are improved when the domestic price variable is restricted to cover only tradables.

The plan of the paper is as follows. In section II we discuss the basic formulations of the import equations we examine, and also briefly, the methods used to construct the price indices for tradable and nontradable goods. Section III reports the results of estimating annual demand equations for total imports for ten industrial countries over the period 1951–1973. The countries in our sample are Austria, Belgium, Canada, Denmark, Finland, Germany, Italy, Sweden, the United Kingdom, and the United States. The principal conclusions are contained in section IV. The definitions and sources of the data used are given in the appendix.

II. SPECIFICATION OF THE IMPORT EQUATION

A. *Alternative Formulations*

Within a general system of demand equations for imports, tradable goods, and nontradable goods, the particular function for imports has the theoretical form

$$M^D = f(PM, PNT, PT, Y/Y^*, Y^*) \qquad (1)$$

where the variables are defined as follows:

M^D = quantity of imports demanded

PM = price of imports
PNT = price of nontradable goods
PT = price of tradable goods
Y/Y^* = ratio of current real income (Y) to its trend value, i.e., the "output-gap"
Y^* = trend level of real income.

The introduction of all relevant prices into the formulation follows naturally from the assumption that individuals make a simultaneous choice between the three types of goods subject to their budget constraint. The aggregation of goods into these relevant categories, and thus the inclusion of the prices of tradable and nontradable goods into the import function, is consistent with the recent literature on the subject.[6] Standard demand theory would indicate that the partial derivatives of the demand for imports with respect to the three prices would have the following signs:

$$\frac{\partial M^D}{\partial PM} < 0; \quad \frac{\partial M^D}{\partial PNT} > 0; \quad \frac{\partial M^D}{\partial PT} > 0.$$

The activity variable in the formulation is split up into the output-gap and the trend level of real income, thus allowing a distinction to be made between the effects of cyclical factors, and those factors that are secular in nature, on the level of imports.[7] The effect of both these variables is expected to be positive.[8]

It should, however, also be mentioned that the use of real income as the relevant activity variable, even when separated into its cyclical and trend components, is itself somewhat questionable. If, for example, imports are primarily finished goods, then perhaps domestic expenditure would be more appropriate than domestic output. The reasoning behind the use of domestic expenditure would be that domestic demand for foreign goods (imports)

---

[6] For a survey see Goldstein and Officer (1979). Other studies dealing explicitly with imports are those by Murray and Ginman (1976), Mutti (1977), and Clements (1977).

[7] For a discussion of this issue and some empirical estimates, see Khan and Ross (1975).

[8] There is, of course, the possibility that the effect on imports may be negative. If imports are viewed as the difference between the consumption and the domestic production of importables, then an increase in both the cyclical and secular values of real income could increase domestic production faster than consumption, thus causing imports to fall. For a discussion of this issue, see Magee (1975) and Goldstein and Khan (1978).

should properly be related to domestic expenditure on *all* goods, rather than to the sum of domestic and foreign expenditures on domestic goods. The use of income involves the latter by definition. On the other hand, if imports are mainly intermediate products sold to productive enterprises, it may be more appropriate to treat imports as a function of domestic output.[9]

The log-linear version of equation (1) is (with time subscripts added to the variables):[10]

$$\log M_t^D = a_0 + a_1 \log PM_t + a_2 \log PNT_t + a_3 \log PT_t \\ + a_4 \log (Y/Y^*)_t + a_5 \log Y_t^*. \quad (2)$$

The assumption of homogeneity in prices, or absence of money illusion, in equation (2) would involve the imposition of the restriction on the price elasticities,

$$a_1 + a_2 + a_3 = 0,$$

and thus yield the restricted equation:[11]

$$\log M_t^D = b_0 + b_1 \log (PM/PT)_t + b_2 \log (PNT/PT)_t \\ + b_3 \log (Y/Y^*)_t + b_4 \log Y_t^*. \quad (3)$$

If in addition to this assumption of homogeneity, it is also postulated that the overall price index (the income deflator) is a Divisia index of the form

$$\log PGDP = \alpha \log PNT + (1 - \alpha) \log PT \quad (4a)$$

---

[9] It should also be noted that if imports are indeed intermediate inputs, then use of equation (1) also involves the assumption that domestic production is "separable" as between intermediate inputs (I) on the one hand, and labor (L) and capital (K) on the other. That is, one is assuming that the relevant production function is of the following form:

$$Q = \min[f_1(I), f_2(L, K)].$$

This mixture of fixed-coefficient and neoclassical production functions implies that to produce a given unit of output (Q) requires a certain quantity of intermediate inputs or imports, $I = f_1^{-1}(Q)$. The quantity of imports demanded is therefore a function of output alone — and not also a function of labor and capital prices. This is the rationale for excluding these prices (wages and the cost of capital) from equation (1).

[10] Khan and Ross (1977) have shown that the logarithmic functional form is preferable empirically to the alternative linear form.

[11] Dividing through by PT is only one of the possibilities, since any of the prices could have been used for this purpose.

Table 1: Relationships between Equations and Summary of Parameter Restrictions

Equation	(2)	(3)	(4)	(5)
(2)	—			
(3)	$a_1 + a_2 + a_3 = 0$	—		
(4)	$a_2 = -a_1\alpha;\ a_3 = -a_1(1-\alpha)$	$a_2 = -a_1\alpha$	—	
(5)	$a_3 = -a_1;\ a_2 = 0$	$a_2 = 0$	$\alpha = 0$	—

where $PGDP$ is the GDP deflator and α is the weight of nontradable goods in total income,[12] then equation (3) simplifies to

$$\log M_t^D = c_o + c_1 \log (PM/PGDP)_t \\ + c_2 \log (Y/Y^*)_t + c_3 \log Y_t^*. \qquad (4)$$

This type of equation, with only one relative price variable, is the standard model found in the literature.[13]

One last possibility is that imports and nontradable goods do not substitute so that the price of the latter is irrelevant in the determination of imports, i.e., $\partial M^D/\partial PNT = 0$. Along with the assumption of homogeneity this would imply the following equation:

$$\log M_t^D = d_0 + d_1 \log (PM/PT)_t \\ + d_2 \log (Y/Y^*)_t + d_3 \log Y_t^*. \qquad (5)$$

Naturally, this equation would be applicable when the elasticity b_2 in equation (3) was equal to zero.

The relationships between equation (2) and the restricted equations (3), (4), and (5) are conveniently summarized in Table 1.

It is apparent that the various models can be viewed as nested, i.e., each succeeding model, (3)–(5), is a restricted version of the prior model, and thus formal statistical tests can be performed to choose empirically among them.

---

[12]This is the so-called "true" cost of living index if the utility function is Cobb-Douglas.
[13]See Leamer and Stern (1970) and Magee (1975).

B. Construction of the Price Indices of Nontradable and Tradable Goods

To begin with, we should point out that our approach to the construction of price indices for tradable and nontradable goods is based on a division of the economy along sectoral lines. The total output of those industries that export their products in significant amount (i.e., as a proportion of their total output) constitutes the economy's production of "exportables." The total output of those industries the products of which compete to a significant degree with imports constitutes the economy's production of "importables." Together, exportables and importables are the country's production of "tradables," and the industries involved are defined as the tradable sector of the economy. The remaining part of GDP is the economy's output of "nontradables," and the industries concerned are designated as the nontradable sector.

For each of the 10 industrial countries in our sample, we made the same allocation of industries into the tradable and nontradable sectors. Specifically, the tradable sector consists of (i) agriculture and related activities, (ii) mining and quarrying, and (iii) manufacturing. The nontradable sector encompasses all other industries in which GDP originates — or, specifically in terms of industry groupings: electricity, gas, and water; construction; wholesale and retail trade; transport, storage and communication; financial, insurance, and real estate services; consumer services; business services; and government services.[14]

As for the actual construction of the price indices themselves, they are obtained in the same manner that the implicit GDP deflator is derived — that is, essentially by dividing GDP at current prices by GDP at constant prices. This is best illustrated by considering the following identities:

$$GDPC \equiv GDPCT + GDPCNT$$
$$Y \equiv YT + YNT$$

where

$$GDPC = \text{gross domestic product at current prices}$$

---

[14] For a comparison of our classification of industries into the tradable and nontradable sectors with that of other writers, see Goldstein and Officer (1979).

$GDPCT$ = output of tradables at current prices
$GDPCNT$ = output of nontradables at current prices
Y = gross domestic product at constant prices
YT = output of tradables at constant prices
YNT = output of nontradables at constant prices.

The implicit GDP deflator is obtained as the ratio of GDP at current prices to constant prices:

$$PGDP = GDPC/Y.$$

Similarly, one can obtain the price indices of tradable and nontradable goods, PT and PNT, as follows:

$$PT = GDPCT/YT$$
$$PNT = GDPCNT/YNT.$$

The basic sources of the data used to construct these price indices are discussed in the appendix.

Having indicated how the series on the prices of tradable and nontradable goods (PT and PNT) were constructed, the next step is to consider their deficiencies, because they too are at best only proxy variables for the true variables. One problem that these indices face, like the GDP deflator, is that they are current-weighted price indices. For the analysis of price movements, a base-weighted price index is often preferred to an equivalent current-weighted index. The tradable and nontradable price measures, however, can be constructed only as the ratio of output at current prices to output at constant prices. Since these outputs are inherently current-weighted, no equivalent base-weighted price index can be obtained.

A second limitation, or deficiency, involves the classification of industries into the tradable and nontradable sectors. Every industry (producing sector) of the economy must be allocated to either the tradable or nontradable sector in order to obtain the tradable/nontradable breakdown of total output (GDP). The problem is that the level of aggregation of the existing data may be too high to permit a clear classification of industries into one sector or the other. As such, one has to allocate an industry to the sector in which the preponderance of its sub-industries (weighted by their value added) would be assigned if more disaggregated data existed. The end result is that some tradable (nontradable) output is bound to be included in the nontradable (tradable) sector — an outcome which by definition cannot occur with the true variables.[15]

There are two reasons why we do not regard the tradable/nontradable classification problem as too serious. First, even a cursory examination of input-output tables for a number of the countries included in our sample reveals that the degree of foreign-trade participation (e.g., the ratio of final imports or exports to total domestic sales) is substantially higher for the tradable sector than the nontradable sector — a finding which at least suggests that our classification scheme is reasonable. Based on input-output data for the year 1970,[16] we were able to compute the ratio of (final) imports to total domestic sales, and the ratio of exports to total domestic sales, in the tradable and nontradable sectors for seven of our sample countries, and in all but one case the ratios for the tradable sector were substantially larger than for the nontradable sector.[17]

Second, simple correlations between the various price indices indicate that import prices are in all cases more highly correlated with prices of tradable goods than with those of nontradable goods. The correlation between import prices and the income deflator lies (as expected) between the other two.[18]

C. Assumptions for Estimation of Models

In order to estimate equations (2)–(5), two assumptions have to be made.[19] The first is that the actual quantity of imports (M_t) is equal to the quantity demanded (M_t^D). This is tantamount to assuming that importers are always on their demand schedules or, perhaps more relevant in our case, that any disequilibrium is corrected within a year.[20] Second, it is implicitly assumed that the supply of imports is infinitely elastic with respect to the price of

---

[15] Of course, one could also argue that the true variables themselves cannot be unambiguously allocated to tradables or nontradables but rather, lie along a spectrum.

[16] The sources are national input-output data.

[17] The exception was the United Kingdom, where such normally nontradables as banking services and insurance traditionally have played an important role in the balance of payments. The basic results, calculated from input-output tables, are available upon request.

[18] The results of these correlations are available from the authors upon request.

[19] Apart from the introduction of stochastic errors (u) into each specification.

[20] Preliminary results obtained with a Koyck-type lag tended to support this hypothesis.

imports, so that the latter can be treated as exogenous, and as such the equation can be estimated by ordinary least squares.

Since simple functions such as we have specified generally display positive serial correlation in their errors,[21] we specify a first-order autoregressive scheme for these as follows:

$$u_{it} = \rho_i u_{it-1} + \epsilon_{it} (i = 1, \ldots, 4) \tag{6}$$

where the u are the original errors, ρ is the coefficient of autocorrelation, and the ϵ are errors assumed to have classical properties.

III. RESULTS

Equations (2) to (5) were estimated by ordinary least squares (using the Cochrane-Orcutt method when necessary to adjust for autocorrelation and to estimate the value of ρ) for the period 1951–73 for ten industrial countries.[22] For each of the equations, we report the elasticities (with their respective t-values in parentheses), the adjusted coefficient of determination ($\bar{R}^2$), the standard error of estimate (S.E.E.), the Durbin-Watson test statistic (D.W.), and the estimated coefficient of autocorrelation (ρ).

A. Individual Equation Estimates

The results for the most general import function, i.e., equation (2) are reported in Table 2. Taking the price elasticities first, we find that the one with respect to the price of imports (a_1) turns out to have the correct negative sign in all but one of the countries, namely, the United Kingdom (U.K.). Despite the fact that most previous estimates of aggregate U.K. imports also have recorded a positive import-export elasticity, we regard this result as too implausible to permit including the United Kingdom without further analysis.[23] For five

---

[21] See, for example, Houthakker and Magee (1969), Khan and Ross (1975), and more recently, Goldstein and Khan (1976).

[22] The sources of the data are contained in the appendix.

[23] For example, see the studies by Khan and Ross (1975), and Goldstein and Khan (1976). When U.K. import demand is estimated on a more disaggregated basis, this problem often disappears. The U.K. price elasticity, while positive, is not significantly different from zero in Table 2. In the more restricted equations, however, the corresponding U.K. price elasticity is indeed significantly positive. These further results for the United Kingdom are available on request.

Table 2: Demand for Imports Equation:
$\log M_t = a_0 + a_1 \log PM_t + a_2 \log PNT_t + a_3 \log PT_t + a_4 \log (Y/Y^*)_t + a_5 \log Y_t^*$

Country	a_0	Price Elasticities			Income Elasticities		$\bar{R}^2$	S.E.E.	D.W.	ρ
		a_1	a_2	a_3	a_4	a_5				
Austria	−8.519	−0.823	0.249	0.503	3.006	1.578	.988	.034	1.69	—
	(3.04)	(5.07)	(0.74)	(1.21)	(11.06)	(6.01)				
Belgium	−8.045	−0.476	−0.056	0.549	1.708	2.015	.998	.028	1.71	—
	(8.78)	(2.91)	(0.29)	(2.97)	(6.73)	(13.02)				
Canada	−2.273	−0.198	0.978	−0.357	2.526	0.596	.994	.034	1.58	—
	(1.11)	(0.67)	(2.51)	(0.83)	(8.47)	(2.16)				
Denmark	−13.799	−0.424	−0.637	0.694	1.647	2.226	.995	.041	2.00	—
	(3.18)	(1.76)	(1.52)	(1.65)	(3.92)	(5.00)				
Finland	−3.150	−0.212	0.927	−0.258	3.566	0.975	.989	.057	2.19	—
	(1.08)	(1.04)	(1.85)	(0.52)	(4.96)	(2.43)				
Germany	−10.866	−0.254	1.384	−1.486	1.170	1.278	.985	.041	1.62	.544
	(2.19)	(1.06)	(1.53)	(1.32)	(3.64)	(3.14)				
Italy	−13.241	−0.446	−0.215	1.035	3.780	1.904	.994	.063	1.85	—
	(2.92)	(2.00)	(0.30)	(2.42)	(3.94)	(2.90)				
Sweden	5.965	−0.843	−0.955	1.281	1.882	−0.164	.978	.044	1.99	.320
	(0.79)	(2.03)	(2.26)	(1.97)	(2.46)	(0.19)				
U.K.	2.507	0.094	0.880	−0.222	1.904	0.293	.982	.027	2.06	.388
	(0.32)	(0.76)	(1.54)	(0.85)	(3.75)	(0.33)				
U.S.A.	3.379	−1.119	2.320	2.095	3.032	−0.575	.996	.023	2.63	.269
	(1.25)	(6.07)	(6.91)	(4.98)	(10.92)	(1.83)				

Note: t-values are in parentheses below coefficients.

countries — Austria, Belgium, Italy, Sweden, and the United States — the import-price elasticity is both negative and significantly different from zero at the 5% level. Insofar as the elasticity with respect to the price of nontradable goods is concerned, it has the hypothesized positive sign in six cases; of these six it is significantly different from zero (at the 5% level) only for Canada and the United States. The tradable-goods price elasticity is also positive in six of the country estimates, but is significant in only three cases — Belgium, Italy, and the United States.[24] One possible reason for observing a greater number of significant elasticities with respect to import prices, as compared to the other elasticities, may be the degree of inter-correlation between the three price indices. The collinearity between PNT and PT is generally greater than

---

[24]The elasticity for Sweden is also significant if the 10% level is used.

between *PM* and the other two indices, and this could very easily result in the inefficient estimates we have observed.[25]

All the cyclical income elasticities in Table 2 are significantly different from zero and indicate, as expected, that imports vary procyclically. Except for Germany, these elasticities are also significantly larger than unity. The result for Germany may be one explanation why it has generally had a better trade balance performance than any of the other countries in the sample. The trend, or secular, income elasticity, also has a positive sign in eight cases, and in the two equations where it is negative (Sweden and the United States), it is not significantly different from zero.[26]

Next we consider the import function with the restriction of homogeneity imposed on the estimates, i.e., $a_1 + a_2 + a_3 = 0$. The results are shown in Table 3. The homogeneity restriction itself was first tested by using a log-likelihood ratio test in which a comparison is made between the values of the log-likelihood functions of the unrestricted case, $L(\lambda_1)$ (equation (2)), and the restricted case $L(\lambda_2)$ (equation (3)). As is well known, twice the value of the difference between these, $2[L(\lambda_1) - L(\lambda_2)]$, is distributed as χ^2 with degrees of freedom equal to the number of restrictions imposed, which in our case is only one. An alternative method, yielding equivalent results, is simply to perform a t-test on the value of $(a_1 + a_2 + a_3)$, utilizing the variance-covariance matrix of the estimated parameters. The results of both tests demonstrated that the homogeneity restriction could be rejected on statistical grounds only for the United States.[27] Therefore we are justified in proceeding sequentially with the analysis only for the remaining eight countries.

Concerning the results reported in Table 3, the import-price elasticity has the correct negative sign for all eight of the countries, and it is statistically significant for five. In comparison with the earlier results, the elasticities for Canada and Denmark increase and are now significant; however, that for Sweden declines and becomes insignificant. There are only four countries

---

[25] The correlation between *PNT* and *PT* ranges from a low of 0.891 for Canada to a high of 0.997 for Denmark and Germany. Since we have not examined this multicollinearity issue in any detail, this should be viewed as only a possible hypothesis.

[26] The elasticity for the United Kingdom, while positive, is also not significant different from zero.

[27] It would also be rejected for the United Kingdom. The country-by-country test results for homogeneity are available from the author upon request.

Table 3: Demand for Imports Equation:
$\log M_t = b_0 + b_1 \log (PM/PT)_t + b_2 \log (PNT/PT)_t + b_3 \log (Y/Y^*)_t + b_4 \log Y_t^*$

		Price Elasticities		Income Elasticities					
Country	b_0	b_1	b_2	b_3	b_4	$\bar{R}^2$	S.E.E.	D.W.	ρ
Austria	−7.953	−0.863	0.271	3.018	1.508	.998	.034	1.62	—
	(3.44)	(7.09)	(0.83)	(11.45)	(8.36)				
Belgium	−8.022	−0.479	−0.062	1.725	2.023	.998	.027	1.71	—
	(9.41)	(3.09)	(0.35)	(11.21)	(16.71)				
Canada	−6.559	−0.816	−0.066	2.417	1.449	.978	.039	2.05	.400
	(3.26)	(2.95)	(0.21)	(5.97)	(8.05)				
Denmark	−9.488	−0.622	−0.462	1.269	1.709	.994	.043	1.94	—
	(2.84)	(3.00)	(1.11)	(3.67)	(5.93)				
Finland	−7.316	−0.174	0.411	3.487	1.570	.988	.059	2.09	—
	(7.37)	(0.84)	(1.08)	(4.70)	(16.49)				
Germany	−10.394	−0.299	1.149	1.323	1.120	.987	.041	1.55	.515
	(2.10)	(1.28)	(1.56)	(4.95)	(3.03)				
Italy	−15.804	−0.410	−0.614	3.425	2.299	.994	.062	1.82	—
	(8.19)	(1.94)	(1.99)	(4.49)	(12.84)				
Sweden	−8.689	−0.143	0.271	1.034	1.601	.989	.084	1.86	—
	(3.37)	(0.59)	(1.42)	(1.58)	(7.42)				
U.S.A.	−24.131	−0.679	−0.008	2.098	2.518	.864	.093	1.49	.856
	(4.43)	(3.33)	(0.02)	(5.61)	(6.37)				

Note: t-values are in parentheses below coefficients.

(Austria, Finland, Germany, and Sweden) where the elasticity with respect to the ratio of nontradable to tradable goods-prices has the hypothesized positive sign. In the other cases it would seem that nontradable goods and imports are complements rather than substitutes. Since the nontradable/tradable elasticity coefficient is not significant at the 5% level for any country, a strong conclusion along these lines should not be drawn.

The cyclical income elasticities in Table 3 are all positive, and with the exception of Sweden, are all significantly different from zero. The secular income elasticities are now significant in all cases, and in most they are substantially larger than before.

When the GDP deflator is used as the only domestic price variable, and the absence of money illusion is assumed, equation (4) is obtained. The results are very similar to the ones reported in the previous set of estimates (see Table 4). The relative price elasticity is always negative, and it is significant in four of

Table 4: Demand for Imports Equation:
$\log M_t = c_0 + c_1 \log (PM/PGDP)_t + c_2 \log (Y/Y^*)_t + c_3 \log Y_t^*$

Country	c_0	Price Elasticity c_1	Income Elasticities c_2	c_3	$\bar{R}^2$	S.E.E.	D.W.	ρ
Austria	−6.573	−0.877	3.001	1.401	.998	.034	1.65	—
	(4.91)	(6.98)	(11.49)	(13.36)				
Belgium	−6.526	−0.520	1.730	1.811	.998	.031	1.57	—
	(7.59)	(2.80)	(9.99)	(14.87)				
Canada	−5.246	−0.353	2.328	1.335	.899	.040	1.92	.778
	(3.78)	(1.50)	(6.91)	(10.56)				
Denmark	−3.805	−0.735	0.894	1.220	.993	.049	1.90	—
	(1.46)	(3.19)	(2.51)	(5.44)				
Finland	−7.925	−0.309	3.213	1.627	.988	.058	2.16	—
	(12.24)	(1.78)	(6.27)	(25.82)				
Germany	−16.451	−0.462	1.375	1.572	.986	.042	1.64	.514
	(8.61)	(2.33)	(5.11)	(10.97)				
Italy	−14.008	−0.036	3.181	2.132	.985	.065	1.90	.311
	(7.78)	(0.18)	(3.38)	(12.75)				
Sweden	−11.316	−0.116	0.666	1.820	.989	.049	1.57	.206
	(4.22)	(0.42)	(1.12)	(8.07)				

Note: t-values are in parentheses below coefficients.

the countries. The income elasticities, both cyclical and secular, all have the correct positive signs and again, apart from the one case of Sweden, all are significantly different from zero.

Since the import elasticity with respect to the price of nontradable goods is insignificant for all the countries in our sample, we next estimated equation (5), which both excludes the price of nontradable goods and assumes homogeneity in the remaining prices. The results for this equation are reported in Table 5.

All of the price elasticities reported in Table 5 have the correct sign, and all but those for Finland, Italy, and Sweden are significantly different from zero. Clearly, removing the price of nontradable goods has improved somewhat the quality of our estimates of the remaining price coefficient. The cyclical income elasticities always carry the correct (positive) sign, and are statistically

Table 5: Demand for Imports Equation:
$\log M_t = d_0 + d_1 \log (PM/PT)_t + d_2 \log (Y/Y^*)_t + d_3 \log Y_t^*$

Country	d_0	Price Elasticity d_1	Income Elasticities d_2	d_3	$\bar{R}^2$	S.E.E.	D.W.	ρ
Austria	−8.561	−0.980	3.067	1.555	.997	.033	1.70	.178
	(5.87)	(5.35)	(10.76)	(13.58)				
Belgium	−7.743	−0.510	1.729	1.983	.998	.027	1.74	—
	(25.04)	(4.11)	(11.53)	(45.03)				
Canada	−6.150	−0.779	2.443	1.412	.977	.039	2.05	.430
	(9.49)	(2.94)	(7.32)	(23.94)				
Denmark	−6.097	−0.754	1.073	1.417	.994	.043	2.11	—
	(4.40)	(4.40)	(3.58)	(11.82)				
Finland	−8.173	−0.277	2.927	1.651	.988	.059	2.15	—
	(13.57)	(1.49)	(5.49)	(28.21)				
Germany	−17.771	−0.469	1.394	1.671	.986	.043	1.66	.507
	(12.17)	(2.18)	(5.15)	(15.22)				
Italy	−13.569	−0.138	3.095	2.092	.985	.043	1.90	.295
	(9.23)	(0.55)	(3.35)	(15.34)				
Sweden	−12.102	−0.118	0.724	1.886	.979	.049	1.67	.235
	(9.72)	(0.40)	(1.18)	(17.81)				

Note: t-values are in parentheses below coefficients.

significant in all cases but for Sweden. The estimated secular income elasticities are all positive and significant.

B. Comparison of Equations

Viewing the results for the four estimated equations together, some interesting conclusions emerge. First, on the criterion of goodness-of-fit, we find that the most unrestricted equation usually yields the lowest standard error of estimate, although there are some exceptions. For example, in the results for Austria and Belgium, the equation that uses the price of tradable goods as the sole domestic price variable appears to give the best fit, while in the German case the equation with two relative prices (equation (3)) has the smallest standard error.

In order to examine this question more formally, we performed log-likelihood ratio tests be tween equation (3) and equations (4) and (5), respectively. Since, as reported earlier, the homogeneity assumption is generally satisfied, this essentially involves testing the restrictions $a_2 = a_1 \alpha$ and $a_2 = 0$, respectively. The results of these tests can be summarized as follows.[28]

As compared to equation (3), the model using the GDP deflator (*PGDP*) was invalid for Belgium, Canada, Denmark and Italy. Excluding nontradable goods prices from the specification, as represented by equation (5), was inappropriate only for Italy. We therefore can reasonably conclude that the model that uses the price of tradables as the only domestic price variable (namely, equation (5)) does as well as the more general import equation (3), and better than the other restricted import equation (4).

Turning to the import price elasticities themselves, it was readily apparent that the model employing only the ratio of import prices to tradable goods prices (shown in Table 5) tends to yield larger elasticities with smaller variances than the unrestricted model.

In conclusion, these results point to the usefulness of disaggregating the domestic price index into its nontradable and tradable goods components so as to increase the statistical power of the results. It also appears to be generally correct to exclude nontradable goods prices from the import demand specification and this limits the domestic price variable to tradable goods prices alone — a finding that weighs against aggregate price indices such as the GDP deflator in aggregate import demand functions. The only exceptions to these results were the United States, where the price of nontradable was found to be a statistically significant determinant of import demand. and the United Kingdom, where the consistent appearance of a positive import price elasticity precluded drawing any meaningful conclusions.

IV. CONCLUSIONS

Almost all existing estimates of the price elasticity for demand for total imports are based on relative-price measures that compare the price of imports to one domestic price — namely, the wholesale price index or the income deflator. The use of either of these indices carries the implication that imports

---

[28] Again, the country-by-country test results for the restrictions are available from the author upon request.

substitute equally with nontradable and tradable goods. In this study, we relaxed this restriction and estimated the aggregate import equation using specially constructed separate price indices for nontradable and tradable goods.

The major finding of this study is that the price of nontradable goods does not appear to be a significant determinant of the demand for imports in most industrial countries. This in turn has two implications. The first is that one should not constrain the price elasticity of demand for imports to be equal as between domestic tradable goods and nontradable goods — a consideration which argues against using, say, the income deflator as a proxy for the price of import substitutes. The second implication is that the assumption of strong separability in the import demand equation that is used to justify the inclusion of only one relative price as a determinant — namely, that between imports and domestic tradable goods — would seem to be consistent with the available empirical evidence, at least for seven of the ten industrial countries considered here. Our results indicated that using only the price of tradable goods as the domestic price variable, while leaving the explanatory power of the equation largely unaffected, generally yielded estimates of the relative price elasticity that were larger and more significant than those obtained when the price of nontradable goods was included in the formulation (with or without the restriction that the effects of the prices of nontradable and tradable goods are identical).

Morris Goldstein, Mohsin S. Khan, and Lawrence H. Officer, "Prices of Tradable and Nontradable Goods in the Demand for Total Imports," *The Review of Economics and Statistics*, 62:2 (May, 1980), pp. 190–199. © 1980 by the President and Fellows of Harvard College. Used with permission of the publisher.

REFERENCES

Armington, Paul S., "A Theory of Demand for Products Distinguished by Place of Production," IMF *Staff Papers* 16 (Mar. 1969), 159–178.

Clements, Kenneth, "A General Equilibrium Econometric Model of the Open Economy," unpublished, University of Chicago, Dec. 1977.

Goldman, Steven M., and Hirofumi Uzawa, "A Note on Separability in Demand Analysis," *Econometrica* 32 (July 1964), 387–398.

Goldstein, Morris, and Mohsin S. Khan, "Large Versus Small Price Changes and the Demand for Imports," IMF *Staff Papers* 23 (Mar. 1976), 200–225.

Goldstein, Morris, and Mohsin S. Khan, "The Supply and Demand for Exports: A Simultaneous Approach," this REVIEW 60 (May 1978), 275–286.

Goldstein, Morris, and Lawrence H. Officer, "New Measures of Prices and Productivity for Tradable and Nontradable Goods," *Review of Income and Wealth* 25 (Dec. 1979), 413–427.

Gregory, Robert G., "United States Imports and Internal Pressure of Demand: 1948–68," *American Economic Review* 61 (Mar. 1971), 28–47.

Heien, Dale M., "Structural Stability and the Estimation of International Import Price Elasticities," *Kyklos* 21, Fasc. 4 (1968), 695–711.

Houthakker, Hendrik S., and Stephen P. Magee, "Income and Price Elasticities in World Trade," this REVIEW 51 (May 1969), 111–125.

Khan, Mohsin S., and Knud Z. Ross, "Cyclical and Secular Income Elasticities of the Demand for Imports," this REVIEW 57 (Aug. 1975), 357–361.

Khan, Mohsin S., and Knud Z. Ross, "The Functional Form of the Aggregate Import Equation," *Journal of International Economics* 7 (May 1977), 149–160.

Leamer, Edward E., and Robert M. Stern, *Quantitative International Economics* (Boston: Allyn and Bacon, 1970).

Magee, Stephen P., "Prices, Income and Foreign Trade: A Survey of Recent Economic Studies," in P. B. Kenen (ed.), *International Trade and Finance: Frontiers for Research* (Cambridge: Cambridge University Press, 1975), 175–252.

Murray, Tracy, and Paul Ginman, "An Empirical Examination of the Traditional Aggregate Import Demand Model," this REVIEW 58 (Feb. 1976), 75–80.

Mutti, John H., "The Specification of Demand Equations for Imports and Domestic Substitutes," *Southern Economic Journal* 44 (July 1977), 68–73.

Officer, Lawrence H., "The Productivity Bias in Purchasing Power Parity: An Econometric Investigation," IMF *Staff Papers* 23 (Nov. 1976), 545–579.

Samuelson, Lee, "A New Model of World Trade," *OECD Economic Outlook: Occasional Studies* (Paris: Organization of Economic Cooperation and Development, 1973).

Taplin, Grant B., "A Model of World Trade," in R. J. Ball (ed.), *The International Linkage of National Economic Models* (Amsterdam: North-Holland Publishing Company, 1973), 177–223.

APPENDIX

Data Definitions and Sources

The data used in this paper are annual observations for the period 1950 to 1973 for all countries. All variables are defined in domestic currency units.

The basic sources of the data are:
- A: International Monetary Fund, *International Financial Statistics*
- B: Organization for Economic Cooperation and Development, *National Accounts of OECD Countries*

Variables

- M: imports (in constant 1970 prices). Source A, line 71 divided by line 75.
- PM: unit-value index of imports, 1970 = 100. Source A, line 75.
- Y: GDP (in constant 1970 prices). Source B.
- $PGDP$: GDP deflator, 1970 = 100. Source B.
- PT: price index of tradable commodities, 1970 = 100. This series is generated by dividing the nominal value of GDP originating in the tradable goods sector by the real value of GDP of that sector. Source B (tables on GDP by type of economic activity). See Officer (1976) and Goldstein and Officer (1979) for further details.
- PNT: price index of nontradable commodities, 1970 = 100. The method of calculating this series is analogous to that for PT; see Goldstein and Officer (1979).
- Y^*: trend level of GDP (in constant 1970 prices). This series was calculated by fitting the equation

$$Y^*_t = Y_0 e^{g\tau}$$

where Y_0 is the initial value of real GDP, g is its growth rate, and τ is a linear time trend.

Part II

Currency Regimes, Exchange Rate Policy and International Policy Coordination

Chapter 4

Market-based Fiscal Discipline in Monetary Unions: Evidence from the US Municipal Bond Market

Morris Goldstein and Geoffrey Woglom

SECTION 1. INTRODUCTION

It is widely accepted that participation in a currency union is inconsistent with independence in the conduct of monetary policy. Indeed, in the ongoing discussions about the path to economic and monetary union (EMU) in Europe, much attention is being devoted both to the establishment of a *central* monetary authority and to securing a mandate for that institution which would give primacy to the goal of price stability. In this sense, there would appear to be an emerging consensus about how to constrain or 'discipline' monetary policy.[1]

Less settled at this stage is what constraints, if any, should be placed on national fiscal policies in a currency union. The debate is influenced by two observations. First, ten years of experience with the European Monetary System (EMS) — during which exchange rate commitments became progressively 'harder' — does not suggest that the exchange rate regime itself will be sufficient to force a convergence around sound fiscal policies. In the words of the Delors

Report (1989, paragraph 3):

> the EMS has not fulfilled its potential. . . . the lack of sufficient convergence of fiscal policies as reflected in large and persistent budget deficits in certain countries has remained a source of tensions and has put disproportionate burden on monetary policy.

Second, if fiscal policy discipline was not forthcoming in an EMU, then the key objective of the union itself could well be threatened. Specifically, if a member of the union accumulated so much debt that it eventually became unable to service it, there would be pressure either on the central monetary institution to monetize the debt or on other members to bail out the errant borrower. In these circumstances, the central bank would find it difficult to credibly commit itself to price stability and other members would find their own incentives for implementing sound fiscal policies distorted. In time, the private sector would incorporate higher inflation expectations into its wage and interest rate contracts. In the end, the social advantages associated with using one money of stable purchasing power would be forfeited.

Reflecting these concerns, there is strong support for including in any EMU treaty explicit provisions prohibiting monetary financing and billing out of budget deficits. Still, debate continues on whether such provisions are all that is required to encourage fiscal discipline. At least three separate schools of thought have surfaced.

One view, echoed in the Delors Report (1989), is that binding *fiscal rules* represent the preferred solution to the problem. These rules would impose effective upper limits on budget deficits and on debt stocks of individual member countries, as well as limit recourse to external borrowing in non-member currencies.[2] In brief, the case against rigid fiscal rules is that they are incapable of taking adequate account of differences in the circumstances of members. For example, the same budget deficit (relative to GNP) is apt to be less cause for concern in a country with a high private saving rate, a low stock of debt, a temporarily high unemployment rate, and a good track record on inflation than in one with the opposite characteristics. There are also questions of effectiveness. In this connection, von Hagen (1991) reports a greater tendency for US states with debt limits and stringent balanced budget requirements to substitute unrestricted for restricted debt (by delegating functions and debt-raising power to off-budget entities and local governments).

A second approach, which finds expression in more recent EC Commission reports (see *Economic and Monetary Union*, August 1990, and *One Market, One Money*, October 1990), also calls for constraints on national fiscal policies, but adopts a more discretionary format. Specifically, it proposes that peer group, *multilateral surveillance* be reinforced to discourage errant fiscal policies of individual member countries; in addition, it suggests that the EMU Treaty incorporate the principle that '. . . excessive budget deficits must be avoided' (EC Commission, 1990a). Suffice to say that this tack too is open to criticism. Multilateral surveillance exercises typically employ a broad set of economic indicators. This sets up the risk that different indicators will send conflicting signals for policy adjustment, thereby allowing an errant fiscal position to continue for too long.[3] Moreover, without previously agreed upon rules available to settle disputes, there is a risk that negotiations, cum pressures for 'solidarity' within the union, could delay unduly the needed fiscal adjustment.

Yet a third — albeit very different — route to fiscal discipline is to entrust private financial markets with that role. Such *market-based fiscal discipline* would take the form of an initially rising default premium on the debt of a member country running excessive deficits. If those deficits persisted, the default premium would increase at an increasing rate, and eventually the offending country would be denied access to additional credit. This increase in the cost of borrowing, along with the threat of reduced availability of credit, would then provide the incentive to correct irresponsible fiscal behaviour. Advocates of the market approach (Bishop *et al.*, 1989) recognize that it will work only if certain conditions are satisfied, namely: (i) capital must be able to move freely, (ii) full information must be available on the sovereign borrower, (iii) the market must be convinced both that there are no implicit or explicit outside guarantees on sovereign debt and that the borrower's debt will not be monetized, and (iv) the financial system must be strong enough to withstand the failure of a 'large' borrower. They do not regard these conditions as unrealistically restrictive. Not surprisingly, those who favor the fiscal rules or surveillance options are less convinced, and point to the developing-country debt crisis of the early 1980s and to the New York City financial crisis of the mid-1970s as graphic illustrations of the limitations of the market's disciplining process.[4] Skeptics also note that high public debts often reflect political polarization or distributional conflicts over the sharing of the fiscal burden — factors that can make fiscal adjustment relatively insensitive to a rise in the cost of borrowing.[5] Presumably, these doubts lie behind the assessments that '... the constraints imposed by market forces might either be too slow and weak or too sudden and disruptive' (Delors Report, 1989, paragraph 30), and that '... the effectiveness of market discipline cannot be taken for granted' (EC Commission, 1990b, p. 100).

In choosing among these alternative mechanisms for achieving greater fiscal discipline, it is natural to seek guidance from the experience of federal states. The experience of the United States is of particular interest for ongoing EMU discussions. For one thing, the viability of the United States as a common currency area is long since firmly established; in operational terms, this implies that one can legitimately disregard expectations of an exchange rate change as contributing to differences in borrowing costs paid by different fiscal jurisdictions. Second, state governments do not have access to central bank financing; as noted above, a similar provision is expected to be included in any EMU treaty. Third, with regard to creditors, US states enjoy immunity from bankruptcy courts, much like a sovereign country does (see English, 1991, and Orth, 1987). Fourth, while many US states have voluntarily imposed their own statutory limits on their deficit-spending and/or borrowing, there are no *federally-imposed* borrowing limits; this provides enough autonomy at the state level to test the market-discipline hypothesis using a cross section of states, while also giving some scope to gauge the influence of fiscal rules on borrowing costs. Fifth, the US capital market is probably closest to the kind of integrated, deep, informationally efficient financial area that Europe seeks to become after 1992. Finally, while individual state and local governments have at times run sizable fiscal deficits, there have been *no* state or municipal defaults on general obligation bonds during the post-World War II period (Davidson, 1990, and Cohen, 1988); (state) fiscal discipline has therefore been more the rule than the exception.

To be sure, there are also significant differences between the United States and Europe that are worthy of explicit mention. As noted by Lamafalussy (1989) and others, in Europe there is a greater concentration of expenditures and, especially, borrowing needs in a few regions; for example, Italy's budget deficit alone — at some 2 percent of EC GDP — is equal to more than half of the aggregate EC deficit. This in turn may mean that a 'no bail-out' pledge will carry less credibility in Europe than in the United States. Another difference is that ratios of debt to total product are much higher — by almost an order of magnitude — in European countries than in American states. Whereas the heavily indebted European countries have (total) debt-to-GNP ratios near and in some cases above 100 percent, their state counterparts in the New England and Pacific regions have ratios on the order of 10 to 20 percent; see Eichen-green (1990).[6] Labour mobility is also much higher in the United States than in Europe[7] — a factor that should make it easier for Americans to discipline higher spending local authorities by fleeing jurisdictions where higher tax burdens are not offset by more generous provisions of public goods.[8] Yet a fourth difference is that the involvement and relative size of the central fiscal authority is much greater in the United States than in Europe. The Community budget is presently about 1 percent of EC GNP and even after creation of the single market, it is not expected to exceed 3 percent; by way of contrast, the federal budget in the United States accounts for roughly a quarter of US GNP. One implication of this difference is that American states do not have as much access (via tax collections) to their residents' incomes as do member countries of the EC; at the same time, region-specific income fluctuations are cushioned to a much greater extent (via variations in tax and transfer payments) in the United States than they are in Europe.[9]

Taken together, these differences imply that the market for EC country debt after EMU may not generate the same default premium for any given risk of default as does the municipal bond market in the United States. But the size of the default premium is not as important as the broader issue of whether changes in the default premium accurately reflect changes in the probability of default, that is, whether interest rates move in response to those aspects of fiscal policy behaviour that alter the probability of default. For if the bond markets do operate in such an informationally efficient manner, then the practical options for leaning more heavily on a 'market-based' approach to fiscal discipline are enhanced. To mention but one possibility, observed relative default premia might be employed as 'indicators' to trigger multilateral surveillance discussions; in this way, the 'incentive' to correct excessive fiscal imbalances could be large even in the face of small increases in the market's cost of borrowing.

The primary purpose of this paper is to provide new empirical evidence on market-based fiscal discipline by estimating the relationship between the cost of borrowing and measures of default risk in the US municipal bond market.

Our efforts are aided by access to a set of survey data on yields of state general-obligation bonds that covers 39 states from 1973 to the present.[10] We believe that this survey data, collected by the Chubb Corporation, offers a richer medium for testing the market discipline hypothesis than has been available heretofore; not only is there a much larger sample of observations, but problems of comparability across bonds with different maturities, call provisions, and coupon yields are effectively eliminated by the survey design.[11]

In addition to testing the market discipline hypothesis, the US state data have implications for the first approach to fiscal discipline, binding fiscal rules. The state data contain a variety of self-imposed fiscal rules. Thus we can test whether financial markets perceive these rules to be effective in limiting default risk. While there may be important differences between voluntarily and involuntarily imposed fiscal rules, the state data allow us to test whether it is possible to credibly 'tie one's own hands'.

The rest of the paper is organized along the following lines. Section 2 reviews the theory of default risk in the context of the supply and demand for state borrowing. Section 3 describes in detail the (Chubb) survey data and the other data used, and reviews the specification issues raised by the theory of default risk. The econometric results are presented in Section 4. Anticipating what follows, we do find evidence that states with larger stocks of debt, larger (current) fiscal deficits, and higher trend rates of growth of debt relative to income, pay more to borrow in the municipal bond market than do states with more conservative fiscal-policy track records. Moreover, we also find that, ceteris paribus, states with more stringent, voluntary, constitutional limits on borrowing face a lower cost of borrowing. Concluding remarks are contained in Section 5.

SECTION 2. THE MARKET FOR STATE BORROWING

The Supply of Funds to State Borrowers

Theories of the supply of funds to states typically assume that any state's borrowing is a small fraction of total borrowing in the capital markets.[12] Consequently, the market interest rate is assumed to be unaffected by any individual state borrowing. Put another way, states are price takers (with respect to the expected, risk-adjusted interest rate) on credit markets. This does not, however, imply that all states face the same promised interest rate (equivalently, yield to maturity). The promised interest rates on state bonds in fact show considerable variability. It is not atypical for the spread between the lowest and highest yields to be over 100 basis points. This section looks at the theoretical reasons used to explain these spreads in spite of a common, market-determined interest rate. The explanations can be separated into two factors: (i) default risk; (ii) risk premia.

Default Risk

Modern capital theory is a theory of the determinants of expected returns. In the case of securities subject to default, the expected return is determined by the stated or promised interest rate and the probability and consequences of default. For example, in the case of a one-period bond on which there is a positive probability of complete default, $(1 - P)$, the relationship between the promised interest rate, R, and the expected interest rate, E, is given by:

$$E = (1 + R)P - 1$$
$$= R - (1 - P)(1 + R) < R \qquad (1)$$

Because of the probability of default, the expected interest rate is less than the promised rate. Therefore, the promised interest rate on these bonds has to be higher than the interest rate on safe assets, which bear the (after-tax equivalent) risk-free rate, R_T. There are two reasons why the interest rate on loans with the possibility of default are higher than the risk-free rate: default premia and risk premia. Default premia compensate a lender for the expected losses from default. Risk premia compensate a lender for the possible increased riskiness of the total portfolio that results from the possibility of default. Unfortunately, many authors use the terms risk premia and default premia interchangeably in this framework.

Finance theory implies that default premia must be positive for assets subject to default risk, but risk premia may be zero even with default risk. The possibility of a zero risk premium on a loan with default risk occurs when the default risk can be diversified away (i.e., when the default risk is unsystematic). In this case, the lending to one risky borrower does not increase the risk of the total portfolio because of diversification. With diversification, the default risk from one loan is combined with offsetting risks on other loans. To focus initially on the determinants of default risk, we start with the case of no risk premia.

With no risk premia, the expected interest rate on a bond with default risk must equal the risk-free rate, or

$$E = (1 + R)P - 1 = R_T \tag{2}$$

Adding one to both sides of (2) yields:

$$1 + E = (1 + R)P = 1 + R_T \tag{2'}$$

Written in this way, the equality of the expected interest rates implies that the expected repayment of principal and interest on the risky and risk-free securities must be the same. The theory of the promised interest rate on risky debt in this case becomes a theory of the determinants of the risk of default, or, in terms of equation (2), the theory of the determinants of P. The relationship between default risk and the rate on risky state debt can be written explicitly by rearranging (2) to yield:

$$R - R_T = (1 + R_T)(1 - P)/P \tag{3}$$

This equation shows that as the default probability increases, the spread between the interest rate on risky state debt and the after-tax, equivalent risk-free rate also increases.

For our purposes, the most interesting determinants of the probability of default are debt variables and current borrowing. In many different contexts, (e.g., Stiglitz and Weiss, 1981, Eaton and Gersovitz, 1981, Metcalf, 1990, and Capeci, 1990), it has been shown that when current borrowing affects the probability of default, the supply curve can be backward bending, as in Figure 1 (a more technical derivation is detailed in the Appendix). At low levels of debt, an increase in borrowing, B, causes the promised rate to rise in order to compensate the lender for the increased probability of default. Notice, however, that the increase in the promised rate, R, also worsens the borrower's financial position by raising the interest expense on new borrowing. Thus, increasing the promised rate, by itself, increases the probability of default.

At some critical interest rate (R_C) and level of borrowing (B_C), the supply curve becomes vertical. At this point with $B = B_C$, any increase in the interest rate would cause the expected rate to *fall* because of the increased probability of default. The only way the promised rate could rise above R_C while fulfilling

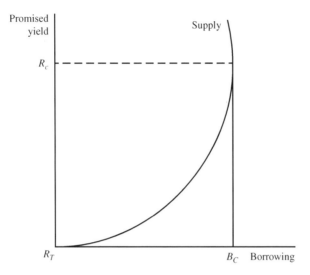

Fig 1: The supply curve of borrowing

(2), would be if the level of borrowing fell below B_C; hence the backward bend to the supply curve. Promised rates above R_C, however, are unlikely to be observed in the market for reasons discussed below.

While the supply curve, at least initially, has the normal upward slope, lenders are *not* being induced by higher *expected* rates to increase their supply of credit. Recall that we began the analysis by assuming that the supply of credit to a state was infinitely elastic because any state's borrowing is a small fraction of total borrowing. That assumption is fulfilled in Figure 1, in spite of the shape of the supply curve. While the promised rate in Figure 1 varies with state borrowing, the expected rate is constant throughout. The slope of the supply curve solely reflects the change in the promised interest rate needed to keep the expected rate constant as the probability of default varies.

While the analysis so far has been very simple, the qualitative results on default risk are more general. For example, while the analysis was done for one-period bonds with the possibility of total default, it generalizes fairly easily for multiperiod bonds and partial defaults. In fact, if the probability of default is constant over time, the analysis immediately generalizes for the case of longer maturity bonds (see Yawitz *et al.*, 1985). In this case, however, one must take account of the fact that only the current deficit must be financed at the current promised rate. As is shown in the Appendix, this complication suggests that the slope of the supply curve increases at an increasing rate the larger the fraction of new borrowing in total borrowing. Thus, positively-valued current deficits may have a strong effect on the cost of state borrowing.

Risk Premia

Risk premia complicate the relationship in equation (2) between the interest rate on risky debt, the risk-free rate, and the probability of default. Most theories of risk premia, however, suggest that premia should either be proportional to default risk, or more than proportional to default risk. Thus while equation (3) no longer holds, the interest spread in (3) provides an upward-biased measure of default probabilities, where this bias increases with the probability of default.

Specifying the risk premia associated with state debt requires a specification of planned holding periods. For example, if most lenders are planning to hold state debt to maturity, the only nominal risk is related to the probability of default. Risk premia arise when this default risk cannot be eliminated through diversification (when default risk has a systematic component). In this case, buying risky state bonds would increase the risk on the total portfolio and financial investors would seek to be compensated for their greater exposure to risk by a higher promised yield. While equation (2) no longer holds, the promised yield would still be a positive function of default probabilities.[13]

Many investors, however, either have shorter holding periods, or are concerned for other reasons with the current market value of risky bonds throughout the holding period. A good example of the latter type of investor is a municipal bond mutual fund, which must 'mark to market' each day. In either case, these financial investors are concerned with the volatility of the market value of the state bond throughout its maturity. This volatility will depend on changes in the current interest rate on the bond (i.e., the secondary market yield). Volatility of secondary market yields can result from two causes: (i) cyclical changes in the risk of default, which are independent of debt variables; and (ii) changes in credit ratings. In both cases, these risk premia are likely to be positively related to default risk.

The relationship between debt variables and promised yields is nonlinear. As discussed above, as debt variables increase, the promised rate is likely to rise at an increasing rate. This suggests that an exogenous increase in default risk caused by a major recession is likely to have a larger impact on heavily indebted states. Thus, the volatility of yields and the associated risk premia are likely to be increasing functions of default risk. Davidson (1990) presents evidence showing that the spread between municipal bond rated by Moody's as Baa and Aaa is more volatile over time than the spread between the Aa and Aaa rates.[14] This evidence is consistent with the hypothesis that risk premia due to cyclical volatility increase with default risk.

Credit-rating changes are also associated with changes in yields. Rating changes are generally regarded as primarily reflecting unanticipated changes in a state's fiscal position.[15] While one can argue that an Aa state is just as likely to experience either a deterioration or improvement in its fiscal position as a Baa state, risk premia from rating changes still increase with default risk. This relationship results from an important nonlinearity between ratings and yields. Many financial intermediaries are prohibited from holding securities rated below investment grade quality (below the Moody's rating Baa, or the S&P rating BBB). With the removal of these large holders, yields would have to rise dramatically to induce the remaining holders to absorb the total supply of debt. Thus, while changes either way in ratings may be equally likely, the *consequences* of a rating downgrade for a Baa state are more severe. An A state, however, faces a greater likelihood of a downgrade below Baa than does a Aaa state. Thus one would expect the risk premia associated with ratings changes to rise with the probability of default.

Conclusions

There are additional factors that affect the interest rates on specific issues of state debt, namely (i) maturity, (ii) callability, (iii) the coupon yield, and (iv) insurance.[16] The complication of these factors, however, can be avoided if interest rates on bonds with identical characteristics with respect to these factors are compared across states. After controlling for these factors, the expected interest rates for all state bonds, after adjusting for risk premia, should be equal to the equivalent after-tax interest rate on Treasuries. The equality of expected interest rates, however, implies that the promised rates, the rates observed directly on financial markets, will differ because of differences in default and credit risk across states. Default and credit risk should be an increasing function of state borrowing.

The Demand for Funds by State Borrowers

The key issue in the states' demand for funds is whether the quantity demanded is sensitive to the cost of borrowing. If it is, the promised yield could never reach R_C in Figure 1. Metcalf (1990) estimates a model of the demand for state borrowing, where states choose between borrowing and tax finance based on demographic factors and the after-tax cost of borrowing. He finds that states do vary their borrowing based on the after-tax cost of borrowing.

This model of the demand for borrowing is important because while states must be price takers with regard to the expected risk-adjusted interest rate, it is implausible to assume that they would be price takers with regard to the *promised* interest rate. The state must recognize that by borrowing more, the promised rate on all new borrowing increases. Specifically, the marginal cost of borrowing one more dollar exceeds the promised rate on this borrowing, and is equal to the promised rate plus the change in the promised rate (which depends on the slope in Figure 1) times the volume of new borrowing. But as borrowing approaches B_C, the change in the promised rate is large for small changes in borrowing (i.e., the slope in Figure 1 goes to infinity). As a result, the marginal cost of borrowing increases without limit as B approaches B_C, and the state has a strong incentive to keep total borrowing below B_C.

While this model is plausible and receives empirical support, it is not consistent with the credit rationing part of the market approach to fiscal discipline. The credit rationing story can be resurrected, however from different models of state borrowing. For example, Eaton and Gersovitz (1981) develop a model for sovereign country borrowing where a country borrows to smooth its consumption stream. In this model, if the state of nature is adverse enough, a country might wish to borrow above B_C. In this case, the credit markets would limit borrowing to B_C at the promised interest rate R_C. The country is credit-constrained because it would be willing to pay a higher promised rate in order to borrow more, but no lender will lend more. In this model, credit constraints arise out of unforeseen, large shifts in the demand curve.

These two models need not be viewed as mutually exclusive. For example, trend borrowing may be determined by Metcalf's interest-sensitive model, with unanticipated variations around trend being explained by the Eaton and Gersovitz model. The data certainly suggest that there can be unanticipated increases in borrowing. Louisiana's experience during the 1980s provides a dramatic example. In December of 1982, Louisiana was an Aa rated state with promised yields below those of Aaa-rated New Jersey. Five years later, Louisiana was Baa1-rated with yields over 100 basis points higher than New Jersey's. During this time period, deficits in excess of 18 percent of state expenditures were incurred by Louisiana. This suggests that while the trend demand for debt is interest-sensitive, unanticipated increases in demand also occur.

In this paper, we are primarily concerned about estimating the *supply curve* of funds to risky state borrowers. Market-based fiscal discipline can work even with interest-insensitive borrowers via credit rationing. In addition, the simultaneity issues, described below, make estimating the demand curve problematic. For estimating the supply curve, the determinants of the demand for state borrowing are important chiefly because of the identification problem.

SECTION 3. DATA AND ISSUES OF ECONOMETRIC SPECIFICATION

Data on Market Yields

The primary data needed to test for the existence of default premia on state debt are market yields on the obligations of the various state governments. States, however, issue two basic types of bonds: revenue bonds and general obligation bonds. General obligation bonds (GOs) are 'full faith and credit' obligations of the state, whereas revenue bonds are only backed by the revenues of the specific project being financed by the bond. For example, the repayment of interest and principal on a Florida Department of Transportation Bond, a revenue bond, could come from toll revenues. Florida State Board of Education bonds, on the other hand, are financed from the general tax revenues of the state. Given our interest in the fiscal position of state governments, we need yield data on general obligation bonds.

The need for market price data on general obligation bonds, however, raises immediate problems because these bonds are not actively traded. For example, J.P. Morgan tracks the yields on over 75 actively-traded tax exempt bonds in their *Municipal Market Monitor*. Of these bonds, only 5 are state GOs. Surprising as it may seem, information is *not* widely available on the market prices of individual state debt.

As previously noted, however, financial market participants, particularly mutual funds, have a need for current market values. This need is met by brokerage firms (e.g., J. J. Kenny) that place values on bonds issues for a fee.

These bond values, however, are not in general transactions prices. Instead, the relationships between the prices on particular issues are specified in what is called a 'pricing matrix'. This matrix uses a relatively small number of transactions prices to infer the values of all the other securities being evaluated. The information that goes into the specification of the pricing matrix is proprietary and not generally available. While it is difficult for an outsider to determine the validity of these matrix prices, it is noteworthy that these pricing services are widely used. In fact, one of the widely-reported municipal bond indices, the Bond Buyer 40, is based on municipal bond 'prices' from these services. Thus, the financial markets' own needs for current market values are not met solely with transactions prices.

Transaction price data and matrix prices suffer from another problem. In addition to default risk, risk premia and tax effects, municipal bond prices and yields are affected by other features that vary by issue. Unless one compares *identical* securities across states, these other features can have a significant impact on yield spreads. For example, a randomly selected issue of J.P. Morgan's *Municipal Market Monitor* (1989) lists the market yields on two Florida State Board of Education Bonds. These market yields are based on the closing bid price at Morgan. On August 24, 1989, the two market yields were 7.05 and 7.27 percent. The bonds were identical, except that the lower yielding bond matured in 2013 as opposed to 2010, was callable at 100 in 1996 as opposed to 102, and bore a coupon of 5 percent instead of 7.25 percent. During the same week, the yield spread between AA and AAA 20-year municipal bonds was reported by Delphis Hanover as 20 basis points. Thus, the yield spread caused by the special features on the two Florida State GOs was wider than the yield spread between two credit-rating categories.

Fortunately, there is a data source that allows us to avoid the problem of comparability on GO bonds, The Chubb Relative Value Study. The Chubb Corporation, an insurance company, has conducted since 1973 a semi-annual survey of 20–25 (sell-side) municipal bond traders. The traders are asked to give the yields on 5, 10 and 20 year maturity GOs for 39 states and Puerto Rico, relative to the yield on a comparable New Jersey state GO. The survey results for December 1989 are reproduced in Table 1. This survey implies that, on average, traders felt that a *comparable* California 20-year GO should have a market yield 14.04 basis points below New Jersey's market yield, while a *comparable* Louisiana 20-year GO should bear a yield 70 basis points higher

Table 1: Chubb Relative Value Study, December 1989. (Basis Point Spread for a 20-year State GO, Relative to a New Jersey 20-year GO.)

	Ranking:	Moody's Rating	Avg. Response	Std. Dev.
1	California	Aaa	−14.04	3.84
2	North Carolina	Aaa	−11.91	4.32
3	Virginia	Aaa	−10.65	4.76
4	Connecticut	Aa1	−9.96	5.09
5	Missouri	Aaa	−8.30	5.28
6	South Carolina	Aaa	−6.74	5.58
7	Georgia	Aaa	−6.39	2.58
8	Maryland	Aaa	−4.65	3.51
9	Tennessee	Aaa	−4.09	5.80
10	New Jersey	Aaa	0.00	0.00
11	Ohio	Aa	1.39	3.41
12	Utah	Aaa	5.57	4.84
13	Maine	Aa1	7.00	4.95
14	Minnesota	Aa	8.13	3.79
15	Montana	Aa	8.39	5.25
16	Delaware	Aa	8.61	4.51
17	Kentucky	Aa	8.70	5.31
18	New Hampshire	Aa1	9.52	3.84
19	Rhode Island	Aa	10.26	3.58
20	Vermont	Aa	11.17	3.56
21	Alabama	Aa	12.09	3.83
22	Wisconsin	Aa	12.13	3.93
23	Pennsylvania	A1	12.91	4.83
24	Mississippi	Aa	13.39	4.49
25	Hawaii	Aa	13.87	3.83
26	Michigan	A1	14.04	4.84
27	New Mexico	Aa	14.48	3.59
28	Illinois	Aaa	14.48	4.67
29	Oregon	A1	16.57	3.59
30	Florida	Aa	17.26	4.11
31	Nevada	Aa	18.74	4.00
32	NewYork	A1	20.39	4.75
33	Oklahoma	Aa	21.61	7.29
34	Texas	Aa	22.74	5.93
35	North Dakota	Aa	22.83	10.11
36	Washington	A1	24.48	3.05
37	Alaska	Aa	27.39	7.49
38	West Virginia	A1	28.22	5.34
39	Puerto Rico	Baa1	48.09	6.99
40	Massachusetts	Baa1	62.39	11.50
41	Louisiana	Baa1	70.00	12.07

than New Jersey's. Most important, for our purposes, the Relative Value Study implies that the yield spreads between comparable California and Louisiana 20-year GOs should be 84.04 basis points.[17] Since the bonds being evaluated are comparable across states, the differences in yield spreads can only reflect default risk, risk premia, and tax effects. Thus while the data are not based on transactions prices, they do solve the problem of special features such as call provisions.[18]

As one would expect, these yield spreads vary over the course of the business cycle: over time, the spread for a particular state can vary considerably. For example, during the recession year of 1982, the spread between the highest and lowest rated states of Oklahoma and Michigan was over 170 basis points: in contrast by 1989, the high-low spread fell by a factor of 2 and Michigan was a higher-rated state than Oklahoma (see Table 1). These yield spreads behave as one might expect if they, in fact, reflect changes over time in default risk.

Other Data

To measure state debt, we used data on net, tax-supported debt as reported by Moody's. This debt figure is calculated each time Moody's issues a Credit Report on a new issue. Net tax supported debt includes all debt serviced from state tax revenues even when the state itself was not the issuer (e.g., Massachusetts Bay Transportation Authority bonds in Massachusetts), and deducts from gross debt, obligations that are serviced from non-tax revenues (e.g., Oregon general obligation debt that is backed by mortgage lending). Moody's publishes the latest available numbers for each state annually. These data reflect the most accurate picture of state's fiscal position from the perspective of one of the two major credit rating agencies. Unfortunately, the numbers are not updated at a uniform time during the year. These data are available from 1981 through 1990. To derive measures of the relative size of debt, the nominal debt numbers were deflated by the implicit GNP deflator for the year and divided by trend Gross State Product (based on Department of Commerce, real Gross State Product data). Bond ratings are the Moody's ratings.

Finally, state 'constitutional' debt limitations were measured by an index devised by the Advisory Commission on Intergovernmental Relations (ACIR, 1987). These limitations can vary from a requirement for the governor to submit a balanced budget to a prohibition on the issuance of general obligation debt. The ACIR index tries to measure in one number the restrictiveness of the various provisions adopted by a particular state. The index varies from 0 in Vermont, a Aa-rated state with no restrictions, to the maximum of 10 in 26 states. These 26 states include 8 of the 9 states with no general obligation debt, 7 of the 11 Aaa-rated states, 10 of the 23 Aa-rated states, and West Virginia, an AI state. For the 5 states (other than West Virginia) rated below Aa, the index ranges from 6 to 3.

The summary statistics for all of our variables are given in Table 2. At first glance the data in Table 2 seem to indicate that debt levels among the US states are orders of magnitude lower than among the European countries. This conclusion is unwarranted, however, because the Federal government is much larger in the United States than it will be in Europe, at least for the immediate future. As a result, states have less access to the incomes of their residents than do the European countries. Thus it is inappropriate to compare relative debt levels of the US states to the relative debt levels of the European countries. A better comparison of the relative importance of government debt between the US states and the European countries is provided by the fraction of total government expenditures accounted for by interest on the debt. During the 1989 fiscal year, interest as a fraction of total expenditures ranged between 1.5 and 10 percent (US Census, 1990) for the 50 states. Bishop (1991) reports statistics that suggest the comparable numbers for the European countries range between 5 and 25 percent. Thus, while debt levels are higher in Europe than among the US states, these differences are not as large as the numbers in Table 2 might suggest.

Table 2: Summary Statistics for Major Variables

	Mean	Minimum	Maximum	Std. Dev.
Yield spread	16.5	−28.4	143.5	23.5
Debt	2.3	0.2	7.1	1.4
'Deficit'	0.2	0.0	2.3	0.3
Trend growth in debt	1.5	−11.9	20.6	6.7
ACIR index of debt limitations	7.6	0.0	10.0	2.8

Note: The yield spread is measured in basis points; debt and deficit in percentage points of trend gross state product, and trend growth in debt is percentage points per annum.

Specification Issues

As outlined earlier, our basic aim is to estimate the relationship between the promised interest rate and default risk, where default risk in turn is related, inter alia, to the quantity of debt — or more generally, to a state's past and prospective fiscal policy behaviour. Put in other words, we hope to be able to trace out the supply curve illustrated in Figure 1.

The dependent variable in all our regressions is the yield spread on a 20-year state, general obligation bond relative to the yield on a 20-year New Jersey general obligation bond. In a cross-section regression, this implies that the constant term can be thought of as capturing New Jersey's yield.

In contrast to earlier empirical studies, we see four aspects of fiscal policy behaviour as potentially impacting on the probability of default. The first of these is the existing stock of debt (relative to income), which summarizes the scale of the state's past borrowing; ceteris paribus, the higher this ratio, the higher the default probability. Our second fiscal policy indicator is the expected growth of relative debt. This is captured in our regressions by the difference for each state between the trend rate of growth in real debt and trend growth in real state product. A state for which this trend variable is positive will have, on average, a rising relative debt, and thus a larger risk of default over the life of a 20-year general obligation bond.

Recall from Section 2 that the theory of default premia suggests that the slope of the supply curve should increase more rapidly the greater the proportion of new borrowing that must be financed at the current interest rate. If new borrowing causes an increase in the promised yield, then a deficit should affect the yield independently of its effect on total debt outstanding. This provides the rationale for our third fiscal policy variable, namely the increase in debt over the preceding year. We give this variable a value of zero if debt falls and a value equal to the deficit when it is a positive number. The expectation is that the deficit will carry a positive sign in the regressions. Last but not least, we have included the stringency of the state's constitutional debt limitations as also affecting default risk. Here, the argument is that stringent constitutional limitations make it more likely that any deviation from responsible fiscal policy will be corrected before it reaches crisis proportions; as such, we expect the constitutional stringency index to appear in the regressions with a negative sign.

So much for the fiscal variables. Next, we need to consider the likelihood that there are additional factors, particular to each state, that should help to explain default risk. Bond ratings are a discrete measure of all the factors (including fiscal variables) in each state that affect default probabilities. Liu and Thakor (1984) have proposed a two-step regression procedure designed to use the information in these, otherwise omitted state-specific factors. For each year, the rating categories are replaced with the average yield spread for the states in that category. A regression is then run for each year that estimates the numerical value of each state's rating category based on the included fiscal variables (i.e., debt, deficit, trend of the debt-to-income ratio, index of constitutional debt limitations). The *residuals* from these regressions, which we will call the ratings residuals, are an estimate of the quantitative importance of the factors that have *not* been captured by the included fiscal variables. In the second stage, the yield spread is regressed on all the variables employed in stage one plus the ratings residual. This procedure allows one to capture the information that is embedded in bond ratings and that is not already accounted for by the fiscal variables.[19]

Two related specification issues are the non-linearity of the relationship between fiscal variables and promised yields and variations in the risk of default over the business cycle. With regard to the first issue, we assumed that the non-linear supply curve in Figure 1 can be approximated by a quadratic function in the debt variables. The problem of the variation in the risk of default with the business cycle was handled with dummy variables. Because the risk of default is higher during a recession year (even with the same debt stock), we included dummies in our regressions to allow the constant term to vary by year. In addition, the non-linearity of the supply curve suggests that the slope may also vary by year. A higher risk of default is likely to change both the location of the supply curve in Figure 1 as well as the slope for any value of borrowing. Thus we included slope dummies in our regressions to allow the effect of an increase in the debt variables on yields to vary by year.[20]

The final specification issue is to account for the simultaneity between the promised interest rate and the debt variables. Recall that the issue of simultaneity arises when the states' demand for borrowing is interest-sensitive. The simultaneity problem is therefore likely to be most severe for cross-sectional differences in trend levels of debt. To account for this possibility, we tested our basic pooled equation against a panel model with fixed effects. The fixed-effects model, however, uses deviations from state sample means to estimate the supply equation. As a result, the time-invariant state variables (viz., trend debt growth and debt limitations) must be dropped from this specification.

The fixed effects model has the advantage of controlling for state-specific omitted variables that we cannot measure quantitatively, but which market participants report are important. For example, Delaware is an Aa-rated state, with GO bond yields typically below the average for all Aa-rated states. Yet, Delaware is one of the 4 states with the largest relative debt. Oregon, on the other hand, is an Al-rated state with a well-below average value for its relative debt, about one-fifth the size of Delaware's relative debt. The larger relative debt in Delaware primarily reflects the fact that the municipal government system is much less well developed in Delaware because of its small size. Therefore, the Delaware relative *state* debt is closer to a measure of the relative size of the *state and local* debt for other states.

These unobserved, fixed effects may impart a downward bias to our estimates for the effects of debt on yields. For example, because financial markets know about Delaware's unique state and municipal system, Delaware is able to borrow at relatively low yields (i.e., the supply curve in Figure 1 is shifted to the right for Delaware). But given these relatively low yields and an interest-sensitive demand, Delaware has a incentive to borrow more. Our supply curve expects to find a *positive* relationship between cross-section differences in relative debt and yields, but the unobserved, fixed effects impart a *negative* relationship between promised yields and relative debt.

With the fixed-effects model, we avoid having to explain why Delaware has a lower yield than Oregon in spite of the higher relative debt. Instead, we must explain how deviations from the mean in debt. The disadvantage of this approach is that we can only include variables that change over time. Therefore, with this approach, we cannot test for the importance of debt limitations, or for importance of the growth in trend debt.

The fixed-effects model solves the simultaneity problem if mean debt levels are interest-sensitive, while the deviations from the means are not (Hsiao, 1986). It is, of course, possible that deviations from the mean in debt and yield variables are simultaneously determined. Therefore, we also estimated the fixed-effects model with two-stage least squares. The problem here, however, is to find appropriate instruments, variables that affect the demand for borrowing, but are unrelated to supply. Finding appropriate instruments presents a problem because virtually all of the instruments that affect demand also affect the probability of default, and thereby also affect supply. Metcalf (1990) argues that demographic factors, such as the percentage of elderly, and current economic conditions are important exogenous factors in the demand for state borrowing. These same factors, however, are also likely to affect the probability of default. Take for example Metcalf's argument that a large population of elderly in a state can lead to a reliance on debt finance. It seems to us that the same argument implies that that state will have a higher probability of default for any level of borrowing. Default places a heavy burden on a state's residents. Defaulting on a newly issued 20-year state GO, when the bond approaches maturity, however, will not adversely affect the current generation of the elderly. While it is not clear how to solve this simultaneity problem, we experimented with lagged values of debt and economic conditions as instruments.

Table 3 presents the basic equation of our pooled regressions along with a pirori implications from the discussion of theory and specification issues.

SECTION 4. EMPIRICAL RESULTS

Our basic regression results for the yield spread are presented in Table 4. These regressions use the largest sample period available with both the Chubb data and the Moody's debt data (i.e., 333 observations).[21] Two versions of our theoretical model are shown. The first one, which we call the full model, includes the current deficit and its squared value, along with all the other determinants of default risk outlined earlier. The second version, which we label the abbreviated model, is identical except that it excludes the deficit variables.

The results in Table 4 offer broad support for our theoretical model. The coefficient on relative debt (the ratio of debt to trend state product) is significant with the expected positive sign, suggesting that debt stocks have a significant influence on borrowing costs. This is a robust finding for our pooled samples, and contradicts Eichengreen's (1990, p. 151) conclusion — based on yield spreads for a single year and on measures of gross state debt — that 'there is weak evidence that higher debt burdens increase the cost of borrowing.' The full model also indicates a significant effect for the current fiscal deficit in increasing a state's promised interest rate. Also, as is suggested by theory, the higher the trend rate of growth of the relative debt, the higher both the default

Table 3: Specification of Full Model and Definitions of Variables

---

Yield spread = $a_0 + a_1$ Debt + a_2 Deficit + a_3 Debt^2 + a_4 *Deficit*^{2} +
a_5 Trend growth in relative debt + a_6 Debt limit + a_7 Ratings residual +
a_{8-14} Year dummies + a_{15-22} (Year dummies) debt + a_{23-30} (Year dummies) deficit

Yield spread is the basis point value of the spread between the yield on a given state's 20-year GO debt and New Jersey's yield.

Debt is Moody's real net tax supported debt as a fraction of the trend value of real gross state product; $a_1 > 0, a_3 > 0$.

Deficit is the change in debt when positive, or zero; $a_2 > 0, a_4 > 0$.

Trend debt growth is the difference between trend growth in real tax-supported debt and real gross state product; $a_5 > 0$.

Debt limit is the ACIR index of the restrictiveness of a state's constitutional limitations on debt; $a_6 < 0$.

Ratings residual is the residual from a regression of the moody's rating for each state regressed against the preceding fiscal variables. The rating category is assigned the average value of the yield spreads for the states in that category; $a_7 = 1$.

Year dummies take on the value of 1 for one year between 1983–1989, and zero otherwise; a_{15-22} and a_{23-30} should be larger the greater the default risk in that year (i.e., during a recession).

---

risk and the cost of borrowing. Taken together, these estimates for the debt variables suggest that states which have implemented relatively conservative fiscal policies are perceived by the market as having a lower default probability and thereby reap a market dividend in the form of a lower borrowing cost.

Interestingly enough, the estimated coefficient on our 'constitutional fiscal rule' variable is also significant and with the expected negative sign. Indeed, and somewhat to our surprise, this constitutional debt limitation variable (measured by the ACIR index of fiscal stringency) was the most consistent performer among all the fiscal policy variables, typically emerging as significant with the expected sign not only in the pooled, time-series results but also in the single-year cross-sections. (We also estimated several pooled regressions where the constitutional debt-limitation variable entered interactively with the debt and deficit variables but the results showed little pattern or reason.)[22]

The implication, for what it is worth, is that states which have voluntarily imposed limitations on their borrowing and debt accumulation are seen by the market as having lower default risk, even after controlling for their past fiscal-policy track records. Using the point estimate in column (1) of Table 4, a state with an 'average' set of constitutional limitations (an index value of 7.6)

Table 4: OLS Estimates for the Abbreviated and Full Models

	Full Model (1)	Abbreviated Model (2)
Debt	8.26	9.98
	(3.51)	(4.92)
Deficit	23.26	
	(2.37)	
$Debt^2$	−0.25	−0.40
	(0.86)	(1.55)
$Deficit^2$	−11.40	
	(2.55)	
Trend debt growth	0.28	0.35
	(2.51)	(3.47)
Debt limits	−1.99	−2.01
	(7.31)	(8.18)
Ratings residual	(0.98)	(0.99)
	(24.0)	(26.7)
Std. error of est.	12.77	11.94
$\bar{R}^2$	0.70	0.74
Number of observations	333	333

Note: Sample Period 1982–90; 't' statistics in parentheses. In addition, each regression contained a constant term, year dummies for 1983–90, and slope dummies for the debt variable for 1983–90. Thus the coefficients on debt and the deficit refer to the 1982 coefficients for these variables. The variables are as described in Table 3.

pays 5 basis points more than a state with the most restrictive set of limitations. Presumably, market participants view these fiscal rules as constraining future fiscal adventurism. Because the ACIR index combines a group of rather diverse restrictions (ranging from the requirement that the governor must submit a balanced budget to an absolute dollar ceiling on the amount of general obligation debt), it would be unwise to read too much into this finding. But it does suggest that the benefits of 'tying one's hands' — so emphasized in the literature on the credibility of monetary policy — may be applicable to certain aspects of fiscal policy as well.

This brings us to the ratings residual, which is highly statistically significant with the excepted positive sign and with a coefficient that is not significantly different from its expected value of one. Our results do therefore support the notion that credit rating categories contain important information about default risk that is *not* captured by the fiscal variables. It also shows why trying to infer the presence of market discipline from eyeball observations of yield spreads and fiscal policy differences, without attempting to hold other things equal' is apt to be misleading. The first-stage regressions that attempt to explain the ratings are not presented, but are qualitatively similar to those estimated in earlier studies.

It would of course be desirable to show not just that default premia increase with looser fiscal policy, but also by how much. This can be calculated — and we in fact do so below — but the estimates, we are afraid, are subject to considerable margins of error. To reflect the theoretically appealing notion that default risk should rise at an increasing rate with higher levels of dept, we attempt to capture the non-linear nature of the supply curve with a quadratic in dept (and in the deficit). Most typically, however, the squared terms appeared in the regressions with the wrong sign and in some cases with a 't' value above 2. This is the case with the estimates for the full model shown in column (1) of Table 4: the estimated coefficient on the squared dept stock is negative but insignificant, while that on the squared deficit term is negative with a 't' value in excess of 2. Nevertheless, this imprecision should not overshadow the strong qualitative conclusion implied by our estimates that promised yields increase with the stock of debt.

Earlier on, we also speculated that default risk could vary over time, perhaps on account of the business cycle. Because we have included year-by-year shift and slope dummy variables, the estimated slope coefficients on debt and the deficit refer to 1982. Because 1982 was a recession year, it is not unreasonable to posit that default risk was then at a peak. In fact, the spread between Baa-Aaa municipal bonds was widest for any year in our sample during December of 1982. Thus it is reassuring that the point estimates (the results for the abbreviated model are shown in Table 5) for all of the slope dummies on debt are negative and 6 out of the eight are statistically significant. The constant term dummies are primarily positive, but none are statistically significant.

While there is broad support for the theoretical model, our attempt to test for the additional effect of new borrowing was not successful, as is shown by a comparison of the estimates for the full and abbreviated models in Table 4. In the results for the abbreviated model in column (2), the relative debt stock, the trend growth of the debt stock, the constitutional debt limitation index, and

Table 5: Time Dummies for the Abbreviated Model (Results for Regression of Column (2), Table 4)

	1983	1984	1985	1986	1987	1988	1989	1990
Constant term dummy:	4.30 (0.84)	8.54 (1.69)	4.44 (0.85)	7.40 (1.43)	3.63 (0.68)	0.67 (0.13)	−1.40 (0.28)	−5.50 (1.11)
Coefficient on debt dummy:	−2.58 (1.36)	−3.88 (2.05)	−4.53 (2.27)	−5.97 (3.04)	−4.23 (2.09)	−4.12 (2.09)	−3.97 (2.11)	−1.19 (0.66)

the ratings residual all appear as statistically significant with the theoretically expected signs. The squared value of the debt stock carries the wrong (negative) sign but has a high standard error.[23] In short, all the same qualitative conclusions apply. It is worth noting that the explanatory power of the abbreviated model (as measured by both the unadjusted and adjusted R-squared) is actually superior to that of the full model.[24] From this, we conclude that our attempts to capture with our deficit variable the additional effects on default risk stemming from new borrowing were unsuccessful (despite the significance of the deficit variable in the regressions for the full model).

Using the estimated coefficients in the abbreviated model, it is possible to calculate some suggestive statistics about the quantitative effect of relative debt on borrowing costs. For example, during the recession year of 1982, relative debt had a mean value of 2.2 percent. An increase in relative debt of one percentage point would have led to an increase in borrowing costs by more than 8 basis points, and the promised yields rise with the relative debt as long as debt was less than 12.3 percent of Gross State Product. The lowest estimates of the effect of debt on yields occurs for 1986, when the slope dummy on debt takes on the largest negative value of −5.97 (from Table 5) with a statistically significant 't' value of 3.0. For this year, our estimates imply that an increase in the relative debt by one percentage point (from the mean value of 2.2 percent) would raise borrowing costs by over 2 basis points and promised yields rise with relative debt as long as relative debt is less than 5.0 percent of Gross State Product.

We also estimated the full and abbreviated models on a cross-section of states for single years. Not unexpectedly, estimated coefficients on the fiscal policy variables were typically much less well determined than in the pooled samples, and the sizes — and sometimes even the signs — of the coefficients

Table 6: OLS Estimates of the Abbreviated Model for Single Year

	1982	1987	1990
Debt	17.12	3.49	−3.45
	(2.65)	(0.59)	(1.84)
Debt^2	−1.63	0.06	1.40
	(1.63)	(0.05)	(5.31)
Trend debt growth	0.88	0.32	0.16
	(1.87)	(1.22)	(1.21)
Debt limits	−3.83	−1.58	−2.23
	(3.59)	(2.39)	(6.72)
Ratings residual	0.95	1.03	0.96
	(9.98)	(10.13)	(14.95)
Standard error of estimate	16.96	10.85	5.26
$\bar{R}^2$	0.791	0.762	0.930
Number of observations	37	37	37

Note: The variables are as described in Table 3.

often changed quite markedly from period to period. For illustrative purposes, we show in Table 6 estimates of the abbreviated model for the years 1982, 1987, and 1990. Note in particular how the estimated coefficient on the debt-to-income variable, as well as that on its squared value, differ across the three years. For example, if one had only the estimates for 1982, it would be concluded that promised yields increased — albeit at a decreasing rate — with the stock of debt, whereas a dramatically different conclusion would emerge from the 1990 results. And if reliance had to be placed on the 1987 estimates, the conclusion would be that there was *no* significant association between promised yields and the stock of debt. In our view, these single-period, cross-section results indicate how constraining it can be to ignore time-series variation in default risk — and even more so — how hazardous it can be to draw conclusions on the market discipline hypothesis from estimates based on a small sample of observations taken at one point in time.

As discussed in Section 3, theory suggests that debt stocks and interest rates should be simultaneously determined. The results discussed so far do not, however, take account of this possible bias. Table 7 presents our attempts to account for this simultaneity. The pooled regression of the abbreviated model (from column (2) of Table 4) is reproduced in column (1) for comparison. The second column gives OLS estimates of the fixed effects version of the

Table 7: Accounting for Simultaneity in the Abbreviated Model

	Pooled OLS (1)	Fixed Effects OLS (2)	Fixed Effects 2SLS (3)
Debt	9.98 (4.92)	8.53 (2.44)	19.7 (3.68)
Debt^2	−0.40 (1.55)	0.11 (0.24)	−1.54 (1.76)
Trend debt growth	0.35 (3.47)	— —	— —
Debt limits	−2.01 (8.18)	— —	— —
Ratings residual	0.99 (26.7)	0.99 (24.3)	1.02 (22.5)
Std. error of est.	11.94	8.42	8.61
R^2	0.74	0.68	0.67
Number of observations	333	333	333
Tests of restrictions:			
Test of Col. (2) over col. (1):			$F(34,277) = 8.11$
Test of fixed effects in col (2):			$F(36,277) = 6.88$
Test of time dummies in col (2):			$F(16,277) = 4.61$
Test of fixed effects and time dummies in col (2):			$F(52,277) = 6.30$

Note: Sample period 1982–90; 't' statistics in parentheses. The regression in column (1) contained a constant term, and each regression also contained year dummies for 1983–90, and slope dummies for the debt variable for 1983–90. Thus the coefficients on debt and the deficit refer to the 1982 coefficients for these variables. The variables are as described in Table 3.

abbreviated model, which are unbiased in the case where mean levels of debt are interest-sensitive, but deviations from the mean are not. The third column gives a two-stage, least-squares estimate of the fixed effects model, where lagged values of debt, debt squared, and the unemployment rate are used as instruments.

The results from Table 7 indicate that simultaneity is important, which is what we would expect for interest-sensitive state borrowers. Notice that in the second column, the squared debt term is still insignificant, but the point estimate is no longer negative. Given the small size of the squared term in the first two columns of Table 7, however, the quantitative effects of increases in debt on yields are very similar. The first 'F' test reported at the bottom of

Table 7 shows that the introduction of 34 extra coefficients in the fixed effects model *does* significantly lower the standard error of the regression over the pooled model of column (1).[25] This result suggests that we must interpret the coefficients on debt limitations and trend debt growth in the pooled sample with care. The significance of these variables in the first column indicates that these variables capture significant information about the cross-state variation in default risk. The rejection of the pooled model in favor of the fixed-effects model, however, indicates (not surprisingly) that there are other cross-state factors that are also relevant. To the extent that debt limitations and trend debt growth are correlated with omitted cross-state factors, the causal effect of these 2 variable on promised yields may be overstated in column (1).

In the third column of Table 7, we employ a two-stage, least-squares estimation to account for possible simultaneity between deviations from state mean debt levels and deviations from state mean yields; again, there are substantial changes in our estimates. In this case, the squared debt term reverts to negative, but there is a substantial increase in the size of the positive coefficient on debt. The two-stage, least-squares estimates of the fixed-effects model imply that during 1982, a 1 percentage point increase in relative debt above its mean value of 2.2 percent would lead to an increase in *over* 12 basis points in the promised yield on that state's debt (as opposed to the 8 basis points implied by the OLS estimates in column (1)). Even in 1986 when the slope dummy for debt again takes on its largest negative value, a one percentage point increase in the relative debt would increase the promised yield by almost 7 basis points. Thus, while our attempts to deal with simultaneity have not resolved the anomaly of nonpositive signs on the squared debt terms, they do point to much larger effects of increases in debt on promised yields.

SECTION 5. CONCLUDING REMARKS

In the ongoing debate on the need for constraints on national fiscal policies in a monetary union, it is perhaps not surprising that *both* sides have claimed the US experience as supporting their position. Proponents of binding fiscal rules are able, for example, to point to the existence of states' own voluntary constitutional limitations on borrowing as demonstrating their usefulness, as well as to allege lags, overreactions, and inconsistencies in yield spreads across states as arguing against heavy reliance on market forces. Likewise, opponents of fiscal rules can highlight the joint absence of (postwar) defaults by state governments and of federally-imposed fiscal rules; they also regard the observed differences in market yields across states with different fiscal stances as illustrating the sufficiency of 'market-based' discipline. Suffice to say that without some empirical evidence on the link between state fiscal policy and state borrowing costs — while holding other factors constant — it is difficult to choose between these competing claims.

In this paper, we have used survey data on yield spreads for general obligation municipal bonds to get a first fix on the empirical regularities involved. On the whole, we see our empirical results as lending qualified support to the 'first half' of the market-discipline hypothesis. Specifically, we do find evidence that US states which have followed 'more prudent' fiscal policies are perceived by market participants as having lower default risk and therefore are able to reap the benefit of lower borrowing costs. In this context, 'more prudent' fiscal policies encompass not only a lower stock and trend rate of growth of debt relative to income, but also relatively stringent (albeit voluntarily imposed) constitutional limitations on the state's borrowing authority. In this latter connection, however, it remains to be shown whether a fiscal policy rule imposed by a higher level of government would carry the same credibility with the market as one initiated voluntarily by the lower-level borrowing authority itself.

On the basis of our point estimates from the abbreviated model in Table 4, we calculate that a (hypothetical) state which has fiscal-policy characteristics that are one standard deviation 'looser' than the mean of our sample would pay roughly 15–20 basis points more on its general obligation bonds than another (hypothetical) state with fiscal policy characteristics one standard deviation 'tighter' than our sample mean.[26] This is in the same ballpark as Capeci's (1990) estimate (for local municipalities in New Jersey) that a one standard-deviation loosening of fiscal policy is associated with an increase in borrowing costs of 22 basis points. In evaluating the size of our fiscal-policy-related default premium, one should keep in mind at least four points. First, there have been *no* defaults on general obligation bonds in the postwar period — a factor that suggests a low probability of default. Second, even if a default did occur, the consequences for borrowers may be much larger than those for creditors. Third, if a state pays say, a 6 percent promised yield on its general obligation bonds, a default premium of say, 20 basis points represent an increase of 3 percent in its nominal cost of borrowing — not necessarily a trivial addition expense. And, as a fraction of its real borrowing costs, the 20 basis point increase would be substantially higher. Fourth, and as noted in the Introduction, it is possible to conceive of (non-market) mechanisms that would magnify the market signal in yield spreads to increase the incentive to discipline errant fiscal policy. But this takes us beyond the scope of this paper and towards the 'second half' of the market-discipline hypothesis, namely, the proposition that authorities faced with increased borrowing costs will rein in their errant fiscal policy behaviour.

APPENDIX THE SUPPLY OF STATE LOANS

To illustrate the possibility of a backward bending supply curve in the simplest context, assume no risk premia and that the probability, P, of no default is:

$$P = P(Z) \quad \text{(A.1)}$$

where $Z = B(1 + R); P(O) = 1; P'(O) = 0; P' \geq 0$; and P is zero for some large, but finite value of Z.

In this case, equation (2) in the text holds for all risky state borrowers, and the variation in interest rates on risky debt can be determined by totally differentiating (2) by B, and R and (using (A.l)):

$$(1 + R)P'[dB(1 + R) + BdR] + dRP = 0 \quad \text{(A.2)}$$

which upon rearranging yields:

$$dR/dB = -(1 + R)^2 P'/[P + (1 + R)P'B] \quad \text{(A.3)}$$

While the exact, detailed relationship between borrowing and the promised rate depends on higher-order derivatives, two key result follows from (A.3): first, the denominator in (A.3) is initially positive, since $P(0) = 1$ when $B = 0$; second, since P becomes zero for some finite Z, the denominator eventually is nonpositive. The convexity of the supply curve in Figure 1, however, does not follow from (A.3) but depends in a complicated way on the second derivative of P.

To illustrate the qualitative nature of the complication of existing debt, consider the case where borrowers have issued some long-term bonds, B, at the rate $\bar{R}$, and only the current (positive valued) deficit, D, is issued at the current rate $\bar{R}$. In this case, the end-of-period financial obligations of the borrower are given by:

$$Z = B(1 + \bar{R}) + D(1 + R) \qquad (A.4)$$
$$\text{for} \quad D \geq 0.$$

In this case, the analogues to (A.3) are given by:

$$dR/dB = -(1 + R)(1 + \bar{R})P'/[P + (1 + R)P'D]$$
$$dR/dD = -(1 + R)^2 P'/[P + (1 + R)P'D] \qquad (A.5)$$

Consequently, the effect of higher debt on the yield differs from the effect of a higher positively valued deficit only to the extent that the current interest rate differs from past interest rates.

While the signs of the second derivatives still depend on P'', one interesting result does follow from (A.5):

$$d^2R/dB^2 = -\{(1 + \bar{R})P'/[P + (1 + R)P'D]\}dR/dB$$
$$+ \text{ other terms proportional to } dR/dB$$
$$d^2R/dD^2 = -2\{(1 + R)P'/[P + (1 + R)P'D]\}dR/dD$$
$$+ \text{ same other terms but proportional to } dR/dD \qquad (A.6)$$

The first-terms on the right-hand sides of (A.6) are both positive and the first term for d^2R/dD^2 is larger, as long as $2(1 + R) > (1 + \bar{R})^2$. The remaining terms will be nearly equal as long as R is nearly equal to $\bar{R}$. All this analysis suggests that $d^2R/dD^2 > d^2R/dB^2$.

NOTES

The views expressed are the authors' alone and do not represent the views of the International Monetary Fund. In addition to colleagues in the Research Department of the IMF, the authors are grateful to Tom Barone, John Capeci, R. B. Davidson III, James Dearborn, Peter Garber, Gilbert Metcalf, Michael Mussa, Carmen Reinhart, Lars Svensson, Thomas Swartz, and Irene Walsh for helpful comments on an earlier draft. Ravina Malkani provided much appreciated research assistance.

1 For a discussion of monetary policy issues in an emerging European EMU, see Frenkel and Goldstein (1991).

2 In some proposals, an additional fiscal rule would be that public borrowing would be permissible only to finance investment.
3 For a fuller discussion of this conflicting-signals problem, see Frankel (1990).
4 In the case of the developing-country debt crisis, interest rate spreads on bank loans to developing countries were slow to rise in the mid-to-late 1970s, and the transition to highly restricted access (in the early 1980s) came abruptly. One explanation for the relatively narrow loan spreads is the perception of a bail-out — either of the indebted countries themselves or of the deposit liabilities of the large international banks extending the loans; see Folkerts-Landau (1985). In the case of the New York City financial crisis, it apparently took some time for market participants to realize that New York City was diverting approved funds and pledging future receipts — both earmarked for other purposes — to meet current operating deficits; see Bishop *et al.*, (1989).
5 EC Commission (1990b).
6 The state debt-to-GNP ratios used in this paper are much lower than the figures cited above because we employ a more restrictive measure of state debt that is more closely linked to default risk; see Section 3.
7 Eichengreen (1990). The difference between Europe and United States on the degree of labour mobility is reduced if one only considers mobility across states, since much of US mobility is apparently within states.
8 Obstfeld (1990).
9 Sala-i-Martin and Sachs (1992). It should be noted, however, that estimates of the 'cushioning effect' of the US federal tax and transfer system on region specific shocks appears to be quite sensitive to the time dimension of the shock — and perhaps also to the level of disaggregation of regions. In this connection, von Hagen (1991) finds a much lower cushioning effect than Sala-i-Martin and Sachs, using a shorter-run definition of shocks and more disaggregated definition of regions.
10 While the municipal bond market includes obligations of cities as well as of states, we consider only the latter in this paper.
11 In a broad survey of the relevance of the US currency union for European Economic and Monetary Union, Eichengreen (1990) estimates the effects of debt variables on yields. Liu and Thakor's (1984) paper is typical of the finance literature on state default risk and fiscal variables. Capeci (1990)

provides a broad survey of the municipal bond literature related to default risk. Most of the studies reviewed, however, are of the local municipal bond market.

12 In credit markets, it is arbitrary on which side of the market the borrowers and lenders are placed. One can talk about the supply and demand for credit, in which case borrowers are on the demand side and lenders on the supply side, or alternatively the supply and demand for debt, which reverses the sides. In this paper, we use the former categories so that lenders supply funds to states and state borrowing leads to a demand for funds.

13 The question of risk premia on sovereign debt is tested empirically in Stone (1990) and Cottarelli and Mecagni (1990).

14 US bonds are given credit ratings principally by Moody's Investor Service and Standard & Poor's. The qualitative description of the Moody's Ratings categories are: Aaa — Best Quality; Aa — High quality; A — Upper medium grade; Baa — Medium grade; Ba — Possess speculative elements; B — Generally lack characteristics of desirable investment; Caa — Poor Standing; may be in default; Ca — Speculative in a high degree; often in default; C — Lowest grade; very poor prospects. In addition to each broad category, a 1, 2, or 3 can be added to the letters to indicate whether the security is in the high, middle, or low end of the ratings category. See Van Horne (1990) for a discussion of the relationship between credit ratings and default risk.

15 The rating agencies, however, try to measure default risk independently of the business cycle. Thus for example, the Baa — Aaa spread widens during a recession instead of the spread remaining constant with fewer Aaa states and more Baa.

16 In principle, the yield on state debt can vary because of taxes. To a state resident, neither federal nor one's own state's securities are subject to state and local taxation. State, general obligation debt, however, is also free of federal taxation, so that the marginal rate of federal taxation for the marginal investor who is indifferent between Treasuries and state debt with appropriate default and risk premia. Various competing theories (summarized in Poterba, 1989) have identified the relevant marginal investor as banks, insurance companies, corporations, or individuals. Poterba (1989) presents empirical evidence in support of the hypothesis that individuals were the indifferent investors during the 1960–88 period, particularly for the case of long-term municipal debt.

In fact, such differences in marginal tax rates are frequently cited for what would otherwise be anomalies in yields across states. For example, Swartz (1989) refers to 'tax related demand' to explain why the yields on Connecticut and California state bonds were consistently among the six lowest during the late 1980s in spite of credit ratings below Aaa. During the same time period, the bonds of at least 5 other Aaa states traded with higher yields. We tested for differences in yields due to differences in average, marginal rates of federal taxation across states, but found anomalous results.

17 The 10 excluded states include the 9 states who have no outstanding GO debt and Arkansas. In addition, we excluded New Jersey, Alaska and Hawaii. The latter 2 states were excluded because of their unique fiscal status.

18 The Chubb Relative Value Survey does not include explicit instructions to evaluate comparable bonds. Tom Swartz of Chubb, however, reports that these instructions are implicit, and that whenever a survey respondent asks they are instructed to evaluate comparable bonds.

19 Cranford and Stover (1988) criticize Liu and Thakor by noting that because the error from the first-stage regression is orthogonal to the fiscal variables, the point estimates of the fiscal coefficients in the second-stage regression will be identical to an OLS regression of yield on the fiscal variables, omitting the ratings variable. In response, Liu and Thakor point out that while the point estimates will be the same, the standard errors will be lower in the second-stage regression. The question then becomes which are the appropriate standard errors. We believe that the standard errors from Liu and Thakor's procedure are more appropriate for our test. The ratings residual allows us to capture the effects of omitted factors, which if not accounted for would mask the statistical significance of the relationship between fiscal variables and yields.

20 Notice that the ratings variable is also capturing variations in the risk of default over the business cycle. For example, the spread between the numerical values assigned to Baa and Aaa ratings in the recession year of 1982 was 153.6 basis points, whereas the same spread during 1989 was less than half as much at 70.9 basis points.

21 The 333 observations derive from observations on 37 states over the 1982–90 period (9 years).

22 There may well be a problem of multicollinearity here given the preponderance of high values for the debt limitation index.
23 In addition to problems of simultaneity there may also be a multicollinearity problem at work as between the debt and squared-debt variables. In this connection, it is worth noting that when the abbreviated model was re-estimated using *either* the level or the squared value of debt-to-income, the estimated coefficients were significant with the expected positive sign.
24 Note that the ratings residual variable is not the same between the two regressions. In the abbreviated model, whatever information there is in the deficit variable is captured by the ratings variable. This adds to our suspicion that the deficit variable is capturing the increased probability of default from new borrowing.
25 The dependent variables for the regressions in columns (1) and (2) are the yields and deviations from state mean yields, respectively. The latter variable has a smaller variance, which accounts for the lower $\bar{R}^2$ reported in column (2) in addition to the lower standard error.
26 The fiscal-policy characteristics included in this calculation are debt, debt^2, the trend of the debt to income ratio, and the constitutional debt limitation index.

Morris Goldstein and Geoffrey Woglom, "Market-Based Fiscal Discipline in Monetary Unions: Evidence from the U.S. Municipal Bond Market," in Mathew Canzoneri, Vittorio Grilli, and Paul Masson, (editors), Establishing a Central Bank: Issues in Europe and Lessons from the US," Cambridge University Press, 1992.

REFERENCES

ACIR (Advisory Commission on Intergovernmental Relations) (1987), *Significant Features of Fiscal Federalism*, Washington, D.C.: US Government Printing Press.

Bishop, Graham, Dirk Damrau, and Michelle Miller (1989), '1992 and Beyond: Market Discipline CAN Work in the EC Monetary Union,' Salomon Brothers, London.

Bishop, Graham (1991), 'The EC Public Debt Disease: Discipline with Credit Spreads and Cure with Price Stability,' Salomon Brothers, London.

Capeci, John (1990), 'Local Fiscal Policies, Default Risk and Municipal Borrowing Costs,' Brandeis University, Department of Economics, No. 259.

Cohen, Natalie R. (1988), 'Municipal Default Patterns,' Enhance Reinsurance Co.

Cottarelli, Carlo, and Mauro Mecagni (1990), 'The Risk Premium on Italian Government Debt, 1976–88,' IMF Working Paper No. 90/38.

Cranford, Brian, and Roger Stover (1988), 'Comment on Interest Yields Credit Ratings, and Economic Characteristics of State Bonds,' *Journal of Money, Credit, and Banking* **20**, 691–95.

Davidson, R. B. (1990), 'Municipal Market Analysis: A Framework for Analyzing Quality Spreads,' J.P. Morgan, 29 March.

Delors Report (1989), *Report on Economic and Monetary Union in the European Community*, Committee for the Study of Economic and Monetary Union, Brussels: EC Commission.

Eaton, Jonathan, and Mark Gersovitz (1981), 'Debt with Potential Repudiation: A Theoretical and Empirical Analysis,' *Review of Economic Studies* **49**, 289–309.

EC Commission (1990a), 'Economic and Monetary Union: The Economic Rationale and Design of the System', Luxembourg: EC Commission.

EC Commission (1990b), 'One Market, One Money — An Evaluation of the Potential Benefits and Costs of Forming an Economic and Monetary Union', *European Economy*.

Eichengreen, Barry (1990), 'One Money for Europe? Lessons from the US Currency Union,' *Economic Policy* **5**, (10), 119–86.

English, William (1991), 'When America Defaulted: American State Debt in the 1840's,' Mimeo, University of Pennsylvania.

Folkerts-Landau, David (1985), 'The Changing Role of International Bank Lending in Development Finance,' *IMF Staff Papers* **32**, 317–63.

Frankel, Jeffery (1990), 'Obstacles to Coordination, and a Consideration of Two Proposals to Overcome Them,' in William Branson, Jacob Frenkel and Morris Goldstein (eds.), *International Policy Coordination and Exchange Rate Fluctuations*, University of Chicago Press for the National Bureau of Economic Research, Chicago, pp. 109–45.

Frenkel, Jacob and Morris Goldstein (1991), 'Monetary Policy in an Emerging European Economic and Monetary Union', *IMF Staff Papers*, forthcoming.

Hsiao, Cheng (1986), *Analysis of Panel Data*, Cambridge: Cambridge University Press.

Lamafalussy, Alexandre (1989), 'Macro-coordination of Fiscal Policies in an Economic and Monetary Union in Europe,' Supplement to Delors Report.

Liu, Pu and Anjan Thakor (1984), 'Interest Yields, Credit Ratings, and Economic Characteristics of State Bonds: An Empirical Analysis,' *Journal of Money, Credit and Banking* **16**, 345–50.

Metcalf, Gilbert (1990), 'Federal Taxation and the Supply of State Debt,' NBER Working Paper No. 3255.

Obstfeld, Maurice (1990), 'Discussion,' *Economic Policy* **5**, (10), 166–69.

Orth, John V. (1987), *The Judicial Power of the United States: The Eleventh Amendment in American History*, New York: Oxford.

Poterba, James (1989), 'Tax Reform and the Market for Tax Exempt Debt,' NBER Working Paper No. 2900.

X. Sala-i-Martin and Jeffrey Sachs (1992), 'Fiscal Federalism and Optimum Currency Areas: Evidence for Europe from the United States', in this volume.

Stiglitz, Joseph and Andrew Weiss (1981), 'Credit Rationing in Markets with Imperfect Information,' *American Economic Review* **73**, 393–410.

Stone, Mark (1990), 'Are Sovereign Debt Secondary Market Returns Sensitive to Macroeconomic Fundamentals?' IMF Research Department Seminar Paper.

Swartz, Thomas (1989), 'State General Obligation Trading Values — Back to the Future,' *Municipal Analysts Forum* 7–10.

Van Horne, James (1990), *Financial Market Rates and Flows*, 3rd edition, Englewood Cliffs, NJ: Prentice-Hall Inc.

Von Hagen, Jurgen (1991), 'Fiscal Arrangements in a Monetary Union: Evidence from the US,' mimeo, School of Business, Indiana University, March.

United States Census (1990), *State Government Finances in 1989*, Washington, D.C.: Department of Commerce.

Yawitz, Jess, Kevin Maloney, and Louis Edderington (1985), 'Texas, Default Risk, and Yield Spreads,' **40**, 1127–40.

Chapter

5

A Guide to Target Zones

Jacob A. Frenkel and Morris Goldstein*

INTRODUCTION

This chapter identifies key issues surrounding the advisability and practicality of adopting "target zones" for the exchange rates of major currencies.[1]

At present there are wide differences of view on the subject of target zones. This reflects at least three factors: first, different assessments of the performance

---

*Mr. Frenkel. Economic Counsellor and Director of the Research Department from January 1987, is a graduate of Hebrew University and the University of Chicago. When this paper was written, he was consultant to the Research Department and the David Rockefeller Professor of International Economics at the University of Chicago.

Mr. Goldstein, Deputy Director of the Research Department from January 1987, is a graduate of Rutgers University and New York University. When this paper was written, he was an Advisor in the Research Department.

Reprinted from Vol. 33, No. 4 (December 1986)
International Monetary Fund
STAFF PAPERS
© 1986 by the International Monetary Fund

[1] At its meeting in Seoul, Korea on October 6–7, 1985, the Interim Committee of the Board of Governors of the International Monetary Fund requested the Executive Board of the Fund " . . . to study the issues raised in these reports [the reports on the international monetary system presented by the Deputies of the Group of Ten and the Deputies of the Group of Twenty-Four] with a view to facilitating a substantial consideration by the Committee at its next meeting." This paper is one of the series of papers prepared in late 1985 in response to that request.

of the existing exchange rate system of managed floating; second, different evaluations of whether a system of target zones could remedy the perceived weaknesses of the existing system; and third, different conceptions of the preferred form of target zones.

The purpose of this chapter is not to make the case either for or against the adoption of target zones. Indeed, we have tried to avoid expressing our own view on this central issue. Rather, the intention is to raise and discuss factors that should be considered in any serious examination of the topic. As such, the paper not only outlines potential strengths and weaknesses of various versions of the target zone approach but also confronts operational questions that would have to be faced if the target zone approach to exchange rate management were adopted.

The chapter is organized as follows. Section I addresses four fundamental questions concerning the definition of and the rationale for target zones: first, what is generally meant by a target zone approach to exchange rate management and how can "hard" and "soft" versions of this approach be defined; second, what are the perceived deficiencies in the existing exchange rate system which motivate the call for the adoption of target zones; third, how might target zones remedy these deficiencies; and fourth, what factors are behind much of the skepticism over and opposition to target zones?

Section II deals with a series of operational questions and issues of a more technical and specific nature that weigh heavily on the practicality of implementing a target zone approach. The issues discussed are the following: how would the target zones be calculated; what currencies would be included in the system of target zones; how wide should the target zones be and how frequently should they be revised; and what policy instruments would be employed to keep actual exchange rates within the target zones, and with what consequences for other policy objectives? A brief postscript appears as Section II of the chapter.

Finally, three caveats relevant to the nature and scope of this study should be mentioned. First, there should be no presumption that advocates of target zones see this as the *only* proposal for improving exchange rate stability. Indeed, most advocates of target zones would also rely on stronger surveillance of a broader nature to help reach that objective. Second, since the chapter does not attempt to compare the target zone proposal to other proposals for improving exchange rate stability, there should likewise be no presumption that the strengths and weaknesses outlined here are more or less significant than those associated with other proposals.[2] Third, since many of the precise operational features of a system of target zones remain largely conjectural (e.g., which currencies would be included, how target zones would be calculated, etc.), the views expressed on these operational features should be seen more as aids to discussion and debate than as definite conclusions.

I. THE MEANING AND RATIONALE FOR TARGET ZONES

What are Target Zones?

Target zones mean different things to different people. Perhaps the easiest way to think of them is as a *hybrid* exchange rate system that combines some of the attributes and characteristics of both pegged and flexible exchange rate systems.[3]

How Does a System of Target Zones Differ from Other Exchange Regimes?

Target zones differ from a pure system of *clean floating* in that the authorities are permitted (and indeed are likely) to intervene in the exchange market, and, more generally, are encouraged "to take a view" on the desirable level of the exchange rate. Target zones differ from the present system of *managed floating* in at least two principal respects:[4] (i) the authorities establish a target zone for the exchange rate for some future period; and (ii) the authorities are expected to keep more of an "eye" on the exchange rate in the conduct of

---

[2]Some other proposals for improving exchange rate stability are analyzed in Crockett and Goldstein (1987).

[3]In the Group of Ten report, target zones are described as follows: " ... the authorities concerned would define wide margins around an adjustable set of exchange rates devised to be consistent with a sustainable pattern of balances of payments" (para. 31). (See International Monetary Fund, 1974b through 1985a.)

[4]Another way of summarizing the difference between a system of target zones and the present system of managed floating would be as follows. Under target zones, authorities must come to a mutually agreed view on the appropriate zones for major currency exchange rates. In contrast, under the present system. authorities have not generally expressed their own view on appropriate zones for exchange rates, let alone come to a common view with other authorities.

monetary policy so as to keep the actual exchange rate within the target zone.[5] Compared to the *adjustable peg system*, target zones need *not* entail a formal commitment to intervene in all circumstances in the exchange market to keep actual rates within the zone. Indeed, the only concrete intervention guideline that is typically mentioned is that the authorities refrain from "destabilizing intervention," that is, buying their own currency when it is above the top of the zone and selling it below the bottom of the zone. This specific guideline was also included in the Fund's 1974 "Guidelines for the Management of Floating Exchange Rates."[6] Finally, target zones differ from a pure system of *rigidly fixed* exchange rates in that, in addition to the lack of a formal intervention obligation, the zones themselves are to be occasionally reviewed and changed if deemed necessary.

How Can "Hard" and "Soft" Versions of Target Zones Be Defined?

In general, various versions of target zones can be distinguished by reference to the following four characteristics:

(i) *width* of the target zone (outside of which the exchange rate is viewed as "out of line"),
(ii) the *frequency* of changes in the target zones,
(iii) the degree of *publicity* given to the zones; in this context, one may distinguish between public announcement of the target zones and confidential disclosure in official circles (for purposes of exchange rate surveillance, intervention, multilateral policy coordination and consultation), that is, "loud zones" versus "quiet zones," and
(iv) the degree of *commitment* to keeping exchange rates within the zone.

---

[5]Target zones are intended to reflect estimates of *real* equilibrium exchange rates because it is the real exchange rate that is most relevant for resource allocation decisions and for balance of payments adjustment: however. it is usually assumed that for operational purposes these real rate calculations would be translated into *nominal* exchange rate zones. The assumption is that the authorities can alter real rates by operating on nominal rates. Also, whereas a breach of the target zone is expected to initiate a review of the whole range of a country's macroeconomic and structural policies, most target zone proposals assume that monetary policy will carry the primary responsibility for managing the exchange rate.
[6]International Monetary Fund (1974b).

Obviously, these characteristics define a *spectrum* of possible approaches to target zones. At one end, a "hard" version of target zones might entail a monetary policy that is heavily geared to maintaining the exchange rate within the narrow, infrequently revised, and publicly announced zone. At the other end of the spectrum lies a "soft" version of target zones that might be characterized by a monetary policy paying only limited attention to the level of the exchange rate, and by zones that are wide, frequently revised and kept confidential. The hard and soft poles, in turn, may serve as useful benchmarks for the analysis and evaluation of intermediate versions of target zones.

The hard version of target zones shares some of the attributes of the existing European Monetary System (EMS). In particular, hard target zones can be considered a close relative of the EMS's fixed but adjustable rates with narrow margins and a "divergence indicator." However, unlike the EMS, hard target zones do not entail a formal commitment for exchange rate intervention; nor need there be an analogue to the credit facilities of the EMS. The soft version of target zones differs from existing Fund surveillance procedures (e.g., the requirement for reporting real exchange rate changes in excess of 10 percent to the Executive Board) in that the former introduces a more explicit and formal framework for defining the appropriate pattern of exchange rates and for establishing the links between exchange rates and macroeconomic policies.[7]

What Considerations Underlie the Call for Adoption of Target Zones?

Proponents of target zones proceed from two basic perceptions: first, that the present system of managed floating has exhibited serious deficiencies; and second, that the adoption of a system of target zones could remedy at least some of these deficiencies. Among the alleged deficiencies, the most attention has been paid to the following considerations.

Exchange Rates Have Been Highly Volatile and Unpredictable

Whether measured in real or nominal terms, bilateral or effective terms, the short-run variability of exchange rates over the period of managed floating

---

[7] Existing procedures do not rely on the assessment of appropriate zones but rather use as a starting point the last occasion on which exchange rate developments were brought to the attention of the Executive Board.

has been high — indeed, significantly higher than during the previous Bretton Woods system. In addition, most exchange rate changes have been *un*predictable (as suggested by market indicators like forward exchange rates). While high short-term volatility and unpredictability of exchange rates is usually deemed to be less serious than longer-term "misalignments," this volatility is still regarded as costly because it generates uncertainty, and hence leads to lower levels of investment and trade. Further, developing countries are alleged to be especially hurt by this volatility because they do not have well-developed financial markets (particularly forward cover arrangements).

Exchange Rates of Major Currencies Have Been Subject to Large and Persistent Misalignments

A second complaint against the present system is that exchange rates of major currencies have been subject to large and persistent "misalignments" over the past dozen years. Such misalignments are commonly measured by cumulative departures from purchasing power parity, or by the sheer magnitude of changes in real exchange rates themselves, or by departures from more comprehensive concepts of the "equilibrium" real exchange rate (e.g., the exchange rate that yields a cyclically adjusted current account balance equal to normal net private capital flows). Not surprisingly, charges of misalignment were particularly pronounced over the period 1981–85. A representative estimate of misalignment is provided by Williamson (1985). He estimated that by the end of 1984 the extent of misalignment in the real effective exchange rate was 39 percent (overvaluation) for the U.S. dollar and 19 percent (undervaluation) for the Japanese yen. Such misalignments are, in turn, deemed costly because they have an adverse impact on resource allocation, induce adjustment costs (including unemployment), distort optimal levels of capital formation, and encourage protectionism.

Under the Existing Exchange Rate System, Macroeconomic Policies in Major Industrial Countries Have Been Undisciplined and Uncoordinated

Perhaps the chief criticism by the proponents of target zones is that the existing system of floating exchange rates lacks an effective mechanism for ensuring policy discipline and coordination.[8] As supporting evidence, the critics cite, inter alia, the doubling of industrial-country average inflation rates as between 1963–72 and 1973–85, and the tripling of the ratio of industrial countries' government fiscal deficits to GNP over the same period. On lack of coordination, they point to the frequent conflicts among the major industrial countries on both the stance and mix of macroeconomic policies, as well as on the need for structural reform. Also, despite the efforts made at coordination, critics emphasize the absence of *binding* agreements during the floating-rate period on either rates of monetary expansion or exchange rate norms. Undisciplined and uncoordinated policies, in turn, are said to be costly because such behavior is incompatible with financial stability and sustainable growth, and also because such policies are the main driving force behind both short-term volatility and longer-term misalignment of exchange rates.

IMF Surveillance Under the Existing Exchange Rate System Has Been Largely Ineffective in Respect of Major Industrial Countries, Resulting in Asymmetry in the International Adjustment Mechanism

Yet a fourth alleged weakness of the existing system is that Fund surveillance has not been sufficiently effective in respect of the very industrial countries whose policies have the most significant "spillover effects" on the world economy, thereby producing, among other things, an asymmetric distribution in the burden of adjustment. As evidence for this position, the critics cite the magnitude and persistence of current account imbalances in the United States and Japan, especially over the past three years. The seeming inability of surveillance to bring about a correction of the structural U.S. budget deficit is regarded as another striking example of this lack of symmetry. Further, it is argued that an inappropriate mix of macroeconomic policies in the major industrial countries during the early 1980s resulted in high real interest rates and in sluggish economic activity. A consequence of this was that developing countries faced (during 1981–83) a sharp increase in debt service requirements,

---

[8] In what follows, coordination may be thought of as encompassing all international influences on domestic policymaking; see Polak (1981).

It might be regarded as the chief criticism because short-term volatility and longer-term misalignment of exchange rates are generally regarded as *manifestations* of the lack of discipline and coordination.

a significant decline in export earnings, a compression of their imports, and unusually slow growth. Thus, so it is argued, adverse spillover effects from poor policies in industrial countries were substantial, and the burden of adjustment fell disproportionately on the developing countries.

How Would the Introduction of Target Zones for the Major Currencies Remedy These Four Perceived Deficiencies of the Existing Exchange Rate System?

A central argument advanced by proponents of target zones (see, for example, Roosa (1984)) is that their introduction would restore some of the useful characteristics of the Bretton Woods system without being subject to the flaws that led to the collapse of that system.

Restoring an Anchor for Medium-Term Exchange Rate Expectations

It is often argued that one reason why exchange rates have been so volatile under the present exchange rate system is that market participants lack an "anchor" for medium-term expectations about exchange rates. In such an environment, new information, rumors, or announcements can lead to large revisions of expectations about the future which in turn induce "large" changes in current exchange rates. Furthermore, under some circumstances, such events may set the stage for the emergence of "bandwagon" effects and speculative "bubbles" that can dominate the evolution of the exchange rate and divorce it increasingly from "fundamentals."

It is claimed that target zones will reduce exchange rate volatility and misalignment on two counts. First, the obligation (albeit an informal one) or the intention to keep the exchange rate within the zone provides market participants with useful information about the likely conduct of future macroeconomic policies, especially monetary policy. The easier it is to make an informed judgment about the future course of policies, the less one can expect the erroneous extrapolation of short-term events and the more forgiving will be the market of short-term deviations of policy. Second, the publication of target zones provides market participants with information on the authorities' collective estimate of future equilibrium exchange rates. Therefore, it is said to reduce the risk that market participants use the "wrong model" in translating (even perfectly foreseen) future policy changes into forecasts of future exchange rates.

Restoring Discipline and Coordination to the Conduct of Macroeconomic Policies

Target zones are said to restore *discipline* to macroeconomic policymaking for two reasons. First, if exchange rates are maintained within the target zones, then macroeconomic policies, again particularly monetary policy, are disciplined by the exchange rate constraint. Second, even if the authorities opt to alter the target zone rather than their policies, they would still be obliged both to negotiate a new zone and to explain why a new zone is appropriate. These obligations themselves are said to introduce stronger peer pressure into policy formation.

Turning to the *coordination* of policies, the following points are noteworthy. The very fact that a system of target zones has to be negotiated and must display mutual consistency of cross exchange rates is said to enhance the degree of international policy coordination. Under a system of target zones, so it is argued, the exchange rate implications of alternative stances and mixes of policies would be directly confronted, thereby ending the undesirable current practice whereby exchange rates emerge as a "residual" of other policy actions of individual countries. Also, the requirement that target zones be negotiated and mutually agreed is said to reduce the risk of competitive devaluations.

And to the extent that target zones do restore discipline and coordination to the conduct of macroeconomic policy, they will reduce misalignment and volatility of exchange rates.

Increasing the Effectiveness of IMF Surveillance and Reducing the Asymmetry in the Adjustment Process

Proponents of target zones argue that the need to negotiate, to ensure consistency, and to revise the zones could provide a natural focal point for multilateral Fund surveillance. Just as important, such surveillance procedures when applied to target zones will be aimed at the policies of the major industrial countries, that, in turn, are likely to constitute the membership of the target zone system. It is alleged therefore that target zones will remove the Achilles heel of the present surveillance procedures, namely, the inability to effect a meaningful change in policies of large industrial countries. Since the asymmetry of adjustment is said to depend critically on policy behavior in industrial countries, more effective surveillance of them would also produce more *symmetrical* adjustment.

The remedial properties of a target zone approach would obviously depend on the particular version adopted. The "harder" versions, by virtue of being closer images of the Bretton Woods regime, clearly offer a stronger dose of external pressure on domestic policy. But, as is discussed in subsequent sections, the alleged benefits associated with the harder versions may also entail higher costs.

Proponents of the "softer" versions of the target zone approach argue that their adoption would enhance the surveillance process for at least three reasons. First, even if the zones were wide and were frequently revised, they would exert some disciplinary force on the most flagrant and persistent cases of inappropriate policies. Thus, while soft target zones may not do much to catch misalignments on the order of 10 percent or less, they will, so their supporters argue, catch the 20–40 percent real exchange rate misalignments that do most damage to the system. Second, even if the zones were not announced to the public, they still are likely to provoke helpful discussion and analysis of policy interdependence among officials of participating members. Also, such "quiet" zones provide another channel for peer pressure against inappropriate policies. Third, since the Fund's current practices in any case involve evaluating the appropriateness of members' exchange rates, supporters argue that even unpublished zones may prove useful in generating a more concrete framework for evaluating exchange rate implications of alternative macroeconomic policies.

Escaping the Same Fate as the Bretton Woods System

Supporters of target zones acknowledge that many of the factors associated with the collapse of Bretton Woods have not gone away (e.g., high international mobility of capital, larger financial resources for private speculators than for central banks, existence of large and suddenly changing interest rate differentials across countries, etc.). Nevertheless, they contend that a system of target zones can survive pressure from "hot money" flows. They argue that so long as policy adjustments are made when necessary or so long as the target zones are revised frequently to reflect inflation differentials and needs for real exchange rate adjustment, expectations of large and discontinuous exchange rate adjustments that provide the motive for speculative attacks will seldom arise. In their view, the viability of the EMS provides testimony that it is possible to operate an adjustable peg system in the 1980s provided that there is sufficient political commitment, active exchange market intervention policies, and a presumptive indicator for adjustment. Since a target zone system shares many of these characteristics, it too is viable.[9]

What Factors are Behind Much of the Skepticism About and Opposition to Target Zones?

Opposition to the adoption of target zones stems from a more sanguine appraisal of the performance of the existing system; doubts about the capacity of target zones to remedy alleged deficiencies; and concerns that target zones would introduce new problems. Each of these elements is discussed in turn.

Has the Existing System Failed?

Exchange rate volatility. While the short-run volatility of both nominal and real exchange rates has indeed been high during the period of managed floating, this begs the question of whether that volatility was "excessive." In this connection, opponents of target zones raise two points.

First, the period since 1973 has witnessed great turbulence in the world economy and great uncertainty about the future course of economic and political events. In this environment, *all* asset prices, not only exchange rates, have shown high volatility. In fact, exchange rate changes have been smaller than changes in prices of other assets (e.g., national stock market prices, changes in short-term interest rates, changes in commodity prices). As such, conclusions about the excessive nature of exchange rate fluctuations depend upon the specific yardstick selected.

Second, they note that there is an intrinsic difference between asset prices on the one hand and wages and goods prices on the other hand. The former are auction prices that depend heavily on expectations about the future whereas the latter are more sticky in the short run, reflecting in large part contractual

---

[9] See Ungerer, Evans, and Nyberg (1983) for a review of the EMS experience during the 1979–82 period.

arrangements made in the past. Thus, wages and prices of national output may not serve as a proper yardstick for assessing exchange rate volatility. Indeed, some would say that it is precisely because wages and prices are so slow to adjust to current and expected economic conditions that it is desirable to allow for "excessive" adjustment in exchange rates.

As regards the *unpredictable* nature of exchange rate changes under the present system, opponents of target zones note that the foreign exchange market is one in which risk can be covered relatively easily (via access to forward markets, options markets, etc.). For this reason, it is argued that it may be preferable to concentrate the disturbances in this market rather than transfer them to other markets, such as labor markets, where dealing with them would be more difficult.

Turning to the *cost* of short-run volatility of exchange rates, opponents point to the sporadic nature of the evidence linking exchange rate volatility to the volume of international trade and investment.[10] They also argue that it is doubtful that the system of pegged rates could have survived in the turbulent environment of the past 15 years without severe limits on trade and capital movements being imposed by many countries.[11] Such restrictions on trade and capital flows, in turn, could well have been more costly for the world economy than the short-run volatility of exchange rates experienced under the present system.

Exchange rate misalignment. Almost all observers, even many staunch opponents of target zones, agree that there have been serious misalignments of major currency exchange rates during the past few years, particularly as regards the sharp real appreciation of the U.S. dollar. Opponents of target zones suggest however that in evaluating both the extent and the cost of such misalignments several factors ought to be recognized.

- Changes in *real economic conditions* requiring adjustments in the relative prices of different national outputs occur all the time (continuing intercountry differences in growth of labor productivity, permanent changes in the terms of trade, intercountry shifts in both the marginal productivity of capital and the propensity to save, etc.). Under a system of pegged rates, relative price adjustments are achieved through the

---

[10] International Monetary Fund (1984a).

[11] See, for example, Bryant (1983) and Obstfeld (1985).

slow changes of national price levels and through occasional changes of parity. Under floating rates, adjustments in the relative price of different national outputs occur rapidly and in anticipation of changes in economic conditions rather than after the need for adjustment has become apparent. In the absence of an explicit specification of relative costs, there is no general presumption that slow adjustment of relative prices is preferable to rapid adjustment, or that price adjustments should not occur in anticipation of events requiring such adjustments. Hence, what may seem to be misalignments may in part represent equilibrating changes.

- Critics of target zones argue that one should not overlook the fact that significant misalignment of major currency exchange rates also occurred during the Bretton Woods period, especially in its later years. In this connection, they caution that misalignment of real exchange rates can derive from too *little* nominal exchange rate flexibility as well as from too much. The frequency of misaligned real exchange rates in countries with "pegged" exchange arrangements, where there is often a reluctance to alter nominal rates in the face of large inflation differentials, should stand as a warning to the dangers involved.

- The size of estimated misalignments in major currency exchange rates is, according to defenders of the present system, highly uncertain. To take but one example, calculations of misalignment done by Williamson (1985) and others are strongly affected by the assumption that "normal" net capital flows are zero for the United States. This assumption is important because the equilibrium exchange rate is defined in such calculations as the exchange rate that would produce a current account balance equal to the assumed normal net private capital flow. But a country that is a "normal" net capital exporter under one set of macroeconomic policies, tax considerations, and political events abroad may become a natural importer under others. In this connection, a judgment that normal net private capital flows for the United States were, say, a $30 billion annual inflow (to reflect high expected profitability, relatively low domestic savings, and safe-haven considerations) rather than zero would reduce the estimated misalignment considerably;[12] yet the theoretical reasons for preferring the latter estimate to the former are, so the critics argue, debatable at best.

---

[12] This assumes that such an order of magnitude is compatible over the long run with a reasonable buildup of debt and with an acceptable maturity profile.

- Defenders of the present system argue that explanations that attribute long-term misalignment to a speculative bubble are highly questionable. They point out that the (narrow) theoretical models that are frequently used to generate a speculative bubble in the exchange rate (i.e., a fully expected continuous price change not justified by fundamentals) also imply that such a bubble could prevail for only a short period of time — certainly not for five years or so.

Discipline and coordination. Defenders of the current exchange rate system question the allegation that it exerts less discipline than regimes with greater fixity of exchange rates. As a theoretical matter, it is pointed out that changes in exchange rates are highly visible and are transmitted promptly into domestic prices. As a result, the consequences of undisciplined macroeconomic policies are readily apparent. In contrast, undisciplined policies under fixed exchange rates show up only in reserve changes, and then usually become public only after a significant delay. Therefore, it is argued, the supposed superior disciplining force of a fixed rate regime is not obvious. Furthermore, as an empirical matter, the 1979–86 policy experience in industrial countries can be viewed as evidence that anti-inflationary discipline can be restored *without* fixed exchange rates. Indeed, the deceleration in growth rates of narrow and broad money that took place in the face of high unemployment in most of the major industrial countries in 1979–82 coincided with relatively high variability of both nominal and real exchange rates.

As for coordination, defenders of the present system note that there have been some successful coordination efforts during the past decade. In this context, they mention the U.S. dollar support package of November 1, 1978, agreements on short-term exchange rate management policies (e.g., intermittent joint countering of disorderly market conditions), the agreements of the Bonn economic summit of 1978, and the Group of Five agreement (of September 22, 1985) in New York on foreign exchange intervention and other policies.[13]

In addition, it can be argued that the optimal degree of coordination is less than complete. For example, the *perception* of independent monetary policy may be necessary in some countries for sustaining confidence that monetary

---

[13] Critics of the present system might reply that the Group of Five agreement was a reaction to the absence of coordination and the large misalignments fostered by the present system.

policy will not be inflationary in the long run (particularly if not all potential partners in a target zone system have a track record of consistently sound monetary policy).[14]

In *sum*, the very point of departure for the proponents of target zones, namely, the overall appraisal that the existing system has failed, is itself not universally accepted. Opponents of target zones acknowledge that the present system has weaknesses but do not see these weaknesses as more serious than those demonstrated by earlier systems. In addition, opponents emphasize that the present system has demonstrated some "valuable strengths." Specifically, exchange rate changes are viewed as having made a positive contribution to securing effective external payments adjustment over the medium to long run. The present system is also credited with having maintained a mechanism of conflict resolution (namely, the foreign exchange market) that has *not* involved either suspension of currency convertibility or large-scale restrictions on trade and capital flows; indeed, supporters of the present system claim that floating rates allowed the removal of certain restrictions. Furthermore, it is argued that independent monetary policy, facilitated by the existing exchange rate system, permitted the application of successful disinflationary policies. Finally, it is argued that *no* exchange rate regime would have emerged unscathed from the combination of shocks, portfolio shifts, and structural and institutional changes that occurred during the years of managed floating.

Would the Introduction of Target Zones Improve Matters?

Would target zones provide an anchor? As noted earlier, one of the central arguments for the introduction of target zones is that such zones would provide an anchor for medium-term exchange rate expectations. But would it, and at what costs? Skeptics make the following points.

- If the absence of an anchor stems from lack of information about future government policies, then it is not clear that publication of target zones, rather than announcement of the future course of policies themselves, is the preferred way to provide that information. Obviously, if the zones are

---

[14]See Solomon (1982) on this point.

not published (i.e., quiet zones), then their adoption will not alleviate the policy uncertainty problem at all.[15]
- If the source of uncertainty is that market participants do not possess information on the model linking government policies with the consequent levels of exchange rates, then target zones (loud zones) do indeed provide the missing information. This presupposes, however, either that the government has superior information about the "true model" or that the government carries enough credibility to convince market participants that it will adjust its policies to consistently maintain exchange rates within the announced zone (i.e., it will adjust its policies to make the exchange rate forecast come true). Opponents of target zones see no evidence that governments have such superior information or knowledge about such a model. Further, they point out that experience with preannounced exchange rate targets in Latin America suggests that countries would probably find it difficult to adhere to such targets.[16]
- Even if the target zones were credible for some period of time, critics argue that the occasional need for revision of the target zones will invite the same type of one-way bet for speculators that ultimately felled the Bretton Woods system. Of course, since governments are not formally committed to defend the target zones, they may choose to allow exchange rates to depart from the zone (while subsequently announcing a revised zone). But in that case, the zones themselves would soon lose their credibility.
- Even if the zones are announced, critics contend that "soft" versions of target zones characterized by wide and frequently revised zones are not likely to provide a strong and reliable anchor because they will not sufficiently narrow expectations about the future rate. Yet such wide and frequently revised zones are said to be necessary (by critics) to account for our measure of ignorance about the equilibrium exchange rate and for changing real conditions.
- Even if the anchor is credible and durable, its introduction may be costly. The argument here is that the volatility or misalignment of exchange

---

[15]Some observers also doubt whether in practice quiet zones could be quiet for long. They argue that it is not possible for the Fund and national authorities to know what target zones are without this information leaking out.

[16]See Calvo (1983).

rates is not the likely source of difficulties but rather a *manifestation* of the prevailing package of macroeconomic policies. Without introducing a significant change into the conduct of policies, a manipulation of exchange rates to satisfy the zones may not improve matters at all. In fact, the absence of the exchange rate as a market gauge for assessing policies will then only confuse matters and reduce the information essential for policymaking.

Would target zones provide discipline? It is widely agreed that misalignment of real exchange rates arises to a large extent from undisciplined and uncoordinated macroeconomic policies. Hence, the ability of target zones to reduce misalignment rests in good measure on their ability to enhance discipline. Skeptics put forward the following points.

- Experience suggests to them that national governments are unlikely to adjust appreciably the conduct of domestic policies so as to satisfy the constraints imposed by the exchange rate regime. Rather, it is argued, it is more likely that the exchange rate regime adjusts to whatever discipline national governments choose to have. As an illustration, it is pointed out that other external pressures aimed at restoring discipline to policy in major industrial countries (e.g., individual Article IV consultations, Fund Executive Board discussions of the world economic outlook, Group of Five surveillance meetings, OECD country reports) have met with only limited success. Why then should target zones succeed where other similar measures have produced such limited results?
- Evidence from earlier periods during which exchange rates were more rigid does not suggest that greater fixity of exchange rates induced either lower average external imbalances, or more rapid adjustment of such imbalances, or greater symmetry of adjustment as between either surplus and deficit countries, or between reserve and nonreserve currency countries.[17] Why then should target zones provide the impetus to discipline when exchange regimes with greater formal commitment have not consistently done so?
- In a related vein, it is argued that by focusing attention on exchange rates rather than on the root cause of misalignment, namely, the stance and mix of macroeconomic policies, one may lessen the pressures for corrective action on the ultimate sources of the problem.

---

[17] See International Monetary Fund (1984c), Tables 2 and 3.

- Critics argue that if the nominal target zones reflect rigid targets for real exchange rates, they can destabilize the price level.[18] Take, for example, the case of a country that experiences an unexpected wage push that raises its price level relative to that abroad. Its real exchange rate will then have appreciated relative to its initial level. If the authorities attempt to restore the original real exchange rate by announcing a more depreciated nominal target zone, then the implied expansion in monetary policy (needed to keep the actual exchange rate within the new target zone) will increase the price level. In short, critics warn that while a rigid real exchange rate may be helpful for preventing trade balance deteriorations due to eroding competitiveness, it can also present new dangers for controlling inflation. More broadly, monetary policy is not the appropriate policy response to *all* types of disturbances.
- Critics also point out that while target zones can supply information on intercountry divergences in policy, they don't provide guidance on the right stance of policy *within* a country. For example, if two countries each have inflation rates of 10 percent, the exchange rate may be stable but few would argue that monetary policy in *either* country was appropriate. Again, so the critics argue, target zones do not ensure discipline.

Would target zones enhance coordination and strengthen surveillance? In appraising the effects of the adoption of target zones on policy coordination and on Fund surveillance, skeptics make the following observations.

- Whatever the exchange rate regime, there are strong barriers to coordination for at least two reasons: (i) exchange rates are by their very nature "competitive" in the sense that one country's gain is frequently another country's loss; (ii) various compromises on growth, inflation, and income distribution at the *national* level often leave little room for further compromise on policies at the international level.[19] Target zones, so say their critics, cannot overcome these barriers.
- The process of negotiating target zones could produce dangerous frictions among the negotiating parties and could lead ultimately to a reduced level of coordination in this and other areas.

---

[18] See Adams and Gros (1986) for an analysis of the dangers for inflation of real exchange rate targets.

[19] See Polak (1981).

- One cannot rule out the possibility that the cumbersome negotiation of target zones would land the system back in the management delays of the latter days of the Bretton Woods system, with adverse effects on the desired flexibility of *real* exchange rates. With target zones, one loses the "safety valve" provided by the marketplace for foreign exchange as a mode of conflict resolution.
- To the extent that the adoption of target zones results in a significant loss in independence in the conduct of domestic monetary policy, the authorities may be tempted to adopt discriminatory trade practices and other measures of protection in order to compensate for the loss of a powerful policy instrument.
- Finally, the use of target zones as a possible focal point for Fund surveillance raises three related potential problems. First, the use of the exchange rate as a primary indicator of disequilibria in macroeconomic policies could send misleading signals. Critics note that the more general Fund practice as applied to adjustment programs and financial programming is to employ a whole *set* of macroeconomic indicators for diagnostic purposes. Would exchange rate movements vis-á-vis the target zone constitute a "sufficient statistic" for monitoring macroeconomic policies? If one believes that the answer to that question is negative, then orienting Fund surveillance around that single indicator, in addition to possibly diverting attention from the root causes of disequilibria, may jeopardize the quality of surveillance.

The second problem raised by skeptics is that the target zone approach is agnostic about which policy instruments should be used to respond to departures of exchange rates from the zone. The usual presumption is that it will be monetary policy.[20] However, if the root cause of the disequilibrium is an inappropriate monetary-fiscal *policy mix*, then an excessive emphasis on monetary policy could produce compliance with the target zones and yet leave the fundamental problem unsolved. In short, critics argue that the calculation of the target zones would have to be based on an appropriate and broad set of

---

[20] Most proposals for target zones (e.g., Williamson (1985)) assume that fiscal policy is not well suited to be an instrument of exchange rate policy because it is too inflexible and because its (alleged) comparative advantage (vis-á-vis monetary policy) is in influencing domestic demand rather than the balance of payments.

indicators to avoid sending false signals about both the need for adjustment and the appropriate corrective measures.

Third, critics contend that target zones do not resolve the problem of how to allocate and enforce the burden of adjustment among member countries. When more than one member's (effective) exchange rate leaves the zone, it will be necessary to specify who does what if an effective and coordinated policy response is to take place. But target zones, so the critics argue, offer no solution to this "N-1 problem."

Could target zones escape the fate of the Bretton Woods system? Opponents of the target zone approach to exchange rate management remain unconvinced that target zones could escape the fate of Bretton Woods. They make essentially three arguments. First, technological advances in transferring funds across national boundaries, in combination with absence of parallel growth in official reserves, means that the capital mobility problem (hot money flows) is now even more formidable than in the early 1970s. Second, difficulties associated with negotiating mutually consistent target zones would, as before, produce large discontinuous changes in exchange rates, thus motivating strong speculation. In addition, if the timing of exchange rate changes were done unpredictably to prevent such speculation, this would destroy the *raison d'être* of the target zone scheme itself. Third, the viability of the EMS owes much to the unusual political commitment behind it, to capital controls imposed by some members, and to the structural characteristics of its members.[21] None of these factors would, according to the critics, necessarily transfer to an exchange rate arrangement among a larger and more heterogeneous group of countries. As such, to them, the viability of the EMS does not imply much about the viability or desirability of a target zone system.

II. OPERATIONAL QUESTIONS ASSOCIATED WITH THE POSSIBLE IMPLEMENTATION OF TARGET ZONES

How Would the Target Zones Be Calculated?

An important implicit assumption in the target zone approach to exchange rate management is that the authorities can approximate the equilibrium (real)

---

[21] See Ungerer (1984) for a discussion of the implications of the EMS for the likely success of a return to a system of fixed but adjustable exchange rates.

exchange rate to a useful degree. But by what methods or techniques? Three methods deserve explicit consideration.

The first is the *purchasing-power-parity* (PPP) approach. If the authorities can identify a base period when the country was in external balance, then the equilibrium value for the nominal exchange rate in the current period is the value of the exchange rate in the base period adjusted for the intercountry difference in inflation rates between the current and base periods. This is equivalent to restoring the value of the *real* exchange rate in the base period. Since the real exchange rate, in turn, is often viewed as a measure of the country's competitive position, the PPP approach can be regarded as an analysis of competitiveness as well.

The exchange rate used for such calculations would typically be an index of effective exchange rates using bilateral trade weights or more sophisticated combinations of trade weights and trade price elasticities (e.g., MERM weights). Inflation differentials could be measured by consumer price indices, or more likely, by indices of either unit labor costs or prices in manufacturing.

The PPP approach carries the advantage of simplicity and ease of computation. Arrayed against this, however, are several rather serious disadvantages for use in a target zone context.

First, PPP will be a suitable indicator of the equilibrium exchange rate when all disturbances between the base and current periods are *monetary* in origin. In this case, general price levels will be altered but relative prices (of imports and exports, or of tradables and nontradables, or of individual tradables like food or fuel) will not. In contrast, when disturbances are *real* and do alter relative prices, then it will be desirable to have a departure from PPP (i.e., a change in the real exchange rate). This point is relevant because there have been numerous real disturbances over the past 13 years of managed floating (e.g., large changes in oil prices, changes in savings and investment propensities), and there is little reason to believe that such real disturbances will not occur in the future. This means that if a PPP formula were used to compute the equilibrium rate in a target zone, there would probably have to be a manual "override option" to permit departures from PPP whenever there were real disturbances to the system. But this override option robs PPP of its simplicity and computational facility.

Another disadvantage of the PPP approach is that actual exchange rates of major currencies during the 1970s and early 1980s have *not* followed the paths implied by PPP — and for both the short and long run.[22] To most observers, the empirical failure of PPP in the short run is attributable to an intrinsic difference between exchange rates and prices of national outputs. The former are jumpy, forward-looking, auction prices that move in anticipation of future events, whereas the latter are sticky, backward-looking, administered prices that may largely reflect previous events. In the long run, structural changes and permanent supply shocks may cause PPP to miss the mark. In any case, the poor empirical track record of PPP suggests that exchange rate forecasts based on PPP might not be credible to market participants.

A third difficulty with PPP is that the results themselves appear to be quite sensitive to the choice among alternative price indices and base periods to the income levels and income growth rates of the countries involved in the comparison (i.e., the so-called productivity-bias in PPP)[23] and to the level of aggregation in the data (manufacturing versus the entire economy).[24] Such sensitivity, in turn, makes it difficult to speak with confidence about all but very large misalignments.

A second method of calculating equilibrium exchange rates for target zones is to employ an *estimated structural model of exchange rate determination* that relates the (nominal) exchange rate to "fundamentals." Two popular such models are the monetary model and the portfolio balance model. In the monetary model, the change in the exchange rate is usually explained by changes in the ratio of home to foreign money supplies and by changes in the ratio of the demand for money at home to that abroad (where the demand for money is a function of, inter alia, real income, nominal interest rates). The portfolio balance model relates the (nominal) exchange rate to the stocks of assets denominated in the home and foreign currencies (where these asset stocks include money supplies as well as interest-bearing securities). Since the stocks of financial assets can be related to cumulative budget deficits, cumulative current account imbalances, open market operations, and exchange market intervention, the portfolio balance model provides a direct role for such

---

[22] See Frenkel (1981a). Of course, to the extent that actual exchange rates have been subject to misalignments, one would not want the actual rates to closely follow a PPP path. However, divergencies from PPP have been so marked and so persistent as to raise doubts about the credibility of exchange rate forecasts based on PPP.

[23] See Balassa (1964).

[24] See International Monetary Fund (1984b).

policies in influencing exchange rates. In the monetary model, such policies affect exchange rates only to the extent that they affect the supply or demand for money.

Given estimates for such a structural model of exchange rates, the equilibrium exchange rate could be defined as the rate corresponding to the *desired* path of the explanatory fundamentals in the equation (i.e., money supplies, real income, interest rates, budget positions). This estimate of the equilibrium nominal exchange rate, combined with some assumed consistent path for prices at home and abroad, could then be translated into an estimate of the equilibrium real exchange rate.

This structural approach has three advantages: (i) it is forward-looking and thus compatible with the intrinsic nature of the price behavior of such assets as securities denominated in different currencies; (ii) it provides a direct link between macroeconomic policy variables and exchange rates; and (iii) it recognizes that in today's world of high international mobility of capital, the proximate determinants of exchange rates, at least in the short run, probably lie in asset markets rather than goods markets. At the same time, the structural exchange rate equation approach is subject to at least two serious deficiencies.

The most serious shortcoming is that *all* known structural models of exchange rate determination have been shown to have very limited forecasting ability. In fact, extensive empirical testing over the past few years has demonstrated that the out-of-sample performance of structural exchange rate models is frequently no better than that yielded by "naive" models (e.g., a random-walk model).[25] With the benefit of hindsight, it seems that an important reason for the poor performance of the various models is the nature of exchange rates as asset prices. As indicated above, exchange rates are very sensitive to expectations concerning future events and policies. Periods that are dominated by rumors, announcements, and "news" which alter expectations are likely to induce a relatively large degree of exchange rate volatility. Since by definition "news" cannot be predicted on the basis of past information, it follows that by and large the resulting fluctuations of exchange rates are unpredictable. In a way, this asset market perspective suggests that one should not expect to be able to forecast accurately exchange rate changes with the

---

[25] Meese and Rogoff (1983) and Isard (1986).

aid of simple structural models. The role of the simple structural models is to account for the *systematic* component of the evolution of exchange rates. In cases where the systematic, predictable component is relatively small, one may expect to account for only a small fraction of the variability of exchange rates. The main message of all this is that target zones based on exchange rate forecasts from such models might not carry sufficient credibility to act as an anchor.

Another problem with the structural exchange rate models is that the explanatory variables can be difficult to measure and interpret on a timely basis. For example, the portfolio balance model requires measurement of asset stocks by currency, by country of issuance, and by residence of the holder. But such data only become available much after the fact and estimates based on extrapolation of benchmark figures may introduce substantial error into the calculations. Similarly, in the monetary model one faces the problems of which monetary aggregate to use (in view of financial market innovations), how to forecast that aggregate over the relevant time horizon, and how to distinguish short-term movements in velocity from trends. For these reasons, the prospects of obtaining timely forecasts (target zones) from these models are not encouraging.

The third method for calculating equilibrium exchange rates is the *underlying balance* approach. In this approach, the (real) equilibrium exchange rate is defined as the rate that would make the "underlying" current account (i.e., the actual current account adjusted for temporary factors) equal to "normal" net capital flows during the next two or three years, given (i) anticipated macroeconomic policies in the subject countries, (ii) the delayed effects of past exchange rate changes, and (iii) a number of other expected developments. Furthermore, the equality between underlying current accounts and normal capital flows must *not* be achieved either by wholesale unemployment, or by artificial incentives to incoming or outgoing capital, or by undue restrictions on trade.[26] If after accounting for these factors, "underlying" current accounts are calculated to be quite different from "normal" capital flows, the implication is that either planned macroeconomic policies or present exchange rates need to change to prevent such undesirable balance of payments scenarios from taking place.

---

[26]This description of the real equilibrium exchange rate is a close relative of those outlined in Nurkse (1945) and International Monetary Fund (1970) and (1985b), par. 69.

This underlying balance approach to exchange rate assessment was developed by the Fund staff in the early 1970s (see International Monetary Fund (1984b)); it similarly serves as the framework for calculation of "misalignments" in Williamson (1985). The inputs for the calculations come from various sources. Estimates of "anticipated macroeconomic policies," and their associated real growth and inflation paths, can be obtained from national projections or from the Fund's world economic outlook projections. Estimates of "normal" net capital flows typically come from an analysis of past trends adjusted for expected future structural developments (e.g., capital liberalization measures). Finally, estimates of the effect of exchange rate changes on current accounts can be derived, for example, from either of the Fund's two operating trade models, namely the multilateral exchange rate model or the world trade model.[27]

For application in a system of target zones, the underlying balance approach carries three advantages. First, it recognizes that judgments about the appropriateness of current exchange rates cannot be divorced from either future anticipated macroeconomic policies, or from delayed effects of past exchange rates that are not yet visible but are likely to emerge in the future, or from particular factors (e.g., dock strikes) that are temporary in nature. In this sense, it not only focuses attention on the root cause of misalignment (i.e., inappropriate policies) but also addresses the "time dimension" in the misalignment problem.

Second, the underlying balance approach appreciates that a desirable or sustainable payments position need not imply a zero current account balance. Specifically, it recognizes that a country with a relatively low domestic savings rate but with relatively attractive domestic investment opportunities can run a persistent current account deficit by drawing on foreign savings if (i) it invests those foreign savings wisely; and (ii) the return on domestic investments is not *artificially* high (because of special incentives for or restrictions on international capital flows, or because of unsustainably high government borrowing).

A third advantage of the underlying balance approach is that, at least in principle, it ensures that the computed equilibrium exchange rates are *consistent* across countries.[28] This is so because the trade models that underlie such exchange rate calculations are specifically designed to be used in a multilateral

---

[27] See Artus and McGuirk (1981) and Deppler and Ripley (1978).

setting. Since target zones must be mutually consistent, this is not a trivial consideration.

Moving to the negative side of the ledger, the underlying balance approach is subject to a number of problems.

First and foremost, the concept of "normal" net private capital flows is a particularly ambiguous one; yet estimates of these capital flows play a key role in the estimate of the equilibrium real exchange rate. The reasons why the concept is so slippery include the following: (i) While private saving rates are reasonably stable over time and across countries, the geographic loci of *perceived* investment opportunities are not; the latter depend on a wide set of expected policies in both the origin and host countries — many of which can change precipitately. (ii) Various controls on capital flows make it difficult to determine what is "normal," especially when these controls change over time. (iii) Acquisition of foreign assets subjects the holder to risks (e.g., expropriation risk) that are fundamentally different from those associated with domestic assets, and therefore consideration of such risks may limit exposure even when average real rates of return on foreign assets are high. (iv) Large changes in government fiscal positions, and drastic shifts in private portfolio composition, can lead to large swings in observed capital flows, the duration of which is highly uncertain. The end result of all this is that estimates of "normal" net capital flows for the likely participants in a target zone system are subject to a considerable margin of error.

A second problem with the underlying balance approach is that it is not well suited to the analysis and diagnosis of the *mix* of macroeconomic policies. In general, macroeconomic policies influence the equilibrium exchange rate in this approach via their effect on anticipated real output and inflation paths over the next two to three years. Thus, the model will produce different estimates of the equilibrium exchange rate for different real output and inflation paths. But it cannot distinguish among policy mixes that yield the same output and inflation paths. This must be regarded as a shortcoming since the cause of misalignment may lie more with an inappropriate mix of policies (e.g., overly loose fiscal policy cum overly tight monetary policy) than with an inappropriate stance of policies (e.g., excessively expansionary monetary and fiscal policy).

---

[28] This advantage must be qualified in view of the large global discrepancy in current account positions. This discrepancy makes it harder to reach agreement on what constitutes an equilibrium pattern of current account positions.

The third difficulty with the underlying balance approach is that it is operationally complex. Data requirements are substantial, computations depend on large-scale trade models, the rationale behind some of the calculations is not transparent, and estimates of some key parameters (e.g., short-run and long-run trade elasticities) are uncertain.[29] All of this, in turn, might be burdensome for agreement on, and continuous revision of, target zones.

Fourth, the large-scale trade models that are likely to be used in this approach do not pay sufficient attention to either financial variables or to the important distinction between expected and unexpected values of key economic variables. These omissions render this approach somewhat remote from the mechanisms usually associated with the determination of *market* exchange rates. Therefore, target zones based on forecasts from the underlying balance approach may again be questioned by market participants.

To *summarize*, each of the three methods of calculating equilibrium exchange rates has strengths and weaknesses. It might, however, not be necessary to follow just one method. Instead, one could construct a "consensus" forecast on the basis of estimates from several methods. Such an exercise would also provide information on the comparative performance of each method which, in turn, could aid in the ultimate selection of the proper calculation method. Finally, in appraising the methods of calculating equilibrium exchange rates, it is important to recognize that such methods are already being applied to some degree whenever the Fund "takes a view" on the appropriateness of major currency exchange rates. In this sense, the problems raised are not new ones. The differences are that in a system of target zones (especially the "harder" versions) the method of calculating equilibrium exchange rates would be more explicit and subject to greater scrutiny, and that the results of such calculations would be shared with the market.

What Currencies Should Be Included in the System of Target Zones?

Another central issue for a system of target zones is the number and choice of currencies to be included. Several considerations seem paramount.

---

[29]See, for example, Goldstein and Khan (1985).

- For *administrative efficiency*, it is desirable that membership should be kept fairly small. This is because the complexity of negotiations, and the danger of conflicts that might bring about a collapse of the system, can be said to increase rapidly as the number of partners rises. This position is consistent with the view that centralized management of exchange rates is feasible only when the number of *decisions* to be made is reasonably small.[30] In this connection, it is useful to recall that although a large number of currencies were managed under the Bretton Woods system, countries took the initiative for par value changes, the Fund could only concur with or object to par value changes proposed by a member, and par values were changed rather infrequently.[31] Similarly, the present system of managed floating is a decentralized system that permits "market-based" decisions to act as a safety valve when more centralized decisions about adjustment responsibilities and exchange rate alignments do not prove possible. In short, since international decision-making on exchange rates is likely to be difficult, one should not unduly burden the system with too many players.
- For a target zone system to have an appreciable impact on conditions in foreign exchange markets, it is desirable that the membership include *major currency countries*. Although the vast majority of countries currently maintain some form of "pegged" exchange arrangements, the largest trading countries maintain either "limited flexibility" (e.g., the EMS) or "more flexible" exchange arrangements, including "independent floating" by four of the largest industrial countries (Canada, Japan, the United Kingdom, and the United States).[32] Reflecting this, it has been estimated that about two thirds to four fifths of world trade is conducted at floating rates.[33] The key to progressing toward more fixity in exchange rates therefore lies not in inducing many countries to adopt constraints on

---

[30] Of course, exchange rates established in a target zone would have clear implications for nonparticipants to which they would have to adjust and/or react.

[31] The Bretton Woods system also had the U.S. dollar as the numeraire. With the dollar as anchor, exchange rate decisions could take place one-at-a-time. When this was no longer the case (e.g., August–December 1971), negotiations over exchange rates were much more difficult. It is not clear what currency or currency basket would serve as numeraire in a target zone.

[32] It is worth recalling that the currencies of EMS members float against currencies of many nonmembers.

[33] See International Monetary Fund (1984c) and (1985a), par. 9.

exchange rate flexibility — this is already a fact of life — but rather in inducing the largest trading countries to accept such constraints. This consideration has no doubt influenced the leading proposals (e.g., Roosa (1984)) that the key members of a target zone be either the three largest industrial countries or the Group of Five (or perhaps Group of Seven) countries.

- A further consideration is the *characteristics of the potential member countries*. These characteristics, emphasized in the literature on so-called optimal currency areas, are relevant not for choosing the right number of countries for a target zone but rather for assessing the likely membership.

The more important country characteristics are the following:

(i) The *openness* of the economy. This criterion suggests that relatively open economies should prefer greater fixity of exchange rates because exchange rate fluctuations induce larger domestic price changes in more open economies, thereby complicating the task of domestic stabilization policies.

(ii) The *size* of the economy. Small economies are said to be more inclined to join currency unions because, in the absence of such monetary integration, their effective economic size would be suboptimal. This of course begs the question of which currency to peg to.

(iii) The degree of *commodity diversification*. Highly diversified economies are deemed more likely candidates for greater fixity of exchange rates because their diversification provides some natural insulation against a variety of shocks; hence, there is less need for the insulation properties of a flexible exchange rate.

(iv) The degree of *factor mobility*. Countries between which there is a high degree of factor mobility are viewed as better candidates for currency unions because factor mobility provides a substitute for exchange rate flexibility in promoting external adjustment. Since factor mobility is in turn likely to diminish with geographic distance, this criterion is often used to justify currency unions between small neighboring states.

(v) *Similarity of inflation rates*. The argument here is that countries with similar tastes for inflation — and more important, similar histories of inflation — will tend to prefer greater fixity of exchange rates. There is, however, a chicken-and-egg problem: do member countries of a currency union have similar inflation rates because they belong to the union, or have they joined the union because of their similar capacities to combat inflation?

Obviously, these country characteristics do not all point in the same direction. For example, the criteria of openness, size, and factor mobility suggest that the United States, the Federal Republic of Germany, and Japan would have relatively weak incentives to join a target zone, relative say, to the smaller European countries that are members of the EMS. On the other hand, the criteria of commodity diversification and similarity of inflation rates lean the other way.

A final consideration is the *relationship to existing currency blocs.* In thinking about the potential membership of a target zone system, it is important to recognize that most countries are already part of a currency bloc, be it via pegging to a single currency or currency basket, or via participation in an arrangement with limited exchange rate flexibility (e.g., the EMS). This raises three points: (i) where members of the target zone system are also members of other (regional) currency blocs, provision would have to be made for ensuring consistency of cross exchange rates and for coordinating intervention practices between the "core" target zone and "satellite" currency blocs; (ii) countries that already have non-exchange-rate linking arrangements (e.g., a customs union) may be reluctant to undertake additional linkages (i.e., target zones) for fear of restricting too tightly their room for independent action; and (iii) if the most natural and profitable opportunities for currency union are exploited first, then it is likely that a target zone system among major currency countries may have to operate with more flexibility (e.g., wider margins and more frequent revision of central rates) than satellite currency blocs.

How Wide Should the Target Zones Be and How Frequently Should They Be Revised?

The equilibrium exchange rate — also sometimes referred to as the *central rate* — represents only one of several parameters that characterize target zones. Two others are the *width* of the zones surrounding the central rates and the *frequency* by which the zones are revised. What considerations bear on the determination of these latter two parameters?

Concerning the *width* of the zones, four factors are relevant. First, the zones must be wide enough to accommodate transitory disturbances that do not alter long-run equilibrium real exchange rates. In this sense, the zone may be viewed as providing a buffer. The buffer not only guards against costly shifts in resources due to excessively frequent changes in central rates but also provides the authorities with breathing space to sort out permanent from transitory shocks. Second, the zone should be wide enough to reflect uncertainties about the equilibrium central rate itself. As noted earlier, there are various approaches to calculating the real equilibrium exchange rate and there are uncertainties about the parameter values in each model. To many observers, little is gained by acting as if equilibrium exchange rates could be assessed with great precision. Recognizing this, some proposals for target zones recommend initial zones on the order of 10 percentage points on each side of the central rate (see, for example, Williamson (1985)). The third factor to be considered is speculation. A well-known weakness of fixed exchange rates is that frequently they offer speculators "one-way bets" about the direction of changes in parities. Target zones must therefore be sufficiently wide to allow for occasional changes in central rates within the zone without provoking one-way speculation. Fourth, if central rates were specified in terms of a numeraire currency, then the width of the target zone linking nonnumeraire currencies will in general be different to that between each currency and the numeraire.

Also, there is no reason why the width of the zones should be constant over time. For example, if uncertainty about the equilibrium real exchange rate and about the nature of disturbances diminished with experience, then narrower zones could be adopted. On the other hand, if turbulence increased over time, wider zones could be adopted. Finally, as a corollary of the above arguments, there is no logical presumption that the width of the zone should be the same for all members. In this connection, it is relevant to note the experience of the EMS in which the currency of Italy, a country that has had relatively high inflation in the past, is subject to wider margins than other currencies. Similarly, it has been suggested that if the United Kingdom were to join the EMS, special provision should be made in the form of wider margins for the pound sterling to reflect the influence of oil price developments on the exchange rate.

Turning to the *frequency* of adjustment, a number of points need to be considered. To begin with, the frequency with which the central rates (and zones around them) are adjusted should reflect the frequency of changes in real economic conditions, as well as, of course, the size of inflation differentials across member countries. Examples of changes in real economic conditions would include permanent changes in the terms of trade, continuing intercountry differences in labor productivity, and intercountry shifts in saving and investment propensities. Because such changes in real economic conditions generally do not occur at close intervals, they are unlikely to induce frequent changes in the target zones. The size of inflation differentials depends primarily on how successful target zones are in inducing harmonization of members' macroeconomic and structural policies, particularly monetary policy. The second factor governing the desired frequency of adjustment is the flexibility of macroeconomic policy instruments. Specifically, since a change in real economic conditions can be reconciled *either* by a change in macroeconomic policies with an unchanged zone or by a change in the zone with unchanged policies, it follows that inflexible policies call for higher frequency of zone adjustment, and vice versa. Third, there is the credibility issue. Frequent revisions in the zones reduce credibility of the zones and thereby reduce their value as an anchor for expectations. On the other hand, frequent changes in macroeconomic policies designed to sustain the zones may also reduce credibility — but this time of the policies.[34] Therefore, the optimal frequency of adjustment from a credibility viewpoint involves balancing between these two considerations. Fourth, some have argued that if target zones are adjusted frequently for inflation differentials and the need for balance of payments adjustment, speculative attacks will be discouraged, since they are motivated by large discrete changes in exchange rates. Fifth, the frequency of adjustment must obviously be constrained by the availability of the data necessary for computations.

How Would Exchange Rates Be Kept Within the Zones and With What Consequences for Other Policy Objectives?

For a system of target zones to operate successfully, it is necessary that exchange rates be kept within the agreed zones, at least most of the time. But *how* would participating countries assure this result? Three policy instruments should be considered.

---

[34] A counterargument is that changes in macroeconomic policies in response to real changes in the economy could act at times to enhance the credibility of policy if they were perceived as responsive to these changes.

- The most obvious instrument is *domestic monetary policy*. Indeed, as indicated in Section I, a differentiating characteristic of target zones is that the authorities pay more attention to the exchange rate in the conduct of domestic monetary policy than they do under the present system of managed floating. What this means is that participating members will have to seek greater *coordination* of monetary policies, with a consequent reduction in the ability to independently control the money supply. For example, a member of the system that sees its nominal exchange rate fall to the bottom of the zone would be expected to slow its money growth rate and to increase its domestic interest rate vis-á-vis those of other members;[35] in this way, it would induce an appreciation in its nominal exchange rate, thereby keeping its exchange rate, within the target zone. Assuming that the pass-through of nominal exchange rate changes into domestic prices is less than complete, the same monetary policy action would allow the member to satisfy its target for the real exchange rate as well.[36]

There is little doubt about the *ability* of major industrial countries to influence nominal and real exchange rates in the medium term using domestic monetary policy.[37] The key question concerns the *willingness* to do so given the implied reduction in their ability to then use domestic monetary policy for internal objectives. To many observers, it is simply naive to believe that the United States, Japan, and the Federal Republic of Germany would be willing to override internal objectives for exchange rate targets in the formulation of domestic monetary policy. Under this view, "soft" target zones are the strongest commitment one can reasonably envisage for the three largest potential

---

[35] It is not clear what form monetary intervention would take. Members could intervene in domestic financial markets (exchanging money for debt of the same currency of denomination) or in international financial markets (exchanging moneys of different currency denomination). If the latter were envisaged, questions could arise about the adequacy of intervention assets and about sterilization operations.

[36] Obstfeld (1985) reports that month-month correlations between nominal and real exchange rates for the 1976–85 period were above 0.95 for the U.S. dollar, the Japanese yen, and the deutsche mark.

[37] In the long run (say, three to five years), the ability to use monetary policy to affect the real exchange rate will be more modest. Also, even in the medium term, this ability will be lower for the smaller, more open, more highly indexed industrial countries than for the larger, less open, less indexed ones. See Goldstein and Khan (1985) for a survey of estimates of these "pass-through" effects.

members. Others argue, however, that the independence of monetary policy is far from complete under the present system, even for those countries classified by the Fund as "independently floating." To take but one recent example, the U.K. authorities reacted to the large decline in the dollar/pound rate in early 1985 by encouraging large increases in domestic interest rates — and this even though there was strong domestic pressure for lower interest rates to help reduce unemployment. For this reason, supporters of target zones argue that all countries already have *implicit* target zones beyond which they are willing to sacrifice internal objectives for the exchange rate. It is argued therefore that the loss of monetary independence *at the margin* would be minimal.

- A second possible policy instrument for keeping exchange rates within target zones is *sterilized exchange market intervention* (i.e., exchange market intervention that leaves the monetary base unchanged). Its main attraction is that, if effective, it would permit the authorities to influence exchange rates while simultaneously maintaining control of the domestic money supply.

Unfortunately, the prognosis for using sterilized exchange market intervention as the primary instrument for controlling exchange rates is not favorable. The Jurgensen Report (1983), for example, supports the view that sterilized intervention by itself is unlikely to be an effective tool for influencing the level of the exchange rate over the medium or long term.[38] Similarly, recent empirical work on exchange rate determination indicates that while domestic and foreign currency assets may well be imperfect substitutes — a necessary condition for sterilized exchange market intervention to be effective — risk premiums in exchange markets are *not* well explained by relative asset supplies (the very variables affected by exchange market intervention).[39] In short, the effects of sterilized intervention on market exchange rates are likely to be small and uncertain in size. Nevertheless, sterilized intervention may have a useful role to play in dampening short-term volatility of exchange rates, in countering disorderly market conditions, in complementing and supporting other policies, and in expressing an attitude toward exchange markets.

---

[38] "Intervention will normally be useful only when complementing and supporting other policies." Jurgensen Report (1983).
[39] See, for example, Dooley and Isard (1983).

- *Capital controls* represent a third instrument for keeping exchange rates within target zones. This is, however, generally not regarded as an attractive option for two reasons. First, even aggressive capital control programs, such as those of the early 1970s, were not able to stem private capital flows, and the subsequent development of offshore banking markets suggests even lower effectiveness today. Second, capital control programs are most effective in altering exchange rates when they cover all types of capital transactions. But in that case, there is no presumption that the resource allocation costs of impeding the international flow of capital would be less serious than departures of exchange rates from the zones themselves.

The preceding discussion suggests that the primary instrument for keeping exchange rates within target zones is likely to be monetary policy. If this is so, then a second relevant question emerges: with monetary policy geared more to external objectives, what policy instruments will be assigned to *internal balance* (i.e., price stability and high employment)?

One logical answer is *fiscal* policy.[40] Here, the key question is not so much whether fiscal policy *can* affect aggregate demand in major industrial countries. Experience suggests that it can. Rather, the issue is whether fiscal policy is a sufficiently *flexible* policy instrument to be used for stabilization policy in a world in which some countries have medium-term targets for reducing the share of government expenditure in overall economic activity, some are contemplating large structural changes in their tax system, some are committed to given levels of social programs and defense spending, some are wedded to preannounced public sector borrowing requirements, and some are facing legislatures that can take years (not months) to enact significant cuts in budget deficits.

A second policy option (favored for example by Meade (1984)) is to use *labor market policy* for internal balance. In brief, the idea is to lower the money wage rate in any sector which has excess supply of labor and to raise it where there is excess demand. The problem, recognized by supporters, is that the implementation of such a policy would involve the substantial reform of labor market institutions. In short, although sound in its internal logic, it begs the central question of *how* to bring such a labor market

---

[40] Fiscal policy also has a role to play in achieving a given real exchange rate on a sustainable basis.

policy into being in advanced industrial economies. The slow progress in reducing structural rigidities in European labor markets bears testimony to the difficulties involved.

In *sum*, because of the limitations of other policy instruments, monetary policy is often called on to serve both external and internal objectives. If a move to target zones were made, it would require shifting more of the emphasis toward external objectives. This might not create a major problem if all members of the target zone geared monetary policy toward price stability; or if coordinated, sterilized exchange market intervention could ease the external obligations of monetary policy; or if fiscal policy could be made flexible enough to deal effectively with internal balance. However, since none of these three outcomes is likely to be fully realized, members of a target zone system would probably still be faced with serious conflicts between external and internal balance. At the same time, the constraints on macroeconomic policies induced by a target zone system might make a contribution to the realization of these three outcomes.

III. POSTSCRIPT

This paper, along with others that examined issues raised in the reports on the international monetary system presented by the Deputies of the Group of Ten and Group of Twenty-Four, was discussed by the Fund's Executive Board in early 1986. Since then, efforts to improve the functioning of the exchange rate system have centered on enhancing economic policy coordination among the largest economies and on strengthening the multilateral setting for Fund surveillance, including the formulation of a set of "objective indicators."

At its meeting on April 9-10, 1986, the Interim Committee agreed that "if better exchange rate performance were to be achieved on a durable basis, it would be of the essence that economic policies be conducted in a sound and mutually consistent way and that exchange rate considerations should play their part in those policies" (International Monetary Fund (1986), p. 115). The Committee also reconfirmed the key role that Fund surveillance needs to play in the functioning of the international monetary system. "To improve the multilateral setting for surveillance, the Committee asked the Executive Board to consider ways in which its regular reviews of the world economic situation could be further adopted to improve the scope for discussing external imbalances, exchange rate developments, and policy interactions among members. An approach worth exploring further was the formulation of a set of objective indicators related to policy actions and economic performance, having regard to a medium-term framework. Such indicators might help to identify a need for discussion of economic policies" (ibid., p. 115).

The leaders of the seven major industrial countries, meeting on May 4–6, 1986 in Tokyo at the twelfth annual economic summit, reinforced this commitment to closer coordination of economic policies. They asked that their finance ministers meet at least once a year "to review their individual economic objectives and forecasts collectively, and that they use a set of quantitative indicators of economic policies and performance with a particular view to examining their mutual compatibility" (International Monetary Fund (1986), p. 145). They welcomed the recent examples of improved coordination among the Group of Five countries — including the Plaza Agreement of September 22, 1985 — but felt that additional measures were needed "to ensure that procedures for effective coordination of international economic policy are strengthened further" (ibid., p. 157). Toward this goal, the leaders, together with the representatives of the European Community participating in the meeting, reaffirmed their intention "to cooperate with the IMF in strengthening multilateral surveillance, particularly among the countries (the Group of 5) whose currencies constitute the SDR" (ibid., p. 157). Further, in conducting such surveillance and in conjunction with the Managing Director of the IMF, they asked that account be taken of "such indicators as growth rates of gross national product (GNP), interest rates, inflation rates, unemployment rates, ratios of fiscal deficits to GNP, current account and trade balances, money growth rates, international reserve holdings, and exchange rates" (ibid., p. 157).

In July 1986, the Fund's Executive Board discussed a staff paper on "Surveillance-Indicators Relating to Policy Actions and Economic Performance."[41] This was followed in September 1986 by the Executive Board's discussion of the staff's world economic outlook exercise, the published version of which appeared in October. In the context of analyzing the medium-term prospects of industrial countries, that exercise contains a section which reviews certain potential sources of tension in the interaction of economic developments and considers their implications for the stance of policies.

---

[41] See Crockett and Goldstein (1987) for a published version of that paper.

When the Interim Committee next met on September 28, 1986 in Washington, it once again focused, inter alia, on the use of indicators in surveillance. The Committee agreed that "a key focus of indicators should be on points of interaction among national economies, in particular developments affecting the sustainability of balance of payments positions, and on the policies underlying them" (International Monetary Fund (1986), p. 309). The Committee also asked the Fund's Executive Board "to develop further the application of indicators in the context both of the period consultations with individual member countries and of the world economic outlook so as to facilitate the multilateral appraisal and coordination of economic policies" (ibid.).

"A Guide to Target Zones" by Jacob A. Frenkel and Morris Goldstein. Reprinted from Vol. 33, No. 4 (December 1986) International Monetary Fund Staff Papers. Copyright © 1986 by the International Monetary Fund. Used with permission of the publisher."

REFERENCES

Adams, Charles, and Daniel Gros, "The Consequences of Real Exchange Rate Rules for Inflation: Some Illustrative Examples," *Staff Papers,* International Monetary Fund (Washington), Vol. 33 (September 1986). pp. 439–76.

Artus, Jacques R., and Andrew D. Crockett, *Floating Exchange Rates and the Need for Surveillance*, Essays in International Finance, No. 127 (Princeton, New Jersey: Princeton University, 1978).

Artus, Jacques R., and Anne Kenney McGuirk, "A Revised Version of the Multilateral Exchange Rate Model," *Staff Papers*, International Monetary Fund (Washington), Vol. 28 (June 1981), pp. 275–309.

Artus, Jacques R., and John H. Young, "Fixed and Flexible Exchange Rates: A Renewal of the Debate," *Staff Papers*, International Monetary Fund (Washington), Vol. 26 (December 1979), pp. 654–98.

Bergsten, C. Fred, and John Williamson, "Exchange Rates and Trade Policy," in *Trade Policy in the 1980s*, ed. by William R. Cline (Washington: Institute for International Economics, 1983).

Bergstrand, Jeffrey H., "Is Exchange Rate Volatility 'Excessive'?" Federal Reserve Bank of Boston, *New England Economic Review* (Boston, September/October 1983), pp. 5–14.

Bryant, Ralph C., "Comments and Discussion" on "Floating Exchange Rates After Ten Years," *Brookings Papers on Economic Activity: 1* (1983), The Brookings Institution (Washington), pp. 71–79.

Calvo, Guillermo, "Trying to Stabilize: Some Theoretical Reflections Based on the Case of Argentina," in *Financial Policies and the World Capital Market: The Problem of Latin American Countries*, ed. by P. Aspe, R. Dornbusch, and M. Obstfeld (Chicago: University of Chicago Press, 1983), pp. 199–216.

Cline, William R., *International Monetary Reform and the Developing Countries* (Washington: The Brookings Institution, 1976).

Crockett, Andrew D., and Morris Goldstein, *Strengthening the International Monetary System: Exchange Rates, Surveillance, and Objective Indicators*, Occasional Paper No. 50 (Washington: International Monetary Fund, forthcoming, 1987).

Deppler, Michael C., and Duncan M. Ripley, "The World Trade Model: Merchandise Trade," *Staff Papers*, International Monetary Fund (Washington), Vol. 25 (March 1978), pp. 147–206.

Dooley, Michael P., and Peter Isard, "The Portfolio-Balance Model of Exchange Rates and Some Structural Estimates of the Risk Premium," *Staff Papers*, International Monetary Fund (Washington), Vol. 30 (December 1983), pp. 683–702.

Dornbusch, Rudiger, "Exchange Rate Economics: Where Do We Stand?" *Brookings Papers on Economic Activity: I* (1980), The Brookings Institution (Washington), pp. 143–185.

Dunn, Robert M., *Exchange Rate Rigidity, Investment Distortions, and the Failure of Bretton Woods*, Essays in International Finance, No. 97 (Princeton, New Jersey: Princeton University, 1973).

Emminger, Otmar, *Exchange Rate Policy Reconsidered*, Occasional Paper No. 10 (New York: Group of Thirty, 1982).

—————, *The Dollar's Borrowed Strength*, Occasional Paper No. 19 (New York: Group of Thirty, 1985).

Ethier, Wilfred, and Arthur I. Bloomfield, *Managing the Managed Float*, Essays in International Finance, No. 112 (Princeton, New Jersey: Princeton University, 1975).

Frenkel, Jacob A. "Reflections on European Monetary Integration," *Weltwirtschaftliches Archiv* (Kiel), Vol. 111 (No.2, 1975), pp. 214–221.

————— (1981a), "The Collapse of Purchasing Power Parities During the 1970s," *European Economic Review* (Amsterdam), Vol. 16 (May 1981), pp. 145–165.

————— (1981b), "Flexible Exchange Rates, Prices, and the Role of 'News': Lessons from the 1970s," *Journal of Political Economy* (Chicago), Vol. 89 (August 1981), pp. 665–705.

—————, "International Liquidity and Monetary Control," in *International Money and Credit: The Policy Roles*, ed. by George M. von Furstenberg (Washington: International Monetary Fund, 1983). pp. 65–109.

—————, "Comments on Exchange Rate Arrangements in the Eighties," in *The International Monetary System*, Federal Reserve Bank of Boston (Boston, May 1984), pp. 119–25.

_____, "Seeking a Solution through Policy Coordination," in *Exchange Rate Targets: Desirable or Disastrous*, ed. by John H. Makin (Washington: American Enterprise Institute, 1986), pp. 10–22.

_____, and Joshua Aizenman, "Aspects of the Optimal Management of Exchange Rates," *Journal of International Economics* (Amsterdam). Vol. 13 (November 1982), pp. 231–256.

Frenkel, Jacob A., and Michael L. Mussa, "The Efficiency of Foreign Exchange Markets and Measures of Turbulence," *American Economic Review* (Nashville, Tennessee), Vol. 60 (May 1970), pp. 374–381.

Genberg, Hans, "On Choosing the Right Rules for Exchange-Rate Management," *World Economy* (London), Vol. 7 (December 1984). pp. 391–406.

Goldstein, Morris, *Have Flexible Exchange Rates Handicapped Macroeconomic Policy?* Special Papers in International Economics, No. 14 (Princeton. New Jersey: Princeton University, 1980).

_____, and Mohsin S. Khan, "Income and Price Effects in Foreign Trade," Chap. 20 in *Handbook of International Economics*, ed. by Ronald W. Jones and Peter B. Kenen (Amsterdam: North-Holland, 1985), pp. 1041–1105.

Group of Thirty, *The Foreign Exchange Markets Under Floating Rates, A Study in International Finance*, by the Exchange Markets Participants' Study Group (New York: Group of Thirty, 1980).

_____, *The Problem of Exchange Rates: A Policy Statement* (New York: Group of Thirty, 1982).

Helleiner, Gerald K., *Towards a New Bretton Woods: Challenges for the World Financial and Trading System: Report by a Commonwealth Study Group* (London: Commonwealth Secretariat. 1983).

International Monetary Fund (1970), *The Role of Exchange Rates in the Adjustment of International Payments: A Report by the Executive Directors* (Washington: International Monetary Fund, 1970).

_____ (1974a), *International Monetary Reform: Documents of the Committee of Twenty* (Washington: International Monetary Fund, 1974).

_____ (1974b), "Guidelines for the Management of Floating Rates," in *Annual Report of the Executive Directors for the Fiscal Year Ended April 30, 1974* (Washington: International Monetary Fund, 1974), pp. 112–116.

_____ (1984a), *Exchange Rate Volatility and World Trade*, Occasional Paper No. 28 (Washington: International Monetary Fund, July 1984).

_____ (1984b), *Issues in the Assessment of the Exchange Rates of Industrial Countries*, Occasional Paper No. 29 (Washington: International Monetary Fund, July 1984).

_____ (1984c), *The Exchange Rate System: Lessons of the Past and Options for the Future*, Occasional Paper No. 30 (Washington: International Monetary Fund, July 1984).

_____ (1985a), "Report of the Deputies: The Functioning of the International Monetary System," *IMF Survey* (Washington), Supplement, Vol. 14 (July 1985), pp. 2–14.

———— (1985b), "Deputies of Intergovernmental Group of 24 Call for Major Changes in Monetary System," *IMF Survey* (Washington), Supplement on Group of 24, Vol. 14 (September 1985), pp. 2–16.

———— (1986), *IMF Survey* (Washington), Vol. 15.

Isard, Peter, "The Empirical Modeling of Exchange Rates: An Assessment of Alternative Approaches" (unpublished, International Monetary Fund, June 6, 1986).

Jurgensen Report, *Report of the Working Group on Exchange Market Intervention* (Washington: U.S. Treasury, March 1983).

Kenen, Peter, "Reforming the International Monetary System" (unpublished, New York Academy of Sciences, September 1985).

McGuirk, Anne Kenney, "Oil Price Changes and Real Exchange Rate Movements Among Industrial Countries," *Staff Papers*, International Monetary Fund (Washington), Vol. 30 (December 1983), pp. 843–884.

McKinnon, Ronald I., *An International Standard for Monetary Stabilization, Policy Analyses in International Economics:* 7 (Washington: Institute for International Economics, 1984).

Meade, James, "New Keynesian Bretton Woods," *Three Banks Review* (Edinburgh), Vol. 142 (June 1984), pp. 8–25.

Meese, Richard A, and Kenneth Rogoff, "Empirical Exchange Rate Models of the Seventies: Do They Fit Out of Sample?" *Journal of International Economics* (Amsterdam), Vol. 14 (February 1983), pp. 3–24.

Mikesell, Raymond F., and Henry N. Goldstein, *Rules for a Floating-Rate Regime*, Essays in International Finance, No. 109 (Princeton, New Jersey: Princeton University Press, 1975).

Mussa, Michael, *The Role of Official Intervention*, Group of Thirty Occasional Paper, No.6 (New York: Group of Thirty, 1981).

———— "Empirical Regularities in the Behavior of Exchange Rates and Theories of the Foreign Exchange Market," in *Theory, Policy. Institutions: Papers from the Carnegie-Rochester Conferences on Public Policy*. ed. by Karl Brunner and Allan H. Meltzer (Amsterdam; New York: North-Holland, 1983), pp. 165–213.

Nurkse, Ragnar, *Conditions of International Monetary Equilibrium*, Essays in International Finance, No.4 (Princeton, New Jersey: Princeton University Press, 1945).

Obstfeld, Maurice, "Floating Exchange Rates: Performance and Prospects," *Brookings Papers on Economic Activity: 2* (1985). The Brookings Institution (Washington), pp. 369–464.

Polak, Jacques J., *Coordination of National Economic Policies*, Group of Thirty Occasional Paper, No. 7 (New York: Group of Thirty. 1981).

Roosa. Robert V., "How to Create Exchange Rate Target Zones." *Journal of Commerce* (New York), June 3, 1983, p. 3.

————, "Exchange Rate Arrangements in the Eighties." in Federal Reserve Bank of Boston, *The lmernational Monetary System: Forty Years After Bretton Woods* (Boston, May 1984), pp. 104–18.

Shafer, Jeffrey R., and Bonnie E. Loopesko, "Floating Exchange Rates After Ten Years," *Brookings Papers on Economic Activity: 1* (1983). The Brookings Institution (Washington), pp. 1–70.

Solomon, Anthony M., "International Coordination of Economic Policies: I. The Role of Economic Summitry; II. Coordinating Monetary Policy?" The David Horowitz Lectures at Tel Aviv University, Tel Aviv and Hebrew University, Jerusalem. March 4 and 5, 1982 (unpublished).

Solomon, Robert, *Reforming the Exchange-Rate Regime*, International Economic Letter, RS Associates. Inc. (Washington), Vol. 3. No. 7 (July 18, 1983).

Tobin, James, *A Proposal for lmernational Monetary Reform*, Cowles Foundation Discussion Paper No. 506. Cowles Foundation for Research in Economics (New Haven, Connecticut: Yale University Press, 1980).

Ungerer, Horst, Owen Evans and Peter Nyberg, *The European Monetary System: The Experience, 1979–82*, Occasional Paper No. 19 (Washington: International Monetary Fund, May 1983).

———, "The European Monetary System and the International Exchange Rate System" (unpublished, International Monetary Fund, January 19, 1984).

Willett, Thomas D., *Floating Exchange Rates and International Monetary Reform*, American Enterprise Institute Studies in Economic Policy (Washington: American Enterprise Institute for Public Policy Research, 1977).

Williamson, John. *The Exchange Rate System, Policy Analyses in International Economics: 5* (Washington: Institute for International Economics. 2nd ed., 1985).

Chapter 6

Managed Floating Plus

Morris Goldstein*

WHAT IS A MANAGED FLOATING PLUS REGIME?

Before making the case for managed floating plus as the "least worst" available currency regime option for emerging-market economies, it is necessary to spell out more concretely what the three aspects of such a regime would entail. First, I call it "managed" floating to indicate that, in contrast to pure floating, the authorities could use various policies to counter some short-term movements in the exchange rate. They would be permitted, for example, to intervene in the exchange market from time to time to "smooth" what they regarded as excessive short-term fluctuations in exchange rates or to maintain market liquidity.

Under managed floating, the authorities would not, however, attempt to use large-scale, sterilized exchange market interventions to alter the trend of the exchange rate, which would be determined by market forces. Nor would they attempt to even out almost all short-term volatility in the exchange rate, because such volatility serves to sharpen participants' awareness of market risk. The timing of interest rate movements decided on domestic grounds could be influenced by the exchange rate. The key constraint on allowing exchange rate considerations to influence interest rate decisions is that such external

---

*Morris Goldstein was the Dennis Weatherstone Senior Fellow at the Institute for International Economics when this paper was written.

considerations *not* put in jeopardy the primary objective of monetary policy: the achievement of a publicly announced inflation target.[1]

Second, I call the regime "floating" to signify that the authorities would have no publicly announced exchange rate target and that market forces would be the main determinant of exchange rates.[2]

Third, the "plus" aspect of managed floating plus has two components: an inflation-targeting regime for monetary policy, and an aggressive set of measures to reduce currency mismatching.

Following Bernanke *et al.* (1999), Mishkin (2000), and Truman (2001), I regard inflation targeting as a framework for monetary policy that constrains discretion in at least four key elements: (1) There is an institutional commitment to low inflation as a primary objective of monetary policy. (2) There is public announcement of a numerical target (or sequence of targets) for inflation, with a specified time *horizon* for meeting that target. (3) The central bank is given enough independence from political pressures and/or government directives that it can set the instruments of monetary policy as it sees fit in pursuit of its mandate. (4) The conduct of monetary policy is subject to transparency and accountability guidelines, so that the public is informed about both the reasons for monetary policy decisions and the extent to which the objectives of monetary policy have been attained.

Following the Financial Stability Forum (2000), I define a "currency mismatch" as a situation in which the currency denomination of a country's or sector's assets differs from that of its liabilities such that its net worth is sensitive to changes in the exchange rate.[3] Note that when considering currency mismatches on the part of financial intermediaries (especially banks),

---

[1] This constraint also applies more generally to efforts by the authorities to counter a perceived "misalignment" of the exchange rate, i.e., a departure of the actual exchange rate from its equilibrium level. When a conflict arises between the domestic and external requirements of monetary policy, the domestic requirement must be "king."

[2] Note that, in contrast to managed floating plus, most "intermediate" currency regimes (including a BBC regime) have a publicly announced target for the exchange rate.

[3] Some analysts combine currency, maturity, and liquidity mismatches into a wider concept of "balance sheet vulnerability" or "international illiquidity" — presumably because of the links among these mismatches in many emerging-market financial crises. E.g., Chang and Velasco (1999) regard international illiquidity as a situation in which actual or potential obligations in foreign currency exceed the amount of foreign currency that can be accessed on short notice; Dornbusch (1998) adopts a similar definition and calls it balance sheet vulnerability.

it is necessary to consider both their direct and indirect exposure to exchange rate changes, particularly the indirect exposure that comes about when their loan customers (nonfinancial corporations and others) have large currency mismatches. A depreciation of the local currency that renders many loan customers insolvent would impose large losses on banks, even if the currency denomination of bank loans matched that of bank deposits.[4]

Measures to discourage or limit currency mismatching span a wide field (see discussion below). They can range from allowing the exchange rate to move enough to continually remind market participants of currency risk, to publishing data on indicators of currency mismatching (e.g., the ratio of short-term external debt to international reserves, or currency composition of interbank loans), to regulatory provisions that limit banks' net open positions in foreign currency, to developing better hedging mechanisms and deeper capital markets in emerging-market economies, to proposing more draconian measures (e.g., prohibiting government borrowing in foreign currency, or making foreign currency obligations incurred by domestic residents unenforceable in domestic courts).[5]

Could one of these two components of the "plus" be discarded in the interest of streamlining the proposed currency regime? I do not think so. Indeed, I would argue that inflation targeting and anti-currency mismatching measures reinforce one another.

If nothing is done to discourage currency mismatching, it is unlikely that exchange rate considerations will consistently play second fiddle to low inflation in an inflation-targeting monetary policy.[6] Given the high degree of openness in most emerging-market economies and the extent to which

---

[4] Although it might be argued that such losses on bank loans should be classified as credit losses rather than currency mismatches, these losses would be regarded as currency mismatches under a broader definition that stresses the sensitivity of net worth (and net income) of banks to changes in the exchange rate.

[5] The theoretical literature on currency mismatching emphasizes several explanations, including lack of monetary policy credibility by the sovereign, implicit or explicit bailouts of mismatched private borrowers by the government or central bank, lack of domestic financial development in an emerging economy, and commitment or signaling problems on the part of domestic firms in an emerging-market economy; see Jeanne (2001).

[6] Mishkin (2000) argues similarly that inflation targeting may not be viable in partially dollarized economies unless prudential or supervisory practices make the system capable of withstanding exchange rate shocks.

liabilities are denominated in foreign currency, it is simply unrealistic to suppose that large exchange rate movements would be ignored. As was suggested above, although some policy actions to counter excessive short-term exchange rate movements can be reconciled with inflation targeting, only one nominal anchor can dominate an inflation-targeting strategy, and that anchor must be low inflation.

Without real progress on reducing currency mismatches, we would likely see a continuation of fear of floating on the part of emerging-market economies. In this connection, the empirical work of Hausmann, Panizza, and Stein (2000) suggests that the greater the dependence on foreign currency borrowing, the greater the fear of floating on the part of emerging economies. Moreover, Hausmann and his colleagues report that currency mismatching explains the cross-country variation in fear of floating better than cross-country differences in the pass-through of exchange rate changes into domestic prices. In short, if we want emerging economies to exercise monetary policy independence in pursuit of a low inflation objective, something has to be done to decrease their vulnerability to balance sheet crises linked to large currency mismatches.

By the same token, the successful implementation of inflation targeting in emerging-market economies should make it easier, ceteris paribus, to reduce currency mismatches. One of the reasons lenders outside the emerging economies seem to be reluctant to denominate a higher share of loans in the borrower's local currency is that this would place excessive currency risk on the lender. In my conversations with a group of large private creditors in the Group of Seven (G-7) countries, they maintained that currency risk was high because many emerging economies did not have a reliable monetary policy framework in place that would limit the prospect of strategic devaluation. Without such a policy framework, it became difficult (in the lenders' view) to price currency risk — more difficult (the lenders say) than pricing credit risk. An inflation-targeting framework that contained a credible commitment to low inflation should be responsive to this concern of foreign lenders. This in turn, should increase the supply of local currency-denominated loans from abroad and decrease the size of the currency-mismatching problem.

In addition, a lower rate of inflation should contribute to the development of greater financial depth in emerging-market economies, thereby potentially increasing the supply of local currency-denominated loans from domestic sources. In this connection, Caprio and Demirgüç-Kunt (1997) document that developing countries suffer from a shortage (relative to industrial countries) of long-term finance and find that one of the leading reasons for this shortage is high inflation and unstable macroeconomic policies. They conclude that "attempts to increase the supply of long-term credit to developing countries without addressing the inflation problem could easily prove to be short-lived or costly".

Similarly, Khan, Senhadji, and Smith (2001) argue that inflation impedes financial development by increasing the severity of adverse selection, moral hazard, and monitoring problems; in the process, higher inflation reduces the extension of bank credit and exacerbates credit rationing. Using a dataset for 168 countries (comprising both industrial and developing countries) and employing alternative indicators of financial depth (i.e., domestic credit to the private sector as a share of GDP, stock market capitalization as a share of GDP, private and public bond market capitalization as a share of GDP, and combinations of the above), and his colleagues find that after controlling for other factors, rates above the 3–6 percent range have a significant, negative threshold effect on financial development.

Last but not least, managed floating plus is meant to be a long-term currency regime for emerging-market economies that are heavily involved with private capital markets. Although, during a crisis, capital controls can create some breathing space within which to make policy adjustments, recent research suggests that over time their effectiveness diminishes and the costs associated with their implementation increase.[7] As such, capital controls are not included as part of the "plus."

THE CASE FOR MANAGED FLOATING PLUS

In advancing the case for managed floating plus, I maintain that even plain vanilla managed floating has some significant advantages that are worth retaining, and more important, that there are grounds for believing that the performance of a managed floating regime can be improved significantly when

---

[7] See Ishii, Otker-Robe, and Cui (2001) and Edison and Reinhart (2001) for supporting evidence on the effectiveness and costs of capital controls. Gupta, Mishra, and Sahay (2001) present evidence that large private capital flows, which can be detrimental to growth in a crisis environment, are beneficial for economic growth in the long run.

the plus elements are added to it.[8] One important advantage of plain vanilla floating — as was noted above — is the deterrent effect that daily fluctuations in the exchange rate should have on currency mismatching. As Mishkin (1996) argued, such fluctuations "have the advantage of making clear to firms, banks, and the government that there is substantial risk involved in issuing liabilities denominated in foreign currencies."

Recent empirical support for Mishkin's proposition has been provided in a paper by Martinez and Werner (2001). They examine the currency composition of corporate debt for firms listed on the Mexican Stock Exchange during the 1992–2000 period. They find that although the share of dollar debt in total debt increased from 34 to 49 percent under the floating rate regime the exposure to depreciation risk for the median firm decreased sharply as the ratio of dollar debt to exports fell from 3.9 in 1994 to 1.6 in 2000. In addition, they report that whereas firm size was the main factor explaining the share of dollar debt during the period of fixed exchange rates (with little attention paid to the distinction between foreign and domestic sales), exports became the only significant variable determining the importance of foreign currency (dollar) indebtedness during the floating rate regime. In short, in the Mexican case, floating seems to have been accompanied by better control of currency risk.[9]

---

[8] Larrain and Velasco (2001) provide a comprehensive review of the track record of floating rates in emerging-market economies.

[9] A very different conclusion on currency mismatching was obtained by Arteta (2001). He examines deposit and credit dollarization and their difference (the currency mismatch) on the part of banks in 40 developing economies and economies in transition during the 1990s. His main result is that, after controlling for other factors, the currency mismatch of banks is higher under floating rate regimes — a result that he seems to attribute to the higher cost of hedging under floating.

I do not find Arteta's conclusion persuasive, for three reasons. First, as is argued above and as is illustrated by the results of Martinez and Werner (2001), when considering currency risk for financial intermediaries, it is necessary to consider not only the direct exposure (measured, say, by the currency composition of bank deposits and bank loans) but also the indirect exposure related to currency risk incurred by bank loan customers (measured, say, by the ratio of dollar debt to exports and by the share of bank credit going to producers of tradables). Arteta's database does not apparently allow him to get a good fix on this indirect currency exposure of banks.

Second, though Arteta does control for whether or not foreign currency loans and deposits are allowed in a country, he does not control for specific prudential regulations for banks that limit currency mismatches; as is shown in Table 2 below, many developing countries have such regulations in effect.

A second advantage of floating rates worth retaining is the helpful "cushioning" role that exchange rate flexibility plays in the face of external real disturbances, including negative changes in the terms of trade. This of course remains a key concern for those developing countries in which primary products account for a large share of exports. In a study of the experience of 74 developing countries during the 1973–96 period, Broda (2000) found that output losses after negative terms-of-trade shocks were much smaller for countries with flexible rate regimes than for those with fixed rates.

A similar conclusion appears to apply to the post-Asian crisis experience. Here, Larrain and Velasco (2001) document that emerging-market economies with flexible rate regimes (Chile, Mexico, and Singapore) had a more favorable growth experience (as a group) in the 1998–2000 period than did the "hard peg" economies (Argentina and Hong Kong) — and this despite the fact that the former group (and especially Chile) was hit by more adverse terms-of-trade shocks. Ortiz (2000) reports that the correlation between (monthly) exchange rate changes and changes in the terms of trade switched from positive to negative when Mexico moved from an adjustable peg to a flexible exchange rate regime.

All this is also consistent with one of the relatively few robust conclusions that has come from bottom-line comparisons of economic performance under different currency regimes, namely, that emerging-market economies with flexible rates have typically shown higher average growth rates and/or lower volatility of economic growth than economies with fixed rates.[10]

Third, floating does seem to increase monetary policy independence. Although they acknowledge that the existing econometric evidence on monetary policy independence in emerging-market economies is mixed, Larrain and Velasco (2001) observe that once the estimating equations take careful note of the differences between de facto and de jure exchange rate flexibility and control for the influence of capital controls, floating does seem

---

Third, as Arteta acknowledges, his data do not cover off-balance-sheet currency exposure by banks; these also could affect the appropriate (more comprehensive) measurement of currency mismatch. Therefore, until we know whether Arteta's findings would be robust to inclusion of these factors, I regard the mainstream view of the link between currency regimes and currency mismatching (i.e., that mismatching will be lower, ceteris paribus, under floating rates) as the most plausible one.

[10]See, for example, Bailliu, Lafrance, and Perrault (2000).

to reduce the need to adjust domestic interest rates in response to interest rate movements abroad. This reinforces the well-known point emphasized above that a key advantage (or disadvantage) of flexible (fixed) rates remains the greater scope they provide for using independent monetary policy to deal with domestic cyclical conditions that differ from those in the reserve currency economy.

Even more to the main point of this book, managed floating plus should be able to deliver better economic performance than plain vanilla floating for emerging-market economies heavily involved with private capital markets. I base this conclusion on four arguments.

DEVALUATIONS AND SEVERE CURRENCY MISMATCHES

The first argument: If one seeks an explanation for the finding (highlighted, e.g., in Calvo and Reinhart 2001) that devaluations in developing countries have typically been more contractionary and have been associated with larger credit-rating downgrades than those in industrial countries, the most likely suspect is severe currency mismatches.[11]

By now, we have a set of theoretical models that demonstrates how the combination of large unhedged financial liabilities denominated in foreign currency (i.e., a large currency mismatch) and a large depreciation can play havoc with balance sheets, lead to a fall in creditworthiness, and produce both an output contraction and a financial crisis.[12] In addition, there have been enough recent real world examples linking currency mismatches to contractions or growth slowdowns to illustrate the connection. And recent empirical work also points to a link between currency mismatches and output contraction.

As is often noted, in the run-up to the crisis, almost all the Asian crisis countries (Indonesia, Malaysia, the Philippines, South Korea, and Thailand)

---

[11] It is worth noting that not all currency crises in emerging-market economies are contractionary. Examining a sample of 195 crisis episodes for 91 developing countries during the 1970–98 period, Gupta, Mishra, and Sahay (2001) found that more than 40 percent of crises have been expansionary; for the large emerging markets, the corresponding (expansionary) share of crises was 30 percent.

[12] See, e.g., Chang and Velasco (1999); Cespedes, Chang, and Velasco (2000); and Krugman (2001).

had relatively large and rising currency or liquidity mismatches (as indicated by ratios of short-term external debt to international reserves and of M2 money balances to reserves); and in 1998, they suffered unprecedented declines in growth rates.[13] Currency or liquidity matches also deteriorated in the run-up to the 1994–95 Mexican peso crisis and contributed to the deep recession experienced by Mexico in 1995.[14] Turkey's banks had a large currency mismatch before their crisis in 2000 and recent projections point to a deep contraction in the Turkish economy in 2001.[15]

In Latin America, currency or liquidity mismatches on the eve of the Asian crisis were on average much smaller and so too was the extent of the growth slowdowns. A plausible explanation for why Brazilian economic growth did not fall off the cliff in 1999 (it rose by 0.5 percent) in the face of a huge depreciation of the Brazilian real is that very large currency mismatches in the private sector had already been much reduced by the time the depreciation took place.[16] Concentrating on currency crises in the 1990s, Cavallo *et al.* (2001) find that output contractions were larger in countries with both large devaluations and high foreign currency debt burdens.

Gupta, Mishra, and Sahay (2001) looked at currency crises for a much larger sample of developing countries and a longer time period (1970–98). They report that output contractions are significantly related to some currency-mismatch or debt variables (short-term debt to reserves) but not to others (the change in the external long-term debt). In this case, however, potential multicollinearity problems may mean that some of the effects of currency mismatches are being picked up by other explanatory variables (e.g., the precrisis level of private capital inflows, much of which probably took the form of debt denominated in foreign currency). Finally, Berg and Patillo

---

[13] See Eichengreen and Hausmann (1999), Goldstein (1998), Change and Velasco (1999).

[14] See Calvo and Goldstein (1996) and Goldstein and Turner (1996) for measures of currency-liquidity mismatch in the run-up to the Mexican crisis.

[15] See Bank of England (2001) for net losses on foreign exchange transactions in Turkish banks. The IMF's *World Economic Outlook* for December 2001 estimates that the Turkish economy contracted by about 6 percent in 2001.

[16] See, e.g., Bevilaqua and Garcia (2000); in addition, Krugman (2000) speculates that the relatively good growth outcome in Brazil probably also reflected the relatively small size of the banking sector there.

(1999) suggest that currency mismatch variables rank relatively high as leading indicators of currency crises in emerging-market economies.

Another factor that probably contributed to the contractionary nature of many past devaluations in developing countries is a sharp decline in both confidence and capital inflows. Part of that decline, in turn, may stem from the problem that once a country was forced to abandon the nominal anchor of the exchange rate peg and had to let the exchange rate float, there was often no new credible nominal anchor to replace it (i.e., a monetary growth target was not viewed as a good commitment mechanism). And without such an anchor, there could only be a weak expectation that monetary stability would soon be restored.

The lesson I take away from this is that currency depreciations would become more expansionary in emerging-market economies if currency mismatches were much reduced in size. Establishing a credible nominal anchor (i.e., inflation targeting) to replace the nominal exchange rate would likely also help. This is of course just what managed floating plus seeks to do.

CURRENCY MISMATCHING AND CRISIS MANAGEMENT

The second argument: We should recognize that, as long as the currency-mismatching problem remains unattended to, crisis management in emerging-market economies — including the role of the IMF — will be in an uncomfortable box. Again, this was driven home dramatically during the Asian crisis. When there is a lot of (unhedged) debt denominated in foreign currency, the appeal of lowering domestic interest rates to alleviate the interest rate burden of highly leveraged firms and to counteract the anticipated contraction in the real economy needs to be weighed against (the worrisome prospect that lower interest rates could initiate a free fall of the currency and spawn a wave of bank failures and corporate insolvencies.

Conversely, raising interest rates to support the exchange rate threatens to exacerbate debt burdens and to reduce aggregate demand in the face of an already weakening economy. But if the currency mismatch is small, the prescription of lower interest rates is much easier to implement, because the adverse balance sheet effects of a lower exchange rate become less relevant than the traditional expenditure-switching effects of a depreciation. Because

Australia was not faced with a serious currency mismatching problem, during the Asian crisis it was able to lower interest rates and to allow the exchange rate to depreciate and to play its buffering role. As a result, the Australian economy grew by more than 5 percent in 1998.

Krueger (2000) has argued that until the international community finds a mechanism for preventing the buildup of foreign currency-denominated liabilities in the domestic financial systems of developing countries, the IMF's crisis role will be complex and difficult. Again, managed floating plus is aimed in good measure at reducing this crisis-management dilemma by addressing directly the currency-mismatching problem.

CURRENCY MISMATCHING AND MARKET IMPERFECTIONS

The third argument: I do not find persuasive the contention that the currency matching problem in emerging-market economies (what Eichengreen and Hausmann 1999 call "original sin") reflects a fundamental market imperfection that is here to stay.[17]

The fact that a thriving market for local currency-denominated borrowing (from abroad) does not presently exist for most emerging-market economies does not mean that such a market could not develop in the medium term. Recent history is replete with financial markets — ranging from asset-backed securities to credit derivatives — that did not exist for long periods but quite rapidly became sizable once they got off the ground. Creditors in industrial countries already engage in a wide variety of high-risk activities, including the purchase and underwriting of junk bonds.

It is hard to imagine that domestic currency lending to emerging-market economies is so "special" that its appropriate pricing will forever remain outside the realm of the feasible — especially if the threat of strategic

---

[17] More precisely, Eichengreen and Hausmann (1999) define "original sin" as "a situation in which the domestic currency cannot be used to borrow abroad or to borrow long term, even domestically" (p. 330). They argue that as long as "original sin" prevails, investments in emerging-market economies will inevitably carry either a currency mismatch or a maturity mismatch. Knight, Schembri, and Powell (2000) and Kenen (2001) conclude (as do I) that the "original sin" hypothesis is excessively pessimistic.

devaluation were reduced by the adoption of inflation-targeting regimes in more of the larger emerging economies and if the ongoing effort to strengthen domestic banking systems in developing countries were to produce more creditworthy counterparties. Australia and South Africa have long been able to borrow internationally in their own currencies (and now run floating rate regimes). It has to be admitted that both countries developed local markets early; but why is it such a great leap of faith to expect that large emerging economies with relatively good credit standings (e.g., Chile, China, Hungary, India, South Korea, Mexico, and Singapore) would soon be able to follow their example? Perhaps it took the Asian crisis to convince emerging-market economies of the high vulnerability associated with heavy reliance on foreign currency-denominated borrowing; indeed, popular indicators of currency mismatching (such as the ratio of short-term external debt to international reserves) now suggest smaller mismatches (in Asia) than in the 1996–98 period.

It should also be recognized that data on the currency composition of debt (which are typically used to document the presence of "original sin" in emerging-market economies) are not synonymous with currency mismatching in the presence of hedging markets. Table 1 (taken from Hawkins and Turner 2000) shows the currency composition of debt for both international bank loans and for international debt securities (as of the end of 1999). Unlike most studies, Table 1 also breaks down external debt by the type of borrower or issuer. It can be seen that emerging economies have much smaller shares of debt denominated in their own currency than do industrial countries, that domestic currency debt is more prevalent in emerging economies for international bank loans than for international debt securities, and that South Africa and Australia do indeed show (relative to the majority of emerging economies) high shares of debt denominated in domestic currency. But note that, for some types of borrowing, Hong Kong, Thailand, the Czech Republic, and Poland also show some nontrivial shares of domestic currency debt.

Even more to the point at hand, Table 1 gives the *original* currency composition of the debt — not the final composition. Suppose, for example, that a Polish or Czech corporation issues debt denominated in US dollars but would really prefer to have a debt denominated in local currency (i.e., Polish zlotys or Czech koruny). It might then swap out of the dollar debt into zloty or koruna debt (using the swap market); alternatively, it could hedge its exposure

Table 1: Share of External Debt Denominated in the Domestic Currency, end of 1999 (Percent)

	Loans From International Banks		International Debt Securities[a]		
Economy	Banks	Other Borrowers	Corporate Issuers	Financial Institutions	Public Sector
Argentina	5	0	3	1	2
Chile	8	0	0	0	0
China	0	9	0	0	0
Colombia	3	0	0	0	0
Czech Republic	23	5	0	0	0
Hong Kong	3	18	14	18	25
Hungary	4	1	0	0	0
India	9	2	0	0	0
Indonesia	0	7	2	0	0
Israel	1	1	0	0	0
Mexico	9	0	0	0	0
Peru	2	0	0	0	0
Poland	14	3	12	0	0
Russia	27	1	0	0	0
Saudi Arabia	4	3	0	0	0
South Africa	30	11	37	73	0
South Korea	2	8	0	0	0
Thailand	3	7	0	28	1
Venezuela	8	1	0	0	0
Memorandum:					
Australia	19	29	13	17	43
Canada	10	28	7	8	19
France	44	75	73	54	63
Germany	61	62	64	56	99
Japan	61	29	44	28	16
United Kingdom	10	26	44	36	13
United States	81	85	78	83	95

[a] By country of residence.

Note: For some emerging-market economies, the figures may be overestimates because it is assumed that all loans not denominated in a major currency are denominated in the domestic currency.

Source: Hawkins and Turner (2000).

by purchasing a forward exchange contract or a foreign exchange option.[18] The original currency composition of debt would then not be a reliable indicator of the ability to avoid a large currency mismatch.[19]

The existence of hedging markets would be only a minor technicality if these markets were tiny relative to hedging demand, if available maturity was very short, and if creditworthiness requirements were so stringent as to qualify only very few emerging-market borrowers. But in conversations with traders and market-makers, I did not get the impression that such a characterization fit what is happening on the ground, at least in some subset of emerging economies.[20] For example, one market participant who specializes in currency hedges for European emerging economies observed that if recent trends continue, the market for hedging instruments in Poland would soon (within a year or two) be larger than that in South Africa.

More broadly, discussions with market participants suggest that there is now a top tier of emerging-market economies where currency hedging facilities have relatively good liquidity and maturity. Without pretending to much precision, this top tier would include Hong Kong, Mexico, Poland, Singapore, and South Africa;[21] for a few of these economies, maturities on swaps could even go out as far as 5 to 10 years. A second tier would include Brazil, the Czech Republic, Hungary, South Korea, and Taiwan, where liquidity and other desirable market characteristics are improving but are not as good as in the top tier. Yet a third tier might encompass Argentina, Chile, Indonesia, Malaysia, Russia, Thailand, Turkey, and Venezuela. And so on.

---

[18] See Morales (2001) for a discussion of derivative instruments in the Czech Republic and Poland.

[19] In evaluating the original sin hypothesis, one also needs to take into account local currency denominated loans made in emerging economies by affiliates of foreign owned banks. These have become much more important relative to international bank loans during the past decade, see Goldstein and Turner (2002).

[20] See Goldstein and Turner (2002) for further discussion of hedging markets in emerging market economies.

[21] According to the most recent Bank for International Settlements survey of foreign exchange and derivative market activity, the emerging-market economy currencies with the highest (total) foreign exchange market turnover in (April) 2001 were (in descending order) Hong Kong dollar, Singapore dollar, South African rand, Mexican peso, Korean won, and Polish zloty. (Bank for International Settlements, "Central Bank Survey of Foreign Exchange and Derivatives Market Activity in April 2001: Preliminary Global Data," press release, Basle, October 2001.)

The hedging instruments that were available and/or are most in use seem to depend, inter alia, on an economy's capital market policies as well as on its macroeconomic and debt histories. For example, wherever emerging-market economies have adopted measures to limit the offshore trading of their currencies or to restrict capital flows, nondeliverable forwards were usually the hedging instrument of choice (rather than instruments that require actual delivery of the currency).[22] Where there has been a recent history of pronounced macroeconomic instability and where inflation rates are still relatively high, there are unlikely to be maturities available beyond, say, 1 year (and often shorter). Where relatively liquid bond and money markets exist and span much of the yield curve, one sees more interaction between currency and interest rate products. And where legal arrangements for attaching collateral and for efficient and creditor-friendly bankruptcy are weak, there is naturally more selectivity in choosing local counterparties for such hedging contracts.

My point is not to claim that the availability and cost of hedging currency risk in emerging markets are anywhere near as good as those in industrial countries. They clearly are not.[23] It is instead to argue that strict interpretations of the "original sin" hypothesis — which suggest that emerging markets find it impossible to hedge currency risk and/or that South Africa is the only emerging-market economy now able to borrow in its own currency — seem far too pessimistic about currency hedging possibilities (present and future).[24]

---

[22] See Ishii, Otker-Robe, and Cui (2001) on the use of such measures in Asian emerging-market economies.

[23] In one of the few studies comparing emerging-market currencies with G-3 currencies, Galati (2001) found that bid-ask spreads on a group of emerging-market currencies during the January 1998–June 1999 period were considerably higher and more volatile than those for the yen-dollar exchange rate. E.g., average spreads for the Mexican peso were about two and a half times higher than for the yen-dollar pair. Drawing on the 1995 Bank for International Settlements survey of foreign exchange market turnover, Koch (1997) reports that whereas about 40 percent of total turnover occurs in spot markets for industrial countries, the corresponding figure for emerging economies is closer to 75 percent (i.e., derivative markets are less developed for emerging economies than for industrial ones). Koch suggests that the share of turnover accounted for by derivative markets should rise over time for emerging economies.

[24] E.g., Eichengreen and Hausmann (1999, 330–31) argue as follows: "Critically, these mismatches exist not because banks and firms lack the prudence to hedge their exposures. The problem rather is that a country whose external liabilities are necessarily denominated in foreign exchange is, by definition, unable to hedge.... Similarly, the problem is not that firms simply lack the foresight to match the maturity structure of their assets and liabilities; it is that they find it impossible to do so." Hausmann, Panizza, and Stein (2000, 16) also observe

Although most of the market participants interviewed described hedging activity as "opportunistic" (i.e., as undertaken mainly on those occasions when participants expected the local currency to come under pressure), in an increasing number of emerging-market economies there seem to be markets and instruments available for those so inclined. Moreover, the distribution of hedging facilities (by liquidity, maturity, etc.) across emerging economies is better described as falling along a spectrum (or as dividing itself into tiers) rather than as conforming to a zero-one pattern (i.e., one or two emerging economies can do it but all others cannot).

Taking the argument a step farther, I do not believe the currency mismatching problem is largely beyond the control of emerging economies. There is a whole set of measures (beyond letting the exchange rate move) that could be taken to reduce the size and/or effects of such mismatches.

To begin with, prudential regulations on banks' open foreign exchange positions (relative to capital) could be tightened and enforced more consistently. As is shown in Table 2, many emerging-market economies have made use of such regulations. Although it is true that modern derivative and capital markets offer mechanisms for those wishing to evade such regulations and that there have been some notable cases of circumvention (see, e.g., Garber 1998), it is far from clear that more rigorous enforcement of those regulations is doomed to failure. Also, as Krugman (2000, 96) points out, there is a seeming inconsistency in arguing (as does the "original sin" hypothesis) that modern-day capital markets are too "imperfect" to hedge local currency risk but "perfect" enough to undo any regulations on foreign currency exposure:

> You can't assert that firms must borrow abroad in dollars because they lack the credibility or institutional means either to borrow in local currency or to hedge their dollar debts, and then at the same time assert that if dollar borrowing is discouraged those firms will borrow in local currency and hedge it back to a de facto dollar debt.

A more telling criticism is that regulations or capital charges on banks' open foreign exchange positions will not necessarily reduce crisis vulnerability

---

that "South Africa is the only developing country with a significant amount of debt securities denominated in its own currency."

Table 2: Foreign Exchange Regulations for Banks

Economy	Foreign Currency Exposure
Argentina	No formal guidelines; K requirement associated with foreign exchange position
Brazil	Limits on bought and sold positions. New policy will relate foreign exchange exposures to K requirements
Chile	Absolute weighted sum of net currency positions less than 20 percent of K, with weights reflecting currency volatility and ratings of the country of issuance
Colombia	OP between 5 and 20 percent
Czech Republic	OP in any currency should = 15 percent of K; OP of nonconvertible currency = 152 percent of K; overall OP = 20 percent of K
Hong Kong	Overnight OP (excluding HK$/US$ position) of local banks over 5 percent of K (15 percent for experienced institutions)
Hungary	Absolute sum of OPs = 30 percent of K
India	Bank must obtain approval for its OP limits
Indonesia	Maximum net OP 20 percent of K
Israel	No formal limits
Malaysia	Each bank has individual net OP limit
Mexico	Limit of 1.83 times core K
Peru	Net liabilities = 2.5 percent of K; net assets = 100 percent of K
Philippines	Maximum short position of 20 percent of K temporarily suspended; maximum long position of 5 percent
Poland	Limit of 15 percent K in any currency; limit of 30 percent for overall net position; limit of 40 percent for absolute sum of OPs
Russia	Maximum OP 30 percent of K
Saudi Arabia	No formal limits
Singapore	No normal limits; banks must establish, monitor, and report self-determined limits
South Africa	Maximum net OP 15 percent of K
South Korea	15 percent of K (overbought or oversold)
Thailand	Maximum overbought position of 15 percent of K; maximum oversold position of 15 percent
Venezuela	Maximum OP of 15 percent of K

K = capital
OP = open position
Source: Hawkins and Turner (1999).

if banks do not carefully monitor their clients' foreign exchange exposure.[25] Banks need to exercise particular oversight of dollar loans to firms in the nontradable sector because the latter do not earn foreign exchange.

In some cases, regulations on banks' currency exposure may induce corporations to borrow foreign currency directly. If corporations have big currency mismatches when a large devaluation takes place, they will become insolvent; and when they cannot pay, they also will not be able to repay their existing bank loans. Indonesia's banks were apparently reasonably hedged on the eve of the crisis, but Indonesian corporations took on heavy dollar exposure themselves; and when the exchange rate started falling, belated simultaneous action to hedge in the spot market only drove the rupiah down faster.

Some analysts have gone farther in advancing proposals to limit currency mismatching in the private sector. Krueger (2000), for example, has put forward two suggestions. The first is for emerging-market economies to make foreign currency obligations incurred by domestic entities within their borders unenforceable in domestic courts. This would shift foreign exchange risk to lenders in the industrial countries that are presumably better able to absorb and to manage that risk.

Krueger's second suggestion is that G-7 authorities could pass and enforce legislation that would require their financial institutions to accept liabilities abroad only if they were denominated in the emerging market's local currency; these G-7 financial institutions could then hedge their foreign exchange risk in the marketplace. My preference would be to see whether more rigorous prudential regulation and credit oversight of currency mismatches by banking supervisors and by commercial banks in emerging-market economies could pare down the size of the mismatching problem before considering the more radical proposals advanced by Krueger.

In some cases (e.g., the Mexican crisis of 1994–95), the primary source of the currency mismatching problem is government borrowing. Dooley (1997) has argued that because tax receipts are denominated in local currency and because the shadow price of increased financial crisis vulnerability

---

[25] Chang and Velasco (1999) argue that regulations forcing banks that borrow in a foreign currency to also lend in a foreign currency will be ineffective in reducing vulnerability to crises if this currency risk is simply passed on to firms in nontradable sector (which borrow in a foreign currency but receive revenues denominated in the local currency).

from currency mismatching is far higher than what could realistically be saved in market borrowing costs by denominating government debt in foreign currency, emerging-market economies should eschew foreign currency borrowing altogether (as do most G-7 countries).

In March of 2001, the IMF issued *Guidelines for Public Debt Management* (IMF 2001). Although this document recommends that debt managers "should carefully assess and manage the risks associated with foreign-currency and short-term or floating rate debt," and "should regularly conduct stress tests of the debt portfolio on the basis of the economic and financial shocks to which the government — and the country more generally — are potentially exposed," the report stops far short of either discouraging emerging markets from issuing foreign currency debt or even of suggesting what might be considered "excessive" reliance on foreign currency-denominated debt.

Before endorsing the more radical (Dooley) proposal of no foreign-currency-denominated foreign borrowing, I would like to see the IMF issue much tougher guidelines that put presumptive upper bounds on foreign currency-denominated borrowing in government debt management and then report on compliance with those guidelines in its Article IV and other surveillance reports. Both Alan Greenspan (1999) and Pablo Guidotti (1999), for example, have suggested that simple rules of thumb for reserve and foreign debt management be considered — such as having countries without a good track record of international borrowing maintain unencumbered foreign exchange reserves equal to meet all repayments and interest on foreign debt falling due during the next year.[26]

Although all such simple rules have problems (e.g., no account is taken of potential capital flight), they have the virtue of establishing a transparent, easily understood target and of focusing attention on noncompliance with that target. In view of the risks involved, the current IMF approach to government debt management seems both too general and too weak.

Dependence on foreign currency borrowing in the corporate sector would presumably be reduced if emerging economies could accelerate the development of domestic bond markets (for both government and private debt). This would increase the supply of local currency-denomination finance. Relative to GDP, bond markets are much smaller (and less liquid) in

---

[26] Guidotti was formerly a senior official in Argentina's Finance Ministry.

emerging-market economies than in industrial countries.[27] However, two of the key factors that have historically inhibited the development of bond markets in Latin America and in Asia — that is, bouts of high inflation and lack of government budget deficits, respectively — are likely to be much less important in the future.

Whereas average inflation rates in Latin America reached more than 600 percent in the second half of the 1980s and still stood at nearly 200 percent in the first half of the 1990s, that average fell to 14 percent for the 1996–2000 period; for 2001, the IMF (*World Economic Outlook*, May and December 2001) projected that average inflation would fall to about 6 percent. And those emerging-market economies in Asia that have suffered a crisis have had to issue large amounts of government bonds to help finance their bank recapitalization programs.[28] Because they serve as benchmarks, larger issues of government bonds ought to make it easier to price corporate debt.

As is detailed in Hawkins and Turner (2000), many emerging-market economies have also taken a variety of measures in recent years to make their bond markets more attractive. These measures include upgrading trading and settlement systems, making tax changes favorable to trading and interest income, introducing standard procedures to originate home mortgages, encouraging the use of international rating agencies, and promoting pension funds (to create natural buyers for long-term paper). It is noteworthy that in 2000 local market instruments accounted for the largest share (35 percent) of trading in emerging-market bonds — more than trading in either eurobonds (33 percent) or in Brady bonds (25 percent).[29]

Mexico's experience in managing a floating rate system during the past 6 years illustrates some of the measures that can be taken by emerging-market economies themselves to limit and to deal with currency mismatching

---

[27] See Karacadag and Shrivastava (2000); e.g., in 1995–97 the average ratio of total bond market capitalization (public plus private) to GDP was 90 percent for 12 industrial countries versus 20 percent for 43 emerging economies.

[28] According to data put together by the Emerging Markets Traders Association (EMTA 2001), only Hong Kong and South Korea appear in the top 10 list of the most-traded emerging-market bonds (and then only in 7th and 9th place, respectively). Note also that relative to Latin America, Asian emerging-market economies have relied more on bank loans and less on bonds in their external borrowing.

[29] See EMTA (2001).

problems.[30] In reviewing this experience, Ortiz (2000) highlights several points. He argues that the volatility of the exchange rate (under managed floating) reduces perceptions by the private sector of implicit guarantees and avoids one-sided bets against the currency. He recommends the development of derivative markets to allow domestic agents to better insure themselves against exchange rate movements. Peso-dollar futures and options are now actively traded on the Chicago Mercantile Exchange, and a domestic derivative market started operating in December 1998.[31]

As evidence that a flexible exchange rate regime increases incentives for firms to internalize the risks involved in foreign currency borrowing, Ortiz (2000) notes that (in August 1999) approximately 70 percent of corporate foreign currency debt was held by firms that export most of their products, and that these firms' annual ratio of sales to foreign debt had increased markedly (relative to that in 1991–94 under the adjustable peg regime). Regulations on foreign currency mismatches of banks were made more stringent, so that loans to nonexporting firms could no longer be accounted as full offsets to foreign currency liabilities; in measuring foreign currency exposure, different weights were assigned to bank assets of different quality.

The development of long-term markets for domestic debt was also encouraged to reduce currency or maturity mismatches. The Mexican government had for many years issued domestic long-term debt linked to the consumer price index, and in 1999 it started issuing domestic nominal debt with 3- and 5-year maturities. The World Bank issued a long-term bond denominated in Mexican pesos, and efforts continue to develop benchmarks for long-term private debt denominated in domestic currency.

The IMF can also do more to discourage large currency mismatches. As proposed in Goldstein (2001), every request for an IMF program should contain data on the extent of currency mismatching in the banking, corporate, and public sectors; analysis of the sustainability of these mismatches (including

---

[30] Mexico's efforts to reduce currency mismatching, though more extensive than those of other emerging-market economies, are not unique. E.g., Chile has long issued local currency indexed bonds, and many Asian emerging economies (in the wake of the Asian crisis) have taken measures to promote a local currency corporate bond market.

[31] Goldstein (1995) argues that the development of hedging instruments is one of the key reasons short-rate exchange rate variability has had such a small effect on trade volumes in industrial countries.

scenarios and stress tests of what the consequences of a devaluation of sizes x and y would be); and explicit conditions for reducing the mismatch (if the existing and/or prospective mismatch is judged to be too large). Furthermore, in its *World Economic Outlook* and its *International Capital Markets Report*, the IMF should be drawing attention on a regular basis to currency mismatches for all countries that have significant involvement with private international capital markets.

The Bank of England's *Financial Stability Review* has presented some summary figures on currency mismatches along these lines, and this work could profitably be extended by the IMF. If the existing data on currency mismatching are not adequate, the IMF or the Bank for International Settlements should immediately initiate plans to fill in those data gaps.[32] The more private market participants are aware of the magnitude of currency mismatching, the better the chances that corrective market pressures will be brought to bear before a crisis erupts.[33]

To sum up, the extent of currency mismatching on the part of emerging markets is not a given dictated by the imperfections of international capital markets. Nor is dollarization the only way to deal with such mismatches. If emerging economies and the international financial institutions regarded the currency mismatching problem as one of sufficiently high priority, the size of the problem could be much reduced. It will not happen overnight, but it can happen. In contrast to the second best approach of dollarization, managed floating plus seeks to address the root causes of balance sheet vulnerability and to pursue the first best policy prescription.

INFLATION TARGETING AS A NOMINAL ANCHOR

My fourth argument is that — though emerging-market experience with inflation targeting is still limited, and though it must be admitted that emerging-market economies face greater challenges in implementation than

---

[32] At present, the main data bottleneck on currency mismatching seems to be in the corporate sector. If banks do not have adequate information on currency risk for their customers, it would be useful to conduct surveys to get a handle on aggregate corporate exposure. Note that this would stop far short of regulating foreign currency borrowing in the private, nonfinancial sector.
[33] King (1999) argues along similar lines that when governments and markets alike are informed of the potential for future financing difficulties, they will have time to take preventive action.

industrial countries — there is good reason to believe that such targeting can serve as a good nominal anchor in most emerging economies that are heavily involved with private capital markets.

Chile and Israel began their transitions to full-fledged inflation targeting in 1990 and 1991, respectively.[34] Since then, a number of other emerging-market economies have joined in, including Brazil, the Czech Republic, Poland, South Africa, South Korea, and Thailand. Some analysts (Corbo, Moreno, and Schmidt-Hebbel 2001; Mishkin and Schmidt-Hebbel 2001; Truman 2001) have also classified Colombia, Mexico, and Peru as either "active" or "transition" inflation targeters. Moreover, the group of emerging markets seen as "potential" candidates for inflation targeting is larger still. For example, Truman's (2001) potential inflation targeting group includes Argentina, China, Ecuador, Hong Kong, Hungary, India, Indonesia, Malaysia, Nigeria, the Philippines, Romania, Singapore, Taiwan, Turkey, and Venezuela.

Those who champion the adoption of inflation targeting by emerging-market economies argue that it has significant advantages over other nominal anchors and competing monetary policy frameworks. Mishkin (2000), for example, points out that (unlike an exchange rate anchor) monetary policy under inflation targeting can respond appropriately to domestic considerations and shocks; that (unlike monetary targeting frameworks) inflation targeting does not presuppose a strong relationship between money and inflation (i.e., the monetary authority can use all available information in forecasting inflation); that (unlike eclectic monetary policy strategies) inflation targeting is highly transparent and more easily understood by the public; that (unlike fully discretionary monetary policy frameworks) inflation targeting avoids the time-inconsistency trap; and that (unlike frameworks underpinned by broad mandates) inflation targeting focuses on what the monetary authority can do (i.e., control inflation) — not on what it cannot do.

Skeptics — though not necessarily rejecting the advantages of inflation targeting — stress that an inflation targeting regime also has disadvantages and that the requirements for the successful implementation of inflation targeting are less likely to be satisfied in many or even most emerging-market economies. As Truman (2001) and others argue, inflation (unlike, say, the monetary base)

---

[34]These are the dates of their announcements of a first inflation target; see Schaechter, Stone, and Zelmer (2000).

is not under the direct control of the central bank — particularly when the authorities are trying to bring it down from a high level. Corbo, Moreno, and Schmidt-Hebbel (2001) acknowledge that it takes much longer for inflation rates to stabilize when the initial inflation rate is high (say, 20 percent or more); for example it took about 9 years from the inception of inflation targeting for the inflation rate to stabilize in Chile; it took about 6 years in Israel.

Many advocates of inflation targeting concede that the long lag between monetary instruments and outcomes blunts the accountability of an inflation targeting framework. Masson, Savastano, and Sharma (1997) maintain that prospects for the successful implementation of inflation targeting are dim in most developing countries because seigniorage remains an important source of fiscal revenue (i.e., contributing to so-called fiscal dominance over monetary policy) and because there is no consensus that attaining low inflation should be the overriding objective of monetary policy; they point out that measures of central bank independence are typically much lower in emerging markets than in industrial countries. Masson and his colleagues also report the results of an IMF staff survey that concluded that (at least in 1997) only 5 of 150 developing economies and economies in transition would be good candidates for inflation targeting.

Continuing the same line of argument, other writers argue that

- the transmission mechanism of monetary policy is less well understood in emerging-market economies than in industrial countries,
- other necessary elements in the institutional preparation for inflation targeting (e.g., monitoring of incoming data, evaluation of inflation forecasts) are also lacking in many emerging economies,
- the relatively high fragility of the financial sector and the relatively high pass-through of exchange rate changes into domestic prices make attainment of low inflation objectives less likely,
- more rapid structural change and partial dollarization impede the ability to forecast inflation accurately,
- the greater concern for exchange rate movements (fear of floating) will prevent the low-inflation objective from being "king" of monetary policy,
- the higher incidence of government-controlled prices and of supply shocks will complicate the choice of appropriate price indices for measuring inflation, and

- short target horizons and narrow bands are likely to produce "instrument instability" and/or excessive output losses.[35]

The response to these criticisms of inflation targeting for emerging markets has taken a variety of forms. It has been argued that many of the problems raised are less serious today than even 5 years ago, and that some of the alleged "required preconditions" for the successful implementation of inflation targeting also apply to other currency regimes and/or monetary frameworks, whereas the importance of some others has been exaggerated (as evidenced by several successful counterexamples). In addition, supporters of inflation targeting note that some accommodation in the design of the inflation targeting framework can be made to lessen the handicaps or special problems of emerging economies, and that "warts and all," the overall performance to date of inflation targeting in these emerging economies has been quite good.

As was noted above, one of the striking developments of the 1990s was the sharp decline in inflation among emerging markets. According to the IMF's figures (*World Economic Outlook*, May 2001), average inflation rates in emerging-market economies fell from triple-digit numbers in the late 1980s to less than 8 percent in 2000; if a few outliers (Bulgaria Indonesia, Turkey, and Venezuela) are excluded, the average inflation rate in 2000 would be 5 percent. This means that most emerging economies considering a move to inflation targeting could begin at an initial inflation rate much lower than 5 to 6 years ago.

Reliance on seigniorage has likewise fallen, reducing the risk of fiscal dominance of monetary policy. And for those emerging-market economies that would have to start from a high inflation rate, Chile's experience should be encouraging: A gradual but consistent application of the inflation-targeting regime (beginning with just inflation projections and then formalizing and tightening the inflation target as credibility was earned) yielded a significant reduction in inflation (from more than 20 percent in 1991 to about 3.5 percent in 1999–2001), while maintaining good growth performance. The greater volatility of inflation rates in emerging economies can be compensated for by

---

[35] Many of these criticisms are discussed in Corbo, Moreno, and Schmidt-Hebbel (2001); Mishkin (2000); Mishkin and Schmidt-Hebbel (2001); Schaechter, Stone, and Zelmer (2001); and Truman (2001). Also see the IMF's *World Economic Outlook*, May 2001.

(at least initially) making the target ranges for inflation somewhat wider than in industrial countries.

Central bank independence in emerging-market economies has increased along with the decline in inflation rates. Mishkin (2000) argues that central bank independence and inflation targeting (with the latter's heavy emphasis on transparency and accountability in monetary policy) have been mutually reinforcing.

As long as the exchange rate does not challenge the primacy of the low inflation objective, emerging-market economies practicing inflation targeting can engage in some smoothing and leaning-against-the-wind operations in the exchange market. Indeed, a few economies (Chile, Israel, and Poland) have even made a successful transition from crawling exchange rate bands to a floating rate combined with inflation targeting.

Although exchange rate pass-through effects are generally found to be significantly higher in emerging economies than in industrial countries the IMF (*World Economic Outlook*, May 2001) and others report that the size of these pass-throughs also fell sharply in the 1990s — to an average of roughly 20 percent during 1 year and perhaps 25–50 percent during 2 years.[36] Output contractions after the devaluation, and relatively low inflation and appreciated real exchange rates before it, seem to explain these relatively encouraging pass-through outcomes.

With some scope under inflation targeting for both smoothing exchange rate movements and paying attention to currency mismatches, and with lower than expected pass-throughs of exchange rate changes, the probability that the implementation of targeting would be thrown off course by exchange rate concerns has been reduced.

Financial-sector fragility and a lack of fiscal prudence are always impediments to the conduct of monetary policy and/or to the performance of the exchange rate regime; there is no reason to believe that inflation targeting is going to be any less successful than competing regimes in the presence of financial-sector or fiscal policy problems. Likewise, and as was argued above, a regime of managed floating plus inflation targeting is likely to cope

---

[36] These pass-through figures apply to the 1990s group averages for the devaluations in Brazil, Indonesia, Malaysia, Mexico, the Philippines, South Korea, and Thailand; see IMF, *World Economic Outlook*, May 2001.

better with external volatility and external shocks than less flexible currency regimes.

Consider, for example, the shocks faced by Brazil (from Argentina and otherwise) during 2001; would any regime (other than managed floating combined with inflation targeting) still be left standing? Rapid structural change in emerging markets will not only make it harder to control and to forecast inflation; it will also make it harder to gauge appropriate monetary growth targets (under a monetary targeting regime) or to calculate the equilibrium exchange rate under publicly announced exchange rate targets (in adjustable peg or BBC regimes).

Potential instrument instability under an inflation-targeting regime can be avoided or minimized in two ways. First, the maturity (length) of inflation targets can be set close to the estimated time lag in the effect of monetary policy on inflation. Second, the target range specified for inflation should not be too narrow.[37]

Although sound underlying conditions and good institutional preparation make any monetary policy or currency regime work better, it is easy to overstate the necessary preconditions for implementation. As Mishkin and Schmidt-Hebbel (2001) note, the Bank of England began implementation of inflation targeting before it had full instrument independence, some countries that use inflation targeting (e.g., Colombia, South Africa) still do not publish inflation forecasts, and Brazil implemented inflation targeting with most of the bells and whistles within 4 months of announcing its intention to do so — and this in the face of both formidable fiscal and debt problems and a good deal of exchange rate volatility.

Schaechter, Stone, and Zelmer (2000) conclude that (relative to industrial countries) emerging-market economies

- have opted for more formal institutional frameworks in support of inflation targeting (e.g., usually granting formal independence to the central bank before adopting targeting),
- have relied less on statistical models in the conduct of monetary policy,
- have intervened more frequently in foreign exchange markets,
- have adopted inflation targets with shorter time horizons, and
- have preferred bands to point (inflation) targets.

---

[37] See Mishkin and Schmidt-Hebbel (2001).

Perhaps most telling, most analytical reviews of inflation-targeting experience in emerging markets give it relatively high marks.[38] More specifically, most studies conclude that countries adopting inflation targeting have been relatively successful in meeting their announced inflation targets; that the track record on meeting inflation targets has been much better than that in meeting announced monetary growth targets; and that inflation targeting is associated with reduced expectations of inflation and with lower inflation forecast errors. They also conclude that countries adopting inflation targeting are not "inflation nutters" (to borrow a term from Mervyn King), that is, they still allow monetary policy to respond to falls in output; that "sacrifice ratios" (i.e., the change in output associated with a 1 percent fall in inflation) are more favorable after the adoption of inflation targeting than before and more favorable than under monetary targeting (but not as good as under exchange rate-based stabilizations); and that inflation targeting has rarely been associated with a subsequent loss of fiscal prudence.

A final piece of evidence supporting the effectiveness of inflation targeting as a nominal anchor comes from a recent study by Kuttner and Posen (2001). Two features of their work differentiate it from other "bottom-line" regime comparisons. First, the authors compare the effects not only of alternative currency regimes (hard fix, soft fix, float) but also of alternative monetary policy regimes (narrow money target, broad money target, inflation targeting, and other) and of different degrees of central bank independence. Second, they measure the effects of alternative monetary frameworks (where such a "framework" is a combination of a currency regime, a monetary policy regime, and a degree of central bank independence) not only on the variability of the nominal exchange rate the average level of inflation but also on the persistence of inflation (where "persistence" refers to the extent to which inflation returns to its target after an inflation shock occurs).

The advantage of looking at currency regimes and monetary policy regimes simultaneously is that it allows their separate effects to be disentangled. The advantage of using inflation persistence as a metric is that (unlike the average inflation rate) it should normalize for the different incidence of shocks across

---

[38] See IMF, *World Economic Outlook*, May 2001; Corbo, Moreno, and Schmidt-Hebbel (2001); Mishkin (2000); Mishkin and Schmidt-Hebbel (2001); and Schaechter, Stone, and Zelmer (2000). Truman (2001) arrives at a more mixed overall verdict.

time periods. Kuttner and Posen's (2001) data sample covers 124 monetary frameworks in 41 countries (including members of the Organization for Economic Cooperation and Development and countries in Latin America and East Asia) during the 1973–2000 period.

Three findings of Kuttner and Posen's (2001) study are relevant Soft pegs reduce the level of inflation and attenuate exchange rate fluctuations but are characterized by large devaluations. Central bank autonomy is associated with both a more stable exchange rate and a lower level of inflation. And inflation targeting is the only monetary policy regime associated with both lower inflation and lower inflation persistence. In the end, Kuttner and Posen conclude that a monetary framework that combined a floating exchange rate, inflation targeting, and central bank autonomy (i.e., two thirds of managed floating plus) might offer the same anti-inflation benefits as an exchange rate peg on its own, without the proclivity to occasional large depreciations.

To sum up, inflation targeting is hardly a panacea for all the ills that currently beset emerging-market economies. Yet on the basis of the experience gained thus far, inflation targeting does appear to be a good nominal anchor and better than either of the leading alternatives (i.e., monetary targeting under a floating rate or an exchange rate peg of one kind or another).

CONCLUDING REMARKS

Given the number of serious currency crises in emerging-market economies during the past 7 years, it makes no sense to talk about reforming the international financial architecture without addressing currency regimes. Adjustable peg and crawling band regimes are just too fragile for a world of large and sudden shifts in private capital flows and of sometime serious slippages in economic policy reform. Currency boards and dollarization solve some problems but are impotent in dealing with Argentina-type crises characterized by recession, an overvalued real exchange, limited flexibility of domestic costs and prices, and too much public debt to permit countercyclical fiscal policy. And plain vanilla floating has limited appeal to many emerging economies because of their balance sheet vulnerability to large exchange rate changes and because of their dissatisfaction with monetary targeting as a nominal anchor.

The best of the currency regime options is managed floating plus. It would give emerging-market economies a deterrent to currency mismatching and to balance sheet vulnerability, a much reduced fear of floating, enough monetary independence to engage in gross-timing of monetary policy to counter recessions, sufficient "flex" to deal with large shifts in capital flows, and a workable nominal anchor to control inflation. If not managed floating plus, tell me what will work better?

"Managed Floating Plus" from *Managed Floating Plus*, by Morris Goldstein, pp. 43–75 (2002). Peterson Institute for International Economics. Used with permission of the publisher.

REFERENCES

Arteta, Carlos. 2001. Exchange Rate Regimes and Financial Dollarization: Does Flexibility Reduce Bank Currency Mismatches? University of California, Berkeley. Photocopy (November).

Bailliu, Jeannine, Robert Lafrance, and Jean-Francois Perrault. 2000. Exchange Rate Regimes and Economic Growth in Emerging Markets. Bank of Canada, Ottawa. Unpublished (November).

Bank of England. 2001. *Financial Stability Review.* Bank of England, London (December).

Berg, Andrew, and Catherine Patillo. 1999. *Are Currency Crises Predictable? A Test.* IMF Staff Papers 46, no. 2 (June): 107–38.

Bernanke, Ben, Thomas Laubach, Frederic Mishkin, and Adam Posen. 1999. *Inflation Targeting: Lessons from the International Experience*. Princeton, NJ: Princeton University Press.

Bevilaqua, Alfonso, and Marcio Garcia. 2000. *Debt Management in Brazil: Evaluation of the Real Plan and Challenges Ahead.* World Bank Policy Research Paper 2402. Washington: World Bank.

Broda, C. 2000. Terms of Trade and Exchange Rate Regimes in Developing Countries. Massachusetts Institute of Technology, Cambridge. Photocopy.

Calvo, Guillermo, and Morris Goldstein. 1996. What Role for the Official Sector? In *Private Capital Flows to Emerging Markets After the Mexican Crisis,* eds. Guillermo Calvo Morris Goldstein, and Eduard Hochreiter. Washington: Institute for International Economics.

Calvo, Guillermo, and Carmen Reinhart. 2001. Fixing for Your Life. In *Brookings Trade Policy Forum 2000: Policy Challenges in the Next Millennium*. Washington: Brookings Institution.

Caprio, Gerard, and Asli Demirgüç-Kunt. 1997. *The Role of Long Term Finance: Theory and Evidence*. Policy Research Department Working Paper. Washington: World Bank.

Cavallo, Michele, Fabrizio Perri, Nouriel Roubini, and Kate Schneider-Kisselev. 2001. Exchange Rate Overshooting and the Costs of Floating. New York University, New York. Photocopy (November).

Cespedes, Luis, Roberto Chang, and Andres Velasco. 2000. *Balance Sheets and Exchange Rate Policy.* NBER Working Paper 7840. Cambridge, MA: National Bureau of Economic Research.

Chang, Roberto, and Andres Velasco. 1999. *Liquidity Crises in Emerging Markets: Theory and Policy.* NBER Working Paper 7272. Cambridge, MA: National Bureau of Economic Research.

Corbo, Vittorio, Oscar Moreno, and Klaus Schmidt-Hebbel. 2001. Assessing Inflation Targeting after a Decade of World Experience. Central Bank of Chile, Santiago. Photocopy (March).

Dooley, Michael. 1997. Governments' Debt and Asset Management and Financial Crises. In *Risk Management of Sovereign Assets and Liabilities,* eds. Marcel Cassard and David Folkerts-Landau. Washington: International Monetary Fund (December).

Dornbusch, Rudiger. 1998. After Asia: New Directions for the International Financial System. Massachusetts Institute of Technology, Cambridge. Photocopy (July).

Edison, Hali, and Carmen Reinhart. 2001. Stopping Hot Money. *Journal of Development Economics* 66, 533–53.

Eichengreen, Barry, and Ricardo Hausmann. 1999. Exchange Rates and Financial Fragility. In *New Challenges for Monetary Policy,* 329–68. Kansas City: Federal Reserve Bank of Kansas City.

Emerging Markets Traders Association (EMTA). 2001. *EMTA Survey, Third Quarter 2001.* New York: EMTA.

Financial Stability Forum. 2000. *Report of the Working Group on Capital Flows.* Basle: Financial Stability Forum.

Galati, Gabriele. 2001. Trading Volumes, Volatility, and Spreads: Evidence from Emerging Market Countries. *Market Liquidity: Proceedings of a Workshop Held at the BIS,* BIS Papers, no. 2. Basle: Bank for International Settlements (April).

Garber, Peter. 1998. *Derivatives in International Capital Flows.* NBER Working Paper 6623. Cambridge, MA: National Bureau of Economic Research.

Goldstein, Morris. 1995. *The Exchange Rate System and the IMF: A Modest Agenda.* Policy Analyses in International Economics 39. Washington: Institute for International Economics.

Goldstein, Morris. 1998. *The Asian Financial Crisis: Causes, Consequences, and Systemic Implications.* Policy Analyses in International Economics 55. Washington: Institute for International Economics.

Goldstein, Morris, and Philip Turner. 1996. *Banking Crises in Emerging Economies: Origins and Policy Options.* BIS Economic Papers 46. Basle: Bank for International Settlements.

Goldstein, Morris, and Philip Turner. 2002. *Currency Mismatching in Emerging Economies.* Bank for International Settlements, Basle.
Greenspan, Alan. 1999. Currency Markets and Debt. Remarks at a World Bank conference on recent trends in reserve management, Washington (29 April).
Guidotti, Pablo. 1999. Remarks at a G-33 seminar, Bonn (April).
Gupta, Poonam, Deepak Mishra, and Ratna Sahay. 2001. Output Responses to Currency Crises. Paper presented at an IMF research conference, Washington (29–30 November).
Hausmann, Ricardo, Ugo Panizza, and Ernesto Stein. 2000. *Why Do Countries Float the Way They Float?* IDB Working Paper 418. Washington: Inter-American Development Bank.
Hawkins, John, and Philip Turner. 2000. Managing Foreign Debt and Liquidity Crises in Emerging Economies: An Overview. In *Managing Foreign Debt and Liquidity Risks.* Basle: Bank for International Settlements.
IMF (International Monetary Fund). 2001. Guidelines for Public Debt Management. *World Economic Outlook* (May). Washington: International Monetary Fund.
Ishii, Shogo, Inci Otker-Robe, and Li Cui. 2001. *Measures to Limit the Offshore Use of Currencies: Pros and Cons.* IMF Working Paper 01/43. Washington: International Monetary Fund.
Jeanne, Olivier. 2001. Why Do Emerging Economies Borrow in Foreign Currency? International Monetary Fund, Washington. Photocopy (October).
Karacadag, Cem, and Animesh Shrivastava. 2000. *The Role of Subordinated Debt in Market Discipline: The Case of Emerging Markets.* IMF Working Paper 00/215. Washington: International Monetary Fund.
Kenen, Peter. 2001. *The International Architecture: What's New, What's Missing?* Washington: Institute for International Economics.
Khan, Mohsin, Abdelhak Senhadji, and Bruce Smith. 2001. *Inflation and Financial Depth.* IMF Working Paper 01/44. Washington: International Monetary Fund.
King, Mervyn. 1999. Reforming the International Financial System: The Middle Way. Bank of England, *Financial Stability Review* 7 (November): 203–11.
Knight, Malcolm, Lawrence Schembri, and James Powell. 2000. Reforming the Global Financial Architecture: Just Tinkering around the Edges? Paper presented at a conference on reforming the architecture of global economic institutions sponsored by the Bank of England, London (5–6 May).
Koch, Elmar. 1997. *Exchange Rates and Monetary Policy in Central Europe: A Survey of Some issues.* Working Paper 24. Vienna: Oesterreichische Nationalbank.
Krueger, Anne. 2000. Conflicting Demands on the International Monetary Fund. *American Economic Review* 90, no. 2 (May): 38–42.
Krugman, Paul. 2000. Crises: The Price of Globalization? In *Global Economic Integration: Opportunities and Challenges.* Kansas City: Federal Reserve Bank of Kansas City.

Krugman, Paul. 2001. Crises: The Next Generation. Paper prepared for the Razin Conference sponsored by Tel Aviv University, Tel Aviv (25–26 March).

Kuttner, Kenneth, and Adam Posen. 2001. Beyond Bipolar: A Three-Dimensional Assessment of Monetary Frameworks. *International Journal of Finance and Economics* 6, no. 4 (May): 369–87.

Larrain, Felipe, and Andres Velasco. 2001. Exchange Rate Policy in Emerging Markets: The Case for Floating. Harvard University, Cambridge. Photocopy (April).

Martinez, Lorenza, and Alejandro Werner. 2001. The Exchange Rate Regime and the Currency Composition of Debt: The Mexican Experience. Paper presented at an National Bureau of Economic Research inter-American seminar on economics, Banco de Mexico, Mexico City (20–21 July).

Masson, Paul, Miguel Savastano, and Sunil Sharma. 1997. *The Scope for Inflation Targeting in Developing Countries.* IMF Working Paper 97/130. Washington: International Monetary Fund.

Mishkin, Frederic. 1996. *Understanding Financial Crises: A Developing Country Perspective.* NBER Working Paper 5600. Cambridge, MA: National Bureau of Economic Research.

Mishkin, Frederick. 2000. Inflation Targeting in Emerging-Market Countries. *American Economic Review* 90, no. 2 (May): 105–109.

Mishkin, Frederic, and Klaus Schmidt-Hebbel. 2001. *One Decade of Inflation Targeting in the World: What Do We Know and What Do We Need to Know?* NBER Working Faper 8397. Cambridge, MA: National Bureau of Economic Research.

Morales, R. Armando. 2001. *Czech Koruna and Polish Zloty: Spot and Currency Option Volatility Patterns.* IMF Working Paper 01/120. Washington: International Monetary Fund.

Ortiz, Guillermo. 2000. Commentary: How Should Monetary Policymakers React to the New Challenges for Global Economic Integration? In *Global Economic Integration: Opportunities and Challenges.* Kansas City: Federal Reserve Bank of Kansas City.

Schaechter, Andrea, Mark Stone, and Mark Zelmer. 2000. *Adopting Inflation Targeting: Practical Issues for Emerging Market Countries.* IMF Occasional Paper 202. Washington: International Monetary Fund.

Truman, Edwin. 2001. *Inflation Targeting and the International Financial System: Panacea or Poison Pill?* Washington: Institute for International Economics.

Chapter 7

The Rationale for, and Effects of, International Economic Policy Coordination

Jacob A. Frenkel, Morris Goldstein, and Paul R. Masson

Coordination of macroeconomic policies is certainly not easy; maybe it is impossible. But in its absence, I suspect nationalistic solutions will be sought — trade barriers, capital controls, and dual exchange-rate systems. War among nations with these weapons is likely to be mutually destructive. Eventually, they, too, would evoke agitation for international coordination.

James Tobin (1987, 68)

I believe that many of the claimed advantages of cooperation and coordination are wrong, that there are substantial risks and disadvantages to the types of coordination that are envisioned, and that an emphasis on

---

Jacob A. Frenkel is the Economic Counsellor and Director of Research at the International Monetary Fund, and a research associate of the National Bureau of Economic Research. Morris Goldstein is Deputy Director of the Research Department of the International Monetary Fund. Paul R. Masson is an Advisor in the Research Department of the International Monetary Fund, and a research affiliate of the National Bureau of Economic Research.
The views expressed are the authors' alone and do not represent the views of the International Monetary Fund.

international coordination can distract attention from the necessary changes in domestic policy.

Martin Feldstein (1988, 3)

1. INTRODUCTION

This paper discusses the rationale and mechanisms for, and the effects of, international coordination of economic policies. Coordination is defined here, following Wallich (1984, 85), as "a significant modification of national policies in recognition of international economic interdependence."[1] The existence of a number of comprehensive surveys of the literature on coordination makes the task easier.[2] This discussion can, therefore, be selective and focus on a number of key issues that impinge on the advisability and practicality of strengthening policy coordination among the larger industrial countries.

This paper is organized as follows. Section 2 covers economic policy coordination in the widest sense and addresses various dimensions of the rationale for, and scope of, coordination. The terrain covered includes the applicability of the "invisible hand" paradigm to decentralized economic policy decisions, barriers to coordination, the range and specificity of policies to be coordinated, the frequency of coordination, and the number of participants to be included in the coordination exercise. Section 3 narrows the discussion to monetary and fiscal policies and turns to the mechanisms or methods of coordination. The emphasis here is on the two broad issues of rules versus discretion and of single-indicator versus multiple-indicator approaches.[3] A brief discussion is also included on the use of indicators in the ongoing Group of Seven (G-7) coordination process.

Section 4 confronts the problem of how to infer the effects of coordination. A number of empirical experiments are carried out using a global macroeconomic model (MULTIMOD) developed in the International Monetary Fund. The policies considered include nominal GNP or money targeting, "smoothing" rules for monetary and fiscal policy that imply only modest international coordination, and more activist "target-zone" proposals that place greater international conditions on national authorities in the conduct of monetary and/or fiscal policies. In one set of "historical" simulations, we compare the results of simulated policies to the actual evolution of the world economy over the 1974–87 period. In the other set of simulations, we analyze the effects of various single shocks to particular behavioral relationships under alternative policy rules.

2. RATIONALE FOR AND SCOPE OF COORDINATION

The most logical starting point is to ask why international policy coordination would be beneficial in the first place. After all, if in the domestic economy the working of the invisible hand under pure competition translates independent decentralized decisions into a social optimum, why should not the same principle apply to policy decisions by countries in the world economy?

The answer is that economic policy actions, particularly those of larger countries, create quantitatively significant spillover effects or externalities for other countries, and that a global optimum requires that such externalities be taken into account in the decision-making calculus.[4] Coordination is then best seen as a facilitating mechanism for internalizing these externalities.

This conclusion can perhaps be better appreciated by emphasizing the departures from the competitive model in today's global economy. Cooper (1987) has identified several such departures, and his analysis merits some extension here.

Unlike the atomistic economic agents of the competitive model who base their consumption and production decisions on prices that are beyond their control, larger countries exercise a certain degree of influence over prices, including the real exchange rate. This of course raises the specter that they will manipulate such prices to their own advantage and at the expense of others. Two examples are frequently cited — one dealing with inflation, and the other with real output and employment. Under floating rates, a Mundellian (1971) policy mix of tight monetary and loose fiscal policy allows an appreciated currency to enhance a country's disinflationary policy strategy — but at the cost of making it harder for trading partners to realize their own disinflation targets. Similarly, under conditions of high capital mobility and sticky nominal wages, a monetary expansion under floating rates leads to a real depreciation and to an expansion of output and employment at home. But the flip side of the coin is that output and employment contract abroad.[5] Seen in this light, the role of coordination is to prevent — or to minimize — such intentional as well as unintentional "beggar-thy-neighbor" practices. Most international monetary constitutions have injunctions against "manipulating" exchange rates or international reserves.

The existence of public goods constitutes a second important point of departure from the competitive model.

When there are N currencies, there can be only $N - 1$ independent exchange rate targets. Similarly, not all countries can achieve independently set targets for current account surpluses. Adherents of decentralized policymaking — sometimes rather inappropriately labelled the "German school" — argue that such inconsistencies provide no justification for coordination. Much as in the competitive model, the economic system will generate signals — in the form of changes in exchange rates, interest rates, prices, and incomes — that will lead to an adjustment of targets such that they eventually become consistent. If, however, the path to consistency involves large swings in real exchange rates, or even more problematically, the imposition of restrictions on trade and capital flows, then reliance on decentralized policymaking may not be globally optimal. Implicit in this conclusion is the notion that a certain degree of stability in real exchange rates and an open international trading and financial system are valued in and of themselves as public goods (in contrast, the market signals that resolve supply/demand inconsistencies in the competitive model, are not regarded as public goods). If that is accepted, there is a positive role for coordination, both to identify target inconsistencies at an early stage and to resolve them in ways that do not produce too little of the public good(s).[6] It is of course possible for groups of countries who value the public good highly to attempt to obtain more of it by setting up "regional" zones of exchange rate stability or of free trade, and some have done just that (including the establishment of the European Monetary System [EMS]).[7] But the essence of a public good is that it will tend to be *under*supplied so long as some large suppliers or users act in a decentralized fashion.

Once the realm of atomistic competitors is left and that of nontrivial spillovers of policies is entered — be it via goods, asset, or labor markets — the possibility arises that choices made independently by national governments would not be as effective in achieving their objectives as policies that are coordinated with other governments.[8] Whereas any single country acting alone may be reluctant to follow expansionary policies designed to counter a global deflationary shock for fear of unduly worsening its external balance, coordinated expansion by many countries will loosen the external constraint and permit each country to move closer to internal balance. In addition, coordination may assist the policymaking process by mobilizing peer pressure to help provide governments with the political will to make difficult choices in the face of opposition from domestic pressure groups. The success of Weight Watchers provides an intuitive parallel: while overweight individuals know what needs to be done to meet their targets and could in principle do it entirely on their own, many apparently find it helpful to subject themselves to peer pressure and to engage the moral support of others in like circumstances.

All of this establishes a presumption that there can be valid reasons for deviating from the tradition of decentralized decision-making when it comes to economic policy, that is, that there is scope for coordination. This presumption is reinforced by two empirical observations. The first is that the world economy of 1990 is considerably more open and integrated than that of 1950, or 1960, or even of 1970. Not only have simple ratios of imports or exports to GNP increased but also — and probably more fundamentally — global capital markets have become more integrated (Fischer 1988; Frenkel 1983,1986). With larger spillovers, there is more at stake in how one manages interdependence. Second, there is by now widespread recognition that the insulating properties of floating exchange rates are more modest than was suspected prior to their introduction in 1973.[9]

But a presumption that cooperation could be beneficial is not the same as a guarantee — nor does it preclude the existence of sometimes formidable *obstacles* to its implementation.

Suppose national policymakers have a predilection for inflationary policies but are restrained from implementing them by the concern that relatively expansionary monetary policy will bring on a devaluation (or depreciation). Yet, as outlined by Rogoff (1985), if all countries pursue such inflationary policies simultaneously, none has to worry about the threat of devaluation. Here, coordination may actually weaken discipline by easing the balance of payments constraint. In a similar vein, as noted by Feldstein (1988) there is the potential risk that a coordinated attempt to stabilize a pattern of nominal or real exchange rates could take place in an inappropriately high aggregate rate of inflation. Equally troublesome would be a coordination of fiscal policies that yielded an aggregate fiscal deficit for the larger countries that put undue upward pressure on world interest rates. The basic point is straightforward: there is nothing in the coordination process in and of itself that reduces the importance of sound macroeconomic policies (Bockelmann 1988). There can be coordination around good policies and coordination around bad ones — just as with the exchange rate regime, where there are good fixes and bad fixes, and good floats and bad floats (Frenkel 1985). Welfare improvements are not automatic.

It is only realistic, too, to acknowledge that there are barriers to the exercise of coordination. Four of the more prominent ones are worth mentioning. First, international policy bargains that involve shared objectives can be frustrated if some policy instruments are treated as objectives in themselves. Schultze (1988), for example, offers the view that it would have been difficult to have reached a bargain on target zones for exchange rates in the early 1980s given President Reagan's twin commitments to increasing defense spending and cutting taxes. In some other countries, the constraints on policy instruments may lie in different areas — including structural policies — but the implications are the same.

Second, there can at times be sharp disagreements among countries about the effects that policy changes have on policy targets. In some cases, these differences may extend beyond the size to even the sign of various policy impact multipliers.[10] The harder it is to agree on how the world works, the harder it is to reach agreement on a jointly designed set of policies.

Third, while most countries have experienced a marked increase in openness over the past few decades, there remain huge cross-country differences in the degree of interdependence. Large countries — the United States being the classic case in point — are generally less affected than small countries by other countries' policies. Coordination — as Bryant (1987) has recently emphasized — is not a matter of altruism. It is rather the manifestation of mutual self-interest. To the extent that large countries are less beset by spillovers and feedbacks than small ones, the formers' incentive to coordinate on a continuous basis may be lower.[11] In this regard, the high degree of trade interdependence shared by members of the EMS can be seen as a positive factor in reinforcing incentives to coordinate in that group.

Finally, as Polak (1981) has reminded us, in terms of national priorities, international bargaining typically comes after domestic bargaining. More specifically, the compromise of growth and inflation objectives at the national level may leave little room for further compromise on demand measures at the international level.

These barriers to coordination should not be overestimated. One of the clearest examples of true coordination — the Bonn Economic Summit of

1978 — occurred just when domestic bargaining over the same issues was most intense.[12] The growing integration of capital markets — of which the global stock market crash of October 1987 is but one reminder — has brought the implications of interdependence home to even large countries, and continued empirical work on multicountry models should be able progressively to whittle down the margin of disagreement on the effects of policies. Still, as readers of Sherlock Holmes will be aware, sometimes the most telling clue is that the hounds *didn't* bark. If the scope for coordination is to expand beyond the efforts of the past, these obstacles will need to be overcome.

Turning from the rationale to the scope for coordination, a key issue concerns the appropriate range and depth of policies to be coordinated.

The case for supporting a wide-ranging, multi-issue approach to coordination is that it increases the probability of concluding some policy bargains that benefit all parties (Putnam and Bayne 1984), that favorable spillover effects are generated across negotiating issues, and that improved economic performance today depends as much on trade and structural policies as on exchange rate and demand policies. Exhibit A is the Bonn Economic Summit of 1978 where commitments to accelerate growth by Japan and the Federal Republic of Germany were exchanged for a commitment by the United States to come to grips with its inflation and oil problems, and where agreement on macro-economic and energy policies has been credited with reinforcing progress on the Tokyo Round of Multilateral Trade Negotiations (Putnam and Henning 1986).

The defense of a narrower approach to coordination rests on the arguments that negotiation costs rise rapidly with the spread of issues under consideration (Artis and Ostry 1986), that prospects for implementation of agreements dim as the number of jurisdictional spheres expands (i.e., finance ministers can negotiate agreements but fiscal policy is typically the responsibility of legislatures, while monetary policy is the province of independent central banks); and that heated disputes on some issues (such as the stance of monetary and fiscal policies) can frustrate the chance for agreements in other areas (like defense and foreign assistance) where coordination might be more fruitful (Feldstein 1988). In addition, a case could be made that coordination is only likely in areas where there is a consensus about the effects of common policies (Cooper 1988).

In view of these conflicting considerations, it is hard to fault present institutional practices on the range of coordination. Those practices entail high-frequency coordination on narrow issues in a multitude of forums (such as the IMF, the Organization of Economic Cooperation and Development [OECD], the Bank of International Settlements [BIS], and the General Agreement on Tariffs and Trade [GATT]);[13] less frequent (say, biannual) and wider coordination at a higher level in more limited forums (such as the IMF's Interim Committee, or the G-7 major industrial countries); and even less frequent (annual), wider-yet coordination at the highest level (heads of state and of governments at the economic summits). Thus, there are occasional opportunities for multi-issue bargaining, but without the exponential increase in negotiation costs that might ensue if this were the order of the day. All in all, probably not a bad compromise.

The "depth" of coordination covers the degree of specificity and disaggregation within a given policy area. Here, two issues arise — one dealing with fiscal policy, and the other with structural policies. A strong implication of recent research is that aggregate measures, such as the central or general government fiscal deficit, are not likely to be a good guide to the effects of *fiscal policies* on macroeconomic variables such as the current account, the exchange rate, and the rate of interest (Frenkel and Razin 1987b). The reason is that such effects depend on *how* the deficit is altered: that is, taxes versus expenditures, expenditures on tradables versus nontradables, taxes on investment versus those on saving, fiscal action by a country with a current account surplus versus a deficit, and anticipated versus unanticipated policies. This suggests that more specificity in coordination — quite apart from its positive effect on the ability to monitor the implementation of agreed upon policies — would be desirable. It is notable that the Louvre Accord of February 1987 among the G-7 specified not only quantitative targets for budget deficits but also some quantitative guidelines for how these overall fiscal targets were to be achieved.[14]

In the area of *structural policies*, a good case can also be made for specificity — but on somewhat different grounds. Here, coordination may often best be interpreted not as the simultaneous application of the same policy instrument in different doses or directions across countries, but rather as the simultaneous application of different policy instruments[15] — with each country adopting the policy best tailored to its particular structural weakness.[16] In some cases, this may imply reducing impediments to labor mobility or to market-determined wages; in others, it may mean increasing incentives for private investment relative to those for private saving; and in still others, it may mean changes in the trade and distribution system. The simultaneous application of the policy measures across countries may be necessary to overcome the blocking tactics of domestic pressure groups and to enhance the credibility of the exercise. Again, the depth or specificity of coordination can be as relevant as the range.

Another salient issue concerns the question of *when* to coordinate. There has been, and continues to be, wide variation in the frequency of coordination across different forums — ranging from one-of-a-kind meetings like the 1971 Smithsonian Conference on exchange rates to the near continuous discussion and decision-making at the executive boards of the IMF and the World Bank.

One position is that, given the constraints, true coordination cannot be expected to be more than an episodic, regime-preserving effort. Dini (1988) has recently argued that international considerations still play only a small factor in policymaking, and that only at times of crisis is a common interest in coordinated action clearly recognized.[17] Some might even go further and argue that the reservoir of international compromise should be conserved for situations where there is a high probability of a policy deal and where failure to reach an agreement would carry a high cost.

Our view is that both the likelihood and effectiveness of coordination will be enhanced when it is a regular, ongoing process — and for at least three reasons. First, the potential for multiperiod bargaining expands the opportunities for policy bargains (by facilitating, for example, phasing of policy measures). What should count in assessing the gains to coordination is the present discounted value of welfare-improving policy agreements over an extended period — not the welfare change in a single period. Second, as suggested in the game-theoretic literature, the existence of repeated bargaining strengthens the role of reputational considerations in coordination.[18] In contrast, when coordination is a once-and-for-all or episodic exercise, there is a higher risk that agreed policies will never be implemented because of the much discussed problem of time inconsistency, that is, the temptation to renege on earlier policy commitments when it later becomes advantageous to do so (Kydland and Prescott 1977; Calvo 1978). To be effective, coordination agreements need to pass through the market filter of credibility, and credibility is more likely if sticking to the agreement enhances reputation, which in turn allows profitable bargains to be struck in the future. Third, once coordination is established as a routine ongoing process, there is apt to be more freedom of policy maneuver for all participants than when negotiations are conducted in a crisis atmosphere and when disagreements — which after all are inevitable — may be inappropriately seen as signaling the collapse of coordination itself.[19]

A final question concerns the size of the coordinating group, that is, *who* should coordinate. Again, existing practice does not provide a definitive answer. Among the industrial countries, we have the Group of Seven and the Group of Ten. For the developing countries, there are the Group of Twenty-Four and the Group of Seventy-Seven. And in the executive board of the Fund — where industrial and developing countries alike are represented — there are twenty-two representatives of various country groupings — a Group of Twenty-Two.

Among the factors that should influence the size of the coordinating group, three would seem to stand out. First, to the extent that the raison d'être of coordination is the internalization of externalities, the group should include those countries whose policies generate the largest externalities. This argues for including the largest industrial countries. Second, there is the general proposition that the costs of negotiation, and conflicts that might endanger the continuity of the exercise, increase significantly with the number of players. This argues for a relatively small group. Third, and pointing in the opposite direction, a small group runs the risk of concluding policy agreements which are beneficial to the direct participants — but which are not satisfactory to those countries not sitting at the coordination table.[20] In this connection, it is relevant that the managing director of the Fund participates in G-7 coordination meetings. Since the Fund's membership includes not only the larger industrial countries but also the smaller industrial countries, as well as most of the developing countries, one rationale for the managing director's participation is that it provides a systemic perspective and evaluation on proposed policy agreements — while still keeping the meeting small enough for administrative efficiency.

3. MECHANISMS OF COORDINATION

This section shifts the focus from whether to coordinate to *how* to coordinate. More specifically, the advantages and disadvantages of alternative mechanisms of coordination are discussed, with particular attention to the issues of rules versus discretion and of single- versus multi-indicator approaches. The use of economic indicators in the ongoing G-7 coordination process is also outlined.

It is not surprising that many of the issues that emerged during the long and continuing debate on the relative merits of rules versus discretion in domestic economic policy should have resurfaced in the dialogue on international economic policy coordination. After all, the present system of managed floating, even as it has evolved since the Plaza Agreement of September 1985, is much closer to a pure discretion than to a pure rules model. In this regard, the gold standard with its automatic specie flow mechanism, the adjustable peg system with its clear implications for the subordination of domestic monetary policy to the exchange rate (except during fundamental disequilibria), the EMS with its parity grid and divergence indicator, target zone proposals with their trigger for coordination discussions whenever the actual exchange rate threatens to breach the zone, and pure floating with its complete prohibition on all official intervention in the exchange market — all can be considered less discretionary than the present exchange rate system.

Those who support a more rule-based approach to international economic policy rest their case on essentially four arguments. First, the most promising route to eliminating any excess demand for coordination in the world economy is not by increasing the supply, but rather by decreasing the demand (or the need) for coordination (Polak 1981; Kenen 1987). That decrease in demand, in turn, can best be brought about by the application of simple policy rules, such as the maintenance of a fixed exchange rate. In the process, one would eliminate — so the argument goes — most of the negotiation costs and burden sharing conflicts that are intrinsic to more discretionary systems. Second, rules are regarded as the only viable mechanism for imposing discipline on economic policymakers who might otherwise manipulate the instruments of policy for their own objectives.[21] Third, rules are regarded as enhancing the predictability of policy actions and thereby improving the private sector's ability to make informed resource allocation decisions.[22] Fourth, rules are seen as a way of preventing destabilizing fine-tuning, and thus of providing protection against the lack of knowledge about how the economy operates.

The main counterarguments in favor of a discretionary approach are the following. First, rule-based adjustment systems often turn out to be less automatic in practice than in theory. For example, the automaticity of the specie flow mechanism under the historical gold standard was often undermined by the proclivity of authorities to offset or sterilize the effect of gold flows (Cooper 1982; U.S. Congress 1982).

Second, rules will impart discipline to the conduct of macroeconomic policy only to the extent that the penalties for breaking the rules are significant enough to ensure that the rules are followed. The Bretton Woods rule that countries should consult with the Fund once there was a cumulative parity change of 10 percent or more, while complied with in a technical sense, fell short in a substantive sense of its original purpose. The discussion surrounding the revision of the original Gramm-Rudman deficit reduction targets in the United States is a more recent case in point. History could in fact be seen as being just as kind to the proposition that the policy regime adjusts to the amount of discipline that countries want to have — as to the reverse (Goldstein 1980, 1984; Frenkel 1982; Frenkel and Goldstein 1986). Also, care needs to be taken to separate the effects of policy rules on economic outcomes from other influences. In this connection, the oft-made argument that the EMS was a major determinant of the 1979–85 disinflation in Europe would seem to be based on shaky ground.[23]

Third, it is by no means clear that rules are necessary to obtain the benefits of greater predictability of policy. For example, the practice of preannouncing money-supply targets — sometimes accompanied by announcements of public sector borrowing requirements — provides the markets with information on the authorities' policy intentions, but stops well short of a rigid rule.

Finally, while rules diminish the risk emanating from fine-tuning, they increase the risk stemming from lack of adaptability to changes in the operating environment.[24] The idea of a "crawling-peg" rule based on inflation differentials drew quite a few supporters in the 1960s as the right antidote for sticky nominal exchange rates. Yet its neglect of the need for real exchange rate changes now seems more serious in light of the real economic disturbances of the early 1970s.[25] More recently, the crumbling of the link between narrow monetary aggregates and the ultimate targets of monetary policy in the face of large-scale financial innovation and institutional change has reminded us anew of the limitations of policy rules.

In light of all this, there may not be any attractive alternative to conducting economic policy coordination in a judgmental way.

Even after the choice is made about coordinating via rules or discretion, there remains the decision of whether to coordinate around a single indicator or a set of indicators.[26]

There are two main considerations that are typically advanced to support the single-indicator approach. One is that it avoids overcoordination of policies by preserving for each country freedom of action over those policies not used to reach the single target variable. Thus, for example, if the exchange rate is the focus of coordination, monetary policy will be constrained, but other policies will be less affected. Implicit in this line of argument is the view that attempts to place many policies under international coordination will ultimately prove self-defeating and may even induce national authorities to compensate by exercising greater independence in *un*coordinated policy instruments, such as trade policy (Frenkel 1975).

The second, and probably more important, defense of a single-indicator approach is that it sends a clear signal to markets about the course of future policy. If, for example, the monetary authorities commit themselves to maintain a fixed exchange rate within a given band, then movements of the exchange rate provide an unambiguous guide for monetary policy. A similar message would derive from a nominal income target for monetary or fiscal policy, with the exchange rate left to determination of the market. In contrast, a multi-indicator approach increases the authorities' scope for discretion since they can appeal to the conflicting messages coming from different indicators. In cases where the authorities' past record of policy performance has been weak and where a single objective of policy is predominant (such as disinflation), a single-indicator framework for coordination can carry significant advantages in the battle to restore credibility to policy.

But relying on a single policy indicator can also carry substantial risks. Perhaps the most serious one is that the single indicator can send weak — or even false signals — about the need for changes in other policies that are not being coordinated. This is perhaps best illustrated by considering the problem of errant fiscal policy under a regime of fixed exchange rates or of target zones.

First, consider fixed rates. With high capital mobility, a fiscal expansion will yield an incipient positive interest rate differential, a capital inflow, and an overall balance of payments surplus — not a deficit. Here, exchange rate fixity helps to finance — and by no means disciplines — irresponsible fiscal policy (Frenkel and Goldstein 1988a). Only if and when the markets expect fiscal deficits to be monetized will they force the authorities to choose between fiscal policy adjustments and devaluation.[27] The better the reputation of the authorities, the longer in coming will be the discipline of markets, that is, the exchange rate will provide only a weak and late signal for policy adjustment. In this connection, it is worth observing that whereas the EMS has produced a notable convergence of monetary policy, convergence of fiscal policy has not taken place (Tanzi and Ter-Minassian 1987; Holtham, Keating, and Spencer 1987).

Next, rerun the same fiscal expansion under a target zone regime, where the zones are to be defended by monetary policy. In such a scenario, the appreciation of the currency induced by the fiscal action will prompt a loosening of monetary policy to keep the rate from breaching the zone. Here, coordination around a single indicator, namely, the exchange rate, will have exacerbated — not corrected — the basic cause of the problems.[28] The single indicator would have sent the wrong signal for policy adjustment.

In contrast, a multi-indicator approach to coordination — assuming that the list of indicators included monetary and fiscal policy variables — would not be susceptible to this weak or false signal problem. This is because such an approach goes directly to the basic stance of fiscal and monetary policies, rather than passing through the medium of the exchange rate. If, for example, the impetus for coordination was a misalignment of exchange rates, and if the root cause of the misalignment was an inappropriate stance and/or mix of monetary and fiscal policies, the multi-indicator approach would be appealing.

But all is not a bed of roses here either. While all effective approaches to coordination require a consistency of policy instruments and targets within and across countries, this requirement of consistency or compatibility can take an added prominence when authorities make public a set of targets and intended courses for policy instruments.

Two aspects merit explicit mention. One is that exchange rate targets — or even concerted views on the existing pattern of exchange rates — must be consistent with the announced course of monetary and fiscal policies. Without that consistency, attempts to provide the market with an anchor for medium-term exchange rate expectations are likely to prove fruitless.

The second point is that the credibility of multiple policy targets also hinges on the constraints on policy instruments. Two such constraints are the striking inflexibility of fiscal policy in almost all industrial countries (Tanzi 1988), and the limited ability of sterilized exchange market intervention to affect the level of the exchange rate over the medium-term, unless of course it provides a signal about the future course of policies (Mussa 1981; Jurgensen 1983). A relevant concern is that limitations on other policy instruments may wind up with monetary policy being asked to carry too heavy a burden — with primary responsibility for maintaining internal and external balance. In such a case, any contribution that a multi-indicator approach to coordination could make to enhancing the predictability of policies would also be diminished. This is so because a shock to the system — such as the October 1987 global stock market crash — might raise in the minds of market participants the question of whether monetary policy would serve its internal or external master.

Some of the broad issues dealing with mechanisms of coordination can be more concretely illustrated by reviewing several of the salient features of the use of indicators in the ongoing G-7 coordination process.

Indicators assist the policy coordination process in at least four ways. First, they are used to help identify likely inconsistencies between prospective policies and targets, as well as among targets themselves — both within and across countries. Second, they serve as a monitoring device to ascertain whether short-term policy actions and performance are "on track" with respect to earlier announced medium-term projections and objectives. Third, indicators are employed to help gauge the international implications of domestic policies and performance for variables such as external payments positions and exchange rates, and to help reach judgments about whether such implications are desirable and sustainable. Finally, indicators serve as a common data base and terms of reference for assessing the current economic situation and policy options; in their absence, policy discussions could become bogged down by disagreements on "what is" — to say nothing about what should be.

The idea of using indicators in multilateral surveillance predates the recent strengthening of coordination. In 1972–74, a working group of the Committee of Twenty on Reform of the International Monetary System examined how objective indicators might be used to allocate the burden of adjustment to international payments disequilibriums (IMF 1974). That work was abandoned with the move to floating exchange rates because it was thought — erroneously, with the benefit of hindsight — that problems of balance of payments adjustment would henceforth be less serious (Crockett

1987). In the wake of the Plaza Agreement, new life was breathed into the use of indicators at the April 1986 meeting of the Interim Committee. Its communiqué suggested, inter alia, that "An approach worth exploring further was the formulation of a set of objective indicators related to policy actions and economic performance, having regard to a medium-term framework" (IMF 1986). The Tokyo Economic Summit of May 1986 gave further support to the use of indicators in the G-7 coordination process. The Tokyo Economic Declaration also specified that the list of indicators should include: GNP and domestic demand growth, inflation, unemployment, trade and current account positions, monetary conditions, fiscal balances, exchange rates, and international reserves.

In terms of our earlier discussion, the application of indicators within the G-7 coordination exercise is better characterized as a discretionary, multiple-indicator approach than as a rule-based, single-indicator one. As hinted at earlier, these two characteristics of the present approach are related: so long as countries have multiple objectives and weight them differently, a multiple-indicator approach may be the only politically feasible one; and once a multiple-indicator approach is adopted, the more likely it is to be discretionary than rule-based. Indeed, there has been widespread agreement in official circles that indicators should be used as an analytical framework for coordination discussions rather than as automatic triggers for policy actions.

Mention should also be made of two recent initiatives in the use of indicators. As proposed at the Venice Economic Summit in 1987 and incorporated in subsequent coordination meetings, aggregate indicators for the G-7 as a whole have been added to the list of individual-country indicators. Aggregate indicators for the group may include such variables as the growth rates of real GNP and of domestic demand, the current account position, and the real exchange rate. Aggregate indicators are intended to fulfill two purposes: to capture the effects of policies of G-7 countries on countries not directly sitting at the table, and to gauge whether the overall stance of policies in major countries is biased toward expansion or contraction. On the first point, alternative policy packages among the larger industrial countries may have quite different implications for developing countries, depending on how they affect such variables as world interest rates, world economic activity, and the volume of world trade. Aggregate indicators are a shorthand mechanism for inferring the magnitude of these linkages between the industrial and developing countries. On the second point, focus on individual-country indicators — for instance, on real exchange rates — does not give a reading on whether aggregate policy is too inflationary or deflationary. In fact, it was this very concern that coordinated policies might lead to either global inflation or global contraction which prompted former U.S. Treasury Secretary Baker and U.K. Chancellor Lawson, at the 1987 Fund-Bank Annual Meeting, to propose a commodity-price basket indicator. This aggregate indicator is intended to serve as a potential "early warning signal" of emerging inflationary or deflationary pressures. The basket includes prices of primary commodities that are traded on world markets and are widely consumed. Issues arise in the construction of the basket about the treatment of oil, the relative weights to be applied to the component commodities, and the currency denomination of the index. Preliminary econometric work suggests that a commodity-price indicator does have some value as a leading indicator of movements in G-7 consumer prices (Boughton and Branson 1988).

4. THE EFFECTS OF COORDINATION

Identifying key issues related to the rationale and mechanisms for economic policy coordination is one thing; attempting to infer its effects is quite another. The latter is obviously an empirical question that requires for analysis some type of quantitative economic model.

Efforts to gauge the effects of international economic policy coordination or of alternative international monetary arrangements fall into two categories. One strand of the literature compares the value of a welfare function where each country maximizes welfare independently with that where the countries maximize a joint welfare function. Two controversial findings are that the gains from coordination are likely to be "small" for the largest countries and that the gains can even be negative if countries coordinate using the "wrong" model of the world economy.[29]

These findings should not be used as an indictment of coordination — for at least five reasons. First, a comparison of optimal uncoordinated with optimal coordinated policies may not be generalizable to the more relevant comparison of suboptimal uncoordinated with suboptimal coordinated policies. In particular, the link between pressures for protectionism on the one hand, and recession and exchange rates on the other, could result in quite a different counterfactual (i.e., what would happen in the absence of coordination) from that assumed in these studies.[30] To take a specific example, in evaluating the effects of the Plaza Agreement of September 1985, one should ask how protectionist pressures in the U.S. Congress might have evolved in its absence. Second, some of the gains from coordination may be unobservable (unwritten pledges to alter policies in the future), or difficult to separate from less ambitious forms of cooperation (exchange of information across countries), or may extend beyond the realm of macroeconomic policy (joint measures to combat terrorism, to harmonize international fare schedules for air travel, and so on). Third, a judgment that gains from coordination are small presupposes some standard of comparison. Would the gains from international coordination be small relative to the gains from coordination of policies across different economic agencies within a national government?[31] Fourth, empirical estimates of gains from coordination have typically compared policies that do not exploit the incentive governments have to adhere to agreements in order to enhance their reputation for consistency. Currie, Levine, and Vidalis (1987) argue, in contrast, that comparison of "reputational" policies shows large gains. Fifth, the danger that coordination may reduce welfare because policymakers use the wrong model(s) is greatest if they ignore model uncertainty. If, however, policymakers recognize that they do not know the true model and take this uncertainty into account, policy may be set in a more cautious fashion, with positive effects on the gains from coordination (Ghosh and Masson 1988).

The second strain of the empirical literature attempts to quantify the effects of specific policy proposals (such as the introduction of target zones) by comparing them either with a baseline that describes the current policy stance, or with historical values for the macroeconomic variables of interest. This typically involves the simulation of a global econometric model. To date, most attention has been paid to rule-based proposals for policy coordination that focus on real effective exchange rates. Two examples of such studies are Edison, Miller, and Williamson (1987) and Currie and Wren-Lewis (1987). They compare simulated outcomes of cooperative policy rules to recent historical experience. Both of these studies, however, are open to the classic Lucas (1976) critique that, due to the endogeneity of expectations of economic agents, as well as other endogenous responses to the policy regime, estimates of "structural parameters" will differ under different policy regimes; in these studies, expectations are formed in a mechanistic fashion — independent of the policy regime.

In this paper, we present some preliminary rule-based simulations derived from a global macroeconomic model developed in the research department of the IMF and called MULTIMOD. Two sets of simulations results are reported. The first set might be called *historical* simulations. Here, we address two questions: (a) whether a smoother path of monetary and fiscal policies would have produced a smoother path for real exchange rates, real output, and inflation than that observed historically; and (b) what the variability of policy instruments would be under a simple or extended "target zone" scheme where the real effective exchange rate is treated as an intermediate target (Williamson 1985 [1983]; Williamson and Miller 1987). In these historical simulations, the "effects" of coordination are generated by comparing the counterfactual simulations to a baseline simulation where MULTIMOD is constrained to replicate the historical data over 1974–87 by including the appropriate residuals in each equation. These same residuals are also used in the counterfactual simulations, each of which postulates that policy would have been different in some way from its historical stance. Our second set of simulations — for convenience, labeled single-shock simulations — disregard the historical record and focus instead on hypothetical individual shocks to particular behavioral relationships in the model. More specifically, we consider shocks to the demand for money, to aggregate supply, to aggregate demand, to export demand, and to portfolio preferences. Responses to these shocks are then examined under alternative policy rules. In addition to the coordinated rules of simple and extended target zones, we also study monetary targeting and nominal GNP targeting. In short, the objective is to see if, when, and how certain rules are likely to perform better than others.

It could be objected that the rules we consider do not constitute "coordination" in the sense of joint utility maximization, which is the focus of the first strand of literature discussed above. While true, there is certainly an element of coordination in such rules, in the usual meaning of the term. In particular, target zones would have to involve agreement concerning a consistent set of targets; because of the $N-1$ problem, targets for real effective exchange rates cannot be chosen independently.

By virtue of using MULTIMOD for the simulations, our approach differs from most earlier work in two important respects. One is that expectations are forward-looking and reflect the stance of policy. This permits expectations to differ across different policy regimes.[32] For instance, if it is known that the monetary authorities will resist movements away from an "equilibrium" level for the exchange rate, then this will condition the value expected for the exchange rate in the future. In this sense, the results are less subject to the Lucas critique than most of previous work.[33] In a related vein, the model attributes complete credibility to the government's policy stance and assumes that the private sector forms its expectations in a fashion that turns out to be correct ex post. Thus, it gives a potentially powerful influence to changes in present and future policies. Second, although this paper concentrates on the larger industrial countries, MULTIMOD contains a fully specified developing country block.

Before proceeding to a capsule summary of MULTIMOD and to the simulations themselves, it is worth emphasizing a caveat. We are in a still early stage of applying MULTIMOD to policy coordination issues. The results should, therefore, be considered tentative, preliminary, and relevant only to a few rule-based proposals. Much more will need to be learned over time about which aspects of the simulations are quite model specific, about the sensitivity of the conclusions to particular parameter values, and about the effects of alternative coordination proposals — including those that rely on a judgmental or discretionary application of policies.[34]

MULTIMOD is documented fully elsewhere (Masson and others 1988), and we will therefore limit ourselves here to describing its main features. The model contains separate submodels for the three largest industrial countries — that is, for the United States, Japan, and the Federal Republic of Germany — for the remaining four G-7 countries as a group (France, the United Kingdom, Italy, and Canada), and for the remaining smaller industrial countries as a group. Developing countries (excluding the high-income oil exporters) are modeled as one region, but with some industrial disaggregation. Each of the country or regional submodels has equations explaining the components of aggregate demand as well as the supply of the various goods produced. The submodels are linked through trade and financial flows. The parameters of the behavioral equations are in most part estimated using annual data available since the early 1960s.

In the case of industrial countries, financial markets are assumed to exhibit both perfect capital mobility and perfect substitutability between assets denominated in different currencies.[35] Consequently, arbitrage conditions link the returns on long- and short-term bonds and on domestic and foreign bonds. Moreover, as suggested earlier, expectations are assumed to be forward-looking and to be consistent with the model's solution in future periods. Thus interest parity holds both ex ante and ex post in model simulations where future variables are correctly anticipated — that is, where there are no "surprises" after the first simulation period.[36] As a result, the change in the exchange rate between two currencies from one period to the next is determined by their interest differential prevailing in the first period.

Similarly, expected long-term bond rates and rates of inflation are also consistent with the model's solutions for future periods in the absence of further shocks. The rate of inflation — unlike prices in financial markets — is not assumed perfectly flexible. Instead, rigidities in wage and product markets make for persistent effects on output as a result of purely monetary shocks; only in the medium to long run will full employment result.[37] Thus, both monetary and fiscal policies of the industrial countries have significant and persistent effects on real variables, both in the country undertaking the policy change and in other countries.

In order to provide some feel for the properties of MULTIMOD, Table 1 shows the effects of monetary and fiscal policies in each of the three major countries on itself, on the other three major countries, and on the remaining G-7 countries.[38] These policy changes are assumed to be *un*anticipated at the time of initiation. Two comments are in order about the results. First, and not surprisingly, policy actions taken by the United States have much larger spillover effects than those undertaken in Japan or in the Federal Republic of Germany. This reflects the large size of the U.S. economy and the fact that, while it is a relatively closed economy to imports, a relatively large share of its imports come from other G-7 countries. Japan is only roughly half as large (in terms of GNP) and obtains more of its imports from outside the G-7 sources. Germany is the most open but is smaller than Japan; the spillovers of its actions primarily affect other European countries. Second, while both monetary and fiscal policies have strong effects on domestic real output over the medium term, fiscal policy has a much larger own-effect on the current account than does monetary policy.[39] This is because the output and relative-price effects go in the *same* direction for a fiscal policy change, whereas they *offset* each other in the case of monetary policy. A fiscal expansion, for example, induces an

Table 1: Spillovers from Changes in Fiscal and Monetary Policies in MULTIMOD

Country Taking Action	Real GDP[a]				Current balance[b]				Real effective exchange rate[a]			
	United States	Japan	Germany	Other G-7 Countries	United States	Japan	Germany	Other G-7 Countries	United States	Japan	Germany	Other G-7 Countries
Government Spending Increase of 1% of GNP in 1988[c]												
United States	1.2	0.5	−0.1	0.2	−13	3	−1	3	1.5	−0.3	−0.1	−0.5
	0.6	0.6	0.1	0.6	−18	6	—	7	1.8	−0.2	−0.4	−0.6
Japan	—	1.5	−0.1	0.1	1	−5	—	2	0.1	0.5	0.1	−0.3
	0.1	0.6	—	0.3	1	−8	1	4	−0.1	0.9	—	−0.4
Germany	0.1	0.1	0.8	0.2	1	1	−6	2	−0.3	−0.2	0.7	−0.2
	0.1	0.2	0.3	0.2	—	2	−5	3	−0.4	−0.3	0.9	−0.2
Increase in Money Supply Target by 5% Relative to Baseline												
United States	1.2	−0.5	−0.3	−0.1	6	5	5	—	−3.8	0.6	1.4	0.6
	0.8	−0.2	−0.1	−0.1	6	5	6	−1	−2.1	0.3	1.0	0.3
Japan	−0.1	1.1	—	—	−1	3	—	−1	0.4	−2.2	0.3	0.6
	−0.1	1.0	−0.1	−0.3	−1	6	−1	−4	0.3	−1.2	—	0.4
Germany	−0.1	—	2.1	—	−1	—	5	1	1.2	0.8	−3.5	1.0
	—	−0.1	1.1	−0.2	—	−1	−1	−1	0.7	0.5	−1.8	0.5

Note: First and second rows for each entry correspond to first and third year domestic and foreign effects.
[a] Percentage deviation from baseline.
[b] Deviation from baseline, billions of dollars.
[c] Temporary; each successive year is 70% of previous year's.

appreciation of the real exchange rate and an increase in domestic demand — both of which lead to a fall in net exports.[40] In contrast, a monetary expansion yields a depreciation of the real exchange rate — which promotes net exports — and an increase in domestic demand — which penalizes them; because the relative-price effect dominates — at least in the case of the United States and Japan — the result is a small improvement in the current account.

4.1. Historical Simulations

One rather minimalist interpretation of coordination is that large countries should use their monetary and fiscal policies in a largely independent decentralized way but should avoid sharp changes in policy stance that would, in turn, generate sharp changes in real exchange rates. Such a concession to internalizing externalities would not affect the ultimate size of the stock adjustment of actual to desired policies but would constrain the speed of adjustment — much in the same spirit that speed limits in boat marinas discourage large boats from producing wakes that would topple smaller boats. One exponent of "smoothing" guidelines is Corden (1986, 431), who states:[41]

> If we accept that the spillover effects of a foreign fiscal policy change can be defined as the adverse effects of the destabilization of the real exchange rate, two implications follow.
>
> The most important implication is that each country benefits the other by maintaining relatively stable policies, meaning policies which will minimize real exchange-rate changes in either direction. Coordination consists essentially of a reciprocal agreement to modify policies that generate real exchange-rate instability.

Figures 1 to 3 summarize developments for some indicators of policy stance since the first full year of generalized floating (1974), while Figure 4 gives a measure of real effective exchange rates for the G-7 countries.[42] There are well-known difficulties in getting good policy indicators, including the problem that each of the series — money growth, the share of government purchases on goods and services in GNP, and the ratio of tax receipts less noninterest transfer payments to net national product and interest receipts — are all endogenous to some extent. It should also be emphasized that this historical period contains several different policy regimes, ranging from targeting of monetary aggregates over much of the earlier part of the period,

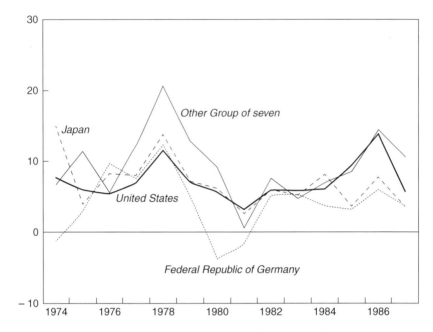

Fig 1: Money growth rates: actual values (percent change)

to the strengthening of international economic policy coordination since the Plaza Agreement of September 1985.

Nevertheless, some useful stylized facts emerge from an examination of historical data. First, money growth rates are quite volatile and appear to be positively correlated across economies. Second, taxes net of transfers seem to exhibit more variation than government spending; evidence of fiscal stimulus in the United States in 1983 is clear. Finally, real exchange rates exhibit large fluctuations, especially for the United States.

To estimate the effects of "smoother" policies, each of the variables in Figures 1 to 3 was replaced by its five-year moving average. Those values then were input as exogenous variables into MULTIMOD, and the values of endogenous variables were calculated.

Table 2 presents the mean and standard deviation of several macroeconomic indicators, comparing their historical values with those resulting from a simulation of smoother policies. Interestingly enough, smoothing of policy variables is nowhere near sufficient to produce smooth values for major macroeconomic variables. On the contrary, such a simple smoothing

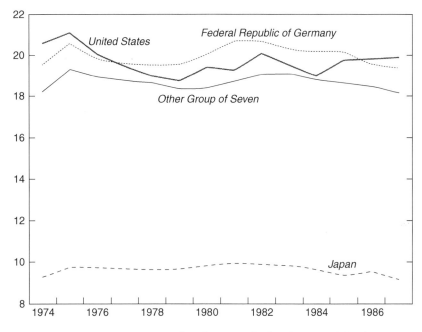

Fig 2: Government spending share: actual values (percent of GNP)

rule tends to accentuate some of the fluctuations in the historical data. For example, though the average growth of real gross domestic product is about the same as in the historical data, its standard deviation is higher in the policy smoothing simulation. Real effective exchange rates are somewhat less variable with smoothing, but real short-term interest rates are considerably more variable.

This simulation illustrates that smoothing policy instruments may lead to less, not more, smoothness in target variables. Other variables exogenous to the model are also a source of variation in output and exchange rates. The model simulation suggests that the random shocks over the historical period, including changes in nonpolicy variables such as oil production, have had a greater influence in producing swings in exchange rates and in economic activity than economic policy variables. The role of policy has been to accommodate partially those shocks. For instance, money growth rates were increased initially after the first and second oil price shocks, but a permanent increase was resisted. The basic point is that the variability of policy instruments has to a large degree been a response to shocks, rather than an exogenous source

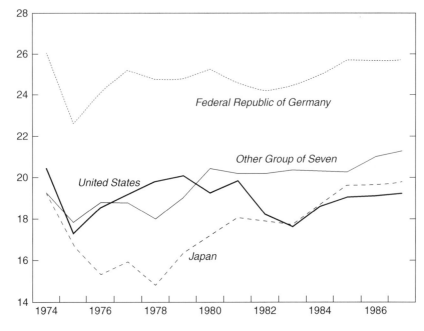

Fig 3: Tax rates: actual values (percent)

of instability;[43] put in other words, the historical period already contains considerable smoothing — albeit of a discretionary rather than rule-based variety — and therefore attempts to impose additional smoothing on top of it do not produce salutary effects.

Note also that real effective exchange rates take on values in this simulation that are very similar to the historical data, though they are somewhat less volatile when policy is smoothed. There seems to be little support here for the notion that exchange rate stability can be achieved solely through the application of simple mechanical smoothing rules. Recall, however, that the smoothing simulation has only considered a change in the path of policy variables — leaving their end points unchanged — rather than a permanent change in those variables. A permanent increase in the rate of money growth or in the shares of taxes or government spending in output might have more powerful effects.

A more activist approach to the coordination of economic policies would go beyond smoothing. One such approach would be to postulate that monetary

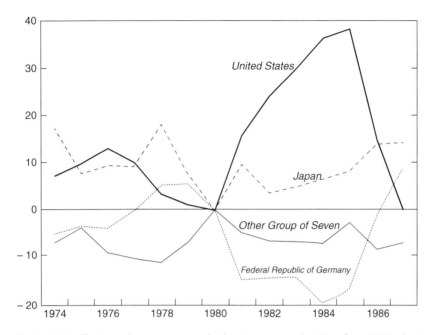

Fig 4: Real effective exchange rates: actual values (percentage deviation from 1980 value)

authorities resist movements of an intermediate variable — in particular the real effective exchange rate — from their long-run equilibrium levels. A system of target zones for exchange rates has been proposed by Williamson (1985 [1983]) and extended by Williamson and Miller (1987). The original proposal calculated "fundamental equilibrium exchange rates" and advocated the use of monetary policies to resist movements away from those rates. As explained by Williamson:

> The basic focus of exchange rate management should be on estimating an appropriate value for the exchange rate and seeking to limit deviations from that value beyond a reasonable range. (1985 [1983, 47])

> While other techniques, like sterilized intervention, may be able to give limited assistance, a serious commitment to exchange rate management leaves no realistic alternative to a willingness to direct monetary policy at least in part toward an exchange rate target. (56)

More recently, Williamson and Miller (1987, 7) supplement the prescription that monetary policies be used to target real effective exchange rates with

Table 2: MULTIMOD Simulations: Comparisons of Historical Policy Stance with Values of Endogenous Variables when Money Growth, Tax Rates, and the Stance of Government Spending in GDP are Smoothed, 1974–1987

Variable	Mean Values		Standard Deviations	
	Historical Values	Simulated Values under Smoothing	Historical Values	Simulated Values under Smoothing
Growth rate of real GDP				
United States	2.5	2.6	2.8	4.6
Japan	3.7	3.8	1.8	2.9
Germany	1.9	2.0	1.9	3.6
Other Group of Seven	2.2	2.4	1.4	3.0
Rate of inflation				
United States	6.5	7.4	3.0	3.0
Japan	5.0	6.5	6.0	5.9
Germany	3.9	4.5	2.1	1.9
Other Group of Seven	10.2	11.4	5.4	6.1
Real effective exchange rate (1980 = 0)				
United States	14.6	16.3	12.9	11.7
Japan	9.4	9.3	5.2	5.1
Germany	−5.4	−5.1	9.1	8.9
Other Group of Seven	−6.6	−8.6	3.0	3.1
Real short-term interest rate				
United States	2.1	2.5	3.6	4.4
Japan	2.7	2.5	3.5	4.6
Germany	2.9	2.7	2.4	3.1
Other Group of Seven	2.3	2.4	5.7	6.8

the assignment of fiscal policies to targets for the growth in domestic demand for the G-7 countries: "The basic argument is that a nominal income target fulfills the same function as a money supply rule, providing a "nominal anchor" to prevent inflation from taking off and a guide to expectations, while avoiding the shocks to demand that come from variations in velocity." In addition, the proposal, or "blueprint," specifies that "the average level of world (real) short-term interest rates should be revised up (down) if aggregated growth of nominal income is threatening to exceed (fall short of) the sum of the target growth of nominal demand for the participating countries." (2)

Earlier simulation studies of target zones have been undertaken by Williamson and Miller (1987, App. C), based on Edison, Miller, and

Williamson (1987). Those studies employed the Federal Reserve Board's multicountry model (MCM), which is characterized by adaptive expectations. As emphasized earlier, MULTIMOD uses model-consistent forward-looking expectations — a difference that should, in our view, produce more firmly grounded answers.

Two simulations were performed — one for the original target zone proposal (labeled "target zones"), and one for target zones augmented by a rule for fiscal policy (labeled "blueprint"). The attempt was made to stay close to the spirit of the original proposals while still making a few minor modifications.

Much of the action in a target-zone scheme centers around the monetary reaction function since it is monetary policy that is typically assigned to the exchange rate. In the standard version of MULTIMOD, the reaction function for short-term interest rates involves resisting movements away from an exogenous target for base money. The demand for base money, in turn, is assumed to depend on real GNP and on its deflator with elasticities close to unity. When the effects of target zones are simulated, this term is retained but with a much lower weight than normal.[44] The "target-zone" element in the reaction function is represented by the assumption that the short-term interest rate deviates from the baseline depending on the cube of the deviation of the real effective exchange rate from its target value (Edison, Miller, and Williamson 1987, 97). Thus, the monetary policy rule used in both the target-zone and blueprint simulations takes the following algebraic form:

$$R = R^b + [(c - \bar{c})/n]^3 + a[\bar{m} - m],$$

where, as in Edison and others (1987), R is the short-term rate, R^b is its baseline value, c is the log of the real effective exchange rate, $\bar{c}$ its target value, and n is half the width of the target zone, (namely, 10 percent); $\bar{m}$ is the target for the (log of the) monetary base, m the long-run demand for the monetary base with baseline interest rates but simulated output and prices, and a is a negative constant.[45]

Targets for the real effective rate were taken from Williamson (1985 [1983]).[46] As in Edison, Miller, and Williamson (1987), an adjustment to the level of the target real effective rate is made to keep it compatible with the definition used in the model, but the constraint is imposed that the translated target exchange rate variable follow the same path as in Williamson (1985 [1983]).[47]

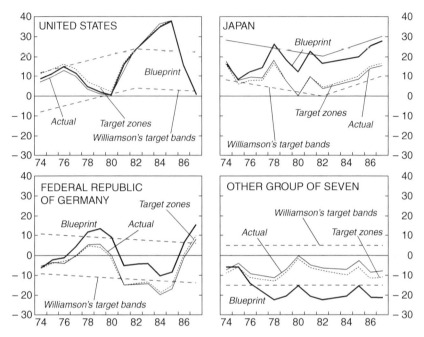

Fig 5: Real effective exchange rates: actual and simulated values (percentage deviation from 1980 value)

As mentioned earlier, the "blueprint" proposes that fiscal policy follow a rule targeted on nominal domestic demand growth. As such, the equations in MULTIMOD for real government spending on goods and services had to be endogenized along such lines. The target paths for nominal domestic demand growth were taken from Williamson and Miller (1987) for the period 1980–87; outside that period, we used their formula to calculate targets.

The main results of interest are portrayed in Figures 5 to 8, where actual (historical) values are compared to simulated values for the target-zone proposal and for the blueprint proposal. The figures cover real effective exchange rates, real GNP growth rates, rates of inflation, and current account balances. Bands 10 percent each side of Williamson's (1985 [1983]) fundamental equilibrium exchange rates have been drawn on Figure 5.

Several interesting — albeit tentative — conclusions emerge from the simulations.

First, there is surprisingly little success in limiting real exchange rate movements away from their targets, especially for the United States.[48] This

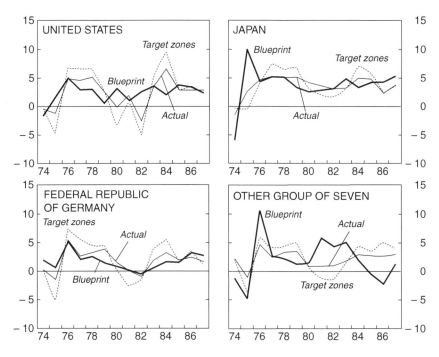

Fig 6: Rate of growth of GNP: actual and simulated values (percent change)

is apparent for both the more limited assignment of monetary policy to target exchange rates and the case where fiscal policy is made endogenous, though not specifically for exchange rate targeting. Also, the cost of resisting exchange rate movements in terms of greater variability of nominal interest rates appears to be quite high in the model. In 1985, the short-term rate in the United States is 370 basis points below its baseline value in the target-zone simulation, and 260 basis points above in Germany. An attempt to increase the feedback onto interest rates of real exchange rates produced explosive behavior in the model and negative nominal interest rates. Why is the movement in real effective exchange rates so small? In the model, this is the result of the long-run neutrality of real variables with respect to monetary policy, of the relatively small impact of interest rates on exchange rates when exchange rates are anchored by perfect foresight, and of the fact that monetary policy changes are anticipated in advance. A nominal depreciation resulting from anticipated monetary expansion leads quite soon to increases in import prices and domestic

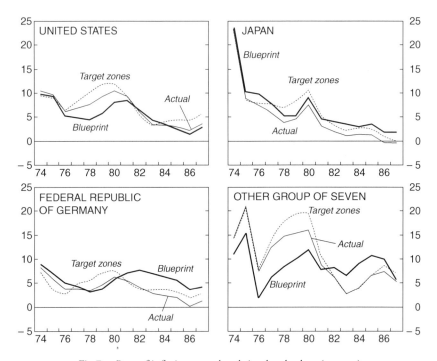

Fig 7: Rate of inflation: actual and simulated values (percent)

inflation, reducing the amount of real depreciation. Such a scenario has been discussed by Feldstein (1988, 7) in the following terms:

> If the United States had agreed in 1983 to stop the dollar's rise, the easiest way would have been for the Federal Reserve to ease monetary policy.... The easier monetary policy would produce inflation and the inflation would cause the dollar's nominal value to decline. In the end, there would have been no change in the real exchange rate or the trade deficit but a higher price level and a high rate of inflation.

With perfect foresight of policy changes, the required movements in monetary policy may be quite large for even small, and transitory, real exchange rate changes. It can be seen from Figure 5 that the dollar's real effective exchange rate is judged by Williamson and Miller (1987) to be undervalued in 1978–80, but overvalued from 1982 to 1985. Thus, interest rates have to rise in the earlier period but fall in the latter (relative to baseline). With perfect foresight, the amount they must rise in the earlier period is amplified because it is known that they will be lower later.[49] Note that monetary policy is effective in the model

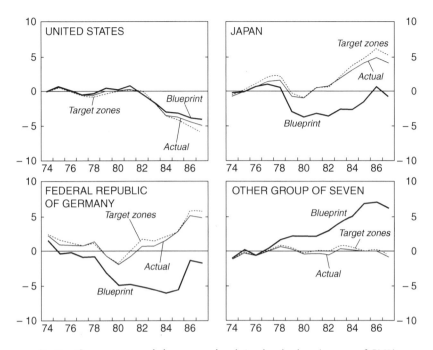

Fig 8: Current account balance: actual and simulated values (percent of GNP)

in the short run, provided that the money supply change is unanticipated. Table 1 indicates that an increase in the money supply of 5 percent causes a real effective depreciation in the first year ranging from 2 percent in the case of Germany to 4 percent in the United States; by the second year, the depreciation has been reduced to 1 to 2 percent. If anticipated beforehand, the extent of the depreciation is further reduced.

A second conclusion is that the use of monetary policy alone to maintain target zones — keeping the same stance of fiscal policy as in the baseline — seems to exacerbate the inflationary pressures of the late 1970s and early 1980s, and to lead to more variable inflation rates; see Figure 7. In this simulation, the United States eases monetary policy to prevent the dollar's appreciation in 1980–85; with perfect foresight of such a policy stance, inflation rises somewhat in the late 1970s in anticipation. Conversely, the dollar's undervaluation in 1987 (according to the calculated fundamental equilibrium exchange rate) requires a tightening of policy, which tends to lower inflation rates in the mid-1980s below baseline levels.

The substantial effects on real variables in the blueprint simulation appear to be the result mainly of the fiscal rule. In the blueprint simulation, GNP growth is smoothed considerably in the United States and the Federal Republic of Germany (see Figure 6). The recession of 1982 and the high growth of domestic demand in the United States in 1984 are both smoothed out; U.S. GNP growth in 1984 is only 2.7 percent, compared to 7.2 percent historically, while the United States no longer experiences a recession in 1982. Moderation of sharp GNP movements is however not so evident for Japan and the other G-7 countries. Indeed, the non-U.S. G-7 countries experience large output variations in 1975–76 in the blueprint simulations. This may be a result of a mechanical application (in the period up to 1980) of the Williamson-Miller formula for calculating nominal demand targets; if adjusted in an ad hoc fashion (as is done in Williamson and Miller 1987 for the second oil shock), a more reasonable path might result.

Third, current account imbalances are reduced for the major three countries in the blueprint simulation, in the sense of being closer to zero; see Figure 8. Most of the effects again come as a result of the changes in fiscal stance. In particular, targets for domestic demand growth in Germany and Japan are consistently above the historical values, and this leads to a much more stimulative fiscal policy in these countries (see Williamson and Miller 1987, Figs. 4 and 5). But again, there is a cost. General government fiscal deficits reach 10 percent of GNP in Germany and 8 percent in Japan in the early 1980s!

By the same token, it is the fiscal stimulus — rather than the monetary policy change — that is the cause of the sizable appreciation of the yen and deutsche mark in the 1980s relative to baseline. Clearly, such large deficits would be neither desirable — nor tolerable politically. It is also noteworthy that the counterpart to the smaller current account surpluses in Germany and Japan is larger surpluses in the other G-7 countries, rather than a reduction of U.S. deficits. This occurs because a weighted average of domestic demand targets for France, the United Kingdom, Italy, and Canada in Williamson and Miller (1987) is consistently lower than actual demand over the period 1974–87.

4.2. Single-Shock Simulations

In our view, the results of the historical simulations are instructive. Still, it is not clear to what extent these results reflect either the specific shocks that were present in the 1974–87 historical episode or the assumption made that all exogenous variables — including the shocks — were known prior to their occurrence. Furthermore, because the historical data contain a great variety of shocks, interpretation of the simulation results is blurred. In what follows we do a set of simpler experiments with the model, where only one shock to a particular behavioral relationship is assumed to occur. The shock, which is assumed to have been unanticipated when it occurred, is an innovation that applies to a single period. Though temporary, the shock nevertheless has persistent effects because errors are serially correlated and because the structural equations of the model include lagged effects. Expectations are assumed to be formed in the model in a way that properly takes into account the subsequent dynamics; that is, once the shock has occurred, perfect foresight is assumed to prevail.

No more than the historical simulations, results from single shocks do not allow a complete evaluation of policy rules. Clearly, the relative variance of various shocks should influence the choice among policy rules (Poole 1970; Henderson 1979). The historical simulations that were discussed above do capture the relative importance of the different shocks, but only for one historical episode. More informative perhaps would be evaluation of policy rules under a series of drawings from the distribution describing the shocks — a subject that we hope to investigate in a forthcoming paper. Nevertheless, analyses of single shocks do permit some intuition to be brought to bear on the issue of policy choice; they should shed some light on when particular rules are likely to perform better than others. Ranking the rules would, however, generally require an explicit objective function that specifies the weights attached to output fluctuations, inflation, and other objectives.

In the simulations reported below, we expand the set of policy rules to include not only simple and extended target-zone schemes, but nominal GNP and money targeting as well. It is implicitly assumed that nominal GNP and money targeting involve less coordination than target zones, although there is no reason to rule out the possibility that nominal GNP (or nominal domestic demand or money) targets might be internationally coordinated. The four policy rules can be compactly summarized as:

1. *Money targeting*: the short-term interest rate is aimed at a target for the monetary base; real government expenditure is exogenous.
2. *Nominal GNP targeting*, using the short-term interest rate. Again, government expenditure is exogenous.

3. *Target zones*, using the short-term interest rate; the level of world interest rates is also adjusted up or down as a function of world nominal income. Government expenditure is exogenous.
4. *Blueprint proposal*: As for target zones, but in addition government expenditure is aimed at a target for nominal domestic demand (i.e., absorption).

To be more precise about the implementation of the alternative policy rules, consider the following equations where lower-case variables denote logs and upper-case variables represent levels. In particular, M is the monetary base (m is its logarithm), u is a random shock to the demand for money, Y is nominal GNP, WY is aggregate nominal income (in dollars) of industrial countries taken together, Q is real GNP, P is the GNP deflator, A is nominal domestic absorption, G is real government expenditure on goods and services, C is competitiveness (the relative price of domestic to foreign output), and R is the short-term interest rate. A b superscript indicates baseline values, which are also assumed to be the target values of the relevant variables. Implicitly then, the simulations start from a position of equilibrium, which is disturbed by the shock being considered. The goal of each of the rules should be to return the economy as quickly and smoothly as possible to the initial equilibrium.

(1) *Money targeting*:

$$R = R^b + 13.5\left[m^d - m^b\right]$$

where m^d is long-run money demand, ignoring the effect of interest rates; m^d is given by:

$$m^d = p + .970q + 5.15u$$

(2) *Nominal GNP targeting*:

$$R = R^b + 25\left[y - y^b\right]$$

(3) *Target zones*:

$$R = R^b + \left[\left(c - c^b\right)/0.1\right]^3 + 25\left[wy - wy^b\right]$$

(4) *Blueprint*:

$$R = R^b + \left[\left(c - c^b\right)/0.1\right]^3 + 25\left[wy - wy^b\right]$$
$$(G - G^b)/Q^b = (A^b - A)/A^b$$

The form of the policy rules requires some explanation, especially since they differ slightly from those performed for the historical period. In general, we have attempted to follow as closely as possible the intentions of their advocates. The form selected resulted from some experimentation that identified inadequacies with alternative specifications or with feedback parameters. In particular, since policy changes have lagged effects on their targets, "instrument instability" may result if one attempts to hit the targets too closely period by period (Holbrook 1972). This applies most forcefully to the interest rate instrument, where caution needs to be exercised not to set the feedback coefficient too high.

Rule (1), for *money targeting*, used the same specification as in the standard version of MULTIMOD. If a money target were exactly achieved, an implication would be an explosive, sawtooth pattern for short-term interest rates. For this reason, equation (1) allows interest rates to equate the long-run demand for money (conditional on observed GNP) to the money stock target. The short-run demand for money can be written as:

$$m = p + .1883q - .0070R - .0074R_{-1} + .8058(m - p)_{-1} + u,$$

where u is an error term. Setting $m = m^b$ and solving for R, on the assumption that $R = R_{-1}$ and $m - p = (m - p)_{-1}$, yields

$$R = -13.5(m^b - p) + 13.1q - 69.4u$$

A rearrangement of this equation, on the assumption that the equation also holds in the baseline, gives rule (1) above.

Nominal GNP targeting has been proposed by Tobin (1980) and others as preferable to money targeting because it avoids an inappropriate tightening or easing of monetary policy in response to velocity shocks. The form that such a nominal GNP target might take has been discussed by Taylor (1985b), Fischer (1988), and Tobin (1980). Rule (2) was specified in terms of a target for the *level* of nominal GNP, rather than its rate of change, because of the potential instability of the latter identified in Taylor (1985b). Some experimentation with feedback coefficients led to a value of 25. Since the interest rate is in percent, this implies that a 1 percent deviation from the nominal GNP target leads to a 25 basis point increase in the interest rate. Such a value yields a flatter aggregate demand schedule (in $Q - P$ space) for nominal GNP targeting than for money targeting (Taylor 1985b). Since the coefficient of real income is approximately unity in equation (1), the money rule can also be framed in terms of nominal GNP with the difference that the error in the demand-for-money equation would then also affect the setting of interest rates.

Target zones, rule (3), follow the form described in Williamson and Miller (1987) and in Edison, Miller, and Williamson (1987). There are some slight modifications relative to the historical simulations, such that the feedback rules are closer to those proposed in the "blueprint." Specifically, the width of the target zone is taken here to be 10 percent, not the 20 percent used in the historical simulation. The problems of nonconvergence that were present in our historical simulations did not surface here, allowing us to increase the reaction of short-term interest rates to deviations from fundamental equilibrium exchange rates. Also, the nominal anchor for prices is the target level of world nominal income — rather than money supply targets. Note that it is the level, not the rate of change of world nominal GNP that appears in the equation, again reflecting Taylor's (1985b) findings. The feedback coefficient on world nominal GNP was taken to be the same as for domestic nominal GNP targeting.

The *extended target zones* or "*blueprint*" proposal, rule (4), contains an equation for government spending that does not hit domestic-demand targets exactly. However, since the first-year multiplier effect on output of G is close to one, the rule allows approximate achievement of domestic-demand targets.

So much for the policy rules. The (transitory) shocks that we consider are the following:

(A) A shock to the *demand for money* — that is, to velocity — in the United States of 2 percent.
(B) An *aggregate supply shock* in the United States; in particular, the residual in the equation for the rate of change in the nonoil GNP deflator is increased by 2 percent.
(C) An *aggregate demand shock* in the United States: a positive innovation in consumption equal to 1 percent.

(D) A *shift in demand* towards U.S. goods, equal to 10 percent of U.S. exports.
(E) A *portfolio preference shift* out of U. S. dollar assets, leading to an increase in the required rate of return on dollar assets by 10 percentage points.

Each of the rules is simulated subject to each of the five shocks, one at a time. Figures 9 to 12 give the main results of interest.

The *money demand shock* is not plotted because the results are straightforward to describe. It is only in the case of money targeting that the money shock has any effect on policy settings and on other endogenous variables (there is a small effect of the money shock on consumption because money is a component of net wealth, but the magnitude is negligible). In the case of money targeting, the positive innovation to money demand leads to temporarily higher short-term interest rates, and as a consequence, to temporarily lower economic activity. Other rules ignore the money demand shock and maintain policy instruments unchanged; macroeconomic variables therefore remain at their equilibrium levels. This points up the superiority of these rules in the face of money demand shocks — an argument similar to that made by the advocates of nominal GNP targeting (Tobin 1980). Of course, if shifts in money demand could be identified, then the rule for targeting money could be modified to target a "shock-corrected" money stock that omitted the term u.

The *aggregate supply shock* (or cost-push inflation shock) yields a variety of responses (Fig. 9). This shock tends to put upward pressure on the domestic output price relative to the absorption deflator, leading to some (short-run) stimulus to consumption as well as higher inflation. As mentioned above, the greater flatness of the aggregate demand curve under nominal GNP targeting — vis-à-vis money targeting — leads to a greater response of interest rates and hence greater short-run output losses but smaller increases in prices. Which of the two rules is preferable depends on the trade-off between the two objectives of output and price level stability, as well as on the discount rate that captures intertemporal trade-offs.[50] There is also a considerable difference between responses under the target-zone and blueprint rules. Using monetary policy to counteract the real appreciation of the U.S. dollar requires *lower*, not higher, U.S. nominal interest rates. However, for both the target-zone and blueprint rules, there is an additional term (with admittedly an arbitrarily imposed coefficient) that tends to raise interest rates if world nominal GNP grows too fast, which is the case here. Under target zones, the result is that U.S.

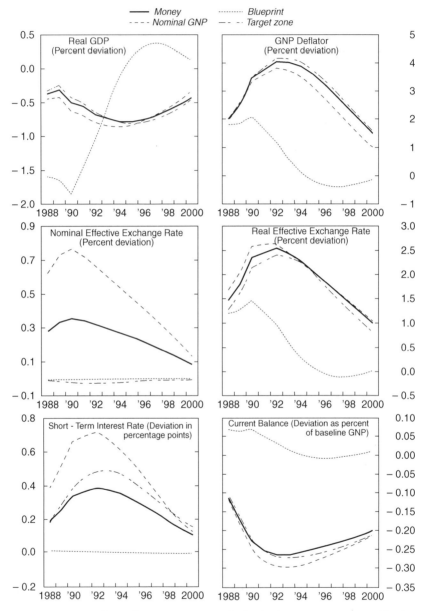

Fig 9: Simulated effects of U.S. aggregate supply shock (deviations of U.S. variables from baseline)

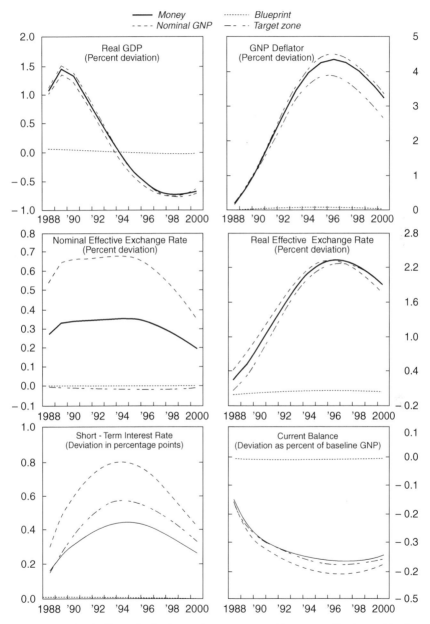

Fig 10: Simulated effects of a shock to U.S. consumption (deviations of U.S. variables from baseline)

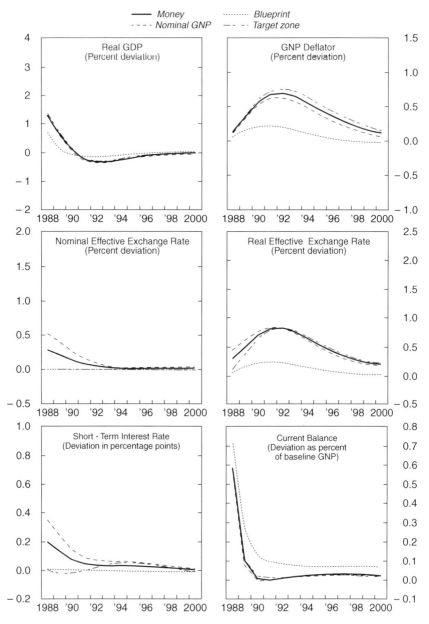

Fig 11: Simulated effects of a shock to U.S. exports (deviations of U.S. variables from baseline)

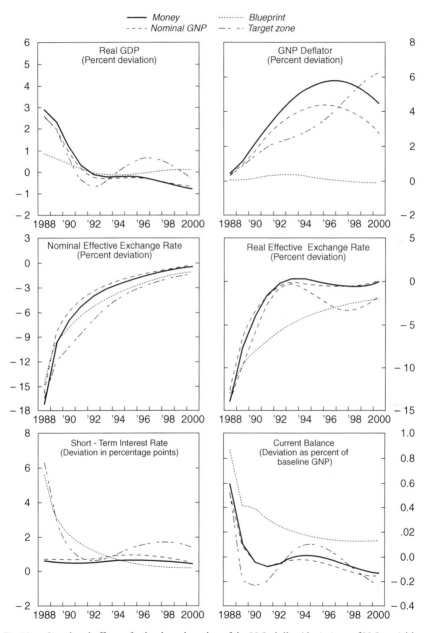

Fig 12: Simulated effects of a shock to the value of the U.S. dollar (deviations of U.S. variables from baseline)

interest rates rise but by somewhat less than interest rates in other industrial countries. This leads to a small nominal dollar depreciation, which tends to add to inflationary pressures but limits output losses. In contrast, under the blueprint rule U.S. government spending contracts to counteract the stimulus to consumption, helping to limit the real appreciation of the dollar. The net effect on output is negative because domestic demand is close to its baseline value, but foreign demand falls. However, output is actually higher after seven years, by which time prices have returned to their baseline levels. The bottom line is that an aggregate supply shock causes a dilemma for the first three rules because one instrument has to wear two hats: that is, monetary policy has not only to resist inflationary pressures but also to neutralize output effects or resist the real exchange rate appreciation in the country experiencing the shock.[51]

Next, consider the *aggregate demand shock*, namely, a 1 percent increase in U.S. consumption (see Figure 10). Again, the effects differ under alternative policy rules. Absent any policy changes, such a shock will increase output and put upward pressure on prices, as well as appreciate the real exchange rate and lead to a decline in the current account. It also generates positive spillovers for the output of other countries. Since nominal GNP rises, as does the demand for money, both rules (1) and (2) cause interest rates to rise; again, given the relative steepness of the aggregate demand curves, the output and price increases are more moderate under nominal GNP targeting. Turning to the coordinated rules, the real appreciation of the U.S. dollar leads to a smaller rise in interest rates in the United States than in other industrial countries under target zones. However, by limiting the interest rate increases in the United States in response to a demand increase, this rule builds in inflationary pressures, which persist longer than for other rules. In contrast, the extra degree of freedom accorded by fiscal policy in the blueprint rule allows the aggregate demand shock to be almost completely offset by lower government spending. As a result, the output, price, and real exchange rate effects are smallest for this rule.

Figure 11 presents results from an aggregate demand shock that corresponds to a shift towards U.S. goods and away from other countries' goods. The positive shock to U.S. exports of 10 percent shows up in lower exports of other countries in proportions that correspond to their shares in world trade;[52] the U.S. current account improves by some $30 billion in the first period. For all policy rules, U.S. real output rises initially, and price increases are relatively small. The contrast is greatest in the behavior of short-term interest rates. Neither real exchange rates nor world nominal GNP change much, so that there is little effect on interest rates under target zones or the blueprint. However, money and nominal GNP targeting resist the rise in activity and prices in the U.S. by raising interest rates.

The final shock is to the *exchange rate of the dollar* (against the yen, the deutsche mark, and other industrial country currencies) brought about by a 10 percent increase in the required return on dollar assets. Output effects are largest for the two uncoordinated rules (money and nominal GNP targeting) and least for the coordinated rule (the blueprint) that uses both monetary and fiscal instruments. The exchange rate overshoots under all four rules, with the U.S. nominal effective exchange rate depreciating by about 15 percent in the first year. Under target zones, the GNP deflator shows no signs of stabilizing (Fig. 12). Under the blueprint, higher domestic demand results from the income effect of higher exports; as a result, government spending must fall to achieve the nominal domestic-demand target. This leads to a *greater* real depreciation of the dollar in the years 1990–96 than under the other rules, and a larger current account balance.

To sum up, there are five basic conclusions that emerge from these simulations of individual shocks.

First, as in the historical simulations, monetary policy is relatively ineffective when its subsequent effects are anticipated. This conclusion seems to follow whether or not the shocks themselves are anticipated. Conversely, fiscal policy — in particular, variations in government spending — seems to be quite powerful in influencing real output, real exchange rates, and current accounts. Clearly, then, a comparison of rules that use both fiscal and monetary policy with those that just use monetary policy will favor the former. But there is a catch. The use of fiscal policy may not have the flexibility that is assumed for it in, say, the blueprint rule. It may be constrained by other objectives — including the need to reduce budget deficits or to limit the importance of government in the economy. As such, fiscal policy may not be able to react immediately to shocks, at least not within the one-year period assumed here.

Second, it does appear that the behavior of alternative policy rules in response to different shocks is quite different. Rules that perform best for some shocks may perform least well for others. In some cases, however, it is clear which rule dominates (or which rules dominate). For instance, if money demand shocks are prevalent, then monetary targeting is not appropriate. Somewhat surprisingly, even when portfolio preference shifts are frequent, our results do not suggest that target zones — implemented through monetary policy changes — would be preferred. Reliance on monetary policy to ensure that real exchange rates remain within target bands may not be effective.

Third, nominal GNP targeting — while it dominates money targeting if velocity shocks are prevalent — may be subject to acute problems of instrument instability, implying that an attempt at close control would involve large swings in interest rates from period to period. Because of the relative ineffectiveness of monetary policy to affect real magnitudes in the model, using monetary policy to target nominal GNP would have to allow for large deviations from targets. It is therefore unlikely to be very precise. As a consequence, the advantages for credibility of framing policy on a single indicator are apt to be diluted by the inability of the authorities to achieve close control of that indicator. Nominal GNP targeting could also make it too easy for authorities to walk away from their targets by citing forces "beyond their control."

Fourth, the simple target-zone proposal is also subject to the ineffectiveness of monetary policy. As a result, target zones that rely solely on monetary policy do not seem capable of maintaining real effective exchange rates within bands that are even 10 percent on either side of the target. While, we have considered only arbitrary shocks, a comparison with estimated variances suggests that they are not out of line with historical experience. This relatively small impact of interest rates on real exchange rates in the model is due in large part to the twin properties that exchange rates are anchored by perfect foresight and that perfect foresight is assumed to prevail following the shocks. If the equilibrium level of the exchange rate were uncertain, or there were extrapolative expectations, then target zones might have greater effectiveness. Another important consideration is that for some shocks — in particular, a supply shock — the target zone would move monetary policy in a perverse direction. By resisting the real appreciation resulting from an inflationary shock, it would exacerbate those inflationary pressures.

Fifth and finally, target zones augmented by the use of the fiscal instrument — as outlined in the blueprint proposal — are more successful in limiting the effects of shocks. Its greater success in limiting movements away from long-run equilibrium real exchange rates derives mainly however from the use of fiscal policy. As suggested earlier, if fiscal policy is constrained by other objectives — or cannot be used flexibly — then the implied ability to counteract shocks may be illusory. Our results are an illustration of the point that it is clearly desirable to improve the flexibility of the budgetary process, whatever the objectives that guide fiscal policy.

NOTES

1. Other definitions of coordination include: "decisionmaking that maximizes joint welfare and thus enables international interdependencies to be positively exploited" (Artis and Ostry 1986, 14); and "agreements between countries to adjust their policies in the light of shared objectives or to implement policies jointly" (Horne and Masson 1988, 261). A more general term is "cooperation," which includes policy coordination, but also extends to exchange of information and consultation among countries. We do not address these issues of terminology in this paper.
2. See the surveys by Artis and Ostry (1986), Cooper (1985), Fischer (1988), Hamada (1979), Horne and Masson (1988), Kenen (1987), Polak (1981), and Wallich (1984).
3. Another key issue relating to mechanisms for coordination is that of hegemonic versus more symmetric systems; on this, see Frenkel, Goldstein, and Masson (1988).
4. Evidence on the size of spillover effects from policy actions by the major industrial countries is discussed in the latter part of this section and in Table 1.
5. The conclusion that a monetary expansion under floating rates affects real output in opposite directions at home and abroad is associated with the Mundell-Fleming model (Mundell 1971; Fleming 1962). For a recent evaluation of this model, see Frenkel and Razin (1987a); a broader survey of the international transmission mechanism can be found in Frenkel and Mussa (1985). Econometric models are more divided on whether a monetary expansion under floating rates has negative transmission effects on real output abroad; see Helliwell and Padmore (1985) and Bryant and others (1988).
6. Corden (1986) has recently argued that there may be a case for asking large countries to slow their speed of adjustment to desired policy targets so as to dampen movements in real exchange rates that could cause difficulties for others (see Sec. 1.4).

7. Another constraint on regional attempts to create more of the public good is that they may divert or discourage its production outside the region; the argument here is analogous to the concepts of "trade creation" and "trade diversion" in the customs union literature.
8. To reach this conclusion, it is necessary to assume that each player does not have sufficient policy instruments to achieve all its policy targets simultaneously, and that coordination alters the trade-offs among policy targets; see Gavin (1986). Without those assumptions, the motivation for coordination would disappear.
9. See Goldstein (1984). This is not to say that the insulating properties of floating rates are inferior to those of alternative regimes. Indeed, it is hard to see any other exchange rate regime surviving the shocks of the 1970s without widespread controls on trade and capital.
10. See Bryant and others (1988) and Helliwell and Padmore (1985) for a comparison of open-economy multipliers from different global econometric models. Frankel and Rockett (1988) illustrate the sensitivity of welfare effects of coordination to the selection of the "right" versus the "wrong" economic model.
11. See Fischer (1988). Dini (1988) goes further to argue that when the incentives to coordinate differ widely among group members, there may be a tendency for bilateral bargains to take place among those who have the most to trade.
12. See Putnam and Bayne (1984). At the same time, the Bonn Economic Summit of 1978 is regarded in some quarters as illustrative of the pitfalls of coordinating macroeconomic policies when the economic outlook is changing rapidly.
13. Another example of high-frequency coordination is that among central banks of the largest countries on exchange-market intervention tactics.
14. For example, the Louvre Communique states that: "The United States Government will pursue policies with a view to reducing the fiscal 1988 deficit to 2.3 percent of GNP from its estimated level of 3.9 percent in fiscal 1987. For this purpose, the growth in government expenditures will be held to less than 1 percent in fiscal 1988 as part of the continuing program to reduce the share of government in GNP from its current level of 23 percent;" see IMF (1987).
15. Because coordination of structural policies typically involves different policy instruments, individual country actions cannot — unlike in the

case of coordination of fiscal policies — be evaluated with reference to an aggregate policy indicator that would be desirable from a global perspective.

16. This is not to deny the helpful role that harmonization of structural policies — ranging from adopting similar tax provisions to implementing common regulations concerning movements of goods, labor, and capital — could play in certain circumstances.
17. Those who hold the view that international factors have minimal influence on policymaking sometimes also argue that countries' policy commitments in coordination agreements represent policies that would have occurred even in the absence of such agreements. Under this view, coordination affects only the timing of policy announcements, with countries delaying such announcements until coordination meetings so that they can present a dowry to the others.
18. See the papers in Buiter and Marston (1985).
19. As Poehl (1987, 19–20) notes: "international cooperation does not necessarily imply that all parties must agree on all details at all times. It is important that we regard it as a process of maintaining stability in our increasingly interrelated world economy. . . . The process of international cooperation may be difficult and burdensome, even frustrating at times, but there is no alternative to it."
20. It is precisely because of the risk of "collusion" among the coordinating countries that Vaubel (1985) favors decentralized decision-making.
21. It is in this context that the problems of time inconsistency and moral hazard often surface.
22. Advocates of rules also argue that once the public knows better what the authorities will do, markets will demand less of a risk premium to hold the authorities' financial obligations.
23. Kenen (1987) cites a regression of the change in the inflation rate between 1979 and 1985 on the level of the inflation rate in 1979 and a zero-one dummy variable denoting participation in the exchange rate mechanism of the EMS. The sample comprised twenty-two industrial countries. The EMS dummy variable was *not* statistically significant, whereas the level of the inflation rate in 1979 was. Note that this finding does not preclude a helpful role of the EMS in disinflation since participation could still have reduced the output cost of disinflation (Giavazzi and Giovannini 1988); but this is a different story.

24. As developed in Polak (1988), the need for rules to guard against the dangers of fine-tuning has receded in any case since economic policy in most industrial countries is now oriented much more toward the medium term. Fischer (1988) makes the complementary point that the state of our knowledge about the effects of monetary and fiscal policy is too rudimentary to justify policy rules. Niehans (1987) expresses doubts that rules could be relied upon to reduce international disturbances.
25. On the limitations of purchasing-power-parity rules, see Frenkel (1981).
26. Multiple indicators can reflect multiple targets and/or multiple instruments employed to reach a smaller number of targets.
27. The literature on "speculative attacks" deals with just this phenomenon; see, for example, Flood and Garber (1980).
28. See Frenkel and Goldstein (1986). This missing link between exchange rate movements and fiscal policy under target zones is being increasingly recognized. Whereas first-generation target-zone proposals spoke only of monetary policy, second- generation proposals have added a policy rule or guideline for fiscal policy; contrast Williamson (1985 [1983]) with Williamson and Miller (1987). Also, see the simulations of simple versus extended target-zone rules in Section 4.
29. See Oudiz and Sachs (1984), McKibbin and Sachs (1988), and Taylor (1985a) for evidence on the size of the gains, and Frankel and Rockett (1988) for the effects of using the "wrong" model.
30. See Schultze (1988) and Bryant and others (1988). As an example of the difficulties associated with identifying the "counterfactual," contrast Feldstein's (1988) appraisal of the likely evaluation of exchange rates in the absence of the Plaza Agreement with that of Lamfalussy (1987).
31. Frankel and Rockett (1988), however, show that, for a set of models compared in Bryant and others (1988), gains from knowing the "true" model (assuming that one is correct) dominate gains from coordination.
32. Another recent paper, Taylor (1986), considers different exchange rate arrangements in a rational expectations model; however, only completely fixed and freely floating exchange rates are compared, and the model is limited to the seven major industrial countries.
33. The model simulations do not, however, allow for two other ways in which private sector behavior may be affected by changes in policy regimes. First, the variance of output, prices, or exchange rates may be different, leading

to different degrees of substitutability among goods or assets. For example, it has been argued that the greater variability of exchange rates has led to a lower level of international trade than would have prevailed under fixed rates. Second, expectations may contain "speculative bubbles" in some circumstances, and hence may not solely reflect economic fundamentals. For example, the rise of the U.S. dollar early in 1985 despite declining interest rate differentials in favor of dollar-denominated assets is hard to explain.

34. Although simulation studies of judgmental coordinated policies are somewhat more difficult to design than analyses of rule-based proposals, a start in this direction has been made in some internal studies by Fund staff.

35. In contrast to the industrial countries, developing countries are not assumed to face perfect capital markets. Instead, the availability of financing reflects their ability to service debt, as measured by a ratio of their inflation-adjusted interest payments to the value of their exports. It is assumed that there is an upper limit to this ratio, beyond which the risk of nonrepayment becomes high, and consequently creditors would refuse to grant further new lending. As a result of the financing constraint, imports by developing countries are also constrained, tending to reduce both consumption and investment. The constraint on financing is, however, not solely based on current developments, but also reflects an assessment of future export prospects of developing countries; expected future exports are made to be consistent with the model's solution for those future exports.

36. This is a feature that will be relaxed in future work — in particular, by imposing shocks to residuals in successive periods.

37. Labor markets do not appear explicitly in the model, but features of wage bargaining, such as those due to overlapping multiperiod contracts, are reflected in the equation estimated for inflation.

38. The properties of MULTIMOD for these policy changes are quite similar to the average for other existing multicountry models; see Fischer (1988, 16).

39. One strong implication of this empirical regularity is that any "assignment rule" that assigns monetary policy to the current account — for example, Williamson and Miller's (1987) blueprint — is going to face problems; on this point, see Genberg and Swoboda (1987) and Boughton (1988).

40. It is assumed here that fiscal expansion is *not* accommodated by an increase in money growth. Current account effects also reflect the impact of interest rate changes on net investment income.
41. Niehans (1987, 215) also stresses the importance of steady policies: "The first, and most promising, step to reducing international disturbances must surely be the avoidance of the policy shifts that produce them. Especially for the dominant economy, the United States, the most important part of cooperation is steadiness."
42. The measure of real effective exchange rate is the country's manufactured export price, divided by a weighted average export price of its competitors, including developing countries. Thus, an increase indicates appreciation.
43. Corden (1986, 431) recognizes this to some extent: "[Coordination] means, incidentally, that if private investment in a country declines there should be some compensating increase in its fiscal deficit to modify the current account effect. It does not necessarily mean that a fiscal policy stance should be stable."
44. The role of this variable is to give a nominal anchor to the system. The inclusion of this term is also consistent with the intent of the blueprint proposal to make the level of interest rates depend (in an unspecified fashion) on the growth of aggregate GNP.
45. In implementing the rule, the value given by Edison, Miller, and Williamson (1987) to n, 10 percent, was initially tried, but the model either would not solve or gave negative nominal interest rates. Consequently, a higher value, 20 percent, was used, implying a lower feedback of exchange rate misalignments on interest rates.
46. Again, we adopt Williamson's (1985) estimates of target or equilibrium real effective exchange rates merely to stay as close as possible to the original proposals. There should be no implication that we agree or disagree with those estimates. For a discussion of some of the difficulties associated with calculating equilibrium exchange rates, see Frenkel and Goldstein (1988b).
47. It should also be noted that MULTIMOD's definition of real effective exchange rates is wider than most measures, since it allows for competition from manufactures produced in developing countries.
48. It is also the case in Edison, Miller, and Williamson (1987), that real exchange rates under a target zone regime differ little from their historical values.

49. Suppose there are three time periods and that interest parity relates interest rates and exchange rates. Suppose also that the exchange rate is unchanged in the third period. In each period, the interest rate differential is equal to the appreciation that is expected for (and actually occurs in) the next period. Thus, in terms of deviations from baseline, $d_t = e_{t+1} - e_t$, where $e_3 = 0$. Then in the second period, the interest differential will have to be equal to the desired change in the exchange rate; if it is overvalued by 5 percent, interest rates will have to be 5 percentage points lower. If in the first period the exchange rate is undervalued by 5 percent, then interest rates will have to be not 5, but 10 percentage points, higher.
50. As shown in Buiter and Miller (1982), if the model has the natural rate property, then the cumulative output losses from different disinflation policies are the same when discounting is ignored.
51. If there is no feedback of inflation onto monetary policy — such as through world nominal income — then the target-zone rule cannot be simulated in MULTIMOD because of the absence of a nominal anchor.
52. The shock is distributed using the weights that serve to allocate the world trade discrepancy in MULTIMOD. As a result, the shock to the United States is also reduced by the U.S. share of world trade, so that U.S. exports rise on impact by 8.6 percent, not the full 10 percent.

Jacob A. Frenkel, Morris Goldstein, and Paul R. Masson, "The Rationale for, and Effects of International Economic Policy Coordination," in William Branson, Jacob A. Frenkel, and Morris Goldstein (editors), International Policy Coordination and Exchange Rate Fluctuations, pp. 9–55 (1990). University of Chicago Press and NBER. Used with permission of the publishers.

REFERENCES

Artis, Michael, and Sylvia Ostry. 1986. *International economic policy coordination.* Chatham House Papers, no. 30, Royal Institute of International Affairs. London: Routledge and Kegan Paul.

Bockelmann, H. 1988. The need for worldwide coordination of economic policies. Paper presented at Conference on Financing the World Economy in the Nineties, School for Banking and Finance, Tilburg University.

Boughton, James. 1988. Policy assignment strategies with somewhat flexible exchange rates. IMF Working Paper no. 88/40.

Boughton, James, and William Branson. 1988. Commodity prices as a leading indicator of inflation. IMF Working Paper no. 88/87.
Bryant, Ralph. 1987. Intergovernmental coordination of economic policies. In P. B. Kenen, ed., *International monetary cooperation: Essays in honor of Henry C. Wallich.* Essays in International Finance no. 169 (December): 4–15. Princeton: International Finance Section, Princeton University.
Bryant, Ralph, and others, eds. 1988. *Empirical macroeconomics for interdependent economies.* Washington, DC: Brookings Institution.
Bryant, Ralph, and Richard Portes, eds. 1987. *Global macroeconomics: Policy conflict and cooperation.* London: Macmillan.
Buiter, Willem, and Marcus H. Miller. 1982. Real exchange rate over-shooting and the output cost of bringing down inflation. *European Economic Review* 18 (May/June): 85–123.
Buiter, Willem H., and Richard C. Marston, eds. 1985. *International economic policy coordination.* New York: Cambridge University Press.
Calvo, Guillermo A. 1978. On the time consistency of optimal policy in a monetary economy. *Econometrica* 46 (November): 1411–28.
Cooper, Richard N. 1982. The gold standard: Historical facts and future prospects. *Brookings Papers on Economic Activity* 1:1–45.
Cooper, Richard N. 1985. Economic interdependence and coordination of economic policies. In R. W. Jones and P. B. Kenen, eds., *Handbook of international economics,* vol. 2, 1194–1234. Amsterdam: North-Holland.
Cooper, Richard N. 1987. International economic cooperation: Is it desirable? Is it likely? Lecture presented at International Monetary Fund (October).
Cooper, Richard N. 1988. U.S. macroeconomic policy, 1986–88: Are the models useful? In Ralph Bryant, and others, eds., *Empirical macroeconomics for interdependent economies,* 255–66. Washington, DC: Brookings Institution.
Corden, W. Max. 1986. Fiscal policies, current accounts and real exchange rates: In search of a logic of international policy coordination. *Weltwirtschaftliches Archiv* 122 (no. 3): 423–38.
Crockett, Andrew. 1987. Strengthening international economic cooperation: The role of indicators in multilateral surveillance. IMF Working Paper no. 87/76.
Currie, David, Paul Levine, and Nicholas Vidalis. 1987. International cooperation and reputation in an empirical two-bloc model. In R. C. Bryant and R. Portes, eds., *Global macroeconomics: Policy conflict and cooperation,* 75–127. London: Macmillan.
Currie, David, and Simon Wren-Lewis. 1987. Conflict and cooperation in international macroeconomic policymaking: The past decade and future prospects. International Monetary Fund (December). Typescript.
Dini, Lamberto. 1988. Cooperation and conflict in monetary and trade policies. Paper presented at International Management and Development Institute, U.S.–European Top Management Roundtable. Milan, February 19.

Edison, Hali J., Marcus H. Miller, and John Williamson. 1987. On evaluating and extending the target zone proposal. *Journal of Policy Modeling* 9 (Spring): 199–224.

Feldstein, Martin. 1988. Distinguished lecture on economics in government: Thinking about international economic coordination. *The Journal of Economic Perspectives* 2 (Spring): 3–13.

Fischer, Stanley. 1988. International macroeconomic policy coordination. In Martin Feldstein, ed., *International economic cooperation*, 11–43. Chicago: University of Chicago Press.

Fleming, J. Marcus. 1962. Domestic financial policies under fixed and under floating exchange rates. *IMF Staff Papers* 9 (November): 369–79.

Flood, Robert, and Peter Garber. 1980. Market fundamentals versus price level bubbles: The first tests. *Journal of Political Economy* 88 (August).

Frankel, Jeffrey, and Katherine Rockett. 1988. International macroeconomic policy coordination when policymakers do not agree on the true model. *American Economic Review* 78, no. 3 (June): 318–40.

Frenkel, Jacob A. 1975. Current problems of the international monetary system: Reflections on European monetary integration. *Weltwirtschaftliches Archiv* 111 (no. 2): 216–21.

Frenkel, Jacob A. 1981. The collapse of purchasing power parities during the 1970's. *European Economic Review* 16 (May): 145–65.

Frenkel, Jacob A. 1982. Turbulence in the market for foreign exchange and macroeconomic policies. The Henry Thornton Lecture, City University Centre for Banking and International Finance, London.

Frenkel, Jacob A. 1983. International liquidity and monetary control. In George M. von Furstenberg, ed., *International money and credit: The policy roles.* Washington, DC: International Monetary Fund.

Frenkel, Jacob A. 1985. A note on "the good fix" and "the bad fix." *European Economic Review* 1–2 (June–July).

Frenkel, Jacob A. 1986. International interdependence and the constraints on macroeconomic policies. *Weltwirtschafliches Archiv* 122 (no. 4).

Frenkel, Jacob A., and Morris Goldstein. 1986. A guide to target zones. *IMF Staff Papers* 33 (December): 633–70.

Frenkel, Jacob A., and Morris Goldstein. 1988a. The international monetary system: Developments and prospects. Paper presented at the Cato Institute Conference, February 1988. *Cato Journal* 8 (Fall).

Frenkel, Jacob A., and Morris Goldstein. 1988b. Exchange rate volatility and misalignment. In *Financial Market Volatility.* Kansas City: Federal Reserve Bank of Kansas City.

Frenkel, Jacob A., Morris Goldstein, and Paul R. Masson. 1988. International coordination of economic policies: Scope, methods, and effects. In Wilfried Guth, ed., *Economic Policy Coordination*, 149–91. Washington, DC: International Monetary Fund.

Frenkel, Jacob A., and Michael Mussa. 1985. Asset markets, exchange rates and the balance of payments. In R. W. Jones and P. B. Kenen, eds., *Handbook of international economics*, vol. 2, 679–747. Amsterdam: North-Holland.

Frenkel, Jacob A., and Assaf Razin. 1987a. The Mundell-Fleming model: A quarter century later. *IMF Staff Papers* 34 (December) 567–720.

Frenkel, Jacob A., and Assaf Razin. 1987b. *Fiscal policies and the world economy.* Cambridge, MA: MIT Press.

Gavin, Michael. 1986. Macroeconomic policy coordination under alternative exchange rate regimes. Federal Reserve Board (September). Typescript.

Genberg, Hans, and Alexander Swoboda. 1987. The current account and the policy mix under flexible exchange rates. IMF Working Paper no. 87/70.

Ghosh, Atish R., and Paul R. Masson. 1988. International policy coordination in a world with model uncertainty. *IMF Staff Papers* 35 (June): 230–58.

Giavazzi, Francesco, and Alberto Giovannini. 1988. Interpreting the European disinflation. The role of the exchange rate regime. *Informacion Comercial Espanola* (May).

Goldstein, Morris. 1980. *Have flexible exchange rates handicapped macroeconomic policy?* Special Papers in International Economics no. 14 (June). Princeton: Princeton University Press.

Goldstein, Morris. 1984. *The exchange rate system: Lessons of the past and options for the future.* IMF Occasional Paper no. 30 (July).

Hamada, Koichi. 1979. Macroeconomic strategy and coordination under alternative exchange rates. In R. Dornbusch and J. Frenkel, eds., *International economic policy: Theory and evidence*, 292–324. Baltimore: Johns Hopkins University Press.

Helliwell, John F., and Tim Padmore. 1985. Empirical studies of macroeconomic interdependence. In R. W. Jones and P. B. Kenen, eds., *Handbook of international economics*, vol. 2, 1107–51. Amsterdam: North-Holland.

Henderson, Dale. 1979. Financial policies in open economics. *American Economic Review* 69 (May): 232–39.

Holbrook, Robert S. 1972. Optimal economic policy and the problem of instrument instability. *American Economic Review* 62 (March): 57–65.

Holtham, Gerald, Giles Keating, and Peter Spencer. 1987. *EMS: Advance or face retreat.* London: Credit Suisse First Boston Ltd.

Horne, Jocelyn, and Paul R. Masson. 1988. Scope and limits of international economic cooperation and policy coordination. *IMF Staff Papers* 35 (June): 259–96.

IMF. 1974. Documents of the Committee of 20. Washington, DC: International Monetary Fund.

IMF. 1986. *IMF Survey* (May 19): 157.

IMF. 1987. *IMF Survey* (March 9): 73.

Jurgensen, Philippe. 1983. *Report of the working group on exchange market intervention.* Washington, DC: U.S. Treasury.

Kenen, Peter B. 1987. Exchange rates and policy coordination. Brookings Discussion Paper no. 61 (October). Washington, DC: Brookings Institution.

Kydland, F., and E. Prescott. 1977. Rules rather than discretion: The inconsistency of optimal plans. *Journal of Political Economy* 85 (June): 473–91.

Lamfalussy, Alexandre. 1987. Current account imbalances in the industrial world: Why they matter. In P. B. Kenen, ed., *International monetary cooperation: Essays in honor of Henry C. Wallich.* Essays in International Finance no. 169 (December): 31–37. Princeton: International Finance Section, Princeton University.

Masson, Paul R., and others. 1988. MULTIMOD: A multi-region econometric model. *Staff studies for the world economic outlook* (July). Washington, DC: International Monetary Fund.

McKibbin, Warwick J., and Jeffrey D. Sachs. 1988. Coordination of monetary and fiscal policies in the industrial countries. In Jacob A. Frenkel, ed., *International aspects of fiscal policy,* 73–113. Chicago: University of Chicago Press.

Mundell, Robert A. 1971. *The dollar and the policy mix.* Essays in International Finance no. 85 (May). Princeton: Princeton University Press.

Mussa, Michael. 1981. *The role of official intervention.* Occasional Paper no. 6. New York: Group of Thirty.

Niehans, Jurg. 1987. Generating international disturbances. In Y. Suzuki and M. Okabe, eds., *Toward a world of economic stability: Optimal monetary framework and policy,* 181–218. Tokyo: University of Tokyo Press.

Oudiz, Gilles, and Jeffrey D. Sachs. 1984. Macroeconomic policy coordination among the industrial economies. *Brookings Papers on Economic Activity* 1: 1–75.

Poehl, Karl Otto. 1987. Cooperation — A keystone for the stability of the international monetary system. First Arthur Burns Memorial Lecture, at the American Council on Germany, New York (November).

Polak, Jacques J. 1981. *Coordination of National Economic Policies.* Occasional Paper no. 7. New York: Group of Thirty.

Polak, Jacques J. 1988. Economic policy objectives and policymaking in the major industrial countries. In WilfriedGuth, ed., *Economic policy coordination*, 1–43. Washington, DC: IMF.

Poole, William. 1970. Optimal choice of monetary policy instruments in a simple stochastic macro model. *Quarterly Journal of Economics* 84 (May): 197–216.

Putnam, Robert D., and Nicholas Bayne. 1984. *Hanging Together: The Seven-Power Summits.* Cambridge, MA: Harvard University Press.

Putnam, Robert D., and C. Randall Henning. 1986. The Bonn summit of 1978: How does international economic policy coordination actually work? Brookings Discussion Papers in International Economics no. 53 (October). Washington, DC: Brookings Institution.

Rogoff, Kenneth. 1985. Can international monetary policy cooperation be counterproductive? *Journal of International Economics* 18 (May): 199–217.

Schultze, Charles. 1988. International macroeconomics coordination — Marrying the economic models with political reality. In Martin Feldstein, ed., *International Economic Cooperation,* 49–60. Chicago: University of Chicago Press.

Tanzi, Vito. 1988. Fiscal policy and international coordination: Current and future issues. Paper presented at Conference on Fiscal Policy, Economic Adjustment, and Financial Markets. Boconni University, January 27–30.

Tanzi, Vito, and Teresa Ter-Minassian. 1987. The European monetary system and fiscal policies. In Sijbren Cnossen, ed., *Tax coordination in the European community,* ch. 13. Series on International Taxation no. 7. Boston: Kluwer Law and Taxation Publishers.

Taylor, John. 1985a. International coordination in the design of Macroeconomic policy rules. *European Economic Review* 28 (June–July): 53–81.

Taylor, John. 1985b. What would nominal GNP targeting do to the business cycle? In K. Brunner and A. H. Meltzer, eds., *Understanding monetary regimes.* Carnegie-Rochester Conference Series on Public Policy 22: 61–84.

Taylor, John. 1986. An econometric evaluation of international monetary policy rules: Fixed versus flexible exchange rates. Stanford University. Typescript.

Tobin, James. 1980. Stabilization policy ten years after. *Brookings Papers on Economic Activity* 1: 19–71.

Tobin, James. 1987. Agenda for international coordination of macroeconomic policies. In P. B. Kenen, ed., *International monetary cooperation: Essays in honor of Henry C. Wallich.* Essays in International Finance no. 169 (December): 61–69. Princeton: International Finance Section, Princeton University.

U.S. Congress. 1982. *Report to the congress of the commission on the role of gold in the domestic and international monetary systems.* Washington, DC: Government Printing Office (March).

Vaubel, Roland. 1985. International collusion or competition for macroeconomic policy coordination? A restatement. *Recherches Économiques de Louvain* 51 (December): 223–40.

Wallich, Henry C. 1984. Institutional cooperation in the world economy. In Jacob Frenkel and Michael Mussa, eds., *The world economic system: Performance and prospects,* 85–99. Dover, MA: Auburn House.

Williamson, John. 1985[1983]. *The exchange rate system.* 2d ed. Policy Analyses in International Economics no. 5. Washington, DC: Institute for International Economics.

Williamson, John, and Marcus H. Miller. 1987. *Targets and indicators: A blueprint for the international coordination of economic policy.* Policy Analyses in International Economics no. 22 (September). Washington, DC: Institute for International Economics.

Part III
Banking, Financial Crises and Financial Regulation

Chapter 8

Banking Crises in Emerging Economies: Origins and Policy Options

Morris Goldstein and Philip Turner

INTRODUCTION

There is a natural inclination to think of financial crises as rare events. Yet banking crises have become increasingly common — especially in the developing world. Lindgren *et al.* (1996) have reported that over the 1980–96 period at least two-thirds of IMF member countries experienced significant banking sector problems. In many regions, almost every country has experienced at least one serious bout of banking trouble. Moreover, the incidence of banking crises in the 1980s and 1990s has been significantly higher than in the 1970s, and much higher than in the more tranquil period of the 1950s and 1960s. Honohan (1996) goes even further, arguing that

---

Mr Goldstein is the Dennis Weatherstone Senior Fellow at the Institute for International Economics, Washington D.C., and a former Deputy Director of the Research Department at the International Monetary Fund. He was a consultant in the Monetary & Economic Department of the BIS when this paper was written. The authors are grateful to Ib Madsen who was responsible for most of the statistical work; thanks are also due to Stephan Arthur, Chris Bennett and Karsten von Kleist. They are also most grateful to the central banks who contributed much of the data. Helpful comments were received from Andrew Crockett, Charles Freeland, Judith Hunter, Carmen Reinhart, Josef Van't dack and Bill White. Christine Mapes and Joyce Ogilvie Steuri typed several drafts most efficiently.
©Bank for International Settlements, 1996. CH–4002 Basle, Switzerland

the frequency and size of financial crashes during the last quarter-century is "unprecedented" — much worse than was experienced prior to 1950.

There are two reasons why banking problems in the emerging economies merit particular attention: first, the serious consequences for the local economies and, secondly, the fallout on other countries as international financial markets have become more integrated.

Banking crises in developing countries have been far more severe during the past 15 years than those in industrial countries. Caprio and Klingebiel (1996a) have recently put together a comprehensive database on banking crises in both industrial and developing countries for this period. According to their estimates of losses or resolution costs, the most severe industrial country banking crisis was that of Spain (1977–85), where estimated losses reached almost 17% of GDP. Next (in descending order) came Finland (1991–93) at 8% of GDP, Sweden (1991) at 6% and Norway (1987–89) at 4%; the US saving and loan crisis (1984–91) cost about 3% of GDP, and the resolution costs of the current bad loan problem in Japan will be high. In the developing world, by contrast, Caprio and Klingebiel identify more than a dozen episodes in which losses or resolution costs exceeded 10% of GDP, including the recent cases of Venezuela (18%), Bulgaria (14%), Mexico (12–15%) and Hungary (10%); in several cases (Argentina, Chile and Côte d'Ivoire), losses were greater than or equal to 25% of GDP. While such estimates are inevitably imprecise, the greater severity of banking crises in developing countries is a common finding of several different studies (see, for example, BIS (1996), Lindgren *et al.* (1996) and Sheng (1996)).

Concern about these banking crises is hardly surprising. Bank difficulties or failures are presumed to generate more serious negative externalities for the rest of the economy than those at either other kinds of financial firms or non-financial firms. These externalities take a variety of forms. The use of public money to recapitalise insolvent banks can seriously handicap efforts to control budget deficits.[1] Even if public expenditure on rescuing banks is viewed as a (domestic) transfer rather than as a real economic cost, it can push the authorities toward less benign ways of financing the deficit (e.g. the inflation

---

[1] Edwards (1995) shows how large-scale public bailouts of banks have complicated efforts at fiscal consolidation in Latin America over the past two decades.

tax); moreover, the rescue itself can sap the incentives for private creditors to monitor the behaviour of banks in the future.

If recapitalisation takes the form of weak banks cutting back lending and widening spreads, the lower availability and higher cost of bank credit can undermine the real economy, particularly for small and medium-sized firms which have fewer alternative sources of financing. In general, a decline in economic activity precedes the outbreak of a banking crisis so that it becomes difficult to isolate the independent effect of the crisis on output during and after the event.[2] Nevertheless, there is widespread agreement that a banking crisis is likely to amplify a downturn;[3] in addition, the worsening of information and adverse selection problems that typically occurs during a financial crisis (as it is the least creditworthy borrowers who will be prepared to pay high interest rates) means that the quality of investment is likely to suffer; that is, saving will not flow to its most productive uses.[4]

Serious banking problems also create difficulties for monetary policy. They may not only distort the normal relationships between monetary instruments and the intermediate and final targets of monetary policy, but they may also compromise the overall stance of monetary policy. Fears of pushing an already strained banking sector over the edge may constrain the monetary authorities from tightening monetary policy to deal with, for instance, a loss of confidence by foreign investors or a rise in incipient inflationary pressures. Banking sector weaknesses explain, as much as anything else, why the Mexican authorities (in April–December 1994) both sterilised so heavily after private capital flows tailed off and engaged in large-scale substitution of lower-yielding, dollar-indexed tesobonos for higher-yielding peso-denominated cetes.[5] Both actions were aimed at limiting the rise in interest rates and buying time for the banks to recover — but, in the end, magnified the decline in international reserves and allowed a currency crisis to widen into a debt crisis.[6] More generally, recent empirical research reveals that banking crises have often been a leading indicator of balance-of-payments crises in emerging markets during the last

---

[2] See Kaminsky and Reinhart (1995), Mishkin (1994) and Sheng (1996).
[3] See Lindgren *et al.* (1996), Johnston and Pazarbasioglu (1995) and Bernanke (1983).
[4] See De Gregorio and Guidotti (1992) and Mishkin (1994).
[5] Between 1991 and mid-1994, the share of non-performing loans in the Mexican banking system doubled — from about 4% to 8%.
[6] See Calvo and Goldstein (1996) and Leiderman and Thorne (1996).

15 years.[7] Finally, banks in developing countries typically operate the payments system, hold the bulk of financial assets, are major purchasers of government bonds, and provide the liquid credit needed by fledgling securities markets.

Banking crises in emerging economies can also be costly for industrial countries, particularly as the importance of emerging countries in the world economy and in international financial markets has grown. Developing countries nowadays purchase about one-quarter of industrial country exports. In 1992–94, they received about 40% of global inflows of foreign direct investment.[8] At end-1995, banks in the BIS reporting area had outstanding claims against developing countries of over $717 billion (about $46 billion more than their liabilities to these countries).[9] Over the period 1990–95, developing countries issued over $133 billion of bonds in international financial markets; at the time of the Mexican crisis, non-residents held about 80% of the tesobonos held outside the banking system.[10] Portfolio equity flows into developing countries in the 1990s approached $128 billion. While still very low (about 2%), the share of emerging markets in the portfolios of industrial country institutional investors has increased sharply over the past five years, and optimal portfolio calculations suggest that this share should continue to rise towards the emerging market share (13%) of global stock market capitalisation.[11] Honohan (1996) estimates that since 1980 the resolution costs of banking crises in all developing and transition economies have approached a quarter of a trillion dollars.[12] Since the late 1970s, all IMF drawings have been made by developing countries. In short, to the extent that banking crises depress developing countries' growth and foreign trade, strain their ability to service and to repay private capital inflows, and eventually add to the liabilities of developing country governments, industrial countries are very likely to feel the repercussions.

---

[7] See Kaminsky and Reinhart (1995).
[8] See Qureshi (1996).
[9] See BIS (1996).
[10] See BIS (1995).
[11] See Levine (1996).
[12] Honohan (1996) arrives at this figure by first regressing resolution costs against bank balance-sheet losses for those countries where data are available for both variables; he then uses that regression to estimate bank crisis resolution costs for those developing countries where data are available only on balance-sheet losses.

This paper therefore discusses the factors responsible for banking problems in developing countries and the policy options that are available for reducing the frequency and severity of these crises. The paper does not address the question of financial fragility more generally; in addition, it concentrates on issues of crisis prevention rather than those of crisis management and bank restructuring.[13] Most of the examples are drawn from the experience of the emerging economies rather than from either the transition economies or the low-income developing countries.

The paper is structured as follows. The next section takes up the origin of banking crises in emerging economies, focusing on eight general problems. The following section then identifies, and comments on, the policy prescriptions that have often been proposed to deal with each of these problems. Examples of recent reforms in some emerging economies are also discussed. Some brief concluding remarks follow in a final section.

FACTORS BEHIND BANKING CRISES

It would be convenient for both diagnosis and prediction if banking crises in emerging markets could be attributed to just one or two factors. But research on the origins of banking crises strongly suggests that this is not the case.[14] The leading culprits that have been identified are the following:

(i) *Macroeconomic volatility: external and domestic*

The very nature of banks makes them vulnerable to large relative price changes and to losses of confidence. Because bankers are presumed to know the creditworthiness of their borrowers better than anyone else, their loans are illiquid and difficult to mark to market. They typically borrow short and lend long. They operate with high leverage (low capital) and on a fractional reserve basis (i.e. hold relatively small amounts of cash). Deposits are redeemable at par, and depositors are assured that they can get immediate access to liquidity—but only if not everyone tries to withdraw funds simultaneously. If volatility sharply

---

[13] Sheng (1996) provides a useful set of principles to guide bank rescue and restructuring efforts.
[14] See BIS (1996), Caprio and Klingebiel (1996b), Folkerts-Landau *et al.* (1995), Gavin and Hausmann (1996), Honohan (1996), Kaminsky and Reinhart (1995), Lindgren *et al.* (1996), Meltzer (1996), Rojas-Suárez and Weisbrod (1995a, 1996b), Sheng (1996) and Sundararajan and Baliño (1991).

alters the relationship between the values of bank assets and liabilities — beyond the ex ante protection provided by bank capital, specific loan loss reserves and reserve requirements against bank deposits — banks can become particularly vulnerable. Volatility in emerging markets derives from several sources — both external and domestic.

One external source is the relatively large fluctuations in the terms of trade. When banks' customers suddenly find that the terms of trade have turned sharply against them, their ability to service existing loans is likely to be impaired. Caprio and Klingebiel (1996a) report that 75% of the developing countries in their sample which experienced banking crises suffered a terms-of-trade decline of at least 10% prior to the crisis (with an average fall of 17%). Kaminsky and Reinhart (1995) likewise identify terms-of-trade deterioration as one of the stylised facts preceding banking crises in small industrial countries and in emerging markets. Hausmann and Gavin (1996) estimate that the standard deviation of changes in the terms of trade in Latin American emerging markets (at roughly 15% per year) is about twice as high (on average) as in industrial countries over the past 20 years. Volatility in the terms of trade is particularly pronounced for countries with high export concentration (e.g. Venezuela, Ecuador); small economies, usually less diversified than larger ones, typically face unusually large fluctuations in their terms of trade (as well as in other sources of volatility). Other things being equal, countries with relatively low export diversification are more susceptible to banking crises.[15]

Volatility in international interest rates, and the induced effect on private capital flows, is another important external factor. Not only do fluctuations in international interest rates affect (either directly or indirectly) the cost of borrowing for emerging markets, but they also alter (at the margin) the relative attractiveness of investing in emerging markets. Indeed, empirical evidence suggests that movements in international interest rates can explain between one-half and two-thirds of the surge in private capital inflows to developing countries in the 1990s.[16] Viewed in a longer-term perspective, the volatility of net private capital flows to developing countries has been marked. For example, Latin American developing countries saw net private capital inflows

---

[15] See Caprio and Klingebiel (1996a) and Gavin and Hausmann (1996).
[16] See Calvo *et al.* (1993) and Dooley *et al.* (1994). Goldstein (1995) provides a survey of these studies.

move from about 6% of host-country GDP in 1981 to practically nil during the 1983–90 period, back up to 4% in 1991, and then even higher, to 5–6% over the 1993–95 period.[17] Similarly, for Asian developing countries which are members of APEC, net inflows in the capital account roughly doubled (as a share of host-country GDP) from 1984–88 to 1989–93.[18] Incompletely sterilised capital inflows boost bank deposits and tempt banks to increase lending even at the expense of lower credit quality. This plants the seeds of trouble when the boom collapses (see below). And when capital flows out unexpectedly as a result of a loss of confidence, there is a danger that a sudden withdrawal of bank deposits will force a "fire sale" of bank assets. Because creditor-country interest rates are driven by economic forces in those countries themselves, some of the volatility in private capital flows facing emerging markets is beyond their control.

Real exchange rates are the third member of the external volatility trio. Real exchange rate volatility can cause difficulties for banks either directly (when there is a currency or maturity mismatch between bank liabilities and assets) or indirectly (when exchange rate volatility creates large losses for bank borrowers). Hausmann and Gavin (1995) report that (owing to highly variable inflation rates) the volatility of real exchange rates of 22 Latin American developing countries has been about twice that of industrial countries over the past two decades. BIS calculations (1996) of the volatility of exchange rates for a sample of Asian and Latin American emerging markets point to a similar conclusion; they also confirm that such exchange rate volatility has been higher in Latin America than in Asia. Recall too that the short-run variability of nominal and real exchange rates for the key-currency (the dollar, the DM and the yen) countries was much greater during the floating rate period (1973–96) than it was during the preceding two decades. Kaminsky and Reinhart (1995) observe that sharp real exchange rate appreciation typically precedes a banking crisis. One reason for this may be the adverse effect on the profitability of the tradables sector. Another may be that the high real domestic interest rates often associated with real exchange rate appreciation or with disinflation encourage residents to denominate their borrowing in foreign currencies, thus exposing themselves to large foreign exchange rate risks.[19]

---

[17] See Hausmann and Gavin (1995).
[18] See Khan and Reinhart (1995).

On the domestic side, both growth and inflation rates are often highly volatile. Assessing credit risk becomes harder when growth and inflation rates fluctuate widely. For example, a company's credit history under hyperinflation may not be a good guide to its performance in a more stable environment. One of the more robust conclusions of the empirical literature on early-warning signals of financial crises is that sharp contractions in economic activity increase the probability of banking (and balance-of-payments) crises. Hausmann and Gavin (1995) calculate that the volatility of growth rates — and particularly the frequency and duration of recessions — in Latin America has been considerably larger over the past two decades than in industrial countries; differences with respect to the volatility of inflation rates are greater still. Caprio and Klingebiel (1996b) report that the volatility of growth and inflation rates was on a rising trend over the 1960–94 period for countries experiencing systemic banking crises over this period, while no such trend was evident for countries experiencing less severe or no banking difficulties.[20] Table 1 shows that emerging markets (particularly those in Latin America) displayed higher volatility in growth and inflation rates than the three largest industrial countries over the 1980–95 period, and that the countries with the most volatile macroeconomic environments were also the ones (on average) with the most volatile behaviour for bank deposits and bank credit (expressed as ratios to GDP).

(ii) *Lending booms, asset price collapses and surges in capital inflows*

According to one school of thought, banking crises are caused by excessive credit creation and unsound financing during the expansion phase of the business cycle; a crisis is triggered when the bubble bursts.[21] Three features of recent experience provide support for this thesis: both bank lending booms and declines in equity prices have often preceded banking crises;[22] those emerging economies that received the largest net private capital inflows have also been

---

[19] See Sheng (1996) on the close association in the 1980s between high real interest rates and banking problems.

[20] Because debt contracts in developing countries are typically of short maturity, an unanticipated decline in inflation would not be expected to directly adversely affect firms' balance sheets. Instead, the trouble comes from the high real interest rates which often accompany disinflation; see Mishkin (1996).

[21] See, for example, Kindleberger (1978).

[22] See Gavin and Hausmann (1996) and Kaminsky and Reinhart (1995).

Table 1: The volatility of macroeconomic indicators and banking aggregates over the period 1980–95[1]

	GDP	Inflation	Bank deposits[2]	Bank credit to private sector[2]
India	2.2	4.1	3.4	4.6
Hong Kong	3.4	3.5	7.9	6.9
Korea	3.5	7.2	5.3	5.6
Singapore	3.3	2.6	5.7	4.6
Taiwan	2.4	5.5	6.4	8.7
Indonesia	2.0	3.1	7.8	20.1
Malaysia	3.0	2.4	8.8	8.4
Thailand	2.7	4.6	6.6	6.5
Argentina	5.5	860.0	23.5	34.4
Brazil	3.7	767.6	20.7	32.8
Chile	5.8	7.5	20.9	21.8
Colombia	1.5	3.9	9.0	9.1
Mexico	4.2	39.4	33.2	22.1
Venezuela	4.9	21.9	12.7	16.0
Memorandum:				
United States	2.1	3.1	4.4	3.4
Japan	1.8	2.0	2.5	2.5
Germany	1.8	1.9	5.4	3.1

[1] Measured as the standard deviation of annual percentage changes.
[2] As a percentage of nominal GDP.

those which experienced the most rapid expansion in their commercial banking sectors;[23] and, finally, part of the capital inflow surge during the 1990s might be regarded as a bubble built on over-optimism about the effects of policy reform in host countries.[24] This argument rests on presumptions that discriminating between good and bad credit risks is harder when the economy is expanding rapidly because many borrowers are at least temporarily very profitable and liquid; that sharp swings in real estate and equity prices intensify these crises because of high loan concentration; and that asset price declines depress the market value of collateral.

---

[23] See Folkerts-Landau *et al.* (1995).
[24] See Krugman (1995).

Nonetheless, the empirical evidence on the effects of lending booms and equity price declines in banking crises has been mixed. Gavin and Hausmann (1996) find that bank lending booms have typically preceded banking crises in Latin America, as well as in some industrial countries (Finland, Norway, Sweden, Japan and the United States). Likewise, Kaminsky and Reinhart (1995) find that lending booms have moderate predictive power for banking crises in emerging markets and small industrial countries. In contrast, drawing on a larger sample, Caprio and Klingebiel (1996b) conclude that, outside Latin America, the link between lending booms and bank crises becomes quite weak.[25] As for sharp declines in equity prices, Kaminsky and Reinhart (1995) find they are among the best leading indicators of banking crises — better than lending booms. Equity prices may act (along with a decline in the terms of trade and the onset of recession) as an exogenous trigger that reduces the profitability of bank debtors, shatters the mood of euphoria and unleashes a downward spiral. Mishkin (1994) also finds evidence that equity price declines are a useful indicator of financial crises, but probably a contemporaneous rather than a leading one. The BIS (1996) reports that the volatility of equity prices in emerging economies has been much greater than that in large European industrial countries over the past decade. Folkerts-Landau et al. (1995) and the BIS (1996) have also emphasised that the large scale of private capital flows relative to the size of equity markets in emerging economies means that these countries may have to live with a significant degree of volatility in equity prices for some time. The Venezuelan banking crisis is but one example of a crisis that was preceded by a violent boom-bust equity market cycle. The lack of consistent data on property prices in developing countries has prevented much systematic examination of their influence;[26] nevertheless, the bursting of property price bubbles has been a feature of many banking crises in industrial and developing countries.[27]

---

[25] Honohan (1996) draws the same conclusion.

[26] This raises the broader question of whether there would be dividends from collecting internationally comparable data on key variables that have a bearing on the health of the banking system (e.g. property prices, loan default rates, interest rate spreads).

[27] See Caprio et al. (1994). The BIS (1996) has also shown that a deflated series of property and equity prices has borne a close relationship with swings in private real credit growth in industrial countries over the last quarter-century.

(iii) Increasing bank liabilities with large maturity/currency mismatches

One indicator of financial deepening as economies develop and mature is a rising ratio of broad monetary aggregates to GDP. Yet not all such increases are benign. If the growth of bank liabilities is very rapid relative to both the size of the economy and the stock of international reserves, if bank assets differ significantly from bank liabilities as to liquidity, maturity and currency of denomination, if bank capital and/or loan-loss provisions have not expanded to compensate for the volatility of bank assets, and if the economy is subject to large shocks to confidence (some stemming from external events beyond its control), then one can have a recipe for increased banking system fragility. Several authors have argued that this is just what has happened over the past two decades or so.

Honohan (1996) notes that, driven by technological innovation and deregulation, the ratio of M2 to GNP for 59 developing countries increased sharply over the 1980–93 period (from 28 to 35% in unweighted terms, and from 32 to 48% in weighted terms) — without a commensurate increase in bank capital. Rojas-Suárez and Weisbrod (1995b) show that on the eve of banking crises, the loan loss reserves of banks of three Latin American countries were no higher than those of large banks in the United States despite the higher risks.

Calvo and Goldstein (1996) argue that advances in technology and information processing, combined with financial liberalisation, have made it much easier for residents of emerging economies to alter the currency composition of their bank deposits.[28] Examining the origins of the Mexican crisis, they note that, as a result of rapidly rising ratios of M2 to GNP over the 1989–94 period and a precipitous decline in international reserves in 1994, the gap between Mexico's liquid banking liabilities and its stock of foreign exchange available to meet those liabilities in case of a run widened progressively. Before the 20th December devaluation, the dollar value of M2 had climbed to a level almost five times higher than the maximum level of international reserves the country had ever recorded. Several other emerging

---

[28] In this regard, the IMF (1995) reports that most of the pressure on Mexico's foreign exchange reserves in 1994, and particularly just before the devaluation, came not from foreign investors but rather from Mexican residents sending their funds abroad.

economies had gaps of one-half to one-third that of Mexico (e.g. Chile and Brazil) and thus, by this measure, were much less vulnerable to attack. Rojas-Suárez and Weisbrod (1995b) document that deposit runs have been much more prevalent during the early stages of Latin American banking crises than those in industrial countries. Dollarisation of deposits will not necessarily solve the problem because depositors will keep funds (dollarised or not) in domestic banks only if they are confident that the banking system has sufficient access to international reserves to cover liquidation into dollars.

When domestic interest rates are high, the temptation for the banking system and bank customers to denominate debt in foreign currency can be particularly strong. For instance, banks may have recourse to short-term, foreign-currency-denominated borrowing in the interbank market to fund longer-term bank loans. Such strategies can come badly unstuck when a devaluation occurs. Sheng (1996) reports that in 1980 developing country banks had a net foreign liability exposure of $81 billion — which subjected them to large revaluation losses from subsequent devaluations under structural adjustment programmes. A more recent example is that of Mexico. Between December 1993 and December 1994, the Mexican peso declined from 3.1 to 5.3 to the dollar and the foreign-currency-denominated liabilities of Mexican banks jumped from 89 billion pesos to 174 billion pesos; at the same time, the credit risk on their loans increased as interest rates rose and as economic activity fell.[29] Bank customers can also find themselves caught by currency mismatches: the BIS (1996) reports the results of a survey which indicated that (at the time of the crisis) almost 60% of the financial liabilities of large and medium-sized Mexican companies were denominated in foreign currencies — even though foreign sales were less than 10% of their total sales.

A large unhedged debtor position in foreign exchange not only makes banks and their customers more vulnerable but also makes it harder to deal with a banking crisis once it occurs. This is because some of the traditional crisis-management strategies — easier monetary policy to reduce real interest rates and currency devaluation to reduce the real value of existing local-currency denominated obligations — will be much less effective when debts are denominated in foreign currencies.[30]

---

[29] See Mishkin (1996), who also highlights the sharp deterioration in the net worth of private Mexican firms attributable to the December 1994 peso devaluation.
[30] See Mishkin (1996).

Similarly, the risks of maturity mismatches are typically higher for banks in the emerging markets because they have less access to longer-term sources of funding (on the liability side) and receive less assistance from securities markets in increasing liquidity and in spreading risks (on the asset side) than do banks in the industrial world. In Germany, for example, 45% of the liabilities of depository institutions are long and medium-term bonds; in Japan, roughly one-third of the financial system's liabilities are classified as insurance reserves, trust funds or bonds.[31] A history of high inflation, currency devaluation and negative ex post real returns on bank deposits has left banks in many developing countries with few sources of longer-term financing. The lack of deep government bond markets can likewise act as a handicap to banks with a pressing need for liquidity. Risk-sharing opportunities for banks may also be more limited. For example, if property companies finance themselves exclusively with bank loans (rather than supplementing bank finance with equity offerings) and if there is practically no securitisation of mortgages, then banks will be more likely to grant loans with loan-to-value ratios that are too high, thus exposing themselves to sharp declines in real estate prices.[32] Nonetheless, a considerable amount of short-term borrowing by banks in emerging economies continues. For example, BIS (1996) figures suggest that (as at end-1995) two-thirds of total bank credit to Asian developing countries were in the form of short-term interbank lines.

(iv) *Inadequate preparation for financial liberalisation*

Few question the long-term benefits of financial liberalisation for developing countries. But such reforms inevitably present banks with new risks which, without the proper precautions, can increase the danger of a banking crisis. When interest rates are liberalised, banks may lose the protection they previously enjoyed from a regulated term structure of interest rates which kept short-term rates below long-term rates. More generally, the volatility in interest rates tends to rise, at least during the transition.[33] Rapid rates of credit

---

[31] See Rojas-Suárez and Weisbrod (1995b).
[32] See BIS (1996).
[33] In this regard, the BIS (1996) reports that the volatility of short-term interest rates in emerging economies was considerably higher than in several large European industrial countries during the past decade.

expansion have often paradoxically coincided with high real interest rates in the wake of financial liberalisation.[34] Lifting restrictions on bank lending often releases pent-up demand for credit in the liberalised sectors (e.g. real estate, securities activities).[35] Lowering reserve requirements permits banks to accommodate increased loan demand — as does the inflow of foreign capital, often attracted by reforming economies. Yet bank credit managers reared in an earlier controlled financial environment may not have the expertise needed to evaluate new sources of credit and market risk. At the same time, the entry of new competitors (foreign and domestic) may well increase the pressures on banks to engage in riskier activities. Easier access to offshore markets may also allow banks to evade domestic restrictions on riskier activities. One example of this is the use of customised derivative contracts in offshore markets to circumvent restrictions on net open positions in foreign exchange. Unless the supervisory and regulatory framework is strengthened before the liberalisation of financial markets, bank supervisors may have neither the resources nor the training needed to adequately monitor and evaluate these new activities.

Some or all of these risks associated with inadequate preparation for financial liberalisation have been linked to banking crises, in Brazil, Chile, Indonesia, Mexico, several Nordic countries, the United States and Venezuela, among others. Kaminsky and Reinhart (1995) note that in 18 of the 25 banking crises in their sample, the financial sector had been liberalised some time during the previous five years. Also, they find that proxies for financial liberalisation (namely, increases in real interest rates and in the size of the money multiplier) helped to predict banking crises.

(v) *Heavy government involvement and loose controls on connected lending*

Both factors have played an important role in the generation of banking crises because they allow the political objectives of governments or the personal interests of bank insiders (owners or directors) to intrude on almost all aspects of bank operations, damaging bank profitability and efficiency. While these

---

[34] See Galbis (1993), Kaminsky and Reinhart (1995) and BIS (1996).
[35] Caprio *et al.* (1994) report that banks tended to expand their real estate lending immediately after financial sector liberalisation or the relaxation of lending guidelines.

intrusions are also present in some industrial countries, the frequency and severity of the problem are generally regarded as being greater in developing countries.

Despite increased privatisation, state-owned banks still retain a significant — and sometimes even dominant — share of bank assets in many emerging economies: see Table 2. In some countries with a federal structure, regional or provincial governments also own banks and operate them in pursuit of their particular objectives. A recent survey of 129 countries carried out by the Basle Committee on Banking Supervision (Padoa-Schioppa (1996)) found that the State had a significant participation in bank capital in nearly half of the countries, with most developing country regional groups reporting extensive government ownership (e.g. 91% for the West and Central African Group; 60–67% for the Gulf Co-operation Council, Seanza Forum and Arab Banking Committee; and 57% for the Central and Eastern European Group). These figures would be even higher if computed under a broader concept of indirect ownership. The same survey also reported that banking systems with relatively high state ownership tend to be more concentrated and less open to foreign institutions, as well as to show greater recourse to the public financing of bank bailouts.

Loan decisions of state-owned banks are much more likely to be subject to explicit or implicit government direction than those of privately owned banks. Most state-owned banks were indeed established to allocate credit to particular sectors of the economy. All too often, however, the creditworthiness of the borrowers does not receive sufficient weight in the credit decision, with the result that loans of state banks can become a vehicle for extending government assistance to ailing industries. Moreover, because these banks are shielded from competition, have their losses covered by the government and are sometimes protected from closure on constitutional grounds, they tend to have lower incentives to innovate, to promptly identify problem loans at an early stage and to control costs. Overstaffing and overextended branch networks are more prevalent. And their loan loss performance is usually inferior to that of their private counterparts. One-third of total loans in Argentina's public banks were non-performing at the end of 1994, compared with 10% for private banks. Of $20 billion in non-performing loans in the December 1994 portfolio of Banespa — owned by Sao Paulo state in Brazil — more than half was owed by the state. Non-performing loans in China, India and Indonesia have also been

Table 2: Indicators of the structure of the banking industry

	Bank share in financial intermediation[1]	Share of state-owned banks[2]	Non-interest operating costs	Net interest margins
	1994		As a % of total assets[3]	
India	80	87	2.6	2.9
Hong Kong	—	0	1.5	2.2
Korea	38	13	1.7	2.1
Singapore	71	0	1.4	1.6
Taiwan	80	57	1.3	2.0
Indonesia	91	48	2.4	3.3
Malaysia	64	8	1.6	3.0
Thailand	75	7	1.9	3.7
Argentina	98	36	8.5	9.2
Brazil	97	48	6.0	6.8[4]
Chile	62	14	3.0	6.1
Colombia	86	23	7.3	8.3
Mexico	87	28	3.9	5.1
Venezuela	92	30	5.7	8.1
Memorandum:				
United States	23	0	3.7	3.7
Japan	79	0	0.8	1.1
Germany	77	50[5]	1.1	1.4

Note: Operating costs and net interest margins are shown before loan loss provisions.
[1] Assets of banks as a percentage of the assets of banks and non-bank financial institutions.
[2] Percentage share of assets. For India, 1993. For Argentina, June 1996. [3] Average of 1990–94.
[4] 1992–94. [5] Not strictly comparable.
Sources: IBCA Ltd. and central banks.

particularly heavy in the state sector.[36] Consistent with this other evidence, the countries in Table 2 with the highest shares of state banks are, on average, also the ones with the higher operating costs and the higher incidence of non-performing loans.

But government involvement in (or implicit taxation of) the banking sector extends well beyond the operation of state-owned banks. Even when banks are privately owned, governments may still influence the allocation of

---

[36] See BIS (1996).

credit to particular sectors, extend favourable loan discounting privileges to certain borrowers, prevent private banks from engaging in certain profitable banking activities, require banks to hold government bonds at below market interest rates, impose high reserve requirements or taxes on banks, and direct banks to borrow in foreign currencies and assume the currency risk.[37] As documented by Folkerts-Landau *et al.*'s (1995) study of APEC developing countries, banks in Indonesia, Korea, Malaysia, the Philippines and Thailand have, at some time over the past two decades, been subject to regulatory requirements or pressures to allocate fixed proportions of their loan portfolios to particular sectors. In Korea, for example, policy loans accounted for almost half of commercial bank loans even ten years after banks were privatised.[38] Increased reserve requirements on healthy banks were used in Argentina in the 1980s to finance lending to troubled institutions; similarly, Mexico used reserve requirements in the 1980s to finance large budget deficits.[39] Banks thus became "quasi-fiscal" agents for the government.[40]

"Connected lending" refers to loans extended to banks' owners or managers and to their related businesses. It is a more common practice among universal banks and development banks. The risks are primarily ones of lack of objectivity (sometimes even fraud) in credit assessment and undue concentration of credit risk. The failure of a few large related borrowers, or a collapse of a particular sector of the economy, can wipe out a bank's capital. De Juan (1996) argues that, because the bank will be unlikely to deal with connected borrowers on an arm's-length basis and because the borrower's access to liquidity will be guaranteed, information flows from the borrower to the creditor will suffer and incentives both to appoint top-quality management in such a company and to identify (and make provision for) bad loans will be low. In his view, such practices contributed to the Spanish banking crisis of the 1980s. Lindgren *et al.* (1996) and Sheng (1996) likewise cite connected lending as a key bank governance problem and one that has contributed to banking problems in Argentina, Bangladesh, Brazil, Chile, Indonesia, Malaysia, Spain and Thailand.

---

[37] Most countries do not offer any remuneration on banks' reserve requirements.
[38] See Nam (1993).
[39] See BIS (1996).
[40] See Honohan (1996) and Lindgren *et al.* (1996).

Most countries have regulations on the maximum exposure that their banks can assume vis-à-vis a single borrower or connected set of borrowers. Table 3 provides a picture of such exposure limits for a group of emerging economies. According to the Basle Committee's recent survey, 90% of countries do not allow lending to a single customer to exceed 60% of a bank's capital, and about two-thirds of countries maintain a stricter standard of 25% of capital. The share of countries with the stricter exposure standard was higher for developing countries than for industrial ones (some of which are in transition to lower percentages).[41] The same survey also indicated that over three-quarters of developing countries report that they apply more severe requirements for exposures to parties related to the bank (connected lending) and almost all regard related borrowers as one risk. The main question is how far exposure limits are effectively implemented in practice. Folkerts-Landau *et al.* (1995) note that monitoring of exposure limits by bank supervisors has in the past been undermined by the use of dummy accounts and fictitious names by borrowers, as well as by a lack of authority for bank examiners to trace the use of funds once deposited in accounts.

(vi) *Weaknesses in the accounting, disclosure and legal framework*

Banks do not operate in a vacuum. To the extent that the institutional structure in which banks carry out their business is weak, their performance will be adversely affected. While there are significant differences across emerging economies, most analysts regard existing accounting systems, disclosure practices and legal frameworks as hindering the operation of market discipline and the exercise of effective banking supervision; these weaknesses also often work to the detriment of bank profitability.[42]

Neither private investors nor bank supervisors will be able to monitor and to discipline errant banks without accurate, current, comprehensive and transparent information on their creditworthiness, as well as on the creditworthiness of their customers. In many countries, the accounting conventions for classifying bank assets as impaired or non-performing are

---

[41] See Padoa-Schioppa (1996).
[42] See BIS (1996), Caprio and Klingebiel (1996a, 1996b), Folkerts-Landau *et al.* (1995), Honohan (1996), Lindgren *et al.* (1996), Meltzer (1995), Padoa-Schioppa (1996), Rojas-Suárez and Weisbrod (1995a, 1995b, 1996b) and Sheng (1996).

Table 3: Rules on maximum exposure to a single borrower

India	25% of capital and free reserves
Hong Kong	25% of capital (group of connected borrowers is treated as single exposure)
Korea	15% of capital
Singapore	25% of capital funds (for locally-incorporated banks: paid-up capital and published reserves; for foreign bank branches: borrowings from head office, other overseas branches and other banks). Group of connected borrowers is treated as a single borrower
Taiwan	3 and 15% of net worth for a natural and a juridical person, respectively
Indonesia	20% of capital for groups of affiliated borrowers; 10% for a single person
Malaysia	30% of capital (paid-up capital, reserves and provisions)
Thailand	25% of (first tier) capital
Argentina	15% of net worth for non-affiliated clients (25% if collateralised). Applies to a single customer as well as to a consolidated group. Loans and other financing for affiliated clients cannot generally exceed the client-owned capital
Brazil	30% of net worth
Chile	5% of capital and reserves (up to 30% if in FOREX for exports and if guaranteed)
Colombia	10% of primary capital (25% if guaranteed by capital other than client's)
Mexico	10% (30%) of net capital for individuals [corporations] (or 0.5% [6%] of net capital of all banks)
Venezuela	10% of paid-up capital and reserves
Russian Federation	50–100% of capital depending on bank's founding date and type
Israel	15% of equity capital
South Africa	Prescribed percentage of capital and reserves. Exposure may not exceed 10% of banks' net qualifying capital and reserves without prior approval from the Board of Directors of the bank or a committee appointed by them for this purpose
Memorandum:	
United States	15% of capital (10–25% state-chartered banks)
Japan	20% of capital (up to 40% including guarantees and exposure through subsidiaries)
Germany	25% of capital (after transition to EU standards)

Sources: Central banks.

not tight enough to prevent banks from making bad loans look good by lending more money to troubled borrowers ("evergreening"). Where loan classification depends only on the payment status — rather than on evaluation of the borrower's creditworthiness and the market value of collateral — it will be easier for bankers and their loan customers to collude in concealing losses by various restructuring, accrual and interest capitalisation devices. If non-performing loans are systematically understated, loan loss provisioning will be inadequate, and the reported measures of bank net income and bank capital will be systematically overstated.[43] Gavin and Hausmann (1996) show that the publicly reported figures on the share of non-performing loans gave little hint of the banking crises in Chile and Colombia in the early 1980s. Similarly, Rojas-Suárez and Weisbrod (1996c) observe that, on the eve of banking difficulties, reported ratios of non-performing to total loans in several Latin American emerging economies were much lower in relation to the size of the subsequent banking problem than were those in Finland and the United States; the same authors found that banks in some Latin American economies were reporting positive net income even during banking crises. In a number of APEC developing countries, loans are classified as non-performing only after the loan has been in arrears for at least six months, and in some cases bank management itself — rather than bank supervisors — set the classification criteria.[44] Such distortions in the identification of "true" non-performing loans may also explain why bank capital by itself does not have higher predictive power for identifying subsequent bank failures.[45] It also explains De Juan's (1996) advice to bank supervisors to focus their attention on the "good" loan portfolio — not the "bad" one.

Distinguishing healthy from unhealthy banks is often hindered by the absence of financial statements on the consolidated exposure of banks, by the lack of uniform reporting requirements for banks within a country, by differences in accounting standards across countries, by the lack of published key financial data on individual banks, by the absence of serious penalties for submitting inaccurate reports to supervisors or the public and by the paucity of private credit ratings for banks in the larger emerging economies. For

---

[43] See Sheng (1996).
[44] See Folkerts-Landau *et al.* (1995).
[45] See Lindgren *et al.* (1996).

example, the Basle Committee's recent survey indicated that 20% of countries still do not consolidate financial and prudential information on banks' global operations.[46]

The legal framework, along with the statutory authority of bank supervisors, also matters. If the legal system makes it difficult and timeconsuming either for banks to seize or to transfer the collateral behind delinquent loans, or for debtors to pledge collateral for bank loans, or to adjudicate cases of corporate or individual bankruptcy, then both banks' credit losses and the cost of borrowing for firms will be (abnormally) high. Rojas-Suárez and Weisbrod (1996c) cite the case of a legal prohibition in Mexico on using movable property (e.g. inventory) as collateral for short-term business loans; as such, borrowers have to pay the (higher) unsecured rate for those loans. Similarly, if bank supervisors lack the statutory authority to issue "cease and desist" orders to banks, or to prevent corporate affiliations that hinder effective supervision, or to specify accounting practices, or to close insolvent banks, then their potential contribution to curtailing excessive risk-taking and to limiting bank rescue costs will be constrained. Several writers have argued that legal uncertainties about the status of creditors in the event of default have likewise constrained the growth of close substitutes for bank deposits (e.g. money market mutual funds, commercial paper) in many emerging economies.[47]

(vii) Distorted incentives...

A system of crisis prevention can be expected to operate well only if the main actors face the proper incentives to discourage excessive risk-taking and to take corrective action at an early stage. Bank owners, managers and creditors, as well as bank supervisors, each need to "have something to lose" if they fail to act in a manner consistent with their mandate. As with banking systems in industrial countries, it has frequently been argued that the present incentive structure in banking in the emerging economies is part of the problem.[48]

---

[46] See Padoa-Schioppa (1996).
[47] See Rojas-Suárez and Weisbrod (1996c).
[48] See BIS (1996), Caprio and Klingebiel (1996b), Goldstein (1996c), Honohan (1996), Lindgren *et al.* 1996), Meltzer (1996) and Padoa-Schioppa (1996).

... for bank owners ...

At least three factors affect the incentives faced by bank owners: bank capital, their share in the costs of any bank restructuring, and the franchise value of the bank. Bank owners (shareholders) will be more likely to appoint good managers and to elect good directors, and so ensure that their agents do not put the bank's solvency in danger, when they have their own funds at risk. Bank capital therefore serves a twofold function: it provides a cushion against unusual losses and it promotes better governance. In a parallel vein, if a bank becomes insolvent, incentives in the future will be affected by who bears the cost of restructuring. Incentives for prudent behaviour will be encouraged if those who benefited from risk-taking absorb most of the costs when that risk-taking goes awry, that is, if shareholders, along with large holders of certain long-term liabilities (e.g. subordinated debt), are the first to lose their money.[49] The franchise value of the bank (i.e. the profitability of a banking licence) is relevant because owners who are enjoying a handsome rate of return from normal banking operations should be less tempted, ceteris paribus, to put that return in jeopardy by engaging in high-risk activities. Weisbrod *et al.* (1992) offer evidence that the franchise value of banks in the United States and Japan has declined over the last few decades, and that this has contributed to excessive risk-taking. In the case of emerging economies, however, the policy implications are less clear: just as too easy entry and too much competition can be harmful to risk-taking incentives, too much concentration in banking may confer monopoly advantages on incumbents (to the detriment of efficiency in banking services).

Table 4 presents risk-based capital requirements and actual risk-based capital ratios for a sample of emerging economies; for comparison, ratios are also presented for the largest industrial countries.[50] Virtually all of the emerging economies listed in the table have adopted a capital requirement that meets or slightly exceeds the Basle minimum standard; only Argentina and Singapore among the countries shown in the table have set a national requirement that is much higher. Turning to actual ratios, banks in several

---

[49] Rojas-Suárez and Weisbrod (1995c) regard this as the first principle of successful bank restructuring

[50] According to a recent survey of the Basle Committee, 92% of countries apply a Basle-like risk-weighted capital approach (although not necessarily the 8% ratio); see Padoa-Schioppa (1996).

Table 4: Required and actual capital ratios
In percentages

	Capital adequacy ratio (national requirements)	Actual risk-based capital ratio (1995)
India	8	9.5[1]
Hong Kong	8[2]	17.5[3]
Korea	8	9.3
Singapore	12[4]	18.7[4]
Taiwan	8	12.2
Indonesia	8	11.9
Malaysia	8	11.3
Thailand	8	9.3
Argentina	12	18.5
Brazil	8[5]	12.9
Chile	8[6]	10.7
Colombia	9	13.5
Mexico	8	11.3
Israel	8	10.5[7]
South Africa	8[8]	10.1
Memorandum:		
United States	8	12.8
Japan	8	9.1

Notes: (1) Several European countries have significantly higher capital ratios. (2) Definitions sometimes differ from those applied by the Basle Committee.
[1] Relates only to public sector banks. [2] 12% for some banks; 16% for some non-banks. [3] Relates to locally incorporated authorised institutions and is on a consolidated basis. [4] Based only on Tier 1 capital. [5] Plus 1.5% on notional value of swap operations. [6] Legislation at present before Parliament. [7] 1994. [8] For some banks, higher ratios.
Sources: Central banks.

emerging economies (Argentina, Colombia, Hong Kong and Singapore) maintain risk-based capital ratios that are both significantly higher than the minimum standard and also higher than the ratios in the larger industrial countries. But all this should not obscure another message from Table 4: banks in most of the emerging economies shown do not appear to have risk-based capital ratios significantly higher than those in the larger industrial countries — despite the higher-risk environment they face. On top of that, some would argue that bank capital ratios in industrial countries may themselves be a poor yardstick; for example, not only did US banks maintain much higher capital ratios before the introduction of deposit insurance, but competitors of banks in the United States (finance companies, insurance companies, etc.) have generally maintained much higher capital ratios — leading some analysts to conclude that banks have (inappropriately) substituted explicit and implicit government guarantees for private capital.[51]

Comprehensive information on the treatment of shareholders during episodes of bank restructuring in developing countries is unfortunately not available. However, Rojas-Suárez and Weisbrod (1996a) conclude that the failure to penalise shareholders was a key shortcoming of some unsuccessful bank restructuring programmes in Latin America in the early 1980s.

There is no consensus on how best to measure the franchise value of banking in the emerging economies. A popular measure (shown in Table 5) is the average return on assets. But some analysts have expressed scepticism about the standard accounting measures of bank profitability. Some also feel that the short-term orientation of financial systems in many emerging economies (especially in Latin America) requires a different definition of franchise value. Rojas-Suárez and Weisbrod (1995) argue instead that the franchise value of banks should be defined as the ability to cover their deposit liabilities with liquid funds. One indicator of this in developing countries is the ability of banks to police the liquidity of their borrowers and to attract deposits. On this argument, banks that maintain low ratios of cash to deposits and high ratios of loans to deposits are viewed as being confident in the liquidity of their assets and thus more serious about policing their borrowers. However, low cash-to-deposit ratios and high loan-to-deposit ratios may simply reflect imprudence, or expectations of too easy access to central bank or government finance in case of trouble.[52] Table 2 above gave some indicators

---

[51] See Meltzer (1996).

[52] Perhaps a better indicator is the ratio of deposits to GNP, with a high ratio suggesting that market participants have confidence in the bank's ability to meet its liabilities. Examining these proxies for franchise value in a set of Latin American developing countries, Rojas-Suárez and Weisbrod (1995) conclude that the franchise value of banks in the region improved between the 1980s and the 1990s. They acknowledge that these ratios would not be good measures of the franchise value of banks in industrial countries but claim that this is because the different financial structure and track record on inflation in the latter does not require banks to be as active in enforcing liquidity among borrowers or in maintaining the confidence of depositors.

of banking efficiency and of the franchise value of banks in some emerging economies and in the largest industrial countries. Great variation across emerging economies makes generalisation hazardous. Nevertheless, banking efficiency (i.e. as proxied by operating costs and net interest margins) in most emerging economies appears lower than in the larger industrial countries (with the difference being considerably greater for Latin American countries than for Asian ones). Concentration, as measured by the share of the five largest banks in total assets shown in Table 5, is higher in most emerging economies than in the largest industrial countries. Judging from the figures on asset returns,

Table 5: Indicators of profitability and concentration in the banking industry

	Average rate of return on assets[1]	Five largest banks' share of deposits or assets[2]
India	−0.2	47.3
Hong Kong	1.7[3]	39.7[4]
Korea	0.6	38.1
Singapore	1.1	39.0
Taiwan	0.7	55.9
Indonesia	0.7	
Malaysia	1.3	34.8
Thailand	1.3	59.6
Argentina	1.4	37.5
Brazil	0.1	54.9
Chile	1.1	46.7
Colombia	2.3	24.5
Mexico	1.3	61.9
Venezuela	1.4	57.2
Russian Federation		29.0
Israel	0.4	85–90
South Africa	0.8	82.0
Memorandum:		
United States	0.8	13.8
Japan	0.1	27.3
Germany	0.2	16.7[1]

[1] Average 1990–94; for Argentina, Hong Kong and South Africa, 1991–94, and for India, 1991–95. [2] In 1994; for Germany and India, 1995 and for Argentina and Singapore, May 1996. [3] Locally incorporated licensed banks only. [4] Total deposits include both domestic and foreign currency deposits.
Sources: IBCA Ltd., OECD and central banks.

there is little to suggest that the franchise value of a banking licence in most emerging economies is currently particularly high.[53]

... for managers ...

Ensuring that banks maintain good credit and internal risk management systems is the job of bank managers and directors: poor management has often been singled out as the leading cause of bank failures. Here, too, poor oversight and imprudent behaviour should in principle incur a cost. In practice, the multiplicity of causes of bank failure — some beyond the control of managers — serves to blur the issue, especially if managers have hard-to-replace experience. However, Caprio and Klingebiel (1996b) found that senior management was changed in the majority of bank restructuring cases in their sample (of mostly developing countries); at the same time, there were some prominent examples of systemic bank failures (e.g. Hungary in the 1990s) where senior managers of restructured banks were merely reassigned to other posts.

... for bank depositors ...

The potential contribution of bank depositors to market discipline in emerging economies is limited by the quality of accounting systems and by the extent of public disclosure. Some analysts have argued that government bailouts have undermined their incentive to monitor the creditworthiness of banks.[54] The main target of such criticism is usually de facto, not de jure deposit insurance. The Basle Committee's recent survey finds that over 70 countries (all but one from the developing world) at present have no formal deposit insurance; among those that do offer deposit insurance, Lindgren *et al.* (1996) report that the typical arrangements offer partial coverage (usually for small retail depositors). Other analysts argue that depositors are probably too small, too dispersed and too financially unsophisticated to exert much discipline.[55] In this perspective, it is discretionary government intervention

---

[53] Again, returns for banks in industrial countries may not be a good yardstick. As noted earlier, some have argued that increased competition from non-banks has forced down the franchise value of a banking licence in the United States and Japan to the point where it encourages excessive risk-taking by banks. In addition, the profitability of banks in Germany — where hidden reserves are important — is not well captured by these figures on average returns. Moreover, the average return figures for Japan presumably reflect the current bad loan problem and therefore are not likely to be representative of returns during more normal periods.

[54] See Meltzer (1996), Caprio and Klingebiel (1996b) and McKinnon and Pill (1994).

to bail out large, wholesale creditors or owners of insolvent banks that is the main problem. Meltzer (1996), for example, cites the case of the Uruguay government which bailed out 28 branches of foreign banks in the 1980s, after their parent banks had refused to renew their loans unless the government provided a rescue.

. . . and for supervisors

Finally, there is the old argument that the political and legal background may encourage bank supervisors to delay the closure of an insolvent bank or the imposition of corrective measures.[56] Given the greater government involvement in banking in emerging economies and the extent of banking or industrial connections, pressures on bank supervisors for regulatory forbearance may well be greater than they are in industrial countries. Not only can closure or restrictions on bank behaviour elicit strong protests from powerful interest groups, but such action can also embroil the supervisor in legal action. Whatever happens, acknowledgement of significant problems at a large bank may subject the supervisor to sharp criticism for not having detected the problem earlier. Yet the costs of delay can be high. For example, the slower supervisors are to close an insolvent bank, the greater the dangers that losses will multiply, as owners or managers "gamble for resurrection". One common answer to potential political pressures is to place supervision in a politically independent government agency or in the central bank. Another possible answer is to reduce the discretion available to supervisors. Some countries (notably the United States) have adopted a more rule-based supervisory regime, where particular corrective actions are mandated once bank capital hits successive capital zone trip-wires.[57] However, many observers do not accept the wisdom of constraining the discretion available to supervisors: some stress the importance of supervisors detecting problems, and encouraging corrective action, well before they have become manifest in below minimum capital levels. Others emphasise the important role that supervisors can play in continuously fostering good risk management practices.

---

[55] See Padoa-Schioppa (1996).

[56] See Kane (1989) and Benston and Kaufman (1988).

[57] The "prompt corrective action" guidelines are contained in the Federal Deposit Insurance Corporation Improvement Act (FDICIA). This is discussed further in the section below. See also Benston and Kaufman (1993).

(viii) Exchange rate regimes

The exchange rate regime can affect vulnerability to speculative attack, the way in which the real value of impaired bank assets is adjusted downwards and the ability of the central bank to act as lender of last resort to illiquid but solvent banks.

A poor track record on inflation and the lack of any obvious alternative to the exchange rate as a nominal anchor led many emerging economies to adopt exchange-rate-based stabilisation plans in the 1970s and 1980s. These plans were often successful in cutting inflation but were also accompanied by significant real exchange rate appreciation. In some cases, heavy market pressure forced a return to greater exchange rate flexibility, often entailing massive devaluation. Gavin and Hausmann (1996) find that unsustainable exchange rate pegs have contributed more to the relatively high volatility of growth rates in Latin American developing countries over the past two decades than any other factor. Also, as noted earlier, sharp appreciation of the real exchange rate has been shown to be a useful leading indicator of banking crises.[58]

Fixed exchange rate regimes have also been criticised for increasing the fragility of the banking system to external adverse shocks. Gavin and Hausmann (1996), for example, argue that, under fixed rates, an adverse shock will lead to a balance-of-payments deficit, a decline in the money supply and higher domestic interest rates. The reduced availability and higher cost of credit will put pressure on banks and their customers and add to any problems associated with the effect of the shock itself on the quality of bank assets. Under flexible rates, by contrast, the shock will be associated with a depreciation of the nominal exchange rate and a rise in the domestic price level, which will serve to reduce the real value of bank assets and bank liabilities to a level more consistent with bank solvency.

With a fixed exchange rate, the central bank must ensure that any liquidity it injects into the system to provide temporary assistance to illiquid but solvent banks does not undermine its exchange rate obligations.[59] A recent noteworthy example was Argentina's response to the large liquidity shock to the banking

---

[58] See Kaminsky and Reinhart (1995) and Goldstein (1996c).
[59] Technically speaking, a currency board cannot create the money it lends as a lender of last resort; it can act as the lender of last resort if the funds are obtained elsewhere (e.g. from official

system that followed the Mexican crisis in early 1995. Because of its currency board arrangement and the specific provisions of the Convertibility Law (80% of the monetary base had to be backed with foreign currency assets), the central bank had to perform a delicate balancing act and ensure enough liquidity to prevent a contagious bank crisis but not so much as to exceed the parameters of the exchange rate commitment.[60] Fortunately, it had some other instruments at its disposal (a decrease in reserve requirements in particular).

POLICY OPTIONS FOR STRENGTHENING BANKING SYSTEMS

Some of the main suggestions for strengthening banking systems in these countries are summarised in this section, mostly following the same sequence as in the previous section.

(i) *Reducing or living with volatility*

Banking systems in emerging economies operate in relatively volatile environments. There are essentially four ways of dealing with this problem: reducing those components of volatility that are under the home country's control; reducing exposure to volatility via diversification; buying insurance against volatility; and holding a larger cushion of financial resources against volatility-induced losses.

More disciplined monetary and fiscal policies help to contain volatility. In this context, it is useful to underline the basic complementarity between macroeconomic and financial stability. One increasingly important aspect of this complementarity is the dependence of terms of borrowing in international capital markets on the perceived creditworthiness of the borrower. The graph illustrates that both interest rate spreads and maturities on international bond issues have differed markedly across countries during the past two years; for example, East Asian borrowers enjoyed in 1995 maturities almost three times longer than, and average spreads about half as large as, borrowers in Latin America. As hinted at earlier, there is a potential virtuous circle at work. With

---

borrowing abroad). Cavallo (1996) has stated that Argentina is in the process of creating an institution that can serve as lender of last resort to the financial system there.
[60] See Fernandez (1996).

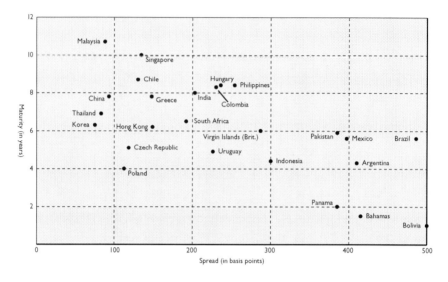

Issuance terms for international bonds, 1994–1996 Q2: maturity and spread
Sources: Euromoney and BIS.

greater macroeconomic stability and fewer bad surprises for asset holders, the structure of the financial system will adapt in ways (e.g. longer maturities, a more diversified structure of financial assets) that make banks less vulnerable to shocks.

A particularly relevant financial aspect of diversification for emerging economies is the role of foreign-owned banks. Because their portfolios are less concentrated in lending to firms in the host country and because they usually have access to external sources of liquidity and foreign exchange (from their parents abroad), they will be able to weather a shock to the local economy better than domestic banks.[61] They may also be more insulated from government pressure. However, their activities have often been concentrated in servicing their compatriot foreign enterprises (with trade credit and the like). A somewhat different argument that is sometimes made is that easier foreign entry may reduce the franchise value of a bank, and may lead some domestic banks to fail.

---

[61] See Gavin and Hausmann (1996).

Table 6: Foreign-owned banks' percentage shares of total assets

India	7.3
Hong Kong	78.0*
Korea	5.1
Singapore	80.0
Taiwan	4.7
Indonesia	3.7
Malaysia	15.9
Thailand	7.1
Argentina	21.7
Brazil	9.4
Chile	21.4
Colombia	3.6
Mexico	1.2
Venezuela	1.2
Russian Federation	2.2
Israel	0.0
South Africa	3.3
Memorandum:	
United States	22.0
Japan	1.8
Germany	3.9

Note: Figures refer to latest available year.
*Refers to all overseas-incorporated authorised institutions.
Sources: OECD, central banks and Ministries of Finance.

Table 6 shows that the share of foreign banks in total banking assets differs widely across emerging economies. In Hong Kong, Chile and Malaysia — which have quite robust banking systems — the share of foreign banks ranges from very high to moderately high; in contrast, the foreign share is quite low in Korea, Mexico and Venezuela. Among the transition economies, the Czech Republic was open to foreign participation early in its reform period. In short, there can be advantages for the stability of the banking system in a volatile environment in not having local banks get all the business. In a similar vein, restrictions that severely limit the portfolios of home banks to the local market work against the principle of diversifying banking risk; these restrictions should therefore be carefully reviewed to see whether they have another compelling rationale that outweighs their diversification liability.

Market instruments that can provide protection against volatility in international interest rates, commodity prices and exchange rates (via swaps, futures, options and the like) have expanded significantly over the past decade, and can reduce risks for creditworthy banks as well as for their customers. This insurance can be expensive just at the times when concern about volatility is the greatest, but this cost has to be weighed against the moral hazard risks associated with inadequate reliance on selfinsurance. The challenge here is often to see that internal risk management systems are reliable enough (including controls over individual traders and the separation of trading from back-office functions) to ensure that these instruments do not themselves generate credit or market risk losses rather than reduce them (recall the unhappy experiences of Codelco, Barings and Daiwa).

Finally, there is the option of banks in emerging economies holding higher levels of capital to compensate for their more volatile operating environment. The Basle risk-weighted standard was always intended as a minimum which national regulations could supplement as circumstances warranted. It is perhaps surprising that the authorities in most emerging economies have thus far chosen not to set national capital standards that are much above the Basle international standard; nor have their banks (with several important exceptions) maintained actual capital ratios much above those found in countries with more stable operating environments.[62] Given the volatility figures reviewed in the above section, it is quite possible that default rates differ greatly between borrowers in industrial countries and those in emerging economies within a given risk-weight class of the Basle standard.[63] Accounting weaknesses and legal impediments to banks' recovery of delinquent loans may also argue for high bank capital ratios in these countries. Higher capital would certainly provide a greater safety margin and better incentives against excessive risk-taking than exist at present. Another possible approach is to more finely differentiate between different risks within the broad asset category. One way to do this is to use the bank's own assessment of the relative riskiness of different loans as embodied by the interest rates it charges. For

---

[62] See Table 4 above, BIS (1996), IMF (1996), Gavin and Hausmann (1996) and Lindgren et al. (1996).

[63] The recent amendment to the Basle standard for market risk may well not capture the kind of volatility most relevant to banking losses in emerging economies.

example, recent Argentine regulations on credit risk impose higher risk weights on loans with higher interest rates. Under these provisions, the risk weights range from 1 (for peso loans with interest rates of 18%) to 6 (for peso loans with interest rates at 78%).[64]

(ii) *Defending against lending booms, asset price collapses and surges in private capital flows*

Proposals for defending against bank lending booms encompass at least two sets of issues. One is how host countries ought to manage macroeconomic and exchange rate policies to best deal with volatile private capital flows. A second is what types of supervisory practices might moderate swings in bank lending and prevent a wholesale deterioration in credit quality.

Macroeconomic policies

On the first issue, Montiel (1996) has recently surveyed and analysed the policy responses of 14 emerging economies which collectively received roughly 70% of total portfolio and direct investment flows to developing countries over the 1989–93 period. Four of his conclusions are particularly relevant for this paper. First, controls or taxes on capital inflows (e.g. quantitative restrictions on foreign borrowing, requiring banks with foreign exchange liabilities to maintain a non-remunerated account at the central bank equal to a specified ratio of such liabilities) did in some cases manage to slow inflows, at least temporarily.[65] Second, many emerging economies have found that substantial capital inflows followed the removal of restrictions on capital outflows; thus, while removal of such restrictions may well have positive welfare implications for the long run, it does not contribute much to the solution of the capital inflow problem. Third, large-scale sterilisation operations — which were employed by 12 of the 14 countries in the group — were capable of restraining

---

[64] Interest rates applying in April 1996.

[65] Gavin *et al.* (1996) conclude that the effectiveness of capital controls diminishes over time — but also that (on the basis of the experiences of Chile and Colombia) perfect effectiveness is not necessary to provide helpful protection against international financial turmoil. The IMF (1995) has likewise acknowledged that temporary controls or taxes on capital inflows may in some circumstances be warranted (as part of a broader policy package to modify the effects of surges in capital inflows).

the growth of the monetary base but were much less effective in insulating asset markets from external financial influences.[66] Indeed, very large increases in equity and real estate prices were often recorded during the periods of heavy inflows. And, fourth, countries which allowed some nominal exchange rate flexibility and kept monetary and fiscal policies tight to limit inflation (e.g. Bolivia, Costa Rica, Indonesia, Korea, Malaysia and Thailand) showed few signs of real exchange rate appreciation and consumption booms — factors that often increase the vulnerability to Mexico-type financial crises. In contrast, those countries which used the exchange rate as a nominal anchor, defended by monetary policy with fiscal policy left basically unchanged (e.g. Argentina, Chile, Colombia, Egypt, Mexico and the Philippines), typically experienced both real exchange rate appreciation and consumption booms. In short, a combination of tight fiscal policy, some nominal exchange rate flexibility, some sterilisation and perhaps some temporary controls/taxes on capital inflows can limit vulnerability to a subsequent crisis.

Reserve requirements, variable capital requirements and other supervisory tools

A key issue is whether bank lending booms are discouraged more effectively by high reserve requirements or by binding capital constraints. Although the trend has been towards lower reserve requirements in emerging economies, deposits at the central bank still represent a high percentage of loans to non-government in a number of countries: see Table 7. Increases in reserve requirements are one of the traditional instruments of monetary control. To take a recent example, strong credit growth following the implementation of the Real Plan in Brazil induced the central bank to increase reserve requirements on almost all liabilities of the financial sector.

Reserve requirements have been criticised as a method of restraining lending booms on two counts.[67] First, because such requirements are costly

---

[66] In line with the general proposition that countries subject to large swings in private capital flows would be well advised to treat all positive developments as temporary and all negative ones as permanent, Summers (1996) advises host countries to be much more restrained in sterilising capital outflows than in sterilising inflows.

[67] Reserve requirements also serve a function as a prudential instrument to counter unexpected liquidity shocks at banks; see the discussion later in this section.

Table 7: Deposits at the central bank as a percentage of loans to the non-government sector

	1994	1995
India	20.3	16.4
Hong Kong	0.1	0.1
Korea	7.5	7.9
Singapore	6.7	6.5
Taiwan	9.9	8.7
Indonesia	0.5	1.1
Malaysia	0.0	0.2
Thailand	1.2	1.4
Argentina	5.8	1.4
Brazil	15.5	11.5
Chile	5.5	5.0
Colombia	27.4	21.8
Mexico	0.0	0.0
Venezuela	48.5	34.9
Memorandum:		
United States	3.2	2.4
Japan	0.6	0.6
Germany	1.7	1.3

Sources: Central banks and IMF *International Financial Statistics*.

to banks, they can encourage substitution of other forms of liquidity for bank deposits, putting banks at a competitive disadvantage with little improvement in monetary control.[68] The empirical evidence is less than conclusive. Rojas-Suárez and Weisbrod (1996b) find no apparent relationship between the level of reserve requirements (on demand and time deposits) in seven Latin American developing countries and the real growth in domestic liquidity. They attribute this result to substitution towards short-term government or central bank securities, important liquid assets in some of these countries. On the other hand, Montiel (1996), drawing on a wider sample of Asian and Latin American emerging economies, reports that increases in reserve requirements were important in keeping the size of the money multiplier under control in host countries during the surge period. Similarly, Reinhart and Reinhart

---

[68] Remunerated reserve requirements can, however, mitigate this.

(1995) find that increases in reserve requirements (used in developing countries as a tool for sterilising the increase in domestic liquidity arising from foreign exchange intervention) have a noticeable temporary effect both in widening spreads between bank deposits and lending rates and in lowering narrow and broad money expansion.

The second criticism of reserve requirements is that they make no distinction between strong and weak banks: they reduce the attractiveness of deposits and loans at all banks. It would be better to focus on preventing lending booms at "weak" banks, that is at banks that are undercapitalised and that do not have good internal systems of credit assessment (e.g. no independent internal oversight of lending decisions by a proper credit review committee).

Binding capital requirements, perhaps supplemented with disaggregated peer group analysis of individual banks, would stand a better chance (so the argument goes) of preventing a sharp decline in credit quality in the face of large capital inflows — without penalising well-run banks.[69] This would be in line with a broader regulatory philosophy that well-capitalised banks require lighter supervision and should be granted more latitude in their activities than undercapitalised ones.[70] Malaysia introduced a two-tier regulatory system along these lines in December 1994. Others are more sceptical that capital requirements can restrain lending booms; instead, they argue that one way or another, the monetary authorities will need to "lean against the wind" to limit credit expansion.[71]

But what about risks specifically linked to the collapse of asset prices or to the emergence of consumption booms? One answer is to discourage the allocation of credit to sectors that are particularly interest rate sensitive (since it is interest rate fluctuations that drive much of the swings in private capital inflows) or that help to fuel the consumption boom. In Hong Kong,

---

[69] Rojas-Suárez and Weisbrod (1996b) support this view. They also show that variations in capital standards across a set of Latin American emerging economies do not show any clear relationship to inter-country differences in real loan growth. They attribute this result, however, not to irrelevance of bank capital for the growth of risky assets, but rather to poor accounting conventions that lead reported bank capital to differ from true capital.

[70] This philosophy is reflected in some of the key provisions of recent US banking legislation (for example, the FDICIA of 1991).

[71] See Gavin and Hausmann (1996), for example.

for example, a recent guideline encourages banks with a property exposure of more than 40% of loans to reduce or to stabilise the proportion. In addition to avoiding undue concentration of credit risk, a realistic valuation of collateral is helpful. Again, the Hong Kong authorities reduced what they regard as acceptable loan-to-value ratios from 80–90% in 1990 to 60–70% by 1993; Taiwan's banks have likewise reduced loan-to-value ratios for property by a similar amount.[72] Bank loans to finance speculative activity in securities markets can be made subject to the same types of risk-protection mechanisms commonly found on organised exchanges (i.e. bankers should hold collateral, frequently marking it to market; require increased margins when the borrower's position deteriorates; and ask for current information on the consolidated exposure of the borrower). Countries as different as Brazil and Singapore have similarly used various types of restrictions (e.g. minimum downpayments, maximum repayment periods) to contain credit-financed consumer booms in recent years. Finally, central bank moral suasion has continued to play a role in both limiting credit expansion and modifying its composition.

(iii) Reducing liquidity/maturity/currency mismatches

Liquidity and maturity mismatches are an intrinsic characteristic of banking. An infrastructure of institutional and regulatory practices has evolved (deposit insurance, an official lender of last resort, an interbank market, liquidity and reserve requirements for banks, etc.) to discourage bank runs and to prevent localised liquidity shocks from leading to a failure of solvent banks. The question is what kind of mechanisms/operating guidelines would be particularly helpful to banks in emerging markets in limiting their exposure to, and vulnerability from, such mismatches.

One option is to keep bank reserve requirements high enough during normal times that they can be reduced to provide a quick source of liquidity to the banking system during episodes of exceptional liquidity strains.[73] One example is Argentina's experience in early 1995 when it was hit with the "tequila effect" of the Mexican crisis. Between December 1994 and March 1995, approximately $7.4 billion left the Argentine banking system (some 16% of total deposits). By reducing in stages what were previously relatively

---

[72] See BIS (1996).
[73] Gavin and Hausmann (1996) have taken this view.

high reserve requirements (from 43% to 30% on sight deposits, and from 3% to 1% on time deposits), the central bank was (by that channel alone) able to move $2.4 billion back into the system.[74] In contrast, because Mexico had (as part of financial liberalisation) already reduced reserve requirements to a very low level, it could not inject liquidity through this channel. A similar line of argument is sometimes put forward for encouraging banks in emerging markets to hold a significant share of government bonds: the banks can respond to a negative liquidity shock by selling government bonds rather than being forced to sell their illiquid loans at "fire-sale" prices.

In some cases, access to liquidity may not be enough and access to foreign exchange may also be needed. As noted in the previous section, it is now much easier for holders of bank deposits in emerging economies to move their funds abroad when they sense an increase in currency or default risk. Also, the greater international integration of capital markets has made it less likely than before that financial disturbances will remain localised in their country of origin. Masson and Mussa (1995) report that roughly one-third of 49 industrial and middle-income developing countries suffered a maximum, monthly reserve loss equal to 100% or more of their IMF quotas during the 1985–93 period. A national lender of last resort will not necessarily be able to meet such needs without an adequate stock of international reserves or ready access to borrowed reserves. As argued earlier, bank creditors can become nervous when bank liabilities are growing rapidly relative to the stock of international reserves. Recent empirical studies suggest that vulnerability to currency and banking crises in emerging economies is inversely related to the country's holdings of international reserves; for example, "early-warning" indicators of financial crises (such as debt-to-GDP ratios, current account imbalances and exchange rate misalignment) appear to send more reliable signals when the country has relatively low holdings of international reserves.[75] A healthy cushion of international reserves appears therefore to have taken on added importance. Co-operative measures among central banks can also help to discourage bank runs or capital flight: one example is the recent repo agreement among a group of Asian central banks to establish mutual lines of assistance (based on holdings of Treasury securities in their reserves).

---

[74] See Fernandez (1996).
[75] See Sachs *et al.* (1996).

Efforts to limit the scale of short-term, foreign-currency-denominated borrowing — by both banks and their customers — should perhaps have even higher priority. As argued by Dooley (1995), because currency and rollover risk in emerging economies can be influenced strongly by events beyond the borrower's control (e.g. changes in international interest rates), because some borrowing countries have a history of devaluation and debt restructuring, and because other constraints in the economy may limit the scope for an aggressive interest rate defence of an exchange rate parity, borrowers (including banks) in emerging economies should be cautious about taking on much foreign currency debt; the variance of borrowing costs over time also counts — not just the average level. Moreover, shifting the risk to bank borrowers by denominating bank loans in foreign currency may just mean swapping currency risk for credit risk. By the same token, a high share of short-term debt makes it easier for creditors to run at the first sign of trouble and gives the authorities little time to react to unfavourable developments in the financial sector. A key challenge in most emerging economies is therefore to build broader and deeper longer-term credit markets. Better macroeconomic performance, pension reform and a strengthening of the legal infrastructure would contribute to the development of such markets. In the meantime, the monetary and regulatory authorities in emerging economies will need to monitor closely any rapid build-up of short-term, foreign-currency denominated borrowing by their banks, and be prepared to limit rapidly growing liquidity or currency mismatches.

(iv) *Preparing better for financial liberalisation*

Of the extensive literature on the appropriate sequencing of financial liberalisation, three points are key for present purposes. First, if entry of new banks or privatisation of formerly state-owned banks is part of the liberalisation process, it is important to ensure that the new owners/managers of those banks pass the "fit and proper" test. Chile's experience of the 1970s provides a cautionary tale.[76] Newly privatised banks were sold to rapidly expanding — and not fully solvent — conglomerates (the grupos), which used them to finance the acquisition of firms. During this process, the new bank owners

---

[76]The account of Chile's experience is based on Edwards (1995).

engaged in risky and financially questionable operations, and accumulated a large stock of bad loans — much of it to interrelated companies owned by the same conglomerate. The public, perhaps because of an implicit government guarantee on deposits, did not distinguish between solid and troubled banks. The episode ended in a major crisis in 1982–83 when some of the largest Chilean banks became insolvent and had to be taken over by the government. To take two more recent examples, a lax entry policy led to a deterioration in credit quality and to bank insolvencies in Poland in the early 1990s, and low capital requirements for new banks in Russia — and the absence of effective penalties/personal liability clauses — probably contributed to the scale of current difficulties.[77]

Second, bank supervision needs to be strengthened before liberalisation. Supervisors need to be trained to be better able to determine which banks have the expertise to cope with the new and expanded activities permitted by liberalisation. They also need to be able to evaluate the risks involved as the expansion of these new activities proceeds. Again, earlier failures are instructive.[78] Up to the late 1970s, Nordic (Finland, Norway and Sweden) banks operated in a highly regulated financial system where there were controls on interest rates and capital flows, and officially directed bank credit. Competition was inhibited and banks earned considerable rents; indeed, in the early 1980s some Nordic banks were among the most profitable in the world. The rise of non-bank financial institutions (e.g. finance companies) that escaped existing regulation, in conjunction with the emergence of new markets, led to pressure for financial liberalisation. The lifting of quantitative restrictions on bank credit and the dismantling of interest rate controls was followed in each country by a significant rise in the ratio of bank lending to GNP, along with a growing concentration of loans on higher-risk activities, including real estate and (especially in Finland) financial market speculation. Bank supervisors were not well equipped to control risk-taking in this new liberalised environment. In Finland, for instance, supervisors were apparently hampered

---

[77] Hong Kong's banking crisis in 1982 also probably owed something to bank entry policies in the late 1970s, and to the effect of intensified competition on risk-taking. As a result of that experience, Hong Kong now applies a minimum asset size of $16 billion for foreign banks, along with stringent authorisation procedures.

[78] The following summary of the Nordic banking crises of the early 1990s is taken from Goldstein *et al.* (1993).

by the opaque status of large financial and industrial groups, by the lack of authority to determine the extent of equity and lending interconnections within the group, and by insufficient staff to conduct adequate and timely bank examinations. Supervisory shortcomings have also played an important role in the overextension of Mexican banks in the liberalised world of the 1990s.

If the decision has been made to go ahead with financial liberalisation before the regulatory and supervisory framework has been upgraded, there is a second-best argument for limiting private capital inflows, or for imposing speed limits on the expansion in bank lending — at least until the quality of the supervisory regime has caught up with the pace of liberalisation.

(v) *Reducing government involvement and connected lending*

Views on the appropriate role of government in the banking sector still differ significantly across countries. Four possible policy options merit explicit mention. One option would be to enhance the transparency of government involvement in, and taxation of, the banking system. Recognising that such quasi-fiscal operations are typically undertaken to circumvent legislative and political constraints on fiscal policy, the IMF (1996) has recently recommended including government subsidies to, or revenues from, involvement with the banking system in central government budget statements. In a similar vein, the opportunity cost of such government involvement would be clearer to the public if figures on the performance of state-owned banks (relative to privately-owned ones) were published; as noted earlier, the incidence of bad loans has typically been greater in state-owned banks than in privately-owned ones, and the public could be made more aware of that difference.

A second option is to get state-owned banks to operate more like commercial enterprises. Many countries have tried this, but with only mixed results. In many cases, the internal culture of such banks exhibits a strong resistance to change. A third option, assuming that some government-directed lending is unavoidable, is to ask the major solvent banks to each "do their bit" by allocating a small percentage of their loans to needs of high political priority. This may be safer and less destructive of incentives to monitor credit quality than concentrating such problems in one institution. This approach has at times been followed in South Africa.

Fourth — and most directly — there is the option of privatising state-owned banks. Even though there may still be some resistance to change in the absence of a competitive domestic structure of the industry, this is the most promising avenue for putting banking on a sounder footing. But much depends on who the new private owners of the banks are. As noted by Honohan (1996), if the new owners are not "fit and proper", the result of privatisation may simply be to exchange public sector inefficiencies for private sector incompetence or even fraud. This reinforces the arguments made earlier for careful screening of banking licences — even if it slows down the pace of privatisation.

Turning to connected lending, most countries already have explicit prudential limits in place. It is noteworthy that New Zealand — which has decided to jettison many traditional regulatory guidelines in favour of increased public disclosure and market discipline (more on this below) — has opted to retain a mandatory prudential limit on connected lending. In order to discourage excessive levels of connected lending, three measures warrant mention. First, countries should work towards ensuring that the accounting and legal framework permits supervisors to verify that reported connected-lending exposure is accurate. Second, greater transparency would make bank creditors more aware of the concentration of credit risk (and possible departure from arm's-length transactions) at individual banks. Chile's banking law, for example, specifies mandatory disclosure of loans to related industrial and commercial groups (also, loans to different members of the group are consolidated).[79] Third, it would be useful to establish threshold reporting limits (to bank supervisors) on connected lending that are below the maximum limit to give supervisors an early indication of high or rising exposure to connected parties.[80]

(vi) *Strengthening the accounting, disclosure and legal framework*

Much of what would be helpful in this wide-ranging area follows from the discussion in the section about existing weaknesses. To begin with, there is a pressing need for stricter asset classification and provisioning practices that reduce the scope for delay in recognising bad loans and that encourage banks to provision adequately against loan losses. Towards this end, more emphasis needs to be given to an evaluation of the borrower's current creditworthiness and less latitude accorded to loans that are being kept current only because

---

[79] See Meltzer (1996).
[80] See Basle Committee (1992).

of the extension of new loans ("ever-greening"). Where the time period over which a loan can be in arrears before it is classified as non-performing is much longer than best practice, that time limit should be reduced (i.e. closer to 90 days).[81] The high volatility of asset prices in emerging economies also makes it more important to take due account of underlying — rather than temporarily inflated — market values and to value conservatively and realistically the collateral underlying bank loans.

Chile's banking law has several features conducive to good provisioning practice: banks classify into four risk groups based on a current assessment of the repayment capacity of the borrower, the borrower's past record, and the value of collateral, rather than on past-due payments. Chilean practice has also moved towards market accounting without accepting the principle as a formal requirement e.g. a bank's net worth is adjusted several times a year to reflect prospective losses and current economic values.[82] The Mexican authorities have recently tightened accounting rules and expect that this will lead to a doubling in the amount of past-due loans reported.

Almost all developing country supervisors report (in the Basle Committee's survey) that they do assess the adequacy of the provisioning made by banks. But where provisioning guidelines are unclear or weak, they should be tightened. Table 8 provides a snapshot of the coverage ratio for bad loans (i.e. the ratio of loan loss reserves to non-performing loans) in a sample of emerging economies. Without pretending too much precision, three observations stand out: (i) there is very wide variation in coverage across countries; (ii) on average, the emerging economies with the highest share of non-performing loans (Mexico, Indonesia and Venezuela) tend to display the lowest provisioning coverage; and (iii) there are some notable exceptions (e.g. Argentina and Malaysia) where coverage in the face of a relatively high incidence of bad loans looks relatively strong.

How far the results of detailed bank supervision should be published is a controversial question. In Chile, inspectors from the Superintendency of Banks and Financial Institutions (SBIF) visit the banks regularly and evaluate the risk of its assets, with the purpose of quantifying estimated losses and monitoring the impact of any non-provisioned losses on the solvency of the bank. The

---

[81] Sheng (1996) cites the case of one South Asian country where, until recently, loans that were not serviced for more than three years were still treated as performing.
[82] See Meltzer (1996).

Table 8: Loan loss reserves and non-performing loans

	Loan loss reserves[1] (A)	Non-performing loans[2] (B)	Coverage ratio i.e. A/B
	as a percentage of total loans		
India	—	19.5[3]	—
Hong Kong	2.2[2]	3.1	0.71
Korea	1.5	1.0	1.50
Singapore	—	—	1.20
Taiwan	1.1	2.6	0.42
Indonesia	2.6	11.2	0.23
Malaysia	9.6	8.2	1.17
Thailand	1.7	7.6	0.22
Argentina	10.2[2]	10.5	0.97
Brazil	1.6	5.9	0.27
Chile	3.5	1.0	3.50
Colombia	1.9	2.5	0.76
Mexico	3.1[4]	14.8	0.21
Venezuela	7.0	17.7	0.40
Memorandum:			
United States	2.7	1.6	1.69
Japan	1.0	3.3	0.30

Note: These figures may not be strictly comparable.
[1] Average 1990–94. [2] Average 1994–95. [3] Relates only to public sector banks. [4] Average 1992–94.
Sources: Office of the Comptroller of the Currency, IBCA Ltd. and central banks.

SBIF then publishes each quarter information on the quality of banks' assets and capital position (e.g. loans and other assets with their estimated losses; provisions; the capital convergence ratio and the credit risk structure). The Superintendency also publishes information on the credit risk rating of all short and long-term securities issued by banks.

The public disclosure of basic information on bank performance, bank income and bank balance sheets needs to become a more widespread and harmonised process. The annex contains two examples of the type of published information that it would be useful to have — both for the banking sector as a whole and on individual banks. The first example shows the aggregate data that are published quarterly for approximately 3,000 national banks in the United

States. The second example shows the quarterly disclosure requirements for individual banks under New Zealand's new supervisory regime.[83] In both cases, the published information allows bank creditors and investors to get a timely picture of bank profitability, bank capital, impaired assets, provisioning and exposure to certain classes of loans. Under New Zealand's new banking law, much of this information is summarised in a one or two-page note that must be displayed prominently in every bank branch — making interpretation easier for small depositors.

New Zealand's disclosure policy for banks raises two other issues that are of wider relevance for emerging economies. One is the contribution that national bank supervisors can make towards monitoring compliance with disclosure requirements, requiring a correction of false or misleading statements, and initiating legal proceedings against banks for issuing false or misleading information. The quality of information is all-important. In this regard, ensuring that more banks (in both industrial and emerging economies) prepare statements according to International Accounting Standards (with a common industry format) would improve the quality of disclosure, as it would facilitate comparisons among banks (both within and across countries).[84]

The second issue concerns the role that credit ratings issued by private credit-rating agencies can play in enhancing market discipline. Note that under the New Zealand regime every bank must prominently display its credit rating (along with any recent changes in that rating); if the bank has not obtained a credit rating, it must disclose that fact. Similarly, government auditors in Chile assign each bank a summary credit rating similar to US CAMEL (Capital, Assets, Management, Earnings and Liquidity) ratings and publish it in major newspapers, while private rating firms offer their appraisal twice a year. Argentina recently required banks to be rated by credit-rating agencies, with ratings displayed with the interest rates offered for different types of deposit. While there continues to be controversy over the leading-indicator value of credit ratings, increased efforts by emerging economies to widen the number

---

[83] Because banks in New Zealand are foreign-owned, and thus subject to home-country supervision overseas, some observers question the applicability of reliance on disclosure to other countries in different circumstances.

[84] A second possibility would be to accept the Generally Accepted Accounting Principles (GAAP) used in the United States; see White (1996) for a comparison of these competing accounting standards.

of banks that receive ratings from independent, internationally recognised creditrating agencies should improve incentives for good management and serious internal risk control.

On the legal side, banks and their supervisors in emerging economies could each do their job better if legal reforms removed outdated impediments to the pledging, transfer and seizure of loan collateral, and enhanced the statutory authority of supervisors to carry out their oversight and corrective action responsibilities.

(vii) Improving incentives for bank owners, managers and creditors, and for bank supervisors

This too is an area that covers a lot of ground. Fortunately, most of the relevant proposals can be grouped into the following five categories: incentives tied to bank capital; greater personal liability for bank directors; steps to limit the disincentive effects of explicit or implicit government guarantees; more rule-based supervisory regimes; and international prudential standards.[85]

As argued earlier, higher capital requirements can improve the incentives for bank owners and implementation of the Basle standards in developing countries. Banks in most emerging economies, given their relatively volatile environment, should probably hold more capital. But capital is typically more expensive to raise than bank deposits (in part because shareholders are less likely to be bailed out when a bank fails than depositors). How can banks be encouraged to increase capital beyond national (minimum) requirements? One incentive can be created by making a bank's range of permitted activities and its regulatory burden a function of the level of its capital. Better capitalised banks could thus be allowed to do more or be subject to less intrusive regulatory oversight. For example, US banks with risk-based capital ratios greater than 10% are permitted to take brokered deposits, whereas those with ratios of between 8 and 10% are prohibited from doing so (except with FDIC approval).

Another possibility is the issuance of subordinated debt, where the purchaser would not expect to be bailed out. Other countries have increased the personal liability of managers and directors.[86] Under New Zealand's

---

[85] Proposals to establish "narrow banks" are not discussed in this paper.
[86] See Caprio and Klingebiel (1996b).

new banking law, the management of a bank is to be replaced when a bank is insolvent or is likely to become so. Under the Federal Deposit Insurance Corporation Improvement Act of 1991 (usually referred to by the acronym FDICIA) in the United States, supervisors are mandated to restrict the pay of bank officers when bank capital falls into the 3–6% range. In New Zealand, bank directors also face serious criminal and civil penalties (including imprisonment, fines and unlimited personal liability for depositors' losses) for false or misleading statements. The objective should be to find an incentive structure that enforces accountability on bank managers and directors but is not so forbidding as to discourage capable individuals from taking up these posts.

There have been several approaches to combating the moral hazard of explicit and implicit government guarantees. One is "co-insurance": de jure coverage of deposit insurance is usually less than complete (i.e. reimbursements are less than 100% or are subject to a ceiling) in industrial and developing countries alike.[87] This is meant to increase the incentive to monitor the health of a bank; some feel that it also helps to build a constituency for strong supervision (since depositors would share the costs of weak supervision).[88] Others doubt that partial deposit insurance coverage significantly strengthens discipline because the de facto treatment of depositors after bank failures is often more generous than de jure arrangements. In addition, partial coverage may delay the closure of an insolvent bank (because of the need to negotiate with depositors). In any case, small depositors may be too dispersed or too unsophisticated to exert much (deposit withdrawal) pressure on weak banks. A second possibility is risk-weighted deposit insurance premiums, whereby riskier banks pay more for insurance. In most cases, however, the difference in insurance premium rates across banks is far less pronounced than differences in actuarial failure rates would imply.[89] A third possibility is to provide deposit insurance through mutual liability (making groups of banks liable for members' losses): this may serve to mobilise peer pressure.[90]

---

[87] See Lindgren *et al.* (1996).
[88] See Honohan (1996).
[89] Benston and Kaufman (1993), for example, level this criticism at risk-weighted insurance premiums for US banks (under FDICIA).
[90] See Caprio and Klingebiel (1996b).

Perhaps the most interesting approach to the moral hazard role of government guarantees is the "structured early intervention and resolution" (SEIR) proposal of Benston and Kaufman (1988) — much of which was ultimately incorporated into recent US banking legislation (FDICIA), and subsequently into that of several other countries. On the assumption that deposit insurance is probably politically inescapable, SEIR structures the regulatory or supervisory response to emerging bank difficulties by seeking to mimic the pressures that the private uninsured bondholders would exert on debtor firms if there were no government guarantees.[91] It does this by imposing a graduated regulatory response (e.g. restrictions on dividends and asset growth, closer monitoring and so on) as bank capital crosses multiple capital zone "tripwires"; see Table 9. If these graduated pressures are unsuccessful, the regulators are required to close the bank before the market value of the bank's capital turns negative. Hence losses to the public are minimised; only the bank's shareholders and uninsured depositors are put at risk.

By making much of the supervisory response mandatory, and thus limiting the supervisor's discretion, the SEIR proposal may also serve to offset the pressure on bank supervisors to delay prompt corrective action. Rules may be particularly welcome to supervisors who operate in an environment of strong political pressures. On the other hand, as Meltzer (1996) has pointed out, such rules may force the closure of some banks that would have become viable later: there are costs in acting too early as well as too late.[92] As shown in Table 9, FDICIA, while requiring US bank supervisors to impose certain sanctions, leaves others to their discretion.[93] Japan also plans to establish a prompt corrective action system from April 1998. Chile's banking law also includes several important pre-commitment features.[94] For example, a bank must capitalise if its net worth falls 40% below its value at the beginning of the year. In addition, a deposit rate 20% above the industry average, three calls

---

[91] FDICIA also seeks to limit disincentive effects by setting mandatory haircuts for uninsured depositors.

[92] It could be argued, for example, that whereas regulatory forbearance aggravated the US saving and loan crisis, it smoothed the resolution of the developing-country debt crisis in the 1980s.

[93] Benston and Kaufman (1993) have criticised FDICIA for being less severe, less mandatory and less prompt than they had suggested.

[94] The following description relies on Meltzer (1996).

Table 9: Summary of prompt corrective action provisions of the Federal Deposit Insurance Corporation Improvement Act of 1991

Zone	Mandatory provisions	Discretionary provisions	Capital ratios (%) Risk based Total	Capital ratios (%) Risk based Tier 1	Leverage Tier 1
1. Well capitalised			>10	>6	>5
2. Adequately capitalised	1. No brokered deposits, except with FDIC approval		>8	>4	>4
3. Under-capitalised	1. Suspend dividends and management fees 2. Require capital restoration plan 3. Restrict asset growth 4. Restrict deposit interest rates* 5. Pay of officers restricted	1. Order recapitalisation 2. Restrict inter-affiliate transactions 3. Restrict deposit interest rates 4. Restrict certain other activities 5. Any other action that would better carry out prompt corrective action	<8	<4	<4
4. Significantly undercapitalised	1. Same as for Zone 3 2. Order recapitalisation* 3. Restrict inter-affiliate transactions* 4. Restrict deposit interest rates* 5. Pay of officers restricted	1. Any Zone 3 discretionary actions 2. Conservatorship or receivership if fails to submit or implement plan or recapitalise pursuant to order 3. Any other Zone 5 provision, if such action is necessary to carry out prompt corrective action	<6	<3	<3

(*Continued*)

Table 9: (*Continued*)

Zone	Mandatory provisions	Discretionary provisions	Capital ratios (%)		
			Risk based		Leverage
			Total	Tier 1	Tier 1
5. Critically undercapitalised	1. Same as for Zone 4 2. Receiver/ conservator within 90 days* 3. Receiver if still in Zone 5 four quarters after becoming critically undercapitalised 4. Suspend payments on subordinated debt* 5. Restrict certain other activities				<2

*Not required if the primary supervisor determines that action would not serve the purpose of prompt corrective action or if certain other conditions are met.
Source: Board of Governors of the Federal Reserve System.

within a year for emergency central bank assistance and any failure to meet a liquidity requirement all trigger a regulatory response.

Finally, there is the broader issue of what can be done to strengthen the political incentives to implement banking reform. A banking crisis itself should lead to the adoption of an improved incentive or supervisory framework: Caprio and Klingebiel (1996b) note a number of prominent cases (e.g. Argentina, Chile and Hong Kong). But their wider analysis of 64 cases of bank restructuring reveals that there have been relatively few success stories.

Another source of pressure for reform can come from host countries where banks want to do business. If the host country is not satisfied that the home country is implementing effective supervision, it can refuse a banking licence. Such pressures have been included both in national legislation and in the Basle Committee's Minimum Standards paper of 1992.[95] This strategy can be very

---

[95] See White (1996) and Padoa-Schioppa (1996).

effective. Nevertheless, such pressure can weaken the principle of preserving home-country leadership of banking supervision; in addition, it could on occasion be used as an excuse to restrict competition.

A third mechanism is voluntary international standards or guidelines (some of which may subsequently become mandatory when embodied in national legislation). Such guidelines are deliberately not all-inclusive but cover only a few key aspects, where different national systems have common ground. Good examples are the Basle Committee's Concordat and its Capital Accord, the G-30's best practice guidelines on internal risk management and disclosure for derivatives, and the IMF's recently agreed Special Data Dissemination Standard. Even if such standards are voluntary, knowledge by market participants of who is, and who is not, meeting the standard establishes market incentives for slow movers. These incentives can help to overcome such local stumbling-blocks to reform as entrenched opposition from interest groups or concerns about the competitive impact of unilateral adoption. At the same time, the specificities of national banking systems are respected.

Some analysts have argued that the banking systems of developing countries need much more extensive standards and that compliance requires more explicit monitoring. Goldstein (1996b) has proposed that the time is ripe for an international banking standard that would go beyond existing Basle Committee agreements (on capital adequacy, consolidated supervision and co-operation between home and host-country banking supervisors) to cover many of the factors most responsible for banking crises in developing countries. Such factors include the high volatility of the operating environment, heavy government involvement, connected lending, intense political pressure on bank supervisors and so on. However, a single standard may not be flexible enough to accommodate the variety of country circumstances. In addition, the approach raises many thorny operational issues: how would the standards be set? If they were to be monitored, who would do the monitoring? What would be the incentives for countries to adopt such standards?

(viii) *Preventing the exchange rate regime from compromising crisis prevention/management*

On the complex issue of a country's choice of exchange rate regime two points are relevant for present purposes. The first is that several emerging economies have avoided the heightened vulnerability associated with a seriously overvalued fixed exchange rate by making a transition to one of several forms of flexibility. Changes in exchange rate arrangements have ranged from a simple widening of bands during periods of heavy capital market pressure to the adoption of a crawling band (à la Chile, Colombia and Israel). Some have changed to managed floating along with domestic inflation targets. The empirical evidence suggests that abandoning rigid exchange rate commitments has not (at least so far) led to any significant deterioration in inflation performance in these countries.[96] The second point is that if the authorities nevertheless decide that a fixed exchange rate or a currency board is the most suitable regime for their circumstances, then they ought to make contingency arrangements for how lender-of-last-resort operations for illiquid but solvent banks can be carried out.

CONCLUSION

Banking crises in emerging economies have multiple causes. The bad news is that there is therefore no single solution. Part of the story is the more volatile environment (external and internal) in which banks in these countries operate — along with a reluctance in many countries, at least so far, to address, or to compensate for, that volatility with diversification, insurance and higher bank capital. Part of it reflects a tendency for banks (much like those elsewhere) to lend too recklessly during the upswing of the business cycle — a tendency that has been exacerbated by large-scale capital inflows that are ultimately intermediated by the banking system. Part of it is a rapid expansion in bank liabilities in a context in which the normal liquidity/maturity mismatches of banks are magnified by an excessively short-term orientation of the financial system, relatively little support from securities markets, a sometimes heavy reliance on foreign-currency-denominated debt and the relatively high variability of international reserves, interest rates and the exchange rate. Part of it results from implementing financial liberalisation before the supervisory and regulatory system has been strengthened sufficiently to manage prudently the new risks involved. Part of it is an accounting, disclosure and legal framework that impedes the potential contribution of market discipline to monitoring and penalising excessive risk-taking. Part of it is an incentive framework

---

[96] See Montiel (1996) and Gavin *et al.* (1996).

that neither gives bank owners, managers and depositors enough to lose if excessive risks are taken nor supervisors enough institutional protection against pressures for delay in implementing corrective action. And part of it is exchange rate arrangements that, whatever other merits they may have, have not been conducive to effective crisis prevention and management in the financial sector.[97]

The good news is that there are several possible policy measures that can significantly reduce the incidence of each of these factors underlying banking crises. Greater macroeconomic stability, a larger role for foreign-owned banks, the wider use of market-based hedging instruments and higher levels of bank capital would all help either to reduce volatility or to make the consequences for the domestic banking system less damaging. Limiting the allocation of bank credit to particularly interest-rate-sensitive sectors, close monitoring of lending by weakly capitalised banks and employing the right mix of macroeconomic and exchange rate policies would similarly limit vulnerability to lending booms, asset price collapses and surges of capital inflows. Maintaining an ample cushion of both liquid assets and international reserves, and adopting a cautious attitude towards short-term, foreign-currency-denominated borrowing can limit banks' liquidity or currency mismatches and discourage runs on both bank and government liabilities. Careful screening of applicants for banking licences along with a prior strengthening of training in, and resources for, banking supervision can reduce the risks that often go hand-in-hand with financial liberalisation. The privatisation of state-owned banks and enhanced efforts to increase the transparency of implicit and explicit government taxation of the banking system should help to put more of the banking system on a commercial footing — with sizable dividends in terms of efficiency and lower loan losses. The more effective implementation of existing restrictions on connected lending would reduce undue concentration of credit risk and discourage favouritism (and fraud) in credit allocation. Stricter asset classification and provisioning practices could reduce the all-too-frequent

---

[97] In a detailed examination of 29 systemic banking crises, Caprio and Klingebiel (1996b) concluded that political factors (government interference and connected lending) were important in at least one-third of the crises, volatility factors (primarily, terms-of-trade deterioration and recession) in one-half to two-thirds of them, and deficient bank management and poor supervision and regulation — broadly defined — in two-thirds to four-fifths of all cases.

"evergreening" of bad loans and provide satisfactory protection against loan losses. Fuller and more internationally harmonised public disclosure of bank soundness and performance — with a greater role for private rating agencies — can help to strengthen market discipline. Considerable scope exists too for tilting the incentives for bank owners, managers and creditors in the direction of bank soundness. In this connection, higher bank capital, higher personal liability for poor management or oversight and increased recourse to coinsurance for depositor losses (with uninsured bank creditors bearing a higher proportion of the losses) would each improve the structure of incentives. The introduction of some rule-based, prompt corrective action elements into the bank supervisory process may, in circumstances where supervisors face strong political pressures for forbearance, enhance supervisory effectiveness.

Several countries are going through a difficult period of banking sector restructuring, and are attempting to address the consequences of, inter alia, earlier failures of prudential oversight. These failures, and the lessons learnt from banking difficulties worldwide, have naturally prompted national authorities almost everywhere to take a good look at their safeguards against banking crises and other systemic financial problems. In some emerging economies, policy measures have been taken to make the domestic banking system more robust and to improve the quality of banking supervision. In many others, these questions are under active consideration. The frequency and severity of banking crises in developing countries over the past decade and a half argue against complacency. Reforms need to be more widely shared and deeply rooted than was the case in the past. Fixing the problems of the banking sector will require a sustained commitment. The ways that international co-operation, in several guises, can encourage or sustain this commitment is clearly an issue that requires urgent consideration.

… 355

ANNEX: TWO EXAMPLES OF DISCLOSURE OF THE FINANCIAL CONDITION OF BANKS

A. *Aggregate positions*: data for national banks in the United States

Income	Balance sheet	Performance ratios
Net income	Assets	Return on equity
Net interest income	Loans	Return on assets
Non-interest income	Real estate	Net interest margin
Non-interest expense	Commercial & industrial	
Loan loss provision	Non-current loans[1]	Loss provision to loans
Gains on securities sales, net	Other real estate owned	Net loan loss to loans
Extraordinary income	Securities not in trading a/c	Non-current loans to loans
Net loan loss		Loss reserves to loans
	Total liabilities	Loss reserves to non-current loans
	Total deposits	
	Domestic deposits	Loans to assets
	Loan loss reserve	Loans to deposits Equity to assets
	Equity capital	Estimated leverage ratio[2]
	Total capital	Estimated risk-based capital ratio

Note: These aggregate data cover around 3,000 banks and are published quarterly.
[1] Ratio of estimated Tier 1 capital to estimated tangible total assets.
[2] Sum of loans and leases 90 days or more past due plus loans not earning the contractual rate of interest in the loan agreement.
Source: Office of the Comptroller of the Currency, *Quarterly Journal*.

B. *Individual positions*: New Zealand's new disclosure regime for banks

The aim of bank supervision in New Zealand is to maintain a sound and efficient financial system. The protection of depositors is not an aim in itself; there is no deposit insurance.

Registration of banks

Bank registration entitles the institution to use the word "bank" in its name; but registration is not required to conduct banking business.[98] The Reserve Bank of New Zealand is responsible for deciding on applications for bank registration subject to certain conditions:

---

[98] However, compliance with disclosure and other requirements contained in the Securities Act is required.

- Total capital of at least 8% of the banking group's risk-weighted credit exposures, of which at least one-half must be Tier 1 capital.[99]
- Group's credit exposure to major shareholders and related entities not permitted to exceed:
    (a) 15% of Tier 1 capital in the case of lending to a non-bank;
    (b) 75% of Tier 1 capital in the case of lending to a bank.
- Locally incorporated banks to have at least two independent directors and a non-executive chairman.

Reserve Bank action when a bank's capital falls below requirements

Recent reforms introduced a more structured approach with the aim of reducing the scope for regulatory forbearance by the banking supervisor.

- If a bank's Tier 1 or total capital falls below the limits noted above, the bank would have to submit to the Reserve Bank a plan for restoring capital, including the following elements:
    (a) no dividends paid until the minimum capital requirements have been complied with;
    (b) no increase in exposure to related parties from the level prevailing when capital requirements first breached;
    (c) if reduction in capital results in a bank being in breach of the limit on related party exposures, the bank would be required to reduce its exposure to a level which complies with the limit.
- If a bank's Tier 1 capital falls below 3% of risk-weighted exposures, gross credit exposures must not be increased from the level which occurred when capital first fell below this limit.

The plan would be published in the bank's public disclosure statement at the first practicable opportunity.

---

[99] At the time of announcement, the Reserve Bank noted, "Although the Bank considers that disclosure alone, without minimum requirements, should provide sufficient incentives for banks to at least adhere to the international norm of 8%, it believes the retention of the capital requirement offers benefits in terms of international credibility, at little, if any, marginal costs to banks".

Form of disclosure

- Quarterly.
- Two main forms, one brief ("Key Information Summary") and the other longer ("General Disclosure Statement"). A Supplemental Disclosure Statement discloses details of any guarantee arrangements and conditions of registration imposed by the Reserve Bank.
- At the half-year and end-of-year, disclosure statements must be published not later than three months after the relevant balance date. In the first and third quarters of a bank's financial year, banks have only two months to publish the disclosure statements, given that in these quarters the disclosure statements are of an abbreviated nature.

Key Information Summary

This one or two page note must be displayed prominently in every bank branch and include:

- Credit rating. If the bank has one, it must disclose the credit rating given to its long-term senior unsecured liabilities payable in New Zealand. It must also disclose the name of the rating agency, any qualifications (e.g. "credit watch" status) and any changes made in the two years preceding the balance date. A bank with no credit rating must disclose prominently that fact.[100]
- Capital adequacy. Risk-weighted capital ratios, as measured using Basle capital requirements.
- Impaired assets. Amount and specific provisions held against them.
- Exposure concentration. Disclosed when exceeds 10% of group's equity; disclosure is based on group's peak lending to individual customers over the accounting period. Disclosed as the number of exposures between 10% and 20% of the group's equity, the number between 20% and 30% and so on.
- Connected lending. Amount of credit exposure to connected persons, based on peak exposure over the accounting period.

---

[100] The initial intention of imposing a mandatory rating on all banks was abandoned in the face of opposition from smaller banks which argued that this would impose unnecessary costs on them.

- Profitability and a statement as to whether liabilities are guaranteed by another party.

General Disclosure Statement

Contains all the information in the Key Information Summary but in greater detail and additional information such as:

- Capital and exposure information. Detailed information on Tier 1 and Tier 2 capital and credit exposures (both on and off balance sheet) for the bank and the banking group.
- Funds management. Information on securitisation, unit trusts, superannuation funds and other fiduciary activities. Explanation of measures in place to minimise risks that might affect the banking group's balance sheet.
- Sectoral information. Credit exposure by industry sectors and geographical areas. Main sources of funds by geographical area, by product and by counterparty type.
- Risk management systems. Description of internal audit function and extent to which systems subject to review.
- Market risk exposures. Banking group's exposure to changes in interest rates, foreign exchange rates and equity prices. Market risk disclosure is for the bank's whole book — both the banking book and the trading book. These disclosure requirements give banks the option of calculating interest rate risk using the Reserve Bank model (based on the Basle market risk model) or using their own model, provided that it produces a result which is at least as conservative as the Reserve Bank model. Both peak and end-of-period exposures must be disclosed.
- Detailed information on asset quality and credit exposure concentration.

Directors' attestations and legal responsibilities

Every disclosure statement must contain attestations signed by every director of the bank. The attestations relate to:

- Whether the bank has adequate systems in place to monitor and manage the banking group's business risks (including credit risk, concentration risk, equity risk, foreign exchange risk, interest rate risk and liquidity risk) and whether those systems are being properly applied;

- Whether the banking group's exposures to related parties are contrary to the interests of the banking group;
- Whether the bank is complying with its conditions of registration;
- That the disclosure statement is not false or misleading.

Directors face serious criminal and civil penalties (including imprisonment, fines and unlimited personal liability for depositors' losses) for false or misleading statements. Directors may also incur common law liability if they allow the bank to continue to accept funds on the basis of a disclosure statement which, although not false or misleading when signed, has become false or misleading as a result of subsequent material adverse developments.

Reserve Bank's responsibilities

Under the disclosure framework, the Reserve Bank:

- Will monitor banks' disclosure statements to maintain a sound understanding of the financial condition of the banking system.
- Will monitor banks' compliance with disclosure requirements and conditions of registration. The Reserve Bank also has the power to require a bank to correct and republish a disclosure statement found to be false or misleading.
- Can initiate legal proceedings against a bank and its directors if a statement is thought to be false or misleading.

The Reserve Bank retains extensive crisis management powers under its Act, including the powers to appoint an investigator, give directives to a bank and recommend that a bank be placed under statutory management.

Sources: Geof Mortlock "A new disclosure regime for registered banks". Reserve Bank of New Zealand *Bulletin* (March 1996) and Peter Nicholl "Market-based regulation". Paper presented to IBRD Conference on Preventing Banking Crises (April 1996).

"Banking Crises in Emerging Economies: Origins and Policy Options", by Morris Goldstein and Philip Turner. Copyright © 1996 by Bank for International Settlements. Used with permission of the publisher.

REFERENCES

BIS (1995): *65th Annual Report*. Basle: Bank for International Settlements.

BIS (1996): *66th Annual Report*. Basle: Bank for International Settlements.

Basle Committee on Banking Supervision (1992): *Report on international developments in banking supervision*. Report Number 8. Basle, September.

Benston, George and George Kaufman (1988): "Regulating bank safety and performance" in W. Haraf and R. Kushmeider (eds.), *Restructuring banking and financial services in America*. Washington: American Enterprise Institute, pp. 63–99.

Benston, George and George Kaufman (1993): "Deposit insurance reform: a functional approach-comment." *Carnegie-Rochester Conference Series on Public Policy*. Vol. 38, pp. 41–49, June.

Bernanke, Ben S. (1983): "Non-monetary effects of the financial crisis in the propagation of the great depression." *American Economic Review*, Vol. 73, pp. 257–276.

Calvo, Guillermo and Morris Goldstein (1996): "Crisis prevention and crisis management after Mexico: what role for the official sector?" in Calvo *et al.*

Calvo, Guillermo, Leonardo Leiderman and Carmen Reinhart (1993): "Capital inflows and real exchange rate appreciation in Latin America: the role of external factors." *IMF Staff Papers* Vol. 40, No. 1, March, pp. 108–150.

Calvo, Guillermo, Morris Goldstein and Eduard Hochreiter (Eds., 1996): *Private capital flows to emerging markets after the Mexican crisis*. Washington: Institute for International Economics.

Caprio, Gerard and Daniela Klingebiel (1996a): "Bank insolvencies: cross-country experience." Washington: World Bank, unpublished, April.

Caprio, Gerard and Daniela Klingebiel (1996b): "Bank insolvency: bad luck, bad policy, or bad banking?" Paper presented to Annual World Bank Conference on Development Economics. Washington: World Bank, April.

Caprio, Gerard, Izak Atiyas and James Hanson (1994): *Financial reform: theory and experience*. Cambridge: Cambridge University Press.

Cavallo, Domingo (1996): "Comment on Gavin *et al.*"

De Gregorio, Jose and Pablo Guidotti (1992): "Financial development and economic growth." IMF Working Paper No. 92/101, Washington: International Monetary Fund, December.

De Juan, Aristobulo (1996): "The roots of banking crises: microeconomic issues and regulation and supervision," in Hausmann and Rojas-Suárez (Eds., 1996a), pp. 83–102.

Dooley, Michael (1995): "Managing the public debt." Paper presented at World Bank conference on "Managing economic reform under capital flow volatility," Washington, 30th May-2nd June.

Dooley, Michael, Eduardo Fernandez-Arias and Kenneth M. Kletzer (1994): "Recent private capital inflows to developing countries: is the debt crisis history?"

NBER Working Paper No. 4792, Cambridge: National Bureau of Economic Research, July.

Edwards, Sebastian (1995): "Public-sector deficits and macroeconomic stability in developing economies," in Federal Reserve Bank of Kansas City, *Budget deficits and debt: issues and options.* Kansas City: Federal Reserve Bank of Kansas City, pp. 307–374.

Fernandez, Roque (1996): "Capital flows and the liquidity shock," in Calvo *et al.* (Eds., 1996).

Folkerts-Landau, David *et al.* (1995): "Effects of capital flows on the domestic financial sectors in APEC developing countries," in Khan and Reinhart.

Galbis, Vincente (1993): "High real interest rates under financial liberalization: is there a problem?" IMF Working Paper No. 93/7. Washington: International Monetary Fund.

Garber, Peter (1995): "Managing risks to financial markets from volatile capital flows: the role of prudential regulation." Economics Department, Brown University, Providence, Rhode Island, unpublished.

Gavin, Michael *et al.* (1996): "The macroeconomics of capital flows to Latin America: experience and policy issues," in Hausmann and Rojas-Suárez (Eds., 1996b), pp. 1–40.

Gavin, Michael and Ricardo Hausmann, (1996): "The roots of banking crises: the macroeconomic context," in Hausmann and Rojas-Suárez (Eds., 1996a), pp. 27–63.

Goldstein, Morris (1996a): "From Halifax to Lyon: what has been done about crisis management?" *Princeton Essays in International Finance No. 200.* Princeton: International Finance Section, Economics Department, Princeton University.

Goldstein, Morris (1996b): "The case for an international banking standard." Washington: Institute for International Economics, unpublished, August.

Goldstein, Morris (1996c): "Presumptive indicators/early warning indicators of vulnerability to financial crises in emerging market economies." Washington: Institute for International Economics, unpublished, January.

Goldstein, Morris (1995): "Coping with too much of a good thing: policy responses for large capital inflows in developing countries." Policy Research Working Paper No. 1507, Washington: World Bank, September.

Goldstein, Morris, David Folkerts-Landau *et al.* (1993): *Exchange rate management and international capital flows.* IMF World Economic and Financial Surveys. Washington: International Monetary Fund, April.

Hausmann, Ricardo and Helmut Reisen (Eds., 1996): *Securing stability and growth in Latin America.* Paris: OECD Development Centre and Inter-American Development Bank.

Hausmann, Ricardo and Michael Gavin (1995): "Macroeconomic volatility in Latin America: causes, consequences, and policies to assure stability." Washington: Inter-American Development Bank, unpublished, July.

Hausmann, Ricardo and Liliana Rojas-Suárez (Eds., 1996a): *Banking crises in Latin America*. Washington: Inter-American Development Bank and Johns Hopkins University Press.

Hausmann, Ricardo and Liliana Rojas-Suárez (Eds., 1996b): *Volatile capital flows: taming their impact on Latin America*. Washington: Inter-American Development Bank and Johns Hopkins University Press.

Honohan, Patrick (1996): "Financial system failures in developing countries: diagnosis and prediction." Washington: International Monetary Fund, unpublished, June.

IMF (1995): *International Capital Markets*. IMF World Economic and Financial Surveys. Washington: International Monetary Fund, August.

IMF (1996): *World Economic Outlook*. IMF World Economic and Financial Surveys. Washington: International Monetary Fund, May.

Johnston, R. Barry and Ceyla Pazarbasioglu (1995): "Linkages between financial variables, financial sector reform, and economic growth and efficiency." IMF Working Paper No. 95/103, Washington: International Monetary Fund, October.

Kaminsky, Graciela and Carmen Reinhart (1995): "The twin crises: The causes of banking and balance of payments problems." Board of Governors of the Federal Reserve System and the International Monetary Fund, manuscript.

Kane, Edward (1989): *The S & L insurance mess: how did it happen?* Washington: The Urban Institute Press.

Khan, Mohsin and Carmen Reinhart (Eds., 1995): *Capital flows in the APEC region*. IMF Occasional Paper No. 122. Washington: International Monetary Fund, March.

Kindleberger, Charles (1978): *Manias, panics and crashes*. New York: Basic Books.

Krugman, Paul (1995): "Dutch tulips and emerging markets." *Foreign Affairs*, Vol. 74, pp. 28–44, July/August.

Leiderman, Leonardo and Alfredo Thorne (1996): "The 1994 Mexican crisis and its aftermath: what are the main lessons," in Calvo *et al.* (Eds., 1996).

Lindgren, Carl-Johan, Gillian Garcia and Mathew I. Saal (1996): *Bank soundness and macroecoomic policy*. Washington: International Monetary Fund.

Levine, Ross (1996): "Stock markets: a spur to economic growth." *Finance and Development*, Vol. 33, March, pp. 7–10.

Masson, Paul and Michael Mussa (1995): "The role of the Fund: financing and its interaction with adjustment and surveillance." Washington: International Monetary Fund.

McKinnon, Ronald and H. Pill (1994): "Credible liberalizations and international capital flows: the overborrowing syndrome." Palo Alto: Stanford University, unpublished.

Meltzer, Allan (1995): "Sustaining safety and soundness: supervision, regulation, and financial reform," Washington: World Bank, December.

Mishkin, Frederick (1994): "Preventing financial crises: an international perspective," *Manchester School*, Vol. 62, pp. 1–40.

Mishkin, Frederick (1996): "Asymmetric information and financial crises: a developing country perspective." Paper prepared for World Bank Annual Conference on Development Economics, Washington, 25th–26th April.

Montiel, Peter (1996): "Policy responses to surges in capital inflows: issues and lessons," in Calvo *et al.* (Eds., 1996).

Nam, Sang-Woo (1993): "Korea's financial markets and policies." Seoul: Korea Development Institute, unpublished, October.

Padoa-Schioppa, Tommaso (1996): Address to the 9th International Conference of Banking Supervisors, Stockholm, 12th–14th June.

Qureshi, Zia (1996): "Globalization: New opportunities, tough challenges." *Finance and Development*. Vol. 33, No. 1, March, pp. 30–33.

Reinhart, Carmen M. and Vincent R. Reinhart (1995): "On the use of reserve requirements in dealing with capital flow problems." University of Maryland at College Park: Center of International Economics Working Paper No. 16, November.

Rojas-Suárez, Liliana and Steven Weisbrod (1995): *Financial fragilities in Latin America: the 1980s and the 1990s.* IMF Occasional Paper No. 132. Washington: International Monetary Fund, October.

Rojas-Suárez, Liliana and Steven Weisbrod (1996a): "The do's and don'ts of banking crisis management," in Hausmann and Rojas-Suárez (Eds., 1996a), pp. 119–57.

Rojas-Suárez, Liliana and Steven Weisbrod (1996b): "Achieving stability in Latin American financial markets in the presence of volatile capital flows," in Hausmann and Rojas-Suárez (Eds., 1996b), pp. 61–92.

Rojas-Suárez, Liliana and Steven Weisbrod (1996c): "Building stability in Latin American financial markets," in Hausmann and Reisen.

Sachs, Jeffrey D., Aaron Tornell and Andrés Velasco (1996): "Financial crises in emerging markets: the lessons from 1995." *Brookings Papers on Economic Activity,* Washington, 1996(1), pp. 147–215. Sheng, Andrew: *Bank restructuring: lessons for the 1980s.* Washington: World Bank.

Summers, Lawrence (1996): "Comments" on Gavin *et al.*

Sundararajan, V. and Tomás Baliño (Eds., 1991), *Banking crises: cases and issues.* Washington: International Monetary Fund, 1991.

Weisbrod, Steven, Howard Lee and Liliana Rojas-Suárez (1992): "Bank risk and the declining franchise value of the banking systems in the United States and Japan." IMF Working Paper No. 92/45. Washington: International Monetary Fund, June.

White, William (1996): "International agreements in the area of banking and finance: accomplishments and outstanding issues." BIS Working Paper No. 38. Basle: Bank for International Settlements, October.

World Bank (1996): *World debt tables.* Volume 1. Washington: World Bank.

Chapter 9

An International Banking Standard: The Time is Ripe

Morris Goldstein

1. This paper puts forward the case for an *international banking standard* (hereafter, IBS).[1] It emphasizes that banking crises in developing countries have been widespread and severe over the past fifteen years, that such banking crises have been costly for the countries involved and increasingly pose risks to others, that existing international agreements do not address the main origins of banking crises in developing countries, and that an IBS offers an attractive route to banking reform.

Four operational questions associated with an IBS are also discussed: should an IBS be a single standard or should it have two levels; what guidelines should be included in an IBS; who would set the standard; and how would compliance with the standard be monitored and encouraged?

2. According to Lindgren *et al.* (1996), over two thirds of the IMF's member countries experienced significant banking-sector problems during

---

[1] The paper summarizes the arguments contained in Goldstein (1997).

the 1980–1996 period; in Africa, in Asia, and in the transition economies of central and eastern Europe, that figure rises to over 90 percent. Moreover, there have been over a dozen developing-country episodes where public-sector resolution costs of these banking crises have amounted to 10 percent or more of GDP.[2] One recent study put these resolution costs of banking crises in all developing and transition economies since 1980 in the neighborhood of $250 billion.[3]

3. Banks in developing countries hold the lion's share of financial assets, operate the payments system, provide liquidity to fledgling securities markets, and are major purchasers of government bonds. In addition, bank liabilities have been growing much faster in developing countries over the past two decades than economic activity. Banking crises exacerbate downturns in economic activity, prevent saving from flowing to its most productive use, reduce the availability and increase the cost of credit to small and medium-sized firms, handicap efforts to control budget deficits, and constrain seriously the room for maneuver in the conduct of monetary policy. Because developing countries are now larger importers, debtors, and recipients of international capital flows than they used to be, and because bank liabilities often turn eventually into liabilities of developing-country governments, there is also an increased risk that banking crises in emerging economies will have unfavorable repercussions on industrial countries.[4]

4. Banking crises in developing countries have multiple origins.[5] Part of the problem is that banks operate within a more volatile environment (terms of trade, real exchange rates, international interest rates, growth and inflation rates) than do their industrial-country counterparts–without compensating

---

[2] Caprio and Klingebiel (1996a, 1996b).
[3] Honohan (1996).
[4] Developing countries currently purchase about 25 percent of industrial-country exports, receive about 40 percent of global inflows of foreign direct investment, have been recipients of almost $260 billion in net portfolio flows (over the 1990–1995 period), have (via their banks) outstanding liabilities to banks in the BIS reporting area of over $717 billion (about $46 billion more than their claims on those banks), and account for virtually all of IMF drawings since the late 1970s; see Goldstein and Turner (1996).
[5] See Caprio and Klingebiel (1996a, 1996b), Folkerts-Landau *et al.* (1995), Goldstein and Turner (1996), Kaminsky and Reinhart (1995), Lindgren *et al.* (1996), and Padoa-Schioppa (1996).

for that volatility by, inter alia, holding more capital.[6] Other major sources of vulnerability include: heavy government involvement in the banking system (i.e., banks become "quasi-fiscal agents" of the government); a high degree of connected lending (with high concentration of credit risk and compromised objectivity in credit assessment); inadequate preparation for financial liberalization; weaknesses in the accounting, disclosure, and legal framework that handicap market discipline; deteriorations in credit quality during lending booms (often stoked in turn by surges of capital inflows); magnification of the normal mismatches of banks (reflecting an excessive resort to foreign-denominated borrowing, a short-term orientation of the financial system, and rapid growth of bank liabilities); an incentive system that doesn't give bank owners, managers, and creditors "enough to lose" when they bring a bank to insolvency and that doesn't provide bank supervisors with enough institutional protection against strong pressures for regulatory forbearance; and fixed exchange rate regimes that can constrain severely the central bank's ability to act as a lender-of-last resort.

5. Existing international agreements on banking supervision — which have been oriented primarily toward G-10 countries — do not address most of the prudential/ supervisory weaknesses in developing countries. And even those areas that are covered (e.g., regulatory capital) do not take into account the particular circumstances of developing countries. For example, under the Basle Accord, a commercial loan carries the same risk weight in say, Venezuela as it does in the United States, even though the variables impacting on credit risk may well be two or three times more volatile in the former than in the latter. Others have argued that remaining weaknesses in asset classification and provisioning practices have greatly reduced the significance of developing countries meeting the 8 percent risk-weighted minimum.[7] In a similar vein, if bank owners in developing countries with high degrees of connected lending

---

[6] On the volatility of the operating environment, see Hausman and Gavin (1995) and the BIS (1996). With several notable exceptions (Argentina, Colombia, Hong Kong, and Singapore), emerging economies neither set national capital requirements much above the Basle minimum, nor do their banks hold actual capital significantly higher than banks in the largest industrial countries; see Goldstein and Turner (1996).

[7] Dziobek *et al.* (1995, p. 19) conclude that "... applying the Basle 8 percent rule without adequate provisioning, as is frequently done, distorts the informational value of the capital ratio and in fact renders the ratio meaningless."

are able to finance their capital contributions with loans from their own bank (or a related party's bank), then they will have none of their own money at stake (in net terms) and capital will not serve its intended function as a restraint on excessive risk-taking.[8]

6. The key question is how can we improve on the international banking agreements we already have, with emphasis on bringing more developing countries more quickly up to a minimum level of sound banking practice and strong banking supervision. A cue might be taken from recent efforts to strengthen other elements of the international supervisory and regulatory regime — particularly, the IMF's recently established Special Data Dissemination Standard, the Group of Thirty's best-practice guidelines for the risk management of derivatives, and the Basle Committee's own 1988 accord on risk-weighted capital standards for internationally-active banks. In each case, it was decided that an international standard offered incentives for countries to make improvements that they might not have been able to implement acting unilaterally — either because of entrenched opposition at home and/or because of considerations of competitiveness with other firms/countries.

7. An IBS would expand existing international banking agreements so as to tackle more of the factors underlying banking crises in developing countries. Although participation in an IBS would be voluntary, knowledge by markets of who has/has not signed on to the standard would establish market penalties for slow movers.[9] Peer pressures should also operate in the desired direction. Other incentives for participating in an IBS might be considered by the official sector to reward crisis prevention measures (e.g., IBS participants might qualify for more favorable terms on loans from the international financial institutions, or for more favorable risk weights in the Basle capital standard).

An IBS, cum a reasonable transition period for implementation, would give those developing countries who are still in the planning stages of banking

---

[8] Rojas-Suarez and Weisbrod (1996) make just such an argument for why bank capital is apt to be a misleading indicator in Latin America.

[9] Countries would be the signatories to an IBS. Their banks (including state-owned banks) would be covered once the IBS was incorporated in national banking legislation. Banks in countries not participating in an IBS might nevertheless want to comply with some IBS guidelines (and advertise that voluntary compliance) to improve their market standing vis-a-vis banks who do not comply.

reform some concrete guideposts and a fixed timetable to follow. For countries that were in the process of reform, it would provide a way of gauging their progress. Countries whose banking systems and supervisory regimes already met or exceeded the standards would not be constrained by them, and would also receive some assurance that their counterparties had taken measures to improve their creditworthiness.

8. Although even a single-standard IBS would be helpful, a two-level standard would be preferable because it could more easily accommodate the significant differences in banking and financial structures and in market orientation among potential participants (e.g., contrast Hong Kong, Chile, and Argentina with say, Russia, China, and India). An arrangement similar to the IMF's new data standards might work for an IBS: an upper level (stricter) standard (level II) that would probably attract countries more heavily involved with international capital markets, and a basic standard (level I) that would apply to all participants. The main incentive to sign on to the higher standard would be the market premium attached to having satisfied more rigorous qualifications.

9. The kind of qualitative and quantitative guidelines that might make up an IBS can be illustrated as follows:[10]

1. *Disclosure* — Participants should be required to publish basic information on bank performance, bank income, and bank balance sheets, prepared in accordance with international accounting standards; if a common format for such disclosure could be agreed, this would be even better. For level II status, banks could also be required to have credit ratings issued by internationally-recognized credit-rating agencies (and to display prominently their most recent rating), as well as to adopt the public disclosure recommendations on the trading and derivative activities of banks and securities firms jointly agreed by the Basle Committee, IOSCO, and the Eurocurrency Standing Committee (Basle Committee, 1996).
2. *Accounting and legal framework* — The aim here should be to move closer to internationally-accepted loan classification and provisioning practices, and to remove undesirable legal impediments both to the pledging, transfer,

---

[10] See Goldstein (1997) for a fuller explanation.

and seizure of loan collateral, and to the statutory authority of supervisors to carry out their oversight and prompt-corrective action responsibilities.

3. *Government involvement* — An IBS could not require governments to reduce their ownership of banks or to end their implicit/explicit taxation of the banking sector. What is more feasible, however, is to have an IBS mandate increased transparency of government involvement in banking. For example, as recently recommended by the IMF (1996), quasi-fiscal operations of governments vis-a-vis the banking system could be included in central government budget statements; in a similar spirit, participants would publish annually data on the share of non-performing loans in state-owned banks (on a basis that permits comparisons with privately-owned banks), along with an annual statement of existing policy on government instructions for the allocation of credit (be it in state-owned or privately-owned banks).

4. *Connected lending* — IBS participants would agree to establish an exposure limit on lending to connected parties, to ensure that related parties not receive credit on terms more favorable than non-related ones, to outlaw practices (e.g., use of fictitious names, dummy corporations, etc.) that make it difficult/impossible for supervisors to verify the accuracy of reported connecting-lending exposure, and to disclose publicly the share of loans going to connected parties. For level II status, participants would agree in addition to establish threshold reporting limits (to bank supervisors) on connected lending that are below the maximum limit (so as to give supervisors some advance warning of rapidly-rising exposure to connected lending).

5. *Bank capital* — Those who sign on to an IBS would agree to adopt the existing 8 percent risk-weighted capital standard for credit risk, along with the recent amendment for market risk. In order to reflect the need for higher capital when the operating environment is relatively volatile, countries wanting level II status would agree further to apply a "safety factor" *if* their recent history of loan defaults, restructured loans, and/or government assistance to troubled banks was significantly higher than the OECD average over say, the past five years.

6. *Political pressure on supervisors and other incentive problems* — Having a stricter capital standard, helpful though that would be, does not answer another important question: what happens when bank capital drops *below* the standard? This becomes particularly important in an environment

where bank supervisors may come under strong pressure to delay the implementation of corrective actions and/or the closure of an insolvent bank. It is precisely for this reason that several countries have gone to a more rules-oriented supervisory regime, where particular corrective actions are mandated once bank capital crosses successive capital zone tripwires. An IBS — at least at level II if not at level I — ought to contain a mandatory "prompt corrective action" requirement (modelled more or less along FDICIA lines in the United States).
7. *Consolidated supervision and cooperation among host and home-country supervisors* — The Basle Committee has been on target in insisting: that all international banks be supervised on a globally-consolidated basis by a capable home-country supervisor; that home-country supervisors be able to gather information from their cross-border banking establishments; that before a cross-border banking establishment is created, it receive prior consent from both the host and home-country authorities; and that host countries have recourse to certain defensive actions (e.g., prohibit the establishment of banking offices) if they determine that these conditions are not being satisfied. Participants in an IBS should therefore agree to implement the 1992 Basle Minimum Standards.

10. The group that sets the IBS should have at least three characteristics: it should have the requisite expertise along with a relatively high degree of political independence; it should be small enough to work together effectively; and it should have adequate representation both from developing countries and from the international agencies that would be involved in monitoring compliance with the standard. If developing countries are not full partners in the drafting of an IBS, it's going to be much harder for champions of banking reform in those countries to sell it to their constituents; and without support from developing countries, an IBS is unlikely to fly. Suppose we regard twenty as the relevant size constraint. Then for purposes of illustration, one might think of a working group with the following composition: 6 representatives from the Basle Committee, 5 banking supervisors from developing countries, 2 representatives each from the IMF, BIS, and the World Bank, and 3 wise men from the private sector.

11. Probably the single toughest operational issue for an IBS is how should compliance with it be monitored? The traditional approach, at least in the field of international banking agreements, is to have international

recommendations ratified by Ministers and Governors, incorporated into national law or regulation, and then monitored/enforced by the national banking supervisor.[11] National supervisors are apt to be more knowledgeable about local banking conditions than an outside group.

The rub is that exclusive home-country control will weaken the credibility of an IBS in those countries where weak banking supervision is part of the problem. For that reason, I don't think one can avoid some type of international monitoring of an IBS. On-site evaluations are crucial to good supervision, and only the IMF and the World Bank have enough troops to make such visits. They could make an appraisal of the health of the banking system — focused around the guidelines in an IBS — part of the normal country-review process. They would hold discussions with the national banking supervisor and with several important banks. Admittedly, there are limits to what can be learned within the space of a two week mission — but at least there would be some outside view on whether a country is living up to the commitments it made when it agreed to participate in an IBS. If the country is not doing so and refuses to take corrective measures (within some reasonable time period), its participation in an IBS would be suspended.

12. To sum up, existing international agreements on banking supervision, helpful as they are, were not designed to deal with many of the major prudential/supervisory weaknesses in developing countries. Nor is it likely that technical assistance and/or market discipline will on their own be capable of motivating serious banking reform.

An international banking standard offers a way to increase the scope and pace of banking reform. An IBS will of course not end banking crises in developing countries; that would not be a realistic objective. But if an IBS contributed to a lower frequency of serious banking crises, the potential payoff would be significant. The absence of superior alternatives suggest to me that we should get on with the job — and with a sense of urgency. This is the time to look for your key where you lost it — not under the lamp post.

Morris Goldstein, "An International Banking Standard: The Time is Ripe," in George C. Kaufman (editor), Research in Financial Services: Private and

---

[11] See White (1996).

Public Policy, Volume 9, pp. 99–106. Copyright © 1997 by JAI Press Inc., Emerald Group Publishing Limited. Used with permission of the publisher.

REFERENCES

Bank for International Settlements. (1996). *66th annual report.* Basle: Bank for International Settlements.

Basle Committee on Banking Supervision. (1996). *Report on international developments in banking supervision,* Report Number 10. Basle: Basle Committee on Banking Supervision.

Caprio, G., & Klingebiel, D. (1996a). Bank insolvencies: Cross-country experience. Washington: World Bank, unpublished, April.

Caprio, G., & Klingebiel, D. (1996b). Bank insolvency: Bad luck, bad policy, or bad banking? Paper presented to Annual World Bank Conference on Development Economics. Washington: World Bank, April.

Dziobek, C, Frecaut, O., & Nieto, M. (1995). Non-G-10 countries and the Basle capital rules: How tough a challenge is it to join the Basle Club? IMF PPAA No. 95/5, Washington: International Monetary Fund.

Folkerts-Landau, D., & Others. (1995). Effects of capital flows on the domestic financial sectors in APEC developing countries. In M. Khan & C. Reinhart (Eds.), *Capital flows in the APEC region.* IMF Occasional Paper No. 122. Washington: International Monetary Fund, March.

Goldstein, M. (1997). *The case for an international banking standard policy analyses in international economics.* Washington: Institute for International Economics, April.

Goldstein, M., & Turner, P. (1996). *Banking crises in emerging economies: Origins and policy options. BIS Economic Papers, 46.* Basle: Bank for International Settlements, October.

Hausman, R., & M. Gavin. (1995). Macroeconomic volatility in Latin America: Causes, consequences, and policies to assure stability. Washington: Inter-American Development Bank, unpublished, July.

Honohan, P. (1996). *Financial system failures in developing countries: Diagnosis and prescriptions.* Washington: International Monetary Fund, unpublished, June.

International Monetary Fund. (1996). *World economic outlook,* IMF world economic and financial surveys. Washington: International Monetary Fund, May.

Kaminsky, G., & Reinhart, C. (1995). *The twin crises: The causes of banking and balance of payments problems.* Board of Governors of Federal Reserve System and the International Monetary Fund. Washington: Federal Reserve Board.

Lindgren, C., Garcia, G., & Saal, M. (1996). *Bank soundness and macroeconomic policy.* Washington: International Monetary Fund, September.

Padoa-Schioppa, T. (1996). *Address to the 9th international conference of banking supervisors.* Stockholm, June 12–14.

Rojas-Suarez, L., & Weisbrod, S. (1996). *Toward an effective regulatory and supervisory framework for Latin America.* Paper presented at IADB conference on "Safe and Sound Financial Systems: What Works for Latin America?" Washington, September 27–28.

White, W. (1996). *International agreements in the area of banking and finance: Accomplishments and outstanding issues.* Paper presented at conference on "Monetary and Financial Integration in an Expanding NAFTA," University of Toronto, May 15–17.

Chapter 10

Origins of the Crisis

Morris Goldstein

Financial crises are seldom generated by one or two isolated factors.[1] The Asian financial crisis is no exception. In what follows, I analyze its multiple origins.

FINANCIAL-SECTOR WEAKNESSES

Each of the ASEAN-4 economies experienced a *credit boom* in the 1990s, that is, the growth of bank and nonbank credit to the private sector exceeded by a wide margin the already rapid growth of real GDP (see part A of Table 1). The credit boom was stoked in part by large net private capital inflows and directed in good measure to *real estate and equities*.[2] As illustrated in part B of Table 1, exposure to the property sector accounted for roughly 25 to 40 percent of total bank loans in Thailand, Indonesia, Malaysia, and Singapore

---

[1] Goldstein and Reinhart (forthcoming 1998) show that in most emerging-market banking and currency crises of the past 25 years, a high proportion of warning signals were flashing.

[2] Montiel and Reinhart (1997) argue that the sterilization policies followed by the host (capital inflow) countries played an important part in setting the stage for the subsequent crisis; specifically, sterilization operations kept domestic interest rates in the host countries higher than would otherwise have been the case, thereby inducing both larger net inflows and a high share of interest-sensitive short-term flows.

Table 1: Growth and Composition of Bank Lending, 1990–96 and 1998

A. Growth of bank credit to the private sector relative to the growth of GDP

	1990–94	1995	1996
Thailand	10.0	11.1	5.8
Indonesia	10.4	4.4	5.7
Malaysia	3.1	10.5	13.1
Philippines	10.7	27.4	31.5
Hong Kong	8.8	8.9	−6.1
Singapore	0.8	7.8	5.7
Korea, South	2.6	2.2	−0.6
Mexico	25.7	−0.6	−36.0

B. Estimates of the share of bank lending to the property sector

	End-1997
Hong Kong	40–55
Singapore	30–40
Thailand	30–40
Malaysia	30–40
Indonesia	25–30
Korea, South	15–25
Philippines	15–20

Sources: Bank for International Settlements (1997); Eschweiler (1998).

and more than that in Hong Kong.[3] Data on exposure of banks to the equity market are harder to come by, but the rising ratio of stock market credit to GDP in Malaysia and the large-scale holdings of equities by South Korean banks have contributed to the strains in these economies.[4]

---

[3] In Thailand, Indonesia, and Malaysia, this exposure was compounded by high (80 to 100 percent) loan to collateral ratios. Also, most of banks' exposure to the property market reflects exposure to property developers rather than to homeowners; see Goldstein and Hawkins (1998).
[4] The highly leveraged state of the Malaysian economy may explain why the authorities have been reluctant to use an aggressive interest rate defense to slow the decline in ringgit. According to estimates reviewed in Eschweiler (1997a), the impact of a rise in the short-term

This overextension and concentration of credit left the ASEAN-4 economies vulnerable to a shift in credit and cyclical conditions. When that shift came, induced initially by the need to control overheating and later on by an export slowdown and by an effort to defend exchange rates with high interest rates against strong market pressures, it brought with it, inter alia, falling property prices and a rising share of nonperforming bank loans.[5] Reflecting the significant amount of office space coming on stream most private analysts conclude that the fall in real property prices in Asian emerging economies has still not fully run its course.[6] Because the credit boom began and ended earlier in Thailand and Indonesia than in Malaysia and the Philippines, the effects were first visible in the former two countries.

While there is considerable variation across the different studies, private-sector estimates of peak and actual nonperforming bank loans point to extreme banking difficulties (that is, shares of nonperforming to total bank loans in the 15 to 35 percent range) in Thailand, South Korea, and Indonesia, and some analysts see Malaysia's banking industry as also in bad shape (see Table 2).[7] The same studies suggest that banks in the Philippines have not been as devastated as in the worst-hit group but nevertheless are much more fragile than the strong banking systems of Hong Kong and Singapore.[8]

In Thailand and Indonesia, vulnerability was also heightened because banks and/or their corporate customers — in seeking to minimize their borrowing costs — agreed to shoulder rollover and currency risk; that is, *too much of their foreign borrowing was undertaken at short maturities and/or*

---

interest rate on GDP is higher in Malaysia than in the other ASEAN-4 economies. Walsh (*Sydney Morning Herald*, 22 October 1997) documents that in 1997 the ratio of stock market credit to GDP in Malaysia was higher than that in the United States just prior to the Great Depression.

[5] See Bank for International Settlements (BIS) (1997). BIS (1997) also provides evidence that property-price booms in Asian emerging economies have tended to be more pronounced than those in larger industrial countries — an outcome that it attributes in part to the rapid pace of industrialization and urbanization in Asia that in turn contributes to an extremely strong demand for new buildings.

[6] See, for example, Eschweiler (1997a).

[7] By "peak" nonperforming loans, I mean estimates of the maximum level of nonperforming loans for the duration of the crisis (usually taken to encompass 1998–99).

[8] Banks in the Philippines hold relatively high levels of capital (see Eschweiler 1998).

Table 2: Estimates of Actual and Peak Nonperforming Bank Loans in Selected Asian Emerging Economies

Study	Thailand	Korea, South	Indonesia	Malaysia	Philippines	Singapore	Hong Kong
Jardine Flemming (1997)							
PNPL/TL	19.3	na	16.8	15.6	13.4	3.8	na
PNPL/GDP	20.0	na	10.8	22.9	7.2	3.8	na
Ramos (1998), Goldman Sachs							
ANPL/TL	18.0	14.0	9.0	6.0	3.0	2.0	2.0
PNPL/TL	>25.0	>25.0	>25.0	12.0–25.0	10.0–15.0	>8.0	>8.0
PNPL/GDP	40.0	34.0	16.0	17.0	7.0	9.0	13.0
Jen (1998), Morgan Stanley							
ANPL/TL	18.0	14.0	12.5	6.0	na	na	na
Peregrine (1997)							
ANPL/TL	36.0[a]	30.0	15.0	15.0	7.0	4.0	1.0
Eschweiler (1998), JP Morgan							
ANPL/TL	17.5	17.5	11.0	7.5	5.5	3.0	1.8
BIS (1997), official estimate for 1996							
ANPL/TL	7.7[b]	0.8	8.8	3.9	na	na	2.7

na = not available
PNPL = Peak nonperforming loans (1998–99)
ANPL = Actual nonperforming loans (1997 or 1998)
TL = Total loans
[a] Includes finance companies.
[b] Estimate for 1995.

denominated in foreign currency.[9] At the time, this was not thought to be such a risky strategy because the Thai baht and the Indonesian rupiah had been stable with respect to the US dollar for many years and because the combination of weak economic activity, a huge stock of bad loans in the banking system, and a public antipathy to bailing out banks seemed to point to the continuation of low interest rates in Japan. Nevertheless, these liquidity and currency mismatches eventually took their toll — in motivating speculative attacks, in magnifying the consequences of subsequent exchange rate changes, and in limiting the authorities' room for maneuver in crisis management.[10]

After the Bank of Thailand drained much of its net international reserves in defense of the baht, the rollover of its large short-term debt obligations became problematic. In Indonesia, the main problem was currency mismatching on the part of corporations.[11] Once the value of the rupiah could no longer be assured, and even more so after the currency was floated, belated efforts by Indonesian corporations to hedge their large short foreign-currency position in the market helped to fuel the rupiah's decline. And, as the rupiah fell, its adverse effect on the debt burden of firms only acted to sap market confidence and to stoke the currency's further decline. In South Korea, too, the rollover of short-term foreign-currency-denominated debt — this time on the part of banks — eventually became the action-forcing event of that crisis.

---

[9]The contention that vulnerability was linked to the composition of external borrowing rather than to the overall external debt burden is supported by cross-country comparisons of the ratios of external debt to GDP and external debt to exports. Specifically, only Indonesia among the five most adversely affected Asian economies has a relatively high debt burden relative to exports — and one that is still lower than those of Argentina and Brazil. Relative to GDP, Thailand and the Philippines have higher debt burdens than their neighbors but not ones outside the range experienced by many developing countries. See Radelet and Sachs (1998) and Goldstein and Hawkins (1998).

[10]Calvo and Goldstein (1996) show that similar liquidity and currency mismatches made Mexico more vulnerable than its Latin American neighbors to attack in 1994. Grenville (1998) emphasizes the differences between the effects of hedged versus unhedged exchange rate changes. Mishkin (1997) makes a persuasive case that heavy reliance on foreign-currency-denominated borrowing not only makes it easier to get into a crisis but also makes it harder to get out of one (because the borrowing country cannot reduce the real value of its liabilities by undertaking a devaluation).

[11]Perry and Lederman (1998) and Ito (1998a) show that the ratio of external debt (owed international banks) to international reserves for the nonbank private sector was much higher in Indonesia in mid-1997 than it was in the other four Asian-crisis economies.

Table 3: Liquidity and Currency Mismatches as of June 1997

	Ratio of short-term Debt International Reserves	Short-term Debt As A Percentage of Total Debt	Ratio of Broad Money to International Reserves
Korea, South	3.0	67	6.2
Indonesia	1.6	24	6.2
Thailand	1.1	46	4.9
Philippines	0.7	19	4.9
Malaysia	0.6	39	4.0
Singapore	na	na	1.0

na = not available
Sources: World Bank (1998); Goldstein and Hawkins (1998); IMF, *International Financial Statistics*.

Table 3 presents several indicators of liquidity/currency mismatch for the Asian emerging economies. Taken as a group, these indicators support the view that South Korea, Indonesia, and Thailand were more "mismatched" than their neighbors in the run-up to the crisis.[12] The contrast would be even sharper if *net* rather than gross international reserves were used in such ratios, because Thailand's commitments in the forward exchange market and South Korea's lending of reserves to commercial banks meant that the figures on gross reserves conveyed a misleading impression of the authorities' usable liquid assets.[13]

The buildup of credit booms and liquidity/currency mismatches in the ASEAN-4 countries would not have progressed so far had it not occurred against a backdrop of long-standing weaknesses in banking and financial sector

---

[12] See also Perry and Lederman (1998) for other indicators of liquidity and currency mismatch, including the ratio of net foreign assets of the banking system to M2 and the ratio of short-term debt owed to international banks to international reserves. They reach a similar qualitative conclusion on the relatively high vulnerability of South Korea, Thailand, and Indonesia — not only within East Asia but also relative to most emerging economies in Latin America.

[13] In this connection, Bhattacharya, Claessens, and Hernandez (1997) estimate that on the eve of the Thai crisis, the ratio of short-term gross external liabilities to net international reserves was on the order of six in Thailand versus less than two in Indonesia and less than one in both Malaysia and the Philippines. Ito (1998a) mentions the lending of South Korean reserves to commercial banks in assessing the adequacy of reserves.

supervision.[14] As in many other emerging economies, loan classification and provisioning practices were too lax.[15] There was too much "connected lending" (lending to bank directors, managers, and their related businesses), with all the attendant dangers of concentration of credit risk and lack of arms-length credit decisions ("crony capitalism"). There was excessive government ownership of, and/or government involvement in, banks.[16] Banks often became the "quasi-fiscal" agents of governments, providing an oblique mechanism for channeling government assistance (off-budget) to ailing industries. In most of these economies (Hong Kong and Singapore are notable exceptions), bank capital was inadequate relative to the riskiness of banks' operating environment.[17] Based on past behavior, there was a strong expectation that, should banks get into trouble, depositors and creditors would get bailed out, and bank supervisors lacked the mandate to counter strong political pressures for regulatory forbearance.[18] On top of all this, the quality of public disclosure and transparency was poor. For example, the 1997 Bank for International Settlements *Annual Report* contains a missing entry for Thailand's share of nonperforming loans in the banking system for 1996, and estimates of

---

[14]See Folkerts-Landau *et al.* (1995) and Lincoln (1997). Common weaknesses in banking supervision in emerging economies are discussed more extensively in Goldstein (1997a), Goldstein and Turner (1996), and IMF (1998a).

[15]A common practice, known in the literature as "evergreening," is to provide a troubled borrower with new loans so that he/she can continue to make payments on the old loan. A good loan classification system would grade a loan according to a forward-looking and comprehensive evaluation of the borrower's creditworthiness — not simply on the payment status of the loan; that is, it would evaluate the loan on the basis of the likelihood that the borrower could meet the next 10 payments, not exclusively on whether the borrower made the last payment. In addition, in several of the crisis countries, loans could be delinquent for 6 to 12 months before they were classified as nonperforming (versus 3 months in the US system). See Goldstein (1997a), Basle Committee on Banking Supervision (1997), and IMF (1998a) for further discussion of good loan classification and provisioning practices.

[16]See Williamson and Mahar (1998) for figures on the size of the state-owned banking sector in selected emerging economies.

[17]See Goldstein and Turner (1996).

[18]Krugman (1998a) and Dooley (1997) stress implicit and explicit government guarantees as a key factor in motivating large capital inflows into these economies. Calomiris (1997) attributes the greater frequency of banking crises in the past several decades primarily to the expansion of the de facto official safety net. Goldstein (1998b) argues that government guarantees need to be viewed in conjunction with financial liberalization and other factors to explain the greater incidence of banking crises during this period. See also the discussion in Chapter 3.

nonperforming loans by outside analysts tended to be on the order of two to three times larger than the last published official figures (see Table 2). In South Korea, the discrepancy between official and private estimates of nonperforming loans was even larger still.

But how did banks and their customers in these countries obtain the external financing that helped to support such lending decisions? After all, it takes two to tango. It is well to recall that the 1990s were a period of *bountiful global liquidity conditions*. During that time, over $420 billion in net private capital flows went to Asian developing countries. Private capital flows rebounded quickly after the Mexican crisis: 1996 was a record year for private net flows to emerging economies; moreover, spreads declined, maturities lengthened, and loan covenants weakened.[19] The nearness of a major financial center — namely, Tokyo — with extremely low interest rates also gave rise to a large "carry trade," where funds could be borrowed directly from Japanese institutions or intermediated via US lenders. Moreover, the Bangkok International Banking Facility (BIBF) — created with incentives to promote Bangkok as a regional financial center and intended to raise funds from nonresidents and lend them to other nonresidents ("out-out" transactions) — turned out to be merely a conduit for Thai banks and firms to borrow abroad ("out-in" transactions).

Last but not least, and much like Mexico "before the fall," the ASEAN-4 economies were widely viewed by lenders to be among the most attractive sovereign borrowers among emerging markets.[20] After all, over the past decade they had integrated themselves into the world economy and had recorded unusually rapid rates of economic growth, high saving and investment rates, and disciplined fiscal positions. The latter factor may also have given lenders confidence that, should local financial institutions encounter difficulties, the public sector would have the resources to provide assistance.[21] In short, (aside

---

[19] One recent study by Cline and Barnes (1997) found that the sharp decline in average spreads on emerging-market Eurobonds between the second quarter of 1995 and the third quarter of 1997 was considerably greater than could be accounted for by improved economic fundamentals the borrowing countries.

[20] South Korea, Malaysia, Thailand, and Indonesia were among the group of 10 developing countries that attracted the largest amounts of net private capital flows during 1990–95; see Goldstein and Hawkins (1998), Grenville (1998) provides a summary of many of the strengths of the ASEAN-4 economies prior to the crisis.

[21] See Claessens and Glaessner (1997).

perhaps from their financial sectors), they were seen as among the best students in "Policy Reform 101."

EXTERNAL-SECTOR PROBLEMS

In 1996, Thailand had a current account deficit equal to 8 percent of its GDP. Over the 1990s as a whole, Thailand had a cumulative current account deficit equal to 36 percent of its 1996 GDP.[22] In 6 of the past 15 years, Thailand's current account deficit equaled or exceeded 6 percent of GDP. The other ASEAN-4 economies have also run relatively large current account deficits in the 1990s, albeit not as pronounced as in Thailand.

Until quite recently, these current account imbalances were widely viewed as benign. Indeed, it was frequently concluded that these were "good" deficits in two respects: first, they did not reflect a saving-investment deficit in the public sector; and second, foreign borrowing was being used mainly to increase investment (rather than consumption), thereby building the capacity to service those debts. In both these dimensions. Asian current account deficits were frequently said to be more sustainable than Latin American current account deficits.

In the run-up to the crisis, however, there were at least five counts on which *concerns about current account imbalances* in the ASEAN-4 countries could well have become deeper.

First, the *quality of investment* in these countries was less impressive than the quantity. Even investment ratios of 30 to 40 percent do not look so attractive when corporate governance is very poor, when so much of private investment is directed toward either speculative activities (e.g., real estate) or industries where overcapacity was likely to be a problem over the medium term, and when too much public investment is directed toward either overambitious infrastructure projects or inefficient government monopolies. In this connection, a recent World Bank report (1998) documents that incremental capital-output ratios (the inverse of which is sometimes taken to be a proxy for the productivity of investme) increased sharply in Thailand and South Korea as between 1985–90 and 1990–96.

---

[22] See Bhattacharya, Claessens, and Hernandez (1997).

Table 4: External Sector Problems

	Real Effective Exchange Rate Overvaluation (versus June 1987 to May 1997 Average)	Current Account Balance (Percentage of GDP)		Merchandise Exports (Annual Percentage Growth)	
	June 1997	1995	1996	1995	1996
Thailand	6.7	−7.9	−7.9	23.1	0.5
Indonesia	4.2	−3.3	−3.3	13.4	9.7
Malaysia	9.3	−10.0	−4.9	20.3	6.5
Philippines	11.9	−4.4	−4.7	28.7	18.7
Hong Kong	22.0	−3.9	−1.3	14.8	4.0
Singapore	13.5	16.8	15.7	13.7	5.3
Korea, South	−7.6	−2.0	−4.9	30.3	3.7
Taiwan	−5.5	2.1	4.0	20.0	3.8

Sources: IMF, *International Financial Statistics*; IMF, *World Economic Outlook*; JP Morgan website, 1998; Council for Economic Planning and Development, Republic of China, *Taiwan Statistical Data Book*, 1997.

Second, the behavior of *real effective exchange rates* over the past two years or so pointed to a deterioration in competitiveness in much of emerging Asia. The currencies of the ASEAN-4 economies followed the US dollar down against the Japanese yen in the first half of the 1990s but then followed the dollar up against the yen thereafter. In the process, they recorded an appreciation of their real (trade-weighted) effective exchange rates relative to trend (where trend is captured by the 1987–97 average). By that measure, at the end of June 1997, the Thai baht stood about 7 percent above its long-term average; the corresponding figures for the Indonesian rupiah, the Malaysian ringgit, and the Philippine peso were 4, 9, and 12 percent, respectively (see Table 4).[23] To be sure, long-term averages of actual exchange rates should be regarded as only a rough proxy for equilibrium exchange rates. Nevertheless,

---

[23] As shown in Table 4, the Hong Kong dollar was, by this measure, the most overvalued currency. It should be noted, however, that recent research Dodsworth and Mihaljek (1997) and Hawkins and Yiu (1995) indicates that the equilibrium rate for the Hong Kong dollar may well have been appreciating over the 1983–94 period because of large productivity differentials (along classic productivity-bias lines) between tradable and nontradable goods (where tradables include financial services). This would make the overvaluation smaller than such deviation-from-trend figures suggest.

such calculations convey the strong impression that the ASEAN-4 countries were *not* experiencing huge misalignments prior to being attacked. At the same time, given that these real appreciations occurred in the context of large current account imbalances, they were a source of increased vulnerability. Here, it is also worth noting that empirical analyses of early-warning indicators of currency and banking crises in emerging economies find that real exchange rate overvaluation has historically been among the very best performing leading indicators.[24]

Third, 1996 was a year in which many emerging Asian economies experienced a significant *slowdown in merchandise export receipts* (see Table 4). In Thailand, merchandise exports were practically flat (0.5 percent increase) in 1996, after rising by 23 percent in 1995. In South Korea, merchandise exports grew by less than 4 percent in 1996 — a big change from the 30-percent-plus growth rate of a year earlier. In Malaysia, Indonesia, and the Philippines an export slowdown was likewise in evidence, albeit on a more moderate scale. It was recognized at the time that some of the export slowdown was attributable to temporary factors, including a decline in the growth of world trade and an inventory glut in the global electronics industry.[25] Still, the 1996 slowdown probably raised doubts about whether emerging Asia's export machine was going to remain the dominant force it had been in the past.

A fourth element of concern was the *competition faced by the ASEAN-4 economies from China*. More specifically, some analysts perceived a shift in regional comparative advantage toward China and away from the ASEAN-4

---

[24] See Kaminsky and Reinhart (1996), Goldstein (1998a), and Goldstein and Reinhart (forthcoming 1998).

[25] According to IMF figures, the volume of world trade grew by 5.6 percent in 1996 — down from over 9 percent in 1995. Developments in the global electronics industry are important because of the high weight of electronics in total exports for the Asian emerging economies. Hale (1997) reports that the electronics sector accounts for 57 percent of Singapore's exports, 49 percent of Malaysia's, 40 percent of the Philippines', and 17 percent of Thailand's. In a similar vein, Fernald, Edison, and Loungani (1998) calculate the share of semiconductors and some related capital goods in the exports of Asian economies to the United States. Singapore tops the list at 83 percent; the corresponding figures for other emerging Asian economies are as follows: Malaysia, 61 percent; Taiwan, 57 percent; South Korea, 54 percent; the Philippines, 54 percent; Thailand, 37 percent; greater China, 19 percent; and Indonesia, 10 percent. The BIS (1997) reports that US dollar prices of semiconductors declined by roughly 80 percent in 1996.

economies.[26] I call it a "perceived" shift because the evidence in favor of this view is less than decisive. For example, Kwan (1997) has noted that the share of Japanese foreign direct investment (FDI) going to China was strongly on the rise between 1992 and 1995–96, whereas the share going to the ASEAN-4 countries was constant. He also notes that analyses of the product composition of exports suggest that ASEAN-4 exports are more "similar" to Chinese exports than are exports of some other Asian economies (South Korea, Taiwan, Singapore) — and this could be seen as disadvantageous to the ASEAN-4 in view of China's relatively low labor costs. On the other hand, Fernald, Edison, and Loungani (1998) have conducted a battery of tests on China's export competition with the rest of developing Asia. They report that there was a strong similarity in export growth between greater China and the rest of developing Asia in the 1994–96 period and conclude that export competition from China is unlikely to have been an important factor contributing to the 1997 Asian financial crisis.

Fifth, looking down the road for 1998 and 1999, some observers may well have seen (in 1997) the sustainability of Asian external deficits threatened by *overproduction* in certain industries and by *intense export competition* among countries. Concerns about global overproduction have recently been voiced over a set of industries, including some (memory chips, automobiles, steel, petrochemicals, lumber, base metals, frozen chickens, etc.) that are important for Asian emerging economies.[27] In addition, the heavy historical dependence of these countries on export-led growth may have painted a picture of slowing overall growth prospects. On the importing side, given exchange rate and cyclical developments, the United States may have looked to many like the logical candidate to absorb a healthy share of emerging Asia's exports. But the United States was on its way to a current account deficit in 1997 of almost $170 billion. Would US import-competing industries, organized labor, and US policymakers accept passively an increase in the US external deficit to say, $230–300 billion in 1998, while ASEAN-4 countries, South Korea, and Japan

---

[26] Thurow (1998), for example, has argued that the swing of the ASEAN-4 economies from trade surplus to deficit is directly traceable to China's decision to concentrate on increasing exports as its engine of economic growth.

[27] See, for example, Farrow (1997).

increased significantly their import penetration of the US market?[28] Couldn't there be a protectionist backlash in the United States against much increased imports from Asia?

When you put it together — large current account deficits, deteriorating quality of investment, appreciating real exchange rates, a marked export slowdown in 1996, worries about China "eating the lunch" of the ASEAN-4 and concerns about overproduction, intense export competition, and potential protectionist pressures — it's not hard to see why external sector developments in the run-up to the crisis constituted a second element of vulnerability.

CONTAGION

Any serious analysis of the Asian currency crisis must also accord a role to contagion of financial disturbances. Past empirical work on contagion has established that contagion is typically greater during periods of turbulence than during more tranquil times, that it operates more on regional than on global lines, and that it usually runs from large countries to smaller ones.[29] On this last count, the Asian currency crisis is unusual, in that it originated in a relatively small country (Thailand) and spread to a wide set of economies, both large (South Korea, Japan, Brazil, Russia) and small.[30]

In addressing the issue of what was driving this contagion, it seems unlikely that the main explanation could be bilateral trade or investment shares with Thailand. Given Thailand's size, these bilateral relationships are simply too small to generate such wide-ranging contagion (see Table 5). In addition, if it were bilateral linkages with Thailand that were paramount for the pattern of contagion, one would have expected to see Malaysia, Singapore, and Taiwan more affected than either Indonesia or South Korea — the opposite of what has in fact taken place.[31]

There are, instead, two more-plausible channels of contagion. One is the *"wake-up call" hypothesis*. In short, it says that Thailand acted as a wake-up call for international investors to reassess creditworthiness of Asian borrowers, and

---

[28] Hale (1997) has argued that the US current account deficit in 1998 might well increase to $300 billion.
[29] See Calvo and Reinhart (1996).
[30] In the case of Japan, however, it would be more accurate to say that lines of causation ran in both directions.
[31] See Goldstein and Hawkins (1998).

Table 5: Bilateral Trade Shares with Thailand, 1996

	Exports to Thailand (As a Percentage of Total Exports)
Korea, South	2.0
Indonesia	1.8
Malaysia	4.1
Philippines	3.8
Singapore	5.7
Taiwan	3.1
Hong Kong	1.0

Sources: IMF, *Direction of Trade Statistics Yearbook, 1997;* Goldstein and Hawkins (1998).

when they did that reassessment, they found that quite a few Asian economies had weaknesses similar to those in Thailand, namely: weak financial sectors with poor prudential supervision, large external deficits, appreciating real exchange rates, declining quality of investment, export slowdowns (in 1996), and overexpansion in certain key industries. As countries were written down to reflect this reassessment of creditworthiness, the crisis spread. Goldstein and Hawkins (1998) show that a weighted average of fundamentals that gives higher weight to those fundamentals where Thailand was relatively weak is more consistent with the ordinal ranking of which Asian economies were most affected by the crisis than are rankings predicated on either the extent of bilateral interdependence with Thailand or the strength of fundamentals irrespective similarities with Thailand.[32]

---

[32] Goldstein and Hawkins (1998) measure the relative impact of the crisis on individual Asian emerging economies by the decline in exchange rates and equity prices in the second half of 1997 and by the revision in forecasted 1998 real GDP growth rates between June and December 1997. Their measures of bilateral interdependence with Thailand include export shares, geographic distance, telephone traffic with Thailand, and export similarity to Thailand. The fundamentals they consider include: excess credit growth, the ratio of short-term external debt to international reserves, the ratio of broad money to reserves, the ratio of external debt to GDP, the banking system's risk-weighted capital ratio, a median estimate of the share of nonperforming bank loans, Moody's financial-strength bank credit ratings, the ratio of the current account deficit to GDP, international reserves, the extent of the 1996 export slowdown, and three alternative measures of overvaluation of the real exchange rate. Further details of this calculation are available from the authors upon request.

I refer to it as a wake-up call because to judge from most market indicators of risk, private creditors and rating agencies were asleep prior to the outbreak of the Thai crisis.[33] Eschweiler (1997a) shows that offshore interest rate spreads on three-month government securities gave no warning of impending difficulties for Indonesia, Malaysia, and the Philippines produced only intermittent signals for Thailand.[34] Sovereign credit ratings issued by the major private credit-rating agencies were even less prescient. As documented in several studies (Radelet and Sachs 1998; World Bank 1998), long-term sovereign ratings issued by Moody's and Standard and Poors remained unchanged during the 18 month run-up to the crisis.[35]

The second channel of contagion results from the *competitive dynamics of devaluation*. As one country after another in a region undergoes a depreciation of its currency, the countries that have *not* devalued experience a deterioration in competitiveness, which in turn makes their currencies more susceptible to speculative attacks. In short, what was an equilibrium exchange rate *before* competitor countries devalue is not likely to remain an equilibrium rate *after* the fact. These competitive dynamics of successive devaluations were a factor in the ERM crisis of 1992–93, and they provide a partial explanation for why some Asian currencies came under increasing pressure after the initial depreciations of the Thai baht and Indonesian rupiah. As shown in Table 6, the Asian emerging economies have important trade links with one another, and they also compete in third-country markets. Indeed, it is because of these competitive pressures that Williamson (1996) has proposed

---

[33]Two alternative explanations for why market signals did not produce much early warning of the crisis are that creditors did not have accurate information on the creditworthiness of Asian borrowers (e.g., external debt turned out to be much larger, and international rescues much smaller, than indicated by publicly available data) and that creditors were awake but expected governments (and/or the IMF) to bail them out in case of trouble.

[34]As regards exchange market pressures, Eschweiler (1997b) notes that there was some indication of concerns in the unregulated options market for Thai baht (in addition to some earlier attacks on the baht) but also that the Indonesian rupiah was trading on the strong side of its intervention band right up to the outbreak of the crisis. Equity prices turned in a more mixed performance (Eschweiler 1997b; Radelet and Sachs 1998). The Thai, Malaysian, Filipino, and South Korean stock markets were in decline prior to the crisis, but in South Korea's case, the decline began so early that its interpretation is ambiguous; also, equity prices were not declining in the case of Indonesia.

[35]The sovereign ratings issued by Euromoney and Institutional Investor did not perform well either. Much the same could be said for stand-alone credit ratings for individual Thai banks.

Table 6: Asian Intraregional Trade, 1996

	Export Share (As a Percentage of Total Exports)	
	Emerging Asia	Japan
Thailand	36.8	16.8
Korea, South	37.8	12.3
Indonesia	26.4	28.8
Malaysia	46.8	13.4
Philippines	25.7	17.9
Hong Kong	47.2	6.6
China	37.3	20.4

Source: Lipsky, Brainard, and Parker (1997).

that these countries adopt a common currency peg. The mechanism of competitive devaluation also explains why questions continue to be asked about whether China will eventually be pressured to devalue (so as to offset the decline in competitiveness linked to the depreciations of the Asian-crisis countries).

Some even go farther (with this competitive devaluation story) and regard the 1994 currency reform cum devaluation of the Chinese yuan as initiating the 1997 round of devaluations. I find this claim unpersuasive. Because of the large share of transactions conducted in the parallel exchange market before the 1994 reform (probably as high as 80 percent), the "effective" devaluation itself was not so large;[36] in addition, China has run higher inflation rates than the (trade-weighted) average of its main trading partners in the 1990s. The bottom line is that China experienced a significant real *appreciation* of its effective exchange rate from the first quarter of 1994 through 1997 (on the order of 50 percent).[37] To the extent that there is evidence of intense export competition between China and the rest of emerging Asia, it takes place in 1989–93 — not since then.[38]

---

[36] See Liu *et al.* (1998) and Fernald, Edison, and Loungani (1998). According to Fernald, Edison, and Loungani (1998), the effective nominal depreciation relative to the US dollar was roughly 7 percent.
[37] See Fernald, Edison, and Loungani (1998).
[38] See Fernald, Edison, and Loungani (1998).

The *contagion to South Korea* is not hard to understand.[39] As noted earlier, South Korea — like Thailand — was an outlier as regards liquidity/maturity mismatches. In addition, it shared with the other Asian-crisis countries long-standing and serious weaknesses in its financial sector and in prudential oversight of banks — much of it tied to government-directed lending to large corporations (*chaebols*), large equity holdings by banks, lax accounting procedures, and a lack of transparency on the part of both banks and corporations. Moreover, the *chaebols* have very high debt-to-equity ratios, and 1996 saw about half of the most important *chaebols* either declare bankruptcy or post losses. By mid-1997, the equity market had already fallen by 60 percent from its previous peak.

Nor can the contagion to *Japan* be considered a matter of financial disturbances elsewhere in the region spilling over to an otherwise healthy economy. Japan has been delinquent in not dealing forcefully and directly with the now-long-standing and massive bad loan problem in its financial sector (recently acknowledged by Japanese authorities to be roughly 80 trillion yen in the banking system). Economic growth in the 1990s has been slower there (on average) than anywhere else in the G-7, and recent projections — including a recent (April 1998) IMF (1998b) forecast of zero growth in 1998 — suggest that recovery (along with a rebound in property prices) is still some way off. The long-running steep decline in the equity market has also meant that Japanese banks, which count unrealized gains in their equity holdings as part of their capital, have on several occasions come under risk of breaching their regulatory capital requirements, with consequences not only for their funding costs in the interbank market (the so-called "Japan premium") but also for concerns about forced asset sales to a declining market.[40]

Against this background, it is not surprising that the crisis in emerging Asia — with its adverse implications for Japanese exports and bank loans to these countries and with its spillover to the Japanese equity market — has taken a toll on Japan. As indicated in Table 7 Japan conducts a larger share of its total trade with the Asian-crisis countries than does any other G-7 country.[41]

---

[39] Young and Kwon (1998) provide an in-depth analysis of South Korea's vulnerabilities prior to the crisis.

[40] For further discussion and explanation for Japan's poor economic performance in the 1990s, see Posen (forthcoming 1998).

[41] The geographic pattern of Japanese foreign trade exaggerates the impact of the crisis *on* Japanese GDP (at least relative to the European G-7 countries) because Japan has much lower

Table 7: Industrial Countries' Merchandise Trade Shares with Asian Economies (as a percentage of total trade)

	ASEAN-4 Countries	Asian Newly Industrialized Economies	Asian Newly Industrialized and Developing Economies	Major Emerging Market Economies
United States	5.0	11.3	21.8	36.7
Japan	12.2	18.2	40.9	43.7
Germany	2.0	3.5	8.6	17.9
France	1.5	2.8	7.4	10.3
Italy	1.4	2.9	6.7	15.0
United Kingdom	2.5	5.2	10.3	14.7
Canada	1.2	2.8	5.9	8.6
G-7 total	4.3	7.9	17.0	24.9

Source: IMF, World Economic Outlook: Interim Assessment, December 1997.

Similarly, the World Bank (1998) has estimated that loans to the Asian-crisis countries account for 43 percent of the capital of Japanese banks (versus 27 percent for the G-7 countries as a group).

And as the number of countries affected by the crisis has grown, the normal channels of trade and capital flow interdependence have also been at work, including some linkages that help to explain the contagion to emerging economies outside the region. For one thing, the crisis-induced growth slowdown in Asia has contributed to a *weakening of primary commodity prices* that puts downward pressure on economies that depend heavily on such goods for exports.[42] For example, Mexico, Venezuela, and Ecuador have been adversely affected by the decline in oil prices. Because more of its total exports go to Asia than do the exports of any other Latin American economy and because copper bulks large in its exports, Chile has also been relatively hard hit by the feedback from the Asian crisis. Less expected, difficulties at South Korean banks have had knock-on effects as far away as Russia and Brazil,

---

ratios of trade to GDP than do the European G-7 countries; see IMF (1997b). In addition, the impact of the crisis on Japan depends, as noted earlier, on whether one includes (as part of the crisis) the depreciation of the yen against the US dollar and European currencies over this period (see Liu *et al.* 1998).

[42] See Perry and Lederman (1998).

because these banks were heavy purchasers of Russian GKOs (government bonds) and Brazilian Brady bonds and because they liquidated much of their holdings during the turmoil. And on and on.[43]

"Origins of the Crisis" from *The Asian Financial Crisis: Causes, Cures, and Systemic Implications* by Morris Goldstein, pp. 1–22 (1998). Peterson Institute for International Economics. Used with permission of the publisher.

REFERENCES

Bank for International Settlements (BIS). 1997. *67th Annual Report.* Basle: Bank for International Settlements.

Basle Committee on Banking Supervision. 1997. *Core Principles for Effective Banking Supervision.* Basle: Basle Committee on Banking Supervision.

Bhattacharya, Amar, Stijn Claessens, and Leonardo Hernandez. 1997. Recent Financial Market Turbulence in Southeast Asia. Washington: World Bank (October). Photocopy.

Calomiris, Charles. 1997. *The Postmodern Bank Safety Net: Lessons from Developed and Developing Economies.* Washington: American Enterprise Institute.

Calvo, Sara, and Carmen Reinhart. 1996. Capital Flows to Latin America: Is There Evidence of Contagion? In *Private Capital Flows to Emerging Economies After the Mexican Crisis*, ed. by Guillermo Calvo, Morris Goldstein, and Eduardo Hochreiter. Washington: Institute for International Economics.

Claessens, Stijn, and Thomas Glaessner. 1997. *Are Financial Sector Weaknesses Undermining the Asian Miracle?* Washington: World Bank.

Cline, William, and Kevin Barnes. 1997. *Spreads and Risk in Emerging Market Lending.* IIF Research Paper No. 97-1. Washington: Institute for International Finance (November). Photocopy.

---

[43]The emphasis in this chapter has been on the underlying vulnerabilities and transmission mechanisms that were responsible for the Asian financial crisis. A different question is whether it is possible to identify clear, short-run triggers for the crisis — much in the same way that the negative outcome of the Danish referendum on the European Monetary Union was a key event for the 1992 ERM crisis or that the Colosio assassination of March 1994 was a key event in the run-up to the Mexican peso crisis. While a host of candidates have been proposed as triggers for the first or second wave of attacks — ranging from heightened expectations of yen appreciation and/or of interest rate increases in Japan in the late spring of 1994, to the devaluation of the new Taiwan dollar in October 1997, to alleged IMF-generated panic associated with its structural policy recommendations for Thailand and Indonesia, and to negative terms-of-trade shocks for key Asian export goods in 1996 and 1997 — I confess to finding each of these factors less convincing as triggers than some key events in the two earlier major exchange rate crises of the 1990s.

Dodsworth, J., and D. Mihaljek. 1997. *Hong Kong, China: Growth, Structural Change and Economic Stability During the Transition.* IMF Occasional Paper No. 152. Washington: International Monetary Fund.

Dooley, Michael. 1997. *A Model of Crises in Emerging Markets.* NBER Working Paper No. 6300. Cambridge, MA: National Bureau of Economic Research (December).

Eschweiler, Bernhard. 1997a. Emerging Asia: The Fallout after the FX Crisis. *Asian Financial Markets.* Singapore: JP Morgan (17 October).

Eschweiler, Bernhard. 1997b. Did the Market See the Asian Crisis Coming? Paper presented at the World Bank Conference on The Asian Crisis, Washington (4 October).

Eschweiler, Bernhard. 1998. *Asian Financial Markets.* Singapore: JP Morgan (16 January).

Farrow, Maureen A. 1997. Asia Unravels. Investment Research. Toronto: Loewen, Ondaatje, McCutcheon Limited (27 November).

Fernald, John, Hali Edison, and Prakash Loungani. 1998. Was China the First Domino? Assessing Links Between China and the Rest of Emerging Asia. Washington: Board of Governors of the Federal Reserve System (March). Photocopy.

Folkerts-Landau, David, Garry Schinasi, Marcel CaSsard, Victor Ng, Carmen Reinhart, and Michael Spencer. 1995. Effect of Capital Flows on the Domestic Financial Sectors in APEC Developing Countries. In *Capital Flows in the APEC Region,* ed. by Mohsin Khan and Carmen Reinhart. IMF Occasional Paper No. 122. Washington: International Monetary Fund (March).

Goldstein, Morris. 1997a. *The Case for an International Banking Standard.* Policy Analyses in International Economics No. 47. Washington: Institute for International Economics.

Goldstein, Morris. 1998a. Commentary: The Causes and Propagation of Financial Stability: Lessons for Policy Makers. In *Maintaining Financial Stability in a Global Economy,* by the Federal Reserve Bank of Kansas City. Kansas City: Federal Reserve Bank of Kansas City.

Goldstein, Morris. 1998b. Banking Crises: International Experience. In *Preventing Banking Crises,* ed. by Gerard Caprio, George Kaufman, and Danny Leipziger. Chicago: Federal Reserve Bank of Chicago; Washington: World Bank. Forthcoming.

Goldstein, Morris, and John Hawkins. 1998. *The Origins of the Asian Financial Turmoil* Reserve Bank of Australia Research Discussion Paper 980. Sydney: Reserve Bank of Australia (May).

Goldstein, Morris, and Carmen Reinhart. 1998. *Forecasting Financial Crists: Early Warning Signals for Emerging Markets.* Policy Analyses in International Economics. Washington: Institute for International Economics. Forthcoming.

Goldstein, Morris, and Philip Turner. 1996. *Banking Crises in Emerging Economies: Origins and Policy Options.* BIS Economic Papers No. 46. Basle: Bank for International Settlements.

Grenville, Stephen. 1998. Exchange Rates and Crises. *Contemporary Economic Policy.* Forthcoming.

Hale, David. 1997. The East Asian Financial Crisis and the World Economy. Testimony before the House Banking Committee, Washington (13 November).

Hawkins, John, and M. Yiu. 1995. Real and Effective Exchange Rates. *Hong Kong Monetary Authority* 5: 1–11.

International Monetary Fund. 1998a. *Toward A Framework for Financial Stability.* Washington: International Monetary Fund.

Ito, Takatoshi. 1998a. Capital Flows in Asia. Paper presented to the NBER conference on Capital Inflows to Emerging Markets, Cambridge, MA, National Bureau of Economic Research, (February).

Kaminsky, Graciela, and Carmen Reinhart. 1996. *The Twin Crises: The Causes of Banking and Balance of Payments Problems.* Board of Governors of the Federal Reserve System and the International Monetary Fund, International Finance Discussion Paper No. 544. Washington: Board of Governors of the Federal Reserve System.

Krugman, Paul. 1998a. What Happened to Asia? Cambridge, MA: Economics Department, MIT (January). Photocopy.

Lincoln, Edward. 1997. Maybe It's the Teacher's Fault: Asian Nations Adopted the Japan Model; Now They're Paying the Price. *U.S. News and World Report* (15 December).

Liu, Li-Gang, Marcus Noland, Sherman Robinson, and Zhi Wang. 1998. *Asian Competitive Devaluations.* Working Paper No. 98-2. Washington: Institute for International Economics (January).

Mishkin, Frederick. 1997. Asymmetric Information and Financial Crises: A Developing Country Perspective. *Annual World Bank Conference on Development Economics.* Washington: World Bank.

Montiel, Peter, and Carmen Reinhart. 1997. The Dynamics of Capital Movements to Emerging Economies during the 1990s. Williams College and the University of Maryland, (July). Photocopy.

Perry, Guillermo, and Daniel Lederman. 1998. Financial Vulnerability, Spillover Effects, and Contagion: Lessons from the Asian Crisis for Latin America, Latin American, and Caribbean Region. Washington: World Bank (March). Photocopy.

Radelet, Steven, and Jeffrey Sachs. 1998. The Onset of the Asian Financial Crisis. Cambridge, MA: Harvard Institute for International Development (February). Photocopy.

Thurow, Lester. 1998. Asia: The Collapse and the Cure. *New York Review of Books* (5 February).

Williamson, John, and Molly Mahar. 1998. A Review of Financial Liberalization. South Asia Region Discussion Paper. Washington: World Bank (January). Photocopy.

World Bank. 1998. *Global Development Finance,* vol. 1. Analysis and Summary Tables. Washington: World Bank.

Young, Soogil, and Jae-Jung Kwon. 1998. The Korean Economy under the IMF Program. Seoul: Korea Institute for International Economic Policy (January). Photocopy.

Chapter 11

Methodology and Empirical Results

Morris Goldstein, Graciela Kaminsky and Carmen Reinhart

Our approach to identifying early warning indicators of financial crises in emerging economies reflects a number of decisions about the appropriate methodology for conducting such an empirical exercise. Key elements of our thinking are summarized in the following guidelines.

Morris Goldstein, Dennis Weatherstone Senior Fellow, has held several senior staff positions at the International Monetary Fund (1970–94), including deputy director of its research department (1987–94). He has written extensively on international economic policy and on international capital markets.

Graciela Kaminsky, visiting fellow, is a professor of economics and international relations at George Washington University. She was assistant professor of economics at the University of California, San Diego (1985–92) and a staff economist at the Board of Governors of the Federal Reserve System (1992–98) before joining George Washington University. She has been a consultant and visiting scholar at the International Monetary Fund and the World Bank, and has published extensively on issues in open economy macroeconomics. In the last few years, her areas of research have been on financial crises, contagion, and herding behaviour.

Carmen Reinhart, visiting fellow, is a professor at the University of Maryland in the School of Public Affairs and the Department of Economics. She is a research associate at the National Bureau of Economic Research. She was vice president at the investment bank Bear Stearns for several years before joining the research department at the International Monetary Fund in 1988. Her work on various topics in macroeconomics and international finance and trade — including capital flows to emerging markets, capital controls, inflation stabilization, currency and banking crises, and contagion — has been published in leading scholarly journals and featured in the financial press.

GENERAL GUIDELINES

First, finding a systematic pattern in the origin of financial crises means looking beyond the last prominent crisis (or group of crises) to a larger sample. Otherwise there is a risk either that there will be too many potential explanations to discriminate between important and less important factors or that generalizations and lessons will be drawn that do not necessarily apply across a wider body of experience.[1] We try to guard against these risks by looking at a sample of 87 currency crises and 29 banking crises that occurred in a sample of 25 emerging economies and smaller industrial countries over 1970–95.[2]

Several examples help to illustrate the point. Consider the last two major financial crises of the 1990s: the 1994–95 Mexican peso crisis and the 1997–99 Asian financial crisis. Was the peso crisis primarily driven by Mexico's large current account deficit (equal to almost 8 percent of its GDP in 1994) and by the overvaluation of the peso's real exchange rate, or by the maturity and composition of Mexico's external borrowing (too short term and too dependent on portfolio flows), or by the uses to which that foreign borrowing was put (too much for consumption and not enough for investment), or by the already-weakened state of the banking system (the share of nonperforming loans doubled between mid-1990 and mid-1994), or by bad luck (in the form of unfortunate domestic political developments and an upward turn in US international interest rates)? Or was it driven by failure to correct fast enough earlier slippages in monetary and fiscal policies in the face of market nervousness, or by a growing imbalance between the stock of liquid foreign-currency denominated liabilities and the stock of international reserves, or by an expectation on the part of Mexico's creditors that the US government would step in to bail out holders of *tesobonos*?[3]

---

[1] One can also view "early warning indicators" as a way to discipline or check more "subjective" and "idiosyncratic" assessments of crisis probabilities for particular economies — just as more comprehensive, subjective assessments can act as a check on the quality of early warning indicator projections.
[2] Our out-of-sample analysis spans 1996–97. Our criteria for defining a currency and a banking crisis is described later in this chapter.
[3] See Leiderman and Thorne (1996) and Calvo and Goldstein (1996) for an analysis of the Mexican crisis.

Analogously, was the Asian financial crisis due to the credit boom experienced by the ASEAN-4 economies (Thailand, Indonesia, Malaysia, and the Philippines), or a concentration of credit in real estate and equities, or large maturity and currency mismatches in the composition of external borrowing, or easy global liquidity conditions, or capital account liberalization cum weak financial sector supervision? Was it the relatively large current account deficits and real exchange rate overvaluations in the run-up to the crisis, a deteriorating quality of investment, increasing competition from China, global overproduction in certain industries important to the crisis countries, or contagion from Thailand?[4] There are simply too many likely suspects to draw generalizations from two episodes — even if they are important ones. To tell, for example, whether a credit boom is a better leading indicator of currency crises than are, say, current account deficits, we need to run a horse race across a larger number of currency crises.[5]

Equally, but operating in the opposite direction, there is a risk of "jumping the gun" by generalizing prematurely about the relative importance of particular indicators from a relatively small set of prominent crises. One example is credit booms — that is, expansions of bank credit that are large relative to the growth of the economy. These have been shown to forerun banking crises in Japan, in several Scandinavian countries, and in Latin America (Gavin and Hausman 1996). Yet when we compare credit booms as a leading indicator of banking crises to other indicators across a larger group of emerging economies and smaller industrial countries, we find that credit booms are outperformed by a variety of other indicators. Put in other words, credit booms have been a very good leading indicator in some prominent banking crises but are not, on average, the best leading indicator in emerging economies more generally. Again, it is helpful to have recourse to a larger sample of crises (in this study nearly 30) to sort out competing hypotheses.

The second guideline is to pay equal attention to banking crises and currency crises. To this point, most of the existing literature on leading indicators of financial crises relates exclusively to currency crises.[6] Yet the costs

---

[4]These alternative explanations of the Asian crisis are discussed in BIS (1998), Corsetti, Pesenti, and Roubini (1998), Goldstein (1998a), Radelet and Sachs (1998), IMF (1997), and World Bank (1998).

[5]Some of these explanations, of course, are not mutually exclusive. For example, large current account deficits may be the outcome of financial liberalization and its attendant credit booms.

of banking crises in developing countries appear to be greater than those of currency crises. Furthermore, banking crises appear to be one of the more important factors in generating currency crises, and the determinants and leading indicators of banking crises should be amenable to the same type of quantitative analysis as currency crises are.[7]

Some policymakers have argued that, looking forward, the emphasis in surveillance efforts should be directed to banking sector problems rather than currency crises. The underlying assumption supporting that view is that as more countries adopt regimes of managed floating, currency crises become a relic of the past. We believe this view to be overly optimistic. It is noteworthy that among all the Asian countries that had major currency crises in 1997–98 only Thailand had an "explicit pegged exchange rate" policy. Indonesia, Malaysia, and South Korea were all declared managed floaters, while the Philippines in principle (but not in practice) had a freely floating exchange rate. Among emerging markets, there is widespread "fear of floating," and many of the countries that are classified as floaters have implicit pegs, leaving them vulnerable to the types of currency crises we study in this book.[8]

We analyze banking and currency crises separately, as well as exploring the interactions among them. As it turns out, several of the early warning indicators that show the best performance for currency crises also work well in anticipating banking crises. At the same time, there are enough differences regarding the early warning process and in the aftermath of crises to justify treating each in its own right.

A third feature of our approach — and one that differentiates our work from that of many other researchers — is that we employ monthly data to

---

[6] See Kaminsky, Lizondo, and Reinhart (1998) for a review of this literature. Among the relatively few studies that include or concentrate on banking crises in emerging economies, we would highlight Caprio and Klingebiel (1996a, 1996b), Demirgüç-Kunt and Detragiache (1998), Eichengreen and Rose (1998), Furnam and Stiglitz (1998), Honohan (1997), Gavin and Hausman (1996), Goldstein (1997), Goldstein and Turner (1996), Kaminsky (1998), Kaminsky and Reinhart (1998, 2000), Rojas-Suarez (1998), Rojas-Suarez and Weisbrod (1995), and Sundararajan and Baliño (1991).

[7] Both Kaminsky and Reinhart (1998) and the IMF (1998c) conclude that the output costs of banking crises in emerging economies typically exceed those for currency crises and that these costs are greater still during what Kaminsky and Reinhart (1999) dubbed "twin crises" (that is, episodes when the country is undergoing simultaneous banking and currency crises). We provide further empirical evidence on this issue in chapter 7.

[8] See Calvo and Reinhart (2000) and Reinhart (2000) for a fuller discussion of this issue.

analyze banking crises as well as currency crises.[9] Use of monthly (as opposed to annual data) involves a trade-off. On the minus side, because monthly data on the requisite variables are available for a smaller number of countries than would be the case for annual data, the decision to go with higher frequency data may result in a smaller sample. Yet monthly data permit us to learn much more about the timing of early warning indicators, including differences among indicators in the first arrival and persistence of signals. Indeed, many of the annual indicators that have been used in other empirical studies are only publicly available with a substantial lag, which makes them plausible for a retrospective assessment of the symptoms of crises but ill-suited for the task of providing an early warning. Hence, we conclude that the advantages of monthly data seemed to outweigh the disadvantages.[10] In the end, we were able to assemble monthly data for about two-thirds of our indicator variables; for the remaining third, we had to settle for annual data.

A fourth element of our approach was to include a relatively wide array of potential early warning indicators. We based this decision on a review of broad, recurring themes in the theoretical literature on financial crises. These themes encompass

- asymmetric information and "bank run" stories that stress liquidity/currency mismatches and shocks that induce borrowers to run to liquidity or quality,
- inherent instability and bandwagon theories that emphasize excessive credit creation and unsound finance during the expansion phase of the business cycle,
- "premature" financial liberalization stories that focus on the perils of liberalization when banking supervision is weak and when an extensive network of explicit and implicit government guarantees produces an asymmetric payoff for increased risk taking,

---

[9] For example, the studies of banking crises in emerging markets by Caprio and Klingebiel (1996a, 1996b), Goldstein and Turner (1996), Honohan (1995), and Sundararajan and Baliño (1991) are primarily qualitative, while the studies by Demirgüç-Kunt and Detragiache (1997), Eichengreen and Rose (1998), and the IMF (1998c) use annual data for their quantitative investigation of the determinants of banking crises.

[10] Private-sector "early warning" analyses likewise seem to be moving in the direction of using monthly data. See Ades, Masih, and Tenegauzer (1998) and Kumar, Perraudin, and Zinni (1998).

- first- and second-generation models of the vulnerability of fixed exchange rates to speculative attacks,[11] and
- interactions of various kinds between currency and banking crises.

In operational terms, this eclectic view of the origins of financial crises translates into a set of 25 leading indicator variables that span the real and monetary sectors of the economy, that contain elements of both the current and capital accounts of the balance of payments, that include market variables designed to capture expectations of future events, and that attempt to proxy certain structural changes in the economy (e.g., financial liberalization) that could affect vulnerability to a crisis.

Once a set of potential leading indicators or determinants of banking and currency crises has been selected, a way has to be found both to identify the better performing ones among them and to calculate the probability of a crisis. In most of the existing empirical crisis literature, this is done by estimating a multivariate logit or probit regression model in which the dependent variable (in each year or month) takes the value of one if that period is classified as a crisis and the value of zero if there is no crisis. When such a regression is fitted on a pooled set of country data (i.e., a pooled cross-section of time series), the statistical significance of the estimated regression coefficients should reveal which indicators are "significant" and which are not, and the predicted value of the dependent variable should identify which periods or countries carry a higher or lower probability of a crisis.

A fifth characteristic of our approach is that we use a technique other than regression to evaluate individual indicators and to assess crisis vulnerability across countries and over time. Specifically, we adopt the nonparametric "signals" approach pioneered by Kaminsky and Reinhart (1999).[12] The basic premise of this approach is that the economy behaves differently on the eve of financial crises and that this aberrant behavior has a recurrent systemic pattern. For example, currency crises are usually preceded by an overvaluation of the currency; banking crises tend to follow sharp declines in asset prices. The signals approach is given diagnostic and predictive content by specifying

---

[11] First-generation models stress poor fundamentals as the cause of the currency crises, while second-generation models focus on shifts in market expectations and self-fulfilling speculative attacks. See Flood and Marion (1999) for a recent survey of this literature.

[12] This approach is described in detail in Kaminsky, Lizondo, and Reinhart (1998).

what is meant by an "early" warning, by defining an "optimal threshold" for each indicator, and by choosing one or more diagnostic statistics that measure the probability of experiencing a crisis.

By requiring the specification of an explicit early warning window, the signals approach forces one to be quite specific about the timing of early warnings. This is not the case for all other approaches. For example, it has been argued that an asymmetric-information approach to financial crises implies that the spread between low- and high-quality bonds will be a good indicator of whether an economy is experiencing a true financial crisis — but there is no presumption that this interest rate spread should be a leading rather than a contemporaneous indicator (Mishkin 1996). Furthermore, the indicator methodology takes a comprehensive approach to the use of information without imposing too many *a priori* restrictions that are difficult to justify.

Finally, we use the signals to rank the probability of crises both across countries and over time. We do so by calculating the weighted number of indicators that have reached their optimal thresholds (that is, are "flashing"), where the weights (represented by the inverse of the individual noise-to-signal ratios) capture the relative forecasting track record of the individual indicators.[13] Indicators with good track records receive greater weight in the forecast than those with poorer ones. Ceteris paribus, the greater the incidence of flashing indicators, the higher the presumed probability of a banking or currency crisis. For example, if in mid-1997 we were to find that 18 of 25 indicators were flashing for Thailand versus only 5 of 25 for Brazil, we would conclude that Thailand was more vulnerable to a crisis than Brazil. Analogously, if only 10 of 25 indicators were flashing for Thailand in mid-1993, we would conclude that Thailand was less vulnerable in mid-1993 than it was in mid-1997. Thus we can calculate the likelihood of a crisis on the basis of how many indicators are signaling. Furthermore, we can attach a greater weight to the signals of the more reliable indicators. Owing to these features, the signals approach makes it easy computationally to monitor crisis vulnerability. In contrast, the regression-based approaches require estimation

---

[13] While this is one of many potential "composite" indicators (i.e., ways of combining the information in the individual indicators), Kaminsky (1998) provides evidence that this weighting scheme shows better in-sample and out-of-sample performance than three alternatives. One can equivalently evaluate the performance of individual indicators by comparing their conditional probabilities of signaling a crisis.

of the entire model to calculate crisis probabilities. In addition, because these regression-based models are nonlinear, it becomes difficult to calculate the contribution of individual indicators to crisis probabilities in cases where the variables are far away from their means.[14]

Guideline number six is to employ out-of-sample tests to help gauge the usefulness of leading indicators. The in-sample performance of a model may convey a misleading sense of optimism about how well it will perform out of sample. A good case in point is the experience of the 1970s with structural models of exchange rate determination for the major currencies. While these models fit well in sample, subsequent research indicated that their out-of-sample performance was no better — and often worse — than that of "naive" models (such as using the spot rate or the forward rate to predict the next period's exchange rate; see Meese and Rogoff 1983). In this study, we use data from 1970–95 to calculate our optimal thresholds for the indicators, but we save data from 1996 through the end of 1997 to assess the out-of-sample performance of the signals approach, including the ability to identify the countries most affected during the Asian financial crisis.

Our seventh and last guideline is to beware of the limitations of this kind of analysis. Because these exercises concentrate on the macroeconomic environment, they cannot capture political triggers and exogenous events — the Danish referendum on the European Economic and Monetary Union (EMU) in 1992, the Colosio assassination in 1994, or the debacle over Suharto in 1997–98, for instance — which often influence the timing of speculative attacks. In addition, because high-frequency data are not available on most of the institutional characteristics of national banking systems — ranging from the extent of "connected" and government- directed lending to the adequacy of bank capital and banking supervision — such exercises cannot be expected to capture some of these longer- term origins of banking crises.[15] Also, because we are not dealing with structural economic models but rather with loose,

---

[14] Of course, ease of application is only one of many criteria for choosing among competing crisis-forecasting methodologies. For example, the signals approach also carries the disadvantage that is less amenable to statistical tests of significance. In addition, some of the restrictions it imposes (e.g., that indicators send a signal only when they reach a threshold) may leave out valuable information.

[15] Indeed, for many countries, detailed data on the state of the banks may not even be available annually.

reduced-form relationships, such leading-indicator exercises do not generate much information on *why* or *how* the indicators affect the probability of a crisis. For example, a finding that exchange rate overvaluation typically precedes a currency crisis does not tell us whether the exchange rate overvaluation results from an exchange rate-based inflation stabilization program or from a surge of private capital inflows.

Nor is the early warning study of financial crises immune from the "Lucas critique": that is, if a reliable set of early warning indicators were identified empirically, it is possible that policymakers would henceforth behave differently when these indicators were flashing than they did in the past, thereby transforming these variables into early warning indicators of corrective policy action rather than of financial crisis. While this feedback effect of the indicators on crisis prevention has apparently not yet been strong enough to impair their predictive content, there is no guarantee that this feedback effect will not be stronger in the future (particularly if the empirical evidence in favor of robust early warning indicators was subsequently viewed as more persuasive).

Much like the leading-indicator analysis of business cycles, we are engaging here in a mechanical exercise — albeit one that we think is interesting on a number of fronts. Moreover, this research is still in its infancy, with many of the key empirical contributions coming only in the last two to three years. In areas such as the modeling of contagion and alternative approaches to out-of-sample forecasting, too few "horse races" have been run to know which approaches work best. For all of these reasons, we see the leading-indicator analysis of financial crises in emerging economies as one among a number of analytical tools and not as a stand-alone, surefire system for predicting where the next crisis will take place. That being said, we also argue that this approach shows promising signs of generating real value added and that it appears particularly useful as a first screen for gauging the ordinal differences in vulnerability to crises both across countries and over time. A family of estimated conditional crisis probabilities will provide the basis of this ordinal ranking across countries at a point in time or for a given country over time.

PUTTING THE SIGNALS APPROACH TO WORK

The signals approach described above was first used to analyze the performance of macroeconomic and financial indicators around "twin crises" (i.e., the joint occurrences of currency and banking crises) in Kaminsky and Reinhart (1999). We focus on a sample of 25 countries over 1970 to 1995. The out-of-sample performance of the signals approach will be assessed using data for January 1996 through December 1997. These are the countries in our sample:

- **Africa:** South Africa
- **Asia:** Indonesia, Malaysia, the Philippines, South Korea, Thailand
- **Europe and the Middle East:** Czech Republic, Denmark, Egypt, Finland, Greece, Israel, Norway, Spain, Sweden, Turkey
- **Latin America:** Argentina, Bolivia, Brazil, Chile, Colombia, Mexico, Peru, Uruguay, Venezuela

The basic premise of the signals approach is that the economy behaves differently on the eve of financial crises and that this aberrant behavior has a recurrent systematic pattern. This "anomalous" pattern, in turn, is manifested in the evolution of a broad array of economic and financial indicators. The empirical evidence provides ample support for this premise.[16] To implement the signals approach, we need to clarify a minimum number of two key concepts which will be used throughout the analysis.

CURRENCY CRISIS

A currency crisis is defined as a situation in which an attack on the currency leads to substantial reserve losses, or to a sharp depreciation of the currency — if the speculative attack is ultimately successful — or to both. This definition of currency crisis has the advantage of being comprehensive enough to capture not only speculative attacks on fixed exchange rates (e.g., Thailand's experience before 2 July 1997) but also attacks that force a large devaluation beyond the established rules of a crawling-peg regime or an exchange rate band (e.g., Indonesia's widening of the band before its floatation of the rupiah on 14 August 1997). Since reserve losses also count, the index also captures unsuccessful speculative attacks (e.g., Argentina's reserve losses in the wake of the Mexican 1994 peso crisis.)

We constructed an index of currency market turbulence as a weighted average of exchange rate changes and reserve changes.[17] Interest rates were

---

[16] See Kaminsky, Lizondo, and Reinhart (1998) for a survey of this literature.

excluded, as many emerging markets in our sample had interest rate controls through much of the sample. The index, I, is a weighted average of the rate of change of the exchange rate, $\Delta e/e$, and of reserves, $\Delta R/R$, with weights such that the two components of the index have equal sample volatilities:

$$I = (\Delta e/e) - (\sigma_e/\sigma_R) * (\Delta R/R) \qquad (1)$$

where σ_e is the standard deviation of the rate of change of the exchange rate and σ_R is the standard deviation of the rate of change of reserves. Since changes in the exchange rate enter with a positive weight and changes in reserves have a negative weight attached, readings of this index that were three standard deviations or more above the mean were cataloged as crises.[18]

For countries in the sample that had hyperinflation, the construction of the index of currency market turbulence was modified. While a 100 percent devaluation may be traumatic for a country with low to moderate inflation, a devaluation of that magnitude is commonplace during hyperinflation. A single index for the countries that had hyperinflation episodes would miss sizable devaluations and reserve losses in the moderate inflation periods because the high-inflation episodes would distort the historic mean. To avoid this, we divided the sample according to whether inflation in the previous six months was higher than 150 percent and then constructed an index for each subsample.[19]

As noted in earlier studies that use the signals approach, the dates of currency crises derived from this index map well onto the dates that would be obtained if one were to define crises by relying exclusively on events, such as the closing of the exchange markets or a change in the exchange rate regime.

BANKING CRISES

Our dating of banking crises stresses events. This is because on the banking side there are no time series comparable to international reserves and the exchange

---

[17] This index is in the spirit of that used by Eichengreen, Rose, and Wyplosz (1996), who also included interest rate increases in their measure of turbulence.

[18] Of course, for a study of market turbulence as well as crisis, one may wish to consider readings in this index that are two standard deviations away from the mean.

[19] Similar results are obtained by looking at significant departures in inflation from a 6- and 12-month moving average.

rate. For instance, in the banking panics of an earlier era large withdrawals of bank deposits could be used to date the crisis. In the wake of deposit insurance, however, bank deposits ceased to be useful for dating banking crises. As Japan's banking crisis highlights, many modern financial crises stem from the asset side of the balance sheet, not from deposit withdrawals. Hence the performance of bank stocks relative to the overall equity market could be an indicator. Yet in many of the developing countries an important share of the banks are not traded publicly. Large increases in bankruptcies or nonperforming loans could also be used to mark the onset of the crisis. Indicators of business failures and nonperforming loans are, however, usually available only at low frequencies, if at all; the latter are also made less informative by banks' desire to hide their problems for as long as possible.

Given these data limitations, we mark the beginning of a banking crisis by two types of events: bank runs that lead to the closure, merging, or takeover by the public sector of one or more financial institutions (as in Venezuela in 1993); and if there are no runs, the closure, merging, takeover, or large-scale government assistance of an important financial institution (or group of institutions) that marks the start of a string of similar outcomes for other financial institutions (as in Thailand in 1997). We rely on existing studies of banking crises and on the financial press; according to these studies the fragility of the banking sector was widespread during these periods.

Our approach to dating the onset of the banking crises is not without drawbacks. It could date the crises "too late" because the financial problems usually begin well before a bank is finally closed or merged. It could also date crises "too early" because the worst of crisis may come later.

To address this issue we also indicate when the banking crisis hits its peak, defined as the period with the heaviest government intervention and/or bank closures.

Identifying the end of a banking crisis is one of the more difficult unresolved problems in the empirical crisis literature — that is, there is no consensus on what the criteria ought to be for declaring the crisis to be over (e.g., resumption of normal bank lending behavior, or a marked decrease in the share of nonperforming loans, or an end to bank closures and large-scale government assistance). In our discussion of the aftermath of crises however, the end of a banking crisis is understood to be its resolution (i.e., the end of heavy government financial intervention), not when bank balance sheets cease to deteriorate.

Other empirical studies on banking crises have focused on annual data and provide no information on the month or quarter in which banking sector problems surface. Hence it is not possible to compare the exact dates with our own analysis. We can, however, compare the dating of the year of the crisis. In most cases, our dates for the beginning of crises correspond with those found in other studies, but there are several instances where our starting date is a year earlier than theirs. Tables 1 and 2 list the currency and banking crisis dates, respectively, for the 25 countries in our sample.

THE INDICATORS

In addition to the 15 early warning indicators originally considered in Kaminsky and Reinhart (1999), we evaluate the ability of nine additional indicators that figure prominently in both the theoretical literature on banking and currency crises and in the popular discussion of these events.

The indicators used in Kaminsky and Reinhart (1999) were international reserves (in US dollars), imports (in US dollars), exports (in US dollars), the terms of trade (defined as the unit value of exports over the unit value of imports), deviations of the real exchange rate from trend (in percentage terms),[20] the differential between foreign (US or German) and domestic real interest rates on deposits (monthly rates, deflated using consumer prices and measured in percentage points), "excess" real M1 balances, the money multiplier (of M2), the ratio of domestic credit to GDP, the real interest rate on deposits (monthly rates, deflated using consumer prices and measured in percentage points), the ratio of (nominal) lending to deposit interest rates,[21] the stock of commercial banks' deposits (in nominal terms), the ratio of broad money (converted into foreign currency) to gross international reserves, an index of output, and an index of equity prices (in US dollars). All these series are monthly. For greater detail, see the appendix. The links between particular early warning indicators and underlying theories of exchange rate and banking

---

[20] The real exchange rate is defined on a bilateral basis with respect to the German mark for the European countries in the sample and with respect to the US dollar for all other countries. The real exchange rate index is defined such that *an increase* in the index denotes a real *depreciation*.
[21] This definition of the spread between lending and deposit rates is preferable to using merely the difference between nominal lending and deposit rates because inflation affects this difference and thus the measure would be distorted in the periods of high inflation. An alternative would have been to use the difference between *real* lending and deposit rates.

Table 1: Currency Crisis Starting Dates

Country	Currency crisis
Argentina	June 1975
	February 1981*
	July 1982
	September 1986*
	April 1989
	February 1990
Bolivia	November 1982
	November 1983
	September 1985
Brazil	February 1983
	November 1986*
	July 1989
	November 1990
	October 1991
Chile	December 1971
	August 1972
	October 1973
	December 1974
	January 1976
	August 1982*
	September 1984
Colombia	March 1983*
	February 1985*
Czech Republic	May 1997
Denmark	May 1971
	June 1973
	November 1979
	August 1993
Egypt	January 1979
	August 1989
	June 1990
Finland	June 1973
	October 1982
	November 1991*
	September 1992*

(*Continued*)

Table 1: (*Continued*)

Country	Currency crisis
Greece	May 1976
	November 1980
	July 1984
Indonesia	November 1978
	April 1983
	September 1986
	August 1997
Israel	November 1974
	November 1977
	October 1983*
	July 1984
Malaysia	July 1975
	August 1997*
Mexico	September 1976
	February 1982*
	December 1982*
	December 1994*
Norway	June 1973
	February 1978
	May 1986*
	December 1992
Peru	June 1976
	October 1987
The Philippines	February 1970
	October 1983*
	June 1984
	July 1997*
South Africa	September 1975
	July 1981
	July 1984
	May 1996
South Korea	June 1971
	December 1974
	January 1980
	October 1997

(*Continued*)

Table 1: (*Continued*)

Country	Currency crisis
Spain	February 1976
	July 1977*
	December 1982
	February 1986
	September 1992
	May 1993
Sweden	August 1977
	September 1981
	October 1982
	November 1992*
Thailand	November 1978*
	July 1981
	November 1984
	July 1997*
Turkey	August 1970
	January 1980
	March 1994*
Uruguay	December 1971*
	October 1982*
Venezuela	February 1984
	December 1986
	March 1989
	May 1994*
	December 1995

* = twin crises

crises are discussed in some detail in earlier papers (e.g., Kaminsky and Reinhart 1999).

Turning to the nine "new" indicators introduced here, four of them are expressed as a share of GDP. These are the current account balance, short-term capital inflows, foreign direct investment, and the overall budget deficit. In addition, we look at the growth rates in the following variables (the first three as shares in GDP and the fourth as a share of investment): general government consumption, central bank credit to the public sector, net credit to the public sector, and the current account balance. The latter measure of

Table 2: Banking Crisis Starting Dates

Country	K & R (1999) and G, K, & R (beginning)	C&K (1996)	IMF (1996 and 1998a & b)
Argentina	March 1980	1980	1980
	May 1985	1985	1985
			1989
	December 1994	1995	1995
Bolivia	October 1987	1986	n.a.
Brazil	November 1985		1990
	December 1994	1994	1994
Chile			1976
	September 1981		1981
Colombia	July 1982	1982	1982
	April 1998		
Czech Republic	1994	n.a.	n.a.
Denmark	March 1987	n.a.	1988
Egypt	January 1980	1980	1981
	January 1990	1990	1990
Finland	September 1991	1991	1991
Greece	1991	n.a.	n.a.
Indonesia	November 1992	1994	1992
			1997
Israel	October 1983	1977	1983
Malaysia	July 1985	1985	1985
	September 1997		
Mexico	September 1982	1981	1982
	October 1992	1995	1994
Norway	November 1988	1987	1987
Peru	March 1983	n.a.	1983
Philippines	January 1981	1981	1981
	July 1997		
South Africa	December 1977	1977	1980
South Korea	January 1986	n.a.	1983
	July 1997		1997
Spain	November 1978	1977	1977
Sweden	November 1991	1991	1990
Thailand	March 1979	1983	1983
	May 1996		1997
Turkey			1982
	January 1991	1992	1991
		1994	1994

(*Continued*)

Table 2: (*Continued*)

Country	K & R (1999) and G, K, & R (beginning)	C&K (1996)	IMF (1996 and 1998a & b)
Uruguay	March 1971		
	March 1981	1981	1981
Venezuela		1980	1980
	October 1993	1994	1993

n.a. = not applicable
K & R = Kaminsky and Reinhart (1999)
G, K, & R = Goldstein, Kaminsky, and Reinhart
C & K = Caprio and Klingebiel (1996b)

the current account was motivated by the view, particularly popular in the wake of the 1994–95 Mexican peso crisis, that large current account deficits are more of a concern if they stem from low saving as opposed to high levels of investment. Recent events in Asia — a region noted for its exceptionally high levels of domestic saving and its even higher levels of investment — have led to a reassessment of that view. We also look at two measures of sovereign credit ratings. As most of the new indicators are not available at monthly or quarterly frequencies, annual data were used.

Table 3 provides a list of the indicators we examine in this book, their periodicity, and the transformation used. We examine the track record of sovereign credit ratings when it comes to "predicting" financial crises. Specifically, we examine the performance of the Institutional Investor and Moody's ratings.

As noted, in most cases we focus on 12-month changes in the variables. This transformation has several appealing features. First, it eliminates the nonstationarity problem of the variables in levels. It also makes the indicators more comparable across countries and across time. Some of the indicators have a strong seasonal pattern, which the 12-month transformation corrects for. For some indicators, such as equity prices, one could contemplate using a measure of under- or overvaluation. However, the empirical performance of most asset pricing models is not strong enough to justify such an exercise.

For the monthly variables (with the exception of the deviation of the real exchange rate from trend, the "excess" of real M1 balances, and the three variables based on interest rates), the indicator on a given month was defined

Table 3: Selected Leading Indicators of Banking and Currency Crises

Indicator	Transformation	Data frequency
Real output	12-month growth rate	Monthly
Equity prices	12-month growth rate	Monthly
International reserves	12-month growth rate	Monthly
Domestic/foreign real interest rate differential	Level	Monthly
Excess real M1 balances	Level	Monthly
M2/international reserves	12-month growth rate	Monthly
Bank deposits	12-month growth rate	Monthly
M2 multiplier	12-month growth rate	Monthly
Domestic credit/GDP	12-month growth rate	Monthly
Real interest rate on deposits	Level	Monthly
Ratio of lending interest rate to deposit interest rate	Level	Monthly
Real exchange rate	Deviation from trend	Monthly
Exports	12-month growth rate	Monthly
Imports	12-month growth rate	Monthly
Terms of trade	12-month growth rate	Monthly
Moody's sovereign credit ratings	1-month change	Monthly
Institutional Investor sovereign credit ratings	Semiannual change	Semiannual
General government consumption/GDP	Annual growth rate	Annual
Overall budget deficit/GDP	Level	Annual
Net credit to the public sector/GDP	Level	Annual
Central bank credit to public sector/GDP	Level	Annual
Short-term capital inflows/GDP	Level	Annual
Foreign direct investment/GDP	Level	Annual
Current account imbalance/GDP	Level	Annual
Current account imbalance/investment	Level	Annual

as the percentage change in the level of the variable with respect to its level a year earlier. This filter has several attractive features: it reduces the "noisiness" of working with monthly data, it facilitates cross-country comparisons, and it ensures the variables are stationary with well-defined moments.

Turning to credit ratings, Institutional Investor constructs an index that rises with increasing country creditworthiness and ranges from 0 to 100; this index is published twice a year and is released in March and September.[22]

---

[22] Since there are two readings of this index per year, in a typical year, say 1995, we would have the percentage change in the rating from September 1994 to March 1995, from March 1995 to September 1995, and the change from September 1995 to March 1996.

Hence we work with the six-month percentage change in this rating index. For Moody's Investor services, monthly changes in the sovereign ratings are used. A downgrade takes on the value of minus one; no change in the rating takes on a value of zero, and an upgrade takes on the value of one. Since Moody's ratings take on values from 1 to 16, we also worked with changes in the ratings that took into account the magnitude of the change.

THE SIGNALING WINDOW

Let us call a signal (yet to be precisely defined) a departure from "normal" behavior in an indicator.[23] For example, an unusually large decline in exports or output may signal a future currency or banking crisis. If an indicator sends a signal that is followed by a crisis within a plausible time frame we call it a good signal. If the signal is not followed by a crisis within that interval, we call it a false signal, or noise. The signaling window for currency crises is set *a priori* at 24 months preceding the crisis. If, for instance, an unusually large decline in exports were to occur 28 months before the crisis, the signal would fall outside the signaling window and would be labeled a false alarm.

Alternative signaling windows (18 months and 12 months) were considered as part of our sensitivity analysis. While the results for the 18-month window yielded similar results to those reported in this book, the 12-month window proved to be too restrictive. Specifically, several of the indicators we use here, including real exchange rates and credit cycles, signaled relatively early (consistent with a protracted cycle), and the shorter 12-month window penalized those early signals by labeling them as false alarms.

For banking crises, we employ a different signaling window. Namely, any signal given in the 12 months preceding the beginning of the crisis or the 12 months following the beginning of the crisis is labeled a good signal. The more protracted nature of banking crises and the high incidence of denial by both bankers and policymakers that there are problems in the banking sector motivate the more forgiving signaling window for banking crises.

---

[23] Of course, normal behavior may change over time, hence, this approach, like other commonly used alternatives (such as logit or probit) is not free from Lucas-critique limitations. For further discussion of this issue, see Kaminsky and Reinhart (1999).

THE THRESHOLD

Suppose we wish to test the null or maintained hypothesis that the economy is in a "state of tranquility" versus the alternative hypothesis that a crisis will occur sometime in the next 24 months. Suppose that we wish to test this hypothesis on an indicator-by-indicator basis. As in any hypothesis test, this calls for selecting a threshold or critical value that divides the probability distribution of that indicator into a region that is considered normal or probable under the null hypothesis and a region that is considered aberrant or unlikely under the null hypothesis — the rejection region. If the observed outcome for a particular variable falls into the rejection region, that variable is said to be sending a signal.

To select the optimal threshold for each indicator, we allowed the size of the rejection region to oscillate between 1 percent and 20 percent. For each choice, the noise-to-signal ratio was tabulated and the "optimal" set of thresholds was defined as the one that minimized the noise-to-signal ratio — that is, the ratio of false signals to good signals.[24]

Table 4 lists the thresholds for all the indicators for both currency and banking crises. For instance, the threshold for short-term capital flows as a percentage of GDP is 85 percent. This conveys two kinds of information. First, it indicates that 15 percent of all the observations in our sample (for this variable) are considered signals. Second, it highlights that the rejection region is located at the upper tail of the frequency distribution, meaning that a high ratio of short-term capital inflows to GDP will lead to a rejection of the null hypothesis of tranquility in favor of the alternative hypothesis that a crisis is brewing.

While the threshold or percentile that defines the size of the rejection region is uniform across countries for each indicator, the corresponding country-specific values are allowed to differ. Consider the following illustration. There are two countries, one which has received little or no shortterm capital inflow (as a percentage of GDP) during the entire sample, while the second received substantially larger amounts (also as a share of GDP). The 85th percentile of the frequency distribution for the low capital importer may be as small as a half a percent of GDP and any increase beyond that would

---

[24] For variables such as international reserves, exports, the terms of trade, deviations of the real exchange rate from trend, commercial bank deposits, output, and the stock market index, for which a decline in the indicator increases the probability of a crisis, the threshold is below the mean of the indicator. For the other variables, the threshold is above the mean of the indicator.

Table 4: Optimal Thresholds (Percentile)

Indicator	Currency crisis	Banking crisis
Bank deposits	15	20
Central bank credit to the public sector	90	90
Credit rating (Institutional Investor)	11	11
Current account balance/GDP	20	14
Current account balance/investment	15	10
Domestic credit/GDP	88	90
Interest rate differential	89	81
Excess M1 balances	89	88
Exports	10	10
Foreign direct investment/GDP	16	12
General government consumption/GDP	90	88
Imports	90	80
Lending-deposit interest rate ratio	88	87
M2 multiplier	89	90
M2/reserves	90	90
Net credit to the public sector/GDP	88	80
Output	10	14
Overall budget deficit/GDP	10	14
Real exchange rate[a]	10	10
Real interest rate	88	80
Reserves	10	20
Short-term capital inflows/GDP	85	89
Stock prices	15	10
Terms of trade	10	19

a. An increase in the index denotes a real depreciation.

be considered a signal. Meanwhile, the country where the norm was a higher volume of capital inflows is likely to have a higher critical value; hence only values above, say 3 percent of GDP, would be considered signals.

Table 5 illustrates the "custom tailoring" of the optimal threshold by showing the country-specific critical values for export growth and annual stock returns for Malaysia, Mexico, and Sweden. A 25 percent decline in stock prices would be considered a signal of a future currency crisis in Malaysia and Sweden but not in Mexico, with the latter's far greater historical volatility.[25]

---

[25] Indeed, as shown in Kaminsky and Reinhart (1998), the volatility pattern for these three countries is representative of the broader historical regional pattern. The wild gyrations in financial markets in Asia in 1997–99, however, may be unraveling those historic patterns.

Table 5: Examples of Country-Specific Thresholds: Currency Crises

Country	Critical Value for Exports (12-month Percentage Change)	Critical Value for Stock Prices (12-month Percentage Change)
Malaysia	−9.05	−15.20
Mexico	−13.10	−38.30
Sweden	−11.25	−20.78

Figure 1 provides another illustration of the country-specific nature of the optimal threshold calculations. It shows for the entire sample our measure of the extent of overvaluation in the real exchange rate for Mexico. The horizontal line is the country-specific threshold, and a reading below this line (recall that a decline represents an appreciation) represents a signal. The shaded areas are the 24 months before the crisis, or the signaling window. Around 1982 the shaded area is wider due to the fact that there was a "double dip," with two crises registering. If the indicator crossed the horizontal line and no crisis ensued in the following 24 months, as it did in early 1992, it is counted as a false alarm. In the remainder of this section we will define these concepts more precisely.

SIGNALS, NOISE, AND CRISES PROBABILITIES

A concise summary of the possible outcomes is presented in the following two-by-two matrix (for a currency crisis).

	Crisis occurs in the following 24 months	No crisis occurs in the following 24 months
Signal	A	B
No signal	C	D

A perfect indicator would only have entries in cells A and D. Hence, with this matrix we can define several useful concepts that we will use to evaluate the performance of each indicator.

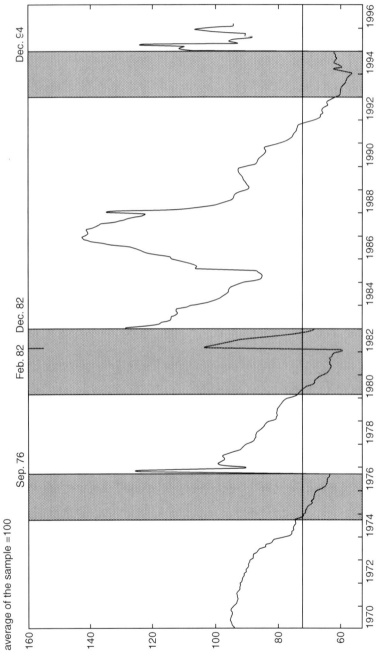

Fig 1: Mexico: Real Exchange Rate, 1970–96

If one lacked any information on the performance of the indicators, it is still possible to calculate, for a given sample, the *unconditional probability of crisis*,

$$P(C) = (A + C)/(A + B + C + D) \qquad (2)$$

If an indicator sends a signal and that indicator has a reliable track record, then it can be expected that the *probability of a crisis, conditional on a signal*, $P(C/S)$, is greater than the unconditional probability. Where

$$P(C|S) = A/(A + B) \qquad (3)$$

Formally,

$$P(C|S) - P(C) > 0 \qquad (4)$$

The intuition is clear: if the indicator is not "noisy" (prone to sending false alarms), then there are relatively few entries in cell B and $P(C|S) \approx 1$. This is one of the criteria that we will use to rank the indicators.

We can also define the noise-to-signal ratio, N/S, as

$$N/S = [B/(B + D)]/[A/(A + C)] \qquad (5)$$

It may be the case that an indicator has relatively few false alarms in its track record. This could be the result of the indicator issuing signals relatively rarely. In this case, there is also the danger that the indicator misses the crisis altogether (it does not signal and there is a crisis). In this case, we also wish to calculate for each indicator the *proportion of crises accurately called*,

$$PC = C/(A + C). \qquad (6)$$

In the next chapter, we employ these concepts to provide evidence on the relative merits of a broad range of indicators in anticipating crises.

Empirical Results

The signals approach was applied to the indicators around the dates of the 29 banking and the 87 currency crises. In what follows, we first compare our results for the 15 monthly indicators to those presented in Kaminsky and Reinhart (1999) and reproduced in Table 6. In addition to presenting our in-sample findings, this exercise allows us to gauge robustness of the signals approach, since the results reported here are derived from a larger sample of countries (25 versus 20.)[26] Moreover, in this chapter we report results for many of the indicators that have been stressed in the financial press surrounding the coverage of the Asian crisis.

THE MONTHLY INDICATORS: ROBUSTNESS CHECK

Tables 6 and 7 summarize the in-sample performance of the monthly indicators along the lines described and presented in Kaminsky, Lizondo, and Reinhart (1998) and Kaminsky (1998). Table 6 covers banking crises, and Table 7 presents the results for currency crises. The variables are shown in descending order based on their marginal predictive power. For banking crises, for instance, the real exchange rate has the greatest predictive power and imports the least. For each indicator, the first column of the tables shows the noise-to-signal ratio.

---

[26]The five countries included here that were not a part of the Kaminsky and Reinhart (1999) sample are the Czech Republic, Egypt, Greece, South Africa, and South Korea.

Table 6: Ranking the Monthly Indicators: Banking Crises

Indicator	Noise-to-signal	Percent of crises accurately called	$P(C\|S)$	$P(C\|S)-P(C)$	Ranking in Kaminsky (1999)	Difference in rank (+ denotes an improvement)
Real exchange rate	0.35	52	24.0	14.1	1	0
Stock prices	0.46	76	23.4	11.2	3	0
M2 multiplier	0.46	63	18.3	9.0	4	0
Output	0.54	90	17.3	7.2	5	0
Exports	0.68	79	14.3	4.7	7	+1
Real interest rate	0.68	96	16.8	4.2	6	−1
Real interest rate differential	0.73	100	15.6	3.7	8	0
Bank deposits	0.73	64	12.9	3.1	9	0
M2/reserves	0.84	72	11.4	1.7	10	0
Excess real M1 balances	0.88	44	11.0	1.2	13	+2
Domestic credit/nominal GDP	0.89	46	10.9	1.1	11	−1
Reserves	0.92	83	10.7	0.8	12	−1
Terms of trade	1.01	92	11.6	−0.1	14	0
Lending-deposit interest rate	1.48	56	8.3	−3.5	15	0
Imports	1.75	64	6.0	−4.1	16	0

Sources: The authors and Kaminsky (1998).

An indicator with a noise-to-signal ratio of unity, such as those in the bottom of the tables, issues as many false alarms as good signals. The second column shows the percent of crises (for which there were data for that indicator) accurately called, while the third column lists the probability of a crisis conditional on a signal from the indicator, $P(C|S)$. The fourth column shows the difference between the conditional and unconditional probabilities, $P(C|S) - P(C)$, the fifth column shows the ranking that the indicator received in the previous signals approach analysis, and the last column calculates the difference between its current and previous rank. Hence, a +3 in the last column would mean that the indicator moved up three notches as the sample was enlarged, while a −2 would reflect a decline in its ranking.

The indicators' rankings based on their marginal predictive power are shown under the heading $P(C|S) - P(C)$. The better the indicator, the higher

Table 7: Ranking the Monthly Indicators: Currency Crises

Indicator	Noise-to-signal	Percent of crises accurately called	$P(C\|S)$	$P(C\|S) - P(C)$	Ranking in K & R (1999)	Difference in rank (+ denotes an improvement)
Real exchange rate	0.22	58	62.1	35.2	1	0
Banking crisis	0.32		46.0	17.0	2	0
Stock prices	0.46	66	47.6	18.3	4	+1
Exports	0.51	80	42.4	15.0	3	−1
M2/reserves	0.51	75	42.3	14.9	5	0
Output	0.57	71	43.0	12.5	6	0
Excess real M1 balances	0.57	57	40.1	12.3	7	0
Reserves	0.58	72	38.9	12.2	8	0
M2 multiplier	0.59	72	39.2	11.6	9	0
Domestic credit/nominal GDP	0.68	57	35.6	8.3	10	0
Terms of trade	0.74	77	35.4	6.5	11	0
Real interest rate	0.77	89	32.0	5.5	12	0
Imports	0.87	59	30.1	2.9	14	+1
Real interest rate differential	1.00	86	26.1	−0.1	12	−1
Lending-deposit interest rate	1.32	63	24.4	−4.8	16	+1
Bank deposits	1.32	43	22.3	−5.2	15	−1

K & R = Kaminsky and Reinhart (1999).
Sources: The authors and Kaminsky and Reinhart (1999).

the probability of crisis conditioned on its signaling — that is, the higher the $P(C|S)$ — and the bigger the gap between the conditional probability $(P(C|S)$ and the unconditional probability $P(C)$. The unconditional probability of a banking crisis (not shown) varies slightly from indicator to indicator because of differences in data availability, since not all indicators span the entire sample.[27] For some indicators the sample is such that the incidence of banking crises (i.e., their unconditional probability) is as low as 9.8 percent or as high as 12

---

[27] As shown in Kaminsky, Lizondo, and Reinhart (1998), the bigger the gap between the conditional probability $(P(C|S)$ and the unconditional probability P(C), the lower the noise-to-signal ratio.

percent. For currency crises, the unconditional probability is clustered in the 27 to 29 percent range.

Several interesting features stand out from Tables 6 and 7.

First, the ranking of the indicators appears to be quite robust across sample selections, as shown in the last column of Table 6. In other words, the results from the 25-country sample closely match the results of the 20-country sample. For currency crises, none of the monthly indicators changes in relative performance by more than one position as the sample is enlarged, and for 10 of the indicators, there is no change at all. For banking crises, the maximum ranking change is two positions and 10 of the monthly indicators show no change in their relative ranking. This is a positive factor for the expected out-of-sample usefulness of the signals approach. Specifically, it suggests that the indicators could well have a similar relative predictive ability for countries that are not included in the sample.[28]

Second, some of the most reliable indicators are the same for banking and currency crises. Deviations of the real exchange rate from trend and stock prices stand out in this regard. Close runners-up are output and exports. A similar statement applies to the least useful indicators; imports and the lending-deposit ratios, for example, do not have any predictive ability for either type of crisis. Several of the low-scoring indicators also carry the weakest or most ambiguous theoretical rationale.[29]

---

[28] We did not include the larger industrial countries (particularly the G-7 countries) in our sample because they have characteristics (such as the ability to borrow in their own currency, a relatively good external-debt servicing history, and high access to private capital markets) that on *a priori* grounds would seem to make their crisis vulnerability different from that of most emerging economies. In addition, data constraints, extremely large structural shifts over time, and difficulties associated with identifying a "normal" period led to the decision to exclude China, Russia, and most of the transitional economies from the sample. Finally, we excluded low-income developing countries from the sample because we wanted to concentrate on emerging economies that had (in addition to the requisite data availability) significant involvement with private international capital markets. In the end, however, one can only tell whether our sample selection results in certain biases by doing further robustness checks on alternative samples of countries.

[29] For instance, lending-deposit interest rate spreads could widen in advance of a crisis due to a deterioration in loan quality or a worsening in adverse selection problems. Alternatively, it could be persuasively argued that ahead of financial crises, banks may be forced to offer higher deposit rates, so as to stem capital flight.

Third, there are some important differences in the ranking of indicators between currency and banking crises. This suggests that currency and banking sector vulnerability takes on different forms. A case in point is the ratio of M2 (in dollars) to foreign exchange reserves, a variable stressed by Calvo and Mendoza (1996) as capturing the extent of unbacked implicit government liabilities. It does quite well (ranks fifth) among the 16 indicators of currency crises, but it is far less useful when it comes to anticipating banking crises. Similarly, the money multiplier, real interest rates, and bank deposits are of little use when it comes to predicting currency crises but do much better in predicting vulnerability to banking crises. This result should not come as a surprise. Both the money multiplier and real interest rates are strongly linked to financial liberalization, which itself helps predict banking crises. As shown in Galbis (1993), real interest rates tend to increase substantially in the wake of financial liberalization. Furthermore, the steep reductions in reserve requirements that usually accompany financial liberalization propel increases in the money multiplier. Bank runs and deposit withdrawals are at the heart of multiple- equilibriums explanations of banking crises (Diamond and Dybvig 1983) yet figure less prominently in explanations of currency crises.[30]

Lastly, banking crises are even more of a challenge to predict than currency crises. For currency crises, the marginal predictive power of 12 of the 16 indicators (column five) is 5 percent or higher; for the real exchange rate, marginal predictive power goes as high as 35 percent. Indeed 9 of the 16 indicators have marginal predictive power in excess of 10 percent. By way of contrast, for banking crisis 11 of the 15 indicators have marginal predictive power of less than 5 percent, and even the top-ranked macroeconomic indicators have marginal predictive power of less than 15 percent. This relative inability of indicators to anticipate crises in sample may be due to two factors. For one thing, for the earlier part of the sample, banking crises were still relatively rare vis-à-vis currency crises — there is a large discrepancy between the number of currency and banking crises studied here. Detecting recurring patterns becomes more difficult in the smaller sample of banking crises. Also, pinning down the timing of a banking crisis requires a tricky judgment about

---

[30] However, some recent models (Goldfajn and Valdés 1995) have highlighted the role of bank runs in precipitating currency crises.

when banking-sector "distress" turns into a full-fledged crisis. As discussed, the timing of currency crises is more straightforward.

The empirical evidence on the "predictability" of banking crises is still limited to a handful of studies. Some have followed the approach pioneered by Blanco and Garber (1986) for currency crises and have attempted to model the probability of banking crises on the basis of domestic and external fundamentals. These studies have encountered some of the same problems highlighted in Table 6 — specifically, the relatively poor predictive power of the models. Moreover, the results in the studies sometimes conflict with one another. Eichengreen and Rose (1998), for example, find that external conditions, specifically international interest rates, play an important role in predicting banking crises. Real exchange rate overvaluations, growth, and budget deficits have predictive power in their regressions. The composition of external debt also seems to matter. Other variables, including credit growth, they conclude, have little or no predictive ability. In contrast, Demirgüç-Kunt and Detragiache (1998) find no evidence in favor of budget deficits, while real interest rates, credit growth, and M2/reserves figure prominently among their significant regressors. Both studies do find, however, that slower economic growth increases the probability of a banking crisis. In any case, it appears that, to improve upon the ability to predict banking crises, we may need to look beyond macroeconomic indicators — an issue that we take up later.

THE ANNUAL INDICATORS: WHAT WORKS?

Tables 8 and 9 present evidence on the performance of eight annual indicators that have been prominent in recent discussions of the causes of financial crises. The indicators include the fiscal variables stressed in the Krugman (1979) model of a currency crisis as well as the short-term debt exposure indicators stressed in recent theoretical and empirical explanations of the Asian crisis (Calvo 1998; Calvo and Mendoza 1996; Goldstein 1998b; Radelet and Sachs 1998). As before, the indicators are ranked according to their marginal predictive power. The first column provides information on the noise-to-signal ratio, the second column lists the percent of crises accurately called, the third column provides information on the probability of crisis conditional on signaling, while the last column provides information on the marginal predictive power of the variable.

Table 8: Annual Indicators: Banking Crises

Indicator	Noise-to-signal	Percent of crises accurately called	$P(C|S)$	$P(C|S)-P(C)$
Short-term capital inflows/GDP	0.38	43	36.8	18.5
Current account balance/investment	0.38	38	36.1	18.4
Overall budget deficit/GDP	0.47	52	26.9	12.1
Current account balance/GDP	0.50	33	29.3	12.1
Central bank credit to the public sector/GDP	0.52	23	23.8	7.6
Net credit to the public sector/GDP	0.72	15	18.3	4.5
Foreign direct investment/GDP	1.05	24	15.6	−0.6
General government consumption/GDP	1.44	15	10.0	−3.8

Table 9: Annual Indicators: Currency Crises

Indicator	Noise-to-signal	Percent of crises accurately called	$P(C|S)$	$P(C|S)-P(C)$
Current account balance/GDP	0.41	56	43.2	19.5
Current account balance/investment	0.49	31	39.0	15.1
Overall budget deficit/GDP	0.58	22	36.4	11.5
Short-term capital inflows/GDP	0.59	29	35.2	10.9
General government consumption/GDP	0.74	15	29.4	5.9
Net credit to the public sector/GDP	0.88	20	26.2	2.4
Central bank credit to the public sector/GDP	0.99	13	23.8	0.1
Foreign direct investment/GDP	1.00	24	21.7	0.1

The top indicator for banking crises is the share of short-term capital inflows to GDP. This is consistent with the results in Eichengreen and Rose (1997) and supports the view that the banking sector becomes particularly vulnerable during cycles of short-term capital inflows. Such short-term inflows are more likely to be intermediated through the domestic banking sector than other types of capital flows, such as foreign direct investment (FDI) and portfolio flows. Indeed, the share of FDI/GDP does poorly as a predictor of banking crises. Two of the fiscal variables — the budget deficit and central bank credit to the public sector — do moderately well, while the third — government consumption — does poorly. Hence the role of the public sector in fueling banking crises is somewhat mixed.

Without overinterpreting the results, it is interesting that the composition of the current account matters, in the sense that the current account as a percentage of investment does better in predicting banking crises than the current account as a share of GDP. It may be that investment is more likely to be financed through the international issuance of bonds and stocks or overseas loans, while consumption is more dependent on local bank credit.

Turning to currency crises, the annual indicators that perform best are those measuring current account imbalances. This finding is not representative of the broader empirical literature. As discussed in Kaminsky, Lizondo, and Reinhart (1998), most of the studies that have attempted to explain the k-period ahead probability of a currency crisis have had mixed results regarding the current account, with most studies finding it insignificant.

The various fiscal indicators do moderately well in anticipating currency crises, lending some support to Krugman-type models. By contrast with banking crises, the composition of capital inflows appears to have relatively little to add to our understanding of what drives a currency crisis. This result, however, may in part be due to the fact that a large share of the currency crises (as opposed to the banking crises) took place in the 1970s in an environment of highly regulated internal and external financial markets, where portfolio flows were negligible.

While our list of indicators is comprehensive, it is by no means exhaustive. The Asian crisis in particular highlighted the importance of currency and maturity mismatches in increasing vulnerability to currency and banking crises. Table 10 presents an indicator of the imbalance between liquid liabilities and liquid assets: namely, the ratio of short-term debt to international reserves. All the emerging economies in this group with debt-to-reserves levels in excess of 100 percent in mid-1997 have been casualties of financial turmoil in recent years (even if not all the speculative attacks ultimately succeeded, as in the case of Argentina.) This suggests that variables such as short-term debt to reserves could be a valuable addition to our list of leading indicators of crisis vulnerability.[31]

---

[31] See Calvo and Mendoza (1996) for an early discussion of this issue. We did not use the ratio of short-term debt to reserves as an indicator in our tests because its relevance was highlighted

Table 10: Short-Term Debt: Selected Countries, June 1997 (Percent)

Country	Short-Term Debt/Total Debt	Short-Term Debt/Reserves
Asia		
Indonesia	24	160
Malaysia	39	55
Philippines	19	66
South Korea	67	300
Thailand	46	107
Latin America		
Argentina	23	108
Brazil	23	69
Chile	25	44
Colombia	19	57
Mexico	16	126

Sources: Bank for International Settlements; *International Financial Statistics*; World Bank.

DO THE INDICATORS FLASH EARLY ENOUGH?

The previous discussion has ranked the indicators according to their ability to anticipate crises while producing few false alarms. Such criteria, however, do not speak to the *lead time* of the signal. From the vantage point of a policymaker or financial market participant who wants to implement preemptive or risk-mitigating measures, it is not a matter of indifference whether an indicator sends a signal well before the crisis occurs or if the signal is given only when the crisis is imminent. Consider for example, the Conference Board's composite indices of business cycle activity for the United States, which are published on a monthly basis. Both financial market participants and policymakers alike find the leading- indicator composite index more valuable than the coincident and lagging indices. Market participants incorporate this information in their investment decisions, while policymakers give it weight in their policy reactions. Over the years, US monetary policy has become increasingly forward- looking and hence preemptive rather than reactive. One

---

mainly by the Asian crisis and we did not want the out-of-sample tests to be biased by its inclusion. In addition, the data were not available for the early part of our sample.

Table 11: How Leading are the Signals? (Average Number of Months from when the First Signal is Issued to the Crisis Month)

Indicator	Currency Crisis	Banking Crisis
Bank deposits	15	8
Beginning of banking crisis	19	n.a.
Domestic credit/GDP	12	7
Domestic-foreign interest rate differential	14	16
Excess M1 balances	15	6
Exports	15	16
Imports	16	11
Lending-deposit interest rate ratio	13	6
M2 multiplier	16	12
M2/reserves	13	14
Output	16	13
Real exchange rate	17	10
Real interest rate	17	16
Reserves	15	10
Stock prices	14	12
Terms of trade	15	18

n.a. = not applicable

could argue that this transition was facilitated by an improvement in our understanding of the business cycle and early signs of its turning points.

In what follows, we tabulate for each of the monthly indicators the average number of months before the crisis when the first signal occurs. This, of course, does not preclude the indicator from giving signals through the entire period immediately preceding the crisis. Indeed, for the more reliable indicators, signals tend to become increasingly persistent ahead of crises. For the low-frequency (annual) indicators, lead time is not much of an issue since some of these are published with a considerable lag and hence tend to be of less use from an early warning standpoint.

Table 11 presents the lead times for our monthly indicators — both for currency and banking crises. In the case of currency crises, the most striking observation is that, on average, all the indicators send the first signal anywhere between a year and 18 months before the crisis erupts, with banking-sector problems (our second-ranked indicator) offering the longest lead time — namely, 19 months. The average lead time for these early signals is 15 months for currency crises. All the indicators considered are therefore best regarded as leading rather than coincident, which is consistent with the spirit of an "early warning system." For banking crises, there is a greater dispersion in the lead time across indicators, and the average lead time is also lower (about 11 months). Furthermore, most of the indicators signal at about the same time, thus the signaling is cumulative and all the more compelling. Thus, on the basis of these preliminary results, there does appear to be adequate lead time for preemptive policy actions to avert crises.

MICROECONOMIC INDICATORS: SELECTIVE EVIDENCE

If, as the previous discussion suggests, banking crises are more difficult to predict on the basis of macroeconomic indicators than currency crises, it appears that the analysis of banking crises may benefit from including a variety of microeconomic indicators of bank health. Gonzales-Hermosillo *et al.* (1997) and Rojas-Suarez (1998) provide some insights in this direction. Rojas-Suarez uses bank-specific data from Colombia, Mexico, and Venezuela and applies the "signals" methodology to this data to glean which items in bank balance sheets are most useful in predicting banking distress.

Her results are summarized in Table 12. They do indeed suggest that bank-specific information could make an important contribution in assessing the vulnerability of the banking sector in emerging markets. More "traditional" indicators, such as liquidity ratios and bank capitalization, turn out to be less

Table 12: Microeconomic Indicators: Banking Crises

Indicator	Percentage of Crises Accurately Called	Noise-to-signal
Bank lending-deposit interest rate spread	73	0.28
Interbank debt growth	80	0.35
Interest rate on deposits	80	0.47
Rate of growth on loans	58	0.72
Net profits to income	60	1.14
Operating costs to assets	40	1.59
Change in banks' equity prices	7	2.00
Risk-weighted capital-to-asset ratio	7	2.86

Source: Rojas-Suarez (1998).

useful indicators in Rojas-Suarez's tests, in large part because they are "noisy" and likely to send many false alarms while missing many of the problem spots. At the other end, bank spreads and the interest rate that banks offer on deposits appear to systematically identify the weak banks.

One possible explanation for why interest rate spreads at the micro level may be more useful indicators of banking crisis than aggregate spreads is that the latter may reflect mainly cross-country differences in the extent of banking competition. In contrast, micro spreads are more likely to be more informative about a bank's risk taking, as all banks within a country are apt to face a more common competitive environment.

Goldstein (1998b) stresses bank exposure to the property sector as an indicator in the context of banking crises. He notes that in many of the affected Asian countries, estimates of the share of bank lending to the property sector exceeded 25 percent. Banking sector external exposure, measured in terms of foreign liabilities as a percentage of foreign assets, also appears to be a worthy addition to the list of sectoral or microeconomic indicators of banking-sector problems.

"Methodology" and "Empirical Results" from *Assessing Financial Vulnerability* by Morris Goldstein, Graciela L. Kaminsky and Carmen M. Reinhart, pp. 11–44 (2000). Peterson Institute for International Economics. Used with permission of the publisher.

REFERENCES

Ades, Alberto, Rumi Masih, and Daniel Tenegauzer. 1998. A New Framework for Predicting Financial Crises in Emerging Markets. New York: Goldman Sachs. December

Bank for International Settlements (BIS). 1998. *The Maturity Sectoral, and Nationality Distribution of International Bank Lending*. Basel: Bank of International Settlements.

Blanco, Herminio, and Peter M. Garber. 1986. Recurrent Devaluation and Speculative Attacks on the Mexican Peso. *Journal of Political Economy* 94 (February): 148–66.

Calvo, Guillerrno A. 1998. Varieties of Capital-Market Crises. In Guillerrno A. Calvo and M. King, eds., *The Debt Burden and Its Consequences for Monetary Policy*. New York: MacMillan Press.

Calvo, Guillerrno A., and Morris Goldstein. 1996. What Role for the Official Sector? In Guillerrno A. Calvo, Morris Goldstein, and Eduard Hochreiter, eds., *Private

Capital Flows to Emerging Markets after the Mexican Crisis. Washington: Institute for International Economics.

Calvo, Guillerrno A., and Enrique Mendoza. 1996. Mexico's Balance-of-Payments Crisis: A Chronicle of a Death Foretold. Journal of International Economics 41, no. 3/4 (November): 235–64.

Calvo, Guillerrno A., and Carmen M. Reinhart. 2000. Fear of Floating. Photocopy. University of Maryland.

Caprio, Gerald Jr., and Daniela Kingebiel. 1996a. Bank Insolvency: Bad Luck, Bad Policy, or Bad Banking? In *Annual World Bank Conference on Development Economics*. Washington: World Bank.

Caprio, Gerald Jr., and Daniela Klingebiel. 1996b. Bank Insolvency: Cross-Country Experiences. Washington: World Bank.

Corsetti, Giancarlo, Paolo Pesenti, and Nouriel Roubini. 1998. What Caused the Asian Currency and Financial Crisis? Part II: The Policy Debate. National Bureau of Economic Research Working Paper 6834. Cambridge, MA: National Bureau of Economic Research.

Demirguç-Kunt, Asli, and Enrica Detragiache. 1998. The Determinants of Banking Crises in Developing and Developed Countries. *IMF Staff Papers*, 45 no. 1:81–109.

Diamond, Douglas, and Phillip Dybvig. 1983. Bank Runs, Liquidity, and Deposit Insurance. *Journal of Political Economy* 91 (June):401–19.

Eichengreen, Barry, and Andrew Rose. 1998. *Staying Afloat When the Wind Shifts: External Factors and Emerging-Market Banking Crises*. National Bureau of Economic Research Working Paper 6370 (January). Cambridge, MA: National Bureau of Economic Research.

Eichengreen, Barry, Andrew Rose, and Charles Wyplosz. 1996. Contagious Currency Crises. National Bureau of Economic Research Working Paper 5681 (July). Cambridge, MA: National Bureau of Economic Research.

Flood, Robert, and Nancy P. Marion. 1999. Perspective on the Recent Currency Crisis Literature. *International Journal of Finance and Economics* 4, no. 1 (January):1–26.

Furman, Jason, and Joseph E. Stiglitz. 1998. Economic Crises: Evidence and Insights from East Asia. *Brookings Papers on Economic Activity* 2 (June):1–114.

Galbis, Vicente. 1993. *High Real Interest Rates under Financial Liberalization: Is There a Problem?* International Monetary Fund Working Paper 7. Washington: International Monetary Fund (January).

Gavin, Michael, and Ricardo Hausman. 1996. The Roots of Banking Crises. The Macroeconomic Context. In Ricardo Hausman and Liliana Rojas-Suarez, eds., *Banking Crises in Latin America*. Washington: Inter-American Development Bank.

Goldfajn, Ilan, and Rodrigo O. Valdés. 1998. Are Currency Crises Predictable?, *European Economic Review* 42 (May): 887–895.

Goldstein, Morris. 1997. *The Case for an International Banking Standard*. Policy Analyses in International Economics 47. Washington: Institute for International Economics.

Goldstein, Morris. 1998a. Early Warning Indicators and the Asian Financial Crisis. Unpublished paper. Washington: Institute for International Economics.

Goldstein, Morris. 1998b. *The Asian Financial Crisis: Causes, Cures, and Systemic Implications*. Policy Analyses in International Economics 55. Washington: Insitute for International Economics.

Goldstein, Morris, and Philip Turner. 1996. *Banking Crises in Emerging Economies: Origins and Policy Options*. Bank for International Settlements Economic Paper 46, (October). Basel: Bank for International Settlements.

Gonzales-Hermosilla, Brenda, Ceyla Pazarbasioglu, and Robert Billings. 1997. Determinants of Banking Systems Fragility: A Case Study of Mexico. *IMF Staff Papers* (September): 295–314.

Honohan, Patrick. 1997. *Banking System Failures in Developing and Transition Countries: Diagnosis and Prediction*. Bank for International Settlements Working Paper 39 (January). Basel: Bank for International Settlements.

International Monetary Fund (IMF). 1997. *International Capital Markets*. Washington: International Monetary Fund.

International Monetary Fund (IMF). 1998a. *World Economic Outlook*. Washington: International Monetary Fund.

International Monetary Fund (IMF). 1998b. *International Capital Markets*. Washington: International Monetary Fund.

International Monetary Fund (IMF). 1998c. *World Economic Outlook*. Washington: International Monetary Fund.

Kaminsky, Graciela L. 1998. *Currency and Banking Crises: A Composite Leading Indicator*. International Finance Discussion Paper Series, 629 (Decemeber). Washington: Board of Governors of the Federal Reserve.

Kaminsky, Graciela L., Saul Lizondo, and Carmen M. Reinhart. 1998. Leading Indicators of Currency Crises. *IMF Staff Papers*, 45, no. 1, (March):1–48.

Kaminsky, Graciela L., and Carmen M. Reinhart. 1998. Financial Crises in Asia and Latin America: Then and Now. *American Economic Review*, 88, no. 2, (May):444–48.

Kaminsky, Graciela L., and Carment M. Reinhart. 1999. The Twin Crises: The Causes of Banking and Balance-of-Payments Problems. *American Economic Review* 89, no. 3, (June): 473–500.

Kaminsky, Graciela L., and Carmen M. Reinhart. 2000. On Crises, Contagion, and Confusion. In *Journal of International Economics*, 51, no. 1 (June): 145–68.

Krugman, Paul. 1979. A Model of Balance of Payments Crises. *Journal of Money, Credit, and Banking* 11 (August): 311–25.

Kumar, Manmohan S., William Perraudin, and Vincenzo Zinni. 1998. Predicting Emerging Market Currency Crises. Credit Suisse First Boston Discussion Paper. London: Credit Suisse First Boston.

Leiderman, Leonardo, and Alfredo Thorne. 1996. The 1994 Mexican Crisis and Its Aftermath: What are the Main Lessons? In Guillerrno A. Calvo, Morris Goldstein, and Eduard Hochreiter, eds., *Private Capital Flows to Emerging Markets after the Mexican Crisis*. Washington: Institute for International Economics.

Meese, Richard A., and Kenneth Rogoff. 1983. Empirical Exchange Rate Models of the Seventies: Do They Fit Out of Sample? *Journal of International Economics* 14 (February): 3–24.

Mishkin, Frederic S. 1996. Understanding Financial Crises: A Developing Country Perspective. *Annual World Bank Conference on Development Economics*. Washington: World Bank.

Radelet, Steven, and Jeffrey Sachs. 1998. The East Asian Financial Crisis: Diagnosis, Rernedies, Prospects. Brookings Papers on Economic Activity 2: 1–90.

Reinhart, Carment M. 2000. The Mirage of Floating Exchange Rates. *American Economic Review*. Forthcoming.

Rojas-Suarez, Liliana. 1998. Early Warning Indicators of Banking Crises: What Works for Emerging Markets? With Applications to Latin America. Photocopy.

Rojas-Suarez, Liliana, and Steven R. Weisbrod. 1995. *Financial Fragilities in Latin America: The 1980s and 1990s*. International Monetary Fund Occasional Paper 132. Washington: International Monetary Fund.

Rojas-Suarez, Liliana, and Steven R. Weisbrod. 1996. The Do's and Don'ts of Banking Crisis Management. In Ricardo Hausman and Liliana Rojas-Suares, eds. *Banking Crises in Latin America*. Washington: Inter-American Development Bank and Hohns Hopkins University Press.

Sundararajan, V., and Tomas Balifio. 1991. *Banking Crises: Cases and Issues*. Washington: International Monetary Fund.

World Bank. 2000. *Global Economic Prospects and the Developing Countries 2000*. Washington: World Bank.

Chapter 12

Measuring Currency Mismatch and Aggregate Effective Currency Mismatch

Morris Goldstein and Philip Turner

A currency mismatch refers to how a change in the exchange rate will affect the present discounted value of future income and expenditure flows. This will depend on two broad elements. One is the currency denomination of financial assets and liabilities: the more sensitive the net financial worth to changes in the exchange rate, the greater, ceteris paribus, the currency mismatch. The

---

Morris Goldstein, Dennis Weatherstone Senior Fellow, joined the Institute for International Economics in 1994 and has held several senior staff positions at the International Monetary Fund (1970–94), including deputy director of its research department (1987–94). He has written extensively on international economic policy and on international capital markets.

Philip Turner has been at the Bank for International Settlements (BIS) since 1989, where he is the head of the secretariat group in the monetary and economics department, responsible for economics papers produced for central bank meetings at the BIS. His research interests include financial stability in emerging markets, banking systems, and bank restructuring in the developing world. He was a member of the Financial Stability Forum's Working Group on Capital Flows. Between 1976 and 1989, he held various positions, including head of division in the economics department of the Organization for Economic Cooperation and Development (OECD) in Paris. In 1985–86, he was a visiting scholar at the Bank of Japan's Institute for Monetary and Economic Studies.

other is the currency denomination of future income and expenditure flows (other than returns to capital assets). Once such a broad perspective is adopted, significant differences in the degree of currency mismatch are revealed both across emerging economies and over time.

As an analytical counterpoint to our proposed definition of currency mismatch, suppose one attempted to gauge aggregate currency mismatch by looking only at the share of international bonds and bank loans denominated in the borrower's local currency — that is, suppose one used measures of original sin as a sufficient statistic for drawing inferences about aggregate currency mismatch. How might the original sin measures lead one astray? It turns out that the answer is helpful in understanding what should be included in a good measure of currency mismatch.

ORIGINAL SIN: A MISLEADING MEASURE

Table 1, taken from Eichengreen, Hausmann, and Panizza (2002), gives three measures of original sin. These measures are defined as one minus the percentage of own currency-denominated securities in the relevant total, so that the closer the ratio to one (zero), the greater (smaller) the original sin and implied currency mismatch. These original sin calculations suggest that currency mismatch is pervasive in all developing country groups, and the mismatch has been persistent over 1993–2001. Another strong implication of Table 1 is that developing countries face a much larger currency mismatch than not only issuers of the five major currencies but also small industrial countries.

Using original sin as a measure of aggregate currency mismatch would be misleading on at least five important counts. First, it ignores cross-country differences in export openness, reserve holdings, and the size of foreign assets more generally, which can be crucial for assessing currency risk. Consider two net debtor countries (A and B) that have identical shares of foreign currency–denominated debt in total external debt. Assume country A has twice as high a ratio of exports to income as country B. Should it then be concluded that the two countries face an identical currency mismatch? Of course not. Both sides of the net income statement and the balance sheet are relevant for gauging the extent of the currency mismatch. For most of the past decade, Argentina and Brazil, for example, have had ratios of exports to GDP that hovered in the 7 to

Table 1: Measures of Original Sin by Country Groupings, Simple Average (Billions of Dollars)

Group	OSIN1 1993–98	OSIN1 1999–2001	OSIN2 1993–98	OSIN2 1999–2001	OSIN3 1993–98	OSIN3 1999–2001
Financial centers	0.58	0.53	0.34	0.37	0.07	0.08
Euroland	0.86	0.52	0.55	0.72	0.53	0.09[a]
Other developed	0.90	0.94	0.80	0.82	0.78	0.72
Offshore	0.98	0.97	0.95	0.98	0.96	0.87
Developing	1.00	0.99	0.98	0.99	0.96	0.93
Latin America and the Caribbean	1.00	1.00	1.00	1.00	0.98	1.00
Middle East and Africa	1.00	0.99	0.97	0.99	0.95	0.90
Asia Pacific	1.00	0.99	0.95	0.99	0.99	0.94
Eastern Europe	0.99	1.00	0.97	0.98	0.91	0.84

a. For 1999–2001, it was impossible to allocate the debt issued by nonresidents in euros to any of the individual member countries of the currency union. Hence, the number is not the simple average but is calculated taking Euroland as a whole.

$$OSIN1_i = 1 - \frac{\text{Securities issued by country } i \text{ in currency } i}{\text{Securities issued by country } i}$$

$$OSIN2_i = \max(INDEXA_i, OSIN3_i)$$

where

$$INDEXA_i = \frac{\text{Securities + loans issued by country } i \text{ in major currencies}}{\text{Securities + loans issued by country } i}$$

$$INDEXB_i = 1 - \frac{\text{Securities in currency } i}{\text{Securities issued by country } i}$$

$$OSIN3_i = \max\left(1 - \frac{\text{Securities in currency } i}{\text{Securities issued by country } i}, 0\right)$$

Notice that $OSIN2 > OSIN3$ by construction and that, in most cases, $OSIN1 > OSIN2$.

Source: Eichengreen, Hausmann, and Panizza (2002).

13 percent range — less than half that of Mexico and Chile and less than a fifth that of typical Asian emerging economies (Table 2).[1] At identical original sin

---

[1] Argentina's ratio of exports to GDP mushroomed in 2002 because of the deep recession and the effects of the sharp fall in the peso exchange rate on both GDP measured in dollars and export earnings.

Table 2: Export Openness, 1994–2002 (Exports as a Percent of GDP)

Region/Country	1994	1995	1996	1997	1998	1999	2000	2001	2002
Latin America[a]	14.4	16.9	17.7	16.9	16.3	18.0	19.5	19.2	22.5
Argentina	7.5	9.7	10.4	10.6	10.4	9.8	12.5	11.5	27.7
Brazil	9.5	7.7	7.0	7.5	7.4	10.3	10.7	13.2	15.8
Chile	29.3	30.5	27.3	27.1	26.3	29.3	31.7	34.7	34.0
Colombia	15.0	14.5	15.2	14.8	15.0	18.3	21.5	20.8	19.7
Mexico	16.8	30.4	32.1	30.3	30.7	30.8	31.0	27.4	27.2
Peru	12.8	12.5	13.1	14.2	13.2	14.7	16.0	15.8	16.1
Venezuela	30.9	27.1	36.5	28.4	19.9	21.6	28.4	22.3	31.4
Asia, large economies[a]	20.8	21.0	20.7	22.6	23.4	23.1	26.4	25.6	28.2
China	22.0	21.0	20.9	22.9	21.7	22.1	25.9	25.1	29.3
India	10.0	11.0	10.6	10.9	11.2	11.8	13.8	14.2	15.2
Korea	27.8	30.2	29.5	34.7	49.7	42.3	44.8	42.8	40.0
Taiwan	43.9	48.5	48.4	49.0	48.4	48.0	54.0	50.2	53.7
Other Asia[a]	37.9	39.6	39.1	44.0	60.4	53.5	60.4	57.5	54.4
Indonesia	26.5	26.3	25.8	27.9	51.2	34.9	42.4	41.1	34.7
Malaysia	89.2	94.1	91.6	93.3	115.7	121.3	124.8	116.3	113.8
Philippines	33.8	36.4	40.5	49.0	52.2	51.5	56.2	49.0	51.7
Thailand	38.9	41.8	39.3	48.0	58.9	58.4	67.0	66.4	64.8
Central Europe[a]	31.8	36.5	36.5	39.4	42.9	42.7	48.8	48.4	45.7
Czech Republic	50.5	53.6	52.5	56.5	58.8	60.6	69.8	70.8	65.2
Hungary	28.9	44.4	48.5	55.1	62.6	65.2	74.9	74.4	64.5
Poland	23.8	25.4	24.4	25.6	28.2	26.1	29.4	28.4	29.6
Russia	27.8	26.9	24.2	23.9	30.6	43.8	44.1	36.2	34.4
Israel	32.6	30.6	29.8	30.4	31.6	36.0	40.6	35.5	36.9
Turkey	21.4	19.9	21.5	24.6	24.3	23.2	24.0	33.7	28.9
South Africa	22.2	23.0	24.6	24.6	25.7	25.7	28.6	30.6	34.0

a. Weighted average of countries shown, based on 1995 GDP and PPP exchange rates.
Note: Exports include goods and services per the national accounts definition, except China and Taiwan, for which the balance-of-payments definition is used.
Sources: IMF's *International Financial Statistics* and national sources.

ratios, Argentina will, ceteris paribus, have a much larger currency mismatch than Mexico or Singapore. The same line of argument about cross-country differences also applies to holdings of international reserves and foreign assets more broadly. Whereas monetary authorities of some emerging economies, such as Korea and Malaysia, have net foreign assets (in 2002) that are five to seven times larger than currency held outside banks, those in others, such as the Philippines, Brazil, and Poland, have much lower ratios (less than three). Likewise, data on net international investment positions taken from the IMF's *Balance of Payments Yearbook* reveal sharp differences among emerging economies. For example, foreign assets (in 2002) accounted for less than 10 percent of foreign liabilities in Ecuador but for 66 and 86 percent in Chile and the Czech Republic, respectively; in Hong Kong and Singapore, foreign assets exceed foreign liabilities (i.e., they are net creditors, not net debtors).[2] Since our preferred measures of currency mismatch consider both assets and liabilities, they are not subject to this pitfall.

Second, and in a similar vein, an original sin measure would ignore changes in foreign-currency receipts and assets over time. Consider a net debtor country where the share of foreign currency–denominated debt in total corporate debt increased from one-third in 1994 to one-half in 2000. According to the original sin measure, its currency mismatch would have increased. But suppose that over the same period its exports increased much more, so that the ratio of foreign-currency debt to exports fell from, say, almost four to one and a half. Clearly, the country's currency mismatch would have fallen, not risen. This is not a hypothetical case. It is in fact a summary of the evolution of (corporate) currency mismatch Mexico (Martinez and Werner 2001). If one leaves out changes in the asset side of the aggregate currency balance sheet, one can miss much of the action in time-series variation of currency risk. When both sides of the balance sheet are considered, aggregate measures of currency mismatch are not nearly as persistent as original sin measures would suggest. The ratio of short-term external debt to international reserves in four Asian-crisis countries was roughly half as high in 1999 as it was in 1996. Another implication is that original sin ratios based on the liability side of the balance sheet are not likely to be good leading indicators of the timing of financial crises in emerging

---

[2] Figures on foreign assets and liabilities don't reveal the currency composition of positions but are suggestive of nontrivial cross-country differences in currency risk.

economies (since such ratios move very little over time).[3] In contrast, and as discussed earlier, currency mismatch measures that capture both sides of the balance sheet (e.g., the ratio of short-term external debt to reserves and the ratios of bank and corporate foreign debt to exports) have done well in leading-indicator exercises of currency and banking crises in emerging economies, and the output costs of such crises have been shown to be higher when currency mismatch (so measured) was large than when it was small.

Third, the original sin measure — like all aggregate measures of currency mismatch — ignores the key question of who bears the currency risk within an emerging economy. This is particularly relevant when produces of nontradables that do not generate foreign revenue to service the debt undertake a significant share of external borrowing. Once again, consider (net debtor) countries A and B with identical original sin ratios. But assume that exporters exclusively undertake country A's dollar borrowing whereas real estate companies that operate exclusively in the domestic economy undertake country B's dollar borrowing. Do these two countries face identical currency mismatches? Certainly not. Country A's mismatch is likely to be much lower than country B's. One of the lessons of the Asian financial crisis of 1997–98 is that using short-term external foreign currency–denominated borrowing to fund long-term real estate investments is hazardous. Similarly, a country where the government does the bulk of external borrowing is apt to have a larger currency mismatch than one where exporters do the bulk of the borrowing because government taxes are typically denominated in domestic currency while most external borrowing is denominated in foreign currency. Going in the same direction, firm-level studies have shown that the investment effects of a currency depreciation are different when firms have export revenues and

---

[3] Measures of dollarization in the *domestic* financial system show more variation across countries and over time than do original sin ratios (of external borrowing). Yet even empirical studies of domestic dollarization have produced quite mixed results. Arteta (2003), for example, finds no evidence that high liability dollarization in the banking system heightens the probability of banking crises or currency crashes in emerging economies or that such crises are more costly in countries where bank liability dollarization is high. Reinhart, Rogoff, and Savastano (2003a) find, inter alia, that dollarization has little impact on the effectiveness of monetary policy, that output fluctuations are fairly similar in countries with different degrees and varieties of dollarization, and that exchange rate–linked government debt increases crisis vulnerability. De Nicolo, Honohan, and Ize (2003) find that financial intermediaries in dollarized financial systems are prone to higher risk.

when they do not. Again, original sin ratios would not pick any of this up. To capture the incidence of foreign exchange risk in the economy, one needs disaggregated data on the allocation of credit and on the characteristics of the borrower. None of the aggregate measures of currency risk will capture this incidence of risk very well. But original sin measures of currency risk can be particularly misleading because they ignore differences across (net debtor) countries and over time in the asset side of the balance sheet; they are thus more likely to miss even gross differences in the tradable/nontradable distinction.

Yet a fourth problem with the original sin measure of mismatch is that it would restrict attention to international bonds and bank loans. It therefore ignores the currency composition and increasing importance of the domestic bond market, the participation of global investors in domestic bond markets, and bank lending by the domestic affiliates of foreign-owned banks operating in emerging economies. It turns out that these exclusions are crucial for drawing conclusions about if and how emerging economies differ from industrial countries as well as about how significant financial activity in domestic currency vis-á-vis that in foreign currency is. What's more, one should guard against any suggestion that only external borrowing by emerging economies (because it involves a transfer of resources to relatively poor countries) should be considered in examining the path to lower financial fragility there; recent research indicates that domestic financial intermediation generates significant benefits and may well reduce some of the vulnerabilities associated with heavy reliance on external borrowing.

Until recently, it was not possible to get comprehensive data on the currency composition of domestic bond markets in emerging economies. In recent years, however, the scope of the Bank for International Settlements' banking and financial market statistics has been broadened to include domestic debt securities in emerging markets, complementing the data on international bond issuance. In a recent paper John Burger and Francis Warnock (2002) summarize and analyze these data (as of end-2001) for 50 countries (Table 3). The key observation is that once the total bond market is considered, the share of the bond market denominated in local currency is not that different between emerging economies and industrial countries. In Asian emerging economies, the local-currency share of the bond market is 88 percent — higher than the local-currency share in Canada (71 percent) and the United Kingdom (74 percent) and identical to the local-currency share in the euro

Table 3: Bond Market Development, end-2001

Region	Bonds Outstanding (Percent of GDP)	Local Currency Denominated (Percent of Total)	Dollar-Denominated (Percent of Total)
Euro area	109	88	5
Japan	116	99	1
United Kingdom	92	74	15
Canada	92	71	23
Latin America	30	47	42
Emerging Asia	41	88	10
Other	59	75	13
Total non-US	85	87	7
United States	142	98	—

Sources: Burger and Warnock (2002). Data on dollar-denominated bonds and notes are from security-level data underlying table 14B (International Bonds and Notes by Country of Residence) in BIS, *International Banking and Financial Market Developments*. Local currency–denominated debt is the sum of the long-term debt component of BIS table 16A (Domestic Debt Securities) and the local-currency portion of Table 14B. Domestic debt for countries not available in table 16A is from the IMF's *Government Finance Statistics Yearbook* and Merrill Lynch (2002). Total non-US includes only the 50 countries in Burger and Warnock's sample.

area (88 percent). It is in Latin America that the local-currency share of the bond market (47 percent) is significantly lower than elsewhere. Since global investors do participate in local bond markets and since local bond markets in all regions (including the industrial countries) represent the largest share of the total bond market, excluding them from the analysis of currency mismatch would be hard to defend.[4] As Burger and Warnock (2002) emphasize, the data in Table 3 suggest that if there is a robust difference between industrial and emerging economies as regards bond markets, it is that the size of the total bond market (relative to GDP) is much smaller in emerging economies than it is in industrial countries — not a difference in the currency composition of the bond market, as the original sin hypothesis (OSH) suggests.

---

[4] Reinhart, Rogoff, and Savastano (2003b, 42) share this view when they argue that "the view that only external debt is a completely separate matter is clearly wrong. Foreigners often hold domestically-issued debt, and domestic residents often hold foreign-issued debt — indeed, the process of liberalization encourages active arbitrage across the two markets."

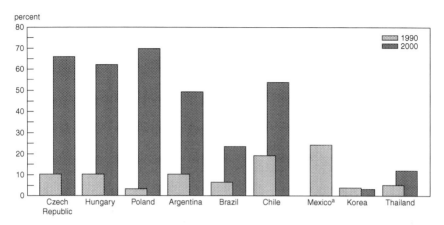

Fig 1: Market share of foreign-owned banks in emerging markets

If the foreign-owned banks that have effective control without holding more than 50 percent of equity are included, the proportion would be over 40 percent in 2000.

Note: Data include banks where foreigners hold more than 50 percent of equity.

Sources: Central banks.

Similarly, a lot of the action in emerging-market finance is missed when one concentrates only on cross-border bank lending in domestic currency. A more comprehensive picture needs to include lending in local currency by foreign affiliates of industrial-country banks operating in emerging economies. Foreign presence in emerging-market banking systems has been increasing in the 1990s and now stands above 50 percent in Hungary, Chile, Poland, and the Czech Republic (Figure 1). Also, lending by foreign affiliates of industrial-country banks has been on a steady upward trend (as cross-border bank lending to developing countries has declined). Indeed, as shown in Table 4, such local claims (denominated in local currency) by foreign affiliates now amount to more than a third of total foreign-bank claims (in all currencies) in developing countries as a group; in Latin America and the Caribbean, the local-claims share is above half. Why might foreign banks prefer to do domestic-currency lending via their foreign affiliates within emerging economies rather than via crossborder flows? One plausible answer is that foreign-bank affiliates take in domestic-currency deposits; as such, the degree of currency risk (for the lending bank) is much lower for local lending than it is for cross-border lending (where there is no obvious offset). This distinction is also reflected in the regulatory

Table 4: Foreign Banks' Consolidated Claims, Local and International, 1990–2003 (Billions of Dollars)

Region	1990	1995	1996	1997	1998	1999	2000	2001	2002	2003 Q3
Developing countries										
Local	52	124	153	251	279	304	434	523	542	575
International	531	752	855	995	938	881	885	838	802	884
Africa and Middle East										
Local	6	14	12	14	16	22	24	27	34	36
International	110	115	111	122	136	140	137	130	134	144
Asia and Pacific										
Local	27	56	65	73	81	95	117	123	143	165
International	134	307	368	421	337	299	278	252	238	282
Europe										
Local	3	9	12	36	39	38	62	87	112	128
International	103	118	135	171	175	165	184	181	202	235
Latin America and Caribbean										
Local	15	44	64	128	144	149	231	287	253	245
International	184	212	242	280	290	277	285	275	228	223

Note: Local claims comprise those of BIS reporting banks' foreign offices denominated in local currency. International claims are the sum of cross-border claims in all currencies and local claims of BIS reporting banks' foreign offices denominated in foreign currency only.
Source: Bank for International Settlements.

capital structure facing international banks: whereas cross-border bank lending in local currency (of the borrower) faces a capital charge for foreign exchange risk, domestic-currency lending by affiliates with domestic-currency deposits is not subject to such a capital charge.[5]

Some might argue that expanding the sources of local currency-denominated finance beyond international bonds and cross-border bank lending to include bank lending by local affiliates of foreign banks and domestic bonds is inappropriate — either because foreign banks merely displace lending by locally owned banks or because domestic bond markets make little use of

---

[5] On this shift, see Hawkins (2003); Wooldridge, Domanski, and Cobau (2003); and Lubin (2003).

foreign saving (and hence do not involve the transfer of real resources associated with cross-border purchases of bonds). We disagree.

Considerable empirical literature now supports the view that lower entry restrictions on foreign-owned banks in emerging economies improve the efficiency of the banking system, are associated with significant upgrades in the quality of regulation and disclosure, and reduce vulnerability to a crisis.[6] Affiliates of foreign banks not only bring with them risk capital but also permit a diversification of risk and can serve as high-quality counterparties in hedging contracts. According to Gerard Caprio and Patrick Honohan (2001), there is no hard evidence that the local presence of foreign banks has destabilized the flow of credit or restricted access to small firms. Entry of foreign banks is thus by no means a zero-sum game for the host emerging economies — especially when it comes to reducing their financial fragility.

Likewise, as Richard Herring and N. Chatusripitak (2001) have convincingly argued, bond markets are central to the development of an efficient economic system, and further development of the domestic bond market in developing countries would offer significant benefits. Bond markets make financial markets more complete by generating market interest rates that reflect the opportunity cost of funds at each maturity; they avoid concentrating intermediation uniquely on banks; and they provide a useful market signal and disciplining device for macroeconomic policy. Having a well-functioning domestic bond market improves the supply of local currency–denominated finance and thus can help to reduce excessive reliance on (largely) foreign currency–denominated external finance. The existence of such a market also benefits those borrowers who rely on banks for finance: banks will be more able to offer long-term credit terms because they can use bond markets to hedge their maturity mismatches. Hence customers of banks, who never directly use bond markets, gain indirectly.

Summarizing a large body of cross-country empirical evidence, Caprio and Honohan (2001) report that there is a strong positive association between the level of financial development and economic growth and that both banking

---

[6]See Barth, Caprio, and Levine (2000). Caprio and Honohan (2001) also show that foreign bank ownership (i.e., the percent of total banking assets owned by foreign banks) has been lower in crisis countries than in noncrisis ones. For a recent review of foreign banks in emerging markets, see CGFS (2004).

and market finance support economic growth.[7] They find that the deeper the financial system, the lower (ceteris paribus) the economic volatility. While legitimate questions remain as to whether it is preferable to first develop a local bond market before relying on the external bond market or vice versa, we are unaware of robust evidence from the empirical literature that indicates that external bond markets offer large benefits for economic growth and crisis prevention but domestic ones do not. It is true that domestic debt markets, especially new ones, tend to be thin and the pricing volatile. This often discourages local debt managers from using these markets. But it is all too often forgotten that the pricing of the sovereign debt of highly indebted borrowers in international markets is also very volatile — witness the sharp swings in Brazilian spreads from mid-2002 to mid-2003. There are reasons to believe — and some evidence — that pricing in local markets improves as debt markets deepen. Accepting volatility in the early stages of local-market development can be regarded as an investment in the future. Just running to international markets "because deals can be done faster" does not constitute such an investment.

Indeed, some analysts have even begun to suggest that the presumption may have begun to shift against unconditional or premature financial globalization (at least for those developing countries in the early phases of financial integration and with relatively poor quality of domestic institutions). In this connection, the conclusions of a recent IMF study (Prasad *et al.* 2003) that reviews and evaluates the empirical evidence on the effects of financial globalization on developing countries are worth noting. Financial integration or globalization is measured in the IMF study in a variety of ways, including by government restrictions on capital account transactions and by the observed size of capital flows crossing the border. The authors conclude: (1) "an objective reading of the vast research effort to date suggests that there is no strong, robust and uniform support for the theoretical argument that financial globalization per se delivers a higher rate of economic growth" (p. 5); (2) "procyclical access to international capital markets appears to have had a perverse effect on the relative volatility of consumption for financial integrated developing economies" (p. 9); and (3) "A number of researchers have now concluded

---

[7] For other studies analyzing the link between financial market development and growth, see King and Levine (1993a, 1993b) and Khan and Senhadji (2000).

that most of the differences in per capita income across countries stem not from differences in capital-labor ratios, but from differences in total factor productivity, which, in turn, could be explained by 'soft factors' or 'social infrastructure' like governance, rule of law, and respect for property rights" (p. 31). In short, no analysis of the path to reduced financial fragility and higher economic growth in emerging economies that concentrated exclusively on external sources of finance would be persuasive. Domestic financial markets in emerging economies should not be compared to some idealized version of cross-border capital flows but rather to their real-world counterparts — warts (sudden stops, cross-country contagions) and all.

An original sin measure of currency mismatch would leave out domestic bond markets. While much smaller relative to GDP than in industrial countries, domestic bond markets in emerging markets are already anything but trivial. By end-2001, outstanding domestic debt securities in emerging markets amounted to over $2 trillion — up from $1 trillion in 1994. Likewise, the volume of emerging-market domestic debt that is tradable now exceeds by a wide margin that of tradable international debt — even though international bonds are still more liquid instruments. According to IMF (2003a) figures for the 1997–2001 period, public-sector domestic bond issuance by emerging economies was 13 times larger than international foreign-currency bond issues; international corporate bond issuance by emerging economies in 1997–2001 amounted to only about half of such bonds issued domestically; and the annual average value of international corporate bond issuance declined slightly between 1997–99 and 2000–01, whereas the corresponding average for domestic bond issuance rose tenfold. While emerging markets have traditionally been viewed as bank-dominated financial systems, local bond markets have now become the single largest source (in terms of flows) of domestic and international funding for emerging economies (Table 5 covers both public- and private-sector financing). Clearly, by looking only at international bonds and cross-border bank loans, one would get a partial and misleading impression of both the key elements of emerging-market financing and of trends in these financing patterns.

While the maturity of financing in emerging economies remains much shorter than is available to industrial countries, the (original version of the) OSH went too far in claiming that emerging economies cannot borrow long-term (domestically) in their own currencies. Mihaljek, Scatigna, and Villar

Table 5: Emerging-Market Financing, All Sectors, 1997–2001 (Billions of Dollars)

Region	Domestic				International			
	Equities	Bonds	Bank loans	Total	Equities	Bonds	Bank loans	Total
Total emerging markets	158	2,367	907	3,432	80	303	214	598
Asia	112	342	883	1,337	63	113	96	272
Latin America	313	1,752	−1	1,784	12	172	103	288
Central Europe	13	273	25	311	6	18	15	38

Note: Emerging markets are Argentina, Brazil, Chile, China, Czech Republic, Hong Kong, Hungary, Korea, Malaysia, Mexico, Poland, Singapore, and Thailand.
Source: IMF (2003a, 78).

(2002) report that 37 percent of domestic-debt securities in Latin America were short-term in 2000 — down from 53 percent in 1995; the percentage of short-term debt for emerging economies in Asia and Central Europe is lower than in Latin America. Moreover, data collected by Salomon Smith Barney (2001) indicate that domestic currency–denominated bonds with maturities extending to 20 years currently exist in India, Malaysia, the Philippines, Poland, South Korea, and Thailand; if long maturity were defined as 10 years, then some domestic currency–denominated bonds in Argentina, Colombia, the Czech Republic, Hong Kong, Hungary, Mexico, and Singapore would also qualify. And in Chile — an emerging economy with original sin ratios close to one — the average maturity of inflation-indexed local currency–denominated corporate bonds now runs 15 to 20 years (up from 10 to 15 years in the first half of the 1990s), and the market for indexed local-currency bonds has tripled in size since 2000 (IMF 2003a). To be sure, some of these long-dated domestic-currency bonds in emerging economies are not as liquid as would be desirable, but this list belies the notion that it is simply impossible for emerging economies to borrow at long maturity from their own citizens unless they denominate this debt in one of the leading reserve currencies; equally important, as argued later, if emerging economies can improve their macroeconomic performance and institutions, they will be able to attract more longer-term finance.

In their latest papers (Eichengreen, Hausmann, and Panizza 2003e; Hausmann and Panizza 2003), Eichengreen, Hausmann, and Panizza construct a measure of "domestic" original sin to complement their external original sin measure; the earlier papers ignored almost completely the domestic bond markets. Domestic original sin is measured by the share of the domestic bond market accounted for by the sum of foreign currency–denominated instruments, short-term domestic currency–denominated fixed-rate debt, and domestic–currency debt indexed to the interest rate. The higher this measure of domestic original sin, the lower the share of long-term fixed-rate and long-term inflation-indexed debt denominated in domestic currency — and the assumed lower stage of "development" of the domestic debt market. Of the 22 emerging economies in their sample, 9 (Taiwan, India, South Africa, Slovak Republic, Thailand, Singapore, Hungary, Poland, and the Philippines) had domestic original sin ratios less than one-half. Perhaps more important, they find that there are *no* countries with poorly developed domestic bond markets that have been redeemed from external original sin — suggesting that domestic bond development is a necessary precondition for a country to borrow abroad in its own currency. Also of interest, seven emerging economies in their sample are free of domestic original sin but still suffer from external original sin — a result that Eichengreen, Hausmann, and Panizza interpret as suggesting that domestic bond market development is not a sufficient condition for a country's being able to borrow abroad in its own currency. But since their bond market figures refer to a single year (1999), another interpretation is that there is simply a time lag between domestic bond market development and the subsequent ability to borrow abroad in one's own currency.

Yet a fifth caveat about using original sin as a measure of aggregate currency mismatch is that the former concentrates on the "original" currency denomination of international bonds and cross-border bank loans; the original borrowers could use derivatives markets to limit their currency risk and/or transfer that risk to other parties (including foreigners). Consider a Polish nonfinancial corporation that issued an international bond denominated in US dollars but preferred to have its risk denominated in Polish zloties. It could use the swap, forward, or options market to switch or hedge its original exposure. In that case, the original currency composition of that corporate bond would not reveal much about the firm's currency mismatch. The IMF (2003a) reports, for example, that virtually all local companies in Brazil that have access to international financial markets raise funds denominated in US dollars but then use the local derivatives market to swap the international financial obligations into the local currency with an interest rate indexed to the overnight rate.

The early work on OSH did not take account of derivatives markets. In the later versions of the OSH, the authors (Eichengreen, Hausmann, and Panizza 2002) address the possibility that currency swaps could distort their measure of original sin. Their adjustment for this is to include all international bonds denominated in an emerging-market currency even if issued by countries other than the home country. They find that this makes little difference to their results since there are not enough local currency–denominated international bonds to sustain a large volume of currency swaps. But this procedure, while moving in the right direction, still suffers from several problems. Currency swaps are only one of many ways of hedging or transferring currency risk. In most of Latin America, for example, there is a greater reliance on forwards than on foreign exchange swaps, while the reverse holds for most of the Asian emerging economies; Eichengreen, Hausmann, and Panizza (2002) consider only currency swaps. Since foreigners also participate in local bond markets, domestic bonds denominated in local currency should also in principle be taken into account in gauging potential currency swap operations; and because (as argued earlier) the volume of domestic bonds outstanding far exceeds that of international bonds, there is no shortage of domestic-currency bonds for swap operations with foreigners.

What makes it difficult to assess the difference derivatives make for the correct measurement of currency risk is that still relatively little is known about who is on the other side of these transactions. Unlike Eichengreen and Hausmann (1999), we do not regard a redistribution of currency risk within an emerging economy as being of little significance, since a transfer of exposures from nontradable to tradable producers could (as argued earlier) generate a sizable reduction in currency mismatch. Still, it would be illuminating to know how prominent foreigners are in these transactions. A recent IMF study (2003a, 66) reports that foreign-investor participation in local derivative exchanges is usually "fairly limited" but has been considerable in Mexico, Hungary, Poland, and the Czech Republic; that in some emerging economies like Singapore, Hong Kong, and South Africa, foreign dealers account for the bulk of turnover in over-the-counter derivatives markets; that "real-money accounts" (both dedicated and cross-over investors) hedge relatively little of their risk exposures in emerging economies while speculative money accounts (hedge funds and proprietary trading desks of commercial and investment banks) use derivatives markets freely for either hedging or speculative position-taking; and that the main sellers of protection in credit derivatives markets are internationally active banks. In our own discussions with market participants, there was a view that internationally active banks and real-money funds were likely to be on the other side of derivatives transactions when locals wanted to short the local currency.

How far derivatives alter the currency exposure implied by the original currency composition of international bonds and bank loans will not be known until there is better information on the identity of counterparties in hedging transactions — both within and across countries. But the wide array of hedging instruments and markets makes it a leap too far to assume that the original currency composition of international bonds and bank loans provides a reliable picture of who is ultimately bearing the currency risk.

SUMMARY

A useful way to sum up this discussion about the original sin measure of currency mismatch is to ask under what set of conditions it would produce a good estimate. Three such conditions are apparent.

Condition number one is that domestic bond and bank flows would either have to be very small relative to international flows or if large, would need to have the same currency composition as international flows. It is clear that condition one is grossly violated. As seen earlier, domestic financial flows are large relative to international flows, and the local currency share of domestic finance is much larger than for international flows.

Condition number two is that the asset side of balance sheets (and the income side of net income statements) would have to be similar across countries and relatively constant over time. If that were the case, then information on liabilities alone would track pretty well both cross-country differences and changes over time in currency mismatch. But, as shown earlier, this condition too is far divorced from what is observed in practise.

Condition number three is that neither the distribution of currency risk within an economy nor the redistribution of currency risk internationally (via the use of derivatives) would matter much. If that were the case, then data on aggregate currency mismatch and the original currency composition of bond and bank flows would be sufficient for gauging currency risk. But as argued earlier, it does matter which entities and sectors within an economy bear the currency risk, and some emerging economies do have enough access to decent derivative and hedging instruments to potentially alter significantly the allocation of currency risk implied by the original currency composition of financial instruments.

Aggregate Effective Currency Mismatch

Our preferred definition of currency mismatch — that is, the sensitivity of net worth or of the present discounted value of net income to changes in the exchange rate — is indeed much harder to measure than original sin. But it offers better guidance to what one should try to measure. Although no single measure captures all the relevant features of currency mismatches throughout the economy, we believe it is possible to get useful rough estimates of mismatch both across countries and for a given country over time by relying jointly on a number of available mismatch variables as well as by constructing a new measure of aggregate effective currency mismatch. Moreover, other potentially valuable indicators of currency mismatch could be obtained in the future — particularly for the corporate sector — if data collection for them were accorded higher priority.

As discussed earlier, empirical work suggests that the ratio of short-term external debt to international reserves has been a useful leading indicator of the probability of getting into a currency crisis. A recent IMF study (Aturupane *et al.* 2004) reports, inter alia, that virtually all emerging economies with access to international capital markets, which experienced a crisis during the January 2000–December 2002 period, had a ratio of short-term debt to reserves of greater than one. The ratio of broad money balances (M2) to reserves also appears to have value in signaling currency crises. These short-run liquidity measures are available for a large group of emerging economies.

Other indicators of currency mismatch — encompassing both sectoral and aggregate measures — are also worth monitoring because they can reveal sectoral mismatch vulnerabilities that may be submerged within the aggregate, or because they permit one to control for factors (like local currency-denominated bonds and bank loans and the responsiveness noninterest income flows to a change in the exchange rate) that ought to affect the severity of crises, or because they cover a wider range of foreign-currency assets and liabilities.

Figure 2, taken from Reinhart, Rogoff, and Savastano (2003a), components that would ideally make up sectoral foreign-currency balance sheets. The rub is that, while data for some of these components (like international reserves, foreign-currency bank deposits held at home, and external foreign-currency debt) are now available for many emerging economies, data on other components (such as foreign-currency cash holdings, foreign-currency credit extended by banks to domestic households and firms, and foreign currency-linked domestic debt) are in much more limited supply.

Tables 6 and 7 — the former for an industrial country (Australia) and the latter for an emerging economy (Thailand) — illustrate how sectoral balance sheets (usually taken from national sources) can be used to gauge currency mismatches and vulnerabilities.

Table 6 provides data on sectoral foreign-currency exposure for the Australian economy as of end-June 2001. The Australian Bureau of Statistics (ABS) collected the data, with the assistance of the Reserve Bank of Australia, as a supplement to the *Survey of International Investment*. According to the ABS (2001), the aim was to capture quantitative and qualitative data about Australian enterprises' foreign-currency exposure and the risk management practices associated with that exposure. More than 230 resident enterprises with significant foreign-currency exposure were approached (including general government entities), and the response rate was 77 percent. Information was requested about foreign-equity assets, foreign currency–denominated assets and liabilities, the notional value of derivative contracts with a foreign-currency component, the policies enterprises adopted on hedging foreign-currency exposure, and foreign currency–denominated receipts and payments expected from trade in goods and services in the following year (i.e., in the 12 months to end-June 2002).

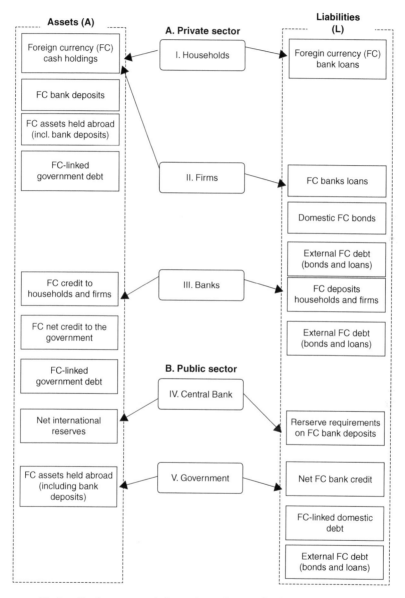

Fig 2: Foreign currency balance sheet of a partially dollarized economy
Source: Reinhart, Rogoff, and Savastano (2003a).

Table 6: Australia: Foreign-Currency Exposure by Financial Sector, End-June 2001 (Billions of Australian Dollars)

Instrument	Banks	RBA and CBAs	Other Financial Corporations	General Government	Other Resident Sectors	Total All Sectors
Foreign currency–denominated financial debt assets	−69.8	−36.9	−33.6	−5.5	−10.6	−156.5
Foreign currency–denominated debt liabilities	186.5	8.8	61.4	4.1	60.1	321.0
equals						
Net debt position	116.7	−28.1	27.8	−1.4	49.5	164.5
Principal of foreign currency—derivative contracts in a bought position	−435.3	−11.3	−69.8	−0.4	−31.7	−548.4
Principal of foreign currency—derivative contracts in a sold position	325.8	32.1	61.8	8.9	34.9	463.4
equals						
Net debt position unhedged after derivatives	7.2	−7.4	19.8	7.2	52.6	79.5
Foreign-equity assets	−30.7	0.0	−84.0	0.0	−113.9	−228.5
equals						
Foreign-currency exposure	−23.4	−7.4	−64.1	7.2	−61.2	−149.0

RBA = Reserve Bank of Australia
CBAs = State and Territory Central Borrowing Authorities
Source: ABS (2001).

Several results in Table 6 are worth highlighting. The general government sector was the only one with a net foreign currency liability exposure, after accounting for hedging activities and foreign-equity positions; its net foreign currency liability position was A$7.2 billion. Although the "banks" subsector had considerably larger foreign currency–denominated financial debt liabilities (A$186.5 billion) than its foreign currency–denominated financial assets

Table 7: Thailand: Intersectoral Asset and Liability Position, End-December 1996 (Millions of Dollars)

	Holder of the Liability (Creditor)				
Issuer of the Liability (Debtor)	General Government and Bank of Thailand	Commercial Banks	Nonbank Sector	Rest of the World	Total
General government and central bank					
(Bank of Thailand)					
Domestic currency		2,394	11,885		14,279
Total other liabilities		5,555		5,152	10,707
Short term		3,616[a]		34	3,650
Medium and long term		1,939[a]		5,118	7,057
Commercial banks					
(including BIBFs)					
Total liabilities	10,327		139,299	48,790	198,417
Deposits and other					
short term:	9,366		131,866	28,858	170,090
In foreign currency			448	28,189	28,637
In domestic currency	9,366		131,417	669	141,453
Medium and long term:	961		7,434[a]	19,932	28,327
Equity (capital)					23,439
Nonbank sector					
Total liabilities		206,715		61,701	268,416
Short term:		555[a]		18,831[b]	18,831
Medium and long term		31,542[b]		42,870[b]	42,870
Equity (capital)				4,745	136,252
Rest of the world[b]					
Total liabilities	38,694	7,029			45,723
Currency and short term	38,694	2,580			41,274
Medium and long term		4,449			4,449
Equity			481		

BIBFs = Bangkok International Banking Facilities
a. In domestic currency.
b. In foreign currency.
Source: Allen et al. (2002).

(A$69.8 billion), its hedging activities in the derivatives markets plus a sizable foreign-equity asset position turned its total foreign-currency exposure into an A$23.4 billion net asset position. Summing the sectoral exposures, Australian resident enterprises had an aggregate net foreign-currency asset position of A$149 billion.

The Australian sectoral balance sheet drives home the point that in countries where residents are widely using derivatives markets to hedge foreign exchange exposures, it is highly desirable to try and obtain information on those hedging activities to measure currency mismatch.[8] The Australian example likewise illustrates the valuable information that can be retrieved from surveys on foreign exchange exposure (including exposure in the nonbank and government sectors), if more governments were prepared to conduct them.

Table 7, taken from Allen *et al.* (2002), provides a picture of sectoral asset and liability positions in Thailand just before its 1997 crisis (end of December 1996). While short-term liabilities to the rest of the world were very small ($34 million) in the government sector, short-term liabilities in foreign currency were huge for commercial banks (almost $29 billion) and the nonbank sector (almost $19 billion). Thailand's aggregate short-term foreign-currency debt was therefore on the order of $48 billion. On the asset side, the monetary authorities — the Bank of Thailand (BOT) — held roughly $39 billion in foreign reserve assets, although the BOT already had some forward and swap obligations not shown in its balance sheet. Table 7 also shows that the banking system's foreign assets were just over $7 billion. Allen *et al.* (2002) estimate that of the $207 billion in claims of the commercial banking system on the domestic nonbank sector, about $32 billion was denominated in foreign currency. In the end, these sectoral balance sheets permit Allen *et al.* (2002) to draw the following conclusions about Thailand's currency mismatch: In December 1996, there was a roughly $10-billion financing gap between the government's foreign reserves and the country's total external foreign-currency liabilities falling due in the short term; the maturity and currency mismatches of commercial banks vis-à-vis nonresidents were enormous (on the order of $26 billion if none of the short-term liabilities was rolled over); and nonbank

---

[8]The ABS (2001) study also includes a detailed breakdown of derivative contracts by type (i.e., forwards, interest rate swaps, futures, and currency options) and by sector, as well as a disaggregation of hedging activities by instrument (i.e., foreign-equity assets, debt liabilities, and fixed-income assets).

corporations and households had perhaps even larger mismatches than the commercial banks. The sectoral analysis also shows that currency risk was essentially being passed on from the commercial banks to the nonbank sector; since the latter had relatively little foreign currency–denominated revenue, the large devaluation that subsequently occurred was sure to generate large-scale insolvencies in the nonbank sector and ultimately sizable loan delinquencies and a systemic banking crisis.

NEW MEASURE OF AGGREGATE EFFECTIVE CURRENCY MISMATCH

At the aggregate level, a rough but nonetheless useful measure of aggregate effective currency mismatch (AECM) can be constructed using the international banking statistics of the Bank for International Settlements (BIS), the IMF's data on the international liquidity position of the monetary authorities and on the claims and liabilities of financial institutions, and some estimates of the currency composition of the total bond and banking markets. The main purpose of such a measure is to provide a shorthand stress test of the consequences for the domestic economy of an aggregate currency mismatch — *if* there were a large depreciation of the local currency. Our AECM measure has three components: net foreign-currency assets, exports (or imports) of goods and services, and the foreign-currency share of total debt.

Specifically, net foreign-currency assets (NFCA) are defined as follows:

$$\text{NFCA} = \text{NFAMABK} + \text{NBKA\$} - \text{NBKL\$} - \text{IB\$} \quad (1)$$

where NFAMABK is net foreign assets of the monetary authorities and deposit money banks, from line 31 of the monetary survey in the IMF's *International Financial Statistics*; NBKA$ is foreign-currency assets of non-banks (cross-border) held with BIS reporting banks; NBKL$ is foreign-currency liabilities of nonbanks (cross-border) to BIS reporting banks; and IB$ is international debt securities (bonds) outstanding, denominated in foreign currency.

Note that NFCA can be either negative (denoting a net liability position in foreign exchange) or positive (denoting a net asset position in foreign currency); a smaller negative figure for NFCA therefore denotes a smaller currency mismatch. When NFCA is negative (positive), a depreciation of the local currency will decrease (increase) net worth. In this book, we are mainly interested in crisis vulnerability, so we concentrate most of our attention on emerging economies with a negative foreign-currency mismatch.

Whereas data on nonbank exposures and international debt securities are collected by currency denomination, those on net foreign assets (as consolidated in the Fund's monetary survey) are not. As such, one has to assume that both foreign assets and liabilities are denominated exclusively in foreign currency; this will tend to overstate foreign-currency liabilities for those few emerging economies with relatively low shares of foreign currency in external liabilities (e.g., the Czech Republic, Poland, and South Africa). A second shortcoming of the data is the limited coverage of the foreign assets of corporations and households. The BIS statistics pick up some assets held with banks abroad, but there are reasons to expect that foreign-currency assets held abroad by corporations and households exceed those figures.

Next, the foreign-currency share of total debt (FC%TD) is written as follows:

$$\text{FC\%TD} = \frac{\text{NBKL\$} + \text{BKL\$} + \text{DCP\$} + \text{IB\$} + \text{DB\$}}{\text{NBKL} + \text{BKL} + \text{DCP} + \text{IB} + \text{DB}} \qquad (2)$$

Here, the suffix "$" refers to debt denominated in foreign currency, and NBKL is liabilities of nonbanks (cross-border) to BIS reporting banks, in all currencies; BKL is liabilities of banks (cross-border) to BIS reporting banks, in all currencies; DCP is domestic credit to the private sector, as reported in line 32 of the monetary survey in the IMF's *International Financial Statistics*; IB is international debt securities (bonds) outstanding, in all currencies; and DB is domestic debt securities (bonds) outstanding, in all currencies.

In the baseline calculations, all domestic bonds and domestic bank loans (domestic credit) are assumed to be denominated in domestic currency — that is, (DB$/DB) and (DCP$/DCP) = 0. FC%TD must fall between zero and plus one.

Finally, let us denote the country's exports and imports of goods and services as XGS and MGS, respectively. These trade variables are a proxy for the response of net-interest income flows to a change in the exchange rate and for the country's ability to service foreign-currency debts.

These elements can be combined to construct an overall currency mismatch variable. Since we have not proposed a formal model of mismatch, the choice of a specific functional form is to some extent arbitrary, in particular the weights attached to each element. One possibility is simply to multiply the elements (NFCA, FC%TD, XGS, and MGS). Accordingly, we define the AECM measure as follows:

$$AECM = (NFCA/XGS)(FC\%TD); AECM < 0 \qquad (3a)$$

Equation (3a) says that an emerging economy's (negative) AECM will be lower if its export receipts are higher and the share of foreign currency in total debt financing is lower. Observe also that equation (3a) is equivalent to expressing the effective mismatch as the product of the ratio of net foreign-currency assets to GDP, the ratio of GDP to exports, and the foreign-currency share of total debt, and is written as

$$AECM = (NFCA/GDP)(GDP/XGS)(FC\%TD) \qquad (4)$$

Equation (4) makes it clear that higher export openness (i.e., a low value for GDP/XGS) lowers the effective mismatch.

While equations (3a) and (4) are appropriate where the economy has a net liability position in foreign currency (AECM < 0), they need to be modified slightly when the economy has a net asset position (AECM > 0). When there is a net liability position, an exchange rate depreciation induces a negative "balance-sheet effect" (net worth falls) and a positive "competitive effect" (exports rise and imports fall); in other words, the competitive effect offsets the balance-sheet effect and makes the effective mismatch smaller. In contrast, when there is a net asset position in foreign currency, the balance-sheet effect (net worth rises) and the competitive effect (exports rise and imports fall) go in the same direction — that is, the competitive effect reinforces the balance-sheet effect and makes the mismatch larger. Replacing exports in equation (3a) with imports when AECM is positive recognizes the different implications of exports and imports for foreign exchange availability and allows an exchange rate- induced fall in imports to make the mismatch larger;[9] as such, when AECM is positive, the expression is written as

$$AECM = (NFCA/MGS)(FC\%TD); AECM > 0 \qquad (3b)$$

Tables 8 to 11 show for a group of emerging economies over the 1993–2002 period key components of the AECM, the effective mismatch indicator itself,

---

[9]This is in the same spirit of using the ratio of external debt to exports to track external debt sustainability, while using the ratio of international reserves to imports to track reserve adequacy.

Table 8: Net Foreign-Currency Assets, 1994–2002 (Billions of Dollars)

Region/country	1994	1995	1996	1997	1998	1999	2000	2001	2002
Latin America[a]	−43.6	−51.1	−66.3	−85.5	−120.5	−131.7	−128.2	−169.8	−182.4
Argentina	−16.7	−24.6	−30.9	−41.2	−54.2	−62.6	−70.4	−103.9	−99.9
Brazil	4.0	6.6	−1.9	−25.4	−40.4	−47.1	−49.1	−64.2	−75.6
Chile	3.7	4.9	5.2	2.0	−0.3	1.3	0.5	−3.8	−6.6
Colombia	3.4	1.0	−1.4	−2.7	−4.4	−4.1	−3.0	−3.5	−4.4
Mexico	−54.2	−57.2	−63.9	−45.4	−46.3	−43.8	−34.6	−18.2	−19.4
Peru	7.0	6.6	8.4	6.8	6.1	6.2	7.9	8.1	8.3
Venezuela	9.2	11.6	18.3	20.4	18.8	18.3	20.4	15.6	15.3
Asia, large economies[a]	139.0	146.9	157.6	185.6	250.0	348.0	442.9	559.6	671.7
China	35.5	52.0	84.5	137.0	155.7	181.5	226.5	304.4	373.5
India	11.4	9.8	12.0	13.7	17.0	22.5	28.4	39.0	60.8
Korea	−3.2	−10.7	−36.8	−58.4	−23.9	16.4	45.0	52.8	46.7
Taiwan	95.3	95.9	97.9	93.3	101.3	127.6	143.0	163.3	190.7
Other Asia[a]	1.2	−13.1	−32.2	−78.0	−37.7	−5.3	5.3	20.1	28.4
Indonesia	−13.5	−14.0	−14.5	−27.8	−19.8	−11.5	−4.7	2.1	8.3
Malaysia	17.1	14.3	9.6	−4.5	8.9	16.1	13.3	12.9	7.9
Philippines	3.4	1.9	−3.8	−12.2	−9.1	−9.3	−11.6	−12.8	−14.6
Thailand	−5.8	−15.2	−23.5	−33.4	−17.8	−0.6	8.3	17.9	26.8
Central Europe[a]	0.7	16.8	18.6	18.2	25.4	28.4	31.4	39.5	39.4
Czech Republic	4.1	8.2	7.4	6.7	10.8	14.0	14.4	18.0	25.1
Hungary	−9.5	−6.2	−6.4	−6.8	−6.2	−4.9	−5.0	−2.3	−4.6
Poland	6.1	14.9	17.6	18.3	20.8	19.4	22.0	23.8	18.9
Russia	13.9	11.1	3.6	−15.0	−34.3	−21.4	1.4	11.0	16.4
Israel	6.0	6.4	9.3	13.6	16.4	15.4	15.9	14.3	14.1
Turkey	−12.3	−10.3	−11.5	−15.0	−19.0	−19.6	−37.2	−39.4	−46.2
South Africa	−10.6	−10.8	−13.4	−11.4	−12.4	−6.1	−5.8	−2.6	3.2

a. Sum of the countries shown.
Note: Net foreign-currency assets equal net foreign assets of the monetary authorities and deposit money banks, from line 31 of the monetary survey in the IMF's *International Financial Statistics* plus foreign-currency assets of nonbanks (cross-border) held with BIS reporting banks minus foreign-currency liabilities of nonbanks (cross-border) to BIS reporting banks plus international debt securities (bonds) outstanding, denominated in foreign currency; outstanding year-end positions shown.
Sources: IMF's *International Financial Statistics,* national sources, and Bank for International Settlements.

Table 9: Foreign-Currency Share of Total Debt, 1994–2002 (Percent)

Region/country	1994	1995	1996	1997	1998	1999	2000	2001	2002
Latin America[a]	22.9	25.3	26.9	26.8	25.6	29.3	29.2	28.7	32.9
Argentina	32.9	36.4	40.2	41.4	43.2	44.7	46.2	49.2	58.9
Brazil	15.1	15.8	16.6	17.1	14.3	18.4	19.6	19.0	23.7
Chile	17.8	17.3	18.7	22.8	23.3	23.7	22.7	24.4	26.8
Colombia	34.7	34.2	36.1	36.3	36.0	35.9	33.0	33.8	34.5
Mexico	26.8	39.4	46.3	40.5	44.4	40.1	37.0	33.9	33.8
Peru	38.6	40.5	44.0	38.7	34.5	29.2	26.3	23.1	24.6
Venezuela	44.6	38.7	44.5	47.4	48.3	48.4	41.6	38.4	47.9
Asia, large economies[a]	10.2	10.6	11.4	12.1	9.0	7.3	6.2	5.5	4.8
China	10.6	9.6	9.0	8.3	6.5	4.8	3.8	3.1	2.1
India	7.5	8.1	8.3	9.2	8.7	7.4	6.3	5.1	4.6
Korea	16.0	18.1	21.9	31.5	19.3	15.9	14.3	12.9	11.5
Taiwan	5.0	4.7	4.5	4.8	4.6	3.9	3.1	4.0	5.5
Other Asia[a]	23.2	26.0	26.1	31.9	25.9	22.8	22.2	20.9	19.8
Indonesia	33.0	32.6	32.9	46.7	42.9	33.1	32.0	28.9	22.5
Malaysia	13.9	13.8	14.6	19.8	17.7	16.9	15.8	15.9	18.2
Philippines	12.4	13.4	17.7	25.3	26.1	29.1	31.9	33.0	35.2
Thailand	26.4	32.8	32.5	35.2	23.3	18.8	17.9	15.7	12.7
Central Europe[a]	19.2	19.6	18.0	19.5	19.2	20.1	19.8	18.0	16.9
Czech Republic	11.5	13.7	14.2	16.8	14.2	13.5	13.5	15.1	13.0
Hungary	30.2	33.8	31.8	32.5	34.5	37.2	34.9	31.8	25.1
Poland	11.8	10.6	8.9	11.3	12.0	13.3	14.6	12.4	13.9
Russia	35.3	26.7	22.1	22.1	47.2	42.1	37.0	34.1	35.5
Israel	3.1	3.4	3.6	4.9	5.5	7.1	7.3	8.5	9.0
Turkey	40.6	35.6	33.0	33.5	31.2	31.2	31.4	24.6	22.9
South Africa	7.2	8.5	10.6	9.8	10.2	9.2	10.4	16.1	13.0

a. Calculated with aggregates of countries shown.
Note: See definition of foreign-currency share of total debt on page 462.
Sources: IMF's *International Financial Statistics*, national sources, and Bank for International Settlements.

Table 10: Original AECM Estimates, 1994–2002 (Assuming Zero Foreign-Currency Share of Domestic Debt)

Region/Country	1994	1995	1996	1997	1998	1999	2000	2001	2002	Foreign-Currency Share of Total Debt (2002)
Latin America										
Argentina	−28.40	−35.79	−43.80	−55.14	−75.09	−100.37	−104.42	−164.91	−207.88	58.30
Brazil	1.22	1.57	−0.60	−7.14	−9.87	−15.72	−14.99	−18.19	−25.14	23.70
Chile	4.56	4.52	4.45	1.86	−0.39	1.58	0.53	−3.99	−7.86	26.77
Colombia	7.07	1.76	−3.54	−6.20	−10.65	−9.37	−5.45	−6.96	−9.64	34.46
Mexico	−20.56	−25.90	−27.67	−15.14	−15.91	−11.90	−7.11	−3.60	−3.80	33.83
Peru	37.42	27.37	36.61	24.02	20.00	20.57	21.69	20.09	21.15	24.51
Venezuela	31.64	26.50	54.12	50.06	44.95	52.55	42.91	27.24	43.30	47.88
Asia, large economies										
China	3.37	3.70	4.95	6.95	6.16	4.59	3.48	3.48	2.42	2.10
India	2.56	1.77	2.21	2.49	2.71	2.69	2.61	2.93	3.84	4.56
Korea	−0.45	−1.31	−5.26	−11.09	−2.93	1.81	3.34	3.98	2.93	11.54
Taiwan	4.66	3.71	3.56	3.37	3.77	3.82	2.75	5.14	8.00	5.47
Other Asia										
Indonesia	−9.53	−8.61	−8.13	−21.57	−16.80	−7.65	−2.33	1.30	3.91	22.50
Malaysia	3.51	2.27	1.54	−0.96	2.34	3.57	2.23	2.39	1.56	18.18
Philippines	1.64	0.78	−1.98	−7.68	−6.95	−6.89	−8.80	−12.09	−13.42	35.15
Thailand	−2.71	−7.11	−10.68	−16.24	−6.29	−0.16	2.09	4.08	4.68	12.70

(*Continued*)

Table 10: (Continued)

Region/Country	1994	1995	1996	1997	1998	1999	2000	2001	2002	Foreign-Currency Share of Total Debt (2002)
Central Europe										
Czech Republic	2.16	3.68	3.09	3.39	4.50	5.56	5.17	6.46	6.97	13.02
Hungary	−23.78	−10.65	−9.33	−8.75	−7.29	−5.87	−5.01	−1.90	−2.69	25.08
Poland	3.37	5.37	4.24	4.82	4.71	5.11	5.61	5.06	4.23	13.94
Russia	7.57	3.60	0.93	−3.23	−18.97	−10.58	0.80	5.16	7.07	35.46
Israel	0.51	0.54	0.77	1.59	2.24	2.40	2.22	2.51	2.66	8.98
Turkey	−17.91	−10.83	−9.68	−10.75	−12.17	−14.25	−24.37	−19.76	−20.17	22.87
South Africa	−2.55	−2.64	−4.00	−3.08	−3.70	−1.65	−1.65	−1.20	1.33	13.05

AECM = aggregate effective currency mismatch
Source: Authors' calculations.

Table 11: Modified AECM Estimates, 1994–2002 (Assuming Nonzero Foreign-Currency Share of Domestic Debt)

Region/Country	1994	1995	1996	1997	1998	1999	2000	2001	2002	Foreign-Currency Share of Total Debt (2002)
Latin America										
Argentina	−69.74	−79.97	−89.64	−108.73	−143.77	−186.56	−189.33	−282.38	−309.58	87.71
Brazil	1.79	2.38	−0.90	−10.73	−15.72	−23.05	−21.44	−26.15	−32.84	30.95
Chile	7.05	7.08	6.74	2.61	−0.54	2.18	0.74	−5.45	−10.39	35.37
Colombia	8.65	2.16	−4.27	−7.44	−12.81	−11.20	−6.60	−8.36	−11.50	41.12
Mexico	−32.48	−34.32	−33.54	−18.91	−19.22	−14.56	−8.74	−4.50	−4.77	42.50
Peru	80.62	56.25	69.84	51.62	47.72	56.11	64.06	66.07	65.51	76.23
Venezuela	31.74	26.62	54.29	50.20	45.08	52.68	43.03	27.33	43.39	47.97
Asia, large economies										
China	4.88	5.52	7.55	10.87	10.61	9.03	7.65	8.71	8.08	7.01
India	2.56	1.77	2.21	2.49	2.71	2.69	2.61	2.93	3.84	4.56
Korea	−0.57	−1.59	−6.16	−12.36	−3.50	2.29	4.37	5.35	4.07	16.02
Taiwan	4.66	3.71	3.56	3.37	3.77	3.82	2.75	5.14	8.00	5.47
Other Asia										
Indonesia	−17.08	−15.49	−14.56	−30.92	−25.31	−13.61	−4.24	2.54	9.13	52.53
Malaysia	3.62	2.34	1.59	−0.98	2.39	3.65	2.29	2.45	1.60	18.59
Philippines	1.64	0.78	−1.98	−7.68	−6.95	−6.89	−8.80	−12.09	−13.42	35.15
Thailand	−3.73	−9.06	−13.65	−20.31	−8.95	−0.25	3.21	6.53	8.14	22.07

(*Continued*)

Table 11: (Continued)

Region/Country	1994	1995	1996	1997	1998	1999	2000	2001	2002	Foreign-Currency Share of Total Debt (2002)
Central Europe										
Czech Republic	5.32	7.68	6.36	6.17	8.39	10.03	9.30	10.86	11.30	21.12
Hungary	−37.77	−15.86	−13.85	−12.81	−10.31	−7.82	−6.80	−2.68	−4.13	38.46
Poland	6.60	11.05	9.89	9.84	9.37	9.58	9.83	9.44	7.30	24.07
Russia	7.81	3.98	1.13	−4.06	−19.61	−11.07	0.84	5.38	7.38	37.04
Israel	2.28	2.23	3.13	5.03	6.52	6.15	5.74	6.00	6.01	20.30
Turkey	−26.52	−17.33	−16.21	−17.73	−21.05	−24.38	−41.70	−38.38	−41.32	46.84
South Africa	−3.01	−3.05	−4.53	−3.53	−4.25	−1.93	−1.89	−1.31	1.49	14.63

AECM = aggregate effective currency mismatch
Source: Authors' calculations.

and a modified version of the effective mismatch indicator that takes account both of the (estimated) share of foreign currency in domestic bank loans to the private sector and of the share of exchange rate-linked instruments in domestic public debt.[10] For purposes of comparison, Table 13 provides Eichengreen, Hausmann, and Panizza's (2002) calculations of original sin ratios for the same countries.

A reassuring feature of the estimates of net foreign-currency assets, shown in Table 8, is how large negative currency mismatches either lead or are contemporaneous with currency and banking crises in this group of emerging economies. In this connection, we draw attention to the large negative net foreign-currency positions in Mexico in 1994–96, the Asian-crisis countries (Korea, Indonesia, Malaysia, the Philippines, and Thailand) in 1997–98, Russia in 1998, Argentina in 2001–02, Brazil in 2002, and Turkey in 2000–02. In terms of dollar values, the largest negative net foreign-currency position by far was Argentina's imbalance in 2001–02 (at around $100 billion); next in line were Brazil ($76 billion), Mexico ($64 billion), Korea ($58 billion), Turkey ($46 billion), Russia ($34 billion), Thailand ($33 billion), and Indonesia ($28 billion). It is also evident from Table 8 that some emerging economies have had positive net foreign-currency positions consistently over the past decade and that some others — including all the Asian-crisis countries except for the Philippines — have turned negative net foreign-currency positions into positive ones. In 2002, China and Taiwan were the economies with the largest positive net foreign-currency positions (at $373 billion and $191 billion, respectively).

Table 9 gives our (baseline) estimates of the foreign-currency share of total debt, under the assumption that both domestic bank loans and domestic bonds are exclusively denominated in domestic currency. Several observations are in order. To begin with, the foreign-currency share of the total debt market is much lower virtually everywhere than the foreign-currency share of cross-border bank loans and international bonds (as represented, say, in original sin ratios). For the larger Asian emerging economies taken as a group (China, India, Korea, and Taiwan), the foreign-currency share of the total debt market is estimated to be less than 5 percent (in 2002). The second observation is that

---

[10] The time-series behavior of the export openness ratio is not shown, as it was presented earlier in Table 2.

the foreign-currency share is much higher in Latin America than in the other emerging-market regions. Foreign-currency shares vary considerably within regional groups with, for example, Argentina's estimated foreign-currency share being higher than others in Latin America; the same could be said of Russia among European emerging economies and of the Philippines among the former Asian-crisis economies. As regards trends over time, Table 9 suggests that the foreign-currency share has risen moderately (over the 1994–2002 period) in Latin America, fallen sharply in larger Asian emerging economies, and fallen less markedly in both the former Asian-crisis countries and Central Europe. Foreign-currency shares have increased notably in Argentina, Brazil, Chile, and the Philippines.

Table 10 presents the baseline AECM estimates. Since our estimates of the AECM "normalize" the nominal net foreign-currency asset positions for variations in both export openness and the foreign-currency share of total debt, they invite time-series and cross-country comparisons of currency mismatch. Going back again to the most prominent crisis episodes within our sample group, we observe that the size of the estimated currency mismatch is typically larger in the run-up to and especially during the crisis; again, see Mexico in 1994–96; Korea, Indonesia, Malaysia, the Philippines, and Thailand in 1996–98; Russia in 1997–99; Argentina in 1999–2002; Brazil in 2001–02; and Turkey in 2000–02. Comparing across crisis episodes, the effective mismatch in the recent Argentine crisis was by a factor of ten the largest one is our sample. Argentina's effective currency mismatch in 2001–02 was huge because the size of the net foreign-currency mismatch itself was so big relative to the size of the economy, because the foreign-currency share of total debt was significantly higher in Argentina than in other crisis episodes, and because its degree of export openness was low (particularly before 2002) relative to that in most other crises.[11] But the estimates in Table 10 actually *understate* the size of the effective mismatch in Argentina in 2001–02 because

---

[11] In some preliminary regression analysis, we found that, ceteris paribus, the *lower* the country's export openness, the higher the foreign-currency share of total debt. This is the opposite of what one would expect to find if there were good risk assessment in place. It is also opposite to what has been found in firm-level studies where firms that export tend to have a higher share of foreign-currency debt. This negative correlation between the foreign-currency share of debt and export openness is suggestive of economywide distortions (perhaps related to the currency regime and/or the official safety net) that create the wrong incentives for hedging currency risk.

the actual foreign-currency share of total debt is even higher than indicated by the estimates in the table. The next largest effective currency mismatches were those for the Mexican crisis, the Brazilian crisis (2002), and the Turkish crisis (2000) — all estimated to be roughly the same order of magnitude. Interestingly enough, effective currency mismatches during the Asian financial crisis are judged to have been significantly smaller (except in the case of Indonesia) — reflecting those countries' high export openness and relatively low foreign-currency share of total debt.[12] Korea's effective currency mismatch in 1997, for example, is estimated at less than half the size of those during the Mexican, Brazilian, and Turkish crises. In 2002, the largest effective currency mismatch was in Argentina, followed in descending order by Brazil, Turkey, and the Philippines.

In Table 11, we revise our AECM estimates to reflect that domestic bank loans and domestic bonds are *not* exclusively denominated in domestic currency in all emerging economies. To get a fix on the share of foreign currency in domestic bank loans going to the private sector, we relied primarily on the estimates given in Reinhart, Rogoff, and Savastano (2003a); for those emerging economies not represented in that paper, we drew on the database in Arteta (2002, 2003). For China, Nicholas Lardy provided us with an estimate of the share of bank loans denominated in foreign currency which he put together from national sources. The five emerging economies in our sample with the highest share of foreign currency in domestic bank loans (1994–99 average) were Peru, Argentina, Turkey, Indonesia, and Hungary; among the economies with very low shares were Brazil, India, Taiwan, the Philippines, Venezuela, Malaysia, China, and Korea. To capture the share of foreign currency-linked instruments in domestic government debt, we again leaned on the estimates in Reinhart, Rogoff, and Savastano (2003a). Unfortunately, their estimates cover only 10 of the countries in our sample; still, the countries covered are generally considered to be the ones with the highest shares of linked debt. Where data on exchange rate-linked domestic public debt were missing, we assumed as a first approximation that the foreign-currency share was zero. The five emerging

---

[12] In contrast, ratios of short-term external debt to reserves would suggest that the aggregate mismatch in some Asian-crisis countries (Korea) in 1997 was larger than recent mismatches in Latin America; this reflects, inter alia, the different nature of the two mismatch indicators, with short-term debt to reserves signaling near-term liquidity strains and the AECM signaling the severity of crises (contingent on a large change in the exchange rate).

economies with the highest shares of exchange rate-linked domestic public debt were Argentina, Peru, Turkey, Brazil, and Russia; those with relatively low shares were China, Thailand, Venezuela, India, Korea, Malaysia, and South Africa.

As expected, the recognition of foreign-currency debt into both domestic credit and domestic bonds serves to increase our estimates of both the foreign-currency share of total debt and the size of the AECM — compare the entries in Table 11 with those in Tables 9 and 10. What is perhaps most interesting is the diversity of changes across countries from this modification in assumptions about the currency composition of domestic (bank and bond) debt. In three emerging economies (Argentina, Peru, and Indonesia), the new assumptions produce a new foreign-currency share of total debt that is equal to 50 percent or higher; indeed, in Argentina and Peru, that share rises to 88 and 76 percent, respectively, while in Indonesia it increases to 52 percent. With much higher foreign-currency shares, the AECM rises as well: in Argentina, the (peak) AECM climbs (in 2002) from 208 to 310 percent of exports, while in Indonesia, the (peak) AECM in 1998 advances from 17 to 25 percent of exports. The change in assumptions also has large consequences for Turkey: the foreign-currency share of total debt increases from 23 to 47 percent, and the (peak) AECM almost doubles in 2000 from 24 to 42 percent of exports. In sharp contrast, the change in assumptions produces very small changes in foreign-currency shares and AECMs in India, Korea, Malaysia, Taiwan, Venezuela, the Philippines, Russia, and South Africa. In the middle of the pack lie Brazil, Mexico, Chile, Hungary, and Thailand, where the rise in peak AECMs is moderate. And finally, in China, the Czech Republic, Poland, and Israel, the increases in foreign-currency shares and AECMs are large but start from a rather low level; these are also economies that have consistently run positive net foreign-currency positions over the 1994–2002 period.

MODIFICATION OF AECM

The estimates in Tables 10 and 11 represent in our view a significant improvement over what has been available heretofore on aggregate currency mismatch; nevertheless, our estimates of AECM should be regarded as only a "first pass" at what could be accomplished. They are based on data that are available for all larger countries, from IMF and BIS sources. National data sources will often be richer. In this connection, several alternative formulations of the AECM could be explored further, four of which are mentioned next.

First, we could attempt to incorporate cross-country and time-series variation in *leverage ratios* into our mismatch indicator. A more general equilibrium treatment of the sensitivity of net worth and net income to a change in the exchange rate would take on board the possibility that the shock causing the exchange rate to change (depreciate) might simultaneously affect (increase) the cost of borrowing. Similarly, the authorities might react to an exchange rate depreciation by increasing interest rates. In both cases, a high degree of leverage would alter the effects of a change in the exchange rate. One would also expect that, ceteris paribus, the larger the total debt relative to the size of the economy, the larger the effect of a currency mismatch in debt markets. Table 12 shows the ratio of total debt to GDP for our sample of emerging economies. It is evident that this debt ratio varies significantly across countries and within countries over time. In some initial experiments, we allowed the ratio of total debt to GDP to increase the mismatch indicator. The main results can be inferred from Table 12. On a regional level, the relatively high leverage in Asian emerging economies tended to increase their AECMs vis-à-vis less-leveraged economies in Latin America, offsetting to some extent regional differences in mismatches attributable to differences in export openness. In Argentina, which has quite a low ratio of total debt to GDP, the leverage adjustment narrowed the gap between the peak mismatch and the rest of the field — for example, the leverage adjustment considerably raised Thailand's peak AECM (in 1997) and also those for Korea (in 1997) and Brazil (in 2000–02). In contrast, Russia's relatively low leverage ratio reduced its peak AECM. In Turkey, the increase in the total debt ratio over the 1994–2001 period contributed to the large aggregate currency mismatch in 2000–01. The pattern of aggregate effective mismatches increasing markedly remained in the run-up to and during financial crises.

Second, instead of using the *stocks* of bank loans and bonds as weights to derive the foreign-currency share of total debt, one could use financing *flows* to weight the various currency shares. This carries some attraction since the stocks of debt can sometimes produce a misleading impression of current financing opportunities — for example, when the domestic banking system is experiencing serious problems, new financing from banks may be close to zero or negative, even if the stock of bank loans outstanding is very large. Some

Table 12: Total Debt as a Percent of GDP, 1994–2002

Region/country	1994	1995	1996	1997	1998	1999	2000	2001	2002
Latin America[a]	**73.0**	**67.9**	**71.0**	**75.1**	**83.8**	**83.7**	**78.2**	**86.5**	**86.7**
Argentina	49.8	51.8	57.1	64.9	73.6	81.3	84.5	90.8	183.0
Brazil	84.3	75.7	84.2	91.7	110.4	118.3	107.6	136.2	118.2
Chile	124.3	115.3	115.3	124.9	130.6	139.4	142.1	155.1	162.4
Colombia	33.7	35.9	44.4	46.1	56.1	62.2	66.9	77.0	74.7
Mexico	81.6	78.2	64.5	61.9	56.5	56.7	50.3	50.6	51.6
Peru	17.4	19.1	21.0	29.4	33.6	41.2	40.1	41.5	39.3
Venezuela	58.3	44.4	38.4	35.8	36.7	36.9	35.4	40.3	50.5
Asia, large economies[a]	**114.0**	**110.8**	**117.3**	**112.6**	**146.3**	**150.9**	**150.4**	**159.1**	**181.7**
China	111.0	108.9	115.7	127.8	148.0	161.9	168.4	172.9	205.6
India	70.7	63.7	70.4	64.8	70.0	76.3	78.8	83.2	91.2
Korea	108.9	108.5	113.6	84.0	181.7	163.7	151.9	176.7	201.6
Taiwan	186.5	184.9	194.0	181.0	218.5	211.0	193.5	205.4	206.0
Other Asia[a]	**104.9**	**108.8**	**118.3**	**101.7**	**172.8**	**147.3**	**133.2**	**138.8**	**136.9**
Indonesia	66.6	67.7	71.7	55.7	119.8	92.8	78.0	76.2	75.5
Malaysia	168.6	176.3	199.8	172.2	238.3	225.0	220.9	238.4	236.7
Philippines	100.7	97.8	113.0	102.4	128.9	118.3	112.3	119.4	116.7
Thailand	120.7	127.3	133.6	120.4	201.3	177.7	150.7	153.7	158.4
Central Europe[a]	**90.0**	**81.6**	**77.5**	**75.8**	**83.5**	**81.9**	**81.9**	**86.4**	**98.5**
Czech Republic	94.0	96.2	91.5	91.8	109.9	107.3	108.2	104.3	114.9
Hungary	154.3	141.3	137.3	123.9	131.2	121.5	122.4	123.4	136.7
Poland	61.3	54.9	53.1	54.6	59.8	60.6	62.2	70.3	79.2
Russia	24.1	32.7	38.1	49.4	36.8	49.3	38.7	35.9	39.6
Israel	203.9	187.0	188.9	183.0	175.9	192.2	184.3	194.1	213.7
Turkey	50.9	50.1	56.2	60.3	69.9	84.5	98.7	150.3	134.1
South Africa	136.5	129.6	119.2	123.2	128.6	133.6	121.3	99.7	148.7

a. Calculated with aggregates of countries shown.
Note: Total debt is equal to liabilities of nonbanks (cross-border) to BIS reporting banks, in all currencies, plus international debt securities (bonds) outstanding, in all currencies, plus domestic debt securities (bonds) outstanding, in all currencies, plus domestic credit to the private sector, as reported in line 32 of the monetary survey in the IMF's *International Financial Statistics*. Outstanding year-end positions shown.
Sources: IMF's *International Financial Statistics*, national sources, and Bank for International Settlements.

simulations were done along these lines using the individual-country data on bond issues and new bank loans. More often than not (at least for the 1997–2002 period), the flow weights tended to produce somewhat lower foreign-currency shares of total debt and hence lower AECMs, but a disadvantage of the flow formulation was that the flows varied so much from year to year that they produced high (time-series) variability in the foreign-currency share of total debt — at least for those emerging economies where the foreign-currency share was quite different across the various financing components. Perhaps some combination of stock and flow weights may ultimately prove to be useful.

Yet a third scenario would employ a different weighting scheme (as between exports and GDP) to scale net foreign-currency assets. In this connection, it could be argued that for larger emerging economies, exports underestimate the share of tradables in GDP, and therefore a somewhat broader scaling variable would be appropriate to capture the sensitivity of noninterest flows to a change in the exchange rate. To cite one possibility, net foreign-currency assets could be scaled by giving exports a weight of two-thirds and GDP a weight of one-third.

Fourth, one could attempt to get a more comprehensive measure of foreign-currency assets and liabilities than is available from our definition of net foreign-currency assets in equation (1). For some emerging economies, debt owed to BIS reporting banks is significantly lower than total debt owed to foreigners; similarly, there are other foreign-currency debt flows, such as trade credit extended by nonfinancial corporations, that are not fully covered in our formulation of net foreign-currency assets. One could obtain a more comprehensive measure by deriving a currency–weighted transformation of a country's net international investment position (NIIP). The problem is that the NIIP data show only liabilities/assets vis-à-vis nonresidents — not assets and liabilities broken down by currency of denomination. Hence, assumptions about the currency composition of each broad component of the external balance sheet would have to be made in order to derive an estimate of the aggregate currency mismatch. Where available, data on the currency composition of external bond and banking flows and benchmarks from portfolio surveys could be used to inform such estimates. Once each major component of the NIIP is assigned a currency denomination, a weighted average estimate of the aggregate currency mismatch could be derived (where the weights are the value of each component in total foreign assets or total foreign liabilities). According to Allen *et al.* (2002), 78 countries now include their NIIPs in their submissions to the IMF's *International Financial Statistics*; from mid-2002 on, all countries that subscribe to the Fund's Special Data Dissemination Standard are expected to disseminate their NIIPs and publish quarterly external debt data. In summary, the use of NIIP data can provide a valuable cross-check on the mismatch variable defined here. One reason such a cross-check is important is that there are major conceptual and statistical discrepancies between debtor-based statistics (usually the international investment position statistics) and creditor-based statistics (e.g., from BIS banking statistics). Efforts to examine and document such discrepancies are important.[13]

For purposes of comparison, Table 13 presents the original sin ratios (calculated by Eichengreen, Hausmann, and Panizza 2002) for the same 22 emerging economies listed in most of the earlier tables.[14] Recall that when the foreign-currency shares of cross-border bank loans and international bonds are both one, the original sin ratio is also one. The results in Table 13 and those in Tables 10 and 11 paint utterly different pictures. In the original sin calculations, there is little suggestion either of large differences in aggregate currency mismatch across emerging economies or of sharp variations in these mismatches over time. These original sin ratios certainly don't hint that aggregate currency mismatches are larger in the run-up or during financial crises, and there is no indication that mismatches diminish in the recovery from the crisis.

Another difference is that the original sin calculations imply that debtor countries must have negative net foreign-currency positions, whereas our approach (as seen in Tables 10 and 11) is consistent both with some emerging-market debtors running consistently positive net foreign-currency positions and with emerging economies switching from negative to positive positions

---

[13] For an exploration of this, see BIS (2002). The origin of this study was that the statistical authorities in some emerging markets noted striking differences between their estimates of external debt and the joint BIS-IMF-OECD-World Bank statistics on external debt, which were heavily based on creditor data sources. For an overview, see von Kleist (2002). The volume contains a comparison of the data for Chile, China, the Czech Republic, India, Latvia, Mexico, the Philippines, Poland, and Thailand.

[14] We chose OSIN2 ratios from Eichengreen, Hausmann, and Panizza (2002) for Table 12.

Table 13: Original Sin Ratio in Emerging Economies

Region/country	1993–98	1999–2001
Latin America		
Argentina	0.98	0.97
Brazil	1	1
Colombia	1	1
Mexico	1	1
Peru	1	1
Venezuela	1	1
Asia, large economies		
China	1	1
India	1	1
Korea	1	1
Taiwan	1	0.62
Other Asia		
Indonesia	0.94	0.98
Malaysia	0.99	1
Philippines	0.98	0.99
Thailand	0.98	0.87
Central Europe		
Czech Republic	0.88	0.84
Hungary	1	0.98
Poland	0.95	0.89
Russia	1	0.98
Israel	1	1
Turkey	1	1
South Africa	0.91	0.76

Source: OSIN2 ratios from Eichengreen, Hausmann, and Panizza (2002).

(or vice versa). Consider, for example, an emerging economy with a negative NIIP (i.e., a debtor). Assume that the bulk of foreign liabilities is direct foreign investment denominated in the domestic currency. In that case, a net debtor might easily have a positive net foreign-currency position, especially if it had recently undergone a sharp increase in its holdings of international reserves.[15]

---

[15] In their latest paper on original sin, Eichengreen, Hausmann, and Panizza (2003e) now acknowledge that a net debtor will have an aggregate currency mismatch when there is a

To conclude on the measurement issue, it is possible to do a lot better (than relying on original sin ratios) in measuring currency mismatches at the aggregate level. Our proposed indicator of aggregate effective currency mismatch — shown in Tables 10 and 11 — is an attempt to buttress that claim with some illustrative calculations. These estimates could be improved further with a moderate increase in resource costs (at the international financial institutions) devoted to measurement and monitoring of mismatches.

At the sectoral level, the lack of data on the corporate sector is the biggest hole in the data needed to measure and assess currency mismatches. Better data on corporate balance sheets would permit a fuller and more systematic analysis of sectoral currency exposures and vulnerabilities. We therefore argue that the collection of such data ought to merit high priority in efforts by the official sector to monitor and provide early warnings of currency and banking crises. Some promising efforts to bring mismatches in the corporate sector into clearer focus are already under way. For example, Mulder *et al.* (2002) used the Worldscope database to construct a ratio of corporate foreign debt to exports for 19 emerging economies and found that this currency mismatch variable was helpful in explaining both the probability and severity of currency crises over the 1991–99 period. In another example, Gray (2002) applied contingent claims analysis already so popular in the pricing of corporate default risk in the largest industrial countries to a growing set of emerging economies. One attraction of contingent claims analysis is that because it relies heavily on forward-looking price information (i.e., information on the value and volatility of equity and junior claims), it is relatively parsimonious in its data requirements for corporate balance sheets yet it can still generate estimates of the vulnerability of various sectors (including the corporate sector) to changes in the exchange rate. While Gray's (2002) analysis is currently available for only a handful of the larger emerging economies, it could be extended to a wider sample.

"Measuring Currency Mismatch: Beyond Original Sin" and "Aggregate Effective Currency Mismatch" from *Controlling Currency Mismatches in Emerging*

---

net debt to foreigners *denominated in foreign currency* (emphasis added); previously, they had asserted (incorrectly) that "countries with original sin that have net foreign debt — as developing countries are expected to have — will have a currency mismatch on their national balance sheet" (Eichengreen, Hausmann, and Panizza 2002, 10).

Markets by Morris Goldstein and Philip Turner, pp. 21–56 (2004). Peterson Institute for International Economics. Used with permission of the publisher.

REFERENCES

ABS (Australian Bureau of Statistics). 2001. Measuring Australia's Foreign Currency Exposure. In *Balance of Payments and International Investment Position, Australia* (December quarter). Canberra: Australian Bureau of Statistics.

Allen, Mark, Christopher Rosenberg, Christian Keller, Brad Setser, and Nouriel Roubini. 2002. A *Balance-Sheet Approach to Financial Crisis.* IMF Working Paper 02/210 (December). Washington: International Monetary Fund.

Arteta, Carlos. 2003. *Are Financially Dollarized Countries More Prone to Costly Crises?* International Finance Discussion Papers 763 (March). Washington: Board of Governors of the Federal Reserve System.

Barth, James, Gerard Caprio, and Ross Levine. 2000. *Banking Systems Around the Globe.* World Bank Policy Research Paper 2325 (April). Washington: World Bank.

Burger, John, and Francis Warnock. 2002. *Diversification, Original Sin, and International Bond Portfolios.* Washington: International Finance Division, Board of Governors of the Federal Reserve System (December).

Caprio, Gerard, and Patrick Honohan. 2001. *Finance for .Growth: Policy Choices in a Volatile World.* Washington and Oxford: World Bank and Oxford University Press.

CGFS (Committee on the Global Financial System). 2004. Report of the Working Group on Foreign Direct Investment in the Financial System of Emerging Economies (Christine Cumming, chair). Bank for International Settlements, Basel (April).

De Nicolo, Gianni, Patrick Honohan, and Alan Ize. 2003. *Dollarization of the Banking System: Good or Bad?* World Bank Policy Research Working Paper 3116. Washington: World Bank (August).

Eichengreen, Barry, and Ricardo Hausmann. 1999. Exchange Rates and Financial Fragility. In *New Challenges for Monetary Policy.* Proceedings of a symposium sponsored by the Federal Reserve Bank of Kansas City, August 26–28, Jackson Hole, Wyoming. Kansas City: Federal Reserve Bank of Kansas City.

Eichengreen, Barry, and Ricardo Hausmann. 2003c. Original Sin: The Road to Redemption. University of California, Berkeley, and Harvard University. Unpublished paper (October).

Eichengreen, Barry, Ricardo Hausmann, and Ugo Panizza. 2002. Original Sin: The Pain, the Mystery, and the Road to Redemption. Paper presented at a conference on Currency and Maturity Matchmaking: Redeeming Debt from Original Sin, Inter-American Development Bank, November 21–22, Washington.

Gray, Dale. 2002. Macro Finance: The Bigger Picture. *Risk Magazine,* June 17–19.

Hausmann, Ricardo, Ugo Panizza, and Ernesto Stein. 2000. *Why Do Countries Float the Way They Float?* IADB Working Paper 418 (May). Washington: Inter-American Development Bank.

Hausmann, Ricardo, and Ugo Panizza. 2002. The Mystery of Original Sin: The Case of the Missing Apple. Harvard University and Inter-American Development Bank. Photocopy (July).

Hausmann, Ricardo, and Ugo Panizza. 2003. On the Determinants of Original Sin: An Empirical Investigation. *Journal of International Money and Finance* 22: 957–90.

Hawkins, John. 2003. International Bank Lending: Water Flowing Uphill? In *From Capital Surges to Drought: Seeking Stability for Emerging Economies,* ed., Ricardo Ffrench-Davis and Stephany Griffith-Jones. Basingstoke, UK: United Nations University/Macmillan.

Herring, R.. and N. Chatusripitak. 2001. *The Case of the Missing Market: The Bond Market and Why it Matters for Financial Development.* Wharton Financial Institutions Center Working Paper, University of Pennsylvania. (An earlier version appeared as an Asian Development Bank Institute Working Paper 11, July 2000.)

IMF (International Monetary Fund). 2003a. Local Securities and Derivatives Markets in Emerging Markets: Selected Policy Issues. In *Global Financial Stability Report,* March. Washington: International Monetary Fund.

Khan, Mohsin, and Abdelhak Senhadji. 2000. *Financial Development and Economic Growth: An Overview.* IMF Working Paper 00/209. Washington: International Monetary Fund.

Khan, Mohsin, Abdelhak Senhadji, and Bruce Smith. 2001. *Inflation and Financial Depth.* IMF Working Paper 01/44 (April). Washington: International Monetary Fund.

King, Robert, and Ross Levine. 1993a. Finance, Entrepreneurship, and Growth: Theory and Evidence. *Journal of Monetary Economics* 32, no. 3: 513–42.

King, Robert, and Ross Levine. 1993b. Finance and Growth: Schumpeter Might Be Right. *Quarterly Journal of Economics* 108, no. 3: 717–37.

Lubin, David. 2003. Bank Lending in Emerging Markets: Crossing the Border. In *From Capital Surges to Drought: Seeking Stability for Emerging Economies,* ed., Ricardo Ffrench-Davis and Stephany Griffith-Jones. Basingstoke, UK: United Nations University/Macmillan.

Martinez, Lorenza, and Alejandro Werner. 2001. The Exchange Rate Regime and the Currency Composition of Corporate Debt: The Mexican Experience. Paper presented at the National Bureau of Economic Research Inter-American Seminar on Economics, July 20–21, Cambridge, MA.

Merrill Lynch. 2002. *Size and Structure of the World Bond Market.* New York: Merrill Lynch.

Mihaljek, Dubravko, Michela Scatigna, and Agustin Villar. 2002. Recent Trends in Bond Markets. In *The Development of Bond Markets in Emerging Economies.* BIS Policy Papers no. 11. Basel: Bank for International Settlements (June–July).

Prasad, Eswar, Kenneth Rogoff, Shang-Jin Wei, and M. Ayhan Kose. 2003. *Effects of Financial Globalization on Developing Countries: Some Empirical Evidence.* Washington: International Monetary Fund (March).

Reinhart, Carmen, Kenneth Rogoff, and Miguel Savastano. 2003a. *Addicted to Dollars.* NBER Working Paper 10015. Cambridge, MA: National Bureau of Economic Research.

Von Kleist, Karsten. 2002. *Comparison of Creditor and Debtor Data on Short-Term External Debt.* Basel: Bank for International Settlements.

Wooldridge, Philip, Dietrich Domanski, and Anna Cobau. 2003. Changing Links between Mature and Emerging Financial Markets. *BIS Quarterly Review* (September). Basel: Bank for International Settlements.

Chapter 13

The Case for an Orderly Resolution Regime for Systemically-Important Financial Institutions

Rodgin Cohen and Morris Goldstein[1]

SUMMARY

The Obama Administration has proposed that the government be given special authority to resolve a nonbank financial institution if its failure could have serious systemic effects. This new Orderly Resolution Regime (ORR) is needed because the existing regime confronts US economic and regulatory authorities with two very unappealing options: allow the institutions to go into corporate bankruptcy, thereby accepting the associated systemic risk, or to weigh in (often over a weekend) with a large government rescue.

Arguments that this new ORR will be over-used and will increase moral hazard are weak for four main reasons. First, the expansion of the (de facto) official safety net that occurred during this crisis took place without any ORR in place. Second, appropriate safeguards have been proposed that should limit its use. Third, as proposed, it is not clear that an ORR will necessarily weaken market discipline and, finally, while the Systemically Significant Financial

---

[1] Rodgin Cohen and Morris Goldstein are members of the Pew Financial Reform Task Force. Mr. Cohen is a Partner, Sullivan & Cromwell LLP. Mr. Goldstein is the Dennis Weatherstone Senior Fellow, Peterson Institute for International Economics.

Institution (SIFI) distinction is often described as similar to the Government Sponsored Entity (GSE) distinction, the latter actually represents a unique set of circumstances.

The chief counter proposal to the ORR, an amendment of the existing corporate bankruptcy code, suffers from four potential flaws. First, corporate bankruptcy is focused almost exclusively on the interests of creditors of the firm, with little concern for "third party" effects such as systemic risk. Second, the restrictions on the claims of creditors inherent in bankruptcy will likely result in counterparties (and employees) refusing to do business with a financial institution either in or approaching bankruptcy. Third, court proceedings are likely to move slowly, as opposed to administrative proceedings like an ORR. Finally, whereas the ORR would permit the government to intervene in various ways before the firm "fails," traditional corporate bankruptcy would not.

Other important considerations include the proposal that any ORR should have a dual mandate (both to seek a least-cost resolution and to minimize adverse spillover effects), provide a system of prompt-corrective-action (PCA), and cover any SIFI not subject to the FDIC's resolution authority. The decision to discuss whether the ORR should be used should be initiated by the firm's prudential regulator or the market stability regulator, with the decision to activate the ORR vested in the Treasury, subject to certain additional requirements. Any ORR should be funded from an assessment and on a pre-arranged line of credit from the Treasury, with the FDIC acting as the operational resolution authority.

INTRODUCTION

The Obama Administration has proposed — as a fundamental part of its comprehensive program for financial regulatory reform — that the US Government be given special authority to resolve a nonbank financial institution if its failure could have serious systemic effects.[2] The FDIC has

---

[2] "Financial Regulatory Reform: A New Foundation," US Treasury Department, Washington DC, June 17, 2009 (referred to hereafter as US Treasury White Paper). Such resolution authority for systemically significant financial institutions might also be introduced as free-standing legislation; see, for example, the draft bill ("Resolution Authority for Systemically Significant Financial Companies Act of 2009") sent to the US Congress in late March, 2009, by the Treasury Department.

long had such resolution authority for banks.[3] Under the proposed new resolution authority, the US Government would be allowed to place a failing, Systemically-Important Financial Institution (SIFI) into conservatorship or receivership, and then to administer its orderly reorganization or wind-down. Any financial institution — be it a securities firm, an insurance company, a hedge fund, a private equity firm, or a bank holding company — which is not now subject to the resolution authority of the FDIC would be covered if its failure poses systemic risk.

In this paper, we provide, in section two, answers to three key questions about such a new Orderly Resolution Regime (ORR) for SIFIs: (i) why is a new ORR for SIFIs needed; (ii) will a new ORR be overused, and will it increase moral hazard; and (iii) could the resolution of failed SIFIs be handled better by amendment of the existing corporate bankruptcy code than by creating a new ORR? Finally, in section three, we offer recommendations and raise some unresolved issues for the design of a new ORR for SIFIs.

THREE KEY QUESTIONS ABOUT A NEW ORDERLY RESOLUTION REGIME FOR SYSTEMICALLY-IMPORTANT FINANCIAL INSTITUTIONS

Why is a new ORR for SIFIs needed?

We need a new ORR because the existing regime for dealing with failing SIFIs has shown itself to be unworkable. Under the existing regime, the impending failure of a SIFI confronts US economic and regulatory authorities with two very unappealing options. Option 1 is to allow the SIFI to go into corporate bankruptcy (Chapter 11 or Chapter 7), and to accept the systemic risks associated with the inflexibility and narrow focus of this traditional bankruptcy process (i.e., the adverse effects on financial markets of creditor stays, lack of attention to third-party effects of insolvency, potentially long delays in obtaining approval of reorganization/liquidation plans, fragmented resolution

---

[3]The FDIC was made the sole receiver for national banks in 1933 under the National Banking Act. In 1987 (under the Competitive Equality Banking Act, CEBA), the FDIC received additional authority to charter a national bridge bank as an alternative to receivership or conservatorship. Under the Federal Deposit Insurance Corporation Improvement Act (FDICIA) of 1991, the FDIC was granted expanded authority to serve as the statutory receiver for state-chartered banks.

authority for complex financial institutions, and inability to intervene prior to insolvency). These risks are inherent in the bankruptcy process because the bankruptcy code was not designed with the challenges of resolving today's large, interconnected, global financial institutions in mind. Option 2 is to weigh in (often over a weekend) with a large government rescue of the failing SIFI so that the financial institution does not default on its obligations and the bankruptcy outcome can be avoided. But such a government rescue often has to be conducted under severe constraints that threaten its effectiveness and raise its financial and political cost. Frequently, the rescue has to be put together so quickly that crisis managers have little time to think through the best resolution strategy, or to carry out appropriate due diligence on the failing institution, or to search out the most suitable purchaser, or to benefit from an eventual rebound of fire sale prices for the failing firm's assets.

The crisis conditions of the past year have also shattered the illusions that financial institutions (other than banks themselves) are so resilient that we needn't worry about their failure, and that such failures are devoid of adverse systemic implications. We have seen that investment banks — like commercial banks — can be subject to "runs," that even collateralized borrowing may be not available during a crisis to financial institutions perceived as insolvent or illiquid, and that large losing bets in the derivatives market can bring a previously AAA-rated and diversified giant nonbank financial company to its knees. It is likewise instructive: that the five largest US investment banks at the start of this crisis have failed, been pushed by market forces to be acquired, or have elected to become bank holding companies regulated by the Federal Reserve (Fed); that the Fed's unprecedented extensions of guarantees and liquidity assistance during this crisis have been directed in large part at the nonbank financial sector (where about half of aggregate US credit flows originate); and that concerns about the systemic effects of an AIG bankruptcy have led both the Bush and Obama Administrations to put over $180 billion of public funds toward its rescue.

The global turmoil that followed the bankruptcy of Lehman is likely to make the bankruptcy option for SIFIs seem even less attractive to policymakers going forward — even if much of that turmoil may have reflected the market reaction to the treatment of Lehman's bondholders as an unexpected change in the unwritten "rules of the game" on resolution, rather than the interconnectedness of Lehman per se. And contrary to what is sometimes suggested, there are SIFIs left. Suppose, for example, that GE Capital, or Metropolitan

Life, or Goldman Sachs, or one of our largest "traditional" bank holding companies were, at some point down the road, to run into serious financial difficulties. Given their size and inter-connectedness in global markets, who among us would feel comfortable recommending that they go into Chapter 11 or Chapter 7 "free-fall" bankruptcy or, alternatively, that the US Government decide over a weekend to mount a massive bailout package.

The proposed ORR for SIFIs offers a "third way." It would give the authorities an additional crisis management tool that combines three desirable characteristics of an effective resolution regime for SIFIs: (i) the ability, when necessary, to continue temporarily the core operations of the firm (possibly, after transferring the assets and liabilities of the failing SIFI to a government-operated "bridge bank"), so as to minimize market lockups and fire sales of assets; (ii) good moral hazard properties (docking shareholders, changing management, and paying off some senior creditors at estimated recovery costs), so to minimize the incentives to repeat the excesses of the past at government expense; and (iii) considerable "flexibility" for the government conservator or receiver to manage the resolution process, so as to minimize damage to the wider economy and to lower taxpayer costs.[4] Such a resolution regime could contribute critically to the successful management of any future SIFI failures.

Won't a new ORR for SIFIs be over-used, and won't it increase moral hazard going forward?

We think not — for at least four reasons: the current safety net, appropriate safeguards, market discipline, and the uniqueness of GSEs.

The current safety net

First, it is important to recognize that the huge expansion of the (de facto) official safety net that has occurred during this crisis took place when there

---

[4]The conservator or receiver of the firm under the ORR for SIFIs would have authority to take control of the operations of the firm, to sell or transfer all or part of the assets of the firm to a bridge institution or other entity, to transfer the firm's derivative contracts to a bridge institution, and to renegotiate or repudiate certain of the firm's contracts, including contracts with certain of its employees. In addition, the conservator or receiver would be authorized to borrow from the Treasury when necessary to finance its activities (with the proceeds of an assessment on bank holding companies and perhaps other financial institutions used to repay the costs of any such loans from the Treasury). See the US Treasury's White Paper.

was *no* ORR for SIFIs. An extraordinary economic and financial crisis was underway and the consequences of throwing banks and SIFIs into resolution/bankruptcy were much feared. Part of the policy response to the crisis was a wholesale and ad hoc expansion of official guarantees and of government recapitalization for financial institutions (including the TARP), along with unprecedented use of the Federal Reserve's emergency lending authority (that is, Section 13(3) of the Federal Reserve Act for extensions of credit to individuals, partnerships, or corporations in "unusual and exigent circumstances").[5] Recall too that the FDICIA resolution regime for banks was created after the US savings and loan crisis, precisely because of the negative reaction to the "regulatory forbearance" and large public bailout costs that occurred when there was no ready and permanent alternative resolution framework either to corporate bankruptcy or to large ad hoc bailout operations for thrifts and banks. The current situation for SIFIs is analogous to the pre-FDICIA situation for banks. The relevant question is whether an ORR will be overused and will increase moral hazard *relative* to the alternative of no ORR.

Appropriate safeguards

The Obama Administration's plan for an ORR for SIFIs contains safeguards that should limit its use. Specifically, the plan calls for the US Treasury to activate this regime only after determining that the firm is in default or in danger of defaulting, that failure of the firm and its resolution under otherwise applicable law would have serious systemic effects, and that use of the ORR would avoid or mitigate these effects. Moreover, the Treasury can invoke resolution authority only after consulting with the President and only upon written recommendation of two-thirds of the members of the Federal Reserve Board and two-thirds of the members of the FDIC Board.[6] These are the same kinds of safeguards against excessive use that are in the systemic risk exemption for bank resolution under FDICIA. This systemic override for

---

[5] The US Treasury's White Paper argues (p. 74) that the federal government's responses to the impending bankruptcies of Bear Stearns, Lehman, and AIG were "... complicated by the lack of a statutory framework for avoiding the disorderly failure of nonbank financial firms." and that in the absence of such a framework, "... the government's only avenue to avoid the disorderly failures of Bear Stearns and AIG was the use of the Federal Reserve's lending authority."

[6] If the firm is a broker-dealer, invoking resolution requires a written recommendation of two-thirds of the SEC.

banks under FDICIA has been only rarely used. The Treasury also emphasizes that bankruptcy should remain the dominant tool for handing the failure of a bank holding company when concerns about systemic risk are not paramount. As for the charge that, once the government intervenes, it will be very reluctant to pull out, we would note that FDIC resolution authority has been used much more frequently to sell or liquidate failing banks than to rehabilitate them; we would expect the same to be true of an ORR for SIFIs.

Market discipline

It is not obvious (at least to us) that designating a limited set of nonbanks as "systemically important or significant," or as "Tier 1 FHCs" (financial holding companies), will automatically weaken market discipline, or give these firms an unfair comparative advantage over nonbanks not so designated, or turn the designated institutions into de facto GSEs.

As suggested earlier, there is nothing in the proposed ORR for SIFIs that prevents the government receiver from forcing a change in management, or from leaving common shareholders of the resolved firm with little or no recovery, or from paying off creditors and counterparties at estimated recovery cost rather than at par; to the extent that these stakeholders of the resolved firm are not "made whole" by the resolution process, market discipline should continue to operate. Also, even if some or all debt holders of the resolved firm are paid more than they would be in the case of bankruptcy, this higher payment may be justifiable if the ORR produces a higher value for the firm than would a liquidation under fire sale prices. Moreover, one should not exaggerate the positive influence of market discipline in the run-up to this crisis. After all, creditors and counterparties of Bear Stearns, Lehman, and AIG did not exert much discipline until near the end — despite well-publicized problems that existed months before those institutions' demise or intervention.

Yes, if some financial institutions are regarded as subject to the ORR, they may be able (at least initially) to fund themselves more readily and on better terms, and they may attract customers who highly value stability and certainty. But is also true that even without official designation as SIFIs, many market participants will regard large and highly interconnected nonbank financial institutions as "too big to fail" (TBTF) and those nonbank financial institutions will reap the benefits linked to that market expectation. Just as relevant, the Obama Administration's financial regulatory plan calls for financial firms designated as Tier 1 FHCs to be subject to more stringent prudential measures and to a higher capital requirement (and perhaps to a special assessment to help fund an ORR).[7] These measures may compensate for much or all of the competitive advantage that designation as an SIFI confers.

On a broader level, there is also a trade-off to be considered in the (joint) decision to announce who is/is not an SIFI, and to subject the designated institutions to tougher prudential standards. If the government identifies the SIFIs ex ante, then it incurs any (additional) moral hazard risks linked to that designation, but it also retains the opportunity to reduce the risk of failure by subjecting the designated SIFIs to tougher regulation/supervision. Alternatively, if the SIFIs are identified only ex post (by the government's rescue efforts), any moral hazard reduction associated with a policy of "constructive ambiguity" is retained, but the government gives up the option of "internalizing the externalities" associated with de facto TBTF (leading to the popular criticism that the present regime privatizes the gains from excessive risk-taking but socializes the losses). After the massive injections of government funds during this crisis to avoid the failure of financial institutions, it appears that the greater risk may lie in pretending ex ante that certain large and interconnected nonbanks may not be TBTF but then acting as if they are TBTF once failure is imminent.

The uniqueness of GSEs

Fourth, the GSEs have long had a unique status among nonbanks because of their hybrid public-private structure, because of the huge size of their balance sheets, because of the important role of housing and home ownership in the economy and in the American Dream, and increasingly because of the large holding of GSE obligations by foreign governments and foreign central banks. The systemic consequences of allowing Fannie or Freddie to fail are of a different order of magnitude than those for other nonbanks. We do not see how designating some nonbanks as SIFIs turns them into de facto GSEs. Plans for the future of the GSEs — including the ultimate resolution regime — will have to be sui generis.

---

[7] Note that, if more stringent prudential measures and/or higher capital requirements are to be imposed on a set of nonbanks, it would be very difficult to keep the identity of those institutions confidential. Moreover, any measures must be carefully calibrated to avoid undue competition or economic harm.

Could the resolution of failed SIFIs be handled better by amending the existing bankruptcy framework (perhaps by adding a new chapter 16 for financial institutions) than by creating a new ORR?[8]

On a theoretical level, it is possible to think of a new special chapter of the bankruptcy code that would be specifically designed for SIFIs and that would contain many of the components of an ORR. In that case, the differences between the proposed new ORR and "bankruptcy" would be, of course, much smaller than at present (almost by definition). On a practical level, however, differences between traditional corporate bankruptcy and special resolution regimes for financial institutions are so fundamental as to make us highly skeptical about taking the bankruptcy route for SIFIs. If there are concerns about the US Treasury plan, they would be better addressed by amending the ORR than by creating a new "fish out of water" chapter of the bankruptcy code.

A comprehensive analysis of the differences between corporate bankruptcy and special resolution regimes for financial institutions has been put forward by Bliss and Kaufman (2006).[9] For our purposes, it is sufficient to summarize four of the distinctions that they emphasize: priorities, stays, management of the process and proactive action.

Priorities

Special resolution regimes for financial institutions typically give considerable attention to the impact of resolution on the wider economy and on financial markets. Put in other words, beyond their immediate objectives (e.g., achieving "least-cost resolution" for the deposit insurance fund, subject to legally-mandated claimant priorities, under FDICIA), such special resolution regimes give weight to "externalities."[10] In contrast, corporate bankruptcy is focused almost exclusively on the interests of creditors of the firm, with little concern for "third party" effects. A regime that ignores externalities and "systemic" effects

---

[8] It is not always clear whether those who prefer handling the impending failure of a systemically significant financial institution within the bankruptcy code want a new chapter only for nonbank financials, or whether they would also favor dismantling the existing FDIC resolution regime for banks. We assume that the FDIC regime for banks is retained.

[9] Robert Bliss and George Kaufman, 2006, "US Corporate and Bank Insolvency Regimes: An Economic Comparison and Evaluation," Federal Reserve Bank of Chicago Working Papers. No. 2006–01, Chicago: Federal Reserve Bank of Chicago, January.

[10] For example, Bliss and Kaufman (2006) note that the FDIC, when conducting asset sales, is directed to "... fully consider adverse economic impact."

seems ill-suited to resolving "systemically important" nonbank financials. This difference between the two regimes reflects the assumption that failure of a bank is potentially more costly for the broader economy than is the failure of a normal corporation. We do not claim that SIFIs are just like banks. But we do argue that large and interconnected nonbank financials engage in many of the same financial activities (and sometimes at similar scale) as do their large and interconnected bank counterparts, that the failure of SIFIs can generate adverse spillovers for the broader economy, and that the resolution of SIFIs raises many of the same challenges as the resolution of systemically-important banks. In this sense, SIFIs are closer to systemically-important banks than they are to many non-systemically-important nonbanks. Put in other words, we think it makes more sense to place a Morgan Stanley or an AIG in a resolution regime that is similar to that which would be used for a Bank of America or a Citibank, than to put it in the Chapter 11 or Chapter 7 bankruptcy regime that would be used for an IBM or an AOL.

Stays

A second distinction between the two regimes is in the treatment of creditor stays. Such stays contribute to the coordination of creditor claims and prevent creditor runs. Although the corporate bankruptcy code has some exemptions from stays for derivative contracts, other creditor claims are subject to such stays and they are a key element in Chapter 11 reorganizations. In contrast, in special resolution regimes for financial institutions, the ability of the receiver to impose such creditor stays is strictly limited. One of the reasons why there is often such pressure to complete over a weekend the purchase and assumption of a failing, systemically important financial institution is to avoid the creditor stays (and its domino effects) that would otherwise be triggered if that institution chose (or were forced) to go into traditional Chapter 11 or Chapter 7 bankruptcy.[11] Financial institutions that are not able to transact continuously with their short-term creditors are not likely to be able to stay in business long. The currency of the realm in financial markets is "trust," and if that trust is lost by restrictions on the claims of creditors, then counterparties (and employees) may soon refuse to do business with a financial institution in a bankruptcy

---

[11] Creditor stays can also make it impossible to implement dynamic hedging strategies that call for continuous access to markets.

process (or even at an earlier stage, causing the business to "fail" even if it is not yet insolvent or even illiquid). Operating a railroad or an airline under Chapter 11 bankruptcy is one thing. Operating a SIFI under Chapter 11 is quite another.

Management of the process

Difference number three relates to the overall "flexibility" that the receiver/trustee has under the two regimes. That flexibility is much more limited under corporate bankruptcy because such bankruptcies are conducted in federal bankruptcy courts, each creditor group must vote to approve the plans of the management and receiver/trustee, and the court must approve the decisions taken by the receiver/trustee. The potential for long time delays is thus considerable. Contrast this with special resolution regimes for financial institutions. As Bliss and Kaufman (2006) explain, these are considered to be administrative proceedings; creditors, management, and shareholders can file claims and request information, but they do not participate in the decision-making process. In effect, once the receiver is appointed, the receiver runs the show. Assuming that adequate financing is available and that the resolution protocol is respected, the receiver then has considerable discretion is managing the resolution of the failed institution. This flexibility cum discretion can be very helpful in minimizing adverse systemic effects or in limiting losses to the taxpayer.

Suppose, for example, that the failed SIFI is a bank holding company with bank, securities, and insurance subsidiaries. Absent an ORR for SIFIs, the resolution process could be highly fragmented and inconsistent — as the FDIC resolved the bank subsidiary, SIPIC resolved certain of the securities subsidiaries, several state insurance departments sought to resolve the insurance subsidiaries, and the bankruptcy court resolved the holding company and all its other subsidiaries. But the receiver of the bank holding company under a new ORR for SIFIs could potentially avoid much of these inefficiencies and competing claims by coordinating the resolution process under a central plan. In a similar vein, the receiver of the new ORR might be able to obtain better prices for the firm's assets by transferring them to a bridge bank and then selling them at a later date when market conditions had improved. Alternatively, the receiver of the new ORR could decide that speed of resolution was essential to limiting adverse spillover and confidence effects of the impending failure and hence could decide to sell the SIFI to a healthier institution over the weekend.

As we know from other "rules versus discretion" issues in economics, granting policymakers wide discretion is a two-edged sword. It can produce good results if the policymaker uses the discretion wisely, but can lead to bad outcomes if that discretion is exercised in a biased or incompetent manner. The discretion/flexibility accorded to a government receiver of an ORR for SIFIs would be no different. But if there are concerns that the government receiver will abuse his discretion — say, because some of his decisions on modification of contracts will be politically motivated, or because he may aim to enhance his influence by seeking to rehabilitate too many SIFIs, or because he will not have sufficient experience dealing with resolution of SIFIs — there are ways to limit that discretion without discarding all the other potential advantages of an ORR.

A few examples illustrate the point. The receiver will have less discretion if the funds he has on hand to manage the resolution process are not unlimited. Although the US Treasury proposal puts no limits on the funds that the ORR could borrow from the Treasury, the Congress could decide to allocate a given initial amount but require the ORR to get Congressional authorization for any additional amounts. Similarly, if the aim is to provide some protection against capricious or politically motivated decisions by the receiver, the bill creating the ORR could subject some decisions of the receiver to ex post judicial review, and the fundamental strategic decisions (e.g., to sell the SIFI) to an intergovernmental collaborative process. And if the concern is inexperience, the Congress could insist that the government agency managing the ORR for SIFIs be one that has demonstrated experience in operating special resolution regimes; the FDIC has such experience — albeit with banks. The first two of these amendments to an ORR would reduce the "flexibility" and "discretion" of the receiver, but they may still be justified on a wider cost-benefit calculus.

Proactive action

Last but not least, whereas special resolution regimes for financial institutions permit the government to intervene in various ways before the firm "fails," traditional corporate bankruptcy does not. Thus, for example, FDICIA lays out a set of "prompt corrective actions" (PCA) that a bank (and the FDIC) should take once bank capital falls below certain pre-specified thresholds.

Unless the systemic risk exemption is activated, FDICIA can also require the receiver (FDIC) to close the bank when it still has positive net worth. None of this is possible under traditional corporate bankruptcy. Again, we see this as an advantage for an ORR because such corrective pre-failure measures could increase the institution's chance of avoiding failure — or at least reduce the cost of such failure if it occurs. Admittedly, the PCA tripwires in FDICIA have not been very effective in this crisis, but improvements to the design of the PCA mechanism — in light of lessons learned during this crisis — should be possible.[12]

RECOMMENDATIONS AND UNRESOLVED DESIGN ISSUES FOR AN ORR FOR SIFIS

If the existing bankruptcy/resolution regime for SIFIs is broken and a new ORR is needed, then the number one operational question is: what should this ORR for SIFIs look like? We think the outline of an ORR for SIFIs provided in the US Treasury's recent White Paper represents a good start on how such a regime might be constructed and how it might operate.[13] In what follows, we offer recommendations on the design of such a new ORR, along with some unanswered questions about its operations. We focus on the ORR mandate, its coverage, a PCA component, initiation of the process, funding, selection of the operational resolution authority, the resolution protocol, and international considerations.

1. <u>Mandate</u> — *The ORR for SIFIs should seek to resolve SIFIs in a way that seeks to minimize both adverse systemic effects on the financial system and the US economy, as well as the cost of resolution to the US taxpayer.*

<u>Commentary</u> — Although a single mandate would provide clearer direction, a dual mandate is more appropriate for such an ORR. Because the resolution authority will be dealing only with systemically-important institutions, least-cost resolution (as under FDICIA) cannot be the sole objective; minimizing adverse spillover effects on the financial system and the US economy is also very important. Likewise, ignoring the cost of resolution to the taxpayer would be misguided given the large size of institutions to be

---

[12] See "Principles for Reforming the US and International Capital Framework for Banking Firms," US Treasury Department, Washington DC, September 3, 2009.

[13] See pp.76–78 in the US Treasury White Paper.

covered by this regime, the need to limit the moral hazard effects of government intervention, and the desire to avoid sticking taxpayers with a large bill for problems that were not of their own making. In seeking to avoid systemic risk, the resolution authority will likely face three types of problems: taking action at the resolved institution (e.g., a total wipeout of shareholders) can cause pressure at other institutions; defaults to creditors and counterparties of the resolved institution can cause other institutions to fail because of their actual and perceived exposure to the resolved firm; and uncertainty about the form and extent of the resolution could cause a systemic freezing of payments and/or credit. The impact of the resolution on taxpayers will depend on many factors, including: whether the resolved firm is liquidated rather than rehabilitated or sold, how much financial assistance the government provides, the form of the government's assistance (e.g., guarantees versus cash liquidity), and the prioritization of the government's claim.

The mandate should also be broad enough to provide the resolution authority with sufficient flexibility to achieve its objectives in the face of considerable diversity and uncertainty across types of financial institutions and economic circumstances. We would also hope that the resolution authority would use this flexibility to address the TBTF problem when doing so would not conflict with its main objectives; for example, it may be easier to break up a very large failing nonbank into smaller parts when the failing institution is being resolved than by confronting TBTF with "size limits" or via a change in the antitrust laws.

2. Coverage — *Any financial institution, the failure of which poses systemic risks, and which is not subject to the FDIC's resolution authority under FDICIA, should be covered by the new ORR for SIFIs. All institutions covered by the ORR would also be subject to whatever tighter prudential standards, including higher capital requirements, deemed appropriate for "systemically-important" financial institutions, i.e., Tier I FHCs — be they banks or nonbanks. There is a strong argument that these standards should be applied on an individual institution basis, rather than arbitrarily and automatically to all SIFIs.*

Commentary — The selection of SIFIs to be included in the new ORR should be based mainly on size and inter-connectedness — regardless of the institution's charter (although banks would still be covered under the existing

FDIC regime).[14] We don't think the government should have to disclose (or be irrevocably bound by) the specific quantitative metrics it uses for these criteria. Some would go further and argue that it will be difficult in advance to develop specific criteria that would cover every institution that should be subject to special resolution and, hence, that the government should have discretion to include some institutions that don't meet the usual criteria. To reflect changes in economic weight and circumstances over time, it must be possible to add/delete institutions from the list.

3. Pre-insolvency intervention — *A system of prompt-corrective-action (PCA), modeled broadly on the PCA for banks under FDICIA, should be created as part of the ORR to improve the odds — both that insolvency can be avoided by corrective actions and, failing such correction, that intervention is undertaken before the cost of the resolution becomes so large. In designing such a PCA for SIFIs, the FDIC or the Treasury should be given the tasks of evaluating the performance of PCA for banks during this crisis under FDICIA, determining whether different tripwires (than used for banks under FDICIA) would be appropriate for SIFIs under a new ORR, and recommending if and how a minimum capital ratio and other financial metrics should be used as the trigger to initiate the resolution process. In addition, consideration should be given to requiring all SIFIs to file and keep current "living will plans," explaining how they would be wound down in case of failure. In that case, such plans would be deemed confidential supervisory material and exempt from public disclosure.*

Commentary — Despite the problems that PCA tripwires for banks have encountered during this crisis, a PCA framework is still probably the best protection one has against excessive regulatory forbearance and against intervening far too late in the game to avoid a large loss to taxpayers. It is not clear, however, whether the existing capital-based tripwires need just some minor modification, or whether a more wholesale revamping is needed (especially for SIFIs). Some would argue, for example, that the principal regulator should be authorized to intervene whenever there is a significant deterioration in the financial condition of the institution, but that neither the conditions that motivate such intervention nor the corrective actions themselves should be specified in advance; others would regard such a move

---

[14]Leverage may also be important.

to greater discretion as destroying the whole motivation and effectiveness of a PCA framework. More thought should be given to how to recognize when an SIFI has "failed." Does a firm fail when its capital falls to a pre-specified threshold, or when the common shareholders are wiped out and management is replaced, or when, in addition, preferred shareholders and debt holders are wiped out or suffer a significant haircut, or when there is an actual liquidation? The preparation of "living will plans" could help to reduce the uncertainty about the resolution process for SIFIs and should also motivate these firms to consider more carefully the adequacy of their cushions and defenses against extreme stress in financial markets.

4. <u>Initiation of resolution</u> — *The decision to discuss whether the ORR should be used for a particular SIFI could be initiated by the firm's prudential regulator or the market stability regulator (the Federal Reserve). We also agree with the view taken in the White Paper that the decision to activate the ORR for an SIFI should be vested in the Treasury, after consulting with the President and only upon the written recommendation of two-thirds of the members of the Federal Reserve and FDIC boards; the primary regulator of the resolved institution (if not the Treasury, the Fed, or the FDIC) should also have to give his written recommendation.*

<u>Commentary</u> — Because the institutions to be covered by the new ORR are all required to be "systemically important," it makes sense to have the input and views of all the relevant government departments in deciding whether to invoke the ORR for a particular failing firm (as opposed to allowing it to go into Chapter 11 or 7 bankruptcy). In addition to their systemic responsibilities, the Treasury, the FDIC, and the Fed also represent the most likely sources for financing the resolution.[15] One potential problem with requiring so many government bodies to "sign off" on invoking the ORR is that a divergence of views among them will prevent them from acting, and that such inaction will prove costly. One way around this problem would be not to require unanimous agreement but instead agreement by the Treasury and either the Fed or the FDIC. The counter-argument to this proposal is that the primary risk is that resolution authority will be invoked too often when it is not needed, and that the unanimity requirement will limit its use to cases that are clearly "systemically important." Some would also argue that the decisions

---

[15] A line of credit from the Federal Reserve would probably be considered only if all other options for financing the resolution were not available.

of the Federal Reserve on these matters are apt to be less politically influenced than those of the Treasury, and hence, a Federal Reserve sign-off is essential to maintain the requisite objectivity. And if the FDIC is chosen to be the resolution authority, it may seem odd to prevent it from voting on whether such the resolution regime should be activated.

5. Funding for the new ORR — *The new ORR for SIFIs should be funded from two sources: an assessment on the designated SIFIs and a pre-arranged line of credit from the US Treasury.*

Commentary — We favor a dual financing structure for the new ORR because the amounts needed are likely to be too large (in the hundreds of billions of dollars) to be satisfied by (exclusively) assessing a limited number of SIFIs. It seems preferable therefore to have the SIFIs bear the loss up to a designated amount, and to arrange a government line of credit for the ORR's remaining financing needs. Some argue that any limit on the funding for a new ORR would be artificial and arbitrary, that requiring Congress to approve funding beyond an initial allotment would subject the financial system and the US economy to unacceptable risks of delay (if the request for additional funds were turned down), and that the only guideline should be to provide the resolving authority with whatever funds it sees as necessary to meet the ORR's objectives. The counter-argument is that there is a tradeoff between reducing systemic risk on the one hand, and upholding accountability and limiting excessive discretion on the part of the resolution authority on the other, and that the accountability advantages of a limit on Treasury funding outweigh any increased systemic risk. There is also a debate about ex post versus ex ante assessments on SIFIs. One view is that any Treasury funding should be recouped from ex post assessments so that recourse to the Fed's emergency lending authority can be avoided. Others argue that ex ante assessments are to be preferred because ex post assessments would not be risk-sensitive, would be subject to a "falling domino" problem (that is, they would take capital out of the remaining institutions when they could least afford it and possibly jeopardize their future), and would allow the failing institution to escape an assessment.

6. Selection of the operational resolution authority — *The FDIC should be the operational resolution authority for the new ORR for SIFIs. Because the FDIC's expertise is largely limited to banks, it would be desirable to supplement the FDIC's staff with expertise in the main businesses of the SIFIs (insurance, broker-dealing, etc), as well as the Fed's expertise.*

Commentary — The FDIC has more experience in resolution than any of the other candidates. It would therefore take significant time for any other government agency to develop both a staff and the necessary experience, and such a hiatus could well be costly under the still-considerable vulnerability of the financial system.

7. <u>The Resolution Protocol</u> — *The protocol should be guided by three principles. First, resolution authority should be activated only under extreme conditions (of systemic risk) but, once activated, the resolution authority should be accorded sufficient "flexibility" to get the job done. This is necessary so that the authority can respond to the variety of circumstances that will inevitably exist; less recognized, the same flexibility can reduce moral hazard. A second principle is that the authority must be able to utilize the basic types of resolution, namely, sale, rehabilitation through a conservatorship, liquidation, and if necessary, ad hoc types. This is desirable because each type of resolution has advantages and disadvantages that can be decisive in particular situations. And a third principle is that any assistance provided by the government during the resolution should have a priority over, at least, existing claims. This is consistent with the mandate of the ORR to minimize cost to the taxpayer.*

Commentary — Flexibility should also permit different resolution procedures to be applied at the operating company and holding company levels. In addition to sale, rehabilitation through a conservatorship, and liquidation, the resolution authority should have the authority to renegotiate or repudiate certain of the firm's contracts (just as in a bankruptcy proceeding); such modifications in contracts may be necessary, for example, to put a rehabilitated firm on a path to sustainability. If there is concern that such an authority will be misused (say, for political purposes), an "arbitrary and capricious" standard can be used to for judicial review of these contract modifications. More than one type of resolution may be used in an individual case; for example, there could be a sale of some parts of a resolved SIFI and liquidation of others. Also, one type of resolution (conservatorship) could evolve into another (liquidation).

8. <u>International considerations</u> — *Because virtually every SIFI will have substantial international operations and international "connectivity," there is inevitably going to be an international dimension to any ORR for SIFIs. The main priority here is to avoid application of a "ring fence" concept that can frustrate otherwise sensible resolution plans, and also invite retaliation from other countries.*

Commentary — The Lehman bankruptcy demonstrated that a strengthened resolution process in any single country will have only limited efficacy if there is no strengthened international resolution process. For this reason, it is essential that the Basle Committee on Bank Supervision expedite its work on developing recommendations for cross-border resolution. Although this is our last point in the chronology of this paper, it has the very highest priority and importance.

CONCLUSION

The Obama Administration's proposed ORR is needed because the existing regime confronts US economic and regulatory authorities with two very unappealing options: allow the institutions to go into corporate bankruptcy thereby accepting the associated systemic risk, or to weigh in (often over a weekend) with a large government rescue to attempt to mitigate the systemic risk. Arguments that this new ORR will be over-used and will increase moral hazard are generally weak; notably, the relevant question is whether an ORR will be overused and will increase moral hazard *relative* to the alternative of no ORR. While theoretically possible, the chief counter-proposal to the ORR, an amendment of the existing corporate bankruptcy code, is inferior to the ORR in fundamental ways, including that corporate bankruptcy is focused almost exclusively on the interests of creditors of the firm, with little concern for "third party" effects such as systemic risk. Finally, while workable as proposed, the ORR, as proposed by the Obama Administration, could be improved along several dimensions, including the adoption of a dual mandate to both ensure a least-cost resolution to protect taxpayers, as well as to mitigate spillover effects.

"The Case for an Orderly Resolution Regime for Systemically-Important Financial Institutions" by Rodgin Cohen and Morris Goldstein. Copyright © 2009 by The Pew Charitable Trusts. Used with permission of the publisher.

Chapter 14

The 2014 EU-wide Bank Stress Test Lacks Credibility

Morris Goldstein

Results from last month's EU-wide stress test are reassuring, especially for countries at Europe's core. This column warns against a rosy interpretation. The test relies on risk-weighted measures of bank capital ratios that have been shown to be less predictive of bank failure than unweighted leverage ratios — a metric already adopted by the US Fed and Bank of England. In addition, many experts recommend much higher leverage ratios than currently required. The ECB must do more to fix undercapitalisation.

On October 26th 2014 the European Central Bank (ECB) and the European Banking Authority (EBA) released the results of the latest EU-wide stress test and the accompanying asset quality review (AQR).[1]

The 2014 stress test encompasses four key findings:

- The aggregate capital shortfall for the 123 banks participating in the test is €24.6 billion;

Published on VOX, CEPR's Policy Portal (http://www.voxeu.org)
[1] Earlier EU-wide stress tests were conducted in 2009, 2010, and 2011.

- Only 24 of the 123 banks are undercapitalised, as indicated by their inability to meet transitional common equity tier one capital ratios of 5.5 and 8.0% in the baseline and adverse scenarios, respectively;[2]
- The undercapitalised banks are all in Italy, Greece, and Cyprus; and
- The largest banks in France and Germany have ample capital.[3]

These conclusions are simply not credible. To understand why, consider the following facts and arguments.

- Over the past five years, a solid body of empirical work has shown that bank capital ratios employing unweighted total assets in the denominator — so-called leverage ratios — are far more effective in distinguishing sick from healthy banks than risk-based measures that use risk-weighted assets in the denominator.[4] The 2014 test (like its three predecessors) used only a risk-based measure of bank capital. This is not technical hair-splitting but rather an issue that cuts to the very heart of the credibility of stress tests.
- In the run-up to the global financial crisis of 2007–2009, risk-based capital measures were indicating that the largest US and EU banks were well-capitalised; by contrast, leverage ratios were indicating that these banks had thin capital cushions (Hoenig 2013, Pagano *et al.* 2014). Since many of these banks wound up needing official support during the crisis, it is clear which metrics were sending good signals and which were not.
- During the 2011 EU-wide stress test (the last one conducted before the 2014 test), the bank deemed the safest by its very high risk-based ratio, Irish Life and Permanent, had to be placed in a government restructuring program in 2012. Dexia (a French-Belgian bank) and Bankia (based in Spain) also passed the 2011 test, only to require rescue at taxpayer expense a short time after. A revealing study by two European economists showed that if a 3% leverage ratio had been used as the hurdle rate in the 2011

---

[2] If capital raising during 2014 is taken into account, the aggregate capital shortfall declines to €9.5 billion, and the number of banks with a shortfall to 14.

[3] The report on the outcome of the 2014 stress test (EBA 2014) indicates that the AQR resulted in a 40 basis point reduction in the weighted average common equity tier 1 capital ratio. Here I focus on the implications of excluding a leverage ratio from the tests because the quantitative impact of that decision on the size of the aggregate capital shortfall and on the country pattern of shortfalls easily overwhelms the impact of the AQR.

[4] See, for example, Haldane and Madouros (2012) and Blundel-Wignal and Roulet (2012).

test, 26 banks would have failed instead of three (Verstergaard and Retana 2013). Among the failures would have been some large German and French banks, including Deutsche Bank, Commerzbank, BNP Paribas, and Société Générale. A 4.5 leverage ratio would have caught all the banks that subsequently failed. No value of the risk-based measure would have done so while still allowing some banks to pass the test (Vestergaard and Retana 2013).

- Beware of claims by executives from the largest French, German, and Dutch banks emphasizing the credibility of the 2014 stress test results and belittling the results of stress tests done by outside analysts using alternative metrics, including leverage ratios.[5] They may well just be talking their book. Because large French, German, and Dutch banks have low leverage ratios and low ratios of risk-weighted assets to total assets, they invariably look better under a test that uses risk-based measures rather than leverage ratios. Indeed, Martin Wolf shows that the gap between leverage ratios and the risk-based capital metric used in the 2014 test is wider for Dutch, French, and German banks at the 'center' of the euro area than it is for Greek, Portuguese, Irish, Italian, and Spanish banks on the 'periphery'.[6]

- Ever since Christine Lagarde (2011), the IMF's managing director, put a spotlight in August 2011 on the need for "urgent capitalisation" of Europe's banks, a host of estimates by independent analysts has suggested a significant undercapitalisation of Europe's banks. Quite a few of these studies use leverage ratio benchmarks — sometimes supplemented with measures of systemic risk — to gauge the extent of undercapitalisation. Acharya and Steffan (2014), for example, continue to find an EU-wide capital shortfall of hundreds of billions of euros — a far cry from the €25 billion EU-wide shortfall arrived at in the 2014 stress test. Moreover, the largest part of that aggregate shortfall resides with large French banks.

- The US Federal Reserve has been employing a leverage ratio test in its annual stress tests since 2012. The Bank of England announced that it likewise plans to do so in its own stress tests, due later this year. In discussing

---

[5] See, for example, letter by Société Générale's Phillippe Heim, "Alternative Stress Tests Cannot Compare with Those of the ECB," Letters in the *Financial Times*, October 31, 2014.

[6] Martin Wolf, "Europe's Banks are Too Feeble to Spur Growth," *Financial Times*, October 28, 2014.

the heralded resilience of Canadian banks during the 2007-2009 crisis, Mark Carney has testified that "if I had to pick one reason why Canadian banks fared as well as they did, it was because we had a leverage ratio."[7]

- Last but not least, two popular defences of the existing level of capitalisation in EU banks should be discarded.

    o The first claims that large EU banks are adequately capitalised if they have approximately the same capital ratios as large US banks. This contention overlooks the 'too-big-to-fail' problem, which is more severe in the European Union than in the United States. EU bank concentration — if properly measured at both the individual-country and EU-wide levels — is higher than in the United States. In addition, bank credit accounts for a higher share of total financial intermediation in Europe (see Goldstein and Veron 2011, Pagano *et al.* 2014). Large EU banks should therefore be holding more capital than their US counterparts — not less, as recent data on leverage ratios indicate.[8]

    o The second defence suggests that large EU banks have enough capital if their capital ratios are similar to those of their global peers, broadly defined. But bank capital ratios are almost surely too low everywhere. Drawing on both theory and empirical evidence, Admati and Helwig (2013) make a persuasive case for higher bank capital requirements.[9] In a similar vein, 20 distinguished professors of finance (including two Nobel laureates) concluded (in a November 2010 letter to the *Financial Times*) that bank leverage ratios ought to be about 15% and that achieving such a target would generate substantial social benefits, with minimal if any social cost.[10] This target is far from the 3% minimum

---

[7] "Mark Carney Sees Logic in Tougher Cap on Banks' Leverage," *Independent*, September 29, 2014.

[8] Pagano *et al.* (2014) compare mean leverage ratios, corrected for differences in international accounting standards, for globally-systemically-important banks (G-SIBs) in the European Union and the United States. The averages for the second quarter of 2013 were 3.9% for EU banks versus 4.5% for US banks.

[9] Although Admati and Helwig (2013) strongly prefer to measure bank capital by a leverage ratio rather than by a risk-based metric, their overall conclusion about bank capital being way too low also applies to risk-based capital measures.

[10] "Healthy Banking System is the Goal, not Profitable Banks," *Financial Times*, November 9, 2010. See also Admati and Helwig (2013) on why higher minimum requirements for bank capital have a very favorable benefit-cost ratio.

for the leverage ratio established under Basel III and far from actual leverage ratios maintained by large banks around the world. All of this suggests that the capital hurdle rates used in the 2014 EU-wide stress test are more likely to be too easy (low) than too tough (high).

CONCLUSION

On the eve of becoming the Single Supervisor for Europe's largest banks, the ECB missed an important opportunity to establish trust in EU bank supervision. By refusing to include a rigorous leverage ratio test, by allowing banks to artificially inflate bank capital, by engaging in wholesale monkey business with tax deferred assets, and also by ruling out a deflation scenario, the ECB produced estimates of the aggregate capital shortfall and a country pattern of bank failures that are not believable. This was not a case of 'doing whatever it takes' to establish credibility, but rather one of avoiding the tough decisions and asking the market to 'take whatever'. When it comes to fixing the long-running undercapitalisation of Europe's banking system, what European authorities have delivered will not be enough.

"The 2014 EU-wide bank stress test lacks credibility" by Morris Goldstein. Copyright © 2014 by VOX, CEPR's Policy Portal. Used with permission of the publisher.

REFERENCES

Acharya, V, and S Steffan (2014), "Falling Short of Expectations? Stress Testing the European Banking System", VoxEU, January 17.

Admati, A, and M Helwig (2013), *The Banker's New Clothes: What's Wrong with Banking and What to Do About It*, Princeton: Princeton University Press.

Blundel-Wignal, A, and C Roulet (2012), "Business Models of Banks, Leverage, And the Distance to Default", *Financial Market Trends*, Paris: OECD.

EBA (European Banking Authority) (2014), Results of the 2014 EU-Wide Stress Test. Aggregate Results. London: European Banking Authority.

Goldstein, M, and N Veron (2011), Too Big To Fail: The Transatlantic Debate. Working Paper No. 11-2. Washington: Peterson Institute for International Economics. January.

Haldane, A, and V Madouros (2012), "The Dog and the Frisbee", Paper presented at the Federal Reserve Bank of Kansas City's 36th Economic Policy Symposium, Jackson Hole, Wyoming.

Hoenig, T (2013), "Basel III Capital: A Well-Intended Illusion", Paper presented at the International Association of Deposit Insurers 2013 Research Conference, Basel, Switzerland.

Pagano M, V Acharya, A Boot, M Brunnermeier, C Buch, M Helwig, S Langfield, A Sapir, and L van den Burg (2014), Is Europe Overbanked? Report of the Advisory Scientific Committee, European Systemic Risk Board. June.

Vestergaard, J, and M Retana (2013), *Behind Smoke and Mirrors: On the Alleged Capitalization of Europe's Banks*, Copenhagen: Danish Institute of International Affairs.

Part IV
IMF Policies

Chapter 15

Evaluating Fund Stabilization Programs with Multicountry Data: Some Methodological Pitfalls

Morris Goldstein and Peter Montiel

A noteworthy by-product of the continuing debate over the benefits and costs of Fund conditionality has been the development of a considerable empirical literature on Fund stabilization programs (that is, on stand-by and extended arrangements with the Fund). Furthermore, although the first studies of Fund program experience were carried out almost exclusively by Fund staff (for example, Reichmann and Stillson (1978), Reichmann (1978)), the past seven years have witnessed at least as much quantitative scrutiny of Fund programs from outside the Fund as from within it.[1]

Mr Goldstein, Advisor in the Research Department when this paper was written, is now Advisor in the External Relations Department. He is a graduate of Rutgers University and New York University.

Mr Montiel, an economist in the Developing Country Studies Division of the Research Department when this paper was written, is now in the Macro-economics Division of the Development Research Department, The World Bank. He is a graduate of Yale University and the Massachusetts Institute of Technology.

[1] External studies include Connors (1979), Cline and Weintraub (1981), Williamson (1982, 1983), Gylfason (1983), Killick and Chapman (1982), Killick (1984), and Loxley (1984).

A common practice in many of these studies has been to compare the behavior of one or more key macroeconomic variables (for example, the current account, overall balance of payments, rate of inflation, growth rate of real output, and the like) before the program with the behavior during or after the program. To account for changes in the international economic environment that could alter macroeconomic outcomes independently of the program, it also has become increasingly popular (see Donovan (1982) and Gylfason (1983)) to supplement the "before-after" calculations for program countries with a similar comparison for a reference or "control group" of nonprogram countries.

The primary purpose of this paper is to present and to discuss several methodological problems or pitfalls that can cause "true" program effects to differ from "estimated" program effects when either the before-after approach or the control-group approach is used.[2] Particular attention is paid to the inferences that can properly be drawn about the independent effects of a Fund program from a comparison of program and nonprogram countries. More specifically, we attempt to spell out the conditions under which the observed behavior of macroeconomic outcomes in nonprogram countries can serve as a good predictor of the unobserved behavior of program countries in the *absence* of a program, and to identify the biases in estimates of program effectiveness if these conditions are not satisfied.

Because the issue of program effectiveness is a broad and controversial one, it is worthwhile at the outset to indicate three particular caveats relevant to this study. First, we interpret or define "program effectiveness" as the difference between the actual macroeconomic performance observed under a Fund program and the performance that would have been expected in the *absence* of such a program. As noted by Guitián (1981, pp. 36–37), this is only one of at least three possible measuring rods.[3] Two others, both of which have been used in some earlier studies, are the difference between actual

---

Internal studies include Beveridge and Kelly (1980), Beveridge (1981), Donovan (1981,1982), Kelly (1982), Odling-Smee (1982), and Zulu and Nsouli (1985).

[2] Athough not all of the previous studies of Fund program experience sought to identify the independent effects of Fund programs, this paper evaluates the before-after approach and the control-group approach as estimators of such program effects.

[3] For a thorough discussion of alternative interpretations of "program effects" and of their relative strengths and weaknesses, see Goldstein (1986).

macroeconomic performance under the program and actual performance before the program, and the difference between actual performance under the program and the performance specified in the targets of the program. Obviously, these three alternative performance indicators can yield different verdicts about program effectiveness. Our preference for the first measure, despite its subjective nature, rests on the argument that it is the only one that can provide an estimate of the program's *independent* effect in the real world, where nonprogram factors (for example, oil price shocks, varying rates of economic activity in industrial countries, and the like) are also operating on observed macroeconomic outcomes.

A second caveat is that the interpretation of program effects in this paper depends critically on our definition of a "program." Specifically, a program is defined to be in effect when a country has a formal arrangement with the Fund, and not when a country adopts a "Fund-type" policy package on its own. Under this definition of a program, and using our preferred definition of program effectiveness, a program would be judged to have *no* effect if the country would have adopted the identical set of policies anyway, even though the policies themselves may have substantial impact on the economy and even though these Fund-type policies could be better than some other set of policies.[4] It might be argued that it is the effects of Fund-type policies rather than of Fund involvement that is the more relevant issue. To investigate the effects of Fund-type policies, it is not necessary to differentiate between program and nonprogram countries. Instead, the relevant comparison would be between macroeconomic outcomes under Fund-type policies and those under some other set of policies. Program countries would no doubt be included in the data set, but they would not be identified as such. This approach would have the advantage that the considerable diversity in the policy mix and in country circumstances that characterize Fund programs can be reflected in the analysis. This is not the case with the "on-off" approach typically adopted with large multicountry samples. Nevertheless, much of the existing empirical literature on Fund stabilization programs does make direct comparisons between program and nonprogram countries. It is therefore of

---

[4] In this connection, one would also have to account for the effects of Fund involvement on the availability of additional external resources, either from the Fund itself or through the catalytic effect of Fund involvement on other lenders. For more on this point, see Section II.

some interest to identify what can and cannot be legitimately inferred from such comparisons.

Third, this paper deals exclusively with the *methodology* of estimating program effects. Specifically, we do not offer our own estimates of Fund program effects. We do present (in Section III) some empirical examples of how estimated program effects can differ depending on the methodology used, but these should not be viewed as reliable estimates of program effects themselves. Indeed, it is one of the central tenets of this paper that reliable estimates of Fund program effects from multicountry data must await, among other things, further testing of the issues and pitfalls outlined here.[5] In this sense the calculations presented in this paper should not alter anyone's view about whether Fund stabilization programs "work"; these calculations do, however, have implications for the kinds of evidence that one may want to collect in the future to determine if and how programs work.

The plan of the rest of the paper is as follows. In Section I we introduce a simple but fairly general model of the relationship between macroeconomic outcomes and the presence or absence of a Fund stabilization program. This model not only permits Fund programs to affect macroeconomic outcomes in program countries through a variety of channels, but it also permits prior macroeconomic outcomes to affect the probability that a country will embark upon a Fund program. In addition, the model admits the possibility of stabilizing macroeconomic policy actions in the absence of a Fund program. We then use this model to analyze the conditions under which true program effects would equal estimated program effects under two shorthand calculations: before-after comparisons of (mean) macroeconomic outcomes for program countries alone, and before-after comparisons of (mean) outcomes for program countries relative to those for nonprogram countries. In anticipation of what follows, potentially serious estimation biases are found to exist when the "selection" of program countries is nonrandom and when the determinants

---

[5]The empirical examples in the paper are not reliable indicators of program effectiveness for many reasons. To mention just three, the paper deals with only one (sample-selection bias) of many potential sources of bias in cross-country estimates (for example, we ignore bias associated with interdependence between outcomes in program and nonprogram countries, as well as bias from aggregation across different types of programs); the paper considers only short-term (one-year) effects of programs; and the calculations cover only a few of the wide range of policy instruments actually specified in Fund programs.

of macro-economic outcomes are correlated with the determinants of Fund program selection.

In Section II we outline a procedure (the "modified control-group approach") for removing sample-selectivity bias from control-group estimates of the effects of Fund programs when the selection of program countries is non-random. This modified control-group approach is also capable (in principle) of providing information on *how* total program effects are apportioned among induced changes in policy instruments, induced changes in behavioral parameters, and general "confidence effects." Practical estimation problems associated with the modified control-group approach are discussed.

In Section III we investigate the empirical relevance of the most important methodological pitfalls mentioned above. For this purpose we utilize a sample of developing countries and of Fund stabilization programs over the 1974–81 period. Estimates of Fund program effects are then compared against three alternative estimators — a before-after comparison of mean outcomes for program countries alone, a before-after comparison of mean outcomes for program countries relative to that for nonprogram countries, and a reduced-form regression estimate of program effects that controls for revealed preprogram differences between program and nonprogram countries. The three alternative estimators are demonstrated to produce substantially different estimates of Fund program effects. Conclusions are summarized in Section IV.

I. COMPARING ALTERNATIVE ESTIMATORS OF FUND PROGRAM EFFECTS

In this section we introduce an explicit analytical framework (in the form of a simple four-equation model) for analyzing the effects of Fund stabilization programs.

A Simple Model of Program Effects

For the purposes of this paper, it was desirable for such a model to have four broad features. First, the model should be general enough that the two dominant existing statistical approaches to ex post program evaluation — the before-after approach and the control-group approach — could be treated as special cases of the more general model. In this way the assumptions implicit in the existing methodologies can be identified and evaluated. Second, the model should incorporate nonprogram determinants of macroeconomic outcomes of both an international and a country-specific nature. Third, given that Fund stabilization programs operate primarily by altering the design or stance (or both) of macroeconomic policies, the model should indicate the determinants of indigenous changes in macroeconomic policy so that the macroeconomic outcomes expected in the *absence* of a program can be explicitly defined. In other words, we want a model in which the policy instruments and not just macroeconomic outcomes are endogenous. Finally, the model should indicate what objective factors, if any, determine the probability that a country will have a Fund program during a given period. The reason for treating Fund program status or program-country selection as an endogenous variable is that this is the only way in which to investigate the consequences of systematic differences between program countries and nonprogram countries. Obviously, if such differences exist before a program period, they need to be taken into account in any subsequent comparison of program and nonprogram countries to the extent that they affect macroeconomic performance. Failure to include such differences would mean that variations in macroeconomic performance between the two country groups could be attributed to the presence or absence of a program, when in reality the differences might in large part reflect other factors.

In equations (1) through (4) below, we set out a model of Fund program effects that contains these basic features:

$$\Delta y_{ij} = \Delta x_i' \beta_{ij} + \Delta W' \alpha_{ij} + \beta_{ij}^{IMF} \Delta d_i + \Delta \varepsilon_{ij} \tag{1}$$

$$\Delta x_i = \gamma [y_i^d - (y_i)_{-1}] + \eta_i \tag{2}$$

$$z_i = [y_i^d - (y_i)_{-1}]' \delta + \pi_i \tag{3}$$

$$d_i = 1 \quad \text{if } z_i > z^*$$

$$d_i = 0 \quad \text{if } z_i \leq z^*. \tag{4}$$

In these equations, y_{ij} is the jth macroeconomic outcome or target variable in country i; x_i is a K-element vector of macroeconomic policy variables that would be observed in country i in the absence of a Fund program; W is an M-element random vector of world nonprogram variables; z_i is a random variable that serves as the index of country-specific characteristics that determines the probability of country i having a Fund program during a given period; d_i is a dummy variable that takes the value of unity if a country has a

Fund program and the value of zero otherwise; y_i^d is the desired value of the vector y_i; z^* is the threshold value of z_i that divides program from nonprogram countries; e_{ij}, η_i, and π_i are unobservable error terms (with zero means and fixed variances) that are serially and (for simplicity) mutually uncorrelated; β_{ij}, α_{ij}, β_{ij}^{IMF}, γ, and δ are constants with the appropriate dimensions; Δ is the first-difference operator; the subscript -1 indicates the previous period; and a prime ($'$) denotes the transpose of a matrix.

The variable y_{ij} in equation (1) should be considered as one of the primary targets of a stabilization program, such as the current account, the overall balance of payments, the inflation rate, the real growth rate, and the like.[6] Equation (1) can then be interpreted as positing that the change in this macroeconomic outcome or target variable will be a function of four factors: (1) changes in macroeconomic policy instruments (for example, the rate of domestic credit expansion; government tax revenues, expenditure, or both; the exchange rate; and the like) that would have occurred in the absence of a program; (2) changes in world economic conditions (such as changes in world oil prices or changes in real economic activity in industrial countries); (3) the total effect of a Fund program if the country has a program in place during that period; and (4) a host of unobservable shocks that are specific to country i.

A special word of comment is appropriate for β_{ij}^{IMF}, which is the coefficient that indicates the effect of a Fund program on macroeconomic outcomes. In our view, this coefficient should incorporate at least three channels or avenues by which Fund programs can affect y_{ij}. First, Fund programs can alter the value of macroeconomic policy instruments from what that value would be in the absence of such programs. Note, however, that since Δx_i is defined as the change in policy instruments that would occur in the *absence* of a program, Δx_i, is directly observable only for nonprogram countries; for program countries, Δx_i, must be estimated (through equation (2)). In any case, the important implication is that a program can affect y_{ij}, by making the actual change in policy instruments different from Δx_i. The second potential channel of program effect is by altering what might be called the general

---

[6] Such an interpretation would be consistent with Guitián's view (1981, p. 30) that the broad objective of a Fund-supported stabilization program is "... the restoration and maintenance of viability to the balance of payments in an environment of price stability and sustainable rates of economic growth."

state of confidence about the economy of country i. Here the successful negotiation of a credible program with the Fund may, for example, have a positive effect on private and official capital inflows into country i that may indeed be quantitatively more significant than the financial resources supplied by the Fund itself in support of the stabilization package. This, like the first channel of effect, is of course an empirical question; suffice it to note here that the measurement of such confidence effects of programs is an extremely difficult task in practice. The third and final channel of potential program effect is by changing the parameters β_{ij} for any given size change in the policy instruments. In other words, programs can work not only by, say, making monetary and fiscal policies more restrictive than they would otherwise be, but also by improving or reducing the effectiveness of any given stance of policy. The ways in which behavioral parameters can shift in response to policy changes have been outlined by Lucas (1976), but here it is enough merely to note that programs can change the expectations of agents in the economy about the future course of x_i and y_{ij}, and these altered expectations can in turn affect β_{ij}.[7] The assumptions in equation (1) that unobservable country-specific shocks have zero expected means and are serially uncorrelated imply that, other things being equal, a negative shock to, say, country i's balance of payments in period t is not expected to be repeated in the next period. In other words, the model contains a regression-to-the-mean characteristic for macroeconomic outcomes that provides for some automatic stabilization. Of course, only the data can decide whether such an assumption is consistent with the recent experience of program and nonprogram countries.

The basic notion represented in equation (2) is that the authorities display a systematic policy reaction to perceived disequilibria in their macroeconomic target variables. More specifically, equation (2) says that the change in country i's macroeconomic policy instruments between the current and previous period will be a function of the difference between the desired value of the macroeconomic target variables in this period, y_i^d, and their actual value in the preceding period, $(y_i)_{-1}$, with γ serving as the coefficient that indicates the

---

[7] For example, an announced new target for the real exchange rate may be viewed as more likely to be adhered to if it is a component of a Fund program than otherwise. In that case, the response of the private sector to a given change in the real exchange rate may depend on whether that change occurs in the context of a Fund program.

responsiveness of the policy instruments to such target disequilibria. For example, in the case of stabilizing policy behavior, equation (2) would suggest that a current account deficit in the preceding period that was large relative to the authorities' target deficit would call for a downward adjustment in, say, the rate of domestic credit expansion in this period. Because Δx_i is defined as the change in policy instruments in country i that would occur in the absence of a program, equation (2) spells out "normal" policy behavior by the authorities and thus provides one approach to estimating the counterfactual for program countries. In addition, so long as γ carries the correct sign, equation (2) also implies that there may well be stabilizing policy action in nonprogram countries. Idiosyncratic, country-specific policy behavior is intended to be captured by the error term η_i, in equation (2).

Equations (3) and (4) constitute perhaps the greatest departure in this model from the earlier literature on program evaluation by suggesting that the presence or absence of a Fund program should itself be treated *endogenously* and, in particular, as a function of observable country-specific characteristics. There are strong a priori reasons for believing that Fund program status is not random. A necessary (but not sufficient) condition for the use of Fund resources is that the country display a balance of payments need.[8] This implies that, among the population of potential claimants for Fund resources, the sample of countries with Fund programs in place at any given time is likely to have displayed less favorable external balance performance before the program period itself than the population at large.

As written, equation (3) uses the difference between the desired values of macroeconomic target variables in this period and their actual values in the preceding period to explain the probability that country i will have a Fund program this period. Under the assumption that the desired target values y_i^d are constant over time but not necessarily across countries, this difference reduces to a formulation in which the actual values of macroeconomic outcomes in the preprogram period, $(y_i)_{-1}$, influence program-country selection. Equation (3) should therefore be capable of capturing systematic selection of program countries by the Fund on the basis of balance of payments need because the vector $(y_i)_{-1}$ will include preprogram values of country i's external accounts.

---

[8] Although there is no explicit formula for judging balance of payments needs, the three indicators given foremost attention are the actual balance of payments, the level of international reserves, and recent changes in the level of reserves.

Note further that such specification of equation (3) deliberately makes for a potentially serious problem. As written, the preprogram outcomes $(y_i)_{-1}$ help to explain program selection in equation (3) and also policy reaction Δx_i in the absence of a program in equation (2). Because both z_i and Δx_i can influence the change in macroeconomic outcomes between the program and preprogram year, it can be seen that our model sets up the troublesome possibility that it will be difficult to separate program from nonprogram determinants of Δy_i. As we shall demonstrate later, this problem will be present so long as the determinants of Fund program status d_i are correlated with the determinants of Δy_i, whether through Δx_i or through any other variable explaining Δy_i. As also discussed later, this problem disappears if program selection is random, since δ in equation (3) will then be zero; that is, it will not be possible to relate program-country selection z_i — hence, ultimately, d_i — to any observable objective factors.

With the general outlines of this model of Fund program effects in mind, we can next proceed to analyze how estimated program effects will differ from true program effects under a variety of shorthand estimation techniques.

The Before-After Approach

This approach to ex post program evaluation has been used both by Fund staff (for example, Reichmann and Stillson (1978)) and by outside observers (for example, Connors (1979), Killick and Chapman (1982)). Although these studies utilized multicountry samples, this approach is not necessarily a cross-sectional technique because the (implicit) parameters estimated are allowed to differ across countries.

Recalling that β_{ij}^{IMF} is the "true" effect of a Fund program on the jth target variable in country i, the before-after approach estimates β_{ij}^{IMF} — call it $\hat{\beta}_{ij}^{IMF,A}$ — as:

$$\hat{\beta}_{ij}^{IMF,A} = \Delta y_{ij}, \quad i \in P, \tag{5}$$

where P denotes the set of program countries. Thus, any change in a target variable in a program country (or in a group of program countries) is attributed *exclusively* to program effects. The estimate, $\hat{\beta}_{ij}^{IMF,A}$, is sometimes subjected to (nonparametric) statistical tests of significance and sometimes not.

The fatal flaw of the before-after approach is that it relies on assumptions of other things being equal that are highly implausible. To see this, let us introduce only equation (1) from the general model of program effects:

$$\Delta y_{ij} = \Delta x'_i \beta_{ij} + \Delta W' \alpha_{ij} + \beta_{ij}^{IMF} \Delta d_i + \Delta \varepsilon_{ij}. \tag{1}$$

Now suppose that the preceding period was one during which there was no Fund program in effect (so that $d_i = 0$ for $t-1$). Then,

$$\Delta y_{ij} = \beta_{ij}^{IMF} + \Delta x'_i \beta_{ij} + \Delta W' \alpha_{ij} + \Delta \varepsilon_{ij} \quad \text{for } i \in P. \tag{6}$$

From equation (5), the before-after approach then gives

$$\hat{\beta}_{ij}^{IMF,A} = \beta_{ij}^{IMF} + \Delta x'_i \beta_{ij} + \Delta W' \alpha_{ij} + \Delta \varepsilon_{ij} \quad \text{for } i \in P. \tag{7}$$

Taking expectations of equation (7), conditional on the presence of a Fund program in country i and on observed changes in the world economic environment, we have

$$E(\hat{\beta}_{ij}^{IMF,A} | i \in P, \Delta W') = \beta_{ij}^{IMF} + E(\Delta x'_i | i \in P, \Delta W') \beta_{ij}$$
$$+ \Delta W' \alpha_{ij} + E(\Delta \varepsilon_{ij} | i \in P, \Delta W'). \tag{8}$$

Thus, the before-after approach would produce an unbiased estimate of program effects — that is, $E(\beta_{ij}^{IMF} | i \in P, \Delta W') = \hat{\beta}_{ij}^{IMF,A}$ — if and only if

$$E(\Delta x'_i | i \in P, \Delta W') \beta_{ij} + \Delta W' \alpha_{ij}$$
$$+ E(\Delta \varepsilon_{ij} | i \in P, \Delta W') = 0. \tag{9}$$

In other words, an unbiased estimate of program effects would require that the nonprogram determinants of y_{ij} would have behaved in such a way as to leave y_{ij} unchanged, on average, between the preprogram and current program periods. Reference to the 1973–81 period — when large changes in world oil prices, large year-to-year changes in industrial country real gross national product (GNP), and significant shifts in real interest rates created serious difficulties for the external positions of developing countries (see International Monetary Fund (1983), Goldstein and Khan (1982), and Khan and Knight (1983)) — gives sufficient reason to doubt that $\Delta W' \alpha_{ij}$ would be zero for most program countries, even over short periods. By the same token, the ex post record of money supply growth and fiscal deficits by developing countries during the same period (see International Monetary Fund (1983) and Gylfason (1983)) generates skepticism that changes in domestic policy instruments would have been such as to offset exactly, on the average, the effects of external and internal shocks for most program countries. In short, we should expect the other-things-equal assumption of the before after approach to be violated in practice. As such, estimates of program effects under this approach are likely to be contaminated by nonprogram factors.

The Traditional Control-Group Approach

A second approach, hereafter called the traditional control-group approach, has a long history in empirical labor economics but appears to have been first applied to analysis of experience with Fund programs by Donovan (1982).[9] More recently, Gylfason (1983) has adopted a more sophisticated version of it.

This technique in effect uses the behavior of a control group (a group of nonprogram countries) to estimate what would have happened in the program group in the *absence* of programs. Thus it implicitly assumes that only the program itself distinguishes the group of program countries from the control group. It is therefore natural to interpret this as a cross-sectional approach. Specifically, in terms of the model, we can drop all the country i subscripts from the coefficients because these are now assumed to be identical across countries. In addition, because we are now dealing with country groups, β_j^{IMF} represents the *mean* effect of Fund programs on the jth macroeconomic target variable. The equation for Δy_{ij} can now be written as

$$\Delta y_{ij} = \Delta x_i' \beta_j + \Delta W' \alpha_j + \beta_j^{IMF} \Delta d_i + \Delta \varepsilon_{ij}. \tag{10}$$

Under the control-group approach, β_j^{IMF} is estimated by

$$\hat{\beta}_j^{IMF,B} = (\overline{\Delta y_j})_P - (\overline{\Delta y_j})_N, \tag{11}$$

where a bar over a variable represents its mean, and N denotes the set of nonprogram countries.

---

[9] Many of the methodological issues discussed in this paper have been analyzed earlier in the literature of labor economics concerning "treatment effects"; for example, see Ashenfelter (1978) and Ashenfelter and Card (1984).

To investigate the properties of this estimator, we again take expectations. Applying this procedure to equation (11) yields[10]

$$E(\hat{\beta}_j^{IMF,B}) = \beta_j^{IMF} + E[(\Delta x_i' \beta_j + \Delta \varepsilon_{ij}) | i \in P]$$
$$- E[(\Delta x_i' \beta_j + \Delta \varepsilon_{ij}) | i \in N]. \quad (12)$$

From equation (12), it can be seen that the condition for $\hat{\beta}_j^{IMF,B}$ to represent an unbiased estimate of the true program effects, β_j^{IMF}, is that

$$E[(\Delta x_i' \beta_j + \Delta \varepsilon_{ij}) | i \in P] - E[(\Delta x_i' \beta_j + \Delta \varepsilon_{ij}) | i \in N] = 0. \quad (13)$$

In other words, the groups of program and nonprogram countries have to be drawn from the same population in the sense that the expected value of the change in nonprogram determinants of y_{ij} must be the same for members of both groups. Comparing equation (13) with equation (9) shows that the control-group approach is *not* necessarily less restrictive than the before-after approach. Although the control-group approach controls for the effect of changes in the global economic environment (that is, the term $\Delta W' \alpha_{ij}$ that appears in equation (9) drops out as a source of bias in equation (13) because such global factors are assumed to affect program and nonprogram countries equally), it does so at the expense of introducing a *new* source of bias — the characteristics of nonprogram countries (that is, the term $-E[(\Delta x_i' \beta_j + \Delta \varepsilon_{ij}) | i \in N]$ appears in equation (13) but not in equation (9)).[11]

The foregoing suggests that the choice between the before-after approach and the control-group approach to estimating program effects ought to depend on one's a priori beliefs about similarities between program and nonprogram countries and about the relationship between domestic and global determinants of Δy_{ij}. Specifically, if program and nonprogram countries are believed to be quite similar on average, and if the domestic determinants of Δy_{ij} are not believed to offset international influences on Δy_{ij}, then equation (13) is more likely to be satisfied than equation (9); hence the control-group approach will provide a better (less biased) estimate of program effects than will the before-after approach. We next proceed to investigate, first, the nature of the

---

[10]To simplify the notation, expectations of group averages in equation (12) and elsewhere in the paper are expressed in terms of the "representative" member of each group; that is, we implicitly assume that all members of a group are identical.

[11]We are indebted to Rüşdü Saracoglu for drawing this to our attention.

bias that is generated by this methodology when the determinants of program-country selection are correlated with the determinants of macroeconomic performance and, second, the nature of the biases in the specific (but probably most relevant) case in which both program-country selection and macroeconomic performance depend on macroeconomic performance before the program period.

Nonrandom Selection of Program Countries

To examine these issues it is helpful to introduce the index of unobservable country-specific characteristics, z_i, that regulates the probability that country i will have a program during any given period. Specifically, we now introduce equation (4) from the general model of program effects:

$$\begin{aligned} d_i &= 1 \quad \text{if } z_i > z^* \\ d_i &= 0 \quad \text{if } z_i \leq z^*, \end{aligned} \quad (14)$$

where z^* is an arbitrary threshold value for z_i. Instead of also introducing equation (3), assume for the moment that $E(z_i) = 0$ and $E(z_i^2) = \sigma_z^2$. Equation (4) says that a country will have a program if its index of country-specific characteristics is greater than z^*; if not, it will not have a Fund program, at least in that period. The probability that a country will have a program is therefore equal to the probability that $z_i > z^*$.

We can now use equation (4) to rewrite the necessary condition, as previously expressed in equation (13), for an unbiased estimator of the program effects under the control-group approach; that is,

$$E[(\Delta x_i' \beta_j + \Delta \varepsilon_{ij})|z_i > z^*] \\ - E[(\Delta x_i' \beta_j + \Delta \varepsilon_{ij})|z_i \leq z^*] = 0. \quad (13a)$$

Recall that both $\Delta x_i' \beta_j + \Delta \varepsilon_{ij}$ and z_i are random variables. Suppose that the correlation between these two variables is given by ρ_{xz} and that the expected value of $\Delta x_i' \beta_j + \Delta \varepsilon_{ij}$ is $\Delta x' \beta_j$. We show in Appendix I that if $\Delta x' \beta_j + \Delta \varepsilon_{ij}$ and z_i have a joint normal distribution, then

$$\begin{aligned} E[(\Delta x_i' \beta_j + \Delta \varepsilon_{ij})|z_i > z^*] &> \Delta x' \beta_j \quad \text{if } \rho_{xz} > 0 \\ &= \Delta x' \beta_j \quad \text{if } \rho_{xz} = 0 \\ &< \Delta x' \beta_j \quad \text{if } \rho_{xz} < 0 \end{aligned} \quad (14a)$$

$$E[(\Delta x_i'\beta_j + \Delta\varepsilon_{ij})|z_i > z^*] < \Delta x'\beta_j \quad \text{if } \rho_{xz} > 0$$
$$= \Delta x'\beta_j \quad \text{if } \rho_{xz} = 0$$
$$> \Delta x'\beta_j \quad \text{if } \rho_{xz} < 0. \quad (14b)$$

In other words, if $\Delta x_i'\beta_j + \Delta\varepsilon_{ij}$ and z_i are correlated ($\rho_{xz} \neq 0$), then our expectation of $\Delta x_i'\beta_j + \Delta\varepsilon_{ij}$ will depend on the value taken by z_i. This result is intuitive. Suppose, for example, that ρ_{xz} is positive. Then, relatively large values of $\Delta x_i'\beta_j + \Delta\varepsilon_{ij}$ are associated with relatively large values of z_i. Thus, if we know that z_i is relatively large for some country i but do not observe $\Delta x_i'\beta_j + \Delta\varepsilon_{ij}$, our expectation is that $\Delta x_i'\beta_j + \Delta\varepsilon_{ij}$ will also be relatively large for this country. Likewise, if ρ_{xz} is negative, then relatively large values of z_i will be associated with relatively small values of $\Delta x_i'\beta_j + \Delta\varepsilon_{ij}$, and observing a large z_i will lead us to expect a small $\Delta x_i'\beta_j + \Delta\varepsilon_{ij}$. In contrast, if $\Delta x_i'\beta_j + \Delta\varepsilon_{ij}$ and z_i are known to be uncorrelated, then observing a large z_i gives no basis on which to expect $\Delta x_i'\beta_j + \Delta\varepsilon_{ij}$ to be either particularly large or particularly small for the ith country.

Because program countries are those for which $z_i > z^*$, program countries as a group will exhibit a relatively large z_i. Likewise, the representative z for the nonprogram group will be relatively small. It follows that if $\rho_{xz} > 0$ the difference between the program and nonprogram groups with respect to the expected change in target variable y_j consists of *both* the effect of the program on the change in y_j *and* the difference between the relatively large $\Delta x_i'\beta_j + \Delta\varepsilon_{ij}$ expected for the program group and the relatively small $\Delta x_i'\beta_j + \Delta\varepsilon_{ij}$ expected for the nonprogram group. Because this second component of the expected difference must be positive, the expected difference will *exceed* the true effect of the program on the change in target y_j. A similar analysis establishes that the expected difference will be *less* than the true program effect when $\rho_{xz} < 0$. When $\rho_{xz} = 0$, it remains the case that z_i is relatively large for program countries and relatively small for nonprogram ones, but this gives no reason to expect that $\Delta x_i'\beta_j + \Delta\varepsilon_{ij}$ will be systematically different between the two groups; therefore, the only difference we are justified in expecting is that attributable to the effects of the program. These considerations imply that

$$E(\hat{\beta}_j^{IMF,B}) > \beta_j^{IMF} \quad \text{if } \rho_{xz} > 0$$
$$= \beta_j^{IMF} \quad \text{if } \rho_{xz} = 0$$
$$< \beta_j^{IMF} \quad \text{if } \rho_{xz} < 0. \quad (15)$$

The relations in expression (15) can be derived formally by substituting expressions (14a) and (14b) in equation (12).

Thus, ρ_{xz} is the crucial parameter in determining the direction of the bias in the control-group methodology. Specifically, if the determinants of program selection (z_i) are *positively* correlated with the determinants of macroeconomic performance that would have occurred in the absence of a program ($\Delta x_i' \beta_j + \Delta \varepsilon_{ij}$), then the control-group estimate of program effects ($\hat{\beta}_j^{IMF,B}$) will *overstate* true program effects (β_j^{IMF}). Conversely, only if the determinants of program selection are uncorrelated with the determinants of macroeconomic performance ($\rho_{xz} = 0$) is the control-group estimator an unbiased indicator of true program effects.

The significance of the preceding analysis is that it permits us to move from the vague statement that "if the program and nonprogram groups are different, then the control-group approach will be biased" — a statement that is *not* correct — to the precise identification of ρ_{xz} as the critical parameter determining both the presence and the direction of bias.[12] In assessing the adequacy of the control-group methodology, the relevant question then is whether there are any reasons inherent in the nature of the problem that would lead us to believe that this correlation (ρ_{xz}) will be nonzero.

The model embodies precisely such a nonzero correlation because *both* the determinants of program status in equation (4) and of normal policy changes in equation (2) are linear functions of macroeconomic outcomes before the program period. To show this formally, first rewrite the model by taking the transpose of equation (2), substituting for $\Delta x_i'$ in equation (1), and making some small changes in notation:[13]

$$\Delta y_i = \beta_{0ij} - (y_i)'_{-1} \gamma' \beta_j + \beta_j^{IMF} \Delta d_i + \Delta \hat{\varepsilon}_{ij} \tag{16}$$

$$z_i = \delta_{0i} - (y_i)'_{-1} \delta + \pi_i, \tag{17}$$

$$d_i = 1 \quad \text{if } z_i > z^*$$

$$d_j = 0 \quad \text{if } z_i \leq z^*, \tag{4}$$

---

[12] Note that, when equation (4) holds but $\rho_{xz} = 0$, the program and nonprogram groups can be quite different *without* implying the existence of bias in the control-group methodology.
[13] We also have dropped the global variable $\Delta W'$ and its coefficient α_{ij} from equation (1) to simplify the exposition.

where

$$\beta_{0ij} = y_i^{d'}\gamma'\beta_j$$
$$\Delta\hat{\varepsilon}_{ij} = \Delta\varepsilon_{ij} + \eta_i'\beta_j$$
$$\delta_{0i} = y_i^{d'}\delta.$$

To determine whether the control-group estimator of program effects will be biased, we again need to examine the correlations between $-(y_i)'_{-1}\gamma'\beta_j$ and z_i and between $\Delta\hat{\varepsilon}_{ij}$ and z_i. These will be determined by the signs of

$$\text{cov}[-(y_i)'_{-1}\gamma'\beta_j, z_i] = \beta_j'\gamma\Sigma_{y-1}\delta \tag{18a}$$

$$\text{cov}(\Delta\hat{\varepsilon}_i, z_i) = \sigma_\varepsilon^2\delta_j, \tag{18b}$$

where Σ_{y-1} is the covariance matrix of $(y_i)_{-1}$, σ_ε^2 is the variance of ε_{ij}, and δ_j is the jth component of δ. These results assume that ε_{ij}, η_i, and π_i are mutually uncorrelated.

The crucial thing to notice about the covariances portrayed in equations (18a) and (18b) is that they can in general be expected to be nonzero — a finding that implies that the control-group estimator of program effects will be biased. The more interesting issue, however, is why this estimator turns out to be biased. Our analysis suggests that the determinants of program status will be correlated with the nonprogram determinants of Δy_{ij} for two reasons.

First, preprogram values of key macroeconomic target variables, $(y_i)_{-1}$, are likely to trigger policy responses, Δx_i, *even in the absence of programs*, as originally suggested in our policy reaction function (equation (2)). In terms of equation (18a), this assumption shows up as a nonzero value for the covariance $\beta_j'\gamma\Sigma_{y-1}\delta$.

Second, negative *transitory* shocks in the preprogram period are by their very nature unlikely to recur during the program period (recall that ε_{ij} has an expected value of zero and is assumed to be serially uncorrelated), with the result that *changes* in macro-economic target variables between the preprogram and program periods, Δy_i, will display regression to the mean with respect to past shocks; in terms of equation (18b), this result shows up as a nonzero value for $\sigma_\varepsilon^2\delta_j$.

We next inquire about the direction of this bias. For that source of bias that arises from regression to the mean, we can provide an unambiguous answer under reasonable assumptions. This is not possible for the bias arising from the existence of policy reaction functions; in this case we can, however, spell out the conditions necessary for that source of bias to disappear.

Consider the bias arising from regression to the mean. Because Fund programs are designed to move target variables in the desired direction, we expect the product of β_j^{IMF} and δ_j to be greater than zero (that is, $\beta_j^{IMF} \delta_j > 0$). The logic is that, if a below-target value of y_{ij} (for example, the current account surplus) causes a country to come to the Fund for assistance ($\delta_j > 0$), the Fund program will seek to *increase* actual y_{ij} (that is, $\beta_j^{IMF} > 0$); hence, $\beta_j^{IMF} \delta_j > 0$. Likewise, for those target variables (for example, the rate of inflation) for which the likelihood of program participation is increased when $(y_i)_{-1} > y_i^d$, then $\delta_j < 0$ and we can expect $\beta_j^{IMF} < 0$; here too, the product $\beta_j^{IMF} \delta_j$ will still be greater than zero. The relevance of $\beta_j^{IMF} \delta_j > 0$ is that, because we know from equation (18b) that the correlation between $\Delta \tilde{\varepsilon}_{ij}$ and z_i carries the same sign as δ_j, we can conclude that regression to the mean contributes to a correlation between the determinants of program status (z_i) and the nonprogram determinants of Δy_{ij} (that is, ρ_{xz}), a correlation that has the same sign as β_j^{IMF}. From our earlier analysis, especially equation (15), we then know that in these circumstances the control-group approach will *overstate* the true effect of a Fund program. In short, if program countries are more likely to have experienced negative temporary shocks in the preprogram period, a comparison of changes in mean macro-economic outcomes between program and nonprogram countries will, under plausible assumptions, overstate the beneficial effect of a program. A negative shock in the preprogram period *simultaneously* increases the probability of program participation and increases the probability of a positive change in y_{ij} in the program period. Thus, attributing all of this improvement in y_{ij} to a Fund program overstates the true independent effect of the program.

The direction of bias arising from the existence of policy reaction functions depends on the characteristics of such functions, which is of course an empirical question. Nevertheless, we can show that the bias will disappear under two conditions.

The first condition is that $\delta = 0$; that is, when Fund program status can no longer be related to observable country characteristics and when all countries therefore have an equal probability of becoming program countries. In this case, the covariance represented by equation (18a) is zero as long as π_i, is uncorrelated with ε_{ij} and η_i. In this case of random selection, both sources of bias disappear because the original premise of the control-group approach — that program and nonprogram countries are similar — is satisfied.

The second condition for the policy-reaction bias to disappear is $\gamma = 0$. Again, this would make the covariance represented in equation (18a) equal to zero under our assumption. In other words, if $\gamma = 0$, the policy reactions of the authorities cannot be systematically related to observable characteristics; that is, we would not observe the systematic policy reaction functions represented by equation (2). Note, however, that even when $\gamma = 0$, the bias in the control-group estimator attributable to regression to the mean would still remain. This is so because $\delta = 0$ eliminates the improvement in y_{ij} that is attributable to nonprogram policy actions but not that improvement attributable to automatic stabilization from reversible country-specific shocks.

To sum up, we have argued in this section that there are strong ex ante reasons for believing that the past procedures used to estimate the effects of Fund programs in multicountry samples are subject to significant sources of statistical bias. Because the nonprogram determinants of macroeconomic outcomes cannot in general be expected to behave in such a way as to leave these outcomes unchanged from year to year, the potential problems with the before-after approach can be readily acknowledged. The problems with the control-group approach are also important, but they are perhaps more subtle. As shown above, comparing mean macroeconomic outcomes between groups of program and nonprogram countries will lead to biased estimates of program effects whenever the determinants of program selection are correlated with the determinants of macroeconomic outcomes that would have occurred in the absence of a program.

II. OBTAINING UNBIASED CONTROL-GROUP ESTIMATES UNDER NONRANDOM SELECTION

In this section, we describe a modified control-group estimator and show why it is capable of producing unbiased estimates of program effects even when program and nonprogram countries are different. Second, we discuss some of the operational problems that would have to be faced in actually using this estimator. Finally, we show how this estimator could be used to obtain information not only on total program effects but also on how these effects are achieved. It must be emphasized that we describe only the modifications required to control for observable differences between program and nonprogram countries. Sample-selectivity bias would remain because of unobservable differences between program and nonprogram countries. Although statistical procedures are available to handle this source of bias, we do not describe them here. Futhermore, the modifications we discuss also cannot manage other potential biases (for example, aggregation effects or interdependence between program and nonprogram countries) that may be intrinsic to multicountry data and that may distort the true effects of programs.

A Modified Control-Group Estimator

Consider the following modified estimator, $\hat{\beta}_j^{IMF,M}$, for Fund program effects:

$$\hat{\beta}_j^{IMF,M} = (\overline{y_j})_P - (\overline{y_j})_N - (\overline{x_P} - \overline{x_N})'\beta_j. \tag{19}$$

Reference to equation (11) reveals that this modified estimator differs from the traditional control-group estimator in two respects: the modified estimator contains the additional term $-(\overline{x_P} - \overline{x_N})'\beta_j$, and it is specified in level rather than in first-difference form.[14]

To investigate the properties of this estimator, write the basic equation for the jth macroeconomic target variable in country i (equation (1)) in level form:

$$y_{ij} = x_i'\beta_j + W'\alpha_j + \beta_j^{IMF}d_i + \varepsilon_{ij}. \tag{20}$$

Taking expectations of equation (19), after substituting from equation (20), we then obtain

$$\begin{aligned} E(\hat{\beta}_j^{IMF,M}) &= \beta_j^{IMF} + E[(\overline{\varepsilon_j})_P - (\overline{\varepsilon_j})_N] \\ &= \beta_j^{IMF} + E(\varepsilon_{ij}|z_i > 0) - E(\varepsilon_{ij}|z_i \leq 0) \\ &= \beta_j^{IMF}. \end{aligned} \tag{21}$$

Thus, the modified control-group estimator will be unbiased so long as the unobservable country-specific determinants of y_{ij} (that is, ε_{ij}), are uncorrelated

---

[14]This is only one of several equivalent modified estimators that could be proposed. Their common feature is that outcomes are measured net of observable nonprogram influences that can be estimated on the basis of preprogram information.

with the determinants of program status (z_i). In such a case, one can set $E(\varepsilon_{ij}|z_i > 0) = E(\varepsilon_{ij}|z_i \leq 0) = 0$ and thereby justify the last equality above.

The reason that the modified estimator is unbiased can be explained intuitively by using the conclusions from Section I. Recall that we established there that the traditional control-group estimator would be biased if the nonprogram determinants of Δy_{ij} (that is, changes in domestic macroeconomic policy and changes in unobservable shocks) differed systematically between program and nonprogram countries (that is, if Δx_i and $\Delta \varepsilon_{ij}$ were correlated with Fund program status, z_i). The modified control-group estimator removes both sources of bias present in the traditional version. By subtracting the term $(\overline{x_P} - \overline{x_N})'\beta_j$, an adjustment is made for any differences in indigenous macroeconomic policy between program and nonprogram countries. As regards the second potential source of bias (regression to the mean), note that systematic differences between program and nonprogram countries with respect to *changes* in unobservable shocks are to be expected only because the program-selection rule makes it more likely that countries with negative shocks in the preprogram period will subsequently adopt programs. But also note that the expected *level* of such shocks — that is, $E(\varepsilon_{ij})$ — is zero for all countries. Thus, under our assumptions about the distribution of ε_{ij}, this source of bias is present in estimators expressed in first-difference form that fail to control for prior shocks but not in those (such as the modified estimator) expressed in level form.

Operational Aspects of the Modified Control-Group Estimator

The traditional control-group estimator has an obvious attraction: estimated program effects require only the calculation of mean changes in macroeconomic outcomes for program and for nonprogram countries; that is, only of $(\overline{\Delta y_j})_P$ and $(\overline{\Delta y_j})_N$. The estimation requirements for the modified control-group estimator, however, are substantially more demanding. Not only do we need values for three additional variables or parameters ($\overline{x}_N, \overline{x}_P$, and β_j), but we also face the problem that two of these ($\overline{x}_P$ and β_j) are not observed directly. Recall that $\overline{x}_P$ is not observed because x_i refers to policies that would have been undertaken in the *absence* of programs; thus, x_i is equal to *observed* policies in nonprogram countries but not in program countries. Hence, implementation of the modified control-group approach requires estimating x_i for program countries (as well as estimating the parameter β_j linking Δx_i to Δy_{ij}).

The policy vector x_i is generated by the reaction function (2). In practice, an important limitation of the modified control-group estimator is that such reaction functions may be highly unstable, both across countries and in a given country over time. On the one hand, in extreme cases of instability the problem of estimating the counterfactual becomes insoluble. On the other hand, if crosscountry instability is dominant, the solution is to abandon multicountry samples in favor of country studies. In any case, the issue is an empirical one. In what follows, we describe the calculation of a modified control-group estimator that is conditional on the existence of stable policy reaction functions.

The first step in estimating x_i for program countries is to fit the reaction function (equation (2)) to observable data for nonprogram countries. The only unobserved variable in equation (2) is the country-specific vector of desired macroeconomic outcomes, y_i^d. If this variable can be assumed to be constant over time, it can be captured by a set of country-specific constants, giving the policy-reaction equation the following final form:

$$\Delta x_i = \gamma_{0i} - \gamma(y_i)_{-1} + \eta_i. \quad (22)$$

The *fitted* values of this equation for program countries constitute the counterfactual Δx_i. In effect, this procedure uses data on observed policy behavior in nonprogram countries to identify normal policy reaction in given policy-target circumstances.[15] This normal policy reaction is then used to estimate what "would have been" in program countries if there had not been a Fund program.

An important caveat is in order about another potential source of systematic differences between program and nonprogram countries. Because both the setting of policy instruments in equation (22) and the acceptance by a country of a Fund program as specified in equation (3) reflect policy decisions of the authorities, any unobservable factors, π_i, that make a given country more likely to go to the Fund for assistance — such as a general commitment to adjustment — may also make that country more likely to have adopted a different policy package in the *absence* of a program, Δx_i, than

---

[15] In a pooled cross-sectional time-series sample, this would include observations in nonprogram periods for countries that are program countries in other periods.

another country facing similar observable (policy-target) circumstances. In this case, the behavior of nonprogram countries would not be a good guide to the counterfactual in program countries — even after observable preprogram characteristics of the two groups are controlled for. Formally, this possibility would manifest itself in the model as correlation between the error terms π_i in equation (3) and η_i in equation (2). If such a correlation is present, then equation (22) will provide a biased estimate of Δx_i for program countries — in essence because it fails to remove this additional source of sample-selectivity bias.[16]

But this additional source of bias can be eliminated, even though both η_i and π_i are unobservable. The reader is referred to Heckman (1979) for a description of the appropriate procedure. For our purposes, we note that the procedure requires the specification and estimation of a model of program participation — that is, of equation (3). Thus, removal of the two sources of sample-selectivity bias we have identified requires the specification and estimation of models of endogenous policy formation (equation (2)) *and* program participation (equation (3)).

With $(\bar{y}_j)_P$, $(\bar{y}_j)_N$, and $\bar{x}_N$ observed directly, and with $\bar{x}_P$ estimated as outlined above, the remaining element necessary for application of the modified control-group estimator is the parameter vector β_j, which links normal policy changes in the absence of programs to changes in the macroeconomic target variables. Until now, this vector has been assumed to be known. For our purposes, any unbiased estimator of β_j will suffice. Perhaps the simplest way to produce such an estimate is to fit the macro-economic outcome equation (20) in level form to a pooled cross-sectional time-series data sample by using *observed* values for the policy vector x_i.[17]

---

[16]The direction of the bias depends in part on the correlation between π_i and η_i. Intuitively, if (for a given set of observable preprogram circumstances) countries that would have pursued "worse" policies are more likely to adopt Fund programs, then the behavior of nonprogram countries would provide an excessively optimistic counterfactual, and the beneficial effects of programs would be understated. Conversely, if programs are more likely to be adopted by countries that would have undertaken "better" policies anyway, then the beneficial effects of programs would be overstated because the favorable effects of the policies would be erroneously attributed to Fund involvement.

[17]If Fund programs induce parameter shifts, then only data on nonprogram countries could be used for this purpose.

If the objective is solely to obtain an unbiased estimate of *total* program effects, we can substitute the policy-reaction equation (2) for Δx_i into the level-form equation (20) and derive

$$y_{ij} = \beta_{0i} - (y_{ij})'_{-1}\gamma'\beta_j - (x'_i)_{-1}\beta_j$$
$$+ W'\alpha_j + \beta_j^{IMF} d_i + (\varepsilon_{ij} + \eta'_i \beta_j). \quad (23)$$

Fitting equation (23) to observable data will then yield an estimate of total program effects through the estimated coefficient β_j^{IMF} on the dummy variable d_i. This procedure does not, however, take into account any sample-selectivity bias arising from systematic differences in reaction functions between program and nonprogram countries. If the error terms in equations (2) and (3) are correlated, then the reduced-form approach has to be augmented by the Heckman (1979) correction in order to obtain unbiased estimates of program effects. This shortcut works because it essentially controls for observable differences between program and nonprogram countries. But it cannot yield information on how total program effects are apportioned between changes in policy instruments and other factors.

Analyzing How Programs Work

To analyze the three different channels by which programs can affect macroeconomic outcomes, it is helpful to introduce some additional notation. Let $x_{i,IMF}$ be the vector of policy instruments adopted under a program, $\beta_{j,IMF}$ the vector of coefficients linking these policy instruments to the target variable y_{ij}, and $CON_{i,IMF}$ any unmeasurable confidence effects on y_{ij} attributable to a program. As before, x_i and β_j will be the values of policy instruments and their coefficients in the absence of a program. We can then express the total effect of a Fund program, β_j^{IMF}, as:

$$\beta_j^{IMF} = (x'_{i,IMF} \beta_{j,IMF} - x'_i \beta_j) + CON_{i,IMF}. \quad (24)$$

Rewriting the level-form equation (20) for y_{ij} with the substitution for β_j^{IMF} yields

$$y_{ij} = x'_i \beta_j + W'\alpha_j$$
$$+ [CON_{i,IMF} + (x'_{i,IMF} \beta_{j,IMF} - x'_i \beta_j)] d_i + \varepsilon_{ij}. \quad (25)$$

It is clear that if separate estimates of $\beta_{j,IMF}$ and $CON_{i,IMF}$ could be obtained, it would be possible to identify the separate channels through which a program affects y_{ij}. Given the estimate of x_i for program countries and the estimate of β_j as outlined above, we next need to estimate the following equation:

$$y_{ij} = x_i'(1 - d_i)\beta_j + x_{i,IMF}' d_i \beta_{j,IMF} + CON_{i,IMF} d_i + \varepsilon_{ij}. \qquad (26)$$

The estimated coefficients on $x_{i,IMF} d_i$ and on d_i will then be the estimates of $\beta_{j,IMF}$ and of $CON_{i,IMF}$ that we seek. Of course, if estimation of equation (26) produces the result that β_j is not significantly different from $\beta_{j,IMF}$, then we can put aside shifts in behavioral parameters as a source of program effects and deal exclusively with $(x_{i,IMF} - x_i)'\beta_j$ and $CON_{i,IMF}$.

To summarize, in this section we have shown that the presence of systematic differences between program and nonprogram countries need not render useless the control-group approach to the estimation of program effects. One way of handling the problem is to account for any differences in indigenous macroeconomic policy between program and nonprogram countries and to use the level of macroeconomic performance in the program period rather than its change. This "modified" estimator, however, is significantly more difficult to calculate than the traditional control-group estimator. Yet one important feature of the more structural version of this estimator is that it can be used to provide information not only on total program effects but also on *how* these effects are apportioned among induced changes in policy instruments, shifts in behavioral parameters, and general confidence effects.[18]

III. SOME EMPIRICAL EXERCISES

Demonstrating that several alternative estimation methods can in theory yield different results about the effects of Fund programs is one thing. Illustrating the empirical relevance of that point with actual data on Fund programs is quite another. In this section we provide an exploratory empirical investigation of the aforementioned methodological pitfalls by comparing

---

[18] If economic and political conditions change markedly at frequent intervals, if governments with different policy-reaction functions appear frequently, or both, then it may not be feasible to identify empirically a "stable" policy-reaction function. But this is a matter for empirical testing.

estimates of Fund program effects against the three estimators discussed earlier: a before-after comparison of mean outcomes for program countries alone (estimator A); a before-after comparison for program countries relative to that for nonprogram countries (the traditional control-group estimator B); and a reduced-form regression estimate of program effects that controls only for observed preprogram differences between program and nonprogram countries (a version of the modified control-group estimator M). The data samples are drawn from the population of Fund stabilization programs over the 1974–81 period.

As suggested earlier, although we think that these empirical results are instructive for testing the *sensitivity* of estimated program effects to alternative estimation methods, we do not think that much confidence ought to be placed in any of the estimates of program effects themselves. We say this because the particular equations tested, even for the modified control-group estimator, accommodate only one of the possible sources of bias outlined in Sections I and II (we have not investigated the empirical relevance of correlations between the unobservable components of policy-reaction functions and the factors affecting program participation); because we do not construct a carefully specified, structural economic model for the macroeconomic outcome variables or for indigenous policy reaction; because we have experimented with only one short time span for program effects (that is, the change from the preprogram year to the program year);[19] and because the goodness-of-fit characteristics of the estimates themselves do not merit such confidence. Having made these qualifications, we should also point out that most of the same deficiencies also plague the earlier empirical literature on program effects using multicountry data.[20]

---

[19]The question of when a program country stops being a program country is a particularly difficult one to answer, yet it can have an important effect on program estimates based on multicountry data. Suppose, for example, that two countries face identical current account deficits. Country A, with a Fund program, undertakes a policy of devaluation with expenditure reduction while country B, without a program, adopts increased trade restrictions. Over a one-year period, the change in the current account could well be quite similar for the two countries. Over a longer period (after the program), one might expect country A to show better growth and external balance performance than country B, but this improvement would not be reflected in one-year comparisons. Indeed, country A would be classified as a *non* program country after the program year.

Data Base

Our estimates were made using a sample that contains observations from 58 developing countries during the 1974–81 sample period. It consists of 397 country-year observations, 68 of which are program-year observations. The 58 countries in the sample are those for which data were available for all relevant macroeconomic variables for at least two consecutive years during 1974–81 (not necessarily for the entire period). Consecutive-year Fund programs, including those classified as extended Fund facility programs, are contained in the sample. (A list of the program countries represented is given in Table 6 in Appendix II.)[21]

Definition of Variables

As in most earlier studies, we have selected some popular indicators of external and internal balance as the appropriate outcome or target variables for Fund stabilization programs. Specifically, the four outcome variables that serve as the empirical counterparts to the y variables of the theoretical sections are: the ratio of the overall balance of payments to nominal GNP, BOP/GNP; the ratio of the current account of the balance of payments to nominal GNP, CA/GNP; the rate of inflation as measured by the consumer price index, $\Delta CPI/CPI_{t-1}$; and the rate of growth of real gross domestic product, $\Delta RGDP/RGDP_{t-1}$. These four summary indicators are of course not the only relevant yardsticks of the success of a Fund program, but it would be difficult to argue that they are not important ones.[22] For the purposes of this study, they also carry the advantage of facilitating comparison with earlier empirical work on program effects.[23]

Recall from Section II that calculation of the modified control-group estimator requires data on the vector of policy instruments for both program

---

[20] In this respect, the attention devoted by Donovan (1982) to both long- and short-term effects of programs, and by Gylfason (1983) to the theoretical channels by which domestic credit can affect economic growth as well as the balance of payments, are particularly commendable.

[21] We also ran some tests on several smaller samples. Because the results were qualitatively similar to those reported here, we did not include them in the text.

[22] In addition to the four indicators mentioned above (measured somewhat differently), Donovan (1982) also examined changes in savings and investment ratios and changes in the growth rate of real consumption.

[23] In some of the earlier studies, the external balance variables were scaled by nominal exports rather than by nominal GNP, but we doubt that this difference has any material effect on the qualitative nature of the results.

and nonprogram countries. For this purpose, we collected data on total domestic credit (D) and on the real effective exchange rate (REX) for each of the sample countries.[24] These measures serve as the empirical counterpart to the x variables of the theoretical sections. Again, it is not difficult to think of other policy instruments that would be pertinent to Fund stabilization programs, but few would deny the key roles accorded these two instruments in most programs.

Finally, to create the dummy variable d_i, that captures the presence ($d_i = 1$) or absence ($d_i = 0$) of a Fund program, we assigned a program to a given year if it was approved (by the Fund's Executive Board) during the first six months of that year. Otherwise, the program was assigned to the following year. Also, the phrase "program countries" is used in what follows to refer to those (country-year) observations during which Fund programs were in effect. The data source for each of the variables is identified in Appendix II.

How the Estimators Were Calculated

All that remains before examining the results themselves is to review briefly how the three alternative estimators of Fund program effects in the tables that follow were actually calculated.

For the simple before-after estimator ($\hat{\beta}_j^{IMF,A}$), we computed the *mean* change across the group of program countries for each of the four macroeconomic outcome variables. In terms of earlier symbols, the before-after estimator becomes

$$\hat{\beta}_j^{IMF,A} = (\Delta \bar{y}_j)_P. \tag{27}$$

For computational convenience, the traditional control-group estimator was calculated by running the following regression equation on the combined sample of program and nonprogram countries:

$$\Delta y_i = \alpha_1 + \alpha_2 d_i, \tag{28}$$

where, as before, d_i is the dummy variable for Fund program status and where α_1 and α_2 are estimated coefficients. The estimate of α_2 will then be the traditional control-group estimator, $\hat{\beta}_j^{IMF,B}$.

---

[24] The real effective exchange rate is an import-weighted index, with the consumer price index (CPI) used as the relevant deflator; see Appendix II for a more precise definition.

Last, we have the modified control-group estimator $\hat{\beta}_j^{IMF,M}$. As suggested in Section II, there are several ways to calculate it. Because our primary purpose here is to determine how sensitive estimated program effects are to alternative assumptions, it seemed acceptable to concern ourselves only with total program effects. We therefore chose to use the reduced-form version of the modified control-group estimator given in equation (23), since it is so much easier to calculate. Again, we did not correct for any possible correlation between the unobservable components of program participation and of the policy-reaction function.

By subtracting $(y_j)_{-1}$ from both sides of equation (23), this equation can be estimated in the form

$$\Delta y_{ij} = \beta_{0i} - \sum_h (y_{ih})_{-1} \lambda_h - (1 + \lambda_j)(y_{ij})_{-1} - (x_i')_{-1} \beta_j$$

$$+ W' \alpha_j + \beta_j^{IMF} d_i + (\varepsilon_{ij} + \eta_i' \beta_j), \quad (23a)$$

where $\lambda = \gamma' \beta_j$, is an $N \times 1$ vector with jth element equal to λ_j. As a proxy for W, the variable which measures the international economic environment, we introduced a set of time dummy variables. Also, the β_{0i} are coefficients of a set of country dummy variables designed to capture intercountry differences in desired target values for the y_{ij}. It is also possible to test formally whether the additional variables peculiar to the modified control-group estimator— that is, the lagged values of the vectors y_i and x_i — make as a *set* a significant contribution to the explanation of Δy. To do so, one performs an F-test on the null hypothesis that the coefficients of these variables are all zero. Observe also that, even if prior statistical tests document that program countries differ systematically from nonprogram countries with respect to these variables, these preprogram period characteristics must show as a group a statistically significant effect on Δy for there to be a bias in the traditional control-group estimator of program effects. If preprogram characteristics are not related to Δy, then the estimates of program effects using the traditional and modified control-group methodologies will yield the same results.[25]

---

[25] Some readers will recognize this as an application of "specification bias due to an omitted variable"; see, for example, Kmenta (1971, p. 391). In brief, if equation (23a) is the "true model" but we estimate equation (28) instead, then the bias attaching to α_2 in equation (28) will be a product of two factors: the correlations between the program dummy d_i and the omitted variables (here, the lagged values of y and x); and the coefficients on the omitted

Results

The results of principal interest are set forth in Tables 1–5. Tables 1 and 2 provide estimates of program effects under the before-after estimator and the traditional control-group estimator, respectively. Table 3 presents the results of a test for differences between program and nonprogram countries in the level of macroeconomic outcomes before the program period. Table 4 gives the estimates of program effects using the modified control-group estimator. Finally, Table 5 presents a summary of the sensitivity of estimated program effects to the estimation methodology.

Table 1, although it is confined to changes in macroeconomic outcomes for program countries alone, already raises some doubts about the quality of estimates based on simple before-after calculations. There is a marked

Table 1: "Before-After" Estimates of Program Effects, 1974–81 (In percent)

Variable[a]	1974	1975	1976	1977	1978	1979	1980	1981	1974–81
$\Delta(BOP/GNP)$	−0.05	−2.78	2.84	1.59	−4.35	4.00	−1.69	−1.69	−0.37
$\Delta(CA/GNP)$	−4.40	−2.41	4.50	2.61	−1.26	−0.69	−1.77	−1.12	−0.28
$\Delta(\Delta CPI/CPI)$	52.45	−32.33	−13.93	−22.90	5.39	5.15	2.61	−1.45	−3.05
$\Delta(\Delta RGDP/RGDP)$	0.02	−0.07	0.05	—[b]	0.00	0.00	−0.02	0.01	−0.09

[a] Here and in Tables 2–4, variables are as defined in Section III of the text (under "Definition of Variables").
[b] The growth effect was negative but negligible.

Table 2: Traditional Control-Group Estimates of Program Effects (In percent)

Mean Change in Outcome Variables	Program Countries	Nonprogram Countries	Difference	t-Statistic
$\Delta(BOP/GNP)$	−0.37	−0.21	−0.16	−0.19
$\Delta(CA/GNP)$	−0.28	−0.72	0.44	0.51
$\Delta(\Delta CPI/CPI_{t-1})$	−3.05	0.95	−4.00	−1.06
$\Delta(\Delta RGDP/RGDP_{t-1})$	−0.09	−0.25	0.16	0.20

variables. If either of these factors is zero, then the α_2 in equation (28) will equal the B_j^{IMF} in equation (23a).

Table 3: Differences Between Program and Nonprogram Countries: Means of Outcome Variables in Preprogram Year (In percent)

Outcome Variables	Program Countries	Nonprogram Countries	Difference	t-Statistic[a]
BOP/GNP	−1.53	1.43	−2.96	−3.58**
CA/GNP	−7.26	−5.26	−2.00	−2.10**
$\Delta CPI/CPI_{t-1}$	41.51	20.44	21.07	3.36**
$\Delta RGDP/RGDP_{t-1}$	3.82	5.23	−1.41	−2.02**

[a] Two asterisks indicate statistical significance at the 1 percent level.

difference in the nature and pattern of estimated program effects from year to year. Note, for example, the difference in estimated program effects between, say, 1976 programs and 1980 programs. Again, whereas it is possible that true program effects really do change markedly from year to year, it seems more likely that this temporal instability arises because the nonprogram determinants of changes in macroeconomic outcomes (for example, oil shocks, foreign demand conditions, agricultural supply shocks, and the like), often change significantly from year to year. Because the before-after methodology does not acknowledge such nonprogram influences on Δy, it cannot control for them in estimating program effects.

Table 2, which conveys the traditional control-group estimates of program effects, illustrates three noteworthy features of the results. First, the size and even the direction of estimated program effects sometimes change quite noticeably from values obtained with the before-after estimator. Specifically, once the performance of nonprogram countries is used as a measuring rod, Fund programs become associated with an *improvement* in the current account and with slightly *better* growth. Second, Table 2 documents the importance of applying tests of statistical significance to observed differences in performance between program and nonprogram countries. Whereas the macroeconomic performance of program countries is always different from that of nonprogram countries in each of the four comparisons shown in Table 2, in none of them could it be legitimately concluded that the observed difference was statistically significant (that is, not the outcome of chance).

As emphasized in the preceding sections, we must suspect that the traditional control-group estimates of program effects will be biased if the

Table 4: Modified Control-Group Estimates of Program Effects

Dependent Variable	$(BOP/GNP)_{t-1}$	$(CA/GNP)_{t-1}$	$(\Delta CPI/CPI)_{t-1}$	$(\Delta RGNP/RGNP)_{t-1}$	$(\Delta D/D)_{t-1}$	REX_{t-1}	d_i
$\Delta(BOP/GNP)^a$	−1.092**	0.056	−0.017*	−0.001	0.001	−00.023	−0.011
	(0.063)	(0.055)	(0.009)	(0.001)	(0.002)	(00.019)	(0.008)
$\Delta(CA/GNP)^a$	−0.141*	−0.702**	0.000	−0.002**	0.001	00.039	−0.001
	(0.072)	(0.063)	(0.000)	(0.001)	(0.003)	(00.022)	(0.009)
$\Delta(\Delta CPI/CPI_{t-1})^b$	−71.990*	32.117	−0.458**	−0.351	0.012	−19.433	3.248
	(35.976)	(31.665)	(0.049)	(0.310)	(0.013)	(10.877)	(4.448)
$\Delta(\Delta RGDP/RGDP_{t-1})^b$	27.504**	−6.192	0.010	−0.969**	−0.001	−3.179	−0.220
	(5.889)	(5.183)	(0.008)	(0.051)	(0.002)	(1.780)	(0.728)

Note: Figures in parentheses are standard errors. Coefficients of time and country-specific dummy variables are not reported. A single asterisk indicates statistical significance at the 5 percent level; two asterisks indicate statistical significance at the 1 percent level.
[a]Measured as fractions.
[b]Measured in percent.

Table 5: Implications of Alternative Statistical Methodologies for Estimates of Program Effects (In percent)

Outcome Variable	Before-After Approach	Traditional Control-Group Approach	Modified Control-Group Approach
$\Delta(BOP/GNP)$	−0.37	−0.16	−1.10
$\Delta(CA/GNP)$	−0.28	0.44	−0.10
$\Delta(\Delta CPI/CPI_{t-1})$	−3.06	−4.00	3.25
$\Delta(\Delta RGDP/RGDP_{t-1})$	−0.09	0.16	−0.22

selection of program countries is nonrandom *and* if these nonrandom characteristics are correlated with macroeconomic performance during the program period. Tables 3 and 4 address these two questions. In particular, Table 3 tests our earlier argument that Fund program status is likely to be related systematically to the country's level of macroeconomic performance before the program period. The results are straightforward and can be summarized as follows. Program countries *do* seem to be different from nonprogram countries. In the year before the inception of a Fund program, program countries experienced (on average) larger balance of payments deficits in proportion to GNP, larger current account deficits in proportion to GNP, higher rates of inflation, and lower rates of real output growth than did nonprogram countries. Each of these differences is statistically significant at the 5 percent level or better. This significance is revealed not only by the *t*-test results shown in Table 3 but also by χ^2 tests for differences in the whole set of mean comparisons. These differences in preprogram conditions between program and nonprogram countries appear in all the samples we examined. Indeed, the existence of these preprogram differences between program and nonprogram countries was the single most robust empirical finding of our tests.

Table 4 takes the analysis one step further by testing whether these revealed preprogram differences in macroeconomic outcomes affect the *change* in macroeconomic performance between the preprogram year and the year of the program. Again the results of interest can be conveniently summarized. First, preprogram levels of macroeconomic outcomes *do* appear to affect the change in these outcomes. For all four equations in Table 4, the change in the outcome variable is related in a statistically significant way to two or more of the four outcome-level variables in the preprogram year. In each case, the outcome-change variable is related to is own lagged level with a *negative* coefficient. This finding can be taken as supporting the notion advanced earlier, that macroeconomic outcomes in both program and nonprogram countries may display a regression-to-the-mean property. For example, the greater is the size of the current account deficit in period $t-1$, the greater is the improvement in the current account between period $t-1$ and period t.

Second, and not surprising, estimated program effects under the modified control-group estimator are quite different from those obtained under the traditional control-group estimator. This can be seen most vividly in Table 5, where the three estimators are shown side by side. In addition, and consistent with our earlier expectations about the direction of bias, we find that estimated program effects, after allowing for preprogram differences between program and nonprogram countries, are almost always less favorable. For example, the improvement in the current account ratio disappears entirely, the deterioration in the balance of payments ratio is magnified, and the favorable outcomes for inflation and growth are reversed. Tests of statistical significance again indicate, however, that observed differences in macroeconomic performance between program and nonprogram countries are not significant.

Finally, although the explanatory power of the regression equations in Table 4 is rather low (in the range of .1 to .2 without country and time dummy variables and .2 to .3 with them), the explanatory power is significantly higher (in a statistical sense) when those variables peculiar to the modified control-group estimator are included in the equations. In this respect, an F-test reveals that, for each of the equations in Table 4, the modified control-group variables (that is, the lagged values of targets and instruments) are statistically significant *as a group* at the 1 percent level. In other words, the modified control-group equations in Table 4 hardly provide a "full" or even a "good" explanation for observed changes in macroeconomic outcomes, but it is hard to argue that preprogram characteristics can be ignored when Fund program effects are estimated from multicountry samples.

To summarize, we have shown in this section, if only in a preliminary way, that it does make a significant difference *how* one estimates the effect of Fund programs from cross-sectional data. None of the estimates reported in Table 5 can be construed as a true estimate of program effects. We have not attempted a vigorous implementation of the modified control-group technique and are not convinced that it would be worthwhile to do so. We have, however, demonstrated that point estimates of program effects are not robust when variables are included that measure the preprogram characteristics of countries, and that the direction of change in estimated program effects is as expected a priori. Thus, some of the theoretical sources of bias outlined in the earlier sections do appear to be of more than academic interest.

IV. CONCLUSIONS

Given the pivotal role assigned to Fund stabilization programs in the past and present economic policy strategies of many developing countries, and given the continuing controversy over the effects of these programs, it is not surprising that there has been strong interest in empirical measures of program effectiveness. Because the large number of such programs makes the case-by-case approach a laborious and time-consuming way to arrive at an estimate of "average" program effectiveness, it is likewise understandable that the cross-country approach to program evaluation has dominated the empirical literature. We have argued in this paper, however, that if the estimated program effects from such a cross-country analysis are to be representative of "true" program effects, then certain methodological pitfalls need to be avoided. At the risk of ignoring some problems and of unduly simplifying others, the main lessons of the preceding analysis can be summarized as follows.

- In comparing the performance of program countries with that of nonprogram countries, it is strongly advisable to subject any differences to tests of *statistical* significance. As brought out in our empirical investigation, it frequently turns out that observed differences in performance between the two groups during the program period would not be judged statistically significant at conventional levels of confidence.
- A before-after comparison of mean macroeconomic outcomes for program countries is unlikely to yield a good estimate of true program effects because the nonprogram determinants of macroeconomic outcomes typically change between the preprogram period and the program period. As such, ascribing all of the observed change in outcomes to the program alone will invariably overstate or understate the true independent effect of the program.

- If the mean change in outcomes for nonprogram countries is subtracted from the mean change for program countries, the bias in program estimates attributable to ignoring the nonprogram determinants of macroeconomic outcomes will be reduced. A new source of bias will be introduced, however, whenever program countries differ systematically from nonprogram countries in some characteristic that is related to subsequent macroeconomic performance. In the particular case in which the determinants of Fund program selection are positively correlated with the nonprogram determinants of changes in macroeconomic outcomes, this traditional control-group estimate of program effects will overstate true program effects. Furthermore, preliminary empirical tests suggest that in practice (at least for the 1974–81 period) program countries did have significantly less favorable macro-economic performance than did nonprogram countries before the program period, and that such preprogram outcomes were significantly related to subsequent performance during the program period itself. Not surprisingly, therefore, estimates of program effects that held constant the preprogram levels of macroeconomic outcomes were quite different from those that did not. In any case, the "moral" is that if the program countries are not selected randomly, then these nonrandom selection criteria must be identified either so that a control group can be found with the same characteristics or so that these group differences can be accounted for in any comparison of outcomes between the two groups.
- Because Fund programs probably work in good measure by changing the stance of policy instruments from what would pertain in the absence of such programs, any estimate of program effects that does not allow for this channel of influence runs the risk of capturing only part of total program effects (for example, only "confidence" effects) and thus of understating true program effectiveness (see, for example, Killick and Chapman (1982)). In this paper we have outlined an estimation procedure that in principle permits calculation of how total program effects are apportioned among induced changes in policy instruments, induced changes in behavioral parameters, and general confidence effects. Central to this procedure is the estimation of "policy reaction functions" for both program and nonprogram countries. Although we would not want to underestimate the practical difficulties associated with obtaining credible estimates of such reaction functions for developing countries (particularly when underlying

economic and political conditions are changing markedly at frequent intervals), we see no other way of estimating the counter-factual for program countries. If *cross-country* stability of policy reaction functions is not observed, then the cross-sectional approach using multicountry samples must be abandoned. If *temporal* stability of such functions does not obtain for individual countries, the country studies may also fail to tell much about program effects per se. We would then be left to analyze the effects of Fund-type *policies* and to speculate in each case about the alternative policies that would have been pursued in the absence of a program.

- On a broad level, the methodological problems we have described lead us to the view that considerable caution is needed in attempting to estimate and interpret the effects of Fund programs by using multicountry data.

APPENDIX I

Bias in the Traditional Control-Group Approach

Equations (14a) and (14b) in the text are crucial for establishing the presence of bias in the traditional control-group approach under nonrandom selection of program countries. In this Appendix we derive these equations.

Denote the variance of $\Delta x'_i \beta_j + \Delta \varepsilon_{ij}$ as σ_x^2. Suppose that $\Delta x'_i \beta_j + \Delta \varepsilon_{ij}$ and z_i, have a joint normal distribution, with the correlation between $\Delta x'_i \beta_j + \Delta \varepsilon_{ij}$ and z_i denoted as p_{xz}. Finally, let φ and Φ represent respectively the standard normal density and distribution functions. For the ith country, it will be true that

$$E\left[z_i | (\Delta x'_i \beta_j + \Delta \varepsilon_{ij})\right] = \rho_{xz} \frac{\sigma_z}{\sigma_x} (\Delta x'_i \beta_j + \Delta \varepsilon_{ij} - \Delta x' \beta_j). \quad (29)$$

The probability that country i will be a program country is then

$$\text{prob}(i \epsilon P) = \text{prob}(z_i > z^*)$$

$$= 1 - \Phi\left\{\left[z^* - \rho_{xz} \frac{\sigma_z}{\sigma_x} (\Delta x_i \beta_j + \Delta \varepsilon_{ij} - \Delta x' \beta_j)\right] / \sigma_z\right\}. \quad (30)$$

In the special case in which ρ_{xz} is zero, equation (30) reduces to

$$\text{prob}(i \epsilon P) = 1 - \Phi(z^*/\sigma_z). \quad (30a)$$

The key difference between equations (30) and (30a) is that, whereas the probability of being a program country is a function of $\Delta x'_i \beta_j + \Delta \varepsilon_{ij}$ in equation (30) and thus will differ across countries, in equation (30a) this probability is the same for all countries in the sample.

The next step toward discovering the direction of bias in the control-group estimate of program effects under conditions of nonrandom program selection is to write

$$E[(\Delta x'_i \beta_j + \Delta \varepsilon_{ij})|z_i > Z^*] = \Delta x'\beta_j + \rho_{xz} \frac{\sigma_x \varphi(z^*/\sigma_z)}{1 - \Phi(z^*/\sigma_z)} \quad (31)$$

$$E[(\Delta x'_i \beta_j + \Delta \varepsilon_{ij})|z_i \leq Z^*] = \Delta x'\beta_j - \rho_{xz} \frac{\sigma_x \varphi(z^*/\sigma_z)}{\Phi(z^*/\sigma_z)} \quad (32)$$

Since σ_x and φ are both positive, and since Φ is bounded between zero and unity, $\sigma_x \varphi/(1 - \Phi)$ and $\sigma_x \phi/\Phi$ are both positive. Equations (14a) and (14b) in the text then follow directly from equations (31) and (32a), respectively.

APPENDIX II

Description of Sample and Data Used

The program countries contained in the sample are listed in Table 6.

The sources of the data used in Section III are as follows: for net foreign assets, *International Financial Statistics* (*IFS*) (Washington: International

Table 6: Program Countries in Sample

Year	Program Countries
1974	Chile, Pakistan, Sri Lanka
1975	Burma, Chile, Israel, Pakistan
1976	Bangladesh, Haiti, Kenya, Rep. of Korea, Philippines, Tanzania
1977	Argentina, Burma, Egypt, Haiti, Israel, Kenya, Mexico, Pakistan, Philippines, South Africa, Zaire, Zambia
1978	Argentina, Jamaica, Kenya, Mexico, Peru, Philippines, Portugal, Sri Lanka, Turkey, Zambia
1979	Burma, Egypt, Haiti, Honduras, Jamaica, Mexico, Peru, Philippines, Sri Lanka
1980	Bangladesh, Bolivia, Haiti, Honduras, Jamaica, Kenya, Rep. of Korea, Malawi, Peru, Philippines, Sierra Leone, Sri Lanka, Turkey, Zaire
1981	Bangladesh, Burma, Haiti, Honduras, Jamaica, Rep. of Korea, Pakistan, Sierra Leone, Thailand, Zambia

Monetary Fund, various issues), line 31n; for nominal GNP, real GDP, and current accounts, Fund staff estimates (Current Studies Division data file); for consumer price indices, *IFS*, line 64; for domestic credit, *IFS*, line 32; for real effective exchange rates, Fund staff estimates (Developing Countries Studies Division data file). The precise definition of the real exchange rate (*REX*) is

$$REX = 100 \cdot \exp\left[\sum_{s=1}^{n} \ln\left(EXI_i/EXI_s\right)W_s - \sum_{s=1}^{n} \ln\left(CPI_s/CPI_i\right)W_s\right],$$

where *EXI* is the nominal exchange rate index; i is the reporting country; s is the partner country; W_s is the import weight for partner country s; and *CPI* is the consumer price index.

"Evaluating Fund Stabilization Programs with Multicountry Data" by Morris Goldstein and Peter Montiel. Reprinted from Vol. 33 No. 2 (June 1986) International Monetary Fund Staff Papers. Copyright © 1986 by International Monetary Fund. Used with permission of the publisher.

REFERENCES

Asenfelter, Orley, "Estimating the Effect of Training Programs on Earnings," *Review of Economics and Statistics* (Cambridge, Massachusetts), Vol. 60 (February 1978), pp. 47–57.

Asenfelter, Orley, and David Card, *Using the Longitudinal Structure of Earnings to Estimate the Effect of Training Programs,* Working Paper 174 (Princeton, New Jersey: Princeton University, Industrial Relations Section, July 1984).

Beveridge, W.A., "Fiscal Adjustment in Financial Programs Supported by Stand-By Arrangements in the Upper Credit Tranches, 1978–79" (unpublished; Washington: International Monetary Fund, July 1981).

Beveridge, W.A., and Margaret R. Kelly, "Fiscal Content of Financial Programs Supported by Stand-By Arrangements in the Upper Credit Tranches, 1969–78," *Staff Papers*, International Monetary Fund (Washington), Vol. 27 (June 1980), pp. 205–49.

Cline, William R., and Sidney Weintraub, eds., *Economic Stabilization in Developing Countries* (Washington: The Brookings Institution, 1981).

Connors, Thomas A., "The Apparent Effects of Recent IMF Stabilization Programs," International Finance Discussion Paper 135 (Washington: Board of Governors of the Federal Reserve System, International Finance Division, April 1979).

Donovan, Donal J., "Real Responses Associated with Exchange Rate Action in Selected Upper Credit Tranche Stabilization Programs," *Staff Papers*, International Monetary Fund (Washington), Vol. 28 (December 1981), pp. 698–727.

Donovan, Donal J., "Macroeconomic Performance and Adjustment Under Fund-Supported Programs: The Experience of the Seventies," *Staff Papers*, International Monetary Fund (Washington), Vol. 29 (June 1982), pp. 171–203.

Goldstein, Morris, *The Global Effects of Fund-Supported Adjustment Programs*, Occasional Paper 42 (Washington: International Monetary Fund, March 1986).

Goldstein, Morris, and Mohsin S. Khan, *Effects of Slowdown in Industrial Countries on Growth in Non-Oil Developing Countries*, Occasional Paper 12 (Washington: International Monetary Fund, August 1982).

Guitián, Manuel, *Fund Conditionality: Evolution of Principles and Practices*, Pamphlet Series No. 38 (Washington: International Monetary Fund, 1981).

Gylfason, Thorvaldur, *Credit Policy and Economic Activity in Developing Countries: An Evaluation of Stabilization Programs Supported by the IMF, 1977–79*, Seminar Paper 268 (Stockholm: University of Stockholm, Institute for International Economic Studies, December 1983).

Heckman, James J., "Sample Selection Bias as a Specification Error," *Econo-metrica* (Evanston, Illinois), Vol. 47 (January 1979), pp. 153–61.

International Monetary Fund, *World Economic Outlook: A Survey by the Staff of the International Monetary Fund* (Washington, 1983).

Kelly, Margaret R., "Fiscal Adjustment and Fund-Supported Programs, 1971–80" (unpublished; Washington: International Monetary Fund, September 1982).

Khan, Mohsin S., and Malcolm Knight, "Determinants of Current Account Balances of Non-Oil Developing Countries in the 1970s: An Empirical Analysis," *Staff Papers*, International Monetary Fund (Washington), Vol. 30 (December 1983), pp. 819–42.

Killick, Tony, *The Quest for Economic Stabilization: The IMF and the Third World* (New York: St. Martin's, 1984).

Killick, Tony, and M. Chapman, "Much Ado About Nothing? Testing the Impact of IMF Stabilization Programmes in Developing Countries," Overseas Development Institute Working Paper 7 (London, March 1982).

Kmenta, Jan, *Elements of Econometrics* (New York: Macmillan, 1971).

Loxley, John, *The IMF and the Poorest Countries: The Performance of the Least Developed Countries Under IMF Stand-By Arrangements* (Ottawa: The North-South Institute, 1984).

Lucas, Robert E., Jr., "Econometric Policy Evaluation: A Critique," in *The Phillips Curve and Labor Markets*, ed. by Karl Brunner and Allan H. Meltzer, Carnegie-Rochester Conference Series on Public Policy, Vol. 1 (Amsterdam: North-Holiand, 1976; New York: Elsevier, 1976), pp. 19–46.

Odling-Smee, John, "Adjustment with Financial Assistance from the Fund: The Experience of Seven Countries," *Finance & Development* (Washington), Vol. 19 (December 1982), pp. 26–30.

Reichmann, Thomas M., "The Fund's Conditional Assistance and the Problems of Adjustment, 1973–75," *Finance & Development* (Washington), Vol. 15 (December 1978), pp. 38–41.

Reichmann, Thomas M., and Richard T. Stillson, "Experience with Programs of Balance of Payments Adjustment: Stand-By Arrangements in the Higher Credit Tranches, 1963–72," *Staff Papers*, International Monetary Fund (Washington), Vol. 25 (June 1978), pp. 293–309.

Williamson, John, *The Lending Policies of the International Monetary Fund* (Washington: Institute for International Economics, 1982).

Williamson, John, ed., *IMF Conditionality* (Washington: Institute for International Economics, 1983).

Zulu, Justin B., and Saleh M. Nsouli, *Adjustment Programs in Africa: The Recent Experience*, Occasional Paper 34 (Washington: International Monetary Fund, 1985).

Chapter 16

IMF Structural Programs

Morris Goldstein

SECTION 1. INTRODUCTION

"Detailed conditionality (often including dozens of conditions) has burdened IMF programs in recent years and made such programs unwieldy, highly conflictive, time consuming to negotiate, and often ineffectual."

"The IMF [International Monetary Fund] should cease lending to countries for long-term development assistance (as in sub-Saharan Africa) and for long-term structural transformation (as in post-Communist transition economies).... The current practice of extending long-term loans in exchange for member countries' agreeing to conditions set by the IMF should end."

— *Meltzer Report* (International Financial Institution Advisory Commission 2000, 7, 8, and 43)

"Both the Fund and the Bank have tried to do too much in recent years, and they have lost sight of their respective strengths. They both need to return to basics... [The Fund] should focus on a leaner agenda of monetary, fiscal,

---

The author is grateful to Masood Ahmed, Mark Allen, Caroline Atkinson, Fred Bergsten, Barry Eichengreen, Martin Feldstein, Timothy F. Geithner, Stefan Ingves, Paul Keating, Mohsin Khan, Robert Lafrance, Carl Lindgren, Robert Litan, Michael Mussa, Yung Chul Park, Jacques Polak, James Powell, Miguel Savastano, Todd Stewart, Ohno Wijnholds, John Williamson, and Yukio Yoshimura for helpful comments on an earlier draft, and to Trond Augdal for superb research assistance. He also wants to thank Stanley Fischer and his colleagues at the International Monetary Fund for sharing with him the fund's data on structural conditions in fund programs.

and exchange rate policies, and of banking and financial-sector surveillance and reform."
— *Council on Foreign Relations Task Force* (1999, 18–19)

"The one common theme that runs through perceptions of ESAF [Enhanced Structural Adjustment Facility] at the country level is a feeling of a loss of control over the policy content and the pace of implementation of reform programs."[1]
— *External Evaluation of the ESAF* (Botchway et al. 1998, 20)

"The IMF should eschew the temptation to use currency crises as an opportunity to force fundamental structural and institutional reforms on countries, however useful they may be in the long term, unless they are absolutely necessary to revive access to international funds."
— Martin Feldstein (1998, 32)

"The IMF's activities are not related to those specified in its charter for the simple reason that the par-value system of exchange rates it was to monitor no longer exists. In the tradition of skilled bureaucracies, the IMF has turned to new areas and has managed to expand substantially its financial resources and, in the process, its influence."
— George Shultz (1995, 5)

"The IMF has not been established to give guidance on social and political priorities, nor has its voting system been designed to give it the moral authority to oversee priorities of a noneconomic nature. Its functions have to be kept narrowly technical... and the Fund has to accept that the authorities of a country are the sole judges of its social and political priorities."
— David Finch (1983, 77–78)[2]

"The IMF programs in East Asia are far from optimal for restoring financial market confidence in the short term.... [T]hey have covered a very wide range of policies beyond the immediate financial crisis.... Most of the structural reforms, however, simply detract attention from the financial crisis. They have

---

[1] ESAF is the Fund's Enhanced Structural Adjustment Facility, established in 1987 to provide long-term concessional assistance to low-income countries facing protracted balance-of-payments problems.
[2] Mr. Finch was then the director of the IMF's Exchange and Trade Relations Department.

taken government expertise, negotiating time, and political capital away from the core issues of financial markets, exchange rate policy, and the like."
— Steven Radelet and Jeffrey D. Sachs (1998, 67–68)

"In view of the size of the current deficits and the difficulties that may arise in private intermediation, the Fund must be prepared, when necessary, to lend in larger amounts than in the past. Also, the structural problems faced by many countries may require that adjustment take place over a longer period than has been typical in the framework of Fund programs in the past."
— International Monetary Fund (IMF), *World Economic Outlook* (1980)

"The Fund approach to adjustment has had severe economic costs for many of these [developing] countries in terms of declines in the levels of output and growth rates, reductions in employment and adverse effects on income distribution."
— *Report by the Group of Twenty-Four* (1987, 9)

"Our prime objective is growth. In my view, there is no longer any ambiguity about this. It is towards growth that our programs and their conditionality are aimed."

"Only the pursuit of 'high-quality' growth is worth the effort. What is such growth? It is growth that can be sustained over time without causing domestic and external financial imbalance; growth that has the human person at its center... growth that, to be sustainable, is based on a continuous effort for more equity, poverty alleviation, and empowerment of poor people; and growth that promotes protection of the environment, and respect for national cultural values. This is what our programs are, more and more, and must aim for."
— From speeches by former IMF Managing Director Michel Camdessus (1990, 2000a, respectively)

"In recent years, some critics of the IMF have gone to the opposite extreme, arguing that the IFIs [international financial institutions] should have done more, especially in the context of the economies in transition to develop an appropriate framework of property rights in support of markets.... [I]n considering the future of the two institutions, their activities need to be geared to strengthening the private sector and the appropriate role of government in relation to it."
— Anne O. Krueger (1998, 2003)

"I do not accept the view that when it comes to our poorer member countries, we should not be lending to them, but should turn it over to someone else.... Is the poverty reduction and growth facility... which we are working on jointly with the World Bank... going to be an improvement in the way we deal with countries? Absolutely. Why? Because... it forces us, in cooperation with the World Bank, to make sure that the macroeconomic framework is consistent with what needs to be done for social reasons. Macroeconomic instability is bad for everyone everywhere.... That is why we should remain in these countries.... But we cannot do that in a way that ignores the fact that poverty is the main problem confronting these countries, and that there must be massive efforts, spearheaded by the World Bank, to reduce poverty in these countries."

— Stanley Fischer, IMF first deputy managing director (2000b)

"A changed IMF is needed for the changed world we now have.... As we look to the future we need to redouble our efforts to find better approaches if not answers to fundamental questions.... How do we balance concerns about intrusiveness in national affairs and a desire to promote national ownership of reform programs with a desire to see governments take bolder steps to, for example, build stronger social safety nets, implement core labor standards, empower civil society groups, reduce the role of government in the economy, and address critical issues related to governance, corruption, and crony capitalism?"

— U.S. Treasury Secretary Summers (1999)

"[T]he proposed eligibility criteria [for IMF lending in the Meltzer Report] are too narrow. Even where they are met, they would be unlikely to protect economies from the broad range of potential causes of crises. The criteria focus on the financial sector, and yet even problems that surface in the financial sector often have their roots in deeper economic and structural weaknesses. One simply cannot predict with confidence what the next generation of crises will be and therefore we need to preserve the IMF's ability to respond flexibly to changing circumstances."

— U.S. Treasury *Response to the Meltzer Report* (2000b, 17)

"A central part of the programs in the Asian crisis countries was an unprecedented body of structural reforms.... The overriding question is whether it was appropriate to place so much emphasis on structural reform measures in the financial and corporate sectors.... The answer is clearly yes."

— *IMF Report* (Lane et al. 1999) on Fund Programs in Indonesia, Korea, and Thailand

"[T]he bottom line of the 'era of the IFIs,' despite obvious shortcomings, has been an unambiguous success of historic proportions in both economic and social terms."

— *Minority Dissent, Meltzer Report* (Bergsten et al. 2000, 111)

As suggested above, an active debate has long been under way — and has intensified in the wake of the Asian crisis — about the appropriate scope and intrusiveness of IMF policy conditionality. In this paper, I take up one key element of that debate, namely, the role of structural policies in IMF-supported adjustment programs. By "structural policies," I mean policies aimed not at the management of aggregate demand but rather at either improving the efficiency of resource use or increasing the economy's productive capacity. Structural policies are usually aimed at reducing or dismantling government-imposed distortions or putting in place various institutional features of a modern market economy. Such structural policies include, inter alia, financial-sector policies; liberalization of trade, capital markets, and the exchange rate system; privatization and public enterprise policies; tax and expenditure policies (apart from the overall fiscal stance); labor-market policies; pricing and marketing policies; transparency and disclosure policies; poverty reduction and social safety-net policies; pension policies; corporate governance policies (including anticorruption measures); and environmental policies.

To set the stage for what follows, it is worth summarizing the main concerns and criticisms that have been expressed about the IMF's existing approach to structural policy conditionally.[3] These typically take one or more of the following forms.

---

[3] Neither these concerns and criticisms, nor the counterarguments outlined later in this section, should be interpreted as my own views. I provide my own summary assessment of past fund structural conditionality in section 6.

First, there is a worry that wide-ranging and micromanaged structural policy recommendations will be viewed by developing-country borrowers as so costly and intrusive as to discourage unduly the demand for Fund assistance during crises (see, e.g., Feldstein 1998). Even though the cost of borrowing from the Fund (the so-called rate of charge) is much lower than the cost of borrowing from private creditors — particularly during times of stress — we observe that developing countries usually come to the IMF "late in the day" when their balance-of-payments problems are already severe.[4] This suggests that developing countries place a nontrivial shadow price on the policy conditions associated with Fund borrowing. The concern is that if these conditions become too onerous, emerging economies will wait even longer to come to the Fund (as Thailand did in 1997) or will turn to regional official crisis lenders that offer easier policy conditionality (e.g., in 1998 Malaysia was one of the first beneficiaries of low-conditionality Miyazawa Initiative funds, and Asian countries could eventually decide to elevate the infant Chiang-Mai swap arrangements into a full-fledged Asian Monetary Fund).[5] The outcome — so the argument goes — would then be even more difficult initial crisis conditions, greater resort to the antisocial behavior that the Fund was established to prevent, and a tendency toward Gresham's Law of conditionality (according to which weak regional conditionality would drive out not only the unnecessary but also the necessary elements of Fund conditionality).

A second concern is that insistence on deep structural reforms in cases of illiquidity (rather than insolvency) will serve only to frighten private investors about the size of the problem, thereby rendering more difficult the restoration of confidence and the rollover of short-term capital flows that are the keys to resolving the liquidity crisis (see Radelet and Sachs 1998). No country (including the Group of Seven [G7] countries) is without some structural weaknesses, but it is argued that, however desirable structural policy reforms may be for the performance of the economy over the longer term, it is a mistake to suggest that such reforms are indispensable to resolving the crisis (when they are not). Among the Asian crisis countries, Korea is identified as a

---

[4] The Fund's rate of charge averaged a little over 4 percent from 1997 through the first half of 2000; in contrast, emerging market bond spreads (relative to U.S. Treasuries) have fluctuated from 375 to 1,700 basis points since the outbreak of the Thai crisis in mid-1997.

[5] See C. Fred Bergsten's "Towards a Tripartite World" (*The Economist*, 15 July 2000, 23–26) on regional financial initiatives in Asia.

case in which solvency was never in question and less emphasis on structural reform both in the diagnosis and the policy prescription would have produced a milder crisis.

Concern number three is with equal treatment of countries — one of the Fund's key operating principles. Here, the argument is that the Fund has been asking for sweeping structural reforms from developing countries that it would not ask of industrial countries were the latter in similar circumstances. As Paul Volcker put it, "When the Fund consults with a poor and weak country, the country gets in line. When it consults with a big and strong country, the Fund gets in line" (Volcker and Gyohten 1992). Although differences across countries in economic and political power are a fact of life, the argument is that requiring developing countries to undertake more structural remedies than would their industrial-country counterparts undermines local "ownership" of Fund programs. It also works at cross purposes from simultaneous efforts to forge a consensus on strengthening the international financial architecture in (mixed developing-country and industrial-country) groups like the Group of Twenty (G20) and the Financial Stability Forum (FSF).

Yet a fourth criticism is that permitting the Fund to stray from its core competence of macroeconomic and exchange rate policies into a host of structural policy areas results in poor crisis management, weakens the Fund's overall reputation for competent analysis and advice (with adverse spillovers for the credibility of its recommendations in core policy areas), and runs counter to a sensible division of labor and an application of comparative advantage among the various international financial institutions (IFIs). In this connection, critics have maintained that the Fund bungled bank closures in Indonesia and precipitated a credit crunch in the crisis countries by requiring an unduly rapid increase in bank capitalization (see, e.g., Stiglitz 1999); that the Fund lacks both the expertise and staff resources to make timely and sound policy recommendations in areas as diverse as corporate governance, trade policy, privatization, poverty reduction, and environmental management; and that "mission creep" on the part of both the Fund and the World Bank, in addition to a blurring of responsibilities between them, reduces the public and legislative support necessary to fund them adequately (see Council on Foreign Relations Task Force 1999). Long-term structural reforms (at least outside the financial sector) and poverty reduction should be the main business of the World Bank — not of the IMF.

A fifth charge is that the way the Fund has been managing its structural policy conditionality is flawed. Specifically, the argument is that multiplication of structural performance conditions, the specification of "micro" policy measures, and the increasing reliance on (qualitative) structural benchmarks and program reviews (as monitors of policy performance) have combined both to increase the uncertainty facing Fund borrowers and to lower the incentive to follow through with structural reform. Performance criteria were instituted not only to assure the Fund that its financial resources were being used for the purposes intended but also to assure the borrowing country that if it undertook certain prespecified policy actions it would be eligible to draw (see Guitian 1981; Polak 1991). Also, because performance criteria were relatively few in number, easily measured, and macro in their impact, they both conveyed a relatively clear message about which policy actions were deemed (by the Fund) to carry the highest priority and provided a fairly predictable link with bottom-line economic outcomes (e.g., improvement in the balance of payments). However, when a Fund program contains, say, on the order of fifty or more qualitative structural policy conditions, when many of these conditions are very micro in nature, and when both fulfillment of these conditions and eligibility to draw require judgmental calls by the Fund, signals, impacts, and incentives will be more muddled. Should meeting thirty of fifty structural policy conditions be interpreted as a "good overall effort" that merits Fund support, or should it be viewed as a significant noncompliance with the program?

Suffice to say that these criticisms of the Fund's structural policy conditionality have not gone unchallenged. Again, in the spirit of motivating the subsequent discussion, it is well to consider the following counterarguments.

Although the structural policy conditions the IMF attaches to its loans are often demanding and threaten vested interests within the country, emerging economies recognize that a Fund program represents their best chance to make real traction on the structural weaknesses that have underpinned their crisis vulnerability. Private capital markets, although they sometimes supply strong disciplining force, are not perfect substitutes for either the Fund's specific policy advice or its financing; indeed, in more than a few cases, private creditors will not extend credit in large amounts until the Fund has blessed a country's policies.[6] Turning the steering wheel over temporarily to an outside party

---

[6] Fischer (2000b, 1) argues that the fundamental reason why one needs an institution like the IMF is that "the international financial system left to itself does not work perfectly, and it

is always costly, but better the Fund than one or two large G7 countries. Ironically, the structural policy measures that have drawn the most critical fire in several of the Asian crisis countries (Indonesia and Korea) were for a long time high on the priority list of domestic reformers, but they could not get those reforms implemented (over the opposition of the ruling elite) in a noncrisis situation.[7] At this point, there is no plan to turn Asian swap or credit arrangements into a serious rival to the Fund with competing policy conditionality. Also, very few crisis countries (in Asia or elsewhere) have seen capital controls as the preferred mode of crisis management. Just as it is not optimal for a host country to establish the weakest regulatory and prudential regime simply because it gives market participants the most freedom of action, it is not optimal (from the viewpoint of developing countries) to make Fund structural policy conditionality too easy or flexible. Fund *gaiatsu* — warts and all — may still be the best option out there for jump-starting structural reform.

The distinction between illiquidity and insolvency is not regarded as particularly helpful in most crisis situations, because the dividing line between the two often rests on the quality of crisis management, and because countries differ from firms both in the nature of the relevant collateral and in their willingness (as opposed to ability) to pay (see Fischer 1999). Although investor panic was an important part of the Asian crisis story, so too were "bad fundamentals" that increased downside risk. For example, in the runup to the Korean crisis, seven of the thirty largest *chaebol* were essentially bankrupt; there were large terms-of-trade losses in 1996 (especially for semiconductors); nonperforming loans in the banking system and leverage in the corporate sector were already high; there was a low return on invested capital; capital inflows were biased toward short-term capital and against foreign direct investment; there was a lack of transparency (including on the country's short-term foreign liabilities); and substantial political uncertainty exacerbated the government's

---

is possible to make it work better for the sake of the people who live in that system." Also, see Masson and Mussa (1995) and Krueger (1998). Rodrik (1995) notes that an experiment in which private creditors attempted to specify and monitor conditionality in Peru was soon discontinued.

[7] See Haggard (2000). On the role of domestic reformers in the Asian crisis countries, he concludes as follows: "it is misguided to see the course of policy solely as a response to external political pressures from the international financial institutions and the United States.... At least in some important policy areas, domestic groups were reaching surprisingly similar conclusions on the need for reform" (12).

credibility problem.[8] Yes, many of these structural problems were of long standing, and despite them Korea had shown impressive growth performance over several decades. And yes, Korea has staged an impressive V-shaped recovery without eliminating all these structural problems. Nevertheless, it does not follow that Korea could have regained market confidence without making a good "start" on structural reform in 1997–98. Fund financing–cum–debt rescheduling and an (eventual) turn to easier monetary and fiscal policies — without any structural policy reform — would not have turned the situation around. Treating only the symptoms and not the (structural) root of the problem is not the way to restore confidence. Looking at precrisis fiscal positions in the crisis countries without considering the contingent government liabilities associated with financial-sector restructuring provides a misleading picture of fundamentals (see Boorman et al. 2000). Moreover, the alleged negative effect of Fund public pronouncements on market confidence is said to be much exaggerated. Once Thailand's fall "woke up" market participants to the poor health of banks and corporates in the rest of Asia and every large Group of Ten (G10) bank and security house in the region was issuing weekly reports on the rising share of nonperforming loans in Asian financial systems, it is very unlikely that a Fund statement claiming it was only a short-term liquidity crisis would have turned the tide (after all, the IMF's then managing director was already telling all who would listen that the crisis was really "a blessing in disguise").[9]

Reflecting, inter alia, their less preferred access (in terms of maturity, currency, and predictability) to international capital markets, their weaker institutional framework (ranging from judicial systems to insolvency regimes), and their track record of higher political instability, developing countries *are* different from industrial countries. Recognizing this difference is not dispensing unequal treatment but seeing the world as it is. If the Asian crisis countries — despite their impressive performance on economic growth, inflation, and macro fundamentals over a long period — were regarded by

---

[8] See Roubini's comments in McHale (2000b). Claessens et al. (1999) also found that (precrisis) the four countries most seriously affected by the Asian crisis ranked low on the quality of the regulatory environment in an international comparison of middle-income emerging economies in East Asia and Latin America.

[9] See Goldstein (1998) and Ahluwalia (2000) on the "wake up" hypothesis as an explanation of the contagion in the Asian crisis.

private financial markets as being just like industrial countries, they could have "done an Australia" and got out of the crisis by lowering interest rates and letting their exchange rates depreciate moderately — and this without any Fund assistance.[10] In the event, they could not do that. Nor will the crisis countries be able to sustain their recoveries if they lapse back into the same structural weaknesses they had before. Consequently, it is not realistic to expect a developing country that gets into a crisis to live by the same structural policy conditionality as would a troubled industrial country.[11] For the foreseeable future, developing countries will have to contend with a history of banking, debt, and currency crises, and restoration of confidence will often require a different dose and mix of macroeconomic and structural policies than would be the case for industrial countries. There is no indication that disagreement over past Fund structural policy conditionality is hampering the work of groups like the G20 and the FSF; on the contrary, those groups are making real progress in areas like the application of international financial standards.

The IMF has developed considerable expertise in dealing with banking and financial-sector problems in developing countries. Over the past five years, more than forty-five specialists (including former bank supervisors) have been added to the staff of the Fund's Monetary and Exchange Affairs Department alone. Admittedly, bank closures in Indonesia did not go well. However, since deposit insurance arrangements were not in place, since the authorities were willing to close only a small share of the insolvent banks, and since there were concerns about the moral hazard effects of a blanket guarantee, there was no easy alternative to that action (see Lindgren et al. 1999). Likewise, if stricter bank capitalization requirements had not been instituted in the crisis countries, we would have seen rampant "double-or-nothing" lending behavior by insolvent lenders and an even higher fiscal bill for the bank cleanup. Evidence on the existence of a credit crunch in the crisis countries in 1997–98 is far from clear-cut (see Lane et al. 1999).

In areas outside the Fund's comparative advantage, the Fund draws heavily on other IFIs with the requisite expertise — and especially on the World Bank. This collaboration is particularly close on poverty reduction and social safety

---

[10] See Krugman (1998) on what the "confidence game" means for monetary and fiscal policies in developing countries during a crisis versus what is asked from industrial countries.

[11] See Eichengreen and Hausmann (1999) on financing differences between developing countries and industrial countries.

net issues but also applies increasingly to corporate governance, privatization, trade policy, and environmental impacts. Eliminating all overlap between the IMF and the World Bank (on fiscal and banking reform) is neither feasible nor desirable. The Fund's major focus in the poor countries remains on the macroeconomic framework — a specialization that no other IFI is as qualified to handle. A merger of the Fund and the World Bank is unappealing, both because it would sacrifice the speed and efficiency that come with a still rather small IMF and because a mega-IFI would have too much power across a wide spectrum of macro and micro-economic issues.

Yes, the Fund has given increased emphasis in recent years to economic growth and to social conditions in the design and implementation of its programs with developing countries, just as it was responsive to the unique opportunity and massive need for institution-building systems in the fledgling market economies and new democracies of Eastern Europe. The world has changed. If the Fund did not change with it, and if the Fund did not embrace the same objectives in its programs as its members pursue in their national economic policies, there would be little chance that IMF programs would be either agreed upon or implemented (see Camdessus 1999b).

Structural policies are not like macroeconomic policies, and indicators of policy compliance have to reflect those differences. Progress on banking supervision or privatization cannot be measured in the same way net domestic credit or international reserves are tracked. Performance benchmarks for structural policies have to be qualitative, and a measure of discretion is needed to evaluate the results. Also, because of the interdependencies among structural policies, a macroeconomic impact will come only if progress is made on many fronts simultaneously. Furthermore, the devil is in the details. It makes a big difference if the borrowing country responds to a Fund condition for a large cut in the budget deficit by slashing expenditure on health and education versus the curtailment of the national car project. Moreover, because both the implementation of and payoff from structural projects take longer than macroeconomic and exchange rate policies, it is necessary to measure progress along the way. All of this produces many detailed structural performance tests and some uncertainty about whether the overall effort will warrant Fund financial support, but there are no shortcuts that would work better.

The rest of the paper elaborates on these issues and sets out some additional arguments and factual material relevant for gauging what IMF structural policy conditionality should be like in the future. In section 2, I ask what, if any, guidance on structural policy involvement can be gleaned from the Fund's charter and guidance notes from its executive board. I then discuss three alternative mandates for Fund lending within which structural policy conditionality might operate — ranging from a narrow one based on correction of balance-of-payments problems and resolution of the current crisis, to broader ones that add avoidance of future crises and pursuit of "high-quality" economic growth to the agenda. Section 3 looks at various dimensions of Fund structural policy involvement and conditionality — both in the Asian crisis countries over the past three years and more broadly over the past several decades. It also offers some tentative conclusions on the effectiveness of that conditionality, with particular emphasis on the compliance with Fund conditionality. Because very little factual material has been published heretofore on fund structural policy conditionality, this section contains a number of tables and charts documenting the patterns in such conditionality. In section 4, I speculate on why the scope and micromanagement of Fund structural policy conditionality have increased in recent years. Section 5 lays out a set of potential approaches to streamlining Fund structural policy conditionality if, as seems increasingly likely, the international community and IMF management were to agree that such streamlining would be desirable. Finally, section 6 provides some brief concluding remarks that summarize my own views on Fund structural policy conditionality.

SECTION 2. STRUCTURAL POLICIES AND THE MANDATE OF THE INTERNATIONAL MONETARY FUND

Scripture and Field Manuals

One starting point for figuring out how involved the IMF should be in structural policies would be to look at the Fund's basic marching orders. These range from the IMF's charter (called the "Articles of Agreement") to specific guidance notes issued by the Fund's executive board to IMF staff.

List A reproduces (from Article I of the Articles of Agreement) the Fund's purposes. Although amendments have been made to other parts of the charter over the past fifty-five years, this is not so with the purposes. Two things are immediately obvious from even a casual reading. There are many purposes, not just one; and there are a number of terms and concepts — such as "confidence," "national and international prosperity," "temporary," and "exchange system" — that are (and indeed, have been) susceptible to multiple interpretations.

LIST A

Purposes of the IMF

1. To promote international monetary cooperation through a permanent institution that provides the machinery for consultation and collaboration on international monetary problems.
2. To facilitate the expansion and balanced growth of international trade, and to contribute thereby to the promotion and maintenance of high levels of employment and real income and to the development of the productive resources of all members as primary objectives of economic policy.
3. To promote exchange stability, to maintain orderly exchange arrangements among members, and to avoid competitive exchange depreciation.
4. To assist in the establishment of a multilateral system of payments in respect of current transactions between members and in the elimination of foreign exchange restrictions which hamper the growth of world trade.
5. To give confidence to members by making the general resources of the Fund temporarily available to them under adequate safeguards, thus providing them with opportunity to correct maladjustments in their balance of payments without resorting to measures destructive of national or international prosperity.
6. In accordance with the above, to shorten the duration and lessen the degree of disequilibrium in the international balance of payments of members.

The Fund shall be guided in all its policies and decisions by the purposes set forth in this article.

It is clear (at least to me) that a primary objective is not only to correct balance-of-payments disequilibria but also to do so in a particular way, that is, in a way that doesn't involve either excessive deflation or unemployment at home or beggar-thy-neighbor policies. This is how I interpret the phrases (in paragraph 5) "without resorting to measures destructive of national and international prosperity" and (in paragraph 3) "to avoid competitive exchange depreciation." Such an interpretation is of course also consistent with the Fund's establishment as a response to the beggar-thy-neighbor and Great Depression problems of the 1920s and 1930s.

There is also clear support for measures that promote openness to international trade and a multilateral system of payments, and opposition to measures that hamper this openness. Capital movements are not mentioned. Again, this is consistent with the perceived (trade-output vicious circle) lessons of the 1920s and 1930s and with the popular view about the perils of destabilizing capital flows.

Although there is no denying that a key task of the IMF at the time of its creation was to oversee a system of fixed but adjustable exchange rates, I interpret the promotion of "exchange stability" (in paragraph 3) as going beyond any particular form of exchange arrangements (be it adjustable pegs, currency boards, floating rates, etc.). Put another way, I don't see the raison d'être of the Fund as having disappeared in the early 1970s along with the arrival of floating exchange rates. If the intention were otherwise, paragraph 3 would presumably have referred to "exchange rate" stability, and there be would no purposes other than that one.

Although Article I makes it plain that the framers regarded "high levels of employment and income" and "development of productive resources" as good things, it doesn't say that the Fund should pursue those objectives by whatever means available. Instead, they specify that the Fund should facilitate "the expansion and balanced growth of international trade" and "contribute *thereby*" to buoyant domestic economic activity.

Where else might one look in the Fund's charter for advice relevant to structural policy conditionality? Many would say the revised (in 1976) Article IV, which deals with general obligations of member countries and with the Fund's surveillance responsibilities. Here, economic growth and, to a lesser extent, international capital movements, get greater play than in the Fund's purposes. Specifically, the new Article IV recognizes specifically that the essential purpose of the international monetary system is to provide a framework that both "facilitates the exchange of goods, services, and *capital* among countries, and that sustains sound economic growth." More noteworthy, member countries assume the general obligation to "endeavor to direct... economic and financial policies toward the objective of fostering orderly economic *growth* with reasonable price stability," and the fund assumes the obligation to oversee the "compliance" of each member country with this obligation.

Since "economic and financial policies" directed toward orderly economic growth potentially covers a lot of ground, the practical upshot of the revised Article IV was that it gave the Fund a much broader license to conduct wide-ranging surveillance and annual consultations with members. Ever since then, the Fund's Article IV consultation reports have covered a host of policy areas, including many that would be designated as structural policies.[12] Even though Article IV carries the title "Obligations Regarding Exchange Arrangements," it embodied the view that you had to look at the underlying domestic policy determinants of a stable exchange rate system to see if countries were meeting their international obligations.[13] Yes, Article IV is about Fund surveillance, not about Fund policy conditionality. However, the fact that the former has been given much wider scope (since at least the mid-1970s) probably has contributed somewhat to a wider field of view in Fund lending arrangements as well (more on that in section 4).

But what about more specific directives relating to performance criteria agreed and issued by the Fund's executive board? In my view, the most relevant document is probably the conditionality guidelines for standby arrangements, issued in 1979; see list B. To make a long story short, although the guidelines permit the number and content of performance criteria to vary with a country's problems and institutional arrangements, guideline 9 specifies, inter alia, that performance criteria will "normally be confined to macroeconomic variables" and that "performance criteria may relate to other variables *only in exceptional cases when they are essential for the effectiveness of the member's program because of their macroeconomic impact*" (italics mine). My interpretation of all this is that, at least in Fund standby arrangements, the intention was to limit the number of structural- policy performance criteria and to avoid "micro" conditionality (that is, measures that don't have macroeconomic impact). Although these guidelines have been revisited many times during later board reviews of conditionality, they have been repeatedly endorsed.

---

[12] For a review and analysis of the content of Fund surveillance, see Crow, Arriazu, and Thygensen (1999).

[13] Eichengreen (1999) has made a similar argument that the Fund cannot expect to be successful at promoting international financial stability without addressing sources of financial instability at the national level.

LIST B

Conditionality Guidelines for Fund Standby Lending

1. Members should be encouraged to adopt corrective measures, which could be supported by use of the Fund's general resources in accordance with the Fund's policies, at an early stage of their balance-of-payments difficulties. The article IV consultations are among the occasions on which the Fund would be able to discuss with members adjustment programs, including corrective measures, that would enable the Fund to approve a stand-by arrangement.
2. The normal period for a stand-by arrangement will be one year. If, however, a longer period is requested by a member and considered necessary by the Fund to enable the member to implement its adjustment program successfully, the stand-by arrangement may extend beyond the period of one year. This period in appropriate cases may extend up to but not beyond three years.
3. Stand-by arrangements are not international agreements and therefore language having a contractual connotation will be avoided in stand-by arrangements and letters of intent.
4. In helping members to devise adjustment programs, the Fund will pay due regard to domestic social and political objectives, the economic priorities, and the circumstances of members, including the causes of their balance-of-payments problems.
5. Appropriate consultation clauses will be incorporated in all stand-by arrangements. Such clauses will include provision for consultation from time to time during the whole period in which the member has outstanding purchases in the upper limit tranches. This provision will apply to whether the outstanding purchases were made under a stand-by arrangement or in other transactions in the upper credit tranches.
6. Phasing and performance clauses will be omitted in stand-by arrangements that do not go beyond the first credit tranche. They will be included in all other stand-by arrangements but these clauses will be applicable only to purchases beyond the first credit tranche.
7. The managing director will recommend that the executive board approve a member's request for the use of the Fund's general resources in the credit tranches when it is his or her judgment that the program is consistent

with the Fund's provisions and policies and that it will be carried out. A member may be expected to adopt some corrective measures before a stand-by arrangement is approved by the Fund, but only if necessary to enable the member to adopt and carry out a program consistent with the Fund's provisions and policies. In these cases the managing director will keep executive directors informed in an appropriate manner of the progress of discussions with the member.

8. The managing director will ensure adequate coordination in the application of policies relating to the use of the Fund's general resources with a view to maintaining the nondiscriminatory treatment of members.

9. The number and content of performance criteria may vary because of the diversity of problems and institutional arrangements of members. Performance criteria will be limited to those that are necessary to evaluate implementation of the program with a view to ensuring that the achievement of its objectives. Performance criteria will normally be confined to (a) macroeconomic variables and (b) those necessary to implement specific provisions of the articles or policies adopted under them. Performance criteria may relate to other variables only in exceptional cases when they are essential for the effectiveness of the member's program because of their macroeconomic impact.

10. In programs extending beyond one year, or in circumstances in which a member is unable to establish in advance one or more performance criteria for all or part of the program period, provision will be made for a review in order to reach the necessary understandings with the member for the remaining period. In addition, in those exceptional cases in which an essential feature of the program cannot be formulated as a performance criterion at the beginning of a program year because of substantial uncertainties concerning major economic trends, provision will be made for a review by the Fund to evaluate the current macroeconomic policies of the member, and to reach new understandings if necessary. In these exceptional cases the managing director will inform executive directors in an appropriate manner of the subject matter of a review.

11. The staff will prepare an analysis and assessment of the performance under programs supported by use of the Fund's general resources in the credit tranches in connection with article IV consultations and as appropriate in connection with further requests for use of the Fund's resources.

12. The staff will from time to time prepare, for review by the executive board, studies of programs supported by stand-by arrangements in order to evaluate and compare the appropriateness of the programs, the effectiveness of the policy instruments, and the observance of the programs, and the results achieved. Such reviews will enable the executive board to determine when it may be appropriate to have the next comprehensive review of conditionality.

However, one must also take note that a variety of other lending arrangements (besides standbys) has been created in the Fund with the support of the membership over the past thirty years (ranging from a facility to assist transition economies in coping with the shift away from state trading to multilateral market-based trading, to one that was to assist countries experiencing liquidity problems related to Y2K). More to the point of this paper, some of those lending windows are directly aimed at protracted balance-of-payments problems and at supporting comprehensive efforts at macroeconomic *and* structural reform. These include the Extended Fund Facility (EFF; established in 1974), and both the Structural Adjustment Facility (SAF; established in 1986) and Enhanced Structural Adjustment Facility (ESAF; established in 1987); eligibility for both the SAF and the ESAF is restricted to low-income countries.[14] For these lending windows, structural policy involvement is at the heart of the exercise, and there is little guidance on how many or what kinds of structural policy measures would be viewed as "out of bounds."

Given the prominence of governance issues in the Asian crisis, a final guidance note worth noting is the one issued in July 1997 by the Fund's executive board on "The Role of the IMF in Governance Issues." Although the note states right at the beginning that "the responsibility for governance issues lies first and foremost with the national authorities," it seems to give the Fund staff quite a wide berth to include governance and corruption measures in Fund conditionality if they can make the case that governance problems have some direct macroeconomic impact. In addition, although the note urges the Fund staff to rely on other institutions' expertise in areas of their purview, it states that the Fund could nevertheless recommend conditionality in those areas (outside the Fund's expertise) if the staff considered that such measures

---

[14] In 1999, the ESAF was reorganized into the Poverty Reduction and Growth Facility (PRGF).

were "critical to the successful implementation of the program." Given the timing and context of this guidance note (just at the outset of the Asian crisis), some IMF staff have expressed the view (to me) that the Fund's board was sending them a signal that they would henceforth not support programs that ignored serious and widespread governance and corruption problems.

To sum up, the Fund's existing marching orders on structural policy conditionality are Janus-faced enough that both supporters of narrow conditionality and those of more comprehensive conditionality can find their own biblical passages to buttress their arguments. On the one side, I don't see in the Fund's charter a broad agenda aimed at high-quality growth. What I see instead is a focus on balance-of-payments adjustment, trade opening, elimination of payments restrictions, efforts to increase the stability of the exchange rate system, and a directive to avoid modes of external adjustment that make recession or deflation deeper than necessary and that impose undue costs on other countries.[15] This is not to deny that the Fund's membership may want to pursue high-quality growth (and poverty reduction) for a variety of reasons, including moral imperatives. It's just that I can't find that commandment on the original stone tablets. In a similar vein, the Fund's conditionality guidelines for standby arrangements appear to have had the intention of limiting the number of structural performance criteria, particularly if they are micro in nature. On the other side of the ledger, the Fund's overall surveillance responsibilities (under the revised Article IV) are quite wide-ranging: as regards structural policies, a succession of specific lending windows has been established over the past twenty-five years or so with an explicit structural policy orientation, and guidance notes on "new" structural policy issues like governance and corruption give the Fund staff considerable leeway to include such measures in conditionality as long as they can make a case that they are critical to the success of the program. Perhaps more telling, I could find no evidence of concern about the scope or intrusiveness of structural policy conditionality in the published summaries (so-called Public Information Notices, or PINs) of executive board meetings on the Thai, Indonesian, and Korean programs over the past three years — even though the number and detail of structural conditions in those three programs are extraordinary (see section 3 below).

---

[15] It's also relevant to note that, unlike the charter of the EBRD, the Fund's charter says nothing about promoting "democracy"; see Polak (1991) for a discussion of political influences on IMF lending.

Three Alternative Mandates

If there is relatively little guidance available about the appropriate intrusiveness of Fund structural policy conditionality from official sources, one might consider what different mandates for the Fund would imply about such conditionality. Here, I consider three possibilities, starting with the narrowest and ending with the broadest (and most ambitious).

Mandate I

The Fund's primary focus would be on macroeconomic and financial stability; its crisis management guideline would be to assist a country to get out of the current crisis as soon as possible (without imposing undue costs on itself or its neighbors).

An announced IMF focus on macroeconomic and financial stability would be similar to the increasing popular practice of national central banks to announce that their primary objective is price stability. It doesn't preclude giving some consideration to other objectives, but it makes clear which objective is king and where the authority's central responsibility lies. The emphasis on getting out of the current crisis would mean that crisis management and resolution — and not crisis prevention — should guide program design. Crisis prevention measures would presumably then be handled by the country on its own *after* the current crisis is resolved.

Would Mandate I preclude Fund structural policy conditionality during a crisis? The answer, I believe, is no. However, the extent of the structural conditions would be limited to measures directly related to resolution of the *current* crisis, and their form would depend on both the nature of the crisis and the institutional structure in place in the crisis country; in addition, the design of essential structural policy conditions outside the Fund's core competence (monetary, fiscal, exchange rate, and financial-sector policies) would need to be handled by other international financial institutions (IFIs). A few examples should suffice to illustrate the point.

Suppose that key contributory factors to a balance-of-payments crisis were an overvalued exchange rate and overly expansionary monetary and fiscal policies. Also assume that correction of relative prices was being thwarted by widespread indexation agreements in wage contracts. Assume that the alternatives to devaluation as an adjustment tool are a more draconian tightening of monetary or fiscal policy (which would drive the domestic economy into deep recession) and a large hike in tariff and nontariff barriers. In that case, reduction or elimination of those indexation provisions could be regarded as essential to external adjustment (without either excessive deflation or beggar-thy-neighbor effects), and a labor-market performance test could be part of conditionality.[16]

Next, consider a case in which the primary source of the external disequilibrium is a large budget deficit. Assume that the necessary fiscal adjustment needs to be large, that the economy is expected to undergo a serious contraction, that the incumbent government is quite unpopular at home (because there is a long history of cronyism and corruption), and that there is no social safety net to speak of. In that situation, it could be argued that the Fund program needs to contain a few structural measures (e.g., the closing of a government cartel or monopoly) to send a visible signal to the public that some patronage is being taken away from well-connected government cronies and therefore that the program will be even-handed — and this even if the structural measures themselves have no macroeconomic impact and lie outside the Fund's core competence.[17] Here, these structural measures might be defended as necessary to establish confidence. Similarly, the creation of an unemployment insurance scheme or some other form of social safety net could be viewed as necessary to sustain popular support for the fiscal correction effort over the one- or two-year program period.

Next, picture a situation in which a banking crisis is under way and no deposit insurance system is in place. Depositors are withdrawing deposits from a group of weak banks, and the government is supporting the weak banks' ability to meet withdrawals by providing liquidity assistance to those banks. The deposit run is spreading, and the liquidity injections are pumping up the monetary aggregates and driving down the exchange rate. It is also known that substantial funds will soon be needed to recapitalize insolvent banks and to increase capital at solvent but still weak banks. Because its debt burden is

---

[16] Another example in which labor market policies could be considered essential to overcoming the current crisis is when a banking crisis cannot be overcome without financial-sector and corporate restructuring, and the latter cannot be accomplished without revision of restrictive laws governing employee layoffs.

[17] Allen (1993, 18) takes such a view: "Structural policies can also help build and maintain the political consensus that will support macroeconomic stabilization — for example, by combating unproductive and politically unpopular rent-seeking activities."

already high, the government cannot fund all the bank cleanup costs on its own. It will need help from private creditors abroad. Here, too, one could defend structural conditions relating to bank closures or to deposit insurance reform as being essential for resolving the current crisis; without them, the authorities will not be able to control monetary policy and to halt the free fall of the currency. If the *immediate* aim of raising funds from abroad is being hampered by restrictions on capital inflows or by poor disclosure that prevents foreign creditors from judging the worth of domestic banks, the removal or correction of restrictions or disclosure practices too might be defended as a legitimate element in conditionality.

In contrast to the above scenarios, consider a crisis situation brought on, say, by a large terms-of-trade shock or a shift in investor sentiment stemming from contagion in a neighboring country. Assume also that there are many structural-policy weaknesses and institutional gaps but that these are not serious enough or linked closely enough to monetary, fiscal, and exchange rate policies to prevent the crisis from being resolved with traditional macroeconomic instruments plus some Fund financing. Here, however desirable structural measures may be for longer-term performance, they would not be included as conditions for the program. A plain vanilla Fund program will do the job.

Another relevant question is whether Mandate I would still permit the Fund to make a contribution to poverty reduction in poor countries. The answer is yes, but only insofar as macroeconomic and financial stability itself contributes to poverty reduction, or because the Fund (in collaboration with the World Bank) sees the incorporation of social safety nets into crisis resolution programs as necessary for the successful implementation of those programs. Longer-term efforts (outside of crises) to fight poverty would then be handled by the World Bank and the regional development banks.

Mandate II

The Fund's primary focus would be (as in Mandate I) on macroeconomic and financial stability: its crisis guideline would be to assist a country not only to get out of the current crisis but also to minimize the chances of getting into another one down the road.

Although the Fund's core competence remains the same in Mandate II as in Mandate I, the big difference is that the fund now incorporates crisis *prevention* as well as crisis resolution in program design. An implicit judgment here is that the country needs to use the crisis as a mechanism to reduce its crisis vulnerability and that it would not be able to do this on its own (i.e., without a Fund program) after the current crisis is resolved. Better, then, to "make hay while the sun shines" and combine crisis resolution and crisis prevention in the current program. If confidence in the crisis economy is very low, the Fund might also argue that investors will not return unless there is evidence that the probability of another (near-term) crisis is low; this in turn requires proof that the old (crisis-prone) system is changing, and structural reform would be part and parcel of such proof.

Mandate II increases substantially the scope for structural policy conditionality, even without going into noncore areas of economic policy. Again, a few examples convey the flavor.

Assume that the country has a long-standing problem of undisciplined monetary policy and that monetary policy excesses are also a key factor in the current crisis. In that case, the Fund might argue that a performance criterion that simply says that monetary policy will be tightened within the existing regime will not be credible. In this situation, the program might contain structural policy conditionality that either specifies granting independence to the central bank or takes the monetary reins out of the central bank's hands by establishing a currency board or single currency.

One could tell a similar story about long-standing weaknesses in fiscal policy that lead a country to accumulate a very heavy external debt burden. When, say, a large negative shock occurs to the terms of trade (e.g., oil prices fall), foreign investors run for the exits and a debt crisis breaks out. Assume that the chronically weak fiscal position owes much to a narrow tax base, to a host of large loss-making public enterprises, and to the absence of proper expenditure-control and budgeting departments in the ministry of finance. In parallel with the immediately preceding example, the Fund might argue that a performance criterion that simply targets a lower fiscal deficit for the next year will not be credible. As such, the Fund program could contain structural conditions for widening the tax base, for privatizing state enterprises, and for establishing new administrative units in the ministry of finance.

Carrying forward the same theme, imagine a banking crisis whose proximate determinants are a sharp contraction of economic activity or a sharp rise in interest rates connected with a defense of a fixed exchange rate.

However, assume also that there was a large backlog of nonperforming loans brought on by the following: state-owned banks that lent without any regard to creditworthiness of borrowers; commercial banks that had long demonstrated a proclivity toward "connected lending"; lax loan classification procedures that encouraged the "evergreening" of bad loans and that grossly overstated the true value of bank capital; a legal framework that made it difficult for banks to seize collateral from bankrupt borrowers; ineffective banking supervision from a bank supervisory agency that had neither the political independence nor the mandate or resources to do its job; and lender moral hazard, stoked by repeated episodes of bailing out bank depositors and creditors. Against such a background, the Fund might maintain that a program that merely specified closing insolvent banks and recapitalizing others to international standards would amount to flushing money down the drain. Even if the current banking crisis were resolved, it wouldn't be long before the same underlying vulnerabilities produced a repetition (thereby exacerbating the problem of "prolonged use" of Fund resources). Better then — so the argument would go — to require structural policy conditions that would change each of these poor banking and supervisory practices.

The same kind of argument could be made about the need for conditions (on bank bailouts and the like) to control moral hazard problems, which, by definition, relate to the effect of inappropriately priced insurance arrangements (extended this period) on the risk-taking behavior of policyholders *next period*. Put in other words, it is precisely the worry about avoiding the next crisis that makes it necessary to put additional conditions on the management of the current crisis.

Mandate III

The Fund's focus would be on macroeconomic and financial stability and on sustainable growth; its crisis guideline would be to assist the country not only to get out of the current crisis and to reduce its crisis vulnerability but also to put in place the conditions for sustainable high-quality growth.

The difference here with respect to Mandates I and II is that high-quality growth now occupies a more central role both in the Fund's overall mandate and in its crisis-fighting strategy. Under this more holistic approach, conditionality would likely encompass measures that are viewed as necessary to improve economic growth and protect the poor and the vulnerable, as well as measures to improve the country's resilience to future crises. A hypothetical country scenario can again help to illustrate the differences involved.

Consider a country that is suffering from persistently weak economic growth, a chronic budget deficit, a weak external position, pervasive state intervention, heavy public ownership, protectionism, and a host of governance and corruption problems. A large, negative terms-of-trade shock or a group of bank failures may have pushed this country into crisis, but for the last decade or more it may never have been very far away from crisis.

Reflecting the focus on economic growth (under Mandate III), the Fund and the country authorities might agree that the program ought to have a three-year rather than a one-year tenure, so that any aggregate demand reductions could be made more gradual and so that there would be more time for structural reform to take hold. In addition, the Fund might ask that the country only make good progress toward external payments viability during the program period rather than actually achieving such viability. In an effort to reduce distortions that create an anti-export bias and that hamper efficient resource allocation, the program might well call for the following: scaling back the extent of price controls and state intervention in marketing of exports, foodstuffs, fertilizer, and petroleum products; the reduction or elimination of surrender requirements and controls on foreign exchange allocation; reduced reliance on quantitative restrictions on imports and a reduction in the level and dispersion of tariff rates; privatization of selected public enterprises and the entering into of "performance contracts" with existing managers of public enterprises; liberalization of interest rates (and other measures to move from state to market allocation of credit); development of financial markets for interbank funds, government securities, and stocks; and the phasing-out of government-owned banks.

To protect the most vulnerable groups, such a program would probably also place conditions on the composition of government expenditure cuts, as well as an overall target for the budget deficit. Specifically, these structural conditions could call, inter alia, for a shift in government expenditure away from military and "showcase" expenditures toward expenditure on primary education and health care; severance pay and retraining for workers released from public enterprises that are being privatized; a gradual (rather than abrupt) reduction of price controls on commodities that loom large in poor people's budgets; and the creation of an unemployment insurance system. There might likewise be provisions for special credit arrangements for agricultural producers and for small and medium-sized businesses, and the differential impact of currency devaluation on urban consumers versus agricultural exporters might be subject to partial compensation. As part of efforts to combat corruption problems, audits and public disclosure of findings might be required of certain financial institutions and of government-sponsored monopolies, and employment practices in the civil service could be subject to review. Additionally, core labor standards might be put forward if there were strong evidence of significant departures from them.

To sum up, what gets included in Fund structural policy conditionality depends in good measure on the nature of the crisis and on the extent of interdependence between traditional Fund macroeconomic policy instruments and structural policies. *But the intrusiveness of conditionality also depends on how broad are the objectives of the Fund and the country authorities.* Trying to get out of the current crisis is one thing. Trying to ward off a future crisis is quite another. And trying to spur high-quality growth in a low-income country with a host of government-induced distortions and large institutional gaps is something else again. Yet another relevant factor, particularly as regards the intensity or degree of detail in Fund conditionality, is how much confidence the IMF and creditor governments have in the willingness of the crisis country to carry through on its policy commitments; the greater the skepticism on that score, the greater is likely to be the number of prior actions and other performance tests included in programs. However, that takes us into the next section.

SECTION 3. THE STRUCTURAL CONTENT OF FUND POLICY CONDITIONALITY AND ITS EFFECTIVENESS

Thus far, I have summarized arguments about Fund structural policy conditionality and discussed how the Fund's mandate might affect the scope and details of such conditionality. However, I have not discussed the available facts on Fund structural policy conditionality, nor the existing literature on the effectiveness of conditionality. That is the subject of this section. First, I ask how commonplace, wide-ranging, and detailed structural policy conditions have been in Fund programs; whether structural policy conditionality seems to be increasing over time; in what policy areas structural conditionality has been most intensive; and what performance tests have been used to monitor this conditionality. Second, I then ask what we know about the effectiveness of that structural policy conditionality, including the track record on compliance with Fund conditionality. Most of these questions are not entirely straightforward to answer, both because the relevant data are available only in pieces and because the counterfactual to Fund policy conditionality (that is, what would happen in the absence of a Fund program) is extremely difficult to know or to estimate.

Structural Policies in Fund Programs

Since there is no comprehensive index of Fund structural policy conditionality that is available over a long time period, one has to rely on a set of statistics to tell the story. In what follows, I review, in turn: (a) data on the number of total structural policy conditions per program year for a sample of twenty Stand-By Arrangements (SBAs) and twelve EFFs for the 1996–99 period; (b) data on the average number of structural performance criteria for all Fund programs over the 1993–99 period; (c) data on the number of structural policy conditions (overwhelmingly structural benchmarks) in recent (1997–2000) Fund programs with three Asian crisis countries (Indonesia, South Korea, and Thailand); (d) data on the average number of structural benchmarks per Fund program for thirty-three transition economies over the 1993–99 period; and (e) data on the number of structural benchmarks in earlier SAF programs. For each body of data, I am interested not only in the scope and intensity of structural policy conditionality, but also in the trend, the differences across different types of Fund programs (SBAs, EFFs, and SAF/ESAF/PRGF programs), and the distribution across structural policy areas.

Before getting to all that, a brief digression on the instruments that the Fund uses to monitor compliance with conditionality is warranted. For the purposes of this paper, four of these are of interest.

Performance criteria (PCs) are meant to provide a direct link between program implementation and disbursement of Fund resources. If the criterion is met on the agreed test date (typically set at quarterly intervals), the member country is assured of disbursement; if the criterion is not met, the country cannot draw unless a waiver is obtained. Waivers are granted when a country's noncompliance with performance criteria is viewed by the Fund as inconsequential or when it reflects significant exogenous developments not foreseen at the time the program was framed.[18] PCs are expected to be under the control of the borrower, capable of being precisely and objectively formulated and monitored, and subject to relatively short (usually less than forty-five days) reporting lags. In the structural area, a PC could, for example, specify that elimination of restriction x on current payments be accomplished by date y, or that three insolvent finance companies be closed by date z. *Prior actions* are policy measures that the country agrees to take before a Fund agreement goes into effect. They are apt to be employed when severe imbalances exist and the country is viewed as having had a poor track record of implementation (in earlier Fund programs). *Structural benchmarks* (SBMs) are indicators that aim to delineate the expected path of reform for individual structural policy measures and that can facilitate the evaluation of progress for these actions. Because many structural policies cannot be expressed in quantitative form, structural benchmarks are usually expressed qualitatively; for example, if the program calls for privatization of the state-owned telephone company, submitting the privatization bill to the legislature by date x could be one structural benchmark. Failure to meet structural benchmarks conveys a negative signal but does not automatically render a country ineligible to draw; instead, a decision about eligibility would be judgmental and would likely be taken in a broader midyear *program review* — itself an instrument of conditionality — with an eye toward the country's overall progress on the structural front. Program reviews, like SBMs, assess implementation of policies not amenable to monitoring via PCs (because of their imprecise or qualitative nature). Reviews are broader than individual SBMs and can be used, for example, to assess whether there needs to be a change in program design.[19]

Number of (Total) Structural Policy Conditions per Program Year

At this point, the most comprehensive measure of Fund structural policy conditionality is that produced by the Fund itself via its so-called MONA database (which stands for Monitoring Fund Arrangements). It is the only

---

[18]Waivers also require that the authorities have taken the necessary action to bring the program back on track if this is necessary to meet its objectives.

[19]When conditionality includes a program review, the text of the arrangement specifies what elements are to be reviewed; the review also assesses whether or not the program's objectives are in jeopardy.

Table 1: Number of Programmed Structural Conditions Per Annum, 1996–99

	SBAs	EFF
Median	9	18
Mean	15	18
Standard deviation	12	12

series available that combines information on all four types of structural conditions, namely, performance criteria, structural benchmarks, prior actions, and conditions for completion of program reviews. When only one of those structural policy conditions is used, there is a danger that you are seeing only one part of the elephant. The Fund's index of programmed structural policy measures is then divided by the length of the period to obtain figures on number of programmed structural policy measures per annum. The rub is that this comprehensive measure is so far available only for the twenty SBAs and twelve EFFs over the 1996–99 period. To my knowledge, this comprehensive measure of Fund structural policy conditions has not been published before.

Table 1 presents the goods. Three conclusions stand out. First, the number of structural policy conditions that would be typical for, say, a three-year EFF Fund program over the last few years is high; specifically, it would be more than fifty (three times the annual average of eighteen measures per annum).[20] For a typical one-year SBA, it would be somewhere between nine and fifteen (depending on whether we used the median or the mean). This is a far cry from the "only in exceptional cases" guideline called for in the (1979) conditionality guidelines for SBAs. Second, the median number of structural policy conditions is much higher (double) for EFFs than for SBAs. This is not surprising. As noted earlier, EFFs *must* have a structural policy orientation; SBAs may have structural conditionality, too, but don't necessarily have to (if structural problems are not viewed as serious or pressing). Note that the difference between SBAs and EFFs vanishes when one looks at the mean number of conditions — a finding that could well reflect the presence of a

---

[20] Because the data in Table 1 are expressed as the number of conditions per annum rather than per program, I need to assume that the number of conditions varies proportionally with time to arrive at conclusions about the number in conditions in a "typical" three-year program.

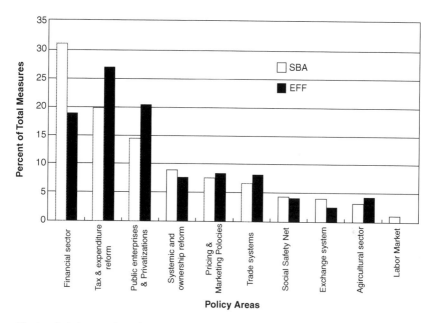

Fig 1: Relative number of IMF structural conditions in different policy areas, 1996–99

few SBAs with very high structural policy content. Third, there is quite a lot of variation across both SBAs and EFFs in the extent of structural policy conditionality. Because these data are thus far available only for the 1996–99 period as a whole, there is nothing that can be said here about trends.

The Fund has broken down its comprehensive measure of structural policy conditions into ten broad policy areas. The results are portrayed in Figure 1. In short, what we see there is that about two-thirds of structural policy conditions are concentrated in three areas: financial-sector policies, tax and expenditure reforms, and public enterprises and privatizations. Since the Fund's core competence is often identified to be monetary, fiscal, exchange rate, and financial-sector policies (see, e.g., Council on Foreign Relations Task Force 1999), this would seem to belie the charge that, on average, most of the Fund's focus in structural policies is far afield from its main expertise — or, to put it in other words, that Fund structural policy conditionality is typically "a mile wide and an inch thick." At the same time, Figure 1 does show that fund structural policy conditionality has reached into a number of "noncore" structural policy areas (e.g., labor markets, social safety nets).

Average Number of Structural Performance Criteria per Program

The Fund's MONA database also contains information on performance criteria (PCs) for the longer 1993–99 period. Tables 2, 3, and 4 present the average number of performance criteria per program for all Fund programs, for ESAF/PRGF programs, and for SBA and EFF programs, respectively; separate figures are also given for the transition economies and (in Table 2) for the Asian economies. In these tables, "quantitative performance criteria" refers to macroeconomic variables (e.g., the nominal value of the fiscal deficit, net domestic credit of the central bank, the stock of net international reserves, etc.) that are used to track compliance with monetary, fiscal, exchange rate, and external debt policies. "Structural performance" criteria are meant to assess compliance with important structural policy commitments. Note that the data here are calculated per program, not per program year. This is more informative in some respects but also carries the disadvantage that the annual figures can be biased upward (downward) if there are more (less) multiyear arrangements agreed in a given year. Note also that because we are dealing only with one component of structural policy conditionality in Tables 2–4, we have to be careful about generalizing about the overall intrusiveness of Fund structural policy conditionality from these figures.

Five main conclusions emerge from Tables 2–6. One is that "structural" PCs are on average less numerous than quantitative macroeconomic PCs — with the notable exception of the three programs for the Asian crisis economies in 1997 (see the upper two panels of Table 2 versus the lowest one). A second conclusion is that the number of structural PCs in the programs with the three Asian crisis economies in 1997 (an average of 14.0 per program) was far above (roughly four times) both the average for all fund programs over the 1993–99 period (an average of 3.3 per program) and for 1997 alone (an average of 7.0 per program); in contrast, the average number of quantitative macroeconomic PCs was actually lower in the Asian economies than for all Fund programs. Finding number three is that the average number of structural PCs in programs with the transition economies was below (not above) the average for all Fund programs over this period. Fourth, there have on average been more structural PCs in ESAF/PRGF programs than in SBA and EFF arrangements (taken together).

Table 2: Summary of Performance Criteria in Fund-Supported Programs, 1993–99

	1993	1994	1995	1996	1997	1998	1999
A. Total Number of Arrangements							
Number of programs approved by year	22	35	30	32	21	21	20
Number of performance criteria	218	373	327	419	328	234	203
Quantitative	186	276	268	297	191	173	150
Structural	32	97	59	122	137	61	53
Number of performance criteria per program	10	11	11	13	16	11	10
Quantitative	8	8	9	9	9	8	8
Structural	1	3	2	4	7	3	3
B. Transition Economies							
Number of programs approved by year	9	8	12	12	7	6	4
Number of performance criteria	82	79	100	156	73	90	37
Quantitative	78	67	100	125	67	64	37
Structural	4	12	0	31	6	26	0
Number of performance criteria per program	9	10	8	13	10	15	9
Quantitative	9	8	8	10	10	11	9
Structural	0.4	2	0	3	1	4	0
C. Asian Economies							
Number of programs approved by year	0	0	0	0	3	1	0
Number of performance criteria	0	0	0	0	59	9	0
Quantitative	0	0	0	0	18	5	0
Structural	0	0	0	0	41	4	0
Number of performance criteria per program					20	9	
Quantitative					6	5	
Structural					14	4	

Notes: Stand-by, extended facility, and SAF/ESAF/PRGF arrangements. Number of performance criteria refers to all performance criteria over the duration of the program. Performance criteria are classified by year of program approval, irrespective of test dates they applied to. Quantitative performance criteria applying to the same variable are counted only once, even if observance was required for more than one test date.

A fifth finding — at least for all Fund arrangements taken together — is that we do observe some upward trend in the average number of structural PCs as we move from the earlier part of the period (2.0 in 1993–95) to the latter part (3.3 in 1996 and 98–99) — even if we exclude 1997; that being said, the straw that stirs the drink in the average of PC numbers is clearly the high figure (14.0 per program) for the three programs with Asian crisis countries in 1997.

Table 3: Summary of Performance Criteria in ESAF/PRGF Arrangements, 1993–99

	1993	1994	1995	1996	1997	1998	1999
A. Total Number of Arrangements							
Number of programs approved by year	7	13	7	14	7	11	9
Number of performance criteria	86	183	116	227	134	132	106
Quantitative	61	102	81	118	72	97	68
Structural	25	81	35	109	62	35	38
Number of performance criteria per program	12	14	17	16	19	12	12
Quantitative	9	8	12	8	10	9	8
Structural	4	6	5	8	9	3	4
B. Transition Economies							
Number of programs approved by year	1	1	0	3	1	3	0
Number of performance criteria	14	14	—	60	17	42	—
Quantitative	10	9	—	33	13	31	—
Structural	4	5	—	27	4	11	—
Number of performance criteria per program	14	14	—	20	17	14	—
Quantitative	10	9	—	11	13	10	—
Structural	4.0	5	—	9	4	4	—

Notes: Number of performance criteria refers to all performance criteria over the duration of the program. Performance criteria are classified by year of program approval, irrespective of test dates they applied to. Quantitative performance criteria applying to the same variable are counted only once, even if observance was required for more than one test date. Dashes indicate no program was assessed for that year.

Unfortunately, there are no directly comparable statistics on average number of structural PCs for earlier periods. An unpublished IMF (1987a) study on SBAs and EFFs during the 1979–97 period does show the breakdown of structural PCs by policy area; if I make the (risky) assumption that there was only one PC per policy area indicated for each country, I get an estimate of 1.3 structural PCs per program for that period — about one-third of the average figure (3.3) for 1993–99 (from Table 2). Polak (1991) reports the average number of total PCs (presumably, quantitative macro-economic PCs plus structural PCs) per program for some earlier periods. Specifically, his figures are less than 6.0 per arrangement for 1968–77, 7.0 in 1974–84, and 9.5 in 1984–87. The comparable figure taken from Table 2 for average (total) PCs per program over 1993–99 would be 11.7. If other monitoring components of Fund policy conditionality (prior actions, SBMs, conditions for program reviews) moved in the same direction over this period — and Polak suggests

Table 4: Summary of Performance Criteria in SBA/EFF Arrangements, 1993–99

	1993	1994	1995	1996	1997	1998	1999
A. Total Number of Arrangements							
Number of programs approved by year	15	22	23	18	14	10	11
Number of performance criteria	132	190	211	192	194	102	97
Quantitative	125	174	187	179	119	76	82
Structural	7	16	24	13	75	26	15
Number of performance criteria per program	9	9	9	11	14	10	9
Quantitative	8	8	8	10	9	8	7
Structural	0	1	1	1	5	3	1
B. Transition Economies							
Number of programs approved by year	8	7	12	9	6	3	4
Number of performance criteria	68	65	100	96	56	48	37
Quantitative	68	58	100	92	54	33	37
Structural	0	7	0	4	2	15	0
Number of performance criteria per program	9	9	8	11	9	16	9
Quantitative	9	8	8	10	9	11	9
Structural	0.0	1	0	0	0	5	0

Notes: Number of performance criteria refers to all performance criteria over the duration of the program. Performance criteria are classified by year of program approval, irrespective of test dates they applied to. Quantitative performance criteria applying to the same variable are counted only once, even if observance was required for more than one test date.

they have — this would point to a significant increase in the monitoring of Fund conditionality over the past thirty years or so.

As regards the distribution of structural PCs across policy areas for earlier periods, the same 1987 IMF study found that the leading categories were the exchange system (12 percent) and the trade system (6 percent). The financial sector, which led the parade in Figure 1, was in third place in 1979–87, and fiscal policy was yet further behind.

Number of Structural Policy Conditions in Recent Fund Programs with Indonesia, South Korea, and Thailand

Since Fund structural policy conditionality in three Asian crisis countries has had a lot to do with reopening the debate on the appropriate scope and detail of conditionality, it makes sense to give those programs a separate look. In Table 5,

Table 5: Number of Structural Policy Commitments in IMF Programs with Three Asian Crisis Countries, 1999–2000

Indonesia	10/97	01/98	04/98	06/98	07/98	09/98	10/98	11/98	03/99	05/99	07/99	01/00	07/00
	28	31	140	109	96	68	62	74	35	33	29	42	41
South Korea	12/08/97	12/05/97	12/24/97	02/98	05/98	07/98	11/98	08/99	11/99	07/00			
	29	33	50	53	51	39	53	83	94	68			
Thailand	08/97	11/97	02/98	05/98	08/98	12/98	08/99	09/99					
	26	24	21	73	50	69	8	9					

Table 6: Number of Structural Benchmarks (SBs) According to Structural Benchmark Groups for Countries in Transition

	Type of Fund Program	Number of Structural Benchmarks
Armenia	SBA	35
Azerbaijan	SBA	26
Belarus	SBA	21
Bulgaria	SBA	19
Macedonia	SBA	19
Romania	SBA	19
Estonia	SBA	18
Georgia	SBA	17
Hungary	SBA	15
Romania	SBA	15
Poland	SBA	14
Kazakhstan	SBA	13
Moldova	SBA	13
Ukraine	SBA	12
Uzbekistan	SBA	12
Croatia	SBA	11
Kazakhstan	SBA	11
Ukraine	SBA	11
Bulgaria	SBA	8
Kyrgyz Republic	SBA	6
Russia	SBA	6
Moldova	SBA	5
Poland	SBA	3
Latvia	SBA	2
Bulgaria	SBA	1
Latvia	SBA	1
Average		13
Kyrgyz Republic	ESAF	35
Albania	ESAF	34
Azerbaijan	ESAF	31
Georgia	ESAF	22
Armenia	ESAF	18
Macedonia	ESAF	17
Average		26
Azerbaijan	EFF	41
Russia	EFF	37
Kazakhstan	EFF	23
Moldova	EFF	16
Lithuania	EFF	11
Croatia	EFF	9
Average		23

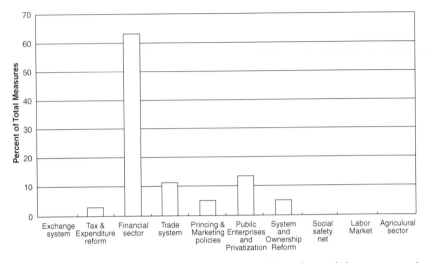

Fig 2: The coverage of structural conditionality in stand-by and extended arrangements in Korea, Indonesia, and Thailand, 1996–99

I provide a running count of the number of structural policy conditions — believed to be overwhelmingly made up of conditions for program reviews and structural benchmarks — contained in successive revisions of the Indonesian, Korean, and Thai programs over the 1997–2000 period. In Figure 2, I present a rough breakdown of the three crisis programs by structural policy areas. In an effort to convey the flavor of the detail in those programs, I have also reproduced in list C the first half of the full SBM matrix for Indonesia as of June 1998. Perhaps it is a hint of one of the main conclusions that it was not practical to attach the full list of structural policy conditions for all three programs: as a group, they are much too long for a paper of this length. The reader should be cautioned that counting the number of structural policy commitments says nothing about which conditions are more important or are more intrusive. Nor does such a count tell us which commitments came at the initiative of the country authorities and which came from the Fund.[21] Moreover, such a count mixes together what might be called formal conditionality (monitored

---

[21] Fund staff note that country authorities often use an IMF letter of intent to underline or to "advertise" policy reforms that have recently been made and those that are expected to be made in the near future — even if those reforms are predominantly "home grown."

by specific performance criteria and structural benchmarks) and informal conditionality (monitored by program reviews).

LIST C

Indonesia: Excerpts from Structural Policy Conditions

Policy Action

Fiscal Issues

Remove VAT exemption arrangements.
Increase proportion of market value of land and buildings assessable for tax to 40 percent for plantation and forestry.
Introduce single-taxpayer registration number.
Increase non-oil tax revenue by raising annual audit coverage, developing improved VAT audit programs, and increasing recovery of tax arrears.
Increase in two stages excise taxes on alcohol and tobacco to reflect exchange rate and price developments.
Raise profit transfers to the budget from state enterprises, including Pertamina.
Raise prices on rice, sugar, wheat flour, corn, soybean meal, and fish meal.
Eliminate subsidies on sugar, wheat flour, corn, soybean meal, and fish meal.
Accelerate provisions under the Nontax Revenue Law of May 1997, to require all off-budget funds to be incorporated in budget within three years (instead of five years).
Incorporate accounts of Investment Fund and Reforestation Fund within budget.
Ensure reforestation funds used exclusively for financing reforestation programs.
Central government to bear cost of subsidizing credit to small-scale enterprises through state banks.
Cancel twelve infrastructure projects.
Discontinue special tax, customs, or credit privileges granted to the National Car.
Phase out local content program for motor vehicles.
Abolish compulsory 2 percent after-tax contribution to charity foundations.
Discontinue budgetary and extrabudgetary support and privileges to IPTN (Nusantara Aircraft Industry) projects.
Conduct revenue review with Fund assistance.

Monetary and Banking Issues

Provide autonomy to BI in formulation of monetary and interest rate policy.

Publish key monetary data on a weekly basis.

Submit to Parliament a draft law to institutionalize BI's autonomy.

Submit draft amendment to banking law to Parliament.

Provide autonomy to state banks to adjust interest rates on credit and deposit liabilities, within any guidelines applying to all banks.

Impose limits on and phase out BI credits to public agencies and public-sector enterprises.

Strengthen BI's bank supervision department and strengthen enforcement of regulations.

Upgrade the reporting and monitoring procedures for foreign exchange exposures of banks.

Appoint high-level foreign advisors to BI to assist in the conduct of monetary policy.

Set minimum capital requirements for banks of Rp 250 billion by end of 1998, after loan loss provisions.

Reduce the minimum capital requirements for existing banks.

Make loan loss provisions fully tax deductible, after tax verification.

Establish program for divestiture of BI's interests in private banks.

Require all banks to prepare audited financial statements.

Require banks to publish regularly more data on their operations.

Lift restrictions on branching of foreign banks.

Submit to Parliament a draft law to eliminate restrictions on foreign investments in listed banks and amend bank secrecy with regard to non-performing loans.

Eliminate all restrictions on bank lending except for prudential reasons or to support cooperatives or small-scale enterprises.

Bank Restructuring

Close sixteen nonviable banks.

Replace the closed banks' management with liquidation teams.

Compensate small depositors in the sixteen banks.

Place weak regional development banks under intensive supervision by BI.

- Provide liquidity support to banks, subject to increasingly restrictive conditions.
- Provide external guarantee to all depositors and creditors of, all locally incorporated banks.
- Establish Indonesia Bank Restructuring Agency (IBRA).
- Determine uniform and transparent criteria for transferring weak banks to IBRA.
- Transfer fifty-four weak banks to IBRA.
- Transfer claims resulting from past liquidity support from BI to IBRA.
- Transfer to IBRA control of seven banks accounting for more than 75 percent of past BI liquidity support and seven banks that have borrowed more than 500 percent of their capital.
- IBRA will continue to take control of or freeze additional banks that fail to meet liquidity or solvency criteria. Where necessary, any such action will be accompanied by measures to protect depositors or creditors in line with the government guarantee.
- Issue presidential decree to provide appropriate legal powers to IBRA, including its asset management unit.
- Take action to freeze, merge, recapitalize, or liquidate the six banks for which audits have already been completed.
- Establish independent review committee to enhance transparency and credibility of IBRA operations.
- Conduct portfolio, systems, and financial reviews of all IBRA banks as well as major non-IBRA banks by internationally recognized audit firms.
- Conduct portfolio, systems, and financial reviews of all other banks by internationally recognized audit firms.
- Announce plan for restructuring state banks through mergers, transfers of assets and liabilities, or recapitalization prior to privatization.
- Ensure that state banks sign performance contracts, prepared by the Ministry of Finance with World Bank assistance.
- Merge two state-owned banks and conduct portfolio reviews of the two banks.
- Draft legislation enabling state bank privatization.
- Introduce private-sector ownership of at least 20 percent in at least one state bank.
- Prepare state-owned banks for privatization.

Develop rules for the Jakarta Clearing House that will transfer settlement risk from BI to participants.

Introduce legislation to amend the banking law in order to remove the limit on private ownership of banks.

Introduce deposit insurance scheme.

Establish Financial Sector Advisory Committee to advise on bank restructuring.

Declare insolvency of six private banks intervened in April and write down shareholder equity.

Issue government bonds to Bank Negara Indonesia at market-related terms to finance transfer of deposits of banks frozen in April.

Initiate first case of an IBRA bank under the new bankruptcy law.

Foreign Trade

Reduce by 5 percentage points tariffs on items currently subject to tariffs of 15 to 25 percent.

Cut tariffs on all food items to a maximum of 5 percent.

Abolish local content regulations on dairy products.

Reduce tariffs on nonfood agricultural products by 5 percentage points.

Gradually reduce tariffs on nonfood agricultural products to a maximum of 10 percentage points.

Reduce by 5 percentage points tariffs on chemical products.

Reduce tariffs on steel/metal products by 5 percentage points.

Reduce tariffs on chemical, steel/metal, and fishery products to 5–10 percent.

Abolish import restrictions on all new and used ships.

Phase out remaining quantitative import restrictions and other nontariff barriers.

Abolish export taxes on leather, cork, ores, and waste aluminum products.

Reduce export taxes on logs, sawn timber, rattan, and minerals to a maximum of 30 percent by 15 April 1998; 20 percent by end of December 1998; 15 percent by end of December 1999; and 10 percent by end of December 2000.

Phase-in resource rent taxes on logs, sawn timber, and minerals.

Replace remaining export taxes and levies by resource rent taxes as appropriate.

Eliminate all other export restrictions.

Remove ban on palm oil exports and replace by export tax of 40 percent. The level of the export tax will be reviewed regularly for possible reduction, based on market prices and the exchange rate, and reduced to 10 percent by end of December 1999.

Investment and Deregulation

Remove the 49 percent limit on foreign investment in listed companies.

Issue a revised and shortened negative list of activities closed to foreign investors.

Remove restrictions on foreign investment in palm oil plantations.

Lift restrictions on foreign investment in retail trade.

Lift restrictions on foreign investment in wholesale trade.

Dissolve restrictive marketing arrangements for cement, paper, and plywood.

Eliminate price controls on cement.

Allow cement producers to export with only a general exporters license.

Free traders to buy sell and transfer all commodities across district and provincial boundaries, including cloves, cashew nuts, and vanilla.

Eliminate BPPC (Clove Marketing Board).

Abolish quotas limiting the sale of livestock.

Prohibit provincial governments from restricting trade within and between provinces.

Enforce prohibition of provincial and local export taxes.

Take effective action to allow free competition in the following:

1. importation of wheat, wheat flour, soybeans, and garlic
2. sale or distribution of flour
3. importation and marketing of sugar

Release farmers from requirements for forced planting of sugar cane.

The tale told by Table 5 and by Figure 2 can be summarized as follows. First, the number of structural policy conditions included in these programs with the three Asian crisis economies is very large (if not totally unprecedented) — many more than you can count using all your fingers and toes.[22] Without claiming any precision, my count from publicly available documents is that

---

[22] I hesitate to call the total number of structural policy conditions in even the Indonesian program "unprecedented" because I am told informally that there was a larger figure (close to 200) in one of Russia's programs with the Fund.

these structural policy commitments summed, at their peak, about 140 in Indonesia, over 90 in Korea, and over 70 in Thailand. Each of these totals is considerably above the average of about 50-plus for all Fund programs over the 1996–99 period. Second, in the programs with Korea and Thailand, the number of structural policy conditions was considerably smaller at the beginning of the program than at its peak — perhaps because the country authorities and the Fund first laid out the main elements of the structural reform package and then filled in the details as they went along, and because implementation of reforms was pretty good (see discussion below). In contrast, the number of structural policy conditions in the Fund program with Indonesia hits its peak pretty early on and then declines as the program period goes on, perhaps reflecting an initial effort to impress the markets with the extent of intended structural reform and then scaling that back as market reaction proved disappointing and as evidence accumulated that implementation capacity or willingness would be lower than anticipated. Third, although financial-sector restructuring and supervision is the dominant policy concentration in all three programs, additional data indicate that the scope of structural policy conditionality is much narrower in the Korean and Thai programs than in the Indonesian one. Putting aside the financial sector, Thai structural policies are mainly focused on tax and expenditure reform and on corporate debt restructuring. In Korea, the non-financial areas getting most attention are corporate governance and restructuring (and some trade and capital-account liberalization). In Indonesia, structural reforms outside the financial sector are more of a mixed bag, with significant commitment clusters appearing for privatization and reform of public enterprises, for trade systems, for pricing and marketing policies, for corporate restructuring, and for tax and expenditure reform; there are also minor clusters for energy and environmental policies and for social safety nets.

Turning to list C, what is striking is the number, scope, and detail of the structural policy commitments made by Indonesia, including in nontraditional areas of conditionality. There are, inter alia, measures dealing with reforestation programs; the phasing-out of local content programs for motor vehicles; discontinuation of support for a particular aircraft project and of special privileges granted to the National Car; abolition of the compulsory 2 percent after-tax contribution to charity foundations; appointment of high-level advisors for monetary policy; development of rules for the Jakarta Clearing

House; the end of restrictive marketing agreements for cement, paper, and plywood; the elimination of the Clove Marketing Board; the termination of requirements on farmers for the forced planting of sugar cane; the introduction of a micro credit scheme to assist small businesses; and the raising of stumpage fees. Enough to say that the great bulk of such measures were *not* included because of their macroeconomic impact; they were presumably included instead for anticorruption reasons, to instill confidence in private investors that the system was changing, to facilitate monitoring of commitments, and (for some commitments) to reflect the structural policy agendas of either other IFIs (the World Bank and the Asian Development Bank) or certain creditor countries (see discussion in section 4).[23]

Number of Structural Benchmarks in Fund Programs with the Transition Economies

Mercer-Blackman and Unigovskaya (2000) have analyzed the use of SBMs in Fund programs for twenty-five transition economies over the 1989–97 period. Their tally, also derived from the Fund's MONA database, is presented in Table 6. Three observations merit explicit mention.

First, the average number of SBMs per program is roughly twice as high in ESAF (twenty-six) and EFF (twenty-three) arrangements and as it is for standby arrangements (thirteen). Second, although the data in Table 7 are not directly comparable with those in Table 1 (not only are the time periods different, but the latter include all structural conditions, whereas the former include only SBMs), the number of SBMs in standby arrangements for the transition economies do not seem far out of line (i.e., higher) with the recent averages for SBAs in all Fund programs — and they are clearly much lower than the averages on SBMs in the three Asian crisis economies. Third, there is more variation for SBAs in the number of SBMs (ranging from one in Bulgaria and Latvia to thirty-five in Armenia) than for either ESAF or EFF arrangements.

Figure 3, taken from Christiansen and Richter (1999), gives the breakdown by policy area of structural policy conditions for the fund's programs

---

[23] Haggard (2000) shares this view.

Table 7: Percentage of IMF Loan Actually Disbursed under Each Arrangements (distribution by quartiles)

	$x < 0.25$ (1)	$0.25 \leq x < 0.50$ (2)	$0.50 \leq x < 0.75$ (3)	$0.75 \leq 1.0$ (4)	Fully Disbursed ($x = 1.0$) (5)	(4)+(5) $0.75 \leq x$ (6)	Number of Arrangements (7)
All arrangements							
1973–77	36.5	7.1	5.9	5.9	44.7	50.6	85
1978–82	19.4	16.1	10.5	12.9	41.1	54.0	124
1983–87	12.9	15.8	19.4	7.9	43.9	51.8	139
1988–92	17.5	15.1	20.6	14.3	32.5	46.8	126
1993–97	27.0	19.1	26.2	11.3	16.3	27.6	141
Full period (1973–97)	21.6	15.3	17.6	10.7	34.8	45.5	615
stand-by	23.1	13.4	15.0	9.5	39.0	48.5	441
EFF	33.9	22.2	19.0	15.9	9.5	25.4	63
SAF/ESAF	9.0	18.9	27.0	12.6	32.4	45.0	111

Source: IMF, *Transactions of the Fund* (1998).

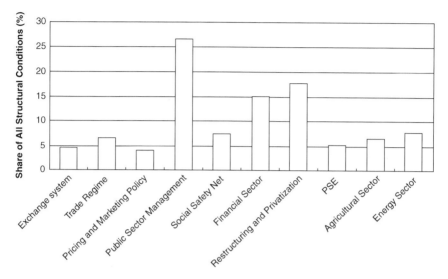

Fig 3: Distribution of structural conditions in IMF-supported programs: Transition economies.

with the transition economies.[24] The main message is that the most frequently occurring structural conditions were in the area of public-sector management (institutional reform, tax and revenue policy, expenditure policy, and public wages and employment). Next in line were restructuring and privatizations, and financial-sector reforms. After that, we see a fairly even distribution across the remaining areas (energy sector, social safety net, agricultural sector, trade regime, exchange system, etc.). The top three categories accounted together for over two-thirds of structural conditions.

Scattered Evidence on Number of Structural Benchmarks in Earlier SAF Programs

An unpublished IMF study (1987) of seventeen SAF arrangements (for low-income countries) in 1986–87 also looked at the number and distribution of structural benchmarks. The main findings were that the average number of

---

[24]The data used to construct Figure 3 are different from those used in Table 8. The former cover (I think) all structural policy conditions (not just SBMs) and they also cover the fund's initial programs with the transition economies under the (lower-conditionality) Systemic Transformation Facility. These differences, however, are not important for our purposes.

SBMs per SAF arrangement was about seven, that there was considerable variation around this average across programs (ranging from three in the program for Bolivia to fifteen for Uganda), and that structural conditions also ranged quite widely across policy areas (covering the exchange system, trade liberalization and tariff reform, public enterprises, tax and expenditure policy, producer pricing and agricultural marketing, and public-sector investment programs).

To sum up, structural policy conditionality is now a common and important element of Fund conditionality. When prior actions, performance criteria, structural benchmarks, and conditions for program reviews are combined, it has been typical (over the past few years) for a one-year standby arrangement to have on the order of, say, a dozen structural conditions and for a three-year EFF arrangement to have, say, fifty of them. About two-thirds of those structural conditions are apt to fall in the areas of fiscal policy, financial-sector reform, and privatization, with the remainder scattered across a fairly wide field. The structural conditions in the Fund's much-discussed programs with three Asian crisis economies (Indonesia, Korea, and Thailand) were much more numerous and detailed than is usually the case. Financial-sector conditions dominated in all three of those Asian programs, but detailed conditions in quite a few noncore structural policy areas were also evident, especially in the case of Indonesia. Although much of the external criticism of Fund structural conditionality has emphasized the wide scope of the Fund's involvement (e.g., some wonder what the Fund has to do with the clove monopoly), our review of the evidence suggests that the number and specificity of conditions in core areas ("micro management") are at least as important an issue.[25]

Those analyzing Fund structural policy conditionality, including researchers both inside and outside the Fund, are unanimous in concluding that there has been a pronounced upward trend in such conditionality over the past fifteen years, and this trend has probably become steeper in the 1990s.[26]

---

[25] Saying that the Fund has micromanaged some structural reforms is not the same as saying that such reforms necessarily lack macroeconomic impact. For example, a condition to reduce significantly the extent of wage indexation could be very detailed but might still carry macro impact.

[26] See, for example, Tanzi (1987), Polak (1991), Killick (1995), James (1998), Krueger (1998), Mussa and Savastano (1999), and Gupta et al. (2000).

The evidence reported in this section (much of it previously unpublished) strongly corroborates this conclusion. Finally, there has also been a shift over time in the instruments used by the Fund to monitor structural conditionality, with resort to structural benchmarks, conditions for program reviews, and prior actions having risen faster than formal performance criteria. Prior to the 1980s, the Fund was hesitant to ask for prior actions, and performance reviews regarding structural policies were exceptional for standby arrangements (see Polak 1991; IMF 1987). Structural benchmarks were apparently not used prior to the establishment of the SAF in 1986. As demonstrated earlier, all this is no longer the case. For example, a comparison of the average number of structural conditions for standby arrangements in 1996–99 in Table 1 with the figures on structural performance criteria in Table 2 suggests that, taken together, structural benchmarks, prior conditions, and program reviews have recently been about five times as numerous as structural performance criteria.

Writing well before Fund programs with the Asian crisis countries, Polak (1991) contrasted the principles put forth in the 1979 Guidelines on Conditionality with actual practice:

> The guidelines do not attempt to change the structure of conditionality: their aim is limited to making that structure less intrusive by limiting the number of performance criteria, insisting on their macroeconomic character, circumscribing the cases for reviews, and keeping preconditions to a minimum. Yet these restraining provisions have not prevented the intensification of conditionality in every direction that the guidelines attempted to block. (61)

Nine years later, it's hard to disagree with that assessment.

The Effectiveness of Fund Structural Policy Conditionality

If we take it as given that the IMF has become more "grandmotherly" or intrusive with regard to its structural policy conditionality, the next question is how effective such conditionality has been.[27] Here, we address just two aspects of that question: the degree of compliance with Fund conditions and the quality of the Fund policy advice implicitly reflected in such structural policy conditionality. Again, much of the available evidence is often not in the

---

[27] The description of Fund conditionality as being "grandmotherly" is from Keynes; see James (1998).

form best suited to the focus of this paper (that is, it refers to compliance with, or the effectiveness of, *all* Fund policy conditions, not just structural policies, or when it deals only with structural policies, it covers only low-income or transition economies). Nevertheless, some conclusions can be put forward. In addition, some of the recent research on compliance with structural conditions in Fund programs with the transition economies is particularly interesting.

Compliance with Fund Policy Conditions

Clearly, Fund policy conditionality cannot have its intended effects if countries do not implement these policies. Two measures of compliance are typically found in the literature: the share of IMF loans actually disbursed, and the degree of compliance with particular Fund policies (e.g., credit ceilings, budget deficits, various structural benchmarks).[28]

Table 7, adopted from Mussa and Savastano (1999), shows the share of Fund lending actually disbursed for 615 Fund programs over the 1973–97 period. Although the authors caution that a low disbursement share could mean the program was so successful — or conditions improved so rapidly — that the country needed to use only a fraction of the committed IMF financing, they conclude that low disbursement cases mainly were ones in which the program went off track (because policies deviated significantly from those agreed upon and subsequent negotiations failed to reach agreement on a modified program).

Here, it is appropriate to highlight three of the Mussa-Savastano findings. First, if we take, say, disbursement of 75 percent or more of the total loan as implying close adherence to IMF policy conditionality, then less than half (45.5 percent) of all Fund arrangements over the entire 1973–97 period would have met that test; see column (6) in Table 7. Second, again using the 75 percent or greater benchmark, the completion rate for standby arrangements (48.5 percent) was notably higher than that for EFF programs (25.4 percent) with higher average structural policy content; the completion rate for SAF/ESAF arrangements, which also have a relatively high structural policy content and deal exclusively with low-income countries, was much higher than for EFFs

---

[28] Another potential measure of compliance would be the share of programs that saw an early conversion of the program to a precautionary arrangement.

and only slightly below that for SBAs. Third, there is a suggestion that the completion rate for Fund programs is declining over time.[29]

A very similar exercise on completion rates was undertaken by Killick (1995) for 305 Fund programs over the 1979–93 period, with results quite close to those obtained by Mussa and Savastano (1999). Killick defines a "completed program" as one that disbursed 80 percent or more of the total Fund loan. He finds on this measure that 47 percent of Fund programs were completed, that the completion rate was higher for SBAs than for EFFs, that the completion rate was declining over time, and that completion rates do not differ (in the expected way) on account of cross-country differences in either per capita income or type of export.[30]

Most earlier studies that looked at compliance with particular Fund policies were restricted to macro conditionality. In brief, Beveridge and Kelly (1980) and Edwards (1989) found that compliance with monetary or fiscal performance criteria was observed in approximately 48–62 percent of Fund programs. Polak (1991) updated these results for SBA, EFF, and SAF programs in the 1980s and found that compliance rates for the 1980s were below those for the 1970s. Killick (1995) cites one unpublished 1991 IMF study that looked at compliance with structural policies in SAF and ESAF programs: slightly over half of all structural benchmarks were observed on schedule (or two-thirds within a few months thereafter), and compliance was relatively high for agricultural producer pricing and marketing and for financial reforms, and relatively low for fiscal provisions (and especially for public enterprise reforms).

Two more recent studies of compliance with fund structural conditionality have been conducted for the transition economies by Christiansen and Richter (1999) and Mercer-Blackman and Unigovskaya (2000).[31] Four of

---

[29] I use the term "suggestion," because Mussa and Savastano (1999) note that the results on completion rates for the 1993–97 period are biased downward due to the inclusion of arrangements with post-1997 expiration dates.

[30] Killick (1995) did find some evidence that completion rates were lower for highly indebted countries and for those that received relatively low access to Fund resources.

[31] A caveat should be noted with respect to studies of the transition economies. Because of the centrality of structural policies to their reform efforts in the 1990s, their experience with structural policy conditionality may be "special" and not necessarily transferable to economies where structural policies occupy a less central role.

their findings are of interest. First, the on-time compliance rate for structural benchmarks as a group averaged 42 percent, with an additional 16 percent of conditions met with delay; the remaining 42 percent of conditions were not met or no information was available. Second, the compliance rate for performance criteria (both macro and structural taken together) was higher than that for structural benchmarks. Third, the correlation between the number of structural benchmarks in a program and the completion rate for those structural policies was negative, although neither large nor statistically significant. Fourth, although there was sizable variation in the compliance rate across structural reform categories, the standard deviation of compliance across countries was more than twice as great as that for compliance by reform category.[32]

To sum up, existing studies suggest that obtaining compliance with Fund conditionality has been a serious problem, including the Fund's structural policy conditionality. The compliance problem has been getting more serious over time. Compliance has been lower for EFF programs than for standby arrangements (but not apparently for SAF/ESAF programs). Compliance has also been lower for structural benchmarks than for performance criteria. Correlations between the compliance rate and the number of structural conditions, along with measures of the variability of compliance across program areas and countries, suggest that greater selectivity both in the countries approved for structurally oriented programs and in the structural measures included in such programs could have a high payoff in terms of compliance rates.[33] Further studies on a broader sample of countries would be useful in sharpening these conclusions, including the important issue of whether or not the product of the number of structural conditions and the compliance rate is approximately a constant.

---

[32] The on-time compliance rate was highest (57 percent) for public wage and employment conditions and lowest (29 percent) for price and marketing conditions. Ukraine had the lowest overall compliance rate (14 percent of structural conditions met on time), while Lithuania had the highest (82 percent).

[33] It is relevant to note that the 1979 "Conditionality Guidelines" suggest that the managing director of the IMF should only recommend that the Fund's executive board approve a Program when it is his judgment that the program... will be carried out"; see Guideline Number 7 in appendix B.

Effectiveness of Structural Policy Conditionality

Even if countries consistently complied with Fund structural policy conditions, this would not necessarily constitute an endorsement for such conditionality unless it can be shown that these are "good" structural policy requirements that lead to "better" economic performance. Evidence relevant for answering that latter query can be gleaned from at least five sources: (a) econometric studies that estimate the effects of IMF programs (as a whole) by comparing program and nonprogram countries or periods; (b) studies that relate either structural policy action within a Fund program or structural policy action more generally (whether in Fund programs or otherwise) to economic growth; (c) studies that relate measures of corporate governance to the extent of exchange rate depreciation or stock market decline during the Asian crisis; (d) a comparison of Fund structural policy recommendations with the "consensus" of the economics profession on what structural policies are good; and (e) a review of the Fund's structural policy recommendations in the Asian crisis countries.

Studies on the Effects of IMF Programs as a Whole. By now, there is an extensive empirical literature on the effects of IMF programs.[34] If one defines "program effects" as the observed outcome (for growth, inflation, the balance of payments, etc.) relative to the counterfactual (that is, the outcome in the absence of an IMF program), then it is clear that most of the early literature had serious methodological flaws (see Goldstein and Montiel 1986). Before-and-after comparisons are not reliable because they attribute all the change in outcomes to a Fund program when exogenous shocks and other influences may really be causing that change. Comparison of program targets and outcomes will not be useful when program targets are set too ambitiously or not ambitiously enough. Simulations of economic models can tell us something about the effect of Fund-type policies but not about the effects of actual Fund programs, and comparisons of outcomes for program and nonprogram countries will not do the job if the two groups differ systematically in ways that matter for economic performance. Over time, most of these methodological problems have been addressed. Nowadays, studies typically seek to identify program effects after controlling both for nonprogram effects and for observed (precrisis) differences between program and nonprogram countries.

---

[34] For a recent survey of this literature, see Haque and Khan (1998).

Still, even the best studies have only indirect implications for the effectiveness of Fund structural policy conditionality since they do not disaggregate the contents of a Fund program into its macro and structural policy components. In any case, what such studies usually find is that Fund programs have a favorable impact on the current account and overall balance of payments, that the effect on inflation is statistically insignificant, and that the effect on economic growth is initially (with the first year) negative but probably turns positive at longer time horizons (see Mussa and Savastano 1999; Fischer 2000a; Conway 1994); too little econometric work has been done on income distribution to say much.[35]

One possible explanation for why such studies do not generate large positive growth effects for Fund programs is that compliance with the policies that matter for medium- to long-run growth is far from complete (as demonstrated above); also, some countries that are in trouble implement their own policies that are not very different from those included in Fund programs. It has also been argued that even nonprogram countries have been influenced by the "silent revolution" in economic thinking on the importance of sound macroeconomic and structural policies and that the Fund has contributed importantly to this revolution (that is, nonprogram countries are not a good "control group" because they too are affected by the policy treatment; see, e.g., Krueger 1998). A second explanation is that the lags associated with the effects of structural policies on economic growth are long and, hence, may show up only after the country has left a Fund program. Yet a third explanation is that the results are right: despite all the rhetoric on "growth-oriented adjustment," Fund programs are still mainly about getting out of financial crises and don't much matter for growth in the medium to long run.

Links between Broad Measures of Structural Policy Reform and Growth. This is a more recent literature, much of it connected with understanding the economic performance of the transition economies.[36]

---

[35]See, however, the recent study by Garuda (2000) who finds that Fund programs improve income distribution and poverty reduction for countries with relatively modest precrisis external disequilibria but worsen them for countries with severe precrisis external imbalances.

[36]There is of course a much broader and older literature on effects of alternative structural-policy strategies (e.g., Balassa's [1983] work on outward-looking vs. inward-looking policy strategies) and on the determinants of growth in developing countries more generally (e.g., Barro [1996]). In addition, there are many studies that take a nonquantitative approach to

One strand looks at whether greater compliance with Fund structural policy conditionality is associated with better growth performance. Here, the recent study by Mercer-Blackman and Unigovskaya (2000) is worth noting. They find that, after controlling for other factors, those transition economies that demonstrated higher compliance with IMF structural performance criteria had better records of sustained economic growth (defined as three consecutive years of positive real GDP growth); in contrast, they could find no significant association between compliance with Fund structural benchmarks and sustained growth. They also report that transition economies that did better on complying with Fund structural performance criteria also showed greater progress on implementing structural reform more generally.[37] One interpretation of their first finding is that the (relatively few) structural policies included as performance criteria are more important for growth than the larger number regarded as structural benchmarks. The authors concede that some of their results are also consistent with other views; for example, countries with better growth performance may find it easier to implement Fund structural conditions, and the unobserved "commitment to reform" may explain *both* Fund program implementation and progress on structural policy action more generally.

The other strand of this literature tests for an association between structural reform — whether achieved within the context of a Fund program or not — and economic growth. A good example is the recent study by Havrylyshyn et al. (1999), which examines the growth experience of twenty-five transition economies over the 1990–97 period. After attempting to hold other determinants of growth constant (including initial economic conditions, inflation, size of government, degree of openness, etc.), they find that the greater was progress on an index of overall structural reform, the higher

---

evaluating Fund structural policies; see, for example, Schadler et al. (1995a), who (looking at Fund programs during the 1988–92 period) concluded that "there was a broad measure of success in accomplishing structural reform" (29).

[37] Progress on structural reform is measured using a structural reform index, derived from De Melo, Denizer, and Gelb [1996] and EBRD Transition reports. This index is meant to capture liberalization of prices and foreign exchange markets, small and large-scale privatization, governance and restructuring reforms, legal reforms, interest rate liberalization, and banking reforms; see Havrylyshyn et al. [1999].

was economic growth.[38] They also tested whether individual components of structural reform aided growth but found that only price liberalization had significant explanatory power when the overall reform index was also included—a finding that they interpret as suggesting that it is the combination of structural policies that is more critical for growth than any single type of policy.

A similar growth exercise for eighty-four low- and middle-income countries during the 1981–95 period is summarized in IMF (1997). In these pooled, cross-section regressions, the authors find that after controlling for other determinants of per capita GDP growth, improved macroeconomic policies and improved structural policies both have significant effects on growth in the expected direction. They also conclude that behavior of growth in ESAF countries does not differ fundamentally from that in other developing countries.

Corporate Governance and the Asian Financial Crisis. As suggested earlier, there has been much discussion of the role that governance and corruption issues played in the Asian financial crisis. A new study by Johnson et al. (2000) provides some interesting empirical results and insights. The authors look at the behavior of nominal exchange rates and stock markets from the end of 1996 through January 1999 for twenty-five emerging economies. Their aim was to see if cross-country differences in measures of corporate governance (e.g., judicial efficiency, corruption, rule of law, protection for minority shareholders, creditor rights, etc.) could do a better job at explaining the extent of exchange rate depreciation and stock market decline than could standard macroeconomic measures (e.g., fiscal and monetary policy, current account imbalances, international reserves, foreign debt, etc.). In brief, they find that the corporate governance horse does better than the macroeconomic horse, particularly for stock market movements. They argue that institutions that protect investor rights are not important as long as growth lasts (because managers do not want to steal). However, when growth prospects decline and there is even a small loss of investor confidence, countries with only weakly

---

[38] Fischer, Sahay, and Vegh (1996) reached a similar conclusion in an earlier paper on the growth experience of the transition economies. Because there are very few transition economies that have not had a program with the IMF, a comparison of program and nonprogram countries is not a viable research strategy.

enforceable minority shareholder rights become particularly vulnerable. This is because outside investors reassess the likely amount of expropriation by managers and adjust the amount of capital they are willing to provide (resulting in a fall of asset values and a collapse of the exchange rate). On some of Johnson et al.'s measures of corporate governance — particularly rights of minority shareholders — several Asian crisis countries (particularly Indonesia and Thailand) ranked low and hence were more vulnerable to the effects of a downturn.

Fund Structural Policy Conditionality and the "Consensus". In 1983 at a conference on IMF conditionality, Richard Cooper [1983] offered the following view: "we could choose any five people present and make a team to work up an economic adjustment program for a particular country other than our own... [and] the program we came up with would not differ greatly from a typical IMF program" (571).

I am more skeptical that we could make the same statement today, at least about Fund programs for the Asian crisis countries. Nevertheless, I would still maintain that the general thrust of the Fund's structural policy recommendations falls squarely in what my IIE colleague John Williamson (1990) has labeled "the Washington policy consensus." Whether it is interest rate deregulation, trade liberalization, tax reform, the currency regime, foreign direct investment, price liberalization, or banking reform, Fund structural policy advice is typically not far from the consensus. Writing fifteen years after Cooper, Anne O. Krueger (1998, p. 1998) offers a similar assessment:

> Many of the lending changes supported by the Bank and the Fund (in, for example, exchange rates, size of fiscal deficits, trade liberalization, agricultural and energy price reforms, privatization, and tax reform) are ones that would be endorsed in broad outline, if not in detail, by almost all economists.

But saying that the Fund's structural policy advice has generally reflected the profession's consensus view does not mean that this advice has not at times gone seriously astray. Three examples illustrate the point. First, along with several of its larger G7 shareholders (particularly the United States and the United Kingdom), the Fund often pushed hard on emerging economies to undertake capital account liberalization without due regard to the adequacy of the host country's regulatory and supervisory framework.[39] In Korea, for instance, the Fund apparently urged liberalization of both short-term and long-term flows. However, when the Koreans said they would only go for the former, the Fund apparently regarded this as better than nothing and accepted it.[40] A second example concerns Fund advice on privatization in transition economies. There, the IMF (2000) acknowledges that privatization runs the danger of producing perverse results in the absence of hard budget constraints, competition, and effective standards of corporate governance. As with capital account liberalization, a more selective approach to privatization with greater attention to sequencing would, with the benefit of hindsight, have been better. Yet a third example was the initial Fund recommendation in Indonesia to go with a limited deposit guarantee for banks rather than a blanket guarantee.[41] In drawing the lessons of the Asian crisis, the Fund (Lindgren et al. 1999) now concludes that in a systemic crisis a blanket guarantee is needed to restore confidence in the financial system.[42]

Fund Structural Policy Conditionality in the Asian Crisis Countries. Because the heart of Fund structural policy conditionality in the Asian crisis countries dealt with the financial sector, and because there is already a separate paper at this conference focused on financial policies in emerging economies, I will confine my remarks on the Fund's structural policy recommendations to four points.

First, I find the underlying rationale for dealing immediately with insolvent and weak banking and finance companies compelling. Without such action, it probably would have been impossible to restore monetary and currency stability (because large-scale liquidity support to insolvent institutions would have worked at cross purposes), and the fiscal tab for

---

[39] One of the few observers who stated publicly his concerns (before the crisis) about the magnitude of short-term capital inflows going into Asian emerging economies was Park (1996).

[40] In appraising Fund structural policy recommendations made in the late 1980s, Schadler et al. (1995a, 31) similarly conclude: "Coordinated programs for structural reforms would have been desirable but were generally not politically or administratively feasible. It is appropriate, therefore, that programs supported the second-best strategy of seizing opportunities for reform on as broad a front as possible. This process cannot give a large role to sequencing considerations, but these are not unambiguous and could unduly slow the process."

[41] A comprehensive guarantee was introduced in Indonesia two months later.

[42] As suggested below, I do not share this view on the use of blanket guarantees, but I think most others do.

bank recapitalization would have been even higher than it has turned out to be (because managers of insolvent institutions would have engaged in more "gambling for resurrection"). Moreover, I don't think confidence could have been restored without some concrete evidence that financial-sector supervision (including transparency and disclosure) was going to be started on a different path for the future than it had been on in the past. Similarly, to show that cronyism and corruption would henceforth be less prevalent, it was important (at least in Indonesia) to take a few visible privileges or sweetheart deals away from those close to President Suharto. Once the crisis deepened and nonperforming loans of banks and corporate insolvencies became larger and more widespread, it also became evident that banks and corporates — particularly in Thailand and Indonesia — would not simply be able to grow out of it without restructuring. Because of strong links between banks and corporates (especially in Korea and Indonesia), as well as the need to cushion somewhat the most vulnerable groups from the effects of the crisis, there was a good case for including some corporate reforms (e.g., reduction of debt-equity ratios by the *chaebol*) and some social safety net provisions in those programs.

Second, notwithstanding the above argument, there were elements of structural conditionality in the three Fund programs with Indonesia, Korea, and Thailand that seem superfluous. I don't find persuasive the argument that trade liberalization measures in the Indonesian and Korean programs were necessary to prevent a slide toward protectionism (see Hamann and Schulze-Ghattas 1999). A better rationale would be that trade liberalization was needed to increase competition and to help discipline inefficient domestic producers. However, that still doesn't explain why trade liberalization needed to be done immediately rather than after the crisis. Likewise, I don't see why the Indonesian program had to be so sweeping with respect to the dismantling of state monopolies and cartels, elimination of restrictive marketing agreements, abolition of showcase projects, and the like, disagreeable as those practices were. For confidence reasons, a few "candies" may have had to be taken away from cronies at the outset, but the rest of the box (and, admittedly, it was a very big box) could have waited for later. In the Korean program, the tax reform and privatization conditions look like they could have waited until after the crisis. Additionally, in Thailand (which had the narrowest of the three programs), it's hard to see why privatization of state enterprises, removal of the real estate tax on foreign purchases of condominiums, and a new land act needed to be part of the Fund's conditions.

Moving from the width to the depth of conditionality, the level of detail reflected in the structural benchmarks for these three programs likewise seems excessive. For example, in Indonesia, was it necessary to have five commitments for reform of oil and gas policy, and eighteen commitments for follow-up actions to the findings of the audit of Bank Indonesia? In Korea, was it essential to have eleven commitments for restructuring, for investment guidelines, and for corporate governance of insurance companies? In Thailand, did six target dates have to be set up to guide the privatization of Bangkok Metropolitan and Siam City banks? More generally, did supervisory and prudential measures for financial institutions in the three crisis countries have to be specified so precisely? Wouldn't, say, a broader commitment to implement the Basel Core Principles of Effective Banking Supervision by date x, along with a few benchmark checks of good progress, be as effective (and less intrusive) and, in addition, carry the seal of approval of the world's key banking supervisors? Couldn't the Fund provide its very detailed views on ways of improving corporate governance as technical assistance, not as conditions in the Fund program? Yes, this would require more faith that the crisis country would want on its own to "do the right thing." However, if it doesn't really want to implement the reforms, then very detailed monitoring via a very large set of structural benchmarks may not push the ball much farther ahead. Besides, unlike performance criteria, failure to meet many of the structural benchmarks does not carry the automatic threat of interruption of fund financing.

Third, I don't agree with either the Fund or many of its critics that the Indonesian experience leads to the lesson that bank restructuring during a systemic banking crisis can only be accomplished successfully if blanket guarantees are issued by the government (see Lindgren et al. 1999). The closing of banks in Indonesia led to runs because the authorities were only willing to close a subset of a much wider group of insolvent banks, because high-level political support (from President Suharto and some others) for the initial bank closures was absent, and because the Fund agreed to a bad compromise. When there are widespread bank insolvencies, the key to restoring confidence is to convince the public that all the bad banks have been closed or resolved, that the remainder are solid, and that small retail depositors (not everybody) will be covered.[43] As a former colleague of mine put it, "people don't run banks that are closed; they run banks that are open that they think will soon be closed." Also, when there is no deposit insurance in place or the insurance system is not viewed as credible, the necessity is for the bank supervisory authority to replace the old management of insolvent banks with a new one (so as to prevent "double-or-nothing" behavior and even larger credit losses), and to eventually dock the shareholders (so as to penalize the owners and to limit moral hazard); such insolvent banks can then be resolved in a variety of ways (even while they honor withdrawals and take deposits). What's not necessary — and can prompt runs — is to board up the teller cages of some banks (while other questionable banks remain open). The real lesson of the Indonesian experience is that a sensible, incentive-compatible deposit insurance system (along the lines of the Federal Deposit Insurance Corporation Improvement Act [FDICIA] in the United States) should be a permanent part of the financial infrastructure in all countries; without it, governments wind up providing ex post deposit insurance, but they do it at higher current cost and with moral hazard effects that increase the likelihood of future banking crises.

In much the same spirit, I disagree with those who say that bank capital requirements should have been phased in even more slowly in the Asian crisis countries so as to prevent a credit crunch. A cutback in lending exposure is an equilibrium response of a bank to a negative shock that reduces its capital. The relevant question is not whether one likes a credit crunch; it is whether one prefers some credit crunch to an expansion of lending — much of which is likely to go to the same insolvent borrowers that were at the root of the banks' difficulties (leading to even larger bank losses). To be sure, there was a fall-off in real credit supply in late 1997 and early 1998 in most of the crisis countries, and undoubtedly some "good" borrowers were also denied credit. However, there was also a fall in real credit demand that apparently was sharper than the fall in supply (at least in Korea and Thailand; see Ghosh and Ghosh 1999; Lane et al. 1999). In addition, there is some evidence that the allocation of bank credit improved (see Borenzstein and Lee 2000). In the end, I doubt we would have obtained a better combined score on economic activity and on bank losses if capital requirements had been less binding during 1998–2000.

---

[43] Ways to limit moral hazard without negating the benefits of deposit insurance are discussed in Financial Stability Forum (2000).

Drawing on a sample of thirty-four countries (twenty-seven of them developing or transition economies) that have experienced significant fiscal costs from bank failures over the 1970–2000 period, Honohan and Klinge-biel (2000) compare "regulatory forbearance" versus "strict" approaches to crisis resolution. They find that unlimited deposit guarantees, open-ended liquidity support, repeated recapitalizations, debtor bailouts, and regulatory forbearance add significantly and sizably to costs. One of their main conclusions bears repeating:

> Our findings clearly tilt the balance in favor of a "strict" approach to crisis resolution, rather than an accommodating one. At the very least, they emphasize that regulatory authorities which [sic] choose an accommodating or gradualist approach to an emerging crisis need to be sure that they have some other way of controlling risk. (19)

Fourth, compliance with the Fund's structural policy conditionality appears to have been much better than the average (for all Fund programs) in Korea and in Thailand but not so in Indonesia. A good deal of progress has been made on financial-sector rebuilding and reform, but much still remains to be done. Moreover, it is still too early to know whether the excessively close relationship between large business and government that has been the source of so much inefficiency and favoritism has changed fundamentally for the better.

It's not easy (especially for an outsider) to measure compliance with structural policy conditions because the Fund programs with the three crisis countries were revised often over the 1997–2000 period and because some structural benchmarks have been dropped or added from one revision to the next. Still, suppose we define "compliance" as having met a condition within, say, three months of the target date. Then my ballpark estimate would be that Korea has complied with about 90 percent of the structural conditions laid out in the Fund's program.[44] The corresponding compliance figure for Thailand would be about 70 percent. Two areas where compliance was weak in

---

[44] During a visit to South Korea in May 2000, I met with many Korean officials who had been involved in the crisis negotiations with the Fund. My overall impression is that most of the structural conditions included in the Fund program had been on the domestic reform agenda for a long time and thus were not viewed as "imposed" on Korea. This may explain in part why the compliance rate with structural conditions has been so high.

Thailand were reform of state banks and privatization of public enterprises. The calculation for Indonesia is subject to the largest margin of error but probably falls in the 20–40 percent range. In Indonesia, compliance with structural conditions has been seriously handicapped by prolonged political instability and by a weak approach by the government toward debtors; compliance has been lower in noncore policy areas than in core areas.

The problem with looking only at the share of structural conditions met is not only that some are more important than others: it is also that most structural policy conditions capture *processes* that do not necessarily have a tight link with outcomes. For example, if the structural benchmark says you must have two outside directors appointed to a corporate board, that can be done, but the outside appointees may not differ much from their predecessors. Or a loan can be restructured, but in a way that doesn't much reduce the present discounted value of the borrower's debt burden. For this reason, it is useful to look at some other, less process-oriented benchmarks for the financial and corporate sectors.

As background, we should recall that the three crisis countries (as a group) experienced a sharp output recovery in 1999 and 2000; inflation is mostly under control, and their current accounts are in surplus (albeit much reduced from the huge current-account surpluses of 1998); see Table 8. In addition, they have much lower ratios of short-term external debt to international reserves than immediately preceding the crisis; they have abandoned publicly declared exchange rate targets; and both nonperforming loans in the banking system and corporate insolvencies are retreating from their peaks. They are moving in the right direction — albeit too slowly — on banking supervision and corporate governance. Additionally, in Korea, the debt-equity ratios for most of the largest *chaebol* have declined sharply. Turning to the negative side of the ledger, equity prices have declined sharply throughout emerging Asia (with the notable exception of China); the expected growth slowdown in the United States meant that export growth of the crisis countries was likely to be much lower (by roughly half) in 2001 than it was in 2000; volatile oil prices are a source of great uncertainty; the high public debt burden in Indonesia and the large fiscal deficit in Thailand limit the scope for countercyclical fiscal policy; bank lending to the private sector has been weak outside Korea; Japan's recovery remains both anemic and fragile; and there has been some political turbulence in the region (the Philippines and Taiwan).

Table 8: Asian Crisis Countries: Real GDP, Consumer Prices, and Current Account Balance

	Real GDP (annual % change)	Consumer Prices (annual % change)	Current Account Balances (as % of GDP)
Indonesia			
1998	−13.0	58.0	4.2
1999	0.3	20.8	3.7
2000[a]	4.5	3.3	6.5
2001[a]	4.2	5.6	5.3
Korea			
1998	−6.7	7.5	12.8
1999	10.7	0.8	6.1
2000[a]	9.0	2.4	2.6
2001[a]	5.0	3.5	1.7
Thailand			
1998	−10.2	8.1	12.7
1999	4.2	0.3	9.1
2000[a]	5.5	1.6	7.7
2001[a]	4.0	2.3	9.4

Sources: 1998 and 1999, IMF (2000); 2000 and 2001, Spencer (2000).
[a] Estimated.

Table 9, taken from Claessens, Djankov, and Klingebiel (1999), provides a summary of financial restructuring in the three crisis countries, at least as of mid-1999. Although there have been later developments, a number of their findings merit mention.

Korea has used a combination of recapitalizations, nationalizations, removal of bad debt, and mergers to strengthen its banking system.[45] However, it was much less active against weak nonbanks and has had to clean up a mess with those investment trusts that rushed in to finance the *chaebol* (especially Daewoo) after the banks cut back. Thailand has closed about two-thirds of its finance companies but has gone more slowly on bank restructuring, asking the banks to raise their own capital and making public money subject to stricter prudential and management changes. Indonesia, after a large, initial liquidity injection to banks, has gotten less far on bank restructuring than the others.

---

[45] In late September 2000, the Korean Government announced that it would be putting in an additional $44 billion of public funds to deal with bad loans of the banking system.

Table 9: Financial Restructuring in Asian Crisis Countries

	Indonesia	Korea	Thailand
1. Initial liquidity support to banks	$ 21.7 billion (18% of GDP)	$23.3 billion (5% of GDP)	$24.1 billion (20% of GDP)
2. Bank shutdowns	64 of 237	None	1 of 15
3. Shutdowns of other financial institutions	n.a.	> 117	57 of 91
4. Mergers of financial institutions	4 of 7 state banks	11 of 26 absorbed by other banks	3 banks and 12 financial companies
5. Nationalizations	12	4	4
6. Public funds for recapitalizations	Plan in place; some bonds issued	Government injected $8 billion into 9 commercial banks; 5 out of 6 major banks now 90% controlled by state	Plan in place; government injected $8.9 billion into private banks and $11.7 billion into public banks
7. Majority foreign ownership of banks	Allowed, 1 potentially	Allowed, 2 completed and 1 near finalization	Allowed, 2 completed and 4 pending
8. Weak financial institutions still in system	Many weak commercial banks	Many weak nonbank financial institutions	Some weak public and private commercial banks
9. Nonperforming loans remaining in banks (% of total loans)	22	18	50
10. Capital shortfall of banking system (% of banking assets)	18	4	8
11. Corporate governance + managements of banks			
a. independent outside directors	None	2/3 of board slots	19
b. changes in top managements, majority-owned domestic banks	None	6 of 11 major banks	3 of 11 banks
12. Corporate restructuring (August 1999)			
a. out-of-court restructured dept/total dept(%)	13	40	22
b. in-court restructured dept/total dept(%)	4	8	7
13. Interest difficulties of firms; percent that cannot cover interest expense from operational cash flows 2000–02 (assuming 1999 interest rates)	53	17	22

(*Continued*)

Table 9: (Continued)

	Indonesia	Korea	Thailand
14. Public debt(% of GDP)			
a. 1997	48	11	7
b. 1999	98	37	40
15. Quality of financial-sector regulation index (4 = best practice, 1 = weakest)			
a. 1997	1.3	2.7	1.0
b. 1999	2.0	3.0	2.7
16. Ownership concentration + legal framework			
a. percent ownership of top 15 families	62	38	53
b. efficiency of judicial system, index (1 = worst, 10 = best)	2.5	6.0	3.2
c. rule of law, index (1 = worst, 10 = best)	4.0	5.4	6.3
d. corruption, index (1 = worst, 10 = top)	2.2	5.3	5.2
17. Market structure changes in financial sector			
a. number of commercial banks: taken over/sold to foreigners/nationalized	4/0/12	5/2/4	0/2/4
b. number of private domestic banks: market share(%)	122(21)	18(37)	13(48)
c. number of state banks: market share (%)	43(78)	10(58)	6(45)
d. number of nonbanks: market share(%)	245(1)	11(5)	22(7)

Source: Claessens, Djankov, and Klingebiel (1999).
Note: In a more recent World Bank [2000] report, it is estimated that nonperforming loans, as of June 2000, account for 30, 10, and 30 percent of total loans in Indonesia, Korea, and Thailand, respectively.

Banks are still undercapitalized — moderately in Korea, more so in Thailand, and extremely so in Indonesia. Nonperforming loans are still very high in Thailand and Indonesia. Korean banks may be able to cover their capital shortfalls from earnings; this is not so with either Thai or Indonesian banks. Korea and Thailand have made some governance and management changes in their banks, Indonesian banks much less so.

Korea and Thailand have restructured about one-half and one-third, respectively, of corporate debt, the bulk of it in out-of-court settlement; the corresponding figure for Indonesia is roughly one-sixth. Although corporations have benefited from the recovery, about one-quarter of Thai firms and over half of Indonesian ones cannot meet interest payments out of operational cash flows.

Despite quite significant increases in foreign direct investment, all three Asian economies have seen their public debt rise appreciably as a result of financial restructuring costs. Public debt is about equal to gross domestic product (GDP) in Indonesia and is more than one-third of it in both Korea and Thailand (having risen from very low precrisis ratios).

Gains have been made in the quality of financial regulation, but it still trails best international practice. So far, Korea and Thailand have come farther than Indonesia on this score. Corporate ownership is still very concentrated among the top fifteen families in all three countries. Corporate governance is changing, but a weak judicial system in Indonesia and a poor bankruptcy law in Thailand have limited the advances.[46]

Last but not least, because of heavy government intervention into the financial system during the crisis (nationalizations, purchase of bad assets, etc.) the government now owns a huge share — about 50 percent on average for the three countries — of total banking assets. Because governments do not do well owning and managing banks, there is a strong need for much larger divestitures (including sales to foreigners) than have occurred to date.[47]

To sum up, studies of the effects of Fund programs show that they have positive effects on the current account and overall balance of payments; effects on growth, inflation, and income distribution have proved to be much harder to pin down with any precision. Those transition economies that have done more on implementing Fund structural performance criteria appear to have done better on economic growth and structural policy reform more generally than those with weaker compliance records. Those emerging economies with better corporate governance structures in place prior to the outbreak of Asian crisis were, on average, hit less hard with currency and stock market declines during the crisis than those with a poorer track record on corporate governance. For the most part, Fund structural policy recommendations reflect the economics profession's consensus of what constitutes sensible structural policy reform, although some serious mistakes on the sequencing of reforms have sometimes taken place. The core of the Fund's structural policy conditionality in the three Asian crisis countries — which focused mainly on financial-sector crisis management and restructuring — was appropriate, with the exception of the bad compromise made on bank closures in Indonesia. That said, the Fund's structural conditionality in the Asian crisis countries (and especially in Indonesia) appears excessive — both in scope and in detail. Thus far,

---

[46] Other analysts (e.g., Root [2000] and Spencer [2000]) have pointed to the low number of affiliate sales by the *chaebol* and the recent rescue of Hyundai Engineering and Construction as disappointments in the Korean reform effort.

[47] See Root (2000) on why a more decentralized approach to financial restructuring in Korea would yield better results than a government-dominated strategy.

compliance with that conditionality has been high in Korea, above average in Thailand, and below average in Indonesia. Looking at a broader array of indicators, progress on restructuring in East Asia is evident but much more needs to be done to put banks and corporates on a sound footing. It is too early to tell whether the past close relationship between government and business has changed fundamentally for the better.

SECTION 4. HOW DID FUND STRUCTURAL POLICY CONDITIONALITY GET TO BE THIS WAY?

If one concludes that Fund structural policy conditionality has become more intrusive than necessary, it is relevant to speculate on how it might have gotten that way. In my view, nine factors have contributed to that trend.[48]

First, in the 1970s and early 1980s, IMF programs came under sharp criticism from many developing countries as being too demand-oriented and too short-run and as not paying enough attention to economic growth, to supply-side reforms, and to income distribution. The disappointing growth performance of developing countries in the early 1980s added to those concerns. Because developing countries increasingly constituted the demand for Fund resources, neither the Fund nor creditor governments could easily dismiss that criticism. New lending windows with higher structural policy content and with lending terms more favorable to low-income countries were created, and monitoring techniques for gauging compliance with structural policy conditions evolved.

Second, the expansion of the IMF's surveillance responsibilities — agreed upon in the mid-1970s under the second amendment of the Fund's charter and given expression in the revised Article IV — permitted Fund Article IV country missions to take a wider field of view in evaluating economic developments and prospects. Structural problems thus came under greater scrutiny. This greater familiarity with structural problems may in turn have led to a greater readiness to include structural policy conditions in programs, at least in those cases in which structural weaknesses were perceived, rightly or wrongly, to have been linked to crisis vulnerability.

---

[48] Several of these factors are discussed in Allen (1993).

Third, the huge transformation task faced by the transition economies — especially in the first half of the 1990s — made structural policies and the building of a market infrastructure the name of the game in that region. And the IMF (along with the European Bank for Reconstruction and Development) was at the center of the technical assistance and policy lending to those transition economies. Again, structural benchmarks came to be relied upon as a way of monitoring structural policy conditionality across a wide front. When structural problems arose in later crises (such as that in Asia), the same monitoring techniques were applied.

Fourth, all the while, the Fund was more and more interpreting its mandate as broader than just promoting macroeconomic and financial stability and helping countries to manage financial crises. From the mid-1980s on, economic growth and, later, high-quality growth were given increased prominence. After the Mexican peso crisis of 1994–95, crisis prevention — with particular attention to strengthening financial systems at the national level and developing international standards and codes of good practice — too moved up on the agenda.

Fifth, crises that involve severe balance sheet problems of banks and private corporations lead to more structural policy intensive fund programs than do those that stem from traditional monetary and fiscal policy excesses — and the Asian crises of 1997–98 had those balance sheet problems in spades. The IMF's executive board also seems to have sent staff the message (in 1997) that lending into serious governance and corruption problems (without any measures to address them) would not receive board support. In the Indonesian program, a decision was made to try to impress the markets with the comprehensiveness of the reform effort.

Sixth, the long-standing and growing problem of obtaining good compliance with Fund programs led over time to greater reliance on prior actions and to more wide-ranging and detailed structural policy conditions, presumably in an effort to penalize poor earlier track records, to thwart evasion, and to detect slippage at an earlier stage.[49] If this broader and more detailed conditionality didn't produce higher compliance and the amount of structural reform hoped

---

[49] Failure to implement earlier Fund recommendations can over time push up structural conditionality even when some of those recommendations come in the form of technical assistance rather than as conditions in Fund programs.

for, maybe the Fund concluded that it was still inducing more structural reform than would obtain with lesser Fund structural policy conditionality. The Fund's Guidelines for Conditionality — which might have reined in excessive structural policy conditionality — came to be viewed by the Fund's executive board as broad principles of intention, not as something to be monitored carefully and enforced.

Seventh, in the meantime, a wide array of legislative groups, non-governmental organizations (NGOs), and even other international financial organizations came to see an IMF letter of intent as the preferred instrument of leverage for their own agendas in emerging economies. Yes, the International Labor Organization (ILO) might be the logical place to push core labor standards, but it doesn't have the teeth of an IMF program. Simultaneously, various G7 governments — and particularly the Fund's largest shareholder — were finding it increasingly difficult to get congressional support for "clean" IMF funding bills. Reflecting this congressional pressure from both major parties, the U.S. executive director at the Fund has been obliged to support with voice and vote a long list of structural policies (ranging from protection of the environment to promotion of economic deregulation and privatizing of industry), and the U.S. Treasury (2000a) is required to report annually to Congress on its compliance with relevant sections of the Foreign Operations, Export Financing, and Related Programs Appropriation Act of 1999. A reading of that report (U.S. Treasury 2000a) confirms that the United States frequently pushed for policies in fund programs that were far from the Fund's core competence. Likewise, in countries where there was prolonged use of Fund resources, IMF letters of intent sometimes became an instrument of leverage that the finance ministry could use in order to push structural reforms on other departments in the government that were opposed. In short, everybody has gotten in on the act.

Eighth, unlike other IFIs, the Fund and the World Bank have sufficient "ground troops" to make on-site visits to all countries. In addition, at least in official circles, the Fund has developed a reputation as being able to act quickly and efficiently. When new structural challenges have arisen, there has therefore been a tendency to say, "give it to the Fund; they go there anyway; have them just add a few specialists on problem x to the mission." The management of the Fund has apparently not said "no" very often to those demands.

Finally, there have been occasions — the Korean and Indonesian programs are important cases in point — when strong pressure from particular G7 governments (during program negotiations) resulted in the inclusion of specific structural policies in a Fund program, and this despite the provision in the Fund's charter (IMF 1988, 42, Article XII, section IV) for each member country of the Fund to "refrain from all attempts to influence any of the [Fund] staff in the discharge of [their] functions."

SECTION 5. APPROACHES TO STREAMLINING FUND STRUCTURAL POLICY CONDITIONALITY

The Fund's new managing director, Horst Kohler, has already indicated that he thinks that the Fund "has been overstretched in the past and needs to refocus" (Kohler 2000c, 3); he has also flagged his intention to end "mission creep," in large part by streamlining structural policy conditionality. To carry out that objective, there are at least eight approaches (not all of them mutually exclusive) worth mentioning.

Structural Preconditions

This radical approach, favored by the majority of the Meltzer Commission (see IFIAC 2000), would jettison ex post IMF conditionality in favor of a small number of preconditions, namely, freedom of entry and operation for foreign financial institutions, regular and timely publication of the maturity structure of outstanding sovereign and guaranteed debt and off-balance sheet liabilities, adequate capitalization of commercial banks, and a proper fiscal requirement.[50] Developing countries that met these preconditions would be eligible immediately for short-term liquidity assistance; those developing countries that did not meet them would not be eligible.

Objections to this approach have been registered on three counts (see Bergsten et al. 2000).

Although meeting these preconditions would reduce the risk of getting into a crisis, they would hardly be sufficient for crisis prevention. Although

---

[50]At present, the only Fund lending window that uses prequalification is the Contingency Credit Line (CCL). However, since its inception in 1999, no country has yet come forward to use it.

many currency and debt crises begin in the banking sector, quite a few others do not, and freedom of entry plus a capital requirement are not good substitutes for the broader range of measures outlined in the Basel Core Principles of Effective Banking Supervision.[51] The fiscal policy precondition is not defined in the report, and making it operational would be subject to the same kind of negotiation and intrusiveness as with present Fund conditionality.

More fundamentally, even if satisfied, these preconditions would not get a country out of a balance-of-payments crisis once it got into one. Without measures to reduce absorption and to switch expenditure from foreign to domestic goods, the crisis country's ability to repay would not improve. Moreover, giving large Fund loans to a country with a runaway inflation or a huge budget deficit would increase moral hazard, not reduce it.

Last but not least, it is highly questionable whether the international community would be willing to exclude completely from IMF financing countries that didn't meet these preconditions, particularly when a new government promised policies different from its predecessor.[52] For this reason, the Council on Foreign Relations Task Force (1999) rejected the "all-or-nothing" approach and opted instead to penalize (reward) countries that have followed poor (good) policies by charging them higher (lower) interest rates when they needed to borrow from the Fund.

Collateralized Fund Lending

Another radical approach to reducing or eliminating Fund structural policy conditionality would have the fund follow the Bagehot (1873) guideline and lend on good collateral (see Meltzer 1999; Feldstein 1999). Good collateral is meant to serve several purposes. It provides a test of whether the borrower is just illiquid rather than insolvent (a solvent borrower has good collateral to pledge; an insolvent one does not); it safeguards the solvency of the lender; and it reduces (borrower) moral hazard by discouraging the borrower from holding risky assets that would not be accepted as good collateral.

---

[51] Garber (2000) has argued that a subordinated debt requirement for banks a la the Meltzer Report could easily be manipulated and evaded.

[52] See Polak (1991). U.S. Treasury (2000b) argues that these preconditions would have precluded the IMF from responding to financial emergencies in the vast majority of its member countries, including all the Asian crisis countries.

Opposition to the collateral proposal emanates from several arguments. If eligible collateral is defined narrowly and strictly (say, holdings of U.S. government securities), then it will not provide much additional advantage in crisis management (since countries so endowed wouldn't need to come to the Fund — they could borrow from private markets). Pledging collateral to the Fund might also run afoul of "negative pledge" clauses in existing loan agreements, and even if it didn't, its favorable impact would be limited because it would raise borrowing costs on the noncollateralized debt. Some would contend too that liquidating the collateral (say, export receipts) in the event of repayment problems (stemming either from bad luck or poor policy performance) would subject the Fund to even harsher criticism from developing-country borrowers than it receives when it interrupts disbursement under a Fund program. Would the United States, for example, have been able politically to cash in the collateral (oil receipts) pledged by Mexico during the 1994–95 peso crisis if things had not worked out so well for Mexico in 1995?

Define Conditionality in Terms of Outcomes, Not Structural Policies or Benchmarks

The idea here would be for the Fund to leave the *process* by which countries respond to crises up to them and instead condition Fund assistance on positive changes in certain outcomes. For example, instead of making changes in the judicial system or the establishment of a new framework for corporate debt restructuring conditions of the program for Indonesia, the Fund could just say that half of the nonperforming corporate debt has to be rescheduled by date x. If the country meets the target, it gets the money; otherwise, it doesn't.

The rub here is that performance criteria are normally confined to variables that are under the control of the borrower. The difficulty with defining structural conditionality in terms of outcomes is that exogenous developments could affect the borrower's ability to meet the target. Consequently, there would be many demands for waivers. In addition, outcomes are often not easy to define for some structural policies (e.g., what is "good" banking supervision, or what constitutes a "restructured" loan). Finally, one of the main purposes of the Fund is to rule certain crisis management processes (e.g., increased resort to trade restrictions) as out of bounds.

Put Restrictions or Penalties on Foreign-Currency Borrowing

If much of structural policy conditionality comes from balance sheet problems of banks and corporates and the latter, in turn, often derive from the buildup of large currency mismatches, why not attack the problem at its source by seeking to discourage foreign-currency borrowing (see Krueger 2000; Dooley 1999)? Presumably, a key reason why Brazil has had a much milder crisis than the Asian countries is that currency mismatching in Brazil was better controlled; hence, when the real crashed, there were many fewer banking and corporate insolvencies. Although (enlightened) government borrowers ought to be able to internalize these externalities, this is not so for private borrowers, who may expect either a government bailout (if things go badly) or who may be driven to take up the cheaper foreign-currency loan because competitors are doing it. Although timely publication of aggregate data on currency and maturity mismatching may improve market discipline, some have proposed going much farther. Krueger, for example, has suggested that foreign-currency obligations incurred by domestic residents of emerging economies be made unenforceable in domestic courts. Others have argued that the currency mismatching problem is a powerful argument in favor of dollarization.

One counterargument is that such measures are too drastic for the problem at hand. If currency mismatching is the problem, why not have the government develop better hedging mechanisms (e.g., futures exchanges), as Mexico has been doing since it moved to a floating rate? Others might say that giving up (via dollarization) the potential advantage of access to easy monetary policy during a severe recession just to minimize the risk of one particular type of crisis is allowing the tail to wag the dog. Enforcement of currency-matching restrictions could also be a problem. In today's world of structured derivatives, what looks like a domestic-currency loan could well have embedded options that amount to an unhedged bet on the exchange rate.

Greater Resort to International Standards

Instead of custom-tailoring structural conditions to a particular crisis situation or particular financial institutions, the fund and its member countries could rely more on generic international standards. For example, if there was a serious problem with data disclosure, or with banking supervision, or with corporate governance, the crisis country could agree to meet international standards in these areas by date x. A potential appeal of the standards is that they represent the consensus on good practice in that area by a group of international experts — not the views of an individual mission chief or even of the Fund (see Eichengreen 2000). Since the fund is already engaged (on a voluntary basis) in evaluating countries' compliance with standards and codes, this approach might also afford more flexibility in the time frame for meeting these conditions.

The disadvantage of the standards approach is that the standards themselves may not be specific enough to address the pressing problems at hand. If the elements of the standards are too vague, monitoring would likely lead to frequent disagreements.

Leaner Structural Conditionality within Present Arrangements

Under this approach, the Fund's executive board would issue a new guidance note calling for "leaner" structural conditionality; henceforth, each structural condition included in a program would have to be directly related to financial stability and would have to carry a macroeconomic impact; in addition, the note might increase the use of formal performance criteria relative to more discretionary structural benchmarks and program reviews. The aim of this new guidance note would be not only to induce mission chiefs to be less wide-ranging and detailed in their structural policy recommendations but also to dissuade *both* creditor and debtor governments from pushing for structural conditions that did not fall within the Fund's core competence ("I'd like to help you, Mr. Deputy Minister, but that just isn't our job"). Associated with this leaner structural conditionality might also be an effort to increase the Fund's leverage for structural policy reform in nonprogram channels. For example, structural weaknesses could be given more attention in published Fund Article IV reports, leaving it more to the private markets to apply pressure for reform. Additionally, much of what now appears as detailed structural benchmarks (in a Fund program) on how to implement a given structural reform could be handled in Fund technical assistance.

Skeptics might argue that the existing guidance note on conditionality that has been around for twenty years or more is perfectly adequate. Why would a new one make much of a difference? To make a difference, management and the Fund's executive board would have to be much more committed to enforcing the new note than they were in enforcing the previous one. However, this would be unlikely to happen unless there was a clear understanding with the G7 and with emerging economies that greater restraint would be exercised than heretofore in assigning the fund new tasks. For example, just within the few months previous to the time of this writing, the G7 requested the IMF to step up its monitoring of money laundering. Questions would also arise on how many structural conditions and how much detail would be appropriate for such a leaner structural conditionally (that is, would it be a big change from prevailing practice, or only a small modification?).

Allowing the Fund to Borrow in the Private Capital Markets

If some G7 legislatures use the Fund's requests for funding (increases in quota, funding for new facilities and debt initiatives, etc.) as points of leverage to impose a variety of (counterproductive and superfluous) conditions on Fund lending practices, it might be argued that the Fund should be given authority to borrow in the private capital markets (thereby increasing its independence).[53] Those who oppose this proposal would contend that the Fund itself, not G7 legislatures, is the main source of excessive structural conditionality; thus, easier funding would reduce "accountability" to the Fund's shareholders and might just as well increase the scope of Fund conditionality as reduce it.

Clearer Division of Responsibility with the World Bank and More Outsourcing of Structural Conditionality in Noncore Areas

The aim here is to retain the advantages of a "comprehensive" approach to crisis prevention and management, sustainable growth, and poverty reduction, while improving the effectiveness of (total) structural policy conditionality by paying greater attention to the different comparative advantages of the various IFIs. Even if the number of structural conditions in Fund programs remained unchanged, the Fund would design and monitor only those conditions that fit within its defined "core competence" (say, monetary, fiscal, exchange rate, and financial-sector policies); anything else would be the responsibility of the World Bank or other IFIs. If one of the other IFIs was not moving fast

---

[53] Another proposal for reducing political demands on the Fund is go to "independent" executive directors — much in the manner of national central banks; see De Gregorio et al. (1999).

enough in drafting a structural policy requirement, the Fund would not be permitted to take over. It would have to stay in its own yard. Under some proposals, the Fund would transfer primary responsibility for running the Poverty Reduction and Growth Facility (PRGF) to the World Bank, although the Fund would still have a sign-off on the adequacy of macroeconomic policies in such programs with low-income countries. Under other proposals (see Kohler and Wolfensohn 2000), the World Bank would get its own new lending window (the Poverty Reduction Support Credit [PRSC]) to support poverty reduction in low-income countries, and the Fund would continue to run and fund the PGRF. Renewed efforts would also be made to improve Fund-World Bank cooperation.

Here, too, there are many potential objections and questions. If the problem is too much and too detailed structural policy conditionality as a whole, why would rearranging responsibilities among the IFIs solve it? If the PGRF is about poverty reduction and if that is supposed to be the main focus of the World Bank, why does the Fund run that facility? If it's true, as suggested by the U.S. Treasury (2000a), that unless the Fund's board has its own money at stake, Fund evaluation of macroeconomic policies in programs with low-income countries won't be done seriously (even with a formal sign-off in programs run by the World Bank), why should we expect other IFIs to be diligent in their evaluation of structural policies in Fund-led programs? Why do we need *two* lending facilities (the existing PGRF in the Fund, and the new PRSC in the World Bank) to support poverty reduction and macroeconomic stability in the low-income countries? Wouldn't one make more sense? How will the IMF and World Bank cooperate more closely with other international organizations (e.g., the Organization for Economic Cooperation and Development, the Bank for International Settlements, the World Trade Organization, the ILO, etc.) under the "contracting-out model" and still meet the demanding time requirements of crisis resolution?

SECTION 6. CONCLUDING REMARKS

I agree with Stanley Fischer's (2000a, 2) assessment that "the IMF.... promotes good macroeconomic and financial-sector policies among its members." However, my reading of the record is that on structural policies the Fund has bitten off more — in both scope and detail — than either it or its member countries can chew. There are limits — no matter how numerous and detailed the Fund's monitoring techniques — to how far the Fund can push a country to undertake structural reforms that it itself is not strongly committed to. Consistent with this view, compliance with fund conditionality has been a serious and growing problem. International Monetary Fund mission chiefs have considerable knowledge and experience in macro-economic and financial policies but not in structural policy areas beyond this core competence. Efforts to include in Fund conditionality everything but the kitchen sink under the loosely defined agenda of pursuing "high-quality" growth have taken the Fund too far from its comparative advantage and have elicited legitimate charges of mission creep.

Among the alternative crisis management guidelines discussed in section 2, the one (Mandate II) that would have the Fund focus on macroeconomic and financial stability and assist a country not only to get out of its current crisis but also to minimize the chances of getting into another one makes the most sense to me. Conditions that lie outside the core areas of monetary, fiscal, exchange rate, and financial-sector policies should be significantly fewer in Fund programs than the average of the past five years and should require strong justification in any program, including having a macroeconomic impact (as called for in the original conditionality guidelines for standby programs). I also read the record as suggesting that the effectiveness of Fund structural conditionality would be increased if a small number of structural performance criteria was substituted for the vast array of structural benchmarks that have characterized many past Fund programs. This would require IMF staff to think harder about which structural conditions merited the highest priority in the reform effort, and about which structural policy changes needed to be made now (during the crisis) and which could wait until somewhat later; putting more weight on a few structural performance criteria would also send a clearer signal to the borrower that failure to meet those performance criteria would likely result in a halt in Fund disbursements.

Last but not least, streamlining and improving Fund structural policy conditionality is about Fund management saying "no" more often than in the past — to requests for Fund assistance where the expectation is low that the country will actually implement Fund policy conditions, to G7 governments when they propose new tasks for the Fund that go beyond the Fund's core competence, to NGOs that seek to use a country's Letter of Intent with the Fund to advance agendas (even if desirable) that lie outside the Fund's mandate and comparative advantage, and to developing-country finance ministries that want to use micro conditions in Fund programs to impose spending discipline on other government ministries that could not be obtained via their national legislatures.

Mr. Kohler's intention to end mission creep at the Fund and to streamline the Fund's structural policy conditionality is welcome. However, it remains to be seen how he will pursue that objective and what the effects will be.

Morris Goldstein, "IMF Structural Programs," in Martin Feldstein (editor), Economic and Financial Crises in Emerging Market Economies, pp. 363–437 (2003). University of Chicago Press and NBER. Used with permission of the publishers.

REFERENCES

Ahluwalia, Pavan. 2000. Discriminating contagion: An alternative explanation of contagious currency crises in emerging markets. IMF Working Paper no. WP/00/14. Washington, D.C.: International Monetary Fund, February.

Allen, Mark. 1993. The link between structural reform and stabilization policies: An overview. In *Coordinating stabilization and structural reform*, ed. IMF Institute. Washington, D.C.: International Monetary Fund.

Bagehot, Walter. 1873. *Lombard Street: A description of the money market.* London: William Clowes and Sons.

Balassa, Bela. 1983. The adjustment experience of developing countries after 1973. In *IMF conditionality*, ed. John Williamson. Washington, D.C.: Institute for International Economics.

Barro, Robert. 1996. Democracy and growth. *Journal of Economic Growth* 1 (1): 1–28.

Bergsten, C. Fred, Richard Huber, Jerome Levinson, and E. Torres. 2000. Reforming the international financial institutions. Minority dissent to the report of the International Institution Advisory Commission. Allan H. Meltzer, Chairman. Washington, D.C.: March.

Beveridge, William A., and Margaret R. Kelly. 1980. Fiscal content of financial programs supported by stand-by arrangements in the upper credit tranches, 1969–78. *IMF Staff Papers* 27 (June): 205–49. Washington, DC: International Monetary Fund.

Boorman, Jack, Timothy Lane, Marianne Schulze-Ghattas, Ales Bulir, Atish R. Ghosh, Javier Hamann, Alexandros Mourmouras, and Steven Phillips. 2000. Managing financial crises: The experience of East Asia. Conference on Public Policy. 10–20 November, Pittsburgh, Penn.

Borenzstein, Eduardo, and Jong-Wha Lee. 2000. Financial crisis and credit crunch in Korea: Evidence from firm-level data. IMF Working Paper no. WP/00/25. Washington, D.C.: International Monetary Fund.

Botchway, Kwesi, Jan Willem Gunning, Yusuke Onitsuka, and Koichi Hamada. 1998. *External evaluation of ESAF.* Washington, D.C.: International Monetary Fund.

Camdessus, Michel. 1990. Remarks before the One-Asia assembly. February, Manila, the Philippines.

Camdessus, Michel. 1994. International cooperation for high-quality growth: The role of the IMF at 50. Washington, D.C.: International Monetary Fund. Available at [http:// www.imf.org/external/np/sec/mds/1995/MDS9521.HTM]. 28 August 2000.

Camdessus, Michel. 1997. Good governance, the IMF's role. Washington, D.C.: International Monetary Fund. Available at [http://www.imf.org/external/pubs/ft/exrp/govern/govindex.htm]. 28 August 2000.

Camdessus, Michel. 1999a. Second generation reforms: Reflections and new challenges. Washington, D.C.: International Monetary Fund. Available at [http://www.imf.org/external/np/speeches/1999/110899.HTM]. 28 August 2000.

Camdessus, Michel. 1999b. Strengthening the link between economic and social policies within the framework of a globalized economy. Washington, DC.: International Monetary Fund. Available at [http://www.imf.org/external/np/speeches/1999/102699.HTM]. 28 August 2000.

Camdessus, Michel. 2000a. Development and poverty reduction: A multilateral approach. Washington, D.C.: International Monetary Fund. Available at [http://www.imf.org/external/np/speeches/2000/021300.HTM]. 28 August 2000.

Camdessus, Michel. 2000b. The IMF and human development: A dialogue with civil society. Washington, D.C.: International Monetary Fund.

Christiansen, Robert E., and Andrea Richter. 1999. The pattern of structural conditionality in Fund programs with EU2 countries. Washington, D.C.: International Monetary Fund, August.

Claessens, Stijn, Simeon Djankov, and Daniela Klingebiel. 1999. Financial restructuring in East Asia: Halfway there? Financial Sector Discussion Paper no. 3. Washington, D.C.: The World Bank.

Claessens, Stijn, Daniela Klingebiel, and Luc Laeven. 2001. Financial restructuring in systemic crises: What policies to pursue? Washington, D.C.: The World Bank-Manuscript, February.

Conway, Patrick. 1994. IMF lending programs: Participation and impact. *Journal of Development Economics*, no. 45:365–91.

Council on Foreign Relations Task Force. 1999. *Safeguarding prosperity in a global financial system: The future international financial architecture.* Carla Hills and Peter Peterson, co-chairs; Morris Goldstein, project director. Washington, D.C.: Institute for International Economics.

Crow, John, Ricardo Arriazu, and Niels Thygensen. 1999. *External evaluation of IMF surveillance.* Washington, D.C.: International Monetary Fund.
De Gregorio, José, Barry Eichengreen, Takatoshi Ito, and Charles Wyplosz. 1999. *An independent and accountable IMF.* Geneva Reports on the World Economy, no. 1. London: Centre for Economic Policy Research Press.
De Melo, M., C. Denizer, and A. Gelb. 1996. Patterns of transition from plan to market. *World Bank Economic Review* 10 (September).
Dooley, Michael. 1999. Debt management in developing countries. University of California at Santa Cruz, Department of Economics. Unpublished manuscript.
Edwards, Sebastian. 1989. The International Monetary Fund and the developing countries: A critical evaluation. *Carnegie-Rochester Conference Series on Public Policy* 31:7–68.
Eichengreen, Barry. 1999. *Toward a new international financial architecture: A practical post-Asia agenda.* Washington, D.C.: Institute for International Economics.
Eichengreen, Barry. 2000. Strengthening the international architecture: Where do we stand? In briefing book from Symposium on Building the Financial System of the 21st Century, 157–96. Bretton Woods, N.H.
Eichengreen, Barry, and Ricardo Hausmann. 1999. Exchange rates and financial fragility. In *New challenges for monetary policy*, 329–68. Kansas City, Mo.: Federal Reserve Bank of Kansas City.
Feldstein, Martin. 1998. Refocusing the IMF. *Foreign Affairs* 77 (March/April): 20–33.
Feldstein, Martin. 1999. A self-help guide for emerging markets. *Foreign Affairs* 78(2): 93–109.
Financial Stability Forum, Working Group on Deposit Insurance. 2000. Background Paper. Basel, Switzerland: Financial Stability Forum, June.
Finch, C. David. 1983. Adjustment policies and conditionality. In *IMF conditionality*, ed. John Williamson, 75–86. Washington, D.C.: Institute for International Economics.
Fischer, Stanley. 1999. On the need for an international lender of last resort. *Journal of Economic Perspectives* 13(4): 85–104.
Fischer, Stanley. 2000a. Presentation to the International Financial Institution Advisory Commission (Meltzer Commission). 28 August, Washington, D.C. Available at [http://www.imf.org/external/np/speeches/2000/020200.htm]. 28 August 2000.
Fischer, Stanley. 2000b. Remarks by Stanley Fischer, acting managing director. Remarks to the Bretton Woods Committee Meeting, 4 April 2000. Washington, D.C. Available at [http://www.imf.org/external/np/speeches/2000/040400.htm]. 17 July 2000.
Fischer, Stanley, Ratna Sahay, and Carlos A. Vegh. 1996. Stabilization and growth in transition economies: The early experience. *Journal of Economic Perspectives* 10(2): 45–66.

Garber, Peter. 2000. Notes on market-based bank regulation. In *Global financial crises: Lessons from recent events*, ed. Joseph Bisignano et al. Boston: Klewer Academic.
Garuda, Gopal. 2000. The distributional effects of IMF programs: A cross-country analysis. *World Development* 28(6): 1031–51.
Ghosh, Swati, and Atish Ghosh. 1999. East Asia in the aftermath: Was there a crunch? IMF Working Paper no. WP/99/38. Washington, D.C.: International Monetary Fund.
Goldstein, Morris. 1998. *The Asian financial crisis: Causes, cures, and systemic implications*. Policy Analyses in International Economics no. 55. Washington, D.C.: Institute for International Economics.
Goldstein, Morris, and Peter Montiel. 1986. Evaluating Fund stabilization programs with multicountry data: Some methodological pitfalls. *IMF Staff Papers* 33 (June): 304–344. Washington, D.C.: International Monetary Fund.
Group of Independent Experts. 1998. *External evaluation of the ESAF: Report by a group of independent experts*. Washington, D.C.: International Monetary Fund. Available at [http://www.imf.org/external/pubs/ft/extev/index.htm]. 13 September 2000.
Group of Twenty-Four. 1987. *The role of the IMF in adjustment with growth*. Washington, D.C.: Intergovernmental Group of Twenty-Four on International Monetary Affairs.
Guitian, Manuel. 1981. *Fund conditionality: Evolution of principles and practices*. Pamphlet Series no. 38. Washington, D.C.: International Monetary Fund.
Guitian, Manuel. 1995. Conditionality: Past, present, future. *IMF Staff Papers* 42(4): 792–835. Washington, D.C.: International Monetary Fund.
Gupta, Sanjeev, Benedict Clements, Calvin McDonald, and Christian Schiller. 1998. *The IMF and the poor*. Pamphlet Series no. 52. Washington, D.C.: International Monetary Fund.
Gupta, Sanjeev, Louis Dicks-Mireaux, Ritha Khemani, Calvin McDonald, and Marijn Verhoeven. 2000. *Social issues in IMF-supported programs*. Occasional Paper no. 191. Washington, D.C.: International Monetary Fund.
Haggard, Stephan. 2000. *The political economy of the Asian financial crisis*. Washington, D.C.: Institute for International Economics.
Hamann, Javier, and Marianne Schulze-Ghattas. 1999. Structural reforms. In *IMF-supported programs in Indonesia, Korea, and Thailand*, ed. Timothy Lane, Atish Ghosh, Javier Hamann, Steven Phillips, Marianne Schulze-Ghattas, and Tsidi Tsikata. Occasional Paper no. 178. Washington, D.C.: International Monetary Fund.
Haque, Nadeem Ul, and Mohsin Khan. 1998. Do IMF-supported programs work? IMF Working Paper no. WP/98/169. Washington, D.C.: International Monetary Fund.
Havrylyshyn, Oleh, and Donal McGettigan. 2000. Privatization in transition countries. *Post-Soviet affairs* 16(3): 257–86.

Havrylyshyn, Oleh, Thomas Wolf, Julian Berengaut, Marta Castello-Branco, Ron van Rooden, and Valerie Mercer-Blackman. 1999. *Growth experience in transition countries, 1990–98.* Occasional Paper no. 184. Washington, D.C.: International Monetary Fund.

Heller, Peter S., A. Lans Bovenberg, Thanos Catsambas, Ke-Young Chu, and Parthasarathi Shome. 1988. *The implication of Fund-supported adjustment programs for poverty: Experience in selected countries.* Occasional Paper no. 58. Washington, D.C.: International Monetary Fund.

Honohan, Patrick, and Daniela Klingebiel. 2000. Controlling fiscal costs of banking crises. Policy Research Working Paper no. 2441. Washington, D.C.: World Bank.

International Financial Institution Advisory Commission (IFIAC). 2000. Report of the International Financial Institution Advisory Commission (Meltzer report). Allan H. Meltzer, chairman. Washington, D.C.: March.

International Monetary Fund (IMF). 1980. *World economic outlook.* Washington, D.C.: IMF.

International Monetary Fund (IMF). 1987a. Monitoring techniques and experience with their application to structural reform. Washington, D.C.: IMF. Unpublished manuscript.

International Monetary Fund (IMF). 1987b. *Theoretical aspects of the design of Fund-supported adjustment programs.* Occasional Paper no. 55. Washington, D.C.: IMF.

International Monetary Fund (IMF). 1988. *Articles of agreement.* Washington, D.C.: IMF.

International Monetary Fund (IMF). 1993. *Articles of agreement.* Washington, D.C.: IMF.

International Monetary Fund (IMF). 1995. *Financial organization and operation of the IMF.* Pamphlet Series no. 45, fourth ed. Washington, D.C.: IMF.

International Monetary Fund (IMF). 1997. *The ESAF at ten years: Economics adjustment and reform in low-income countries.* Occasional Paper no. 156. Washington, D.C.: IMF. December.

International Monetary Fund (IMF). 2000. *World Economic Outlook.* Washington, D.C.: IMF.

International Monetary Fund (IMF). 2001a. Conditionality in Fund-supported programs: Overview. Washington, DC.: IMF. Available at [http://www.imf.org/external/np/pdr/2001/eng/overview/index.htm]. 20 February.

International Monetary Fund (IMF). 2001b. Conditionality in Fund-supported programs. Policy issues. Washington, D.C.: IMF.

International Monetary Fund (IMF). 2001c. Structural conditionality in Fund-supported programs. Washington, D.C.: IMF.

International Monetary Fund (IMF). 2001d. Trade policy conditionality in Fund-supported programs. Washington, D.C.: IMF. Available at [http://www.imf.org/external/np/pdr/cond/2001/eng/trade/index, htm]. 16 February.

International Monetary Fund (IMF). 2001e. IMF executive board discusses conditionality. Public Information Notice (PIN) no. 01/28. Washington, D.C.:

IMF. Available at [http://www.imf.org/external/np/sec/pn/2001/pnO128.htm]. 21 March.
James, Harold. 1998. From grandmotherliness to governance: The evolution of IMF conditionality. *Finance and Development* 35(4). Available at [http://www.imf.org/external/pubs/ft/fandd/1998/12/james.htm]. 3 August 2000.
Johnson, Simon, Peter Boone, Alasdair Breach, and Eric Friedman. 2000. Corporate governance in the Asian financial crisis. *Journal of Financial Economics* 58(1): 141–86. [http://www.jfe.rochester.edu/99362.pdf]. 13 September 2000.
Killick, Tony. 1995. *IMF programmes in developing countries: Design and impact.* London: Routledge.
Köhler, Horst. 2000a. The IMF in a changing world. Remarks to the National Press Club, 7 August. Washington, D.C.: International Monetary Fund.
Köhler, Horst. 2000b. Streamlining structural conditionality in Fund-supported programs: Interim guidance note. In *Conditionality in Fund-supported programs,* International Monetary Fund (IMF). Washington, D.C.: IMF.
Köhler, Horst. 2000c. Toward a more focused IMF. Address at the International Monetary Conference. 30 May, Washington, D.C.
Krueger, Anne. 1998. Whither the World Bank and the IMF? *Journal of Economic Literature,* December: 1983–2020.
Krueger, Anne. 2000. Conflicting demands on the International Monetary Fund. *American Economic Review* 90(2): 38–42.
Krugman, Paul. 1998. The confidence game. *New Republic* 219(14): 23–25.
Lane, Timothy, Atish Ghosh, Javier Hamann, Steven Phillips, Marianne Schultze-Ghattas, and Tsidi Tsikata. 1999. IMF-supported programs in Indonesia, Korea, and Thailand. Occasional Paper no. 178. Washington, DC.: International Monetary Fund.
Lindgren, Carl-Johan, Tomas J. T. Balino, Charles Enoch, Anne-Marie Gulde, Marc Quintyn, and Leslie Teo. 1999. *Financial sector crisis and restructuring: Lessons from Asia.* Occasional Paper no. 188. Washington, D.C.: International Monetary Fund.
Masson, Paul, and Michael Mussa. 1995. The role of the Fund: Financing and its interactions with adjustment and surveillance. Pamphlet Series. Washington, D.C.: International Monetary Fund.
McHale, John. 1998. Capital account convertibility and capital controls in emerging market countries: Some themes from the first meeting. Cambridge, Mass.: National Bureau of Economic Research. Available at [http://www.nber.org/crisis/capital.html]. 21 August 2000.
McHale, John. 1999. Currency and financial crises: The case of Thailand. A report on the first country meeting of the NBER project on exchange rate crises in emerging market economies. Cambridge, Mass.: National Bureau of Economic Research. Available at [http://www.nber.org/crisis/ThaiSum.html]. 21 August 2000.
McHale, John. 2000a. Brazil in the 1997–1999 financial turmoil. Fourth country meeting of the NBER project on exchange rate crises in emerging market

economies. Cambridge, Mass.: National Bureau of Economic Research. Available at [http://www.nber.org/crisis/BrazilSum.html]. 21 August 2000.

McHale, John. 2000b. The Korean currency crisis. A report on the third country meeting of the NBER project on exchange rate crises in emerging market economies. Cambridge, Mass.: National Bureau of Economic Research. Available at [http://www.nber.org/crisis/KoreaSum.html]. 21 August 2000.

McHale, John. 2000c. The Indonesian crisis. A report of the fifth country meeting of the NBER project on exchange rate crises in emerging market economies. Cambridge, Mass.: National Bureau of Economic Research.

Meltzer, Allan. 1999. What's wrong with the IMF? What would be better? In *The Asian financial crisis*, ed. William Hunter, George G. Kaufman, and Thomas H. Krueger, 241–60. Boston: Kluwer Academic.

Mercer-Blackman, Valerie, and Anna Unigovskaya. 2000. Compliance with IMF program indicators and growth in transition economies. IMF Working Paper no. WP/00/47. Washington, D.C.: International Monetary Fund. Available at [http://www.imf.org/external/pubs/ft/wp/2000/wp0047.pdf]. 13 September 2000.

Mussa, Michael, and Miguel Savastano. 1999. The IMF approach to economic stabilization. IMF Working Paper no. WP/99/104. Washington, D.C.: International Monetary Fund. Available at [http://www.imf.org/external/pubs/ft/wp/1999/wp99104.pdf]. 13 September 2000.

Park, Yung Chul. 1996. East Asian liberalization, bubbles, and the challenge from China. *Brookings Papers on Economic Activity*, Issue no. 2:357–71.

Polak, Jacques J. 1991. The changing nature of IMF conditionality. Technical Paper no. 41. Paris: Organization for Economic Cooperation and Development, August. Available at [http://www.oecd.Org//dev/PUBLICATION/tp/tp41.pdf]. 13 September 2000.

Radelet, Steven, and Jeffrey D. Sachs. 1998. The East Asian financial crisis: Diagnosis, remedies, prospects. *Brookings Papers on Economic Activity*, Issue no. 1:1–74.

Rodrik, Dani. 1995. Why is there multi-lateral lending? CEPR Discussion Paper no. 1207. London: Center for Economic Policy Research.

Root, Hilton. 2000. *Korea's recovery: Don't count on the government*. Miliken Institute Policy Brief no. 14. Santa Monica, Calif.: Miliken Institute, May.

Schadler, Susan, Adam Bennett, Maria Carkovic, Louis Dicks-Mireaux, Mauro Mecagni, James H. J. Morsink, and Miguel A. Savastano. 1995a. *IMF conditionality: Experience under stand-by and extended arrangements. Part I: Key issues and findings*. Occasional Paper no. 128. Washington, D.C.: International Monetary Fund, September.

Schadler, Susan, Adam Bennett, Maria Carkovic, Louis Dicks-Mireaux, Mauro Mecagni, James H. J. Morsink, and Miguel A. Savastano. 1995b. *IMF conditionality: Experience under stand-by and extended arrangements. Part II: Background papers*. Occasional Paper no. 129. Washington, D.C.: International Monetary Fund, September.

Schadler, Susan, Franek Rozwadowski, Siddharth Tiwari, and David O. Robinson. 1993. *Economic adjustment in low-income countries: Experience under the enhanced structural adjustment facility.* Occasional Paper no. 106. Washington, D.C.: International Monetary Fund, September.

Shultz, George. 1995. Economics in action: Ideas, institutions, policies. *The American Economic Review* 85(2): 1–8.

Spencer, Michael. 2000. Asia outlook for 2001. *Deutsche Bank Global Markets Research*, December.

Spencer, Michael. 2001. Economics: Assessing the damage so far. *Deutsche Bank Asia Window*, April.

Stiglitz, Joseph E. 1999. Reforming the global economic architecture: Lessons from recent crises. *Journal of Finance* 54:1508–21.

Summers, Lawrence. 1999. Statement at meetings of IMF interim committee. September 1999 annual meeting of IMF and World Bank Group. 28–30 September, Washington, D.C.

Tanzi, Vito. 1987. Fiscal policy, growth, and the design of stabilization programs, ed. A. Martirena-Mantel, 35–40. In *External debt, savings, and the growth in Latin America*, Washington, D.C.: International Monetary Fund.

U.S. Treasury, 2000a. *Report on IMF reforms.* Washington, D.C.: U.S. Department of the Treasury, March. Available at [http://www.treas.gov/press/releases/docs/imfrefor.pdf]. 13 September.

U.S. Treasury, 2000b. *Response to the report of the International Financial Institution Advisory Commission.* Washington, D.C.: U.S. Department of the Treasury, 8 June. Available at [http://www.ustreas.gov/press/releases/docs/response.pdf]. 13 September.

Volcker, Paul, and Toyoo Gyohten. 1992. *Changing fortunes.* New York: Times Books.

Williamson, John. 1990. What Washington means by policy reform. In *Latin American adjustment: How much has happened?* ed. J. Williamson, 5–20. Washington, D.C.: Institute for International Economics.

Williamson, John. 2000. The role of the IMF: A guide to the reports. International Economics Policy Briefs no. 00–5. Washington, D.C.: Institute for International Economics, May.

World Bank. 2000. *East Asia: Recovery and beyond.* Washington, D.C.: World Bank.

Chapter 17

The Fund Appears to be Sleeping at the Wheel

Morris Goldstein and Michael Mussa

Frustrated with the lack of meaningful exchange rate adjustment by China and some other Asian economies, the US Treasury has called on the International Monetary Fund to be more ambitious in its surveillance of exchange rates and warned that the "perception that the IMF is asleep at the wheel on its most fundamental responsibility — exchange rate surveillance — is very unhealthy both for the institution and the international monetary system".

We agree — even if the criticism comes from an institution that has itself only recently awakened from a long slumber on these issues. But continued acrimony between the IMF and its largest shareholder would not be helpful — especially when the world economy faces critical challenges in reversing large and large and rapidly rising payments imbalances.

Consistent with the IMF's responsibility under its articles of agreement "to oversee the international monetary system in order to ensure its effective operation", the Fund has repeatedly emphasised that the massive US external deficit and the corresponding surplus of the rest of the world must start declining. The IMF has rightly focused on many of the policy adjustments

---

The authors are senior fellows at the Institute for International Economics.

important for reducing payments imbalances in a manner that limits risks of financial turmoil and best sustains prospects for global growth. This includes pressing the US for a more responsible fiscal policy.

But the IMF is also uniquely charged to "exercise firm surveillance over the exchange rate policies of its members, and [to] adopt specific principles for the guidance of members with respect to those policies". Regrettably, the Fund has been retreating from this key mandate at a critical juncture. It has endorsed general calls for China and other Asian economies to adopt "more flexible" exchange rate regimes but has failed to emphasise the need for significant exchange rate appreciation to help reduce global imbalances.

China is now the third largest trading economy. Its overall current account surplus has risen from 3 per cent of gross domestic product in 2003 to 4 per cent in 2004; it is likely to exceed 6 per cent in 2005 and may grow more next year. Many other Asian economies also have substantial overall current account surpluses. Massive, sustained, one-way intervention in the foreign exchange market (averaging 12 per cent of Chinese GDP in 2003 and 2004 and rising in 2005) has kept the renminbi from appreciating meaningfully against the dollar in nominal terms and has induced moderate depreciation in China's real effective exchange rate. Many other Asian economies have also limited the appreciation of their currencies. In contrast, the market-determined exchange rates of European countries and of Australia, Canada and New Zealand have appreciated very substantially against the dollar since early 2002. Reduction of the US external payments deficit from more than 6 per cent of GDP to a sustainable level of about 3 per cent undoubtedly requires substantial real depreciation of the dollar against the trade-weighted average of US trading partners. No significant exchange rate adjustment against Asian currencies means that much larger adjustment will be required against currencies that have already appreciated substantially.

Moreover, large-scale, prolonged, one-way intervention by several Asian countries to resist meaningful appreciation is clearly contrary to the IMF's stated principles for the guidance of members' exchange rate policies. Yet, the IMF has held no special consultations with Asian countries on their exchange rate policies. Nor has it provided explicit and public advice on the extent of necessary policy adjustments. It welcomed the renminbi's tiny appreciation against the dollar in late July without indicating the need for substantial further appreciation.

Against this background, it is simply not credible for Rodrigo de Rato, the Fund's managing director, to claim the IMF has been "well ahead of the curve" in its exchange rate advice to China, that there is "no evidence" that China has been running foul of IMF exchange rate guidelines, and that the IMF should not be "a special pressure group" to induce policy changes.

The key issue is that present exchange rate levels in Asia are not consistent with the need to reduce global payments imbalances in a way that minimises risks of financial disruption and supports sustainable global growth. The IMF has a clear responsibility to address this. More sound bites on the need for "greater flexibility" in currency regimes will not suffice, are not going to cut it. The IMF is the international institution designated to exert pressure on its members' exchange rate policies—not for the benefit of individual members but for the broader needs of the international community.

The Fund should also treat the US Treasury's call for more ambition in IMF exchange rate surveillance as a good opportunity to give substance to its special consultations tool; to publish its own assessment of exchange rates; to review its guidelines on exchange rate policies; and to demand a meaningful role in discussions of exchange rate surveillance by the Group of Seven leading industrial countries.

If the IMF fails in these duties, others will take up the task. This is apparent in the widespread Congressional support for the Schumer-Graham bill that would impose high US tariffs on Chinese imports to offset the estimated undervaluation of the renminbi.

Down this route lies a potential trade war and international chaos. which all nations have a vital interest to avoid. The only viable alternative is to insist that the IMF does its assigned job as the vigorous, competent, unbiased, international umpire of exchange rate policies.

"The Fund appears to be sleeping at the wheel" by Morris Goldstein and Michael Mussa. Originally published in the Financial Times, October 2, 2005.

Chapter 18

Currency Manipulation and Enforcing the Rules of the International Monetary System

Morris Goldstein

Concern has been growing, at least in some quarters, that large-scale, prolonged, one-way intervention in exchange markets to limit or to preclude currency appreciation — primarily in China but also in some other Asian economies during the past two to three years — has been both thwarting global payments adjustment and violating the rules of the international monetary system (Goldstein 2004, 2005b).[1]

In its communiqués of October 2004 and of February and April 2005, Group of Seven (G-7) finance ministers and central bank governors stated that "more flexibility in exchange rates is desirable for major countries or economic areas that lack such flexibility to promote smooth and widespread adjustments

---

Morris Goldstein is the Dennis Weatherstone Senior Fellow at the Institute for International Economics. The author is grateful to C. Fred Bergsten, Nicholas Lardy, Michael Mussa, and Ted Truman for helpful comments on an earlier draft, and to Anna Wong for excellent research assistance.

[1] See also C. Fred Bergsten's testimony before the Senate Committee on Banking, Housing, and Urban Affairs titled "The IMF and Exchange Rates," August 22, 2005.

in the international financial system, based on market mechanisms." On April 6, 2005, 67 US senators voted to support an amendment, cosponsored by Senator Charles E. Schumer (D-NY) and Senator Lindsey Graham (R-SC), that called for imposing an across-the-board tariff of 27.5 percent on China's exports to the United States if negotiations between China and the United States on the value of the renminbi proved unsuccessful. In a May 2005 report to the US Congress, the US Treasury (2005, 2) summed up its evaluation of China's exchange rate policies: "current Chinese policies are highly distortionary and pose a risk to China's economy, its trading partners, and global economic growth. . . . If current trends continue without substantial alteration, China's policies will likely meet the statute's technical requirements for designation" as an economy that is manipulating its currency. On July 27, 2005, the US House of Representatives passed, by a 255-168 margin, a bill sponsored by Representative Phil English (R-PA) that would not only extend countervailing duty or antisubsidy law to nonmarket economies (China among them) but also place additional requirements on the US Treasury Department in its reporting to Congress on the practice of currency manipulation. Many analysts argued that the Central American Free Trade Agreement (CAFTA) would not have passed the US House of Representatives later that same day (and then by only a two-vote margin) had not the bill sponsored by Representative English been approved immediately before it. And on September 23, 2005, Timothy Adams, the under secretary of the US Department of the Treasury for monetary affairs, emphasized that "the perception that the IMF is asleep at the wheel on its most fundamental responsibility — exchange rate surveillance — is very unhealthy for the institution and the international monetary system" and urged the IMF to be "far more ambitious" in its surveillance of exchange rates.[2]

In the remainder of this chapter, I argue that a strong case can be made for having international codes of conduct on exchange rate policies, that several popular arguments denying that currency manipulation has recently taken place are flawed, and that the IMF needs to take its monitoring and

---

[2] In the *Financial Times* of October 3, 2005 ("The Fund Appears to Be Sleeping at the Wheel"), Michael Mussa and I agreed with Adams's criticism of recent IMF surveillance over exchange rates; in addition, we concluded that if the IMF does not do its assigned job as the vigorous, competent, unbiased umpire of exchange rate policies others would take up the task with adverse global consequences.

enforcement responsibilities in this area more seriously than it has in the past. I also put forward several specific suggestions for strengthening the IMF's role in this crucial area of surveillance.[3]

DISCOURAGING BEGGAR-THY-NEIGHBOR EXCHANGE RATE POLICIES

A key reason for establishing the IMF was to discourage beggar-thy-neighbor exchange rate policies. After all, the world had just gone through an unhappy experience with the competitive depreciations of the 1920s and 1930s, and there was a global consensus that the new rules of the road should prohibit such practices.[4] When the Fund's charter was amended (for the second time) against the backdrop of the more diversified exchange rate system of the 1970s, the new Article IV placed important obligations relating to exchange rate policy on member countries and on the Fund itself.

Specifically, Article IV, section 1, paragraph 3 of the IMF's Articles of Agreement stipulates that each member country shall "[a]void manipulating exchange rates or the international monetary system in order to prevent effective balance-of-payments adjustment or to gain unfair competitive advantage over other member countries."

For its part, the IMF is directed in Article IV, Section 3 of these same Articles of Agreement to "oversee the compliance of each member with its obligations" [and] "exercise firm surveillance over the exchange rate policies of members" [and] "adopt specific principles for the guidance of members with respect to these policies."

In 1977, the Fund laid out principles and procedures for its surveillance over countries' exchange rate policies (IMF 1977). In that document, a number of developments are identified that might indicate the need for discussion with the country. The first such development is "protracted, large-scale intervention in one direction in the exchange markets." Other developments cover official or quasi-official borrowing, restrictions on trade and capital flows, monetary

---

[3]This paper builds upon the earlier analysis contained in Goldstein (2005b).

[4]In the Fund's original Articles of Agreement and under the par value system then in existence, member countries were supposed to obtain the approval of the Fund for proposed changes in exchange rates larger than 10 percent, and the Fund was to concur if it was satisfied that the change was necessary to correct a fundamental disequilibrium.

and domestic financial policies, and behavior of the exchange rate that appears unrelated to underlying economic and financial conditions.

I think the Fund intended these developments to be a set of presumptive indicators, or "pointers," of (inappropriate) efforts to manipulate the exchange rate or to maintain the "wrong" exchange rate.[5] The interpretation of these pointers was not intended to be mechanistic but rather judgmental within the framework of a comprehensive analysis of the general economic situation and economic policy strategy of the country.

Having the wrong real exchange rate has long been known to impose costs on both the home country and its trading partners: When this important relative price gets far out of line, it distorts resource allocation within the country as well as the pattern of international trade among countries. Significantly overvalued exchange rates have also been linked to currency crises in emerging economies, with large attendant costs in terms of real economic growth; and large undervaluations typically generate excessive accumulation of international reserves that, in turn, can threaten financial instability at home and protectionist responses abroad.

It is unlikely that the costs of misaligned real exchange rates are lower today than when the Fund's founders established the Bretton Woods architecture. The higher international mobility of capital implies that speculative capital flows now respond more rapidly and more strongly to perceived one-way bets in exchange markets. The widespread rise in trade openness means that changes in net exports now have the potential to contribute more to real output changes than they did before. With the progressive lowering of tariffs and other barriers to trade, exchange rates have taken on a larger component of competitive advantage. In addition, the large and increasing weight of emerging economies in both global output and in global trade flows has given the industrial countries a greater incentive to monitor more carefully the exchange rate policies adopted by emerging economies and has also given the emerging economies an increased responsibility to take the global interest into account in formulating their own policies.[6]

---

[5] By the wrong exchange rate, I mean a real exchange rate that differs from the equilibrium rate implied by economic fundamentals.

[6] Looking at 11 large emerging economies, Boyer and Truman (2005) report that these 11 made up more than 31 percent of world GDP (at purchasing power parity exchange rates) and 34 percent of global international reserves in 2004.

On top of these longer-term trends, the current conjuncture has heightened concerns about currency manipulation in at least two respects.

First, the need to deal with an excessively large and rising US current account deficit has — in addition to putting the spotlight on the savings-investment imbalance within the United States — focused attention on exchange rate policies and reserve developments in trading partners of the United States, particularly those in Asia. The US current account deficit — at $660 billion or 5.8 percent of GDP in 2004 and expected to be even larger in 2005 — is approximately twice as large as is likely to be sustainable over the medium term. To bring the US current account down to a sustainable level at reasonable cost requires, inter alia, that the US dollar depreciate in real, trade-weighted terms by another 15 to 25 percent from its current value. But it will be difficult to realize the needed further depreciation of the dollar unless the Asian emerging economies plus Japan — whose currencies have a combined weight in the dollar index of roughly 40 percent — participate in the appreciation of nondollar currencies.[7] Although the euro, the Canadian dollar, and the Australian dollar among some others appreciated strongly in the first wave of dollar depreciation (from the dollar peak in February 2002 until now [late 2005]), the Asian currencies — with the notable exceptions of the Korean won and the Singapore dollar — did not; in fact, they often depreciated in real, trade-weighted terms despite large current account surpluses (Goldstein 2005c). If the Asian currencies do not lead the way in the second wave of dollar depreciation, either the resulting overall dollar depreciation will be too small to promote global payments adjustment or the appreciation of nondollar currencies will be skewed toward those economies where economic circumstances would be poorly served by further large appreciation.

Second, evidence of currency manipulation has become increasingly obvious during the 2003–05 period. The leading case in point is China.

---

[7]This being said, one should not exaggerate the likely impact of Asian currency appreciation on the US current account imbalance. A 20 percent appreciation of all Asian currencies would likely reduce the US current account deficit by approximately $80 billion. This rein forces the basic point made above that the United States itself needs to take decisive action — including measures to lower its structural budget deficit — to reduce its savings-investment imbalance. The least-cost strategy for reducing the US current account deficit is to employ both expenditure-reducing and expenditure-switching policy tools (Mussa 2005, Goldstein 2005c).

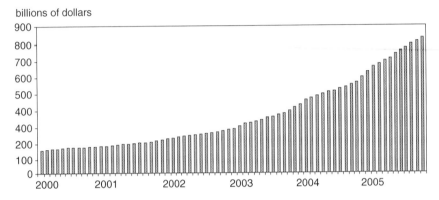

Fig 1: China's foreign exchange reserves, 2000–2005Q3.
Source: China State Administration for Foreign Exchange.
Note: After December 2003, foreign exchange figures are adjusted to reflect a $45 billion transfer to the Bank of China and the China Construction Bank. After April 2005, foreign exchange figures are adjusted to reflect a $15 billion transfer to the Industrial and Commercial Bank of China.

As shown in Figure 1, China has been engaging in large-scale, prolonged, one-way intervention in exchange markets for the better part of three years. In 2003 and 2004, the increase in China's accumulation of foreign exchange reserves averaged nearly 12 percent of GDP — this at a time when China's domestic economy was overheating, when its overall current account position was in substantial and rising surplus, and when the real, trade-weighted value of the renminbi was depreciating.[8] Thus, at a time when the dictates of both internal and external balance pointed toward the desirability of an appreciating renminbi, the Chinese authorities were systematically thwarting adjustment by intervening heavily in the exchange market to keep the real value of the renminbi low and falling. All indications are that China's external imbalance and reserve accumulation will be even larger this year — with the trade balance for the first half of 2005 already larger than for all of 2004 and with some respected China analysts like UBS's Jon Anderson (2005) projecting both a

---

[8] China's economy grew by more than 9 percent in both 2003 and 2004, and its overall current account surplus (relative to GDP) was 3.3 percent in 2003 and 4.2 percent in 2004. According to JP Morgan's index of real, trade-weighted exchange rates, the renminbi depreciated (in real terms) by 10 percent from February 2002 to December 2004. Citigroup's index of real, trade-weighted exchange rates places the real depreciation of the renminbi over this period at 12 percent.

current account surplus in the range of 8 to 10 percent of China's GDP and reserve accumulation of roughly $25 billion per month.[9] China's decision in late July 2005 to revalue the renminbi by 2 percent relative to the dollar and to move de jure from a dollar peg to a currency basket have so far done little to affect its de facto behavior in exchange markets.

Japan intervened heavily in exchange markets — to the tune of $200 billion in 2003 and an unprecedented $150 billion more in the first quarter of 2004 — before suspending such intervention beginning in the second quarter of 2004; according to Takatoshi Ito (2004), Japan's intervention in the 15 months from January 2003 to March 2004 was larger than the cumulative intervention in the preceding 12 years. In recent years Malaysia and Taiwan also have engaged in large-scale, exchange market intervention without extenuating circumstances such as weak domestic demand growth or the presence of current account deficits. From February 2002 to October 2005, the real, trade-weighted values of the Malaysian ringgit and the Taiwanese dollar depreciated by 13 and 8 percent, respectively; the corresponding figure for the Japanese yen was a depreciation of 9 percent.

When current account imbalances become excessively large, changes in real exchange rates in both deficit and surplus countries are a necessary (albeit not sufficient) element of effective and least-cost adjustment. No exchange rate system can function effectively if surplus countries take measures to prevent real appreciation of their currencies.

FALLACIES ABOUT CURRENCY MANIPULATION

Not everyone agrees, of course, that currency manipulation has of late become a serious problem for the international monetary system or that China's use

---

[9] Growth of China's real GDP is likely to exceed 9 percent in 2005 although tentative signs show that growth of final domestic demand is slowing. Reflecting, inter alia, the recent, real, trade-weighted appreciation of the US dollar, the real, trade-weighted exchange rate of the renminbi has also appreciated in 2005 — by roughly 10 percent under the JP Morgan index and by 3 percent under the Citigroup index. If the February 2002 — October 2005 period is taken as a whole, the renminbi has depreciated in real, trade-weighted terms by approximately 1 percent under the JP Morgan index and by a much larger 9 percent under the Citigroup index. If one concludes, as I do, that the dollar will have to fall (in real, trade-weighted terms) over the medium term to help correct the large US current account deficit, then any dollar appreciation in 2005 will prove to be temporary and its reversal in subsequent years will, ceteris paribus, induce a depreciation in the renminbi as well, unless the renminbi appreciates relative to the dollar.

of large-scale, protracted, one-way intervention in exchange markets should be regarded as manipulation.[10] At least four fallacious arguments have often been put forward to rebut claims of manipulation.

The first argument is that because IMF rules permit countries a wide choice of currency regimes and because defense of a fixed exchange rate frequently involves exchange market intervention, there can be no manipulation for countries maintaining a fixed-rate regime.

This argument confuses choice of the currency regime with efforts to maintain a disequilibrium real exchange rate. The former is fully consistent with IMF rules of the game; the latter is not. IMF members are free to pick fixed rates, floating rates, or practically any currency regime in between. They are also permitted to intervene in exchange markets, especially when they encounter disorderly market conditions. What is not permitted under IMF rules is engaging in a particular kind of intervention — namely, large-scale, protracted, one-way intervention. That type of intervention is prohibited because it is typically symptomatic of a disequilibrium real exchange rate, and such a disequilibrium rate can impose serious costs on both the home country and its trading partners.

China can thus legitimately maintain that its choice of a currency regime — be it a fixed rate or a managed float — is a matter of national sovereignty. But it cannot legitimately maintain that it alone gets to decide as a sovereign matter what the exchange rate between the renminbi and the dollar should be (within that currency regime) for long periods regardless of the economic signals about whether that rate is or is not an equilibrium rate, just as the United States cannot decide unilaterally what the dollar-renminbi rate should be. Exchange rates are by definition two-sided variables. When it becomes increasingly apparent that the exchange rate is out of line, it becomes incumbent upon the home country to change it lest it thwart the international adjustment process.

---

[10] I use the term "currency manipulation" to describe socially inappropriate exchange rate policy because that term used in the IMF charter and in some key IMF surveillance guidelines. But the economic logic about what is and what is not appropriate exchange rate policy would be similar if we replaced the words currency manipulation with the perhaps less charged term of "thwarting international adjustment."

A second frequently heard argument is that, because "to manipulate" is an active verb, a country that has maintained the same parity for an extended period cannot be guilty of manipulation because it has not done anything.

What this line of argument fails to see is that what matters for countries' competitiveness is the real, trade-weighted exchange rate (that is, the average trade-weighted nominal exchange rate, corrected for differences in inflation rates across countries) and that the appropriateness of such a real exchange rate should be evaluated against the backdrop of the country's overall balance-of-payments position. Viewed from this perspective, a misalignment of the real exchange rate can come about just as easily from non-movement of the nominal exchange rate as it can from excessive movement. This same perspective also suggests that a given real and nominal exchange rate may be fine when the balance of payments is in deficit but will no longer be appropriate, say, when the balance of payments goes into substantial surplus. As applied to China's circumstances, the renminbi-dollar parity of 8.28 may not have been a problem when China was running either a very small payment surplus or when the real, trade-weighted exchange rate of the renminbi was appreciating, but that same parity became a problem when China simultaneously exhibited both a large external payments surplus and a depreciating real, trade-weighted exchange rate.[11]

Fallacious argument number three is that even protracted, large-scale, one-way exchange market intervention to hold down the real exchange rate should be permitted if the country needs an undervalued exchange rate to generate sufficient employment in its traded-goods industries to ensure social stability. In this connection, China faces a particularly difficult employment challenge because of the large migration out of agriculture and the large employment losses in many state-owned industries.

The rub here is that many countries have full employment objectives and it would be difficult to elevate some countries' concerns in this area over other countries' concerns. Should, for example, one additional worker hired in the export industry of China count more than one in Bangladesh or one in Egypt? Wholesale application of this rationalization for currency manipulation would

---

[11] Many commentators seem to forget that the real, trade-weighted value of the renminbi appreciated by nearly 30 percent between 1994 and early 2002, a period during which annual real economic growth still averaged about 9 percent.

make it next to impossible to provide the right incentives for discouraging competitive depreciation in the international monetary system as a whole; indeed, the likely outcome would be continued conflict over exchange rate policy and greater resort to protectionist trade measures.[12]

Yet a fourth argument for downplaying concerns about currency manipulation is that whatever the country's choice of currency regime and whatever actions it takes with respect to the nominal exchange rate, it will in the long term exert little control over the real exchange rate — and it is real rate that matters for competitive advantage. Thus, if some counties use large-scale exchange market intervention to maintain an under-valued exchange rate, their domestic inflation rates will eventually rise enough to bring their real exchange rates back to equilibrium.

Key phrases here are "in the long term" and "eventually." The fact is that surplus countries can typically resist adjustment and maintain a disequilibrium real exchange rate for longer than deficit countries can. In addition, low-inflation countries may be able to resist real appreciation pressures for a considerable period.[13] In China's case, for example, the undervaluation of the renminbi in 2003 and 2004 did induce much larger capital inflows chasing an expected revaluation of the renminbi. In addition, the Chinese economy did experience during those years a "blowout" of bank credit expansion as well as a marked increase in inflationary pressures (Goldstein 2004). In the end, it took the implementation of strong administrative controls on bank lending, investment project approvals, and land use along with heavy sterilization operations to regain control of the credit and monetary aggregates. Therefore, China did pay a price in terms of domestic financial instability for seeking to

---

[12] If there were a widespread protectionist response to currency manipulation, employment could fall in the export industries of the country doing the manipulating. Also, longer term issues associated with chronic undervaluation are relevant for stabilization policy and employment; Eswar Prasad (2005), for example, has argued that moving towards domestic demand-led growth would help put China on a more sustainable growth path. Goldstien and Lardy (2005) point out that the very large undervaluation of the renminbi is a relatively recent phenomenon and argue that seeking to maintain a large undervaluation of the renminbi is not a sensible development policy for China. Moving toward greater flexibility in the exchange rate also of course carries implications for the independence of monetary policy and for the use of monetary policy as a tool of stabilization.

[13] See Mohanty and Turner (2005) on the domestic consequences of exchange market intervention in emerging economies.

maintain an undervalued exchange rate, and the (temporary) rise in China's inflation rate did reduce somewhat the real depreciation of the renminbi. The larger the scale and duration of exchange market intervention, the greater presumably would be the pressures on the real exchange rate to rise. Nevertheless it is important to note that the real, trade-weighted value of the renminbi did depreciate in both 2003 and 2004. It is asking a lot — I would say too much — to expect the rest of the world to absorb much of the costs of a misaligned real exchange rate (especially for the third-largest trading nation in the world) if the transition to an equilibrium real exchange rate takes years, not months.

In the end, the set of arguments suggesting that currency manipulation is not a serious problem either today or for the future does not withstand close scrutiny. Proponents of these arguments would have us believe that the international monetary system can function effectively as a free-for-all, without an agreed code of conduct. That view was firmly rejected by the experience during the 1920s and the 1930s, and recent conflicts over exchange rate policy imply that the international monetary system will not manage itself in our time either. Why should international codes of conduct for exchange rate policy be any less necessary than those for policy? Through the rulings of adjudication panels in the World Organization — in contrast with what has happened on exchange rates issues — a body of international case law is unfolding, making it clearer what is not internationally acceptable trade policy on everything from bananas to steel to domestic tax systems. Why isn't a similar exercise going on for exchange rate policy?[14]

ENFORCING THE RULES: THE IMF AS AN UMPIRE FOR THE EXCHANGE RATE SYSTEM

If it is accepted that international codes of conduct for exchange rate policy are both necessary and desirable, the next relevant question is who should monitor and enforce those codes. The founders of the IMF and the framers of the new Article IV in the IMF's charter had a ready answer: the IMF. Not only does the IMF have an obligation to exercise "firm surveillance"

---

[14] I say similar (rather than identical) because formal disputes about currency manipulation are likely to be less frequent, subject to a wider margin of error, and resolved according to a broader set of principles than the more detailed disputes about trade policy.

over the exchange rate policies of its member countries, it is also the only international organization with the unique mandate to oversee the functioning of the international monetary system.

But no rules, codes, or mandates can be expected to have much impact if they are not enforced, and the reality is that neither the IMF nor its major shareholders have shown an inclination to get much involved in deciding what is and is not internationally acceptable exchange rate policy. Three observations are revealing.

First, although the IMF's surveillance guidelines permit the Fund's managing director to initiate and conduct an "ad hoc consultation" with a country whenever there is a concern about its exchange rate policy, the Fund has conducted such special consultations only twice (Sweden in 1982 and South Korea in 1987) during the past 26 years and never at all during the past 17 years! Is it credible to argue that there have been no exchange rate problems throughout the world during the past 17 years that were of sufficient concern to justify a country visit by the IMF with the express purpose of investigating more thoroughly whether a serious infraction of the surveillance guidelines had taken place?

Second, even today, after three years of enormous reserve accumulation in China, the IMF has made no public statement indicating either that China might have been engaged in currency manipulation or that the renminbi is undervalued.[15] Instead, the IMF has simply argued over and over again that it would be in the interests of both China and the global adjustment process if China's currency regime showed greater "flexibility." A call for greater flexibility of the renminbi is not the same as either a call for a more appreciated renminbi or a call for less exchange market intervention by the Chinese authorities: If the renminbi depreciated substantially (counter to the needs of the global adjustment process), it would have become more flexible; likewise, continued or even larger exchange market intervention could contribute to a further real depreciation of the renminbi, again making it more flexible. I am not of course suggesting seriously that the Fund believes either that (further) renminbi (real)

---

[15] Goldstein (2004) and Goldstein and Lardy (2004; 2005; *Asian Wall Street Journal* of September 12, 2003; *Financial Times* of July 22, 2005) have maintained for some time that the renminbi is significantly undervalued — on the order of 15 to 25 percent. The undervaluation of the renminbi is likely even larger in 2005 than it was in 2003 or 2004 (Goldstein 2005a).

depreciation would be desirable or that China should reduce the influence of market forces in the determination of its exchange rate. Instead, I am just highlighting the point that the Fund has been very timid and purposely noncommittal on both the appropriate level of China's exchange rate and the intervention measures that China has taken to support the current and recent levels of the exchange rate. The IMF has been willing to say only that the preferred currency regime in China should be one of greater flexibility; it has not defined by how much or when the renminbi would need to change to meet the standard of greater flexibility.[16]

Third, in recent comments about his conception of the role of the Fund,[17] the current managing director, Rodrigo de Rato, indicated that he did not think the Fund should act as a "special pressure group" for changes in country policies, presumably including exchange rate policies.[18] How the Fund is going to exercise firm surveillance and induce corrective action — without pressure — in countries that have prima facie tipped one or more of the pointers of currency manipulation is not clear. The Fund has followed an approach of using quiet diplomacy toward China's exchange rate policies over the past two to three years and at least so far the results have been meager.

In defense of the Fund, one might argue that its major shareholders did not seem to be pressing it much to take on a more activist role in identifying and discouraging currency manipulation. Only the United States has been willing to speak out publicly on this issue; it has addressed the issue almost exclusively on a bilateral basis, and its procedures for identifying manipulation are at best inconsistent.[19]

---

[16] In the *Financial Times* of July 22, 2005 ("China's Revaluation Shows Why Size Really Matters"), Nicholas Lardy and I argued that the initial revaluation of the renminbi included in the currency reform of late July 2005 was far too small.

[17] See Leslie Wroughton, "Under Fire, IMF's Rato Wants to Get the Job Done," Reuters, July 29, 2005; Daniel Altman, "IMF Chief Draws Fire over Style as Leader," *International Herald Tribune*, July 27, 2005.

[18] Ibid. My reaction to de Rato's comments was similar to that of my IIE colleague, Mike Mussa, who remarked: "It's one thing to be a conscientious objector; its another to be a conscientious objector when you have recently been appointed commandant of the Marine Corps".

[19] There have been occasional public criticisms of China's exchange rate policy in other G-7 countries but not, I think, public criticisms charging China with engaging in the M-word (that is, manipulation).

Since 1988, the Omnibus Trade and Competitiveness Act has required the US Treasury Department to report to the US Congress any countries engaging in "exchange rate manipulation." The US Treasury named several Asian economies as manipulators during the 1988–94 period (including China in 1992–94), but the Treasury Department has cited no country since 1994 — including in 2003 and 2004 when, as indicated earlier, there was strong evidence of manipulation by China and several other economies. If China was meeting — or was close to meeting — the technical requirements for manipulation, as argued by the US Treasury Department in May 2005 (US Treasury 2005), then these same technical requirements were also being met during most of the past 24 to 36 months. The criteria used by the US Treasury to evaluate manipulation and exchange rate misalignment are also partly flawed: Specifically, the Omnibus Trade and Competitiveness Act seems to require that bilateral US trade imbalances with partner countries be part of the analysis when these have no sound analytical basis for the purpose at hand; if you want external imbalances to enter the exercise, overall current account positions are what you should look at.[20]

The fact that the US Treasury Department has been dragged kicking and screaming into the currency manipulation debate by the US Congress says something relevant: If there is a widespread perception that no one is minding the store in enforcing the rules of the international monetary system, pressure for doing something about it does not disappear; instead, it gets funneled into calls for corrective action at the national level, where protectionist threats are apt to be greatest and where the analytical tool kit for identifying currency manipulation can be subject to outside pressures. In other words, if the IMF were minding the store, there would be less bilateral freelancing.

The message that I take away from this lack of enforcement of codes of conduct for exchange rate policy is the following: The IMF seems to have accelerated its retreat from the role its founders intended it to have as an umpire for the international monetary system — just at the time when such an umpire is increasingly needed and when there are no other promising candidates to

---

[20] As suggested earlier, looking at overall current account positions should send up a warning flare for China: Its overall current account surplus (relative to GDP) was more than 3 percent in 2003, more than 4 percent last year, and is likely to be at least 7 to 8 percent in 2005. Those who maintain that China's overall current account position has been modest during the past few years have just not been watching the data carefully.

take up that role. Yes, the IMF has other roles to play — coach, banker, crisis manager — but I submit that looking forward none of those roles will be more important than that of umpire.[21]

True, the calls that the IMF will be asked to make will often be controversial — be it ruling on whether China is manipulating its exchange rate or ruling on whether Argentina was acting in good faith in negotiating with its private creditors during its recent debt restructuring.[22] Sometimes the calls made by the IMF will be wrong. But not making those calls at all will be worse for the functioning of the system because the incentives will then become tilted over time toward beggar-thy-neighbor policies, and these in turn will induce retaliation of one kind or another.

The emerging economies, which have perhaps the most to gain from a further integration into the global economy, have a strong interest in supporting objective enforcement of the rules of the game by the IMF because, without such an umpire, they will become increasingly vulnerable to nationalist policies in the advanced countries aimed at "leveling the playing field." In a similar vein, the legitimate desire of emerging economies to obtain more "chairs and shares" in the forums where global economic initiatives are formulated and where countries' economic policies are evaluated will likely be frustrated if there is a perception that their gains in market share have not been fairly obtained.

A MODEST PROPOSAL FOR DISCOURAGING CURRENCY MANIPULATION

Despite the disappointing track record, it is not yet too late for the Fund to reclaim its rightful place in exercising firm surveillance over countries' exchange

---

[21] Mervyn King, governor of the Bank of England, in remarks at a February 4, 2005, London conference on advancing enterprise, set out a similar view: "I believe that we need to rethink the role of the IMF in the international monetary system. I encourage the Fund to articulate a positive vision of the management of the international monetary system in its forthcoming strategic review. I am convinced that the future of the Fund is primarily as an occasional international lender of last resort for middle-income countries suffering financial crises."

[22] See Truman "Overview on IMF Reform", *Reforming the IMF for the 21st Century*, Edwin M. Truman, ed. Institute for International Economics Special Report 19, April 2006, pp. 31–126, on why the IMF should have been more involved as an umpire-adviser than it was during the recent Argentine debt restructuring exercise.

rate policies. Toward that end, I would suggest that the Fund should undertake the following three initiatives.

First, the Fund should begin issuing its own semiannual report on exchange rate policies, in which it would not only discuss exchange rate developments of interest but also identify cases where there are concerns about potential currency manipulation practices. If, as I believe, the Fund is the institution that has a comparative advantage in monitoring and enforcing codes of conduct on exchange rate policies, its views on these matters should not appear, as has often been the case, as a one-sentence summary in the US Treasury Department's reports to Congress. The IMF should issue its own report, with the best objective analysis it can muster. The report should cover industrial countries as well as developing countries. Because a finding by the Fund that a member has been engaging in currency manipulation would be seen as authoritative and as less influenced by national political pressures, it could be expected to act as a deterrent to engaging in currency manipulation in the first place. Over time, case law would develop that would help define what are and what are not internationally acceptable exchange rate policies. The G-7 should signal its support for this exercise by inviting the Fund to become a full and active participant in its discussion of G-7 exchange rates during G-7 meetings.

Second, the Fund should make more frequent use of the special or ad hoc consultations whenever either Fund staff or another member country raises a serious concern about potential currency manipulation. Such consultations would also give the member country involved an initial opportunity to defend its currency policy and explain why there may have been extenuating circumstances in its use of, say, large-scale, prolonged intervention. The dialogue and information obtained during such special consultations would also serve as an input into preparation of the Fund's semiannual reports on exchange rate policies. I make no presumption about how frequently such special consultations would take place or about how many countries would be involved — only that to be relevant they would have to take place more often than never in the past 17 years. Circumstances will dictate when such consultations should be activated.

And, third, the Fund should review as soon as possible its existing guidelines for surveillance over countries' exchange rate polices to see whether they warrant any modification, particularly regarding the pointers that might be indicative of inappropriate exchange rate policies. I think the existing pointers are reasonable, but it is certainly possible that improvements can be made. Until such time as agreement is reached on an amended set of guidelines, the existing guidelines should be enforced.

None of this is likely to make much of an impact unless both the Fund's larger shareholders and the managing director of the Fund give such enhanced surveillance over exchange rate policies the support and leadership it needs. It is about time that they do.

"Currency Manipulation and Enforcing the Rules of the International Monetary System" by Morris Goldstein from *Reforming the IMF for the 21st Century*, Edwin M. Truman, editor, pp. 141–155 (April 2006). Peterson Institute for International Economics. Used with permission of the publisher.

REFERENCES

Anderson, Jon. 2005. China by the Numbers. *UBS Asian Economic Monitor* (August 22).

Boyer, Jan, and Edwin M. Truman. 2005. The United States and the Large Emerging-Market Economies: Competitors or Partners? In *The United States and the World Economy: Foreign Economic Policy for the Next Decade*, ed. C. Fred Bergsten and the Institute for International Economics. Washington: Institute for International Economics.

Goldstein, Morris. 2004. *Adjusting China's Exchange Rate Policies.* Working Paper 04–1. Washington: Institute for International Economics.

Goldstein, Morris. 2005a. RMB Controversies. Paper presented to conference on monetary institutions and economic development, sponsored by Cato Institute, Washington (November 3).

Goldstein, Morris. 2005b. The International Financial Architecture. In *The United States and the World Economy: Foreign Economic Policy for the Next Decade*, ed. C. Fred Bergsten and the Institute for International Economics. Washington: Institute for International Economics.

Goldstein, Morris. 2005c. *What Might the Next Emerging-Market Financial Crisis Look Like?* Working Paper 05-7. Washington: Institute for International Economics.

Goldstein, Morris, and Nicholas Lardy. 2004. *What Kind of Landing for the Chinese Economy?* International Economics Policy Brief 04-7. Washington: Institute for International Economics.

Goldstein, Morris, and Nicholas Lardy. 2005. *China's Role in the Revived Bretton Woods System: A Case of Mistaken Identity.* Working Paper 05-2. Washington: Institute for International Economics.

IMF (International Monetary Fund). 1977. Surveillance over Exchange Rate Policies (April 29). Washington.

Ito, Takatoshi. 2005. The Yen and the Japanese Economy, 2004. In *Dollar Adjustment: How Far? Against What?* ed. C. Fred Bergsten and John Williamson. Washington: Institute for International Economics.

Mohanty, M. S., and Philip Turner. 2005. Intervention: What Are the Domestic Consequences? In *Foreign Exchange Market Intervention in Emerging Markets: Motives, Techniques, and Implications.* BIS Papers 24. Basel: Bank for International Settlements, Monetary and Economic Department.

Mussa, Michael. 2005. Sustaining Global Growth While Reducing External Imbalances. In *The United States and the World Economy: Foreign Economic Policy for the Next Decade*, C. Fred Bergsten and the Institute for International Economics. Washington: Institute for International Economics.

Prasad, Eswar. 2005. Next Steps for China. *Finance and Development* 42, no. 3 (September).

Truman, Edwin M. 2006. *Reforming the IMF for the 21st Century*, Special Report 19. Washington: Institute for International Economics.

US Treasury. 2005. Report to the Congress on International Economic and Exchange Rate Policies (May). Washington.

Part V
China's Exchange Rate Policies

Chapter 19

Two-Stage Currency Reform for China

Morris Goldstein and Nicholas Lardy

It was the unstoppable force meeting the immoveable object. During his recent visit to Beijing, U.S. Treasury Secretary John Snow stated that his objective was to get China to commit to moving to a "free-floating" currency, while senior Chinese officials stressed the contribution that a "stable" yuan had made to economic stability and development in China, Asia and the world. How then to square the circle that seems to call for three objectives: a near-term revaluation of the yuan, greater stability of the yuan in the medium term and greater flexibility and market determination of the yuan a little later down the road?

Most proposals for Chinese currency reform fall prey to one of two problems. If revaluation of the yuan has to wait until China is willing to undertake full capital-account liberalization, then the rest of the world has to live for too long with a misaligned yuan. Alternatively, if China is asked to free float the yuan and adopt capital-account convertibility before it puts its domestic financial sector on a firmer footing, it would be casting aside one of the main lessons of the Asian financial crisis.

Our answer to this dilemma is that China should view reform of its currency regime as a two-step process. The first step should be a medium-size (15% to 25%) revaluation of the yuan, a widening of the currency band

---

Messrs. Goldstein and Lardy were senior fellows at the Institute for International Economics when this paper was written.

(to between 5% and 7%, from less than 1%), and a switch from a unitary peg with the dollar to a three-currency basket peg, with weightings of roughly a third each for the dollar, euro and yen. Step two should be adoption of a managed float, after China strengthens its domestic financial system enough to permit a significant liberalization of capital outflows.

The Chinese leadership implicitly recognizes the yuan is undervalued. But they apparently believe the disequilibrium in the foreign-exchange market can be ameliorated by selective liberalization of current- and capital-account transactions while leaving unchanged the current fixed parity with the dollar.

The authorities recently increased the amount of yuan that Chinese tourists can convert to foreign currency and began to allow Chinese firms with certain types of foreign-exchange earnings to retain them rather than surrender them to the central bank. They have given the green light for a state-owned bank to issue its first dollar-denominated bond on the domestic market and have already signaled that requests for outward foreign direct investment are now more likely to be approved.

They are also discussing a reduction in the value-added tax export rebate rate to 11%, down from its current level of 15%. And they may allow mainland residents and certain financial institutions to purchase limited amounts of foreign securities. The authorities hope that these steps will either increase demand for, or reduce supply of foreign exchange, thus relieving the upward pressure on the currency.

While the go-slow approach presumably appeals to the leadership because of its limited short-run effect on China's exports, incoming FDI, and trade-related jobs, it is likely to do little to remove the misalignment of the yuan that has pushed China's overall balance of payments into a larger surplus, fed a huge reserve accumulation over the past 18 months, and increasingly concerned many of China's trading partners, including the United States, Euroland, Japan and South Korea. Very small adjustments could simply stoke further capital inflows by persuading market participants that speculation on the yuan is a one-way bet. Although the low interest rates paid on domestic central bank bonds has meant that sterilization of international reserves has so far been less onerous in China than in many other emerging economies, experience shows that sterilization becomes more costly and less effective the larger it is and the longer it goes on.

With its mountain of bad loans, China cannot afford to let capital inflows exacerbate the already excessive expansion in bank lending, money-supply growth and investment. The recently announced increase in reserve requirements for banks indicates that overextension of the financial system is now clearly visible on the central bank's radar screen.

In contrast, consider the advantages of our proposal for a medium-size revaluation. This would immediately deal with the existing undervaluation of the yuan and remove the incentive for further speculative capital inflows and reserve accumulation. No longer would the foreign component of the money supply be working at cross-purposes with the needs of domestic stabilization. It would show trading partners that China is not attempting to manipulate its exchange rate, thereby lessening the threat of protectionist measures against China's exports. It would make the yuan part of the solution to the global pattern of payment imbalances — not part of the problem.

In doing so, it would add to the plaudits that China received during the Asian financial crisis for conducting a responsible exchange rate policy and for taking the wider interest of the region into account. It would also increase the odds that Japan and emerging economies elsewhere in Asia would be willing to allow their exchange rates to appreciate, reducing the burden on the euro contributing to the needed downward adjustment of the dollar and limiting the deterioration in China's competitiveness. By adopting a wider band, China would gain valuable experience in allowing the exchange rate to be more responsive to market forces.

Just as important, by moving to a three-currency basket peg, China would increase the stability of its overall trade-weighted exchange rate. In a context where the dollar needs to depreciate further to help reduce the unsustainable U.S. current-account deficit, a basket peg would permit the dollar to depreciate against the yuan without a series of yuan parity changes. That could not happen if China retains its present unitary peg to the dollar.

The key to reconciling China's desire for exchange-rate stability with the need for the yuan to play its proper role in global balance of payments adjustment is to recognize that a fixed rate for the yuan need not be at the present parity. Stability of China's exchange rate should be interpreted against a wider set of reserve currencies than the dollar alone. The transition from "fix" to "flex" need not occur in one fell swoop, since liberalization of the capital account will proceed in stages.

Looking farther down the road, China will find it in its interest to move to a regime of managed floating because capital mobility in and out of China will increase and because it will want to exercise greater monetary-policy independence for stabilization purposes. It would be unwise to float now because the domestic financial system is still far too fragile to rule out large-scale capital flight in response to bad news. In addition, the government still dominates foreign-exchange transactions to a degree that precludes the market functioning properly. But these obstacles to floating the exchange rate should lessen as China reduces its large stock of nonperforming loans in the banking system, government involvement in the credit-allocation process declines in favor of market forces, and the progressive dismantling of restrictions on international capital flows widens and deepens the scope and liquidity of foreign-exchange trading.

As a host of emerging-market crises of the past decade have demonstrated so dramatically, high capital mobility vastly increases the vulnerability of a publicly announced target for the exchange rate. With China's public debt burden rising under the weight of bank recapitalization and assumption of pension liabilities, fiscal pump priming will be more constrained and monetary policy is likely to take on an increased share of stabilization duties. Thus China will want to increase the flexibility of its exchange rate regime.

But this need not mean slavish adherence to a pure float. If and when market forces push the yuan beyond the levels consistent with its economic fundamentals, China, like other countries, should retain the option to manage the float by intervening in the exchange market — so long as that intervention is not prolonged and not just in one direction. In short, a managed float should be the preferred regime choice for the second stage of reform.

The currency regime that has served China well in the past is not the currency regime that will serve China best today or in the future. Likewise, if the U.S. wants to persuade China to reduce the serious undervaluation of the yuan and to play a larger role in the global adjustment process within the next year or so, it too will have to alter its opening negotiating position by dropping the suggestion that China move in one great leap forward to a free float and completely open its capital markets. With some compromise by all parties and with the right sequencing of China's currency reform, a workable solution is in sight.

"Two-Stage Currency reform for China" by Morris Goldstein and Nicholas Lardy. Originally published in the Wall Street Journal, September 12, 2003.

Chapter
20

China's Exchange Rate Policy Dilemma

Morris Goldstein and Nicholas Lardy

This paper summarizes key aspects of China's exchange rate policy, outlines the problems it creates for both China and the global economy, and proposes a feasible policy compromise.

CHINA'S CURRENCY REGIME

On July 21, 2005, China announced a 2.1-percent appreciation of the renminbi (RMB) against the U.S. dollar, a move to a managed float, and a number of other "reforms." Most of these reforms simply reiterated long-standing arrangements; since 1994, China has identified its currency regime as a managed float and has set a 0.3-percent, per day, fluctuation limit (in either direction) for the RMB against the dollar (vis-à-vis the central parity).

The July 2005 announcement, however, did pledge two potentially important alterations: (a) the RMB was, henceforth, to be managed "with reference to a basket of currencies" rather than being pegged to the dollar; and (b) the exchange rate was to become "more flexible," with its value based more on "market supply and demand."

Goldstein: Institute for International Economics, 1750 Massachusetts Avenue, NW, Washington, DC 20036-1903 (email: HYPERLINK "mailto:mgoldstein@iie.com" mgoldstein@iie.com; Lardy: Institute for International Economics, 1750 Massachusetts Avenue, NW, Washington, DC 20036-1903 (email: nlardy@iie.com).

In practice, the July 2005 reforms have had little visible effect. As of mid-December 2005, the RMB-dollar rate was 8.07, a further appreciation of only 0.5 percent. There is also little evidence of pegging to a basket; rather, the RMB continues to track the U.S. dollar closely. And the central bank's monthly intervention in the foreign exchange market in August and September remained huge, at $18 billion per month — only slightly smaller than the $19 billion per month in the first half of 2005. In short, China's exchange rate system remains a heavily managed peg to the dollar — and at a dollar exchange rate very close to the level prevailing before the July reform.

IS THE RMB UNDERVALUED?

There are several approaches to evaluating the misalignment of the RMB. The "underlying balance" approach asks what level of the real, effective (trade-weighted) exchange rate would produce an equilibrium in which the "underlying" current-account position is approximately equal, and opposite in sign, to "normal" net capital flows.[1]

During the 1999–2002 period, before there was any expectation of a currency appreciation, China ran an average capital-account surplus equal to 1.5 percent of GDP. Take this as our measure of normal net capital flows.

Next, define the "underlying" current account as the actual current-account position, adjusted for both cyclical movements that make the demand for imports unusually high or low, and the lagged trade-balance effects of recent exchange rate changes.

China's 2005 current-account surplus will probably be in the neighborhood of 7 to 9 percent of GDP. The underlying current-account surplus should be somewhat lower — say 5 to 7 percent of GDP — because (buoyant GDP growth rate notwithstanding) domestic demand growth has slowed and in 2005 the RMB has appreciated in real trade-weighted terms.

If China's underlying current-account surplus is now in the range of 5 to 7 percent of GDP, while what is required to offset normal capital flows is an underlying current-account deficit equal to 1.5 percent of GDP,

---

[1] Goldstein (2004) provides fuller discussion of this approach. There could be cases where some increase in reserves was desirable, or where only some share of the external imbalance was to be eliminated within a given time period. Nevertheless, the basic premise is that a large discrepancy between normal capital flows and the underlying current-account position signifies a misalignment of the real equilibrium exchange rate.

then China's current account needs to deteriorate by a whopping 6.5 to 8.5 percent of GDP to restore (strict) balance-of-payments equilibrium. If one does a set of simulations with a small trade model to calculate what size real, effective appreciation of the RMB would be necessary to produce such a large turnaround in the current account — taking into account the high import content of China's exports, using a plausible range for price elasticities of demand and supply, and making alternative assumptions about the second-round effects of income changes on the demand for imports — the answers congregate in the upper part of the 20 to 40 percent range. This is somewhat larger than the estimated undervaluation for 2003–2004.[2]

We would not want to go to the stake for the precision of our estimates of RMB undervaluation: after all, there is uncertainty about the underlying parameters, other methodologies yield somewhat different estimates, and China is in the midst of a nontrivial revision of its GDP accounts. Still, with huge reserve accumulation in each of the past three years; with persistent surpluses on both the current and capital accounts; with the real, trade-weighted RMB showing a cumulative depreciation since the dollar peak in February 2002; with the Chinese economy running at full steam, or close to it, for most of the past three years; and with Asian currency appreciation needed to reduce the excessively large U.S. current-account deficit, we submit that it is difficult to arrive at a credible estimate that shows anything but a sizeable undervaluation for the RMB.[3]

PROBLEMS WITH THE CURRENT REGIME

China's current exchange rate regime has created problems for China and the global economy.

First, the (de facto) fixed-dollar exchange rate limits the independence of China's monetary policy and has contributed, thereby, to the pronounced macroeconomic fluctuations of recent years. In 2003–2004, when investment was booming and the rate of price inflation was accelerating, the central bank

---

[2] Goldstein (2004) and Lardy (2005). To estimate the undervaluation of the RMB with respect to individual currencies, one needs a multi-country model. William R. Cline (2005) does such an exercise and estimates that as of November 2005, the RMB was undervalued with respect to the U.S. dollar by 43 percent.

[3] Taking a broad view of the evidence across several methodologies, it looks to us like the RMB is undervalued in real, trade-weighted terms by 20 to 35 percent.

was reluctant to raise domestic lending rates, in part because it feared that, despite controls, higher rates would attract capital inflows. As a result, the real rate of interest to corporate borrowers (proxied by the one-year bank-lending rate minus the change in the corporate goods price index), fell from 8 percent in 2002-Q3 on the eve of the investment boom to negative 4 percent during April through September 2004; that, in turn, contributed to an excess demand for loans.

Second, China's undervalued currency has contributed to growing trade surpluses and, at least in some years, to very large portfolio capital inflows, which appear motivated by an expectation of appreciation. Mammoth exchange market intervention, amounting to 11, 12, and 14 percent of GDP in 2003, 2004, and the first half of 2005, respectively, has been necessary to prevent currency appreciation.

The central bank sterilized much of this reserve accumulation through increases in reserve requirements and open market operations. Since mid-2004, the central bank also used administrative controls to limit bank credit creation. This approach is costly in several respects. There have been episodes when the barn door was locked only after the horses had left. In 2003 and the first half of 2004, there was a bank credit blowout, with the ratio of the increase in bank credit to GDP hitting an all-time high. This led to an investment boom, with long-term consequences for excess capacity in a number of sectors, for downward pressure on operating margins in these sectors, and potentially for nonperforming loans in banks that lent heavily to support such projects. In 2005 we again witnessed a substantial buildup of bank liquidity, reflected in growing excess reserves and declining money market rates.

Increased use of administrative controls on lending is inconsistent with the government's long-term policy of requiring state-owned banks to operate on commercial principles. When the central bank specifies lending ceilings and sectoral lending priorities, the development of a credit culture is slowed. And when money market interest rates are depressed by excess liquidity, bank profitability suffers, since banks are net lenders in the money market.

Third, a highly undervalued RMB encourages excess investment in tradable goods. Eventually, the real exchange rate will appreciate and will lower profitability in tradable goods industries, again with adverse implications for banks.

Fourth, China is accumulating a large exposure to potential capital losses. China's foreign exchange reserves will, at year-end 2005, be in the neighborhood of 40 percent of GDP. A 20-percent revaluation of the RMB against the major reserve currencies would impose a capital loss equivalent to 8 percent of GDP.

Finally, China's prolonged, large scale, one-way intervention in the foreign exchange market — along with its large and growing global current account surplus — fuels protectionist pressure in the United States and elsewhere. One reflection is the Schumer-Graham bill in the U.S. Senate, which could lead to a uniform 27.5 percent tariff on all Chinese imports. Another is the ill-considered congressional action subjecting a potential China National Offshore Oil Corporation (CNOOC) purchase of Unocal to a special congressional review. Since over half of China's exports go to the United States, Euroland, and Japan, and since China has a long-term interest in investing abroad, such protectionist threats ought not be taken lightly.

In sum, the costs to China of maintaining an undervalued currency are already significant and are likely to rise over time. Moreover, unlike some others (e.g., Michael Dooley *et al.*, 2004), we do not see the growth and employment benefits of an undervalued RMB as exceeding its costs (Goldstein, 2006; Goldstein and Lardy, 2005).

China's inflexible currency regime and its undervalued RMB also handicap the adjustment of global imbalances and increase the risk of a hard landing for the dollar and the U.S. economy, with adverse global spillovers.

The U.S. current-account deficit is now running at about 6.5 percent of GDP — an all-time high. If the U.S. current-account deficit is not reduced, U.S. net foreign debt relative to GDP will rise to a worrisome level and U.S. assets will eventually lose their attractiveness relative to alternative investment opportunities — resulting in some combination of a fall in capital flows to the United States, higher interest rates on U.S. liabilities, and a decline in the dollar. If these adjustments were large and disorderly, they would depress U.S. growth significantly, with adverse spillovers for U.S. trading partners.

As Michael Mussa (2005) has emphasized, the inevitable correction of the U.S. external imbalance will necessarily involve a depreciation of the dollar against most currencies, and domestic demand growing more slowly (faster) than domestic output in the United States (rest of the world). The first channel is the expenditure-switching channel, while the second is the expenditure-changing channel. Both are needed. That is why both a more ambitious program of fiscal consolidation and a tightening of U.S. monetary conditions are essential — along with policies that stimulate domestic demand growth in major U.S. trading partners.

The real, trade-weighted U.S. dollar needs to fall by an additional 15 to 25 percent from its current level to support external adjustment. The currencies of Japan, China, and the rest of emerging Asia have a combined weight of roughly 40 percent in the Federal Reserve's dollar index. If the Asian currencies do not participate, either the overall depreciation of the dollar will be too small or the appreciation burden will fall too heavily on economies where a further, large appreciation would not be warranted. In the wave of dollar depreciation starting in February 2002, the euro, the Canadian dollar, and the Australian dollar, among other market-determined currencies, experienced strong, real appreciation, whereas the Asian currencies — with the notable exceptions of the Korean won and Indonesian rupiah — did not.

China remains a prime candidate for leading wider Asian currency appreciation because of its large external imbalance and because the RMB's behavior can influence — for better or worse — the attitude that other Asian economies have toward pressures for appreciation in their own currencies.[4] In this sense, it is important that China be part of the international solution to the adjustment of large external imbalances — and not part of the problem.

POLICY CONSTRAINTS AND A COMPROMISE SOLUTION

China's willingness and ability to deal with the shortcomings in the current exchange rate regime are heavily constrained by at least three important factors.

First, China's banking system, although improving, remains fragile. Households, which have bank deposits equivalent to almost 100 percent of GDP, have had little opportunity to diversify the currency composition of their financial assets and could be susceptible to capital flight if they thought risks of repayment had worsened. Thus, any adjustment of China's exchange rate regime will have to maintain most existing capital controls until the domestic banks are further strengthened.

Second, the degree of undervaluation of the RMB is now so large that it would take a long time to correct if it were done in a series of small steps.

---

[4] In contrast, Barry Eichengreen (2004) has argued that other Asian currencies would not necessarily follow the RMB upward if China revalued.

But this is apt to exhaust the patience of the international community. Also, the greater the expectation that each RMB appreciation will be followed by another, the larger is the scale of capital inflows and the larger the sterilization problem.

And third, China's current leadership, even more than its predecessor, appears to prefer an incremental approach to dealing with the current exchange rate dilemma. They highly value growth and stability. They worry that letting market forces freely determine the exchange rate could result in too much RMB appreciation, slowing exports, employment, and growth and, thereby, contribute to increased social instability.

How then to square the circle? Absent the aforementioned constraints, the policy solution would be straightforward: China could simultaneously and immediately remove the restrictions on capital flows and let the market determine the value of the RMB. The constraints mean the search is for second-best policy options.

All things considered, we believe the preferred course of action is a compromise along the following lines.[5] China would make a credible down payment on removing the large undervaluation of the RMB by immediately revaluing it by 10 to 15 percent, relative to the currency basket; it would widen the band to 5 to 7 percent on each side of the new parity; it would simultaneously implement fiscal expansion; and it would leave in place most capital controls. The 10- to 15-percent revaluation of the RMB would help to reduce China's very large current-account surplus and should persuade those in the U.S. Congress, and in other G-7 legislatures, that China was finally getting serious about controlling its growing external imbalance. A 10- to 15-percent revaluation would be a much more tangible sign of progress than the meager 2.5-percent revaluation registered thus far.

A significant widening of the band would give China some increased independence for monetary policy, would allow scope for some further appreciation of the RMB, and would give China some practical experience in managed increased flexibility. It would also give some substance to China's repeated claim that "market supply and demand" would increasingly determine the RMB's value.

---

[5]This is close to our original formulation of the "two-stage" approach to China's currency reform (Goldstein and Lardy, 2003).

Fiscal expansion is needed to offset some of the contractionary effects of the RMB revaluation. The fiscal expansion needs to be expenditure-based, because direct tax receipts in China — like the agricultural tax and the income tax — are currently far too small to provide a meaningful boost from a tax reduction. Increased government expenditures should strengthen the social safety net because one of the main factors behind China's very high household savings rate is precautionary savings against potentially high out-of-pocket expenses for health care, education, and retirement.[6]

Keeping in place the bulk of existing controls on capital flows is a prudent measure against potential capital flight, should there be bad news about the state of the still-fragile banking system.

True, this would leave a sizeable, real appreciation of the RMB to be carried out later, over, say, the next two years, with all the expectations-cum-capital flow problems that such a phased adjustment entails. Indeed, that is why we pushed for China to remove, in one step, the undervaluation in 2003–2004.[7] But that window of opportunity has passed — now that the undervaluation of the RMB is larger and domestic demand growth has slowed. While speculative inflows have recently declined from the record pace of 2003–2004, one cannot be confident that they would not revive; in such a case, the authorities would need to choose between an acceleration of the RMB appreciation and a temporary recourse to tighter controls on capital inflow.

In the final stage of currency reform — when China's banking system is on firmer footing — China would float the RMB and remove the remaining controls on capital flows. Appropriate sequencing of capital-account liberalization would prevent currency reform from undermining the continued strengthening of the banking system.

Admittedly, this is not such an elegant plan. But if it avoids the international train wreck that would otherwise take place, it merits consideration.

Morris Goldstein and Nicholas Lardy, "China's Exchange Rate Policy Dilemma," *American Economic Review*, Vol 96, No. 2, pp. 422–426, 2006. Used with permission of the publisher.

---

[6] Olivier J. Blanchard and Francesco Giavazzi (2005).
[7] Goldstein and Lardy (2004).

REFERENCES

Blanchard, Olivier J. and Giavazzi, Francesco. "Rebalancing Growth in China: A Three-Handed Approach." Massachusetts Institute of Technology, MIT Department of Economics Working Paper: No. 05–32, 2005.

Cline, William R. "The Case for a New Plaza Agreement." Institute for International Economics, HE Policy Brief: No. PB05–4, 2005.

Dooley, Michael P.; Folkerts-Landau, David and Garber, Peter. "The Revived Bretton Woods System." *International Journal of Finance and Economics*, 2004, 9(4), pp. 307–13.

Eichengreen, Barry. "Chinese Currency Controversies." Center for Economic Policy Research, CEPR Discussion Papers: No. 4375, 2004.

Goldstein, Morris. "Adjusting China's Exchange Rate Policies." Institute for International Economics, IIE Working Paper: No. 04–1, 2004.

Goldstein, Morris. "RMB Controversies." *Cato Journal*, 2006, 26(2).

Goldstein, Morris and Lardy, Nicholas R. "China's Role in the Revived Bretton Woods System: A Case of Mistaken Identity." Institute for International Economics, IIE Working Paper: No. 05–2, 2005.

Goldstein, Morris and Lardy, Nicholas R. "Two-Stage Currency Reform for China," *Asian Wall Street Journal*. September 12, 2003.

Lardy, Nicholas R. "Exchange Rate and Monetary Policy in China." *Cato Journal*, 2005, 25(1), pp. 41–47.

Mussa, Michael. "Sustaining Global Growth While Reducing External Imbalances," in C. Fred Bergsten, ed., *The United States and the world economy: Foreign economic policy for the next decade*. Washington, DC: Institute for International Economics, 2005.

Chapter 21

Challenges Facing the Chinese Authorities under the Existing Currency Regime

Morris Goldstein and Nicholas Lardy

An equilibrium exchange rate for the renminbi can be measured in a number of ways. It could be the exchange rate that produces a "balance" in China's global current account position (i.e., in the sum of trade transactions, investment income, and transfers). It could be the exchange rate that produces a "balance" in its basic balance of payments (i.e., the sum of the current account and long-term capital flows). Or it could be the exchange rate that results in a balance

---

Morris Goldstein, Dennis Weatherstone Senior Fellow since 1994, has held several senior staff positions at the International Monetary Fund (1970-94), including deputy director of its research department (1987-94). He is a member of the Council on Foreign Relations, the Bellagio Group, and the Pew Task Force on Financial Regulatory Reform. He received his BA from Rutgers University in 1966 and PhD from New York University in 1971, both in economics.

Nicholas R. Lardy has been a senior fellow at the Peterson Institute since 2003. He was a senior fellow in the Foreign Policy Studies Program at the Brookings Institution from 1995 to 2003. He was the director of the Henry M. Jackson School of International Studies at the University of Washington from 1991 to 1995. From 1997 through the spring of 2000, he was the Frederick Frank Adjunct Professor of International Trade and Finance at the Yale University School of Management.

in China's overall balance of payments position (i.e., the sum of the current and capital accounts).

By any of these three metrics the renminbi is significantly undervalued and probably by an increasing margin at least through the end of 2007. As we noted in the introduction, an increasingly undervalued exchange rate, a rapidly expanding current account surplus, and the concomitant accelerating buildup of foreign exchange reserves pose several economic challenges for the Chinese authorities. In this chapter, we discuss those challenges for the independence of monetary policy, the rebalancing of the sources of economic growth, the continuing efforts to reform China's banking system, and China's external adjustment and its contribution to correcting global payments imbalances.

INDEPENDENCE OF MONETARY POLICY

A fixed exchange rate regime typically imposes a substantial constraint on a country's monetary policy for the simple reason that if domestic interest rates diverge too much from foreign rates, the country could be subject to destabilizing capital flows. This is particularly likely for small countries that are price takers in international goods and capital markets. Capital controls, in theory, could prevent large inflows (outflows) when domestic interest rates are higher (lower) than foreign rates, but in practice it is difficult to maintain effective controls over time, particularly in an economy that is very open to trade.

Even when controls are effective in limiting capital inflows or outflows, a country with an undervalued exchange rate and thus a large current account surplus will face the challenge of sterilizing the incipient increase in the domestic money supply that results from the large-scale purchase of foreign exchange (i.e., the sale of domestic currency). Otherwise, the growth of liquidity in the banking and financial system leads eventually to inflation and an appreciation of the real exchange rate. Even when sterilization is used successfully to control the growth of domestic liquidity, the authorities need to sell greater quantities of sterilization bonds (reflecting the increasingly undervalued nature of the currency). This, in turn, eventually causes an increase in the interest rate the central bank must pay on these bonds. Eventually, that interest could exceed the earnings from the bank's holdings of interest-bearing foreign currency-denominated financial assets, imposing a substantial financial constraint on sterilization operations.

Views on the extent to which China's exercise of monetary policy is handicapped by its undervalued exchange rate vary widely. One school of thought is that China differs substantially from the small open economy model in which a fixed exchange rate means that a country's monetary policy is determined abroad. According to Jonathan Anderson (2004), "China can run an independent monetary policy under any renminbi regime." He believes China's capital controls are relatively effective and that sterilization, implemented mainly via the sale of central bank bills and increases in the required reserve ratio for banks, has been successful and can be maintained indefinitely. Thus, increases in China's international reserves — whether generated by a growing current account surplus, by the capital account (motivated variously in different periods by the expectation of currency appreciation, rising Shanghai property prices, or a booming domestic stock market), or by errors and omissions in the balance of payments — "have had virtually no impact on domestic liquidity conditions" (Anderson 2006a, 19).

Stephen Green of Standard Chartered Bank holds a similar view. He has carefully tracked the sterilization operations of the People's Bank of China and has shown that even in the first half of 2007, when inward capital flows through various channels increased dramatically, the central bank had little difficulty retaining control of the growth of the domestic money supply (Green 2007a, 2007b).

The alternative school of thought is that China's (quasi) fixed exchange rate already has diminished the effectiveness of monetary policy and that this erosion is likely to continue. Thus, increased currency flexibility is needed to reduce the risks of macroeconomic instability, whether of domestic or external origin (Goldstein and Lardy 2006b; Lardy 2006; Prasad, Rumbaugh, and Wang 2005; Prasad 2008; Yu Yongding 2007b). There are several strands to this argument.

First, central bank control of the growth of monetary aggregates in some periods has depended on the imposition of quotas on the amount of loans banks could make and on various types of "window guidance" on bank lending, rather than on the use of interest rates. These much blunter instruments, rather than market signals, may lead to a much less efficient allocation of credit (Goldstein and Lardy 2004, 7–8; Goodfriend and Prasad 2006, 24). Moreover, this alternative school of thought believes that the resultant policy mix left China with an interest rate structure that was far from optimum.

On the lending side, real interest rates were unusually low for a rapidly growing economy. For example, in late December 2007 the central bank adjusted upward the one year benchmark bank lending rate to 7.47 percent. But inflation, as measured by the corporate goods price index, averaged 9.3 percent in the first quarter of 2008, making the real lending rate −1.8 percent in an economy expanding at more than 10 percent in real terms.[1] A low or, as in early 2008, a significantly negative real lending rate contributed to an underlying excess demand for credit. As a result, in 2008 the authorities were forced to resort to credit quotas to control the growth of lending from the banking system.

From the point of view of savers, deposit rates were also quite low. In 2008 the central bank fixed the ceiling that banks could pay on demand deposits at only 0.72 percent and on one-year deposits at 3.33 percent.[2] But headline consumer price index (CPI) inflation of 7.9 percent inflation in the first half of the year and a 5 percent tax on interest income (reduced from the previous 20 percent rate in late July 2007) meant that the real, after-tax return on demand deposits was −7.22 percent and on one-year deposits −4.74 percent. Low or negative real returns on bank savings may have been a major factor contributing to the boom in the residential property market, as a growing share of housing was sold to "investors" rather than owner-occupiers. The authorities responded in September 2007 by doubling to 40 percent the required downpayment for an individual taking out a mortgage for the purchase of a second or third property.[3]

The more than fivefold increase in equity prices on the Shanghai stock exchange between July 2005 and October 2007 also may have been fueled in part by negative returns on demand deposits. Before the inevitable equity market correction began after mid-October, companies listed domestically were trading at a relatively lofty 38 times estimated 2007 earnings. Even more problematic, half of the earnings growth of companies in the first six months

---

[1] The corporate goods price index is a more relevant indicator of inflation for firms than the CPI, in which food has a weight of about one-third.
[2] On October 8, 2008, the central bank announced adjustments that reduced the rate on one-year deposits to 3.15 percent, effective October 15.
[3] The downpayment requirement was raised to 30 percent for all mortgages financing properties exceeding 90 square meters but remained at 20 percent for owner-occupied properties under 90 square meters (People's Bank of China and China Banking Regulatory Commission 2007).

of 2007 reportedly came not from company core operations but from profits from stock trading (Anderlini 2007).

In short, while the level of real interest rates in China can move significantly with large changes in the inflation rate and, albeit less so, with occasional changes in administered nominal interest rates (as, for example, in the second half of 2008), China is still a prototypical example of the general pattern that low exchange rates require low interest rates (Eichengreen 2004b). As in other countries maintaining an undervalued exchange rate, the Chinese authorities frequently have been slow to raise the general level of interest rates for fear of attracting higher levels of capital inflows that could prove more challenging to sterilize. But one consequence is periodic real estate and stock market booms that heighten financial risk.

A second strand to the argument that increased exchange rate flexibility would enhance the effectiveness of monetary policy concerns the hidden costs and risks in the central bank's successful sterilization of the increase in the domestic money supply associated with the buildup of foreign exchange reserves. These include the risk of a capital loss on dollar assets in the event of eventual appreciation of the renminbi (Goldstein and Lardy 2006b; Dunaway 2009, 11).

Equally important, the sustained large-scale sale of low-yielding central bank bills and the repeated increases in required reserves both hinder the transition of China's banks to operation on a fully commercial basis (Yu Yongding 2007a, 18). In 2003, the central bank, having sold all of its holdings of treasury bonds, began to issue bills to sterilize increases in the domestic money supply associated with its foreign exchange operations. By the end of June 2008, total outstanding central bank bills held by banks reached RMB4.24 trillion (People's Bank of China, Monetary Policy Analysis Small Group 2008,11). From mid-2003 through June 2008, the central bank also raised the required reserve ratio for banks by 50 or 100 basis points on 21 occasions, increasing the ratio from 6 percent of deposits to 17.5 percent. This increase compelled banks to deposit with the central bank RMB5.2 trillion more than if the required reserve ratio had remained at 6 percent.[4]

---

[4] The increase in required reserves over this period was 11.5 percentage points. Total renminbi deposits at the end of June 2008 were RMB44.02 trillion (People's Bank of China 2008).

These changes imposed a substantial tax on banks. The average yield on central bank bills at end-March 2008 was only about 4 percent and the central bank pays only 1.89 percent on required reserves, a rate that has remained unchanged since it was fixed in February 2002. From the perspective of the banks, the alternative use of these funds would be to finance additional loans. Because the benchmark interest rate on a one-year loan, the most common term, at mid-2008 was 7.47 percent and the actual average interest rate on a one-year loan was 8.47 percent, the RMB9 trillion increase in bank holdings of these low-yielding central bank bills and required reserves represented a huge implicit tax on Chinese banks, well in excess of RMB400 billion in 2008.[5] Indeed, the estimated implicit tax on the banking system that stems from the massive sterilization campaign required to tightly control and limit the pace of appreciation of the renminbi approached the after-tax profits of the entire Chinese banking system in 2007.[6]

However, offsetting this large implicit tax is the banks' access to cheap deposits. As noted above, the central bank prohibits banks from competing for deposits by maintaining ceilings on the rates that banks may pay on deposits of various maturities.[7] These nominal interest rates are generally low and, in periods of inflation, are adjusted upward by less than the increase in the price level. Thus, in effect, in periods of inflation households are particularly heavily taxed (we discuss this in some detail in the next section). The key point is that between 2002, when the CPI fell by 0.8 percent, and the first half of 2008, when it rose by 7.9 percent, the implicit tax imposed on households by the decline in the real interest rate on their bank savings deposits was RMB690 billion.[8]

---

[5] Abstracting from the issue of risk and assuming holdings of these two categories of assets by the banks at mid-year 2008 is equal to the average holding of these assets during the year, the implicit tax on the banking sector can be estimated as RMB4 trillion times 3.47 percent (the difference between the 7.47 percent benchmark lending rate and the 4 percent interest banks receive on central bank bills) plus RMB5 trillion times 5.58 percent (the benchmark lending rate minus the 1.89 percent interest banks receive on required reserves), or RMB418 billion.

[6] The after-tax profits of the entire Chinese banking system in 2007 were RMB446.7 billion (China Banking Regulatory Commission 2008, 31).

[7] Banks may offer demand as well as term deposits of three months, six months, one year, two years, three years, and five years. The central bank sets a separate ceiling rate that banks may pay on demand deposits and for each maturity of term deposits.

[8] This tax fell by the second half of the year because CPI inflation fell by more than the reduction in the interest rate paid on demand deposits. The tax, however, remained significant since for

Last but not least, it is one thing to argue that sterilization operations can be continued indefinitely because the interest rate on China's reserve assets exceeds that on its sterilization bills. It is another thing entirely to argue that sterilization can be continued indefinitely while simultaneously reducing China's large external surplus. Large-scale sterilization blocks the monetary, interest rate, and relative-price mechanisms that would otherwise operate (via their effects on the savings-investment balance and on net capital flows) to reduce China's external imbalance. Michael Mussa (2008), for example, argues that when large-scale sterilization produces a negative growth rate in the net domestic assets of the People's Bank of China while the demand for base money is growing briskly, that demand will be satisfied solely through an increase in the net foreign assets of the central bank — and this is of course equivalent to an increase in international reserves.[9] In short, China can either continue its large-scale intervention and sterilization operations or significantly reduce its large external surplus. It cannot do both.

There is no definitive method to measure which of the two views on the independence of monetary policy is correct. It appears to be a matter of judgment. Supporters of the status quo point to studies showing that capital controls provide some degree of independence to China's monetary authority (Ma and McCauley 2007). And they are not persuaded that the resulting interest rate structure leads to excess investment. Despite China's uniquely high rate of capital formation in recent years, some studies show no evidence of a decline in the rate of return to capital (Bai, Hsieh, and Qian 2006). Some go even further, arguing that financial repression is positive since it allows the low-cost bank financing of infrastructure and other strategic public investments that underpin China's economic expansion (Keidel 2007).

In contrast, those who believe China should allow greater exchange rate flexibility acknowledge that sterilization so far has limited the usual inflation and credit growth consequences of large and rapid reserve accumulation but emphasize the negative aspects of the resulting financial repression. Low interest rates associated with financial repression contribute to growing risks

---

the year as a whole CPI inflation was 5.9 percent and in November 2008 the rate Paid on demand deposits was cut to 0.36 percent.

[9] For further elaboration of "monetary approach" to the recent evolution of China's balance of payments, see the discussion later in this section on alternative explanations for the post- 2003 surge in China's net exports.

in property and stock markets and subsidize capital-intensive industries with adverse effects on the environment and the pace of job creation. They also note that although the rate of return on capital through the middle of the decade may have been high, this does not necessarily refute the charge that the rate of investment in China has been excessive. The years 2002–07 were an extraordinary boom era, the only five-year period in the reform era in which China's growth was continuously 10 percent or more and higher in each successive year; but the appropriate measure of the return on capital is not limited to periods of high and accelerating growth, when profits are invariably high, but over an entire business cycle, including both up and down years. Finally, as we discuss below, an insufficiently flexible exchange rate and the resulting financial repression make it more difficult for China to transition to more balanced and sustainable growth.

REBALANCING ECONOMIC GROWTH

Since late 2008, China's top political leadership has embraced the goal of rebalancing the sources of domestic economic growth. They envision transitioning to a growth path that relies more on expanding domestic consumption and less on burgeoning investment and a growing trade surplus (Lardy 2006). Expanding personal consumption is consistent with President Hu Jintao's emphasis on creating a "harmonious society" and a "new socialist countryside" as well as on reducing the pace of growth of energy consumption (associated strongly with investment spending), thus curtailing emissions of greenhouse gases and sulfur dioxide.

Successful rebalancing of the sources of economic growth, away from investment and exports and toward consumption, would also be reflected in changes in the structure of output. Since investment goods, such as machinery and equipment, are produced in the industrial sector, a smaller role for investment in generating economic growth would imply that the share of GDP originating in the manufacturing sector would decrease. Similarly, since almost all of China's exports are manufactured goods, less reliance on the expansion of net exports would also imply that over time the share of GDP originating in the manufacturing sector would decrease.[10] And since services

---

[10] In 2007, 95 percent of China's exports were manufactured goods (National Bureau of Statistics of China 2008a, 164).

account for about a third of personal consumption outlays, an increasing role for consumption in generating economic growth would suggest that the share of GDP originating in the services sector would increase over time as compared with an investment- and export-driven growth path.[11]

China could use numerous policy instruments to promote domestic consumption demand as a source of economic growth. We focus on four domains: fiscal, financial, exchange rate, and price policy.

Fiscal policy options include cutting personal taxes, increasing government consumption expenditures (i.e., outlays for health, education, welfare, and pensions), and introducing a dividend tax on state-owned companies. Cutting personal taxes would raise household disposable income and thus, for any given household saving rate, increase consumption expenditures as well. Increasing government consumption expenditures would both raise consumption demand directly and, by reducing household precautionary demand for savings, lead indirectly to greater private consumption expenditure. A dividend tax would reduce corporate saving and investment, thus reducing the national rate of investment, and would provide additional budgetary revenues to increase government outlays on social programs.

Financial reform would reduce financial repression in China by paying higher real deposit rates to savers, thus increasing household income and consumption as a share of GDP. Throughout the reform period the authorities have controlled interest rates in a manner that has led to a relatively low average real rate of return on household bank savings (Lardy 1998, 10). In effect depositors have been taxed so that borrowers, traditionally mostly state-owned firms, would have access to cheap credit. And the authorities have adjusted interest rates on bank deposits relatively slowly so that when consumer price inflation picks up the real rate of return (the nominal interest rate minus inflation) on savings falls.[12] The result is that household interest earnings are far less than they would be in a more liberalized financial environment where market forces play a greater role in determining interest rates. Since interest income is an important source of household income in China, financial

---

[11]The estimate of the services share of household consumption expenditures is based on urban and rural household surveys conducted annually by the National Bureau of Statistics China.
[12]Exceptions to this pattern occurred in the late 1980s and again from mid-1993 through mid-1996 when the authorities indexed the interest rates for some types of savings deposits to the rate of inflation. See Lardy (1998, 106–15) for details.

repression means that the growth of household income has been less than that of a more liberalized financial environment.

Appreciation of the renminbi could contribute to China's desired transition to a more consumption-driven growth path in two ways. First, currency appreciation would reduce the growth of exports and increase the growth of imports, reducing China's external surplus.[13] Second, as already discussed, a more flexible exchange rate policy in the short run would allow the central bank greater flexibility in setting domestic interest rates and would also pave the way for the introduction of more market-determined interest rates. These developments could lead to lending rates that are higher in real terms than in recent years, reduce China's extraordinarily high rate of investment, and thus contribute to the leadership goal of reducing China's dependence on investment as a source of economic growth. Greater interest rate flexibility would also allow the central bank to mitigate macroeconomic cycles by raising lending rates to moderate investment booms, thus reducing the cyclicality of economic growth.

Price reform offers a fourth policy arena for rebalancing economic growth. Land, energy, water, and utilities are not priced in accordance with relative scarcities and the environment (He and Kuijs 2007). These inputs are more important for manufacturing than for services so more appropriate pricing, as well as enforcement of environmental standards, would reduce investment in manufacturing, particularly the most energy-intensive industries, and increase investment in services. Appropriate pricing at a minimum means full cost recovery; more ambitiously it would mean marginal opportunity cost pricing — including the cost of environmental damage in both production and consumption as well as the opportunity cost of resource depletion (World Bank 2007b).

CHINESE POLICIES FOR PROMOTING CONSUMPTION: THE RECORD TO DATE

In the fiscal arena, the government has adopted a number of tax and expenditure policies to promote consumption. The authorities reduced the agricultural tax significantly in both 2004 and 2005 and eliminated it entirely

---

[13] See the discussion later in this chapter on the effectiveness of renminbi appreciation.

by 2007.[14] The monthly income level exempt from the personal income tax on wages was doubled from RMB800 to RMB1,600 in 2006 and then raised again to RMB2,000 in 2008. The authorities cut the tax on interest income households earn on savings deposits by three-quarters, from 20 to 5 percent, in August 2007 and then abolished it entirely in October 2008. These cuts together raised household disposable income by about 1 percent of GDP per year above the level it would otherwise have attained, contributing modestly to higher levels of household consumption than would otherwise have been achieved (Bergsten et al. 2008,121).

The government also began to collect dividends from some state-owned companies in 2007, but the number of firms required to pay was so small and the rates so modest that the dividends scheduled for collection were only RMB17 billion, a trivial 0.07 percent of GDP. Moreover, the introduction of the dividend tax coincided with a reduction in the general corporate income tax rate. Domestic firms had long complained that they faced a tax burden of 33 percent while foreign firms and joint ventures enjoyed a preferential rate of only 15 percent. After years of debate the government decided to unify the rate paid by both types of firms at 25 percent. This reform reduced the corporate taxes paid by domestic firms in 2007 by RMB134 billion, an amount almost eight times the dividend tax imposed on some state-owned firms. The net result is that retained earnings of the corporate sector continued to expand in 2007. Thus the cumulative effect of tax reform in 2007 was to increase corporate retained earnings and thus corporate savings and investment, the opposite of what is needed to rebalance China's sources of economic growth. Unfortunately, this situation changed little in 2008 when the dividend tax was slated to rise to about RMB30 billion, a trivial 0.1 percent of GDP (Wang Ting 2008).

On the other hand, the increase in government expenditures on social Programs has been far more robust (Table 1). Combined fiscal outlays in 2008 on education, health, and social security and employment were

---

[14]The revenue category "agricultural and related taxes" includes six specific taxes: agricultural tax, livestock tax, farmland occupancy tax, tax on special agricultural products, deed tax, and tobacco leaf tax. The reforms of 2004–06 eliminated the agricultural tax, the livestock tax, and the tax, on special agricultural products, but the government continues to collect the other three taxes.

Table 1: Government Social Expenditures, 2002–08 (Billions of Renminbi)

Year	Education	Health	Social Security and Employment	Total
2002	300.6	66.3	268.9	635.8
2003	335.2	83.1	271.2	689.5
2004	385.4	93.6	318.6	797.6
2005	452.8	113.3	378.7	944.7
2006	546.4	142.1	439.4	1,128.0
2007	712.2	199.0	544.7	1,455.9
2008	893.8	272.2	677.0	1,843.0

Sources: Xinhua News Agency (2008); National Bureau of Statistics of China (2008b, 264); Ministry of Finance (2009).

RMB1,843 billion, well over twice the level of 2004. The growth of social expenditures increased sharply in 2007 and 2008. Thus two-thirds of the increase in these outlays between 2004 and 2008 came in 2007–08. That suggests that, after a somewhat slow start in 2005 and 2006, the government is now rapidly rebuilding the social safety net, which had frayed dramatically in the 1990s as the government drastically restructured state-owned firms and many workers lost access to company-provided social services.

In rural areas the most impressive gain has been the expansion of a new rural cooperative medical system, first introduced in some localities on a trial basis in 2003. This voluntary health insurance program, financed by contributions from individuals, local governments, and the central government, provides partial reimbursement of health care costs (about 30 percent for inpatient care) (World Bank 2008, 89). Central government outlays on this program rose to RMB11.4 billion by 2007, a twenty-fold increase compared with 2005, raising the number of rural residents covered by the program to 730 million by 2007, quadruple the number covered in 2005. By 2007 the program was available in 86 percent of China's county-level administrative units, a sevenfold increase compared with 2004 (Bergsten et al. 2008, 122). In addition to this initiative to improve rural health conditions, the government in 2006 and 2007 eliminated tuition and miscellaneous school fees for 150 million rural primary school students.

In urban areas the number of workers covered by basic retirement, health, unemployment, workers compensation, and maternity insurance in 2008 expanded by 35, 122, 17, 101, and 109 percent, respectively, compared with 2004 (National Bureau of Statistics of China 2008b, 896; 2009). These impressive increases resulted in a substantial rise in the share of urban workers covered by these programs — for example, the share covered by the basic health program doubled from about a third to two-thirds.

The government unveiled a further commitment to provide health care in early 2009 (Chinese Communist Party Central Committee and State Council 2009, State Council 2009). This initiative, which will cost RMB850 billion over three years (2009–11), is designed to provide health insurance to an additional 400 million Chinese, bringing coverage to 90 percent of the population by 2011. Funding will also be provided to build 34,000 health clinics in towns and townships and 2,000 new hospitals in county-level administrative units. Per capita government contributions to the rural cooperative medical insurance scheme are to rise to RMB120 by 2010 compared with RMB80 in 2008 and RMB40 in 2007. Thus presumably the share of total costs of inpatient treatment that will be reimbursed will rise. The net result of this initiative is that the government will directly pay for half or more of all health outlays, up substantially from only 16 percent in 2001.

In addition to accelerating the rebuilding of the social safety net, the government is rapidly increasing transfer payments in both pensions and programs to support low-income households. For example, the State Council in August 2007 approved a three-year program to substantially increase old age pensions to those workers retired from enterprises; monthly pension payments, which averaged RMB963 in 2007, were raised to RMB1,063 beginning in January 2008 and to RMB1,173 in January 2009.[15] The cumulative increase of 22 percent was twice that of consumer prices in 2007–08.

Another example of growing transfer payments is the government's minimum living standard guarantee program, which began in urban areas in the mid-1990s with the provision of a guaranteed minimum income to fewer than a million people. By the early 2000s the program had expanded to cover more than 20 million urban residents, and then it further expanded in two dimensions. First, the average monthly subsidy to eligible urban residents

---

[15] "This Year Basic Old Age Pension Payments Are Planned to Rise by RMB110," http://finance.sina.com.cn (accessed on November 18, 2008).

increased dramatically, from about RMB50 in 2002 to RMB140 by 2008. Second, the program was extended to rural areas and grew rapidly to cover more than 40 million individuals by 2008. As a result annual expenditures on this program in urban and rural areas rose to RMB60 billion in 2008, a vast increase compared with only RMB3.45 billion in 2000 (Ministry of Civil Affairs 2008, 8–10; 2009, 3).

The record is less encouraging in the financial arena. The government has discussed but not yet adopted financial and banking reforms to support the transition to consumption-led growth. From the perspective of households the financial system in recent years has become more — not less — repressive, a development that is evident in the decline in the real rate of interest that banks pay households on their savings deposits. We measure the decline from 2002 for two reasons. First, the central bank set the rate that banks can pay on demand deposits in February 2002 and left it in place until November 2008. Second, the real rate of interest on bank savings deposits in 2002 was positive when measured in real terms; for example, the demand deposit rate was 0.72 percent while the consumer price index declined 0.8 percent in 2002, making the real rate of interest on demand deposits 1.52 percent.

However, consumer price inflation rose after 2002 and nominal interest rates either were adjusted upward by only small amounts or, in the case of demand deposits, remained unchanged. In the first half of 2008 consumer price inflation was 7.9 percent, meaning that the real rate of return on demand deposits had fallen to −7.18 percent, a decline of 8.7 percentage points. The central bank did increase the nominal interest rate that banks could pay on term deposits of various maturities; for example, the rate on one-year deposits by mid-2008 was 4.14 percent, but in real terms that was −3.76 percent, a decline of 6.54 percentage points compared with the real return on one-year deposits in 2002.

An aggregate measure of financial repression faced by households in an environment where deposit rates rose much less than inflation is the calculation of how much more households would have earned on their savings if the real rates in the first half of 2008 had been the same as in 2002. Household savings in the first half of 2008 averaged RMB18,680 billion, almost two-fifths in demand deposits and the balance in term deposits of various maturities ranging from 3 months to 5 years.[16] If these deposits had earned the same real rates as in 2002, total household income in the first half of 2008 would have been RMB690 billion greater than it actually was, an amount equal to 5.3 percent of China's GDP in the first half of the year. That means growing financial repression significantly retarded the growth of household income and thus reduced the contribution of household consumption to economic growth.

A third policy instrument to promote rebalancing is appreciation of the exchange rate of the currency. The Chinese authorities allowed the renminbi to appreciate 21 percent vis-á-vis the dollar between July 2005 and the end of 2008 (the currency appreciated only slightly less on a real, trade-weighted basis). However, after the 2005 change in currency policy, China's current account surplus continued to expand rapidly, more than doubling in absolute terms between 2005 and 2007 and then expanding more slowly (by 15 percent) in 2008. The more moderate expansion in 2008 appears to be as much due to the slowdown in growth in China's major export markets as to the appreciation of the renminbi. In short, compared with mid-2005 when the new currency policy was adopt ed, China's goods became significantly more competitive in global markets and its currency became more undervalued through 2007. As suggested by Figure 1, the degree of undervaluation probably lessened in 2008 as the currency appreciated more rapidly on a trade-weighted basis, but it is difficult at this point to disentangle the factors that contributed to the slowing of the current account surplus growth in 2008.

Given China's large and growing current account surplus, it is hardly surprising that through 2007 the country became increasingly dependent on the expansion of net exports of goods and services to sustain high growth.[17] Net exports jumped from $50 billion (2.5 percent of GDP) in 2004 to $125 billion (5.4 percent of GDP) in 2005, $210 billion (7.5 percent of GDP)

---

[16]This is the average of the end-December 2007 amount of RMB17,575 billion and end-June 2008 amount of RMB19,781 billion.

[17]In recent years net exports of goods and services have accounted for the vast majority China's net current account position while net foreign income and profit and net current transfers have been much smaller components. In 2007, for example, the shares of these three components in the net current account were 83, 7, and 10 percent, respectively (State Administration of Foreign Exchange, Balance of Payments Analysis Small Group 2008a, 9).

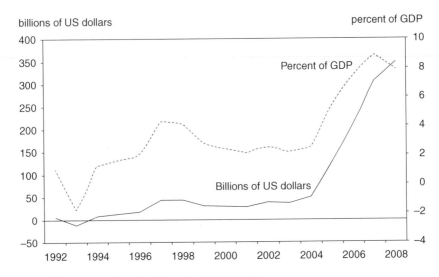

Fig 1: Net exports of goods and services, 1992–2008.
Sources: National Bureau of Statistics of China (2008b); ISI Emerging Markets, CEIC Database; People's Bank of China, Montetary Policy Analysis Small Group (2009a).

in 2006, and $305 billion (8.9 percent of GDP) in 2007 (Figure 1). As a consequence, the contribution of net exports to economic growth increased dramatically, from an average of only 5 percent (0.35 percentage points of GDP growth) in 2001–04 to more than 20 percent (2.4 percentage points of GDP growth) in 2005–07 (National Bureau of Statistics of China 2008a, 36).

In 2008 net exports of goods and services expanded much more slowly to reach $349 billion (8 percent of GDP) (State Administration of Foreign Exchange, Balance of Payments Analysis Small Group 2009, 10), and the contribution of expanding net exports to economic growth shrank to only 9.1 percent (0.8 percentage points of GDP growth). By the first quarter of 2009 net exports reduced China's growth by 0.2 percentage points.[18]

The fourth major policy arena for the government to facilitate a rebalancing of economic growth is the pricing of critical items such as power (fuels and electricity), water, and land. Underpricing of these inputs raises profitability in activities that use them intensively and, if it persists, will lead

---

[18] Li Xiaochao, press conference on 2009 first-quarter economic situation, April 16, 2009, www.china.com.cn (accessed on April 16, 2009).

firms to invest more in these activities, even in an economy where the prices of goods and services are overwhelmingly market determined.[19] To a remarkable degree the subsidies provided through underpricing of fuels and electricity accrue in China to the manufacturing sector rather than to transportation or to households. This is because industry accounts for almost two-thirds of final energy consumption, compared with about one-quarter in the United States (Bergsten et al. 2008, 142).

Energy is one of the most important areas in which the state has retained price-setting power. For example, in the 1980s the state set the price of crude oil at a small fraction of the world price, continuing a policy inherited from the prereform era. But at the end of the 1980s China moved gradually to raise the domestic price of crude to the international level. By 1998 convergence was complete and the government adopted a formal plan to adjust monthly the domestic price of crude to keep it in line with the international price. Retail prices gradually reflected the principle of full-cost pricing and in mid-2000 the government adopted a formal program to adjust these prices monthly as well so that refined product prices reflected the cost of crude (Lardy 1992, 90–94; 2002, 26). Thus while the prices of both crude and refined products were government controlled, they diverged only slightly from market prices.

But as the cost of crude on the global market began to rise rapidly in 2004, the Chinese government began to modify its pricing policies. The domestic price of crude oil was still adjusted monthly with the international price, but only part of the rising cost of crude was reflected in retail prices of major refined products such as diesel and gasoline. By 2005 the government was paying subsidies to Chinese refiners to partially compensate them for their refining losses.

This problem recurred on a much larger scale in the first half of 2008, when global oil prices rose further and retail prices in China for gasoline and diesel fuel were the lowest of any oil-importing emerging market.[20] China Petroleum & Chemical Corporation (Sinopec), the country's largest oil refiner, saw its net profits plunge by three-quarters in the first half of 2008 as its profits in other lines of business together with government refining subsidies barely offset its

---

[19] By the late 1990s 95 percent of retail commodities, 83 percent of farm products, and 86 percent of producer goods were sold at market-determined prices (Lardy 2002, 25).

[20] The average retail price for gasoline and diesel for a group of 65 emerging-market countries in July 2008 was $1.15 per liter; in contrast, the price in China was $0.78 per liter, the lowest of all of the 47 oil-importing countries in the group (Anderson 2008a).

massive refining losses.[21] Although in June 2008 the Chinese government finally did raise the retail price of gas and diesel by almost one-fifth, that adjustment did not eliminate the operating losses of the refiners and left them with no return on capital employed in refining. This situation eased in the second half of the year as the international price of oil fell precipitously while the National Development and Reform Commission held the domestic price of gasoline and diesel fuel unchanged until mid-December, when it cut prices slightly. Thus by the closing months of 2008 the underpricing of gasoline and diesel fuel had ended.

More importantly, in January 2009 the government instituted fuel price reforms that partly restore the earlier full-cost pricing policy. Under the new regime, there will be full-price pass-through when the global price of crude is under $80 per barrel (i.e., prices of gasoline, diesel, and other refined products will move in step with global crude prices). However, if the global price of crude rises above $80 per barrel, retail prices of refined products will rise less than would be required under full-price pass-through (this will be achieved by cutting distribution margins); if it rises above $130 per barrel, retail prices will likely be adjusted upward but with a lag and subject to ceilings (Stanway 2009). Thus, as long as the global price of crude remains below $80 per barrel the state will not subsidize domestic users of fuel.

Initially, a similar pattern of government price intervention applied to electric power. Through mid-decade full-cost pricing was in effect, companies generating electric power were profitable, and few consumers of electricity were subsidized.[22] But in 2007 and 2008, as the price of coal rose on the domestic market, coal mines were reluctant to fulfill long-term supply contracts that had been struck earlier when prices were much lower. Generators therefore

---

[21] Sinopec lost RMB46.0 billion on its refining operations in the first half of 2008 compared with profits of RMB5.7 billion in the first half of 2007; and its overall operating profits plunged from RMB53.6 billion in the first half of 2007 to RMB7.2 billion in the first half of 2008. "Sinopec Corp. Announces 2008 Interim Results/' available at http://english.sinopec.com (accessed on October 20, 2008).

[22] Local governments reportedly provided subsidized electric power to some firms. It is not clear whether local governments covered this subsidy from fiscal revenues or forced the power-generating and/or power distribution companies to sell at prices less than the official tariff schedule.

had to buy a growing share of their coal on the spot market, where prices were much higher than the contract price. But the price that the generating companies received for delivering power to the grid remained unchanged since 2006, leading to plummeting margins. To draw attention to their plight, some generating companies curtailed production, causing localized electric power shortages. In June 2008 the government responded by raising the price of power delivered to the grid by 5 percent.

This price increase turned out to be far too modest. The price of coal fell in the second half of 2008 compared with the peaks of the first part of the year, but China's economic slowdown led to much slower growth in the demand for electricity, indeed in September, October, and November 2008 electric power production declined in absolute terms. Through the end of 2008, the lower usage rate more than offset the reduction in the price of coal. The result was that, in the first 11 months of 2008 the five largest power-generating companies, which account for about two-fifths of China's power generation, posted losses of RMB30 billion and the profits of the power industry as a whole fell 84 percent compared with 39 percent growth in the same period the previous year (Li Qiyan 2009). Moreover, China's grid companies were not allowed to pass the June 2008 on-grid price increase to consumers, so the price adjustment simply reduced the losses of the generators at the expense of the distributors. For example, the profits of the State Grid Corporation of China, responsible for the distribution of electric power in 26 of China's 31 provincial-level administrative units, fell by 80 percent in 2008 compared with 2007 (State Grid Corporation of China 2009).[23] Thus electric power remains subsidized for both household and industrial consumers.

Chinese Premier Wen Jiabao (2009), in his report to the National People's Congress in March 2009, indicated that more comprehensive reform of pricing of resources such as coal, electric power, and water would be undertaken in a timely fashion. Promised reforms, all of which would raise prices, would incorporate in power prices the cost of environmental

---

[23]The sharp decline was the result not only of the margin squeeze but also of severe winter storms and the major earthquake in Sichuan Province.

damage in power production. Premier Wen also promised that China would carry forward market-based reform of interest rates, suggesting that the extent of financial repression would be eased and perhaps even eventually eliminated.

Thus the record to date on policies to promote increased domestic consumption is mixed. In the fiscal domain, tax cuts for individuals have been modest and tax increases on firms, in the form of the new dividend tax, inconsequential. But on the expenditure side, the government's fiscal initiatives to rebuild the social safety net are very impressive, particularly in health care. In recent years, increases in government transfer payments, such as pensions and support for low-income individuals, have also been substantial. In the financial arena, policy thus far has been anemic, but Premier Wen's promised market-based reform of interest rates could ease the high implicit tax burden on households and thus contribute to increased consumption expenditure. The much more rapid appreciation of the exchange rate in 2008 compared with 2006 and 2007 is also a very positive development, which, if continued, will contribute significantly to rebalancing. Price reform is a mixed picture so far, but if Premier Wen's promised reforms of the pricing of water, electricity, and so forth are implemented, they will contribute toward rebalancing the country's sources of economic growth.

While China has taken a number of important steps toward more consumption-driven growth, the results of these efforts are not yet evident in China's GDP expenditure data. Investment growth did moderate somewhat in 2005–07, in line with the government objective of reducing the extraordinarily high share of resources going to investment. But the decline, shown in Figure 2, was only slight and, according to preliminary data, was reversed in 2008. Thus since 2003, the share of China's GDP going to investment has been continuously above two-fifths of GDP, well above the share of GDP going to investment in Japan, Korea, and Taiwan during their high-growth periods. Moreover, the large increases in net exports since 2004 have meant that the consumption share of GDP has fallen significantly, as shown in Figure 3. In 2008 government and personal consumption combined accounted for less than half of GDP, the lowest share of any economy in the world. China is particularly an outlier in terms of personal consumption, which in 2007 accounted for only 35 percent of GDP (National Bureau of Statistics of China 2008a, 35). In contrast, household consumption in Brazil and India in the

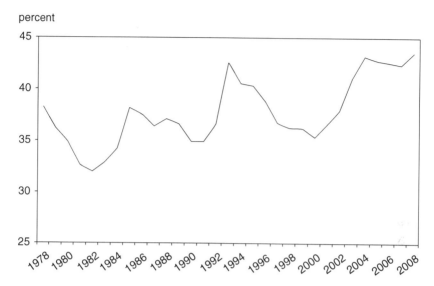

Fig 2: Investment as a share of GDP, 1978–2008.
Sources: National Bureau of Statistics of China (2008b); People's Bank of China, Monetary Policy Analysis Small Group (2009a).

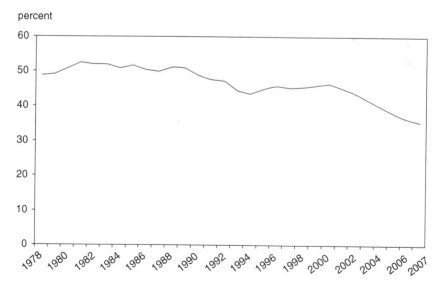

Fig 3: Household consumption as a share of GDP, 1978–2007.
Source: National Bureau of Statistics of China (2008b).

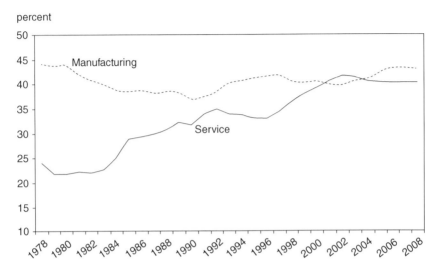

Fig 4: Services and manufacturing as a share of GDP, 1978–2008.
Sources: National Bureau of Statistics of China (2008b); ISI Emerging Markets, CEIC Database.
Note: Manufacturing includes mining, and utilities but not construction.

same year accounted for a much larger share of those countries' GDP, 61 and 54 percent, respectively.[24]

The efforts to rebalance the economy also are not yet reflected in the structure of output. As shown in Figure 4, in the first two decades of economic reform the share of output originating in the services sector roughly doubled, from about 22 percent in the early 1980s to 42 percent in 2002. This trend conforms to the usual pattern of economic growth in which the services share of GDP increases in rapidly growing developing economies. But after 2002, the services share in China initially fell slightly and then basically stagnated at 40 percent in 2005–08. This six-year absence of growth in the services share of GDP in a fast-growing developing economy is extremely unusual, if not unprecedented. In contrast, after 2002 the manufacturing share of GDP rose by almost 4 percentage points to 43 percent in 2006–08, equal to the peak levels of the late 1970s and early 1980s. This too is an unusual pattern for a developing economy.

---

[24]World Bank, *World Development Indicators*, available via subscription at www.worldbank.org/data (accessed on May 28, 2009).

POTENTIAL EFFECTS OF RENMINBI APPRECIATION ON CHINA'S BANKING SYSTEM

There is considerable agreement both in and outside China about the evolution of the country's banking system and of efforts to reform it. Analysts recognize, for example, that the high share of bank deposits in household financial wealth and the dominance of bank loans in enterprises' external financing make the performance of the banking system in China more important than in most other economies — with significant impacts on, inter alia, the growth of total factor productivity, household consumption, the size of public debt, the transmission of monetary policy, and prospects for capital account convertibility. Most observers also believe the central elements of China's banking reform have moved the system in the right direction. These reform elements include:

- large-scale (over $300 billion) public recapitalization of the state-owned commercial banks to remove a huge overhang of nonperforming loans from bank balance sheets;
- implementation of tougher asset classification and provisioning guidelines;
- creation of an energetic bank supervisor (the China Banking Regulatory Commission);
- large reductions in the number of branches and employees in China's four largest banks;[25]
- increase in foreign participation in the banking system as a result of commitments to financial liberalization made as part of China's accession to the World Trade Organization (WTO);
- listing of four large state-owned commercial banks on stock exchanges;[26] and
- sale of bank shares to strategic foreign partners.

But the banking system still has some serious deficiencies and faces a number of formidable challenges going forward. Wendy Dobson and Anil

---

[25] The Industrial and Commercial Bank of China, the Bank of China, China Construction Bank, and the Agricultural Bank of China.
[26] The Industrial and Commercial Bank of China, the Bank of China, China Construction Bank, and the Bank of Communications.

Kashyap (2006) bemoan the still dominant (albeit declining) share of the state-owned banks in total bank lending and the continuing government pressure on these banks to direct too much credit to less profitable state-owned enterprises for the purpose of supporting employment. As a result, small and medium-scale enterprises are underserved by the formal banking system and rely on the informal credit market, where they must pay substantially higher interest rates (Li Jianjun 2008). Similarly, Richard Podpiera (2006) concludes that, despite the central bank's de jure removal of the ceiling on loan interest rates in the fall of 2004, pricing of bank loans remains largely undifferentiated and large state-owned banks do not appear to take enterprise profitability into account when making lending decisions. And Jonathan Anderson (2006b) emphasizes the still relatively low profitability of China's state-owned banks, the high dependence of bank profitability on the huge gap between lending and deposit interest rates, and the likelihood that this interest rate gap will narrow markedly in the period ahead as financial liberalization and globalization proceed.

There is much less agreement about how a more appreciated and more flexible exchange rate for the renminbi would affect banking reform. Moreover, the effects of currency reform have too often been confused with the effects of further capital account liberalization.

One popular view is that going much beyond the existing gradualist approach to currency reform would be too dangerous for the still fragile banking system. Mindful of financial crises in other emerging economies over the past dozen years, proponents of this view argue that a large renminbi appreciation could generate serious currency mismatches for banks and their customers. They worry as well that appreciation could bring in its wake a sharp reduction in growth (on top of the effect of the global financial and economic crisis), making it much harder to maintain the trend decline in banks' nonperforming loans. And they point out that China's financial infrastructure does not yet have hedging instruments adequate for protecting market participants against a marked increase in exchange rate volatility. Their bottom line is that further strengthening of China's banking system — and of its financial system more broadly — is a necessary precondition for bolder currency reform (Zhang 2004, 9–10,19–20).

Others take a nearly opposite tack — seeing bolder currency reform as the ally rather than the enemy of banking reform. They observe that China's banks and their customers are much less vulnerable to currency mismatches than were their counterparts in earlier emerging-market financial crises (Goldstein 2007b). After all, China is a substantial net creditor, not a net debtor, in its overall foreign exchange position. Exporters have lower debt-equity ratios than firms in other sectors. Most of China's largest exporters are foreign owned and do not raise the bulk of their financing in the domestic market. Where the authorities require bank capital to be held in US dollars, reports indicate that the associated currency risk is hedged.[27]

Currency reform advocates also emphasize that the excessive accumulation of international reserves that has accompanied the increasingly undervalued renminbi has put Chinese monetary authorities in a no-win dilemma, with increasing risk to the banking system.[28] If the authorities did not sterilize the large increase in reserves, the resulting explosion of bank credit and of monetary aggregates would probably have been so large as to generate a flood of nonperforming bank loans and domestic inflation. Indeed, even with the ambitious sterilization efforts of the past five years, there were costly bank credit booms in 2003, in the first quarter of 2004, and in the first half of 2006. In 2004, consumer price inflation also hit nearly 5 percent, while producer prices rose by 8 percent. With sticky nominal interest rates on deposits and loans, sharp increases in inflation translate into low (and sometimes negative) real interest rates, which in turn can fuel overinvestment, slow or even negative growth in bank deposits, and speculative runs in equity and property markets.

Alternatively, the authorities can take the high sterilization route. But then the increase in inflation, which would otherwise appreciate the real exchange rate, is cut off. Similarly, if the growth rate of net domestic assets of the central bank is kept too low in a fast-growing economy, the excess demand for money

---

[27] The Bank of Communications, the China Construction Bank, the Industrial and Commercial Bank of China, and the Bank of China all received capital injections from Central Huijin as part of their restructuring prior to public listing. The injections were in the torm of foreign exchange and the banks were not allowed, at least initially, to convert these funds into renminbi. That could have meant that the banks would suffer a reduction of their capital if the renminbi appreciated, possibly reducing their capital adequacy below the levels mandated by the regulator, the China Banking Regulatory Commission. However, Central Huijin sold options to these banks giving them the right to convert their foreign exchange back into renminbi at a fixed exchange rate.

[28] Yu Yongding (2007b) puts it succinctly: "In summary, to achieve simultaneously the objectives of the maintenance of a stable exchange rate, a tight monetary policy, and a good performance of the commercial banks is impossible."

will induce the very expenditure patterns and balance of payments inflows that will perpetuate the economy's external imbalance. Also, as suggested earlier, the need both to place large amounts of low yielding sterilization bills with the banks and to repeatedly raise bank reserve requirements (which likewise pay low interest rates) imposes a "tax" on the banks that is not captured in standard calculations of the "cost of sterilization." If the banks absorb this tax themselves, then their profitability, which is already low by international standards, is further compromised; if instead they pass on the cost of sterilizing to depositors in the form of lower deposit rates, then depositors have an incentive to put their money elsewhere. Without adequate growth of bank deposits, bank loan growth will be unduly constrained. And if the authorities rely on window guidance instead of sterilization to control how much and to whom banks lend, then the longer-term objective of teaching credit officers how to evaluate creditworthiness and of developing a "credit culture" in China's banks would be undermined.

As indicated earlier, low exchange rate flexibility — even with remaining controls on capital flows — also means that interest rate decisions will often be delayed beyond what would be desirable for domestic stabilization purposes, for fear that more decisive interest rate policy would trigger large capital flows that would put undue pressure on the exchange rate. Delaying needed decisions about interest rates is not good for banks. Effective central banking involves taking preemptive interest rate action to ward off both sharp growth slowdowns and inflation excesses. If, for example, the authorities wait too long to move interest rates in response to an overheated economy, monetary tightening may have to be much greater than if they acted earlier; the more volatile the operating environment facing banks, the higher the risk that bank credit growth will be too rapid or too slow. Similarly, if the monetary authorities constantly tinker with export taxes, restrictions on incoming and outgoing capital flows, and the pace and volatility of the exchange rate crawl — as substitutes for more independent monetary policy and a more market-determined exchange rate — it is unlikely that the need for banks and their customers to hedge against this policy uncertainty will be less costly than hedging against greater exchange rate volatility on its own.

Champions of the view that bolder currency reform should not be held hostage to the pace of financial-sector reform do not maintain that the remaining fragility of the Chinese banking system is irrelevant for the sequencing of other reforms. Rather they contend that it is capita account convertibility, not currency appreciation and flexibility, that should await further strengthening of the banking system (Prasad 2007, Goldstein and Lardy 2003b, Williamson 2003). Here the argument is that so long as restrictions on capital outflows are reduced gradually rather than precipitously, the authorities will have adequate room for maneuver in countering, say, an unanticipated setback on banking reform or an unexpected large fall in China's growth rate. In contrast, if bank fragility is paired with the potential for large-scale capital flight, then, as other emerging economies have discovered, the management of such a crisis is inherently much more difficult. Yu Yongding (2007b) observes that if Chinese households and firms decided for whatever reasons — rational or irrational — to suddenly increase the share of their assets invested abroad, capital outflow could quickly grow to as much as $500 billion, with very unpleasant consequences for the Chinese economy.

Under this view, the right sequencing of reform is to continue with banking reform and to move now to reduce significantly both the undervaluation and the inflexibility of the renminbi, but to wait until China's financial system is on stronger footing before opening up too widely the doors on capital outflows.

Looking ahead, the conundrum facing China's banking system can be summarized as follows. The authorities have indicated, quite sensibly, that they wish to expand the role of commercial paper, bond, and equity markets to diversify (away from banks) the sources of external financing available to firms. In addition, they have expressed an understandable intention to gradually lift restrictions on capital outflows, in part to offer savers a higher rate of return and in part, given China's large global current account surplus, to reduce upward pressure on the renminbi. But such moves in the direction of further financial liberalization and globalization are likely to have the competitive effect of reducing the 350 to 400 basis point spread between deposit and loan interest rates, since both Chinese investors and savers will then have more alternatives to domestic banks. As Anderson (2006b) points out, even a 100 basis-point decline in the deposit-loan spread would have wiped out all the profits of state-owned banks in 2005.

How, then, to square this circle? Yes, costs may be reduced further by larger cutbacks in the number of branches and bank employees. Yes, maybe Chinese banks can increase somewhat the share of profits from fees to partially offset the fall in interest income. But in the end, two things are probably required. First, credit allocation decisions will have to be improved further so less income is spent on dealing with bad loans. This in turn would seem to imply that the influence of political factors on loan decisions will have to be reduced vis-á-vis the influence of arm's-length commercial considerations. Can this be done without further reducing the share of state ownership? We doubt it. Second, it will be necessary to lower the burden increasingly imposed on bank profitability by the sterilization requirements of defending a seriously undervalued renminbi. Can this be done other than by reducing the amount of intervention in the exchange market? Again, we doubt it.

EXTERNAL ADJUSTMENT, GLOBAL IMBALANCES, AND THE RISING RISK OF PROTECTIONISM

China's exchange rate policy also carries important implications for the country's own external adjustment, the correction of global imbalances, public policy toward sovereign wealth funds, the operation of the international exchange rate system, and efforts to maintain forward momentum on globalization. In this regard, among the most interesting issues are the following:

- Given the wide range of estimates of renminbi misalignment, can one be confident that the renminbi really is seriously undervalued?
- If China did implement a sizable revaluation/appreciation of the renminbi, would it be effective in reducing substantially the country's large global current account surplus?
- Would the costs of a large renminbi revaluation be prohibitively high?
- What explains the large surge in China's current account surplus between 2004 and 2007?
- Would the effect of renminbi revaluation on global imbalances be larger (smaller) than sometimes assumed because it will (not) lead to sympathetic revaluations in other Asian and emerging-market currencies?
- With China's reserves topping $1.9 trillion at the end of 2008 and with the establishment of its own sovereign wealth fund, what will be the impact and what principles should guide the fund's operations?
- Should the International Monetary Fund (IMF) have regarded China's large-scale, prolonged, one-way intervention in exchange markets since 2003 as

currency manipulation and how should IMF exchange rate surveillance be conducted going forward?
- Were several currency bills introduced in the US Congress a serious threat to open markets or are they a "third-best" policy response to a beggar-thy-neighbor exchange rate policy?

RENMINBI UNDERVALUATION

Some argue that China should not have been expected to appreciate the renminbi earlier and more forcefully because no one really knows the "right" or "equilibrium" exchange rate.[29] They note that studies yield a wide range of estimates of misalignment. An IMF study by Steven Dunaway and Xiangmin Li (2005), for example, maintains that estimates of renminbi undervaluation range from zero to nearly 50 percent. Furthermore, in a subsequent study these authors, together with Lamin Leigh, argue that a more definitive answer is unlikely to emerge soon because of data problems, instability in the underlying economic relationships, and lack of consensus on the proper methodology (Dunaway, Leigh, and Li 2006).[30]

Others (e.g., Goldstein 2004, 2007b) find; the evidence in support of a large renminbi undervaluation increasingly robust and, by 2007, simply overwhelming: China's global current account surplus grew without interruption from 1 percent of GDP in 2001 to 11 percent in 2007 before falling to a still large estimated 9.8 percent of GDP in 2008; China's net capital account position also has been in surplus throughout this period; the real trade-weighted value of China's currency through the end of 2007 was less (i.e., more depreciated) than in early 2002; China's intervention in the foreign exchange market has been persistent, one way, and through the third quarter of 2008 very large; and through 2007 China's domestic economy was growing at or above its potential.

---

[29] Some in this camp (Mundell 2004) also maintain that a fixed exchange rate has served China well, that it could continue to do so, and that claims of "overheating" of the economy are misguided.

[30] Dunaway's view seems to have evolved. In 2009, after he retired from the IMF, he characterized China's exchange rate as "increasingly undervalued" and acknowledged that the resulting competitive pressure China poses caused other Asian countries to seek to limit appreciation of their own currencies (Dunaway 2009,10).

Taking these developments together, any reasonable back-of-the-envelope calculation to determine the level of the renminbi that would eliminate China's global current account surplus would generate a large (and growing) estimate of renminbi undervaluation. Given that studies suggest that each 10 percent change in China's real effective exchange rate is associated with a 2 to 3.5 percent change of GDP in the country's global trade balance (Goldstein 2007b),[31] a reasonable "ballpark" estimate is that a 2.5 percent GDP reduction in China's global current account is linked to each 10 percent real effective appreciation of the renminbi.[32] Thus, for example, eliminating China's 2007 global current account surplus of 11 percent of GDP would require about a 45 percent real effective appreciation of the renminbi.[33] Just to cut the surplus in half from its 2007 level (say, reducing it by 6 percent of GDP) would imply the need for an appreciation of about 25 percent. Of course, for earlier years (e.g., 2003 and 2004) when China's global surplus was much smaller, the implied undervaluation would be lower, but still not small.

The IMF's most recent projection for China's global current account surplus (expressed as a share of its GDP) in 2009 is 10.3 percent (IMF 2009b). If we again assume that each 10 percent real effective appreciation of the renminbi would reduce China's current account surplus by 2.5 percent of GDP, then elimination of the 2009 surplus would require roughly a 40 percent appreciation of the renminbi. But one should also take into account recent movements in the renminbi that have not yet had time to be fully reflected in the observed current account figures; after all, exchange rates operate on trade with a lag. In this connection, suppose that we assume that none of the 15 percent real effective appreciation of the renminbi observed between February 2007 and February 2009 has yet been reflected in the published current account data; by the same token, let us assume that all of the observed

---

[31] Similarly, Ahearne et al. (2007) find that renminbi appreciation of 5 to 25 percent would be required to reduce China's global current account surplus by 3.5 to 6.5 percent of GDP.

[32] Cline (2008) uses an impact multiplier of 3 percent of GDP for each 10 percent real effective appreciation of the renminbi. We prefer the lower figure of 2.5 because we regard the high import content of Chinese exports as reducing the size of the impact multiplier relative to Cline's estimate.

[33] The same type of calculation suggests that almost a 40 percent real effective appreciation is needed to eliminate the estimated global current account surplus of 9.8 percent of GDP in 2008.

5 percent real effective appreciation of the renminbi between June 2005 and February 2007 has been so reflected. Because of the 15 percent effective appreciation of the renminbi that is still "in the pipeline," this would imply that instead of requiring a 40 percent appreciation of the renminbi to eliminate the 2009 surplus, a 25 percent real effective appreciation would do the job (that is, 40 percent otherwise needed real effective appreciation minus the 15 percent real effective appreciation in the pipeline). By analogy, if we used a multiplier of say 3.3 (instead of 2.5) for the effect of each 10 percent real effective appreciation of the renminbi on the current account, appreciation in the pipeline would reduce the needed real effective appreciation from 30 to 15 percent.[34]

The conclusion that the real effective exchange rate of the renminbi remains significantly undervalued in 2009 by somewhere between say 15 and 25 percent does not of course tell one how much the renminbi needs to appreciate vis-à-vis individual currencies, particularly the US dollar. To answer that question, one requires a multilateral model that imposes consistency of current account targets across countries as well as consistency across needed changes in bilateral and effective exchange rates. For example, if China revalues the renminbi by 20 percent against the dollar but other Asian countries follow suit, then the real effective appreciation of the renminbi will be substantially smaller than the renminbi's appreciation against the US dollar since the renminbi will not have appreciated (much or at all) against some of China's trading partners.

Fortunately, William R. Cline and John Williamson (2009) have undertaken such a consistent multilateral exercise for 30 non–oil exporting countries — including China. Although Cline and Williamson employ different assumptions than we do about, inter alia, the target change in China's global current account surplus, the pipeline effects of earlier renminbi appreciation, and the impact multiplier of changes in the renminbi on China's current account, they too find that the real effective exchange rate of the renminbi remains significantly undervalued — by 21 percent — as of March 2009. They

---

[34] By the same reasoning, pipeline effects also help to explain why the estimated undervaluation of the renminbi was likely larger in 2007 than in either 2008 or 2009; not only did China's current account surplus hit a peak (relative to GDP) at 11 percent in 2007 but there was also relatively little renminbi appreciation in the pipeline.

also find that the real effective exchange rate of the US dollar was significantly overvalued — by 17 percent — as of the same date. Because Cline and Williamson conclude that the US dollar needs to go down (depreciate) against practically all US trading partners and that simultaneously the renminbi needs to go up (appreciate) on average against China's trading partners, their model yields the conclusion that the renminbi should appreciate much more against the dollar — by roughly 40 percent — than against other currencies — if the called for 21 percent real effective appreciation of the renminbi is to be achieved.[35] In short, the Cline and Williamson message is that if the dollar does go down over the next few years to help reduce the US current account deficit, China should not ride the dollar down if China expects to achieve the real effective appreciation of the renminbi that would be consistent with reducing substantially (much less eliminating) China's still very large global current account surplus.[36]

Recall that until the second half of 2008 China's large current account surpluses occurred when the domestic economy was booming, which means that China was in what James Meade (1951) called a "nondilemma" situation, where exchange rate appreciation moves the economy simultaneously closer to both external and internal balance. One notable consequence of the sharp decline in growth in 2008 is that this long period of a "nondilemma" situation for exchange rate appreciation has ended — that is, additional real effective appreciation of the renminbi would still move China closer to external balance but farther from internal balance (since the Chinese economy in late 2008 and early 2009 was operating far below potential growth).

Those who claim that the renminbi is clearly undervalued concede that the relevant empirical literature has spawned a wide range of estimates but argue that this reflects largely a lack of comparability across studies. Some studies (Goldstein and Lardy 2006b) assume that the objective is to eliminate entirely China's external imbalance while others (Ahearne et al. 2007, Cline

---

[35] Using March 2009 as their base, Cline and Williamson (2009) calculate that this 40 percent appreciation of the renminbi against the US dollar would result in a bilateral exchange rate of RMB4.88 against the dollar (versus a bilateral rate of RMB6.83 to the dollar at the time of this writing).

[36] As noted earlier, the magnitudes of the real effective and nominal bilateral (vis-à-vis the US dollar) appreciations of the renmindi have been quite similar over the June 2005–March 2009 period as a whole, albeit not for some other periods.

and Williamson 2008b) assume that only part of this imbalance should or could be eliminated within the specified period. Some studies (Goldstein and Lardy 2006b) assume that the adjustment of the trade balance in response to exchange rate changes is spread out over a year or two while others (Cline and Williamson 2009) implicitly assume that the adjustment is more rapid. Some analysts assume that exchange rate revaluation would be undertaken on its own, while others assume that revaluation would be paired with macroeconomic policy that maintained a constant level of aggregate demand. In the former case, the contractionary effect of revaluation reduces the demand for imports in the second round, while in the latter case there is no second-round effect on import demand.

Some studies explicitly model the high import content of China's exports, while others ignore it; when the import content of exports is taken into account, renminbi revaluation leads to a smaller export-price increase than when it is not so assumed. Some studies assume higher export and import price elasticities of demand for China's trade than do others. Because China's imports and exports have been growing faster than the GDP, its traded goods sector is much larger now than it was even half a dozen years ago. Therefore, ceteris paribus, a smaller exchange rate change will be needed to achieve a given trade balance target than when the traded goods sector was smaller. This, in turn, can produce different estimates of renminbi misalignment when the studies are done at different points in time (even when the same methodology is employed).

Some authors obtain point estimates that show very large renminbi undervaluation but do not regard the confidence level on that estimate as sufficiently strong to warrant a conclusion of undervaluation (Cheung, Chinn, and Fujii 2007); others obtain similar estimates and accept the point estimates. And finally, there are several methods for inferring exchange rate misalignments — ranging from the macroeconomic balance approach, to various structural models of exchange rate determination, to a whole family of purchasing power parity models — and different authors have not always chosen the same method, even if some approaches are regarded as more reliable than others.[37]

---

[37] See IMF (2006b) for a discussion of different methods for assessing misalignment of exchange rates.

The contention of the large undervaluation school is that if one "standardized" the misalignment exercise and restricted attention to the better methods and more reasonable assumptions, the large undervaluation verdict would emerge even more clearly. Cline and Williamson (2008a) in a survey found that only one of 18 studies concluded that the renminbi is overvalued. The average estimate indicates substantial undervaluation — on the order of 20 percent for the real effective exchange rate and 40 percent for the nominal renminbi-dollar exchange rate. They also find that renminbi undervaluation was increasing over time, from 17 percent effective appreciation needed in studies using 2000–04 data to 27 percent for studies based on 2005–07 data.

The large undervaluation school also points out that some of the initial agnostics on renminbi undervaluation have come around. In its 2004 Article IV consultation report for China, the IMF (2004,12) concluded that "it is difficult to find persuasive evidence that the renminbi is undervalued." Two years later the Fund's conclusion was quite different: "All of these developments point to the currency [the renminbi] as being undervalued and that this undervaluation has increased further since last year's Article IV consultation" (IMF 2006a, 17). By 2008 the Fund's Managing Director Dominique Strauss-Kahn went even further, publically characterizing the renminbi as "substantially undervalued."[38]

Finally, the large undervaluation school believes that appropriate policy direction for China does not depend on unanimity on the precise degree of undervaluation of its currency. All indicators show that since the early part of this decade the currency has needed to appreciate to reduce a large and growing external imbalance. The best approach is simply to adopt a genuinely more flexible regime and reduce the degree of official intervention so that the market can determine the equilibrium exchange rate. This, of course, is the policy the Chinese officially claimed to have adopted in mid-2005. But, as we have noted, the much advertised increased role for the market in the determination of the exchange rate of the renminbi has been substantially delayed.

---

[38] Reuters, "IMF's Chief Says China Currency 'Significantly Undervalued,'" June 24, 2008, available at www.reuters.com (accessed on April 20, 2009).

EFFECTIVENESS OF RENMINBI APPRECIATION

Another issue is whether a renminbi appreciation would have much effect on China's global current account position. Pessimists cite several factors likely to reduce the effectiveness of exchange rate action: low wages and high profit margins, which together would permit exporters to absorb the cost of appreciation without raising export prices; a high import content of exports; and low price elasticities of demand for imports and exports.[39]

Optimists see it differently. They agree that manufacturing wages in China are very low relative to those in, say, the United States but point out that Chinese productivity is also very low vis-à-vis the US level — and it is the combination of the two (unit labor cost) that matters for competitiveness (Lardy 2006). If wages alone matter, why was Germany, with the highest wages, the world's largest exporter for so many years?[40] And why are some very low-wage countries, for example, most of the countries in Sub-Saharan Africa, extremely modest exporters? Profit margins in China's traditional export industries (e.g., textiles, electronics, machinery, toys, sporting goods, furniture) are modest (in the low to mid-single digits), reflecting strong competition in domestic and external markets. True, profit margins are higher in the newer and faster-growing export industries (e.g., aircraft parts, autos, ships, and telecom equipment), but there is so far little evidence that profit margins move systematically to offset the effects of nominal exchange rate changes on export prices. Anderson (2007b) observed that broad indices of China's export prices rose over the past two to three years, in contrast to falling export prices over the previous three-year period.

As mentioned above, the average import content of exports in China is high — on the order of 30 to 35 percent.[41] Since renminbi appreciation will

---

[39] Some (Bosworth 2004) also argue that there is no obvious channel by which a renminbi Evaluation would correct China's saving-investment imbalance.

[40] China's exports, on a monthly basis, surpassed those of Germany starting in the fall of 2008.

[41] In 2007 processed exports (i.e., export goods assembled from imported parts, components, and assemblies) were $617 billion, accounting for 51 percent of China's total exports of $1,218 billion. Processing imports (i.e., the parts, components, and assemblies used to assemble processed exports) were $369 billion. Thus the import content of processed exports was 60 percent and that of all exports averaged 30 percent. The import content of processed exports has declined gradually as domestic suppliers have displaced imported parts and components. Processed exports as a share of total exports reached a peak in 1997 and 1998 when they

lower the cost of imported inputs (such as parts, components, and assemblies), a given amount of appreciation will produce a smaller increase in China's export prices than if exports had no import content. But this does not imply that renminbi appreciation would be ineffective — only that the exchange rate change needs to be larger to achieve a given trade balance objective. China's role as a regional processing center does distort the meaning of its bilateral trade imbalances with some industrial countries like the United States, since goods previously exported directly from other Asian countries now get assembled in China and thus show up in US trade data as imports from China. But these imported inputs wash out when looking at China's global trade imbalance.

Because the manufactured goods that China exports are typically quite price elastic (around the world) and because many of the goods it imports are also produced domestically, it is highly likely that the Marshall-Lerner condition for an effective revaluation is satisfied. Although econometric studies of China's trade flows are still limited and have to contend with poor price data, relatively short sample periods, and large structural and cyclical changes, more and more researchers are finding significant price elasticities of demand, strongly suggesting that renminbi appreciation will reduce China's global current account surplus.[42]

Optimists also make the point that if the demand for China's exports really was price inelastic, then the authorities should hardly be fearful of revaluation since higher export prices would then increase, not decrease, export revenue.

COSTS OF A MORE APPRECIATED RENMINBI

Even if a significant renminbi appreciation/revaluation reduced China's large external imbalance, some analysts, including many in China, claim that the internal economic cost of such a policy would be too high (Fan Gang 2008).

---

accounted for 57 percent of total imports. Taking these factors into account, the import content of all exports in 2002, for example, was 38 percent.

[42] Kwack et al. (2007) estimate a consistent set of import equations for both China and trading partners. From these estimates they conclude that China's import price elasticity of demand is 0.5 while its export elasticity of demand is 0.7. Goldstein (2007b) provides a summary of price elasticity estimates. In view of the difficulties of estimating the price elasticities for China's trade, some analysts choose instead to simply assume reasonable values for those elasticities. For example, Cline (2005) assumes that the import and export elasticities of demand are each unity. Anderson (2006a) assumes that the sum of the elasticities is just slightly above one.

While the argument is usually couched in terms of the adverse impact of revaluation on China's overall economic growth, employment, and social stability, in some cases the arguments are advanced by sectoral interests that benefit from an undervalued exchange rate. Officials from the Ministry of Commerce, for example, fairly consistently emphasize that the profitability of export industries is very low and that the pace of renminbi appreciation should be limited. Bo Xilai, who was minister of commerce from 2004 through 2007, argued that "RMB appreciation has substantially lowered the profit of export-oriented enterprises, especially labor-intensive ones, whose profit was already very low."[43] His successor, Minister Chen Deming, has also spoken out against rapid appreciation of the Chinese currency.[44]

The counterargument supporting more appreciation sooner has two parts. The first part of the counterargument is that defenders of an undervalued currency all too frequently exaggerate the costs of a large renminbi appreciation, but they rarely, if ever, acknowledge several important observations. First, the last time China's real effective exchange rate exhibited a large appreciation, namely, between 1994 and early 2002, when it appreciated by 30 percent, the country's growth did fall but still averaged 9 percent per year and in no single year did it drop below 7.5 percent. Estimates point to a 10 percent real effective revaluation of the renminbi lowering economic growth by roughly 1 percent a year over a two- or three-year period (Shu and Yip 2006, Anderson 2006a). If this modest decline in growth were seen as too contractionary, revaluation could be paired with a further increase in the rate of growth of government expenditures for health, education, and pensions. This would reduce the need for precautionary savings and contribute to a reduction in China's external imbalance.

Second, while domestic opponents of more rapid currency appreciation cite job losses as a potential cost of rapid appreciation, they fail to note that employment growth in China has been noticeably slower during the present decade, when investment and export-led growth have been most pronounced, than when China's economic growth was oriented more toward consumption

---

[43]"How will RMB exchange rate affect trade?" *People's Daily*, June 2, 2006, http://english.peopledaily.com.cn (accessed on October 10, 2008).
[44]"Rapid appreciation of RMB not good for world," *China Daily*, December 12, 2007, www.chinadaily.com.cn (accessed on October 6, 2008).

(Lardy 2007). China's export industries employed an estimated 45 million workers in 2007, about a third of manufacturing employment (Anderson 2007d, 4); but this accounts for only 6 percent of China's workforce, not 30 or 40 percent. Tens of millions of Chinese workers lost jobs when state-owned enterprises were reformed in the mid- to late 1990s; if there was no social meltdown then, why should there be one after a renminbi revaluation? If the concern is with income losses by workers in low-margin traditional export industries, why not introduce a trade adjustment assistance package to assist displaced workers in industries that are contracting because of a renminbi revaluation?

Third, defenders of the status quo argue that more rapid appreciation will adversely affect the incomes of more vulnerable elements of Chinese society or may even exacerbate income inequality more generally. But if the concern is that farmers and other rural inhabitants will be hurt by the lower cost of food imports after a revaluation, why can't the authorities take fiscal measures to cushion the impact on that sector's standard of living? And since China's exports are produced primarily in the high-income coastal provinces rather than elsewhere, exchange rate action that reduces profitability in export industries should not exacerbate income inequality — indeed it is more likely to ameliorate it.

The second part of the counterargument to the "go slow" approach to currency revaluation is that there are potentially high costs to appreciation but excessive delay almost certainly makes the ultimate costs of adjustment even higher. The reason is that currency undervaluation is a price distortion that affects the allocation of investment resources. The longer the price distortion persists, the more investment resources are misallocated. An undervalued exchange rate tends to raise the profitability of producing tradable goods, which in China's case are overwhelmingly manufactures rather than raw materials or agricultural products. Simultaneously, undervaluation reduces profits in the sector that produces nontradable goods (i.e., services). Other things being equal, one would thus anticipate that renminbi undervaluation would increase the share of investment going to manufacturing and reduce the share going to services.

Figure 5 shows this is precisely what happened as China's currency became increasingly undervalued after the very early part of this decade. The share of investment in urban areas going to manufacturing doubled from 15 percent

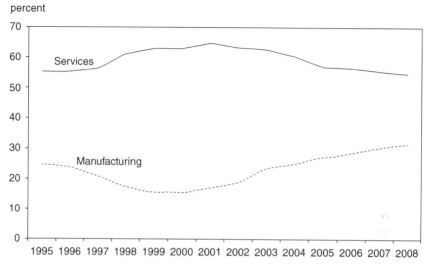

Fig 5: Investment in manufacturing and services in urban China, 1995–2008.
Sources: National Bureau of Statistics of China, *China Statistical Yearbook 2005, 2006,* and *2007;* ISI Emerging Markets, CEIC Database.
Note: Manufacturing does not include mining, utilities, and construction.

in 1999–2000 to 31 percent in 2008.[45] Over the same period the share of investment flowing to the services sector declined from 63 percent to about 55 percent. Some of the increase in the manufacturing share of investment was due to cyclical factors, rather than the increasing undervaluation of the currency that emerged after the early part of the decade. Average GDP expansion slowed to an average of only 8 percent during China's growth slump of 1998–2001. But the slowdown was particularly pronounced in

---

[45] The coverage of these data is manufacturing, narrowly defined (i.e., exclusive of the mining, utilities, and construction subsectors, which generally do not produce traded goods). Ideally, this analysis should be based on the shares of investment in the entire country, not just in urban areas, but surprisingly, data for the whole country do not appear to be available for the years prior to 2003. For 2003–07, when data are available for both urban areas and the whole country, investment in manufacturing in the entire country was 2.2 to 3 percentage points above the share in urban areas. The increase between 2003 and 2007 in the manufacturing share was 6.0 percentage points in the entire country and 6.75 percentage points in urban areas. Thus the sectoral distribution of investment in urban China appears to be a very good proxy for the sectoral distribution of investment in the entire country.

manufacturing, presumably depressing manufacturing investment proportionately more than investment in services.[46] But some portion of the doubling in the manufacturing share of investment and the decline in the services share is due to currency undervaluation, which raised returns to manufacturing investment at the expense of services. This helps to explain the rise in the share of manufacturing and the slight decline in the share of services in GDP after 2002 (Figure 4).

Because China's manufacturing sector is heavily exposed to international trade, significant further currency appreciation, which would reduce both export and import prices measured in terms of domestic currency, would reduce profits in manufacturing and would push some, perhaps many, firms into bankruptcy.[47] This is hardly a persuasive argument for indefinitely delaying appreciation of an undervalued currency since the longer currency undervaluation persists, the longer investment flows are biased toward manufacturing and the greater the potential cost of future adjustment when the exchange rate moves toward equilibrium.

EXPLAINING THE SURGE IN CHINA'S GLOBAL TRADE SURPLUS

One of the mysteries on the external front is what was primarily responsible for the upsurge in China's global trade (and current account) surplus between 2004 and 2007? What is the explanation for an almost quadrupling of net exports of goods and services as a share of GDP, from 2.5 percent in 2004 to 8.9 percent in 2007?[48] Several hypotheses — not mutually exclusive —

---

[46] Peak to trough, the pace of real growth of manufacturing fell by three-fifths, from 21.2 percent in 1992 to 8.7 percent in 2001, whereas the decline in the real growth of services was only a third, from 12.4 percent in 1992 to 8.4 percent in 1998 (National Bureau of Statistics of China 2007b, 59). Thus the slowdown in manufacturing was both more severe and more prolonged than that in services.

[47] In 2006 manufactured exports and imports of RMB7.336 trillion and RMB6.0433 trillion, respectively, accounted for one-quarter and one-fifth, respectively, of the gross value of manufactured output of RMB27.457 trillion (National Bureau of Statistics of China 2007b, 502, 724, 726–27).

[48] As noted earlier, the explosion of the global current account surplus was similar, from 3.6 percent of GDP in 2004 to 11.0 percent of GDP in 2007.

have been put forward, with different implications for China's exchange rate policy.

One hypothesis is that differential growth in total factor productivity between traded and nontraded goods may have made Chinese goods more competitive in international markets than is suggested by conventionally calculated real effective exchange rates (Lardy 2007).

The "real" adjustment in the JPMorgan index of the real effective exchange rate of the renminbi is based on the rate of inflation of core prices for finished manufactured goods (excluding food and energy) in China compared with the same prices in its trading partners. But this method may be a poor measure of the change in the prices of China's exports. Despite an 18 percent appreciation of the renminbi vis-à-vis the US dollar between June 2005 and March 2008, the price of Chinese goods imported to the United States rose only 2.5 percent (US Department of Labor, Bureau of Labor Statistics).[49] The available evidence does not support the view that Chinese firms producing exports cut their margins in order to avoid passing through the renminbi appreciation to US consumers. If anything, profit margins in Chinese industry, which produces almost all of China's exports, increased (World Bank 2007a, 7).

The most likely explanation is that productivity growth in industries that export to the United States was sufficiently large that firms could absorb the adverse effect of the rising value of the renminbi. The combination of a nominal appreciation of the renminbi vis-à-vis the dollar of 18 percent and a 2.5 percent increase in the price of Chinese imports in the United States suggests that total factor productivity growth in China's export industries was 15 percent between June 2005 and March 2008. Over that period, prices in China's major trading partners rose about 8 percent. Thus the Chinese currency would have had to appreciate in nominal terms by almost a quarter to maintain the initial level of competitiveness of its exports. But the rate of nominal appreciation of the renminbi against its trading partners was only 7 percent, so Chinese goods became much more competitive. This calculation suggests that taking into account the rapid productivity growth in export manufacturing, China's real effective exchange rate depreciated by about 15 percent over this period. In contrast, the standard calculation in indices of

---

[49] These estimates by the BLS International Price Project are not based on unit values of imports but take into account the changing composition and quality of import goods.

the real exchange rate is based on either consumer prices (Citi and BIS indices) or a broad index of manufactured goods (JPMorgan index) and hence shows appreciation of the renminbi of 11 percent between June 2005 and the end of March 2008.

The alternative approach outlined above is certainly more consistent with the rapid increase in China's current account surplus in 2005–08. It is also worth noting that a key implication of this "differential Chinese export productivity" story is that if positive differential productivity growth in the export sector were to continue, the renminbi would need to appreciate by a much larger degree than in the recent past if exchange rates are going to contribute to a deterioration in China's global competitive position and a substantial reduction in its external surplus.

Some analysts find this differential productivity story unpersuasive because it is based only on prices of China's exports to the United States (about a fifth of total exports) and these may not be representative (e.g., on product mix) of total Chinese exports. In particular, Jonathan Anderson (2007b) notes that China's export prices for both traditional exports (like clothing and toys) and information technology (IT) electronics have been rising by 3 to 4 percent a year since 2004, whereas they were falling by 3 to 4 percent a year in 1995–2003.[50] He also wonders why, if rising productivity is responsible for the net export surge, there hasn't been more of a continuous move toward increased domestic sourcing in labor-intensive export industries. He speculates that China's now large export market share in some products (toys, footwear, and other low-end products) permits Chinese exporters to pass on their increased costs to overseas buyers. This cannot go on indefinitely if rising wages and renminbi appreciation persist, but he thinks it was a factor in the middle part of the decade.

A second hypothesis is that the large and growing trade surplus was primarily cyclical, with little relation to exchange rate developments. Anderson (2007c) argues that any good theory about China's surging trade surplus has to confront several facts: The shift in the trade balance occurred primarily in the heavy industrial sector, it involved more of a collapse in imports than a jump

---

[50] Anderson's analysis is based on Chinese export price data and Hong Kong data on prices of goods of Chinese origin that are reexported from Hong Kong. Unlike the price data analyzed in Lardy (2007), both of these are calculated from unit values.

in exports, the net export shift was highly correlated with domestic demand swings, the swing was concentrated in metals and industrial materials, and profit margins in heavy industry fell during the initial increase in the trade surplus.

His explanation is as follows: The 2000–03 period witnessed a boom in property, housing construction, and auto sales, brought on by rapid structural changes in homeownership and new consumer finance instruments; and with sharply rising profits in industrial materials and machinery sectors, local governments and state enterprises invested heavily in smelting, refining, and machinery production. The boom soon turned into a bubble, and by early 2004, the authorities drastically curtailed lending for real estate and construction; but the central government could not slow the pace of investment in heavy industry. As a result, productive capacity grew much faster than domestic demand for the next three years; as profits fell, China began to aggressively absorb its surplus capacity by cutting way back on imports and by becoming a sizable net exporter in a few industrial categories. It was as if a large stock of new excess capacity had sprung out of the ground and played havoc with China's balance of payments. Anderson expected the excess capacity problem to abate quickly; indeed, in March 2007 he argued that "China's trade surplus is already peaking and should begin to fall by the latter part of the year" (Anderson 2007a, 35). He saw China returning to a more balanced trade position in the course of 2008 and 2009.

But questions also arise about this "cyclical, excess capacity" view of the surge in China's trade balance. Most fundamentally, unless one understands what is driving investment decisions in industries that end up with excess capacity, it is difficult to either forecast when excess capacity will contract/expand or to apportion influence among many plausible factors. Thus, for example, Anderson (2007c), writing in July 2007, acknowledged that there was no sign of stabilization of the trade balance, that excess capacity in the steel industry (which accounted for about a quarter of the trade surplus surge) showed no sign of a slowdown, and that after-tax profit margins in overall heavy industry had risen, in part because Chinese firms were doing a better job of exploiting export opportunities. Furthermore, even though the exchange rate allegedly had practically no role in the origin of the net export surge, Anderson (2007b, 9) recommended renminbi appreciation "as the only real tool left available to the authorities to offset the effects of excess capacity creation...."

But how do we know that Chinese producers didn't take the expected level of the exchange rate into account when making investments in tradable goods industries? As already noted, an undervalued exchange rate raises the profitability of tradable goods by offering the safety valve of better access to overseas markets if domestic demand proves less buoyant than expected. Similarly, doesn't an increasingly undervalued exchange rate and the spur it gives to exports help explain why investment and profits at least through mid-2008 slowed much less in this investment cycle than in earlier ones? And why should the same Chinese producers who Anderson alleges paid no attention to the exchange rate in 2004–06 in making investment decisions begin to do so in 2007?

Yet a third explanation for the post-2003 net export surge comes from Mussa (2008). He notes that China operated under a fixed exchange rate regime until July 2005 and that it has been in a quasi-fixed regime since then. He maintains that application of the monetary approach to the balance of payments can help to explain not only the net export surge but also the corresponding and seemingly bizarre improvement in China's national savings-investment imbalance despite exceptionally rapid growth in investment, as well as the large and undesirable bias of investment toward tradable goods — i.e., manufacturing — and the resulting surge in the share of manufacturing in GDP.

Mussa observes that China has an exceptionally high ratio of base money to GDP, about 37 percent of GDP in 2006 (compared with about 7 percent in the United States). With nominal GDP growing at a very rapid rate of 16 percent, annual growth in demand for base money in China was large, about RMB1.24 trillion in 2006 (almost 7 percent of GDP); in contrast, the increase of base money in the United States amounted to less than 0.1 percent of GDP. Unlike the United States and many other countries, however, the Chinese central bank does not expand its holdings of net domestic assets to meet the rising demand for base money. Instead, it reduces its net domestic assets (to more negative levels) in order to "sterilize" the monetary effect of a substantial fraction of foreign exchange reserve inflows and to keep the domestic money supply from exploding. The result is that Chinese residents are forced to reduce their spending below their income by an amount corresponding to the central bank's accumulation of foreign exchange reserves less private capital inflows. For 2006, this amounted to 9 percent of GDP.

The reduction in spending, however, is not uniformly distributed over the Chinese economy. Businesses, especially in the tradable goods sector, may experience little or no constraint on their investment spending because they enjoy favorable access to domestic credit and to foreign capital inflows. In contrast, Chinese consumers (and many of the businesses that serve them) do not enjoy such favorable access and their spending is seriously constrained. The result is that overall domestic spending is suppressed and the spending that does take place is strongly tilted toward investment, particularly in tradable goods. Favorable access to capital operates as a subsidy to output and investment for firms that enjoy it, especially for capital-intensive firms in the tradable goods sector. Strong investment by these firms translates into rapidly rising labor productivity and falling unit labor costs. This, in turn, means (as emphasized above in the hidden productivity hypothesis) that the real effective exchange rate of the renminbi is significantly more depreciated than appears from standard indices that use relative consumer price levels rather than the economically more meaningful comparisons of relative unit labor costs in tradable goods industries. And this exchange rate effect is further enhanced by policies that keep domestic energy prices low and impose limited controls on pollution, thereby creating effective subsidies to energy-intensive, pollution-generating enterprises, which account for a substantial portion of the tradable goods sector.

The main policy implication of the monetary approach is that as long as the authorities continue to engage in heavy sterilization while economic growth and demand for base money are increasing rapidly, they will perpetuate the large external surplus by creating a monetary disequilibrium.[51] If they want to reduce the large surplus, they should cut back both on sterilization and on their massive exchange market intervention.

This monetary explanation too leaves some questions unanswered. Would the predictions of the monetary approach be consistent with reserve, current

---

[51] The thrust of the argument here is similar to the conclusion that large-scale sterilization of reserve increases perpetuates external disequilibrium for a country with a large capital inflow because it prevents that inflow from lowering the interest rate and thereby discouraging further capital inflows.

account, and investment behavior in China over a longer period? Would this monetary approach be helpful in explaining the variation in international reserves in other Asian economies, some of which have had even larger sterilization operations than China's? If an excess demand for base money in China led to a weakening of consumption demand during the last few years, why was the lower rate of import growth concentrated in heavy industrial sectors? Is this postulated excess demand for base money in China consistent with the observed saving behavior of the corporate sector over this period?

RENMINBI REVALUATION AND GLOBAL IMBALANCES

There is lack of agreement about the contribution a renminbi appreciation could or should make to the correction of global payments imbalances, particularly the large US current account deficit, which peaked at $788 billion (6 percent of GDP) in 2006 and then moderated somewhat, falling to $673 billion (4.7 percent of GDP) in 2008. The IMF forecasts a further fall to 2.8 percent of GDP in 2009 (IMF 2009b).

One school maintains that China's potential and fair contribution to this international problem is quite limited. After all, China's weight in the Federal Reserve's trade-weighted index for the dollar is about 15 percent. A unilateral 20 percent renminbi appreciation by itself would thus translate into only a 3 percent depreciation in the trade-weighted dollar, a move that would perhaps reduce the US global current account deficit by $40 billion to $55 billion, hardly a major contribution. The United States should instead adopt policies to raise its own low national saving rate — and particularly decrease government dissavings over the medium to long run — if it wants to significantly reduce future US current account deficits and net foreign indebtedness (Roach 2007). Claims that foreigners will tire of adding dollar assets to their portfolios underplay the decline of "home bias" in investment decisions, the attraction of the US capital market, and the moderate size of the US external financing needs relative to the large stock of financial wealth in US trading partners (Cooper 2005).

The large bilateral US trade deficit with China should not be a matter of concern since it is a country's global current account position that matters. Also, the share of the US global trade deficit with emerging Asia has fallen over the past several years: The share with China has increased significantly while the share with other Asian economies has fallen more sharply, a pattern consistent with China's emergence as a major regional processing center. A renminbi revaluation will merely induce a substitution away from Chinese products toward other low-cost producers, with little effect on total US imports.

China's large global current account surplus and the current renminbi exchange rate cause no major damage to either the US or global economy. Indeed it was once argued that the United States benefited from China's large surplus since it provided the funds that China in turn lent back to the United States, helping to finance the large US external deficit. Until the subprime and credit crisis began in mid-2007, the US economy was operating at full employment; the trend decline of employment in US manufacturing was long running (beginning well before any evidence of renminbi undervaluation); US consumers were benefiting from low-cost imports from China; and US borrowers were benefiting from low interest rates that would be higher if China were not purchasing as many US government and other dollar-denominated securities in its exchange market intervention operations (Corden 2009).

If renminbi appreciation had generated a wider and more rapid depreciation of the US dollar in 2005 and 2006, there would not have been enough slack in the economy to accommodate the expansion in US net exports without generating inflationary pressures. If there is a competitive benchmark for currencies in Asia, it is more apt to be the Japanese yen than the renminbi (Park 2007). Other countries benefit from the rapid growth of their exports to China. And China also benefits from this "Bretton Woods II" arrangement since the low value for the renminbi assists China in dealing with its formidable employment problem and in attracting enough foreign investment to build a world-class capital stock for tradable goods (Dooley, Folkerts-Landau, and Garber 2003).

Chinese exchange rate policy had very little influence on the US credit crisis, the primary origins of which were in the excessively loose US monetary policy in the run-up to the crisis (Taylor 2009); grossly inaccurate assumptions about the future path of US housing prices (Baily 2008); shifts in the composition of bank mortgage lending toward less creditworthy borrowers (Gramlich 2007); a major failure of US financial regulation and supervision, along with too much of a hands-off policy by central banks toward the pricking of asset-price bubbles (Goldstein 2008); excessive complexity in a class of securitized instruments, along with incentive problems in the originate-and-distribute model (Calomiris 2008); and unwarranted optimism about the continuous availability of borrowed liquidity (Counterparty Risk Management Policy Group III 2008). Neither China's share of the total balance of payments surplus for all surplus countries (Corden 2009) nor its share of total purchases of US government securities by foreign central banks (Bergsten et al. 2006) are high enough to support claims that China's exchange rate policy significantly pushed down US interest rates in the run-up to the US crisis. Likewise, the shortage of perceived investment opportunities in emerging economies (associated with the "savings glut" hypothesis) and "search for yield" in industrial countries go much beyond China's macroeconomic and/or exchange rate policies.

The opposing view sees much less justification for complacency about global payments imbalances or the undervalued renminbi. True, a unilateral revaluation of the renminbi wouldn't much affect the real effective exchange rate of the dollar. But China is a competitive benchmark for many others and if other Asian economies had followed China's lead by revaluing their currencies, the effects on the dollar and on the US current account deficit would be anything but trivial. Emerging Asia plus Japan has roughly a 40 percent weight in the Fed's trade-weighted dollar index. A 20 percent real appreciation in all Asian currencies would translate into an 8 percent real depreciation of the dollar and probably a $100 billion to $140 billion improvement in the US current account deficit (Goldstein 2007b). This is not small if the objective in 2006–07 was to cut the US deficit, say, roughly in half. If China and Japan hadn't acted to correct the large undervaluation of their currencies, the worry was that other Asian economies that had allowed their currencies to appreciate significantly (e.g., Korea) might reverse course and use large-scale intervention to lower the value of their currencies (Park 2007). Besides, the dollar was still regarded as overvalued to a considerable degree (Obstfeld and Rogoff 2006, Cline and Williamson 2008b).

More specifically, Cline and Williamson (2008b) estimated the US dollar to be overvalued by about 10 percent in February 2008; but according to the JPMorgan index of real effective exchange rates, by the end of the year the dollar had strengthened about 14 percent. All such calculations, however, are now more difficult to interpret given the very strong short-term cyclical effects of the ongoing financial and economic crisis on current account positions.

Implicit in the view that the dollar is still significantly overvalued — despite the recent narrowing of the US current account deficit — is the expectation that the US external imbalance will widen again after the US recovery from the crisis is firmly established. A similar methodology concludes that the renminbi is probably still undervalued (though clearly less so than in, say, October 2007) despite the large cumulative appreciation of the renminbi's real effective exchange rate since July 2005.

If the aim is to eliminate China's estimated global current account surplus of 9.8 percent of GDP in 2008, then (using the rule of thumb that each 10 percent real effective appreciation reduces China's global current account by 2 to 3.5 percent of GDP) even the 20 percent real effective appreciation of the renminbi since July 2005 would be insufficient to eliminate the undervaluation. For example, suppose one assumes that each 10 percent real effective appreciation reduces China's current account surplus by 2.5 percent of GDP, then it would take a 40 percent appreciation to eliminate China's 9.8 percent of GDP global surplus — and the cumulative real effective appreciation of the renminbi since July 2005 would still leave about 20 percent appreciation to go. This probably understates the degree of undervaluation since the current account effects of some of the earlier exchange rate changes had already run their course by the end of 2008. For example, if we only considered real exchange rate changes that occurred over the past two years as having effects on the current account that were still "in the pipeline" (that is, not yet reflected in the published current account figures), then the relevant cumulative real effective appreciation of the renminbi would be about 15 percent, not 20 percent, and the estimated undervaluation would be 5 percent higher than suggested above (25 percent instead of 20 percent). Moreover, one might argue that a good part of the particularly rapid rate of renminbi appreciation in 2008 might be reversed once some of the key currencies that have depreciated strongly vis-à-vis the renminbi over this period rebound from the cyclical and confidence effects of the global financial crisis.

Alternatively, if one posits that only about half of China's 2008 global current account surplus should be eliminated as part of any further cooperative effort to reduce global payments imbalances (as in Cline and Williamson 2008b) and that the rapid renminbi appreciation in 2008 is not likely to be reversed any time soon, then, depending on which index of real effective exchange rates one chooses, one may conclude that the renminbi at the end of 2008 was much less undervalued. For example, Cline and Williamson (2008b) estimated that the renminbi was undervalued in real effective terms by 19 percent (as of February 2008). One can calculate that the renminbi appreciated from 3 to 7 percent between February 2008 and the end of 2008, implying that by year end the renminbi was undervalued by only 12 to 16 percent.

Failure of Asian currencies to share appropriately in the needed real effective depreciation of the dollar would imply one of two undesirable scenarios: Either other currencies (e.g., the euro, the Canadian dollar, and the Australian dollar) would have to appreciate unduly when by the late summer of 2007 they already had made an important contribution (having risen in real effective terms since the dollar peak in February 2002 by 26, 20, and 48 percent, respectively)[52] or the total amount of dollar depreciation would be too small to produce a meaningful reduction in the US global deficit (Truman 2005). The heavy reliance of the United States on official lenders and on short maturity instruments to finance its global current account deficit — with much of the proceeds going to stoke consumption rather than investment — was also regarded as worrisome (Summers 2004).[53]

Another popular position, again before the financial crisis, was that the United States should implement a credible medium-term plan for fiscal consolidation to help raise the low US national saving rate. But satisfactory resolution of the global imbalance problem should not be an "either-or" choice. Both US fiscal action and a better alignment of key exchange rates, including the renminbi, were needed to correct global payments imbalances in the least costly way in terms of economic growth or inflation for deficit and surplus countries alike (Mussa 2005).

---

[52] According to the JPMorgan index, between February 2002 and December 2008 the euro appreciated in real effective terms by 32 percent and the Australian dollar by about 20 percent; in contrast, the Canadian dollar depreciated by 5 percent in real effective terms. The recent behavior of the Canadian and Australian dollars reflects the general decline in currencies of primary commodity-producing countries since the advent and intensification of the global economic and financial crisis.

[53] Setser (2007), writing in early October 2007, reported that almost all of the financing of the US current account deficit over the previous four quarters was financed by central banks in developing countries.

The market for US government securities is very large, deep, and liquid. When Japan suddenly ceased its exchange market intervention in the second half of 2004 after having intervened (cumulatively) to the tune of about $320 billion in 2003 and the first quarter of 2004, there was no major run-up in US interest rates.[54] Emerging economies that have an export basket broadly similar to that of China do suffer a competitive disadvantage from the "export subsidy" (to echo Federal Reserve Chairman Ben Bernanke's 2006 characterization) that a highly undervalued renminbi imparts to China; some US industries are adversely affected as well. Seeking to maintain a highly undervalued renminbi as an investment and export-led growth strategy is not a sensible development plan for China (Lardy 2007), and many of the assumptions made in support of the Bretton Woods II story (e.g., about the importance of the export sector in growth and employment, the role of FDI in financing total investment, the US share of China's total trade, the ownership of export industries) simply do not fit the specifics of the Chinese economy (Goldstein and Lardy 2005a).

The 2002–07 experience with the effect of the renminbi on other countries' exchange rates in Asia would seem to contradict two polar assumptions. The Bretton Woods II thesis is that Asian economies as a group share a strong self-interest in maintaining an undervalued fixed exchange rate (since, among other benefits, it supports employment in their export industries). But if one looks at the evolution of real effective exchange rates for Asian economies from the dollar peak in February 2002 to late summer 2007 the record was diverse.[55] Whereas Indonesia (35), Singapore (29), Korea (22), Thailand (22), and the Philippines (19) — call them the "movers" — registered large appreciations in their real effective rates, Hong Kong (–25), Japan (–15), Malaysia (–14), Taiwan (–4), and China (–3) — the "stickers" — recorded real effective depreciations. If self-interest is revealed by behavior, the "movers" must have decided that the benefits of resisting real exchange rate appreciation, emphasized in Bretton Woods II, were considerably less than the costs.

At the same time, the diversity of real exchange rate behavior in Asia also casts doubt on the assumption that unless China allows its currency to

---

[54] See Ito (2004) for a full discussion of the motives for Japan's large intervention during this period.
[55] This diversity in real exchange rate behavior continued through 2008.

appreciate, nobody else in Asia will do so. Clearly, there must be other factors (e.g., the strength of domestic demand, pressures from capital inflows, inflation threats, costs of sterilization) besides remaining competitive with China that affect Asian exchange rate policy.

Global payments imbalances, including the recycling of China's large global surplus into investment in US assets, may not have been the primary cause of the US credit crisis but they contributed to it. In this connection, a recent IMF (2009c, 8) study on the initial lessons of the crisis concluded that "global imbalances played a role in the buildup of systemic risk. They contributed to low interest rates and to large capital inflows into US and European banks. As we argued earlier, these two factors then contributed to a search for yield, higher leverage, and the creation of riskier assets." It has been estimated that the 10-year US Treasury yield would have been 90 basis points lower (in 2006) had there been no foreign official flows into US government bonds over the previous year (Warnock and Warnock 2006). If US long-term interest rates had been higher, the US housing bubble may not have reached such a dangerous proportion; similarly, it will be much harder to prevent excessive leverage from arising in the future if timely exchange rate adjustments are not made to smooth the elimination of large and unsustainable payments imbalances — and particularly, to rein in large capital outflows from surplus economies. Its other achievements notwithstanding, the recent London G-20 summit was a failure in addressing the global imbalance problem (Setser 2009).

The Bretton Woods II thesis about the long-term mutual benefits for Asia and the United States of large Asian surpluses, undervalued Asian exchange rates, and large US net capital inflows now lies in tatters, confirming the misgivings of skeptics (Goldstein and Lardy 2005a). The Bretton Woods II model did not last for decades; it endured three to five years at most. As documented in this volume, China has not clung to a policy of resisting any sizable appreciation in the real effective exchange rate of the renminbi. The Bretton Woods II strategy has not prevented an unprecedented decline in Asian exports over the past year, along with associated employment declines in export industries. And, as the current credit crisis illustrates vividly, the United States does not have an unambiguous interest in having large capital inflows from Asia push down US long-term real interest rates.

MANAGEMENT OF CHINA'S INTERNATIONAL RESERVES

In September 2007, China formally established the China Investment Corporation (CIC) to manage a portion of the country's massive foreign exchange reserves, which at the time stood at US$1.3 trillion. Many questions have been raised about the implications of CIC's management of cross-border assets (Truman 2008). Will CIC be motivated by political considerations rather than conventional risk and rate of return?[56] Because of its potentially large size and method of operation, could CIC contribute to uncertainty and turmoil in international financial markets? These concerns prompted a leading economic official of the European Union to warn in September 2007 that the European Union was likely to take steps to restrict investments by sovereign wealth funds that are not transparent.

Although CIC could become the world's largest sovereign wealth fund, initially it is smaller than the sovereign wealth funds of the United Arab Emirates, Singapore, Norway, and Kuwait. Since it is investing primarily within China, CIC is probably more accurately described as a holding company than a sovereign wealth fund (the latter typically invests entirely offshore) since it has incorporated Central Huijin Investment Limited (Central Huijin) as a subsidiary.[57] Central Huijin is the conduit through which the government has transferred foreign exchange reserves to domestic financial institutions as part of their recapitalization and restructuring. By the time CIC was created, these injections of capital in domestic banks and securities firms amounted to $66.4 billion. In December 2007 the government, via Central Huijin, injected $20 billion in the China Development Bank. And on November 20, 2008 the government injected, again via Central Huijin, $19 billion in the Agricultural Bank of China as part of its restructuring and presumed eventual public listing. Since the initial funding of CIC is only $200 billion, these domestic investments by Central Huijin absorbed about half of CIC's initial financial resources.

---

[56]Summers (2007) contrasts the investment motives of sovereigns and private investors and discusses the problems that this could generate.

[57]China Jianyin Investment (Limited) was taken over and became a part of Central Huijin in September 2004, before the creation of CIC.

In addition, CIC created Stable Investment Corporation, responsible for both strategic and portfolio international investments. Direct strategic investments will presumably be concentrated in energy, resources, and commodities. Some strategic investments may take the form of loans to Chinese domestic companies seeking to expand abroad. The management of some if not most of the portfolio investments is likely to be outsourced. The magnitude of these international investments is likely to be limited since there are no concrete plans to transfer additional funds from the state's official reserves to CIC and the ongoing flow of foreign exchange purchased by the central bank since the creation of CIC has been added to state official reserves rather than going to CIC.

Those who worry about the prospective size of CIC argue that to limit potential economic and political conflicts with its trading partners, CIC should reject the approach (taken by many state-controlled investors in Asia and the Middle East) of keeping information secret and should instead adopt the Norwegian model of full transparency and accountability.[58] Such an approach would ensure both that political intentions are known and fully communicated and that financial and economic disturbances are minimized.

Others argue that transparency is only secondary and could even pose a threat to other priorities as the disclosure of essential information about assets, investment strategy, or performance could sacrifice some control over the administration of a sovereign wealth fund. Furthermore, CIC management may be concerned that, despite the success of the Norway Pension Fund, full transparency could lead to inferior returns or greater volatility in domestic financial markets. These kinds of arguments have been made by similar state-owned investment firms like Singapore's Government Investment Corporation (GIC). Senior officials at GIC have maintained for years that "it is not in the nation's interest to detail our assets and their yearly returns"[59] and that "publishing this information would make it easier for would-be speculators to plan their attacks."[60]

---

[58] El-Erian (2007) argues that in encouraging transparency and disclosure for sovereign wealth funds, politicians in industrial countries should focus on issues of governance, process, and risk management.
[59] Interview with Lee Kuan Yew, *Wall Street Journal*, April 26, 2001.
[60] Lee Hsien Loong, speech at the Parliament, Singapore, May 16, 2001.

In this connection, Edwin Truman (2008) has proposed a set of best practices for sovereign wealth funds that would cover four elements: structure, governance, transparency and accountability, and behavior. He has also developed a scorecard that rates 32 sovereign wealth funds according to those criteria. The maximum score is 25 points. The average score was just over 10 points, with Norway's sovereign wealth fund at the top (with 24 points) and two Abu Dhabi funds at the bottom (with a 0.5 score). China Jianyin Investment scored well below average (6 points); there was not enough public information on CIC to assign it a score.

CURRENCY MANIPULATION AND IMF EXCHANGE RATE SURVEILLANCE

Another issue is whether China, a member of the IMF, is living up to its obligation (as contained in Article IV, Section I of the Fund's charter) to "avoid manipulating exchange rates or the international monetary system in order to avoid effective balance of payments adjustment or to gain unfair competitive advantage over other member countries." But there is also a question of whether the IMF itself is living up to its obligations to "oversee the compliance of each member country with its obligations" and to "exercise firm surveillance over the exchange rate policies of members."

Some observers have answered one or both of those questions with a resounding "no." C. Fred Bergsten (2005, 2007), Desmond Lachman (2007), Goldstein (2004, 2006a, 2006b, 2007a, 2007b), Goldstein and Mussa (2005), Mussa (2008), and Ernest Preeg (2003), among others, have argued that China's persistent, large-scale, one-way intervention in the exchange market — while its global current account surplus was large and growing and while the real value of its currency remained below that of February 2002 — constitutes strong evidence of currency manipulation. Here, currency manipulation can be interpreted to mean persistent policy efforts either to push the real effective exchange rate away from its equilibrium or to prevent it from returning to equilibrium. Those same authors, along with Timothy Adams (2006), David Dodge (2006), Mervyn King (2006), and the IMF's Independent Evaluation Office (IEO 2007), among others, have also suggested that the IMF has been found wanting or worse ("asleep at the wheel," to use Adams' characterization) in its implementation of exchange rate surveillance. In some analyses, the criticism of the Fund explicitly or implicitly focuses on the China case, while in others it is more wide-ranging.

Other economists — including Anderson (2006a, 2007c) and Jeffrey Frankel (2006) — regard the renminbi as misaligned (undervalued) but do not regard China's exchange rate policy as meriting a "manipulation" finding. In its semiannual *Report to the US Congress on International Economic and Exchange Rate Policy*, the US Treasury has become increasingly critical of China's exchange rate policy but has refused to name China a manipulator because it could not establish "intent" to manipulate. In its consultation reports on China the IMF has moved from criticizing China's currency regime as insufficiently "flexible" to acknowledging that the renminbi is also "undervalued" (IMF 2004, 2006a), but it has never accused China of manipulating the value of the renminbi.[61] This view is consistent with IMF Managing Director Rodrigo de Rato's (2006) repeated statements that he does not think it would be appropriate for the Fund to serve as a global "umpire" for the exchange rate system and that the Fund should not operate as a special pressure group. Some commentators (Eichengreen 2007) concede that IMF exchange rate surveillance has probably been too timid but emphasize that there are limits to how much leverage the Fund can exert on large, surplus countries that do not borrow from it.

In June 2007, the Fund obtained agreement from its membership to revise its 1977 Principles for the Guidance of Members' Exchange Rate Policies (IMF 2007a, 2007b), which the Fund felt were out of date and did not give it enough authority to be more activist in discouraging antisocial exchange rate policy. While the antimanipulation principle was maintained without alteration as a membership obligation, a new principle was added, recommending that members avoid exchange rate policies that result in "external instability." This new principle was regarded as helpful because it is based on outcome, not intent, and because it would give the Fund the latitude to label a

---

[61]The IMF did name China as a currency manipulator in 1992–94; see Lardy (1994, 86–90), Frankel and Wei (2007), and Henning (2007). We cannot yet say anything about the characterization of China's currency policy in the Fund's 2007 Article IV report on China. In the normal course of events that report would have been considered by the Executive Board of the IMF in the early fall of 2007 and been made public shortly thereafter. However, apparently because of objections by the Chinese government, as of mid-2009 the report had not been presented to the Executive Board.

currency as "fundamentally misaligned" without going the full monty to call it manipulation.

While the ongoing debate on the consistency of China's exchange rate policy with IMF surveillance guidelines has many facets, the main lines of argument can be summarized as follows.

China's exchange rate policy is being unfairly singled out for criticism. China is not the only country either to have recorded large percentage or absolute dollar increases in reserves in recent years, or to have a large global current account surplus relative to its GDP, or to have had a depreciation in its real effective exchange rate (Keidel 2005). Analysis by the US Treasury Department (2005, appendix) shows that different single indicators produce different orderings of manipulated currencies. The problem is not with Chinese policies that have led to a strong renminbi but rather with US policies that have led to a weak dollar (Fan Gang 2006, 2008). The Fund's charter permits members a wide choice of currency regimes, including fixed exchange rates, and defense of a fixed exchange rate can involve heavy exchange market intervention. A country that maintains exactly the same parity over an extended period, as China did from October 1997 to July 2005 — even resisting pressures to devalue during the Asian financial crisis — can't be "manipulating" since it hasn't taken any active measures to obtain an unfair competitive advantage. Requiring China to undertake a large revaluation of the renminbi would risk social instability and would infringe unduly on China's national sovereignty. Bowing to international pressure and agreeing to an excessive revaluation would condemn China to the same mistake Japan made in the 1980s, with a consequent lost decade of negligible economic growth (McKinnon 2007). The concept of currency manipulation itself is ill defined and nonoperational since many government policies affect exchange rates and the intent of these policies cannot be identified clearly.[62] If a question arises on policy intent, the strong benefit of the doubt should go to the country.

After having weighed the evidence, neither the IMF nor the US Treasury has found China guilty of currency manipulation.

The IMF was timely in its criticism of the inflexibility of the renminbi, and labeling China as a currency manipulator would only have discouraged

---

[62] Crockett (2007) argues that the macroeconomic policy mix can affect the exchange rate, just as exchange market intervention can.

reform. Unlike the WTO, the IMF has no penalties (other than the extreme and unlikely one of expulsion) for noncompliance with a member's obligations. No country has been found in violation of its Article IV obligations since the second amendment of the Fund's Articles of Agreement in the early 1970s, and the requirement to prove intent under the 1977 guidelines on exchange rate surveillance would not have supported a more activist stance on China's exchange rate policies. The term "manipulation" has a conspiratorial connotation that makes it unworkable for negotiations involving sovereign nations. The Fund needed to rebuild relations in Asia after the Asian financial crisis and a confrontation with China over exchange rate policy would not have been well received in the region and might even have renewed calls for an Asian Monetary Fund as an alternative to the IMF. The Fund means the Fund's Executive Board, and there was no consensus among the Fund's major shareholders for a more aggressive stance toward China's exchange rate policy. On a broader level, the Fund should not seek to serve as global "umpire" for the exchange rate system because such a role would conflict with its role as trusted adviser to its members. In any case, charges of manipulation and fundamental misalignment of the renminbi are now moot since China has permitted its real effective exchange rate to appreciate significantly since October 2007, bringing the cumulative appreciation from July 2005 to end-2008 to 17 to 20 percent.

Critics of both China's exchange rate policy and Fund surveillance of that policy do not find the arguments summarized above to be persuasive.

China's exchange rate policy came under international criticism because it thwarted external adjustment, because it ran counter to China's international obligations as a Fund member, and because until 2008 China was moving too slowly to change it. It is unprecedented for a country of China's size to run a global current account imbalance (of either sign) of 10 percent or more of GDP. There was no other case of a systemically important country that met all four of the following criteria: It had intervened in the exchange market to the tune of roughly 10 percent of its GDP for several years running; its global current account surplus relative to GDP over this period had almost quadrupled to reach 11 percent; the value of its currency was less than in the base period; and its domestic economy had been booming (Goldstein 2007b). Unlike major oil exporters, China's rapidly rising international reserves do not reflect the conversion of wealth from nonrenewable resources underground into financial assets above ground (Truman 2008).

The IMF charter and guidelines do not prohibit exchange market intervention, but they do discourage prolonged, large-scale, one-way intervention because it is symptomatic of a disequilibrium exchange rate that is costly to both the home country and its trading partners.

Depending on what is happening to a country's balance of payments, a misalignment of the real exchange rate can occur just as easily from nonmovement as from excessive movement of the nominal exchange rate; similarly, a given level of the nominal exchange rate may be fine when a country's global current account is in deficit or in small surplus but can be problematic when there is a persistent, very large surplus. Blocking needed real exchange rate movement by intervening to keep the nominal rate fixed or quasi-fixed can therefore legitimately be classified as currency manipulation (Goldstein 2004, 2006c, 2007a).

Accepting the argument that currency manipulation should be permitted for domestic employment reasons would make it impossible to have meaningful international guidelines discouraging competitive depreciation. Japan's lost decade of the 1990s had little to do with the fact that the Plaza Accord led to a 70 percent appreciation of the yen over three years and a lot to do with too much fiscal and monetary stimulus and weak banking supervision, both of which led to property and equity price bubbles that subsequently burst (Kuroda 2004, Kanamori and Zhao 2005).

One of the key indicators of manipulation is prolonged, large-scale one-way intervention in exchange markets and this pointer (unlike some others) does not carry the qualification of "for balance of payments purposes" because there is no plausible non-balance of payments reason for such a policy (Mussa 2008). More generally, if one accepted the Fund's (or the US Treasury's) standard of proof for "intent" to manipulate, there could never be a violation, short of a confession by the manipulating country, and surely this cannot be what the framers of Article IV had in mind. Judging whether China's exchange rate policy qualifies as manipulation is not a close call that involves giving the benefit of the doubt to the country. It is, in contrast, as clear a case of manipulation as arises outside of textbooks.

The Fund has done serious damage to its reputation both by not identifying earlier the growing undervaluation of the renminbi and by failing to enforce its regulatory responsibility for discouraging currency manipulation.[63] Had IMF management and staff been warning the Chinese authorities, say since 2003, that their persistent, large exchange intervention was thwarting external adjustment and was in danger of breaching China's obligations, the Fund would have enhanced its credibility both in and outside China, as evidence mounted of the internal and external costs of an inflexible and increasingly undervalued renminbi. Major IMF shareholders (not just the United States) could perhaps have been persuaded to support this policy line if Fund management and staff had made the effort. But Fund leadership on the China exchange rate issue was not there (Mussa 2008). Indeed, Managing Director de Rato gave the game away early on by characterizing the issue not as potential manipulation violation but instead solely as a difference of opinion on the optimal speed of renminbi appreciation.

Whereas the WTO, through its rulings, has helped to define what is and what is not internationally acceptable trade policy, the Fund, by rejecting its regulatory role, can claim no such clarification on exchange rate policy. "WTO compatibility" means something; no one speaks of "IMF compatibility" because no one knows what it is. A finding of manipulation by the Fund would exert more pressure for a change in Chinese exchange rate policy than has "a difference of opinion" between China and the Fund on the optimal speed of adjustment to greater exchange rate flexibility — both because countries are sensitive to alleged breaches of their international obligations and because such a finding from the Fund could aid chances of success for cases taken to the WTO for exchange rate-related reasons (e.g., Article XV frustration cases).[64]

There was nothing missing in the 1977 guidelines for exchange rate surveillance that would have prevented the Fund from enforcing its principle against currency manipulation. The June 2007 revision added a new principle on avoiding "external instability," but unlike the antimanipulation guideline (which comes directly from the Fund articles), the new guideline is only a recommendation, not a membership obligation, and hence may

---

[63] In recent years, the Fund's forecasts for China's global current account surplus have also been systematically too low, seemingly damaging the Fund's diagnosis and policy prescription for exchange rate policy.

[64] See Subramanian and Mattoo (2009) on how the Fund and the WTO could cooperate against currency manipulation.

have little effect. The term "currency manipulation" comes from the IMF Articles of Agreement and accurately describes what has been going on in Chinese exchange rate policy; but one could easily substitute another (more neutral-sounding) term for it — say, destabilizing exchange market intervention — without changing the substance of Fund surveillance. The Fund will not rebuild its image in Asia by refusing to supply one of the key public goods in its mandate: an internationally agreed code of conduct for exchange rate policies. Two-thirds of China's exports go outside Asia; it would make no sense for China to withdraw from the international institution that sets the rules on international monetary relations with some of its most important trading partners.

Last but not least, the critics assert that by rejecting its regulatory role as global umpire for exchange rates and by not enforcing its guidelines on exchange rate surveillance, the Fund has set the stage for national legislatures (e.g., the US Congress) to step in to fill the breach, with a higher risk of tit-for-tat protectionist trade policy. Under this argument, perceived "fairness" in exchange rate policy is a sine qua non for a win-win "grand bargain" between the industrial countries and the emerging economies on market access and power sharing in the governance of the international economy — but this perceived fairness will not take root without the Fund serving as an unbiased, competent global umpire (Goldstein 2006a).

CONGRESSIONAL CURRENCY BILLS

Increasingly frustrated with the uninterrupted rise in China's bilateral (with the United States) and global trade surpluses as well as the failure of bilateral negotiations to produce a faster and larger appreciation in the renminbi, the US Congress has from time to time threatened to pass currency laws that would penalize any US trading partners that have "manipulated" and/or "fundamentally misaligned" currencies. These bills would replace the part of the Omnibus Trade and Competitiveness Act of 1988 that requires the US Treasury to issue biannual reports to Congress on whether US trading partners are manipulating their currencies, with new legislation that both has more "teeth" to induce compliance and limits the discretion of the US Treasury to avoid a designation of manipulation by arguing that there is insufficient evidence to prove intent to manipulate.

The first such currency bill to gain attention was introduced by Senators Charles Schumer (D-NY) and Lindsey Graham (R-SC) in the fall of 2003. This was a China-specific bill that would have authorized a 27.5 percent tariff on imports from China if negotiations were unsuccessful in eliminating the undervaluation of the renminbi. While 67 senators expressed their intention to vote for Schumer-Graham, its sponsors never brought the bill to a formal vote, delaying a vote several times to see if new bilateral negotiations with China would produce evidence of greater progress and finally, in early 2007, agreeing to join with Senators Max Baucus (D-MT) and Charles Grassley (R-IA) in sponsoring new legislation.

Since then, three prominent currency bills were introduced. The Senate Finance Committee bill (S. 1607) was sponsored by Senators Schumer, Grassley, Graham, and Baucus (hereafter, the SGGB bill), and the Senate Banking Committee bill (S. 1677) was sponsored by Senators Christopher Dodd (D-CT) and Richard Shelby (R-AL) (hereafter, the DS bill). There was also a House bill (H.R. 2942), sponsored by Representatives Duncan Hunter (R-CA) and Tim Ryan (D-OH) (hereafter, the RH bill).

The SGGB bill was voted out of the Senate Finance Committee by an overwhelming 20–1 vote; similarly, the DS bill was endorsed by the Senate Banking Committee by a 17–3 margin. In March 2007, testifying before the Senate Finance Committee, Senator Schumer predicted that the SGGB bill would garner bipartisan support in this session and would be "veto proof." In the event, however, none of these three bills were voted on in Congress during the Bush presidency.

The main features of these three bills are discussed in Hufbauer and Brunei (2008). Here, it is sufficient to note that

- the US Treasury would continue to provide biannual reports to Congress, identifying countries with manipulated or fundamentally misaligned currencies;
- the criteria for judging a currency to be manipulated draw heavily on the pointers identified in the 1977 IMF guidelines on exchange rate surveillance (and in the US 1988 Omnibus Act), with the exception that proof of intent is not required and that the US bilateral trade imbalance with that country is an additional pointer;
- where fundamental misalignment replaces manipulation, a distinction is made (in the SGGB bill) between misalignment attributable to a

list of specific government policy actions (like those used to identify manipulation) and misalignment attributable to other causes (presumably, including market failure), with penalties much greater for the former than the latter;
- penalties for noncompliance are usually graduated (as the period of noncompliance gets longer); for example, they may begin with negotiations with the US Treasury and a call on the IMF to initiate a "special consultation" with the country; later (e.g., after 30 or 180 days), the US Executive Director at the Fund would be asked to oppose any rule change that benefits the country (e.g., an increase in its quota, any IMF financing), the country would not be able to qualify for "market economy" status, and the country's goods would not be eligible for purchase by the US federal government; further down the road (e.g., after 270 or 360 days), trade policy measures of various kinds would kick in (e.g., the Treasury could file a WTO Article XV frustration case, or a misaligned exchange rate would be actionable as a countervailing subsidy, and/or the United States would initiate a WTO dispute settlement case and would consider remedial intervention); and
- there may be a presidential waiver of the penalties in cases of vital economic and security interests, although some bills (e.g., the SGGB bill) provide for a congressional override.

Not surprisingly, the bills provoked a heated debate about their desirability and likely effectiveness both within the United States and abroad. Those opposing the bills offered the following arguments. Such legislation would usurp the authority of both the IMF and the US Treasury (the Executive Branch) to deal more effectively and less confrontationally with international disputes involving exchange rate policy The IMF revised and strengthened its guidelines on exchange rate surveillance and those new guidelines should be given a chance to work. The Strategic Economic Dialogue (SED) with China has made progress the old-fashioned way, through consultation and discussion. The US Congress has neither the objectivity nor the expertise to render sound judgments on other countries' exchange rate policies. Whatever their original intent, these currency bills would ultimately become instruments of protectionism — much like the US experience with antidumping legislation.

Including indicators like the bilateral trade imbalance in determinations of misalignment or manipulation illustrates the weakness of the underlying analysis. Econometric analysis by Jeffrey Frankel and Shang-Jin Wei (2007) found that "political" variables like the bilateral trade imbalance and the US unemployment rate (in presidential election years) have played as important a role in earlier Treasury manipulation findings as have legitimate economic variables such as the global current account imbalance, the estimated degree of currency misalignment, and the size of changes in international reserves. Although the three currency bills (unlike the original Schumer-Graham bill) may be technically "WTO compatible," the odds that the United States would actually win these cases before a WTO panel are low because the bills pursue arguments of dubious legal merit (Hufbauer and Brunei 2008). Inserting currency matters in the WTO adjudication process would risk politicizing the WTO dispute settlement process and weakening support for it around the world.

Moreover, these three congressional currency bills would not be effective in producing a faster and larger appreciation of the renminbi or in reducing the US global and bilateral trade deficits. Policymakers in China who favor bolder currency reform would find their influence weakened by US legislation because among the Chinese the reform would look like capitulation to the demands of the US Congress. The IMF would likewise find it harder to enforce its new currency guidelines because it would look as if it were acting as a surrogate for the US government rather than as an objective international umpire. These bills contain no measures to improve the US savings-investment imbalance. They also run the risk of igniting trade policy retaliation and copycat currency bills abroad; suppose, for example, China passed a bill imposing trade penalties on the United States if it didn't meet some Chinese-imposed target for a reduction in the US budget deficit. If other countries enacted their own national currency bills, there would soon be a completely unworkable and inconsistent network of exchange rate policy guidelines.

Those defending these currency bills offered a different perspective. The currency oversight process was badly broken — both internationally and in the United States. The IMF hasn't sent even one special consultation to investigate exchange rate policy abuses in 20 years — much less made a finding of currency manipulation. As indicated earlier, the Fund has been asleep at the wheel in identifying and discouraging currency manipulation in China. In a similar vein, the US Treasury did not enforce the currency manipulation provisions of the 1988 Omnibus Act in the face of overwhelming evidence that China has been thwarting external adjustment. The bilateral diplomacy championed by Treasury Secretaries John Snow and Henry Paulson produced insufficient renminbi appreciation. Yes, if both — or even either — the Fund and the US Treasury had exercised their currency oversight responsibly, congressional action would be unnecessary. But even a "third-best" policy response to a serious problem is better than no response at all. Congress was not attempting to usurp anything. The US Constitution gives Congress the authority over currency matters and Congress has seen fit to delegate that authority to the Executive Branch (the Treasury), but such delegation is conditional on the Treasury performing well (Henning 2007). If currency oversight is neglected, it is perfectly reasonable for the US Congress to reassert its authority in this area — at least temporarily until the Fund and the US Treasury show signs of better performance. It is not "protectionist" for the US Congress to complain that another country (China) is not taking seriously its obligations on exchange rate policy as a member of the Fund, any more than it is protectionist for the United States to complain about China's lack of enforcement of intellectual property rights. Condoning currency manipulation and allowing a "free for all" in the global exchange rate system is not the friend of open markets.

Defenders of these bills might also have argued that it remains to be seen whether congressional currency bills could be effective in inducing faster appreciation of the renminbi. The US government does not refrain from publicly criticizing China's human rights abuses for fear it will slow reform; what is different about exchange rate policy? The United States also had conditions for supporting China's entry into the WTO and those issues were solved in bilateral negotiation. Similarly, congressional currency bills were part of the negotiation on exchange rate policy and they may alter (in the desired direction) the cost-benefit calculations in Beijing about how fast to move on renminbi appreciation.

Morris Goldstein and Nicholas Lardy, "Challenges Facing the Chinese Authorities Under the Existing Currency Regime," in Morris Goldstein and Nicholas Lardy, The Future of China's Exchange Rate Policy, pp. 27-82 (2009). Peterson Institute for International Economics. Used with permission of the publisher.

REFERENCES

Adams, Timothy D. 2006. The IMF: Back to Basics. In *Reforming the IMF for the 21st Century*, ed. Edwin Truman. Washington: Institute for International Economics.

Ahearne, Alan, William Cline, Kyung Tae Lee, Yung Chul Park, Jean Pisahi-Ferry, and John Williamson. 2007. *Global Imbalances: Time for Action*. Policy Briefs in International Economics 07-4 (March). Washington: Peterson Institute for International Economics.

Anderlini, Jamil. 2007. "China's Strong Earnings Growth Inflated by Stock Market Bull Run," *Financial Times*, August 28, 13.

Anderson, Jonathan. 2004. *China: Reminders on the RMB*. UBS Investment Research, Asian Economic Comment (November 5).

Anderson, Jonathan. 2006a. *The Complete RMB Handbook*, fourth edition. UBS Investment Research, Asian Economic Perspectives (September 16).

Anderson, Jonathan. 2006b. *The Sword Hanging Over China's Banks*. UBS Investment Research, Asian Focus (December 15).

Anderson, Jonathan. 2007a. *The New China: Back to the Real World*. UBS Investment Research, Asian Economic Perspectives (March 1).

Anderson, Jonathan. 2007b. *No Really, How Competitive Are China's Exports?* UBS Investment Research, Asian Focus (April 16).

Anderson, Jonathan. 2007c. *The Real Case for Revaluation*. UBS Investment Research, Asian Focus (July 13).

Bai Chong-En, Chang-Tai Hsieh, and Yingyi Qian. 2006. *The Return to Capital in China*. NBER Working Paper 12755 (December). Cambridge, MA: National Bureau of Economic Research.

Baily, Martin. 2008. The Financial Crisis: What Caused It? Speech prepared for American-European Conference, Brookings Institution, Institut Montaigne, and Institut de l'enterprise, April, Paris.

Bergsten, C. Fred. 2005. "An Action Plan to Stop the Market Manipulators Now," *Financial Times*, March 14.

Bergsten, C. Fred. 2007. The Chinese Exchange Rate and the US Economy. Testimony before the Hearing on the Treasury Department's Report to Congress on International Economic and Exchange Rate Policy and the Strategic Economic Dialogue, Committee on Banking, Housing, and Urban Affairs, Washington, January 31.

Bergsten, C. Fred. 2008. A Partnership of Equals: How Washington Should Respond to China's Economic Challenge. *Foreign Affairs* 87, no. 4: 57–69.

Bergsten, C. Fred, Bates Gill, Nicholas R. Lardy, and Derek Mitchell. 2006. *China: The Balance Sheet — What the World Needs to Know Now about the Emerging Superpower*. New York: PublicAffairs.

Bergsten, C. Fred, Charles Freeman, Nicholas R. Lardy, and Derek Mitchell. 2008. *China's Rise: Challenges and Opportunities*. Washington: Peterson Institute for International Economics and Center for Strategic and International Studies.

Bosworth, Barry. 2004. Valuing the RMB. Paper presented to Tokyo Club Research Meeting, February.
Calomiris, Charles. 2008. The Subprime Turmoil: What's Old, What's New, What's Next? August 22. Available at vox.eu.org (accessed on May 1, 2009).
China Banking Regulatory Commission. 2007. *2006 Annual Report*. Beijing. Available at www.cbrc.gov.cn (accessed on September 14, 2007).
China Banking Regulatory Commission. 2008. *2007 Annual Report*. Beijing. Available at www.cbrc.gov.cn (accessed on July 2, 2008).
Cheung, Yin-Wong, Menzie D. Chinn, and Eiji Fujii. 2007. *The Overvaluation of Renminbi Undervaluation*. NBER Working Paper 12850 (January). Cambridge, MA: National Bureau of Economic Research.
Chinese Communist Party Central Committee and State Council. 2009. *Opinion on Deepening the Reform of the Healthcare System* (March 17). Beijing. Available at www.gov.cn (accessed on April 9, 2009).
Cline, William. 2005. *The United States as a Debtor Nation*. Washington: Institute for International Economics.
Cline, William. 2008. *Estimating Consistent Equilibrium Exchange Rates*. Working Paper 08–6. Washington: Peterson Institute for International Economics.
Cline, William, and John Williamson. 2008a. Estimates of the Equilibrium Exchange Rate of the RMB: Is There a Consensus and If Not, Why Not? In *Debating China's Exchange Rate Policy*, eds. Morris Goldstein and Nicholas R. Lardy. Washington: Peterson Institute for International Economics.
Cline, William, and John Williamson. 2008b. *New Estimates of Fundamental Equilibrium Exchange Rates*. Policy Briefs in International Economics 08-7 (July). Washington: Peterson Institute for International Economics.
Cline, William, and John Williamson. 2009. *2009 Estimates of Fundamental Equilibrium Exchange Rates*. Policy Briefs in International Economics 09-10 (June). Washington: Peterson Institute for International Economics.
Cooper, Richard. 2005. *Living with Global Imbalances: A Contrarian View*. Policy Briefs in International Economics 05-3 (November). Washington: Institute for International Economics.
Corden, W. Max. 2009. China's Exchange Rate Policy, Its Current Account Surplus, and the Global Imbalances. *Economic Journal* (forthcoming).
Counterparty Risk Policy Management Group III. 2008. *Report of the CRMPG III*. (August). New York.
Crockett, Andrew. 2007. The International Financial Architecture and Financial Stability. Dinner speech at the 50th anniversary celebration of the Bank of Ghana, August.
de Rato, Rodrigo. 2006. A Call for Cooperation: What the IMF and its Members Can Do to Solve Global Economic Problems. Speech at the Peterson Institute for International Economics, Washington, April 20.
Dobson, Wendy, and Anil K. Kashyap. 2006. The Contradiction in China's Gradualist Banking Reforms. *Brookings Papers on Economic Activity* (Fall): 103–48.

Dodge, David. 2006. The Evolving International Monetary Order and the Need for an Evolving IMF. Speech at the Woodrow Wilson School, Princeton University, Princeton, March 30.

Dooley, Michael, David Folkerts-Landau, and Peter Garber. 2003. *An Essay on the Revived Bretton Woods System*. NBER Working Paper 9971 (September). Cambridge, MA: National Bureau of Economic Research.

Dunaway, Steven. 2009. *Global Imbalances and the Financial Crisis*. Council Special Report no. 44. New York: Council on Foreign Relations.

Dunaway, Steven, and Xiangming Li. 2005. *Estimating China's Real Equilibrium Exchange Rate*. IMF Working Paper 05/202 (October). Washington: International Monetary Fund.

Dunaway, Steven, Lamin Leigh, and Xiangming Li. 2006. *How Robust are Estimates of Equilibrium Real Exchange Rates for China?* IMF Working Paper 06/220. Washington: International Monetary Fund.

Eichengreen, Barry. 2004b. *Chinese Currency Controversies*. CEPR Discussion Paper no. 4375. London: Centre for Economic Policy Research.

Eichengreen, Barry. 2007. A Blueprint for IMF Reform: More than Just a Lender. *International Finance* 10, no. 2: 153–75.

El-Erian, Mohamed. 2007. "Foreign Capital Must Not Be Blocked," *Financial Times*, October 3.

Fan Gang. 2006. *Currency Asymmetry, Global Imbalances, and Rethinking Again the International Currency System*. Beijing: China National Economic Research Institute (April).

Fan Gang. 2008. Renminbi Revaluation and US Dollar Depreciation. In *Debating China's Exchange Rate Policy*, eds. Morris Goldstein and Nicholas R. Lardy. Washington: Peterson Institute for International Economics.

Frankel, Jeffrey A. 2006. On the Yuan: The Choice Between Adjustment Under a Fixed Exchange Rate and Adjustment Under a Flexible Exchange Rate. In *Understanding the Chinese Economy*, ed. Gerhard Illing. Munich: CESinfo Economic Studies.

Frankel, Jeffrey A., and Shang-Jin Wei. 2007. Assessing China's Exchange Rate Regime. Paper prepared for the 44th Economic Policy Panel Meeting II, hosted by the Federal Reserve Bank of New York, New York, February 12.

Goldstein, Morris. 2004. *Adjusting China's Exchange Rate Policies*. Working Paper 04-1. Washington: Institute for International Economics.

Goldstein, Morris. 2006a. "Exchange Rates, Fair Play, and the 'Grand Bargain'" *Financial Times*, April 21.

Goldstein, Morris. 2006b. Renminbi Controversies. *Cato Journal* 26, no. 2 (Spring/Summer): 252–66.

Goldstein, Morris. 2006c. Currency Manipulation and Enforcing the Rules of the International Monetary System. In *Reforming the IMF for the Twenty First Century*, ed. Edwin Truman. Washington: Institute for International Economics.

Goldstein, Morris. 2007a. The IMF as Global Umpire for Exchange Rate Policies. In *C. Fred Bergsten and the World Economy*, ed. Michael Mussa. Washington: Peterson Institute for International Economics.

Goldstein, Morris. 2007b. *A (Lack of) Progress Report on China's Exchange Rate Policies.* Working Paper 07-5 (June). Washington: Peterson Institute for International Economics.

Goldstein, Morris. 2008. A Ten Plank Program for Financial Regulatory Reform. December. Speech before the National Economists Club, Washington, December 18.

Goldstein, Morris, and Nicholas Lardy. 2003b. "Two-Stage Currency Reform for China," *Asian Wall Street Journal*, September 12.

Goldstein, Morris, and Nicholas R. Lardy. 2004. *What Kind of Landing for the Chinese Economy?* Policy Briefs in International Economics 04-7 (November). Washington: Institute for International Economics.

Goldstein, Morris, and Nicholas Lardy. 2005a. *China's Role in the Revived Bretton Woods System: A Case of Mistaken Identity.* Working Paper 05-2 (March). Washington: Institute for International Economics.

Goldstein, Morris, and Nicholas Lardy. 2006b. China's Exchange Rate Policy Dilemma. *American Economic Review* (May): 422–26.

Goldstein, Morris, and Michael Mussa. 2005. "The Fund Appears to Be Sleeping at the Wheel," *Financial Times*, October 3.

Goodfriend, Marvin, and Eswar Prasad. 2006. *A Framework for Independent Monetary Policy in China.* IMF Working Paper 06/111 (May). Washington: International Monetary Fund.

Gramlich, Edward. 2007. *Subprime Mortgages…American's Latest Boom and Bust.* Washington: Urban Institute.

Green, Stephen. 2007a. *This…is…Sparta!!!* Standard Chartered On the Ground — Asia (April 12).

Green, Stephen. 2007b. *China: Calling all PBoC FX Sterilization Geeks.* Standard Chartered On the Ground — Asia (June 18).

He Jianwu and Louis Kuijs. 2007. Rebalancing China's Economy — Modeling a Policy Package. World Bank China Research Paper No. 7 (September). Beijing: World Bank. Available at www.worldbank.org.cn.

Henning, C. Randall. 2007. *Congress, Treasury, and the Accountability of Exchange Rate Policy: How the 1988 Trade Act Should Be Reformed.* Working Paper 07-8 (September). Washington: Peterson Institute for International Economics.

Hufbauer, Gary, and Claire Brunel. 2008. The US Congress and the Chinese Renminbi. In *Debating China's Exchange Rate Policy,* eds. Morris Goldstein and Nicholas R. Lardy. Washington: Peterson Institute for International Economics.

IEO (Independent Evaluation Office, International Monetary Fund). 2007. *An IEO Evaluation of the IMF's Exchange Rate Policy Advice, 1999–2005* (May). Washington: International Monetary Fund.

IMF (International Monetary Fund). 2004. *People's Republic of China: 2004 Article IV Consultation.* IMF Country Report 04/351 (November). Washington.
IMF (International Monetary Fund). 2006a. *People's Republic of China: 2006 Article IV Consultation.* IMF Country Report 06/394 (October). Washington.
IMF (International Monetary Fund). 2006b. *Methodology for CGER Exchange Rate Assessments* (November). Washington.
IMF (International Monetary Fund). 2007a. *Review of the 1977 Decision — Proposal for a New Decision* (May 22). Washington.
IMF (International Monetary Fund). 2007b. *IMF Surveillance — The 2007 Decision on Bilateral Surveillance* (June 21). Washington.
IMF (International Monetary Fund). 2009c. *Initial Lessons of the Crisis* (February). Washington: International Monetary Fund.
Ito, Takatoshi. 2004. The Yen and the Japanese Economy. In *Dollar Adjustment: How Far? Against What?* eds. C. Fred Bergsten and John Williamson. Washington: Institute for International Economics.
Kanamori, Toshiki, and Zhijun Zhao. 2005. *Renminbi Revaluation: Lessons and Experiences.* Asian Development Bank Research Policy Brief no. 18. Tokyo: Asian Development Bank Institute.
Keidel, Albert. 2005. *China's Currency: Not the Problem.* Policy Brief 39 (June). Washington: Carnegie Endowment for International Peace.
Keidel, Albert. 2007. *China's Financial Sector: Contributions to Growth and Downside Risks* (January 25). Washington: Carnegie Endowment for International Peace. Available at www.carnegieendowment.org (accessed on August 31, 2007).
King, Mervyn. 2006. Speech to the Indian Council for Research on International Economic Relations, New Delhi, India, February 20.
Kuroda, Haruhiko. 2004. The "Nixon Shock" and the "Plaza Agreement": Lessons from Two Seemingly Failed Cases of Japan's Exchange Rate Policy. *China & World Economy* 12, no. 1: 3–10. Available at en.iwep.org.cn (accessed on September 7, 2007).
Kwack, Sung Yeung, Choong Ahn, Yeung Lee, and Du Yang. 2007. Consistent Estimates of World Trade Elasticities and an Application to the Effects of Yuan (RMB) Appreciation. *Journal of Asian Economics* 18, no. 2: 314–30.
Lachman, Desmond. 2007. "Complacency at the IMF," *Gazeta Mercantil*, October 3.
Lardy, Nicholas R. 1994. *China in the World Economy.* Washington: Institute for International Economics.
Lardy, Nicholas R. 1998. *China's Unfinished Economic Revolution.* Washington: Brookings Institution.
Lardy, Nicholas R. 2002. *Integrating China into the Global Economy.* Washington: Brookings Institution.
Lardy, Nicholas R. 2006. *China: Toward a Consumption-Driven Growth Path.* Policy Briefs in International Economics 06-6 (October). Washington: Institute for International Economics.

Lardy, Nicholas R. 2007. *China's Consumption Drive Growth Path*. Peterson Institute for International Economics, Washington. Unpublished manuscript.

Li Jianjun. 2008. At RMB10 Trillion Informal Credit Completely Offsets the Tightening Gap. *China Management Report* (July 6). Available at http://china.zjol.com.cn (accessed on June 5, 2009).

Li Qiyan. 2009. "Power: Stymied Coal Talks Point to Power Reform," *Caijing*, February 4, available at http://english.caijing.com (accessed on April 14, 2009).

Ma Guonan, and Robert McCauley. 2007. *Do China's Capital Controls Still Bind? Implications for Monetary Autonomy and Capital Liberalisation*. BIS Working Papers 233 (August). Basel: Bank for International Settlements. Available at www.bis.org.

McKinnon, Ronald. 2007. Why China Should Keep Its Dollar Peg. *International Finance* 10, no. 1: 43–70.

Meade, James E. 1951. *The Balance of Payments*. London: Oxford University Press.

Ministry of Civil Affairs. 2008. *Report on Statistics and Development in Civil Affairs Work in 2007*. Beijing. Available at http://cws.mca.gov.cn (accessed on April 16, 2009).

Ministry of Civil Affairs. 2009. *Report on Statistics and Development in Civil Affairs Work in 2008*. Beijing. Available at http://cws.mca.gov.cn (accessed on January 12, 2009).

Ministry of Finance. 2009. *A Summary of the Fiscal Expenditure Situation* (May 5). Beijing. Available at www.mof.gov.cn (accessed on May 11, 2009).

Mundell, Robert. 2004. China's Exchange Rate: The Case for the Status Quo. Paper presented at the International Monetary Fund Seminar on the Foreign Exchange System, Dalian, China, May.

Mussa, Michael. 2005. Sustaining Global Growth While Reducing External Imbalances. In *The United States and the World Economy: Foreign Economic Policy for the Next Decade*, ed. C. Fred Bergsten and the Institute for International Economics. Washington: Institute for International Economics.

Michael. 2008. IMF Surveillance over China's Exchange Rate Policy. In *Debating China's Exchange Rate Policy*, eds. Morris Goldstein and Nicholas R. Lardy. Washington: Peterson Institute for International Economics.

National Bureau of Statistics of China. 2007b. *China Statistical Yearbook 2007*. Beijing: China Statistics Press.

National Bureau of Statistics of China. 2008a. *China Statistical Abstract 2008*. Beijing: China Statistics Press.

National Bureau of Statistics of China. 2008b. *China Statistical Yearbook 2008*. Beijing: China Statistics Press.

Obstfeld, Maurice, and Kenneth Rogoff. 2006. The Unsustainable US Current Account Position Revisited. In *G7 Current Account Imbalances: Sustainability and Adjustment*, ed. Richard Clarida. Chicago: University of Chicago Press.

Park, Yung Chul. 2007. Comments delivered at the conclusion of a Workshop on Policies to Reduce Global Imbalances, sponsored by Bruegel, the Korea Institute for International Economic Policy, and the Peterson Institute for International Economics, Washington, February 8–9.

People's Bank of China. 2008. *Overall Monetary Equilibrium in the First Half of 2008* (July 14). Beijing. Available at www.pbc.gov.cn (accessed on July 16, 2008).

People's Bank of China, Monetary Policy Analysis Small Group. 2008. *Report on Implementation of Monetary Policy, Second Quarter 2008* (August 15). Beijing. Available at www.pbc.gov.cn (accessed on August 18, 2008).

People's Bank of China, Monetary Policy Analysis Small Group. 2009a. *Report on Implementation of Monetary Policy, Fourth Quarter 2008* (February 23). Beijing. Available at www.pbc.gov.cn (accessed on February 24, 2009).

Podpiera, Richard. 2006. *Progress in China's Banking Sector Reform: Has Bank Behavior Changed?* IMF Working Paper 06/71 (March). Washington: International Monetary Fund.

Prasad, Eswar S. 2007. Is the Chinese Miracle Built to Last? Cornell University, Ithaca. Unpublished manuscript.

Prasad, Eswar S. 2008. Monetary Policy Independence, the Currency Regime, and the Capital Account in China. In *Debating China's Exchange Rate Policy*, eds. Morris Goldstein and Nicholas R. Lardy. Washington: Peterson Institute for International Economics.

Prasad, Eswar, Thomas Rumbaugh, and Qing Wang. 2005. *Putting the Cart before the Horse? Capital Account Liberalization and Exchange Rate Flexibility in China.* IMF Policy Discussion Paper 05/1 (January). Washington: International-Monetary Fund.

Preeg, Ernest. 2003. Exchange Rate Manipulation to Gain an Unfair Competitive Advantage. In *Dollar Overvaluation and the Global Economy*, eds. C. Fred Bergsten and John Williamson. Washington: Institute for International Economics.

Roach, Stephen. 2007. *Playing with Fire.* Morgan Stanley, Global Economic Forum (April 30).

Setser, Brad. 2007. Central Banks Came Close to Financing Almost All of the US Current-Account Deficit Over the Past Four Quarters. Brad Setser's Blog, Roubini Global Economics, New York, October 2. Available at www.rgemonitor.com/blog/setser.

Setser, Brad. 2009. Imbalance of Powers. *Foreign Policy* (April). Available at www.foreignpolicy.com (accessed on April 1, 2009).

Shu, Chang, and Raymond Yip. 2006. Impact of Exchange Rate Movements on the Mainland Economy. *China Economic Issues* 3/06 (July). Hong Kong: Hong Kong Monetary Authority.

Stanway, David. 2009. Fuel Prices: New, Improved — and Higher. *China Economic Quarterly* (March): 10–12.

State Administration of Foreign Exchange, Balance of Payments Analysis Small Group. 2008a. *Report on China's 2007 International Balance of Payments* (June 5). Available at www.safe.gov.cn (accessed on June 5, 2008).

State Administration of Foreign Exchange, Balance of Payments Analysis Small Group. 2009. *Report on China's 2008 Balance of Payments* (April 4). Available at www.safe.gov.cn (accessed on April 24, 2009).

State Council. 2009. *Notice on Near Term Key Points for Implementing Medical and Health Care Reform (2009–2011)* (March 18). Available at www.gov.cn (accessed on April 7, 2009).

State Grid Corporation of China. 2009. *2008 Corporate Social Responsibility Report of State Grid Corporation of China.* Available at http://csr.sgcc.com.cn (accessed on May 9, 2009).

Subramanian, Arvind, and Aaditya Mattoo. 2009. From Doha to the Next Bretton Woods. *Foreign Affairs* (January/February): 15–26.

Summers, Lawrence. 2004. The United States and the Global Adjustment Process. Third Annual Stavros Niarchos Lecture, Institute for International Economics, Washington, March 23.

Summers, Lawrence. 2007. "Funds That Shake Capitalist Logic," *Financial Times,* July 29.

Taylor, John. 2009. "How Government Created the Financial Crisis," *Wall Street Journal,* February 9.

Truman, Edwin. 2008. The Management of China's International Reserves: China and a Sovereign Wealth Fund Scoreboard. In *Debating China's Exchange Rate Policy,* eds. Morris Goldstein and Nicholas R. Lardy. Washington: Peterson Institute for International Economics.

US Treasury Department. 2005. *Report to the Congress on International Economic and Exchange Rate Policies* (May). Washington.

Wang Ting. 2008. This Year Central Enterprises Anticipate Paying RMB30 Billion in Dividends. *China Securities Journal* (September 10). Available at www.cs.com.cn (accessed on October 29, 2008).

Warnock, Francis, and Veronica Warnock. 2006. *International Capital Flows and US Interest Rates.* Federal Reserve Board, International Finance Discussion Paper no. 840 (September). Washington: Federal Reserve Board.

Wen Jiabao. 2009. *Report on Work of the Government* (March 5). Beijing. Available at www.npc.gov.cn (accessed on April 13, 2009).

Williamson, John. 2003. The Renminbi Exchange Rate and the Global Monetary System. Lecture at the Central University of Finance and Economics, Beijing, October.

World Bank. 2007a. *China Quarterly Update* (September). Washington. Available at http://siteresources.worldbank.org (accessed on September 12, 2007).

World Bank. 2007b. *Water Supply Pricing in China: Economic Efficiency, Environment, and Social Affordability.* Policy Note (December). Washington.

World Bank. 2008. *Mid-Term Evaluation of China's 11th Five Year Plan.* Washington.

Yu Yongding. 2007a. Global Imbalances and China. *Australian Economic Review* 40, no. 1: 3–23.

Yu Yongding. 2007b. Ten Years after the Asian Financial Crisis: The Fragility and Strength of China's Financial System. *IDS Bulletin* 38, no. 4 (July): 29–39.

Zhang Jialin. 2004. *The Debate on China's Exchange Rate Policy — Should or Will It be Resolved?* Essays in Public Policy. Palo Alto: Hoover Institution on War, Revolution and Peace.

Printed in the United States
By Bookmasters